Third Edition

Emotional and Behavioral Disorders

Theory and Practice

Margaret Cecil Coleman
The University of Texas at Austin

Allyn and Bacon
Boston • London • Toronto • Sydney • Tokyo • Singapore

Vice President, Education: Nancy Forsyth
Senior Editor: Raymond Short
Editorial Assistant: Christine Shaw
Executive Marketing Manager: Kathleen Hunter
Production Administrator: Marjorie Payne
Editorial-Production Service: Chestnut Hill Enterprises, Inc.
Composition Prepress Buyer: Linda Cox
Manufacturing Buyer: Aloka Rathnam
Cover Administrator: Suzanne Harbison

Copyright © 1996, 1992, 1986 by Allyn & Bacon
A Simon & Schuster Company
Needham Heights, MA 02194

Library of Congress Cataloging-in-Publication Data

Coleman, Margaret Cecil.
    Emotional and behavioral disorders : theory and practice / Margaret
Cecil Coleman.—3rd ed.
        p.   cm.
    Previous eds. published with title: Behavior disorders.
    Includes bibliographical references and index.
    ISBN 0-205-16632-6
    1. Problem children—Education. 2. Behavior disorders in
children. 3. Special education. 4. Teaching. I. Coleman,
Margaret Cecil. Behavior disorders. II. Title.
LC4801.C58   1996
371.93—dc20   95-5505
                                                               CIP

Printed in the United States of America
10 9 8 7 6 5 4 3 2   00 99 98 97 96

Contents

Preface   ix

1 A Historical Perspective   1

Orientation   1
Overview   1
Ancient Views: Greeks and Romans   2
Early Middle Ages–1600s (Segregation Phase)   3
1700s-1800s (Transition Phase)   5
Early 1900s (Service Phase)   6
Mid–1900s   7
   Research and Emergence of Model Programs   7
   National Trends   8
1960 to 1980   9
   Model Programs and Research   10
   Legislation and Litigation   11
1980s to Present   12
   Current Status   13
   Emergence of Interagency Collaboration   14
Conclusions   15
Key Points   16
Additional Readings   16

2 Definition and Identification   17

Orientation   17
Overview   17
How are Emotional/behavioral Disorders Defined?   18
   Factors Influencing Concepts of Deviance   19
   Defining Emotional/behavioral Disorders   22
   Utility of Definitions   22

What are the Characteristics of Students with Emotional/
    behavioral Disorders?   *25*
    Public Law 94-142 (IDEA) Definition   23
    Problems with the Federal Definition   24
    Factors of Disordered Behavior   25
    Dimensions of Emotional/behavioral Disorders   26
    Intellectual and Academic Functioning   28
    Prevalence and Sex Ratio   29
How are Emotional/behavioral Disorders Identified?   *31*
    Identification Procedures   31
    Instruments Used for Identification   33
    Team Decision Making   36
    Multicultural Considerations   37
    Systematic Screening for Emotional/behavioral Disorders   38
    The Role of the Special Education Teacher in Identification   38
Conclusions   *40*
Key Points   *40*
Additional Readings   *41*

3   Biophysical and Psychodynamic Models   43

Orientation   *43*
Overview   *43*
Biophysical Model   *44*
    Definition and Basic View   44
    Etiology and Development of Disordered Behavior   44
    Typical Evaluation Procedures   48
    Applications of Biophysical Theory   50
Psychodynamic Model   *53*
    Definition and Basic View   53
    Etiology and Development of Disordered Behavior   55
    The Psychodynamic Goal: Healthy Development   59
    Typical Evaluation Procedures   60
    Educational Application   65
    Summary of the Psychodynamic Model   71
Conclusions   *72*
Key Points   *73*
Additional Readings   *73*

4   Behavioral and Ecological Models   75

Orientation   *75*
Overview   *75*
Behavioral Model   *76*
    Definition and Basic View   76

Etiology and Development of Disordered Behavior   77
Typical Evaluation Procedures   79
Educational Application   81
Cognitive-Behavioral Model   *88*
Cognitive-Behavioral Techniques   91
Ecological Model   *92*
Definition and Basic View   92
Etiology and Development of Disordered Behavior   93
Typical Evaluation Procedures   96
Educational Applications   97
Summary of the Ecological Model   103
Conclusions   *103*
Key Points   *104*
Additional Readings   *105*

5   Internalizing Disorders   107

Orientation   *107*
Overview   *107*
Depression   *108*
Definition and Prevalence   108
Characteristics and Symptoms   110
Related Conditions   111
Etiology and Development of Depression   112
Intervention and Treatment   116
Anxiety Disorders   *119*
Definition, Prevalence, and Characteristics   120
Physical, Behavioral, and Cognitive Symptoms of Anxiety Disorders   122
Etiology and Development of Anxiety   123
Treatment and Intervention   125
A Note on Social Withdrawal   *129*
Definition and Characteristics   130
Interventions   130
Implications for Teachers   131
Conclusions   *131*
Key Points   *132*
Additional Readings   *132*

6   Externalizing Disorders   135

Orientation   *135*
Overview   *135*
Attention-Deficit Hyperactivity Disorder   *136*
Definition and Prevalence   136
Characteristics and Symptoms   137

Assessment Procedures   139
Etiology and Development   140
Intervention and Treatment   143
Conduct Disorders   147
Definition and Prevalence   147
Etiology of Conduct Disorders and Aggression   150
Intervention and Treatment   157
Conclusions   160
Key Points   161
Additional Readings   161

7   Assessment and Instruction   163

Orientation   163
Overview   163
Evaluation in the Identification Process   164
Assessment for Instruction   166
Methods for Individualizing Instruction   166
What to Teach: Academic and Social Skills   167
What to Teach: Step 1: Identify Curriculum Domains   167
What to Teach: Step 2: Develop Instructional Objectives   172
The Individualized Education Plan (IEP)   176
How to Teach: Test-Teach-Test   177
Curricula for the Social Competence Domain   182
Curricula for the Affective/emotional Subdomain   183
Curricula for the Social Skills Subdomain   184
Curricula Addressing All Three Subdomains   186
Issues in Social Skills Training   191
Conclusions   192
Key Points   193
Additional Readings   193

8   A Systems Perspective 195

Orientation   195
Overview   195
The Family System   196
Understanding Parent-Child Dynamics   197
Involving Parents   201
Conferencing Skills   207
The Education System   211
A Continuum of Services   211
Reintegration   215
Social Systems   217
Social/Welfare System   217

Juvenile Justice/Correctional System   218
Mental Health System   221
Systems Changes   223
The Teacher's Role   *225*
Teacher as Consultant   225
Teacher as Liaison   227
Teacher as Part of a Social System   229
Conclusions   *230*
Key Points   *230*
Additional Readings   *231*

9   Adolescents   233

Orientation   *233*
Overview   *233*
Defining Adolescence and Emotional/behavioral Disorders
    in Adolescence   *234*
Developmental Changes   234
The Adolescent with Emotional/behavioral Disorders   238
Dealing with Adolescent Issues in the Schools   *239*
Dropping Out   239
Sex-related Problems   240
Sex Education   243
Substance Abuse   244
Substance Abuse Education   248
Gangs, Delinquency, and the Juvenile Offender with Emotional/behavioral
    Disorders   251
Self-Destructive Behavior   254
Interventions with Adolescents with Emotional/behavioral Disorders   *257*
Career Education and Prevocational Training   258
Behavioral Interventions   261
Counseling Techniques and Classroom Groups   262
Conclusions   *264*
Key Points   *264*
Additional Readings   *265*

10   Severe Behavior Disorders   267

Orientation   *267*
Overview   *268*
Defining Severe Disorders   *268*
Autism   269
Schizophrenia   273
Programming for Students with Severe Disorders   *277*
Deciding What to Teach   277

Deciding How to Teach   282
Special Issues   289
Self-stimulating and Self-injurious Behavior   289
Communication/language Development   292
Vocational/independent Living Programming   294
Working with Families of Individuals with Severe Disorders   299
Family Stressors   300
Roles for Educators   301
Conclusions   302
Key Points   302
Additional Readings   303

11 Special Issues   305

Orientation   305
Overview   305
Substance-Exposed Infants and Young Children: Behavioral Effects   306
Prevalence   306
Effects of Substance Exposure   307
The Importance of the Psychosocial Environment   310
Substance-Exposed Young Children   310
Intervention   311
Implications for Teachers   312
Sexual Abuse of Children and Adolescents   312
Definition and Incidence   312
Who Abuses and Who is Abused?   313
The Dynamics of Abuse   314
Effects of Sexual Abuse   314
Mediating Factors and Treatment   316
Implications for Teachers   317
Suspension, Expulsion, and Full Inclusion of Students with E/BD   319
The Legality of Suspension and Expulsion   319
Legal Issues and Inclusion   321
Caring for Students with E/BD Amidst School Reform   322
Conclusions   328
Key Points   329
Additional Readings   329

References   331
Index   369

Preface

A major change in the third edition of *Behavior Disorders: Theory and Practice* is reflected in the new title *Emotional/Behavioral Disorders: Theory and Practice*. This change reflects the movement of the field toward a more inclusive term that encompasses both affective and behavioral manifestations of disorders in children and adolescents. Also, as this third edition went to press, changes to the federal definition of serious emotional disturbance were being negotiated, but had not been completed. Therefore, the definition presented in this edition is the federal definition originally contained in Public Law 94-142 in 1975, with some minor changes.

The basic structure of the third edition of this text is the same as the second edition, with one exception: I have added a Special Issues chapter to cover three basic issues that have an impact on students with emotional/behavioral disorders: effects of substance exposure, effects of sexual abuse, and issues around suspension, expulsion, and full inclusion. These issues are timely, and enough information is presented on each to provide a basis for further exploration and class discussions. In response to requests from reviewers, I have also included information on topics such as gay and lesbian issues (Chapter 9), multicultural issues (Chapters 7 and 8), and the effects of increasing violence among our youth today (Chapter 9).

One theme throughout all three editions has been a systems perspective. It delights me to be able to report, in this current edition, on many systems changes that are occurring across the country in dealing with children and adolescents with emotional/behavioral disorders. We have been giving "lip service" to the need for true interagency collaboration for many years now, and we finally seem to be actively collaborating in many communities, to the benefit of the children (Chapter 8). We may have been slow, but we are moving in the right direction.

Contributors

Sue N. Baugh, M.Ed., Coordinator of Rehabilitation Services, The Devereux Foundation, Victoria, Texas

Rebecca Brown, M.A., Therapist, and Beth Dennis, MSSW-CSW, Therapist and Grant Coordinator, Austin Child Guidance Center, Austin, Texas

Caryl Dalton, Ph.D., Psychologist, Austin, Texas

Jim Gilliam, Ph.D., Associate Professor of Special Education, The University of Texas at Austin

Debbie Gorence, M.Ed., Behavioral Consultant, Austin Independent School District

Ann Kelley, Doctoral Candidate in School Psychology, The University of Texas at Austin

Michael Kirby, Ph.D., School Psychologist, Mapleton Public Schools, Denver, Colorado

Vicki Knowles, M.A., Licensed Professional Counselor, Austin, Texas

Rich Simpson, Ph.D., and Brenda Myles, Ph.D., Department of Special Education, University of Kansas, Kansas City, Kansas

Sarah Sims, M.Ed., Psychological Associate, The Devereux Foundation, Victoria, Texas

Dona Stallworth, Ph.D., Program Consultant for E/BD, Education Service Center Region XIII, Austin, Texas

Kevin Stark, Associate Professor of Educational Psychology, The University of Texas at Austin

Jo Webber, Ph.D., Associate Professor of Special Education, Southwest Texas State University, San Marcos, Texas

Michael Weber, Ph.D., Superintendent, Glenwood City Schools, Glenwood, Wisconsin

Barbara Yonan, Ph.D., School Psychologist, Dallas, Texas

Dedicated to the memory of my grandparents,
Rev. I. L. Sharpe and Edith Cecil, who dedicated their lives
to helping others

Chapter *1*

A Historical Perspective

Historical Views of Deviance:
From Persecution and Segregation to Treatment

Development of Educational Services:
Model Programs, Pioneering Individuals, and Political Trends

Orientation

Throughout history, humans have sought to explain and to treat behavior that was considered deviant. For those of you who are preparing to teach students labeled as emotionally disturbed or behavior disordered, knowledge of the historical development of services for this population can provide perspective about your own niche—where you and your efforts fit into the overall chronology of events. However, more important than knowledge of specific people and events is the realization that deviance has always been a political and social issue, and that services for this population are a reflection of the political and social climate of the times.

Overview

Human fascination with the concept of insanity or mental disturbance can be traced to prehistoric cultures. Survival was difficult during these times, as humans were learning to cope with the natural elements. Mere physical survival was the major goal for thousands of years, and survival of the fittest was paramount to the perpetuation of the human race. Humans who were physically fit and most likely to adapt and survive were valued; the physically unfit were often shunned, left to die, or even put to death. In those early years of human existence, survival of the fittest also applied to the behaviorally deviant. A form of social Darwinism prevailed, in which survival of the group or the culture was valued above the life of the individual. Deviants, whether physically or behaviorally different, were considered a detriment to group survival and were not valued.

During the era when humans were essentially helpless and exerted little control over their environment, they invented superstitious beliefs in an effort to explain and control the ills that plagued them. Supernatural causes were evoked to explain illness, disease, and various disasters of nature such as floods, famines, earthquakes, and volcanic eruptions. Routine natural phenomena such as lightning, thunder, and fire were also attributed to supernatural causes.

Demonology, or belief in possession by demons, was common in ancient times and is prevalent in the early writings of many cultures. A logical extension of superstitious beliefs, demonology was an explanation for aberrant behavior. Both good and evil spirits were believed capable of entering the human person. Possessed individuals were accorded varying treatments. Some were beaten, ostracized, or put to death, while others were elevated to the priesthood. Individuals whose demeanor suggested possession by good spirits were accorded respect and preferential treatment. If the spirits were judged to be evil, however, rites of exorcism ranging from prayer and exhortation to cruel and barbaric measures were performed to drive the evil spirits out of the body.

By creating explanations for natural phenomena and aberrant behavior, humans were able to establish some systematic attempt to manipulate the environment, thereby instilling a meager sense of control. Historians have noted that superstitious beliefs prevail in times and societies in which humans are unable to explain scientifically the environment or to exert a degree of control over the environment because of social or political restraints. Conversely, superstition is minimal in cultures in which scientific thought, political freedom, and the rights of individuals are championed. The following historical perspective demonstrates this inverse relationship, as superstitious beliefs about aberrant behavior are shown to wax and wane over the centuries. The Greeks and Romans give us the first written accounts attributing deviant behavior to purely natural causes; however, during the Middle Ages, when most scientific inquiry was effectively repressed and the church imposed tight social control, superstition again prevailed.

Historically, treatment of deviant individuals falls into three very broad phases:

1. *segregation phase* (Early Middle Ages–1600s): The primary concern was to isolate deviants from the rest of society; hospitals and asylums were established to care for physical needs but psychological needs were essentially ignored;

2. *transition phase* (1700s–1800s): A number of vocal advocates were successful in implementing humane treatment and establishing training schools;

3. *service phase* (1900s–present): Attempts are made to help individuals become functional members of society.

Ancient Views: Greeks and Romans

Although pre-Hellenic civilizations had attempted scientific thought, most historians agree that "their science was indistinguishable from theology" (Durant, 1961, p. 51). It is the ancient Greeks who are credited with enlightening their contemporaries about natural causes of mental and behavioral disorders. Chief among the early Greek contributors were the physician Hippocrates and the philosophers Plato and Aristotle. Hippocrates became a clinical observer of human behavior and was responsible for the first medical writings that systematically classified mental problems and attributed them to natural causes. He attacked the commonly accepted notion that human ailments were caused by gods and insisted that philosophical theories have no place in medicine. His most widely known theory of mental disorders concerned the four "bodily humors": Hippocrates stated that mental imbalance was the result of a disturbance in one or more of the humors—black bile, yellow bile, blood, or phlegm. Hippocrates further proposed that the cure for mental disturbance was to restore the imbalance among the humors, a precursor to modern endocrinology or the study of endocrine secretions.

Plato hypothesized three main sources of human behavior: desire (instinct), which is primarily sexual in nature and is seated in the loins; emotions, located in the heart; and knowledge (reason), located in the head. According to Plato, humans have varying degrees of these qualities, which partially account for differences in personality and styles of behavior. Plato also anticipated modern psychoanalysis by almost two thousand years in insisting that dream interpretation was a key to personality. "In all of us, even in good men, there is such a latent wild beast nature, which peers out in sleep" (cited in Durant, 1961, p. 23).

Aristotle also ventured his opinion about the causes of mental distress; he believed that very hot bile caused both amorous and suicidal impulses. Although such theories represent advanced thinking for the age in which they appeared, they hardly constituted a basis for effective treatment. As Durant summarized the scientific contributions of the Greeks:

> *Greek science went as far as could be expected without instruments of observation and precision, and without experimental methods. It would have done better had it not been harassed by religion and discouraged by philosophy (Durant, 1939, p. 348).*

The Greeks did influence the thinking of several physicians who advanced naturalistic theories in later centuries. Notable among these is Aretaeus of Cappadocia, who claimed that many mental disorders were merely extreme manifestations of normal mental processes or personality dispositions. He also devoted attention to differential diagnosis of illnesses with similar clinical symptoms. Galen, another Greek physician who lived in Rome, is best known for his principle that a physical symptom could occur in a part of the body separate from the actual diseased area, which led to treatment of the illness rather than the symptom. Galen also proposed that the major causes of mental illness could be divided into either mental or physical categories.

Early Middle Ages–1600s (Segregation Phase)

The science of mental health took a giant step backward during the Middle Ages, as demonology and other superstitious beliefs once again prevailed. Scientific explanations of the Greeks and Romans were rejected; popular thought reverted to demonology and again attributed abnormal behavior to unnatural and unscientific causes. An increase in abnormal behavior also occurred toward the latter part of the Middle Ages. One notable manifestation was group hysteria, which occurred in the form of dance manias. Historians believe that mass hysteria occurred as early as the tenth century, and descriptive accounts of dance manias were recorded in the thirteenth century. These accounts indicate that during Saint Vitus' dance, as it was commonly called, large groups of people jumped about excitedly and danced themselves into frenzies. These frenzies reached epidemic proportions in the fifteenth and sixteenth centuries but apparently faded during the seventeenth century.

In early medieval times, monasteries were havens for people afflicted with mental disorders. The clergy generally were kind to afflicted individuals, providing shelter and protection, and treating them with prayer or other rites. However, as theologians began to promote the doctrine of inherent evil and possession by demons, methods of treatment became progressively more severe. A reversion to the unpleasant methods of the ancients occurred. Coleman describes it thus: "Flogging, starving, chains, immersion in hot water, and other tortuous methods were devised in order to make the body such an unpleasant place of residence that no self-respecting devil would remain in it" (1964, p. 32).

During the latter part of the Middle Ages, most forms of mental illness were considered to be signs of consorting with the devil, and elaborate torture devices were devised to extract confessions from persons accused of practicing witchcraft. With the full support of the church and the state, hundreds of thousands of heretics and witches were beheaded or burned at the stake. Even those who dared question the existence of witches or the methods used during trials were in danger of being declared heretics and meeting the same fate. Although these trials were primarily instruments of religious and political persecution and were not aimed at the insane populace, they did provide an avenue for accusation and punishment of those exhibiting abnormal behaviors. Witch hunting peaked during the sixteenth and seventeenth centuries in Europe and spread to some American colonies. In Salem, Massachusetts, where the most notorious colonial witch trials were held, a mood of paranoia prevailed as neighbor turned against neighbor, and the slightest aberration in behavior was cause for accusation and trial.

Despite the risk of being labeled a heretic, many writers and scientists in the sixteenth century began to question openly the concepts of witchcraft and demonology. With the establishment of mental hospitals, the mentally ill were viewed as wretched creatures and victims of fate but were no longer accused of perpetrating evil through witchcraft. These early hospitals or asylums were attempts to segregate the mentally ill and were little more than penal institutions with deplorable conditions.

The first and most famous of these asylums, the Hospital of St. Mary of Bethlehem, was established in 1547 in London. Due to colloquial pronunciation it became popularly known as Bedlam, the modern meaning of which stems from the noise emanating from the London asylum. Asylums such as Bedlam were viewed by the public with great curiosity; Shakespeare even referred to the "lunatics of Bedlam" in one of his plays. The gradual shift in the view of mental illness that was occurring during this period is captured by Despert:

> *Another questionable form of entertainment was the accepted custom of taking the children to visit the mentally ill at Bedlam and other asylums. . . . As is well*

known, the mentally ill were chained, starved, beaten and kept in filth and darkness. The visit was a routine holiday program akin to a visit to the zoo in our days. The difference is that strict rules apply to the teasing and tormenting of animals, whereas of the period we speak, teasing was not only legitimate, but considered more or less a duty since the insane were thought to be more or less possessed. (Despert, 1965, p. 89)

1700s–1800s (Transition Phase)

During the 1700s in Europe, a number of changes were occurring that eventually led to humanistic reforms in both child care and treatment of persons with mental illness. Until the latter part of the century, children were treated more as commodities than individuals. Infant and child mortality rates were extremely high. At the age of seven, and oftentimes younger, children were expected to carry the workloads of adults; they had no rights and paternal authority was absolute (Despert, 1965).

During the middle of the eighteenth century, European writers and philosophers began to champion the rights of children and adults as individuals in society, and the French and American revolutions gave new impetus to the concepts of freedom and individual rights. Soon after the end of the French Revolution, the French physician Philippe Pinel undertook a daring experiment: he removed the chains from some of the patients at La Bicetre, a hospital for persons with mental illness in Paris. Pinel wanted to test his hypothesis that these patients would respond when treated with kindness and respect rather than cruelty and imprisonment. Fortunately for Pinel, the experiment was dramatically successful and some patients showed nearly miraculous improvement. This humane treatment was called *moral therapy* or *moral treatment* and was widely adopted both in Europe and America during the early part of the nineteenth century.

Beginning in the mid-1700s, anecdotal writings describing aberrant behavior in children began to appear. These writings were usually case studies or diaries. The most notable case study was written by Jean Itard, a student of Pinel's, who described his efforts to educate Victor, the "wild boy of Averyon." Victor had been found roaming the forests of southern France; it was believed that he had been abandoned at an early age and had managed to survive without human contact. He exhibited many bizarre behaviors and was labeled an idiot, but Itard believed that Victor was capable of learning many skills, including speech. Although Victor never learned more than a few words, Itard was successful at teaching him some social and practical skills. Itard's work was emulated by his contemporaries and is heralded today as one of the first systematic attempts to teach an individual who had mental and behavioral handicaps.

Another individual who furthered the cause of humanistic treatment of children was Dr. Benjamin Rush of Philadelphia. Known as the father of U.S. psychiatry, Rush was a supporter of public education for all children and an advocate of kind and humane disciplinary methods. His writings furthered the implementation of moral therapy in U.S. asylums in the early nineteenth century and established him as an important writer in the transition between two eras.

Despite the efforts of a few advocates of humane treatment for children, few practical advances were made prior to 1800. In the mid-1800s, reforms emerged in the treatment of individuals with mental illness and mental retardation, largely due to the efforts of a few crusaders. Chief among these reformers were Dorothea Dix and Samuel Gridley Howe. Dix, a vocal proponent of the rights of the incarcerated, waged a 40-year campaign during which she appealed not only to the general public but also to legislatures in over 20 states. Her reforms reached Canada, Scotland, and other countries. Before her career ended, Dix was responsible for the establishment of 32 mental hospitals (Coleman, 1964). Howe was renowned as a pioneer in education for deaf-blind children and served as director of the Perkins Institution for the Blind before he convinced Massachusetts to establish a public school for "feebleminded children." His influence was felt throughout New England, as he was instrumental in establishing other training schools that were based on a model developed in France and brought to the United States by Edouard Seguin around 1850.

By the mid-nineteenth century, many training schools and educational programs in asylums for the insane (mental illness) and the idiotic (mental retardation) were being established. The majority of programs were based on the concept of moral treatment, of which education was an integral part. In public schools, the passage of legislation was eventually to have an enormous impact on services for this population. Toward the end of the century, compulsory school attendance laws were enacted in a number of states. Beginning with Rhode Island in 1840, many states followed suit with compulsory attendance laws, and by the turn of the century nearly all states had enacted compulsory education legislation (Aiello, 1976). Although originally intended as a means of socializing thousands of children immigrating to the United States during this period, compulsory attendance laws had the effect of encouraging educators in public schools to deal with all categories of less able children. The subsequent planning for these children may be viewed as the beginning of the field of special education; many cities established ungraded classes for children who did not flow easily into the mainstream of public education.

Writings of this period began to focus on etiology or causes of disturbance or disorders in children. In Europe, textbooks on the concepts of childhood mental disorders offered many diverse etiologies, ranging from degeneracy and masturbation to religious preoccupation (Kanner, 1962). Although the causes proposed in such writings seem amusing today, these textbooks represent the earliest attempts to collect and solidify a body of literature focusing specifically on childhood mental disorders.

In summary, sociological changes beginning in the eighteenth century finally culminated in the late 1800s in a new awareness of children as individuals with rights and of children with emotional and behavior disorders as deserving recipients of humane treatment and special schooling. However, the picture at the beginning of the twentieth century was still rather bleak. Although attitudes about these children were beginning to change, in practice the majority were receiving little more than custodial services and cursory attempts at education.

Early 1900s (Service Phase)

The first three decades of the twentieth century hosted a number of significant events as well as the establishment of national organizations dedicated to the welfare of individuals with mental disorders. One of the most significant of these was the establishment of the National

Committee for Mental Hygiene, founded primarily by Clifford Beers and the psychologist William James. In 1908, Beers, a young Yale graduate, published his autobiography, *A Mind That Found Itself,* which was a personal account of his mental breakdown and subsequent poor treatment in three institutions before his eventual recovery in the home of a sympathetic attendant. Beers mounted a campaign to enlighten the general public about poor conditions and the need for improved treatment for persons with mental illness. Largely as a result of his personal campaign, the National Committee for Mental Hygiene was created in 1909. Establishment of this organization is often viewed as the beginning of the mental health movement in the United States, which had a widespread influence on public awareness of mental health problems and led to the establishment of clinics and mental health programs for children in the public schools. By 1930, many such programs had been instituted across the country, and in 1931, the first children's psychiatric hospital was founded in Rhode Island.

During this period, other national organizations which focused on the study and education of children with disabilities were founded. The Council for Exceptional Children (CEC), a lobbying organization composed primarily of educators and parents of children with disabilities, was created in 1922. Members of CEC have crusaded for the rights of children and youth with disabilities, and, particularly since World War II, have been instrumental in the passage of favorable legislation. In 1924, the American Orthopsychiatric Association was formed. As the name *orthopsychiatric* implies, this organization is dedicated to research and procurement of information on childhood behavior disorders.

In 1930, an event occurred which demonstrated that both the general public and the federal government were showing increased interest in the welfare of children with disabilities. This event was the White House Conference on Child Health and Protection, a milestone in the field of special education because it marked the first time that special education was nationally recognized as a legitimate part of education (Aiello, 1976). In addition to the national publicity afforded by the conference, the participants' recommendation that the Office of Education include a department of special education was enacted in the early 1930s.

Mid-1900s

Research and Emergence of Model Programs

It was also in the 1930s that systematic attempts to delineate etiology, therapy, and prognosis for children with severe disorders were set in motion. However, these attempts focused on the condition of childhood schizophrenia and were plagued by philosophical differences over the feasibility and utility of classification systems (Kanner, 1962). Notable among these early attempts at definition were Kanner's (1949) description of early infantile autism, Mahler's (1952) description of symbiotic infantile psychosis, and Bender's (1954) attempt to classify childhood schizophrenia into three distinct clinical types.

While some researchers emphasized classification schemes of youngsters with severe disorders, others were turning their attention to descriptions of milder emotional/behavioral disorders. A classic monograph entitled *Children's Behavior and Teachers' Attitudes* was published by Wickman in 1928. This study contrasted the attitudes of public school teachers and mental health clinicians toward 50 problem behaviors. Wickman's results suggested that, whereas clinicians were more interested in withdrawing and other nonsocial forms of behavior, teachers were more concerned with classroom management and authority problems (Wickman, 1928). The Wickman report touched off a controversy that raged for the next 30 years, mainly due to his view that teachers should adopt a hierarchy of attitudes toward behavior more consonant with that of clinicians (Beilin, 1959). This controversy was fueled by widespread misinterpretation of the results; for example, many descriptions of the study failed to report that teachers and clinicians were responding to two different sets of instructions; nonetheless, the study was cited as justification for adding coursework in mental health to teacher education programs across the country.

Beginning in the 1930s and continuing through the 1950s, model education programs for children with severe emotional disorders were established. Lauretta Bender, a distinguished psychiatrist at Bellevue Hospital in New York, was responsible for setting up classrooms for children with emotional/behavioral disorders at Bellevue in 1935. A decade later in Chicago, Bruno Bettelheim established the Orthogenic School for youth with emotional/behavioral disorders and pioneered the concept of a *therapeutic milieu,* a contrived environment conducive to treatment. In 1946, New York City opened the "600" schools, which were programs for this population. Around the same time, Fritz Redl and David Wineman opened Pioneer House in Detroit. This residential treatment center was for delinquent and aggressive boys, later dubbed "the children nobody wants" by Redl and Wineman (1957). Treatment at Pioneer House centered around the therapeutic milieu; Redl and Wineman chose to forego psychiatric treatment in favor of group therapy and a structured, psychologically sound environment. Pioneer House operated less than two years due to lack of financial support, but it became a model for numerous programs throughout the country, and its treatment principles continued to influence services for these children.

Another model program, the League School, was founded by Carl Fenichel in New York City in 1953. Based on his conviction that residential placement is not the ideal solution for youngsters with emotional and behavior disorders, Fenichel opened a day school "to work exclusively with children who had been turned down by every school and agency except mental institutions" (Fenichel, 1974, p. 55). From a modest beginning in a Brooklyn brownstone with one teacher and two children, the League School soon expanded to capacity and by the mid-1970s was serving over 120 youngsters (Fenichel, 1974). The program at the League School incorporated the basics of most current model programs: individually tailored educational plans, a multidisciplinary team approach, and an underlying philosophy aimed at the ultimate goal of teaching students self-control.

National Trends

The postwar era gave new impetus to the general special education movement, as thousands of disabled veterans returned to the United States to be integrated into society. As the federal government sought to provide financial aid and rehabilitation services to the veterans, parents of children with disabilities became more visible and more willing to seek help. Consequently, a number of parent organizations were founded in the late forties and early fifties. The National Association for Retarded Citizens was formed in 1950, and partially due to its lobbying power, all states had passed laws pertaining to education of individuals with mental disabilities by 1956. However, services for students with emotional and behavioral disabilities lagged behind other special populations. Among the reasons proposed for this lack of development were the reluctance of parents to become advocates because of meager economic resources and feelings of guilt (Hoffman, 1974), and a lack of direction among educators due to confusion over definition, etiology, and intervention methods. It was not until the mid-1960s that national organizations for parents and educators of children with behavior disorders were established. In 1964, the Council for Children with Behavioral Disorders, a division of CEC, was founded, and in 1965, the National Society for Autistic Children was organized as a parent advocacy group.

1960 to 1980

Model Programs and Research

Beginning in the early 1960s, the scattered information on educating students with emotional/behavioral disorders was molded into a cohesive body of literature. Although much of the groundwork had been laid prior to that time, it was only after 1960 that the literature began to outline specific classroom practices. The following section is an overview of model programs and works of major contributors to the field, but it is by no means an exhaustive review of the accomplishments of this era.

A highly specific description of classroom procedures for children with behavior problems was published by William M. Cruickshank and colleagues in *A Teaching Method for Brain-Injured and Hyperactive Children* (Cruickshank, Bentzen, Ratzeburg, & Tannhauser, 1961). Although the children in the experimental classroom were labeled "hyperactive" or "brain-damaged," terms that Cruickshank linked to learning disabilities, many of the youngsters experienced severe emotional problems. As Cruickshank and colleagues observed:

> *If a child has a healthy body, but one that will not do what he wants it to—if he has eyes that see, but that do not see things the way other eyes see them—if he has ears that hear, but they have not learned to hear the way other ears do—he cannot tell anyone what his difficulty is: it just seems to him that he is always wrong. No one can see that he is not like everyone else, so he is expected to act like everyone else. These are the things that happen to such children. This is the kind of behavior in a learning situation which the teacher will have to understand if she is to help the child (Cruickshank et al., 1961, p. 131).*

Drawing heavily from the landmark work of Strauss and Lehtinen (1947) with brain-injured children, Cruickshank set up a pilot demonstration project housed in three elementary schools in Montgomery County, Maryland. The initial success of the program was attributed to a high degree of structure and an absence of excessive auditory and visual stimuli in the learning environment. The study specified physiologically based symptoms that interfere with learning (for example, distractibility and perseveration) and gave concomitant instructional strategies that inspired a new confidence in teaching children with such problems. However, subsequent data were not as encouraging; the overall strategy for classroom organization was questioned after the third year (Bentzen & Petersen, 1962).

In 1962, Norris Haring and Lakin Phillips published a book describing their efforts to establish successful experimental classrooms for children with emotional/behavioral disorders in the public schools of Arlington, Virginia. In *Educating Emotionally Disturbed Children,* Haring and Phillips provided explicit instructions for replication of their program. Classrooms were organized according to behavioral principles and Cruickshank's concept of a structured environment, and the total program stressed the child's interactions both at home and in school.

Pearl Berkowitz and Esther Rothman co-authored *The Disturbed Child* in 1960 and thus formed a professional liaison which produced numerous publications over the next two decades. Having received training at the Bellevue school founded by Bender, Berkowitz and Rothman initially favored a heavily psychoanalytic approach. However, their later writings reflected a more moderate approach as they moved toward a model in which both therapy and positive educational experiences were viewed as equally important to the child's developing ego and self-concept (Berkowitz, 1974). Due to their extensive research and continued involvement in several treatment settings in the New York City area, Rothman and Berkowitz are considered pioneers in the development of services for children and youth with emotional and behavioral disorders.

One of the first instruments designed to screen children with emotional problems in the schools was published in 1962. *A Process for In-School Screening of Children with Emotional Handicaps* (Bower & Lambert, 1962) is based upon teacher, peer, and self-ratings. The authors cautioned that it is to be used for screening only and *not* for identification or classification purposes. The instrument was based on several years' research by Bower and his colleagues in California and, for quite some time, was the only instrument available for such purposes. Ironically, the aspect of Bower's work with the most pervasive effect was not the screening instrument but the definition of emotional disturbance that accompanied the research. This definition was adopted in the federal regulations of Public Law 94-142 in 1977 and today constitutes the basis for most state definitions.

Nicholas Hobbs is the name most often associated with the development of Project Re-ED. Funded by the National Institute of Mental Health and the states of Tennessee and North Carolina in 1961 as a demonstration project, pilot residential schools were established by Hobbs in Nashville and Durham. The Re-ED programs operate from an ecological philosophy, which posits that all social systems of the child must be taken into account if treatment is to be effective. In accordance with this strategy, interventions in the home, school, and community are carried out by liaison teachers. Intervention in the residential program is carried out by teacher-counselors who focus on two major goals: (1) helping the child develop competence and experience success in academic areas, and (2) helping the child learn adaptive behaviors that will aid transition back into the home environment. As Hobbs states: "teacher-counselors work in a coordinated effort, not to cure the child, which we believe is a meaningless concept, but to make the ecological system . . . work" (1974, pp. 155–156). Today there are 16 agencies nationwide that base their treatment programs on the Re-ED model.

In the mid-sixties, another model program emerged. Originally known as the Santa Monica Project, Frank Hewett's *engineered classroom* epitomizes the behavioral approach.

Although a clinical psychologist by training, Hewett developed his model out of a need for pragmatism during his teaching experiences. The engineered classroom emerged from his beliefs that:

- You have to have structure (avoid failure by engineering the environment).
- You have to have motivation (use reinforcers).
- You have to have something to say (set up specific educational goals). (Hewett, 1974, pp. 117-127).

Translated to classroom practice, *structure* involves use of activity centers and specific times for specific subjects; *motivation* involves an elaborate check system as reinforcement; and *something to say* involves establishing a hierarchy of educational tasks. Hewett's model and Project Re-ED represent two distinctly different but highly successful approaches to educating students with emotional or behavioral disorders.

In 1965, the classic *Conflict in the Classroom* was published by Nicholas Long, William Morse, and Ruth Newman. Consisting of a collection of writings from the most prominent educators of the time, this book was one of the first attempts to put together under one cover the widely divergent views of psychoanalytic, psychodynamic, and behavioral theory. Moreover, topics included identification and assessment, modes of therapy, model programs, and management techniques relevant to educational planning; consequently, *Conflict in the Classroom* was widely adopted as a textbook in teacher-training institutions and retains its status as a classic and bestseller in the field.

The 1970s saw much progress in educating children with severe disorders, including those with autism and schizophrenia. Research on etiology yielded no clear-cut answers, but research on instructional methodology became definitive. With the use of operant conditioning techniques, students with severe disorders were taught speech and language (Hewett, 1965; Lovaas, 1966; Lovaas, 1977); eye contact and elimination of self-stimulation behaviors (Foxx, 1977, Foxx & Azrin, 1973); and attention to instruction in large groups (Koegel & Rincover, 1974). Successful classroom programs were reported by Kozloff (1975) and Donnellan-Walsh (1976). Parenting programs specifically for parents of children with autism were also established (Kozloff, 1973). Techniques and model programs for this population are treated in detail in Chapter 10.

Legislation and Litigation

Another trend of the sixties and seventies was the demand for rights of the individual by most any group that perceived itself a minority: women, African Americans, Mexican Americans, gays, and numerous other activist groups literally stormed the streets in protest. This period of unrest and activism was unprecedented in our history and undoubtedly influenced individuals with disabilities to press for rights sanctioned by law. Although numerous court cases were decided and several federal laws enacted that have affected the education of individuals with disabilities, only the three most significant of these will be reviewed.

1. *Mills versus Board of Education of District of Columbia* (1971). This court case expanded the right to education to all children with disabilities and ordered that school systems develop due process procedures for parents and comprehensive plans for identification, assessment, and placement of students with disabilities. This case laid the groundwork for Public Law 94-142, passed in 1975.

2. *Public Law 93-112 (Rehabilitation Act of 1973).* This piece of legislation focused on three key issues: provision of services for persons with severe disabilities, an emphasis on research and training, and delineation of special responsibilities of the federal government. The most significant parts of this law are contained in Sections 503 and 504, which require affirmative action toward persons with disabilities by employers and administrators of any programs receiving federal funds. The latter phrase pertains to colleges and universities receiving federal funds, thereby extending certain rights to college students with disabilities.

3. *Public Law 94-142 (Education for All Handicapped Children Act, 1975).* This law has guided the direction of special education since its passage in 1975. Its most basic provision was that all children with disabilities between the ages of 5 and 18 inclusive must be provided a free, appropriate public education. An important requirement of the law was a multidisciplinary planning process culminating in the individual education plan, the IEP, which is a blueprint for each student's educational goals and services. In 1990, P.L. 94-142 was reauthorized as *Public Law 101-476 (Individuals with Disabilities Education Act, IDEA).* This law extended the idea of a participatory planning process to the system level. IDEA requires that "multiple stakeholders" be involved in development of all special education programs. Subsequent to this requirement, the Office of Special Education Programs has rededicated itself to developing a national agenda that will focus attention on avenues for assisting and supporting schools across the country in achieving better outcomes for children and youth with emotional and behavioral disorders.

In summary, the period beginning in 1960 was most productive for educators of children with emotional and behavioral disorders. Research became more definitive, and instructional and management methods were better defined. These advances were reflected in highly successful model programs and more sophisticated literature. In the 1970s, litigation and legislation designed to procure and protect the rights of individuals with disabilities became powerful enough to direct the course of special education through the following decades. A summary of the milestones in the development of services for students with emotional and behavioral disorders during the twentieth century is shown in Table 1-1.

1980s to Present

Another significant piece of legislation, the Americans with Disabilities Act (ADA), was passed in 1990 and took effect in 1992. ADA prohibits private employers and state and local governments from discriminating against qualified individuals with disabilities in hiring, firing, advancement and other conditions related to employment. ADA has implications for all individuals with disabilities, including those with emotional and behavioral disorders, as they seek employment in a competitive job market.

In addition to this landmark legislation, the 1980s and 1990s have been marked by (a) efforts to document our current status nationwide in educating students with emotional/behavioral disorders and (b) the emergence of interagency collaboration as a service delivery model for students with emotional/behavioral disorders.

TABLE 1-1 20th Century Milestones in Development of Services for Students with Behavior Disorders

	EVENTS		MODEL PROGRAMS		PUBLICATIONS	
	Year	Event	Year	Program	Year	Publication
Early 1900s	1909	National Committee for Mental Hygiene			1908	Beers publishes *A Mind That Found Itself.*
	1922	Council for Exceptional Children			1928	Wickman surveys teachers' attitudes toward problem behaviors.
	1924	American Orthopsychiatric Association	1931	Children's psychiatric hospital established in Rhode Island.		
	1930	White House Conference on Child Health and Protection				
Mid-1900s			1945	Bettelheim's Orthogenic School (Chicago)	1943–1954	Kanner, Mahler, and Bender attempt to define and classify severe emotional disorders.
			1946	New York City's "600" Schools		
			1946	Redl and Wineman's Pioneer House (Detroit)		
			1953	Fenichel's League School (New York City)		
1960s to present	1964	Council for Children with Behavioral Disorders	1960	Hobbs' Re-ED schools (Nashville, TN, and Durham, NC)	1961	Cruickshank and colleagues publish *A Teaching Method for Brain-Injured and Hyperactive Children.*
	1965	National Society for Autistic Children	1962	Haring and Phillips' public school ED classrooms	1962	Bower and Lambert publish *A Process for In-School Screening of Children with Emotional Handicaps.*
	1971	Mills v. Board of Education of D.C.	1964	Hewett's Engineered Classroom (Santa Monica)	1965	Long, Morse, and Newman publish *Conflict in the Classroom.*
	1973	P.L. 93-112 (Rehabilitation Act of 1973)	1984	NIMH offers CASSP grants to states to develop service delivery models.	1970s	Successful instructional techniques reported with autistic children by Foxx, Kozloff, Lovaas, and others.
	1975	P.L. 94-142 (Education for All Handicapped Children Act)			1989	Knitzer et al. publish *At the Schoolhouse Door.*
	1990	P.L. 101-476 (Individuals with Disabilities Education Act, IDEA)				
	1990	Americans with Disabilities Act (ADA)				

Current Status

A large step in determining our current status was taken by Knitzer and her colleagues in a national study entitled *At the Schoolhouse Door: An Examination of Programs and Policies for Children with Behavioral and Emotional Problems* (Knitzer, Steinberg, & Fleisch, 1989). Based on the assumption that it is difficult to know what to change until we know what's wrong, this study was a comprehensive attempt to collect data on the current status of services and gaps in services to these children. Data were collected through national surveys to special education and mental health agencies, site visits to programs in several states, phone surveys to staff of programs, and a survey of parents of children with emotional and behavioral disorders. The major findings were:

1. *Parent Advocacy and Support*—Parents of students with emotional and behavioral disorders are frequently not effectively involved with their children's educational needs, partly due to the stigma of the label *seriously emotionally disturbed*. There is no strong parent advocacy or self-help movement for these parents.

2. *Identification*—There is no consensus for a definition of serious emotional disturbance, resulting in continuing underidentification and disparity among states in identification procedures. The exclusion of socially maladjusted youth continues to pose problems. Knitzer et al. question whether the "right" children are the ones being identified: "Data indicate that whether or not a student is identified has as much to do with local tolerances for difficult behavior, attitudes toward special education and resources as it does with a student's needs" (Knitzer, Steinberg, & Fleisch, 1989, p. 2).

3. *Delivery of Needed Services*—Even for students with emotional/behavioral disorders being served in special education, services may be inadequate or inappropriate. Access to therapy for these students is often lacking or, if offered, is usually either short-term or paid for by parents. Although federal law mandates educational services for this population, no parallel federal law mandates mental health services. Further, there is no true continuum of school, day treatment, and residential services for these children, which may result in overreliance on the more restrictive residential placements.

4. *Interagency Cooperation*—Although it is generally agreed that a coordinated interagency effort is essential in meeting the complex needs of students with emotional and behavior disorders, such efforts are thwarted by bureaucratic entanglements. Mental health, social services, education, health, juvenile justice, recreation, and vocational rehabilitation systems all interact with these youth; however, the roles of these various agencies are rarely defined, leading to turf issues and to these children "falling through the cracks."

5. *Training*—There is a shortage of qualified teachers for this population; specifically lacking are qualified males and individuals from ethnically or culturally diverse backgrounds. A lack of support on the job often leads to burn-out and a high turnover rate, which exacerbates the shortage. Also needed is better training for parents and mental health professionals working with children with emotional and behavioral disorders.

6. *Research*—The existing empirical bases for services for children with emotional and behavior disorders are not adequately disseminated or applied. Many programs have not evaluated results due to insufficient resources to conduct thorough evaluations and other relevant research. There is a lack of federal support for research and demonstration activities for this population. Applied research with practical implications should be encouraged, e.g., the impact of various strategies on school competence, vocational skills, and the general coping ability of these students.

Knitzer, Steinberg, and Fleisch concluded their report with ten major recommendations that require local, state, and federal involvement in policy changes needed to rectify these problems. Chief among these recommendations are:

1. A federal mandate (similar to IDEA) for mental health agencies to provide services
2. Designation, in each student's individual education plan, of a lead agency responsible for coordinating services
3. Development of a full continuum of educational and mental health services
Such changes in our current delivery system are sorely needed, and in many states are beginning to be implemented.

Emergence of Interagency Collaboration

In the 1990s, special educators have witnessed an extraordinary movement from talking about the need for interagency collaboration to actually *collaborating* in many states. A technical assistance program, CASSP (Child and Adolescent Service System Program), has been instrumental in the adoption of interagency collaboration models across the nation. Sponsored by the National Institute of Mental Health in 1984, CASSP grants were available to states interested in developing models for effective services delivery to these children and their families. CASSP promotes itself as a philosophy because its specifics vary from locale to locale, depending upon resources. The core values of the philosophy are that services should be *child-centered* and *community-based,* meaning that the needs of the child should dictate the mix of services to be delivered, and that services should be provided at the community level. A multi-agency approach is viewed as a necessity to provide the range of services that is needed. CASSP is described more fully and an example of a CASSP model is given in Chapter 8 under "Systems Changes."

Conclusions

Historically, deviance has always been defined by its societal context. The routine treatment of persons who were socially or behaviorally deviant in previous centuries is appalling to us today. However, a historical perspective of such treatment gives us an appreciation not only of the reformers who have helped shape humane treatment of individuals with emotional and behavioral disorders, but also of the strides that have been made in services for this population in the latter half of this century. Although changes of this magnitude may occur slowly—perhaps imperceptibly—it is important to remember that progress continues in working with students with emotional/behavior disorders.

Key Points

1. Superstitious beliefs about deviant behavior have been created by humans through-out history to give themselves a sense of control over the environment.
2. Not until the 1700s were children recognized as individuals with rights, and prior to 1800, few services for children with emotional disorders existed.
3. The philosophy of humane treatment for persons with mental illness was promoted by Pinel in Europe and by Rush in America in the early 1800s.
4. Reformers such as Dorothea Dix and Samuel Gridley Howe were instrumental in at-taining rights and better treatment for individuals with mental retardation and mental illness in the 1800s.
5. The enactment by states of compulsory school attendance laws by the turn of the cen-tury forced educators to deal with all categories of less able children.
6. In the early part of the twentieth century, the autobiography of Clifford Beers and the founding of the National Committee for Mental Hygiene had a profound influence on public awareness of mental health.
7. Although services for children with emotional/behavioral disorders lagged behind services for other categories of exceptionality, by the middle of the twentieth century a number of model programs were being established.
8. In the 1970s, legislation and litigation established the right to education for all chil-dren with disabilities, ushering in a new era of special programming backed by fed-eral mandates and funding.
9. In the 1980s and '90s, much attention has been directed toward a) determining the current gaps in services nationwide, and b) establishing working interagency partner-ships to fill these gaps.

Additional Readings

A mind that found itself: An autobiography, by Clifford Beers. New York: Longmans, Green, 1908, for an autobiographical account of experiences with mental institutions in the early part of this century.

Conflict in the classroom, edited by Nicholas Long, William Morse, & Ruth Newman, (1st edition), Belmont, CA: Wadsworth, 1965, for a marvelous collection of readings on emotional disturbance that served as the only textbook for educators for several years.

Personal perspectives on emotional disturbance/emotional disorders, Edited by Benjamin Brooks and David Sabatino, Austin, TX: Pro-Ed, 1995, for a book of readings about the history and the current status of educating children with emotional/behavioral disorders according to leaders in the field today.

Definition and Identification

Defining Emotional/behavioral Disorders:
Concepts, Characteristics, and a Definition

Identification Procedures:
Tests, Team Meetings, and Roles

Orientation

> "Along with the hazards of street crime, drunk driving, and Christmas shopping is that of defining what is meant by 'emotional disturbance' . . . Emotion is nonrational, nonlinear, and so far has been pretty elusive to being pinned down by precise prose" (Bower, 1982, pp. 55–56). Eli Bower uses humor to describe what is in reality a very complex and frustrating problem for all professionals who work with students with emotional/behavioral disorders. Although federal regulations have provided some direction for definition and evaluation, the identification procedures for these students are complicated by many factors, including differences among professionals in tolerance levels, terminology, training, and adherence to theoretical models. As teachers, you should be aware of your own personal and professional biases and be prepared to participate in the team process.

Overview

This chapter explores a number of issues in the process of defining emotional/behavioral disorders and identifying students under this category of special education. Three basic questions are addressed:

1. How are emotional/behavioral disorders defined? The difficulties in defining deviance and the need for a definition are explored. The federal definition is presented and critiqued.

2. What are the characteristics of students with emotional/behavioral disorders? Research on characteristics of disordered behavior, prevalence, and sex ratio is presented. A typical case example is described.

3. How are students with emotional/behavioral disorders identified? This section addresses legal requirements for identification procedures and research on what instruments are used and how decisions are made. Issues in the identification of multicultural students with emotional/behavioral disorders are discussed. The chapter concludes by presenting a model for identification and by defining the optimum role of the special education teacher in identification.

How are Emotional/behavioral Disorders Defined?

Since its appearance more than 50 years ago, *emotional disturbance* has been an umbrella term for such varied conditions as schizophrenia, autism, psychosomatic disorders, phobias, withdrawal, depression, anxiety, elective mutism, aggression, antisocial behavior, and a host of other pathologies. This variation in terminology reflects concepts that are unique to particular professions or theoretical positions. Although educators have made great strides in other areas, the field continues to be plagued by a lack of consensus on definition and terminology. The next section of this chapter is devoted to clarification of several factors that contribute to the difficulties in defining disturbed or disordered behavior.

Factors Influencing Concepts of Deviance

A number of related factors influence personal and professional decisions about which behaviors are acceptable and which behaviors are unacceptable. Among these factors are:

- Variation in individuals' tolerance ranges for behavior
- Differences in the theoretical models from which professionals operate
- Differences in terminology associated with emotional problems
- Sociological parameters of behavior

Tolerance Ranges
Everyone has preferences for certain types of behavior and aversions to other types. Teachers also differ radically in their opinions of what is acceptable in the classroom, and it is not unusual for teachers to prefer teaching certain types of students. Although the literature consistently reports teacher preference for passive or conforming students and unfavorable teacher attitudes toward aggressive students, individual teachers' tolerance ranges as well as their reactions to specific individuals vary widely. For example, dependent behavior may elicit sympathy and concern from one teacher, no reaction from another, and a negative attitude from a teacher who places a premium on independence and self-initiation. Teachers' potential for interaction with students has been found to be a function of their tolerance levels for behaviors exhibited by those students (Algozzine & Curran, 1979).

Hewett and Taylor (1980) hypothesize that teachers have two general ranges of tolerance, one for academic differences and one for behavioral differences. They further propose that the tolerance for academic differences is much broader: if a student falls within the expected range for behavior, then she is more likely to be maintained in the regular classroom despite serious academic problems. Other researchers have found that behavioral and academic expectations are interactive: if a teacher has low behavioral expectations for a student, then cognitive or academic expectations will also be lowered (Good & Grouws, 1972). One study revealed that teachers' perceptions of their students' reading abilities were more closely related to ratings of classroom behavior than to actual reading achievement or performance on reading tests (Brown & Sherbenou, 1981). While the exact relationship between academic and behavioral expectations remains unspecified, it is clear that teachers do react differently to various types of behavior exhibited in the classroom. This state of affairs led Algozzine (1977) to question whether emotionally disturbed students are not better described as "disturbing" rather than "disturbed."

Theoretical Models

A second factor influencing concepts of deviance is the number of conflicting theories of how emotional and behavior problems develop. Each theory has unique terminology, identification procedures, and a preferred mode of treatment. Although many classification schemes for theories of disordered behavior have been developed, Rhodes and Tracy (1974) grouped the numerous theories of emotional/behavioral disorders under five major conceptual models: behavioral, biophysical, psychodynamic, ecological, and sociological. While there are some common elements, each model promotes a different view of definition, etiology, identification procedures, and intervention methods. A variation of these models will be discussed in detail in Chapters 3 and 4. All professionals, whether they articulate it or not, operate from beliefs that are based on one or more of these models. Personal perceptions of deviance and subsequent decisions about definition and identification are heavily influenced by such theoretical beliefs. These beliefs depend, in part, on the theoretical and philosophical persuasion of the training program from which an individual graduates. Physicians, psychologists, social workers, and educators emerge from a wide variety of training programs that emphasize different theoretical views, diagnostic tools, and treatment procedures. These theoretical orientations are further reinforced in the work setting. A multidisciplinary team charged with making decisions about an individual student may represent several theoretical stances and thus may view the student in very different ways. The team may fail to agree on whether the student has a disorder or what diagnostic instruments and procedures should be used in the evaluation. They may even use entirely different terms to describe the same symptoms and problems. According to Hobbs (1975b), a particular child "may be regarded as mentally ill by a psychiatrist, as emotionally disturbed by a psychologist, and as behavior disordered by a special educator" (p. 57).

Terminology

A third factor influencing personal perceptions of deviance is the terminology associated with emotional/behavioral disorders. There is little agreement among educators on the basic term that most aptly describes deviant behavior in children. Additionally, educators have asserted that the jargon used by mental health professionals has little application to the school setting (Hobbs, 1975a). An examination of psychiatric and educational terminology should prove helpful in understanding why such confusion exists. The psychiatric terminology encountered in psychological evaluations and records of students with emotional/behavioral disorders is usually based on a classification system developed by the American Psychiatric Association. The sourcebook—the *Diagnostic and Statistical Manual—Revised* (DSM-IV) (American Psychiatric Association, 1994)—is a comprehensive classification scheme that allows assignment of a diagnostic label based on symptomatology. The DSM-IV sourcebook contains ten major headings under "Disorders of Infancy, Childhood or Adolescence." Listed below are the ten headings and some examples of subclassifications:

1. Mental Retardation
2. Learning Disorders

     reading disorder
     arithmetic disorder
     disorder of written expression

3. Motor Skills Disorder

     developmental coordination disorder

4. Communication Disorders

     expressive language disorder
     expressive/receptive language disorder
     phonological disorder
     stuttering

5. Pervasive Developmental Disorders

     autistic disorder
     pervasive developmental disorder (not otherwise specified)

6. Attention-Deficit and Disruptive Emotional/behavioral Disorders

     attention-deficit hyperactivity disorder
     oppositional defiant
     conduct disorder
     disruptive behavior disorder

7. Feeding and Eating Disorders

     pica
     rumination

8. Tic Disorders

     transient tic
     chronic motor or vocal tic
     Tourette's disorder

9.   Elimination Disorders

enuresis
encopresis

10.   Other Disorders of Infancy, Childhood, or Adolescence

separation anxiety
selective mutism
stereotypic movement disorder (American Psychiatric Assocation, 1994).

This classification system was devised to facilitate communication among the medical, psychological, and psychiatric professions and to codify recommendations for medication and therapy. It has few implications for educational services, nor was it intended to do so. However, in order to foster communication between the education and mental health communities and to ensure systematic classification of emotional/behavioral disorders, some states have adopted the DSM-IV system for identification of students with emotional/behavioral disorders in the schools.

The use of differing terms by educators to denote disorders does little to clarify the concept or to promote understanding among professionals. Although the concept of emotional/behavioral disorders has undergone an evolution of labels in the past 50 years, *seriously emotionally disturbed* is the term promoted for special education services by federal regulations stemming from Public Law 94-142 (now referred to as IDEA). *Emotionally disturbed* historically has been used more frequently than other terms in research (F. H. Wood, 1979). Some states adopted this term or a similar one, such as *emotionally impaired* or *emotionally handicapped,* while other states have adopted the term *behavior disordered* to describe this category within special education. Both the term and the definition outlined in federal regulations are advisory; states may therefore adopt their own, provided that neither varies significantly from those provided in the federal regulations (Wood et al., 1991).

The term *behavior disordered* is often seen as less stigmatizing, less severe, more socially acceptable, and more practical than the term *emotionally disturbed.* The term behavior disordered grew out of the behavioral model which posits that teachers can see and describe disordered behavior but cannot easily describe disturbed emotions. Many educators seem to prefer behavior disordered because it seems more plausible to deal directly with disordered behavior than with disturbed emotions.

In the early 90s, the Council for Children with Behavioral Disorders lobbied to have the federal terminology changed to reflect both positions by using the term *emotional/behavioral disorders.* However, the movement met with opposition from administrators and was being negotiated as of 1994. In this text, the terms are used interchangeably in keeping with the models and popular usage, but emotional/behavioral disorders (E/BD) is the term of choice.

Sociological Parameters of Behavior
Sociological parameters constitute a fourth factor that influences personal views of deviance. Behavior which causes a child to be labeled as disordered rarely occurs in isolation; rather, it arises from interactions that are influenced by subcultural and social role factors.

U.S. society comprises a strata of subcultures: racial and ethnic groups, socioeconomic levels, religious denominations, and geographic regions are examples of various subculture boundaries. Whether explicit or implicit, each subculture has its own provisions for membership, standards of behavior, and moral codes. For example, fighting and stealing may be adaptive behaviors for streetwise, inner-city adolescents and may be condoned by their community. The same behaviors would probably be viewed as totally unacceptable by the community at large or by another subculture with different standards. Thus, subcultural expectations are one factor in setting parameters for how behavior is viewed.

Social-role expectations are another sociological parameter of behavior. Sociologists believe that a large portion of an individual's behavior can be predicted and explained on the basis of the individual's status in society and the social roles associated with this status (Brophy, 1977). Behavior that fails to conform to these expectations may be considered deviant. Age and sex roles are major factors: certain behaviors are acceptable for a certain age level or gender, but may be considered highly inappropriate for an older age or the opposite sex. For example, consider the age or gender expectations attached to the following behaviors: thumb sucking, temper tantrums, enuresis, tattling, fistfighting, and use of explicit sexual language. Each of these behaviors is generally considered normal for a certain developmental period but may alarm parents and other adults if continued in excess beyond that period. In addition, many of the behaviors are considered more acceptable for one sex than for the other.

To summarize, four factors influencing individuals' concepts of deviance are: (1) differences in personal tolerance ranges, (2) differing theoretical models, (3) terminology, and (4) sociological parameters of behavior. These factors influence personal definitions of normalcy versus deviance and, subsequently, perceptions of problem behavior.

Defining Emotional/behavioral Disorders

While recognizing that numerous factors influence personal concepts of deviance, professionals still must establish a common ground for working with students with emotional/behavioral disorders. Defining the population to be served is the first step in reaching a workable consensus. This section explores the need for defining emotional/behavioral disorders and analyzes the definition promoted by federal law.

Utility of Definitions

Defining emotional/behavioral disorders is useful for a number of reasons, including determination of prevalence, provision of services, research, and accountability for services provided. However, one mistaken notion is that definitions have utility in identification of specific individuals to be served by programs. Definitions may describe a general population but are not specific enough to allow individuals to be identified; instead, state and local education agencies must create regulations which outline specific criteria for identification purposes. Definitions allow description of students in broad, general terms, but are much too obscure to be used as criteria for selecting individual students (Hammill, 1976).

Public Law 94-142 (IDEA) Definition

The definition of emotional disturbance specified in Public Law 94-142 and its accompanying regulations was first proposed by Eli Bower in 1957. This definition has been adopted in some form by many state departments of education:

> *Seriously emotionally disturbed is defined as follows: (i) the term means a condition exhibiting one or more of the following characteristics over a long period of time and to a marked degree, which adversely affects educational performance: (a) an inability to learn which cannot be explained by intellectual, sensory, or health factors; (b) an inability to build or maintain satisfactory interpersonal relationships with peers and teachers; (c) inappropriate types of behavior or feelings under normal circumstances; (d) a general pervasive mood of unhappiness or depression; (e) a tendency to develop physical symptoms or fears associated with personal or school problems. (ii) The term includes children who are schizophrenic. The term does not include children who are socially maladjusted, unless it is determined that they are seriously emotionally disturbed (Federal Register, 1981).*

Bower (1982) points out that one or more of the noted characteristics could be observed in almost all so-called normal children to some extent at some point; therefore, the crucial difference in his research was that emotionally disturbed children exhibited such characteristics to a marked degree over a period of time. Bower made this observation about 207 students designated as emotionally disturbed:

> *The emotionally disturbed children were poor learners, although potentially able to learn; they had few if any satisfactory interpersonal relationships; they behaved oddly or inappropriately; they were depressed or unhappy and developed illnesses or phobias. It was also noted that one or more of these characteristics were true of almost all nondesignated students to some extent at different times. The crucial differentiation was based on the observation and assessment that in the emotionally disturbed child the characteristics existed to a marked degree over a period of time. (1982, p. 57)*

Bower believes that this definition is practical in educational settings because it avoids presumptions about the child's "intrapsychic condition" or "clinical designation"; it stays within an observable setting and within the conceptual range of school personnel; and it assumes that behavior may vary from setting to setting.

Despite Bower's attempt to stay within a practical, school-oriented framework, the definition has been the focus of considerable discussion. Bower himself (1982) takes issue with the modification of his original wording by the addition of the word *seriously* to the term *emotionally disturbed* and the exclusion of children deemed socially maladjusted. If only seriously emotionally disturbed students are to be served, the implications are that mildly or moderately emotionally disturbed students are to be excluded and, further, that educators are able to distinguish degrees of disturbance on a continuum of severity. This is only one of the many questions raised by educators who wish to make the definition operational for program planning.

Problems with the Federal Definition

The lack of direction provided to states by the federal definition prompted the Executive Committee of the Council for Children with Behavioral Disorders to write a position paper (Council for Children with Behavioral Disorders, 1987). Among the problems identified were:

1. A variety of state definitions exist, resulting in diverse identification procedures. Such diversity in procedures causes a discrepancy between states in the number of children who are identified. Therefore, it is conceivable that many children and adolescents who would be identified and served in one state would not qualify for services in another state.

2. Since it is difficult to operationalize the current federal definition, professionals continue to rely on subjective clinical judgment rather than replicable objective data. Subjectivity in the identification process leads to disagreement, confusion, and lack of consensus on whom we are supposed to be serving.

3. The third and most controversial point of contention with the federal definition is its exclusion of the "socially maladjusted" from the definition of "seriously emotionally disturbed." Social maladjustment is often equated to conduct disorders. The supposed exclusion of students with conduct disorders from special education classrooms is in direct contradiction to practice, as the majority of students referred for and served in special education classrooms for emotional/behavioral disorders score high on measures of conduct disorders (Wood et al., 1991). According to the Executive Committee, the exclusion clause in the definition is based on several assumptions. First, it assumes that a population exists whose antisocial behavior does not represent a disabling condition. Second is the assumption that these students can be differentiated from students with emotional/behavioral disorders who have a disability. Third is the assumption that it is not appropriate for special education to serve groups of youth who have been tagged by other systems such as the juvenile justice system.

The second assumption is especially suspect because "there appears to be a consistent body of professional literature illustrating the interrelated nature of those behaviors described as 'disturbed' or 'disordered' with the behavior commonly thought to constitute 'social maladjustment.' " (Council for Children with Behavioral Disorders, 1987, p. 12). It therefore may not be defensible to attempt to differentiate between an emotional/behavioral disorder with social maladjustment and an emotional/behavioral disorder without social maladjustment.

Additional opposition to this exclusionary practice was voiced by the General Assembly of the American Psychological Association in 1989; their resolution specifically opposed efforts by states to exclude children and youth with conduct disorders from special education services. Thus, it appears that a concerted effort to change this part of the federal definition is underway.

The CCBD Committee concluded its position paper by recommending that the federal definition be revised to "a functional educational definition of this handicapping condition" that does not eliminate the socially maladjusted (p. 16). In addition, the committee suggested that the revised definition delineate the needed sources of data collection rather than focusing on a certain profession (psychology or psychiatry) or the DSM-IV classification system. A new definition was proposed, and in early 1995, was still being negotiated.

What Are the Characteristics of Students with Emotional/behavioral Disorders?

This section highlights research on characteristics of students identified as having E/BD. Included are: factors of emotional/behavioral disorders established in research, dimensions of abnormal behavior that distinguish it from normal behavior, academic characteristics, and prevalence and sex ratio. A brief case study which illustrates several characteristics also is presented.

Factors of Disordered Behavior

A useful framework for conceptualizing deviant behavior is that of *internalizing* versus *externalizing* behaviors. Although these terms have been popularized by Achenbach and Edelbrock (1978, 1983), the basic dichotomy is not new. Peterson (1961) used the terms *personality problem* versus *conduct problem,* and Miller (1967) used the terms *inhibition* versus *aggression* to describe the same concepts.

Internalizing and Externalizing

The internalizing factor represents problems of an introverted nature, i.e., problems with self that include worries, fears, somatic complaints, and social withdrawal. This factor also has been called overcontrolled, overinhibited, shy-anxious, and personality disorder (Achenbach & Edelbrock, 1978).

The externalizing factor represents extroversive behaviors including aggression, over-activity, disobedience, temper tantrums, and delinquency. Externalizing also has been referred to as undercontrolled, aggressive, acting out, and conduct disordered (Achenbach & Edelbrock, 1978). It has also been suggested that internalizers tend to be more reflective and externalizers tend to be more impulsive.

These two basic styles of behaving are shaped by environmental as well as biological factors; they represent pervasive differences in children's reactions to stress. Some evidence indicates that among both normal and disordered populations, males tend to be externalizers and females tend to be internalizers (Achenbach & Edelbrock, 1981). It also has been established that externalizers have a poorer prognosis for treatment than internalizers. However, Achenbach and Edelbrock (1983) warn that these are not distinctly separate factors; rather, they represent "contrasting styles of behavior that are not mutually exclusive" (p. 33). In fact, these researchers have found a clear positive association between the two factors and therefore suggest that perhaps a general underlying factor exists among individuals with behavioral difficulties, much the same as a general (g) factor is thought to exist for intelligence tests. Nonetheless, internalizing and externalizing can be useful terms in understanding deviant behavior.

Internalizers and Externalizers Among Students with E/BD

Three basic behavioral profiles of children and adolescents with emotional/behavioral disorders have been consistently identified over the past 25 years. The classic study of Quay, Morse, and Cutler (1966) established these factors, which subsequently have been supported (Conners, 1970; Kaufman, Swan, & Wood, 1979; Quay, 1966). Quay and his colleagues analyzed teacher ratings of the behavior of 441 children in public school classes for E/BD and found students exhibiting three major profiles:

1. Conduct disorder, characterized by "aggressive, hostile and contentious behavior" (Quay et al., 1966, p. 297)

2. Personality problem, characterized by "anxious, withdrawn, introvertive behavior" (Ibid., p. 29)

3. Inadequacy-immaturity, a less distinct factor involving "pre-occupation, lack of interest, sluggishness, laziness, daydreaming and passivity." (Ibid., p. 298). This factor has also been linked to lack of interest in or awareness of the environment and other autistic-like behaviors.

A fourth factor of deviant behavior that closely approximates social maladjustment was also found. Quay (1972, 1975) identified this cluster of behaviors, called "socialized delinquency." Most of these behaviors relate to participation in subgroups or gangs who break rules or laws such as those against truancy, stealing, and curfew violation. Thus, students characterized as socialized delinquents behave in ways that their peer group condones but society rejects.

These basic profiles of E/BD students can easily be classified into the internalizing-externalizing framework: personality problem and inadequacy-immaturity clearly represent internalizing behaviors. Conduct disorder and socialized delinquency clearly represent externalizing behaviors. Some of the specific behaviors identified in the studies by Quay and Kaufman are presented in Table 2-1.

More recent research also supports that students in classrooms for emotional/behavioral disorders tend to be externalizers (Smith, Wood, & Grimes, 1988; Walker et al., 1988). The internalizing-externalizing dichotomy will be used as a framework to present characteristics in Chapters 5 and 6. Anxiety, depression, and social withdrawal will be presented as internalizing behaviors. Conduct disorders and hyperactivity will be presented as externalizing behaviors.

Dimensions of Emotional/behavioral Disorders

The dimensions of *chronicity, frequency,* and *severity* are essential elements in determining whether behavior is normal or abnormal. Severity or extremeness of behavior is usually readily apparent because of its negative impact or shock value; a behavior such as masturbation in the classroom will immediately receive a great deal of negative attention. However,

TABLE 2-1. Variables of Disordered Behavior Identified by Quay et al. (1966) and Kaufman et al. (1979)*

INTERNALIZING BEHAVIORS	EXTERNALIZING BEHAVIORS
shy, withdrawn	defiant, disobedient
inferiority	aggression toward property, rules and other children
self-conscious, overly sensitive	demands excessive attention
fearful, anxious	swears
avoids participating in groups	distrusts, blames others
sad, moody, irritable	destructive
apathetic	hyperactive
preoccupied, inattentive	temper tantrums
	jealous

*The current author has labeled these variables as internalizing or externalizing: Quay and Kaufman each found three factors of disordered behavior.

chronicity and frequency of behavior are not so apparent and may require some record-keeping on the part of school personnel.

The federal definition stipulates that the student's condition be present "over a long period of time" (chronicity) and "to a marked degree" (severity and/or frequency). The goal of such stipulation is to exclude temporary or moderate behavior problems that may be reactions to situational stress or normal developmental difficulties. Indeed, it has been established that, at some point in their lives, the vast majority of children exhibit behaviors that could be classified as disturbed or pathological (Bower, 1982; Kanner, 1957; Kessler, 1966). As Kessler asserts, "There is no abnormal behavior which cannot be found in normal individuals at certain ages and under certain conditions" (p. 69). Although no objective criteria have been established for determining what constitutes "a long period of time" or "a marked degree," there are some obvious implications. *Chronicity* refers to a pattern of behavior which has been relatively stable over time; it may even disappear for short periods of time but reappear at intervals to interfere with normal or adaptive functioning. *Frequency* and *severity* are related in that the more severe the behavior, the less often it has to occur before being construed as indicative of disturbance. Consider the following examples: A junior high student loses his temper and verbally threatens the teacher; if this behavior had occurred only once during the student's otherwise clean school record, it would likely be treated as an isolated incident and dismissed with a disciplinary action. If, however, it occurred two or three times a week, the student would likely be referred for some type of psychological services as well as school disciplinary measures. Another junior high student makes a bomb threat; in this instance, the single occurrence will probably be considered serious enough to warrant instant disciplinary action, and perhaps referrals to juvenile authorities and to psychological services.

The classroom teacher should use an objective measure to help determine the chronicity, severity, and frequency of problem behaviors. It often proves very difficult for the teacher to distinguish disturbed from disturbing behavior, especially when the behaviors are particularly obnoxious, disruptive, or personally displeasing. In those instances, the teacher's discomfort may result in unintentional exaggeration of the severity of a problem or in overestimation of the number of times the behavior occurs. Behavior recording or the use of checklists or rating scales may be necessary to provide an objective estimate of how often the behavior actually occurs or how abnormal it is in comparison to other students' behavior. Classroom observations by a third party can also help the teacher distinguish disturbed from disturbing behavior.

Intellectual and Academic Functioning

Research indicates that the majority of students with emotional/behavioral disorders (excluding psychotic and autistic) fall within the low–average range on intelligence measures. In a review of 25 studies assessing the academic and intellectual characteristics of a variety of populations with emotional/behavioral disorders, Mastropieri and her colleagues reported average IQs ranging from 89.5 in a public school E/BD sample to 96.5 in an outpatient psychiatric sample (Mastropieri, Jenkins, & Scruggs, 1985). Research over the past 25 years is consistent in that no investigators have found average IQ scores over 100 with these youngsters. Although no causal links between emotional problems and intelligence have been established, it appears that, as a group, students with emotional/behavioral disorders do score lower on intelligence measures and therefore would be expected to experience some degree of academic difficulty.

Indeed, failure to achieve in school is one of the major characteristics of students with emotional/behavioral disorders (Bower, 1961; Foley & Epstein, 1992; Mastropieri, Jenkins, & Scruggs, 1985; Schroeder, 1965). Even when compared to expected achievement based on intellectual functioning, the majority of students with E/BD show academic deficits (Bower, 1969; Forness, Bennett, & Tose, 1983). Learning disabilities also co-exist with emotional/behavioral disorders. One study revealed that of a sample of 124 students admitted to a psychiatric hospital for behavioral/emotional problems, 38 percent had a concomitant learning disability, and 18 percent had a significant learning problem (Fessler, Rosenberg, & Rosenberg, 1991).

Investigators have sought to determine whether E/BD students experience more difficulty in one academic area than another. Although some have found more extreme deficits in math (e.g., Epstein, Kinder, & Bursuck, 1989; Reilly, Ross, & Bullock, 1980) or math and spelling (e.g., Forness, Frankel, Caldon, & Carter, 1980), results are mixed, and at present, inconclusive. In their review, Mastropieri et al. concluded that "research findings tend to support the notion that behaviorally disordered students are deficient in all areas of academic functioning, with some individual investigations reporting more serious deficits in math" (p. 99).

It should be noted that most states have adopted regulations stipulating that academic deficits be part of the criteria for placement of students as E/BD. This stipulation is in keeping with the provision of the federal definition that "the term means a condition . . . which adversely affects educational performance." If academic problems are usually a criterion for placement, then one might logically expect that all E/BD students would exhibit academic deficiencies. However, the populations represented in these studies include such diverse groups as students with emotional/behavioral disorders in public schools, psychiatric inpatients and outpatients, and youthful offenders; not all these groups are under the auspices of special education regulations. In addition, several relevant studies were conducted prior to the passage of Public Law 94-142 in 1975, so academic deficits would not have been a placement criterion for these groups.

In summary, although wide variation exists among individuals, students with emotional/behavioral disorders as a group consistently have scored lower than average on both IQ and achievement measures. Some investigators have found math achievement to be lower than reading, but this finding is not consistent across investigations. While the specific relationship between emotional and intellectual functioning remains to be clarified, teachers of these students should expect them to be experiencing academic difficulties as well as socioemotional problems.

Prevalence and Sex Ratio

Accurate estimation of the prevalence of youth with emotional/behavioral disorders is hampered by differences in data gathering and definition. Bower (1969), in his definitive work with disturbed pupils in California, estimated that about 10 percent of the school-aged population needed intervention for behavioral or emotional problems. However, more recent studies indicate that between 17 and 22 percent of the child and adolescent population in this country suffer from a diagnosable mental/emotional problem requiring intervention (National Institute of Mental Health, 1990). Even the more conservative 12 percent that is often quoted translates into 7.5 million youth under age 18, half of whom are presumed to be severely disabled by their condition (National Institute of Mental Health, 1990). Given these figures, perhaps the most reasonable estimate of children and youth needing special education services for behavioral/emotional problems is between 6 and 10 percent.

In sharp contrast to these needs, the U.S. Office of Education established a prevalence level of 2 percent of the school-aged population to be served in classrooms for the seriously emotionally disturbed. Under 1 percent of the public school population is being served under the category of emotional/behavioral disorders (U.S. Department of Education, 1993; Wood et al., 1991), indicating that this category is underserved even when compared to the extremely conservative cap of 2 percent.

While the exact sex ratio of pupils receiving services for emotional/behavioral disorders has not been established, it has been determined that boys are decidedly more "at risk" than girls (Rubin & Balow, 1971; Schultz, Salvia, & Feinn, 1974; Werry & Quay, 1971). It has also been established that the incidence of autism is four times more common in boys than in girls (Ritvo & Freeman, 1977). Estimations of the sex ratio in classes for emotional/behavioral disorders range from 6:1 to as high as 8 or 9:1, males to females (McClure, Ferguson, Boodoosingh, Turgay, & Stavrakaki, 1989; Reinert, 1976). Researchers have proposed an explanation for this disparity: behaviors that are more typical of boys are more likely to be labeled as disordered. Schlosser and Algozzine (1979) found that behavior problems typically exhibited by boys were rated by teachers as more disturbing than those typically exhibited by girls. Other researchers have found that as boys grow out of childhood and into their teens, they tend to show conduct problems and immaturity, whereas girls tend to show personality problems characterized by withdrawal or neurotic symptoms (Clarizio & McCoy, 1976; Schultz et al., 1974). As mentioned earlier in this chapter, conduct problems and immaturity are more prevalent in classrooms for emotional/behavioral disorders, thereby suggesting that these types of behaviors are likely to be considered disordered.

Jim, the case example in Box 2-1, represents a typical referral to services for students with emotional/behavioral disorders for three reasons: (1) he is male, (2) he is from a lower socioeconomic family, and (3) he exhibits aggressive and disruptive behaviors. Social class is a factor because more aggressive and acting-out behaviors have been found in families of lower socioeconomic status (Graubard, 1973), and these type behaviors are more likely to become classified as disordered. A number of studies have shown that behaviors described as aggressive or socially defiant are consistently more bothersome to teachers (Coleman & Gilliam, 1983; Gersten, Walker, & Darch, 1988; Mooney & Algozzine, 1978). Studies of actual classroom interactions between teachers and these students demonstrate that teachers tend to respond more intensely, more dominantly, and less effectively than with other types of student behavior (Rich, 1979; Rohrkemper & Brophy, 1979). Walker and Buckley (1973, 1974) summarize a number of studies of classroom interactions between teachers and aggressive or disruptive students thus: that such interactions are more likely to be negative than positive, that the teacher is much more likely to reprimand inappropriate behavior than to approve of appropriate behavior in these interactions, and that disruptive children tend to monopolize the teacher's time. Walker further states that these studies are illustrative of the frustration teachers usually encounter in dealing with acting-out children:

> *It often appears that the harder a teacher tries to control an acting-out child's behavior, the less effective he/she is. This process can be physically and emotion-*

BOX 2-1   Jim

Jim is an 11-year-old fourth grader from a lower socioeconomic minority family. He failed second grade and is perilously close to repeating the fourth grade because he doesn't turn in assignments or complete work in class. He has been a constant source of frustration to the teachers at Willough Elementary since transferring from across town last year. His reputation as a difficult and disruptive student preceded him to his new school and appears to be well-earned.

Although Ms. Perkins, his current teacher, tries to handle most discipline problems herself, she has been so exasperated by Jim that she has sent him to the principal's office for disciplinary measures an average of three times a week since the beginning of school. Jim has been involved in several fights in school and on the bus; one was serious enough to get him suspended because the other student had to receive medical attention. On one occasion he pulled a knife but did not use it, and on other occasions he has told Ms. Perkins to "get off his back" and to "go to hell."

Although Ms. Perkins says these occurrences both-

ered her at the time, it is Jim's emotional state that upsets her most; she describes him as often "sullen and hostile," and when he gets in these moods, he talks out in class, refuses to work, and becomes disruptive in any number of ingenious ways. As intervention methods, Ms. Perkins has tried reasoning, punishment by revoking privileges, and ignoring his outbursts whenever possible. She has talked to his parents, who were nice but not very supportive of the disciplinary methods suggested and, she suspects, not very capable of carrying them out. The school psychologist recommended a positive reinforcement system for nondisruptive behavior, but Ms. Perkins doesn't have the time necessary to institute it and she doesn't really feel that Jim should be rewarded for "something he should be doing anyway." She believes that Jim can best be served by someone who is trained to deal with emotional problems, such as the special education teacher. She has been keeping notes on his behavior and talking to Jim's previous teacher as well as the principal because she wants to be able to defend her referral.

ally exhausting . . . and the child's behavior is a constant reminder that the classroom atmosphere is not what the teacher would like it to be. (Walker, 1979, p. 18)

In summary, research on disordered behavior indicates that students who evidence one or more of the following patterns over a long time and to a marked degree are likely to become labeled as emotionally/behaviorally disordered: conduct problems (especially aggression), withdrawn and introvertive behavior, or inadequate/immature behaviors. The majority of these students are male and manifest academic deficiencies. Estimates of youth needing intervention for emotional/behavioral problems range from 12 to 22 percent, but less than 1 percent are being served in special education classrooms. The next section describes how this 1 percent is identified as E/BD.

How are Emotional/behavioral Disorders Identified?

Federal legislation mandates that comprehensive procedures be used in the identification of all students for special education. However, states and local school districts choose to implement these guidelines in ways that vary widely from locale to locale. In this section we will explore the federal guidelines, instruments most commonly used, team decision making, a systematic screening that looks promising, and the role of the special education teacher in identification. First, however, let us turn our attention to a procedure that many school districts implement prior to even making a referral for special education services: prereferral intervention.

Identification Procedures

Prereferral Interventions

Although not required by federal law, prereferral intervention systems are being implemented by many school districts as the first step in the special education referral process. Prereferral interventions are based on the ecological or systems premise that learning and behavior problems should be viewed within the classroom context. The goals of prereferral intervention are to (1) provide regular classroom teachers with needed assistance and suppport, (2) reduce inappropriate referrals for testing, and (3) reduce inappropriate special education placements (Graden, Casey, & Bonstrom, 1985). Most prereferral interventions are based upon consulting services to the regular classroom teacher in order to provide information, support, and/or materials that will aid in her working successfully with the "problem" child. One study that field-tested such a system in six schools reported mixed but encouraging findings (Graden, Casey, & Bonstrom, 1985). Perhaps the most important finding was that system characteristics that mediated success in some of the schools could be pinpointed, yielding information on which types of systems would likely be most successful with prereferral interventions. For further information on rationale and implementation of prereferral systems, refer to articles by Graden and her colleagues that are listed under Additional Readings at the end of this chapter. Box 2-2 is a personal account

BOX 2-2   Prereferral Intervention at Lukenbach School District [1]

Four years ago, the assessment staff at Lukenbach School District became concerned that too much time was being spent on evaluation of students referred to special education as candidates for classes for the emotionally disturbed. Out of 172 students evaluated that year, only 44 percent eventually qualified for placement. In addition to the excessive amount of time spent by teachers and assessment personnel in the evaluation process, it seemed that school personnel were perhaps overreferring due to a lack of understanding about multiple causes of problem behavior such as situational stress, neurological involvement, and developmental differences.

For the past three years, Lukenbach has implemented a prereferral system called ED Screening. When teachers want to make a referral under this system, they contact the school psychologist who takes relevant information, reviews any test data, and does classroom observations and/or interviews the student. Parents and teachers may be asked to complete checklists, and parents may be involved in a consultation. After collecting enough data to make some decisions, the school psychologist then offers feedback and makes recommendations to the referring teacher and other involved school personnel such as principals and counselors.

The goals of this system are twofold: (1) to reduce the number of inappropriate referrals for ED; and (2) to introduce a consultation and support system for teachers. In the first two years, the emphasis was primarily on reducing the number of inappropriate referrals without sacrificing accurate identification of any students actually needing services. Results were certainly encouraging for the first year: the number of evaluations dropped to 117, and the placement rate was 60 percent.

In addition to the ED Screening procedures, an intensive effort was undertaken to educate all school personnel about the definition and specific criteria related to the category of emotionally disturbed. The chronic component of the definition, "over a long period of time" was heavily emphasized, as was the definitional requirement of problems occurring across settings. We discovered that very few of the referrals were totally inappropriate; the students were having difficulty learning due to stress or problems at home. And although we are proud that our special education services are seen as desirable options for children with problems, special ed can't and shouldn't try to serve all students experiencing stress in their lives.

With increased support for teachers and counselors in the regular education system, we believe that the second goal is being reached: consultation is being welcomed in the schools. The extra time spent on behavioral plans and in increasing awareness of alternative explanations for emotional problems has paid off.

Our system is not perfect. Sometimes teachers try recommendations such as shortened assignments but drop them before positive results can be seen. Many of our counselors are burdened with so many duties that they do not have time to counsel children in stress on a regular basis. These and other factors will probably continue to contribute to the number of inappropriate referrals.

Across the board, however, we believe that our ED Screening system has been successful. In addition to the advantages already mentioned, it has reduced the evaluation load and decreased turn-around time on the evaluations that are necessary. Also, the system enables us to track children's progress across years and across campuses. Perhaps the best testimonial is that when it was suggested that the ED Screening program had met its goals and therefore should perhaps be discontinued, there was strong objection to the proposal.

Although the system is not without limitations, we believe that it enables us to provide as many services to as many children as we can, but with appropriate, least restrictive alternatives at every step.

Contributed by Caryl Dalton, Ph.D, former School Psychologist for a school district in central Texas.
[1] Lukenbach is a fictitious name for a suburban school district in central Texas.

of a prereferral intervention system specifically for behavioral referrals that was in its third year of implementation.

Federal Guidelines

Prior to the passage of P.L. 94-142 in 1975 (now called IDEA) it was not uncommon for students to be evaluated with a single test and recommended for special education services by a single evaluator. In order to ensure a more comprehensive evaluation procedure involving more decision makers, a number of mandates about evaluation were laid out in the law:

1. *Nondiscriminatory testing.* State and local education agencies must establish guidelines to ensure that identification procedures are not culturally or racially discriminating. The child must be evaluated in the native language or the one normally used by the child or the child's parents.

2. *Parental involvement.* Parents have the right to participate in making decisions regarding the education of their child, including placement decisions and development of the individualized education plan (IEP).

3. *Multiple criteria and team decisions.* No single test or criterion shall be used in making placement decisions, and a team or committee shall be charged with making the final decision.

4. *Test validity.* Tests must be valid for the purposes for which they are used.

From these basic mandates, state agencies have adopted regulations and guidelines to assist local school districts in devising appropriate identification procedures. Although specific regulations vary from state to state, a few commonalities exist. In the case of a student to be considered for services under the category emotional/behavioral disorders, many states require that a licensed or certified mental health professional (e.g., psychologist or psychiatrist) be responsible for the evaluation. Most states require that eligibility be determined by a multidisciplinary team based on information from a comprehensive assessment in a number of areas such as language, cognitive-intellectual, emotional-social, medical-physical, and behavioral. In addition, some determination of academic functioning or educational level usually is required. Illustrated in Box 2-3 are the identification procedures for Richard, a fourth grader referred for psychological evaluation by his teacher, who believed him to be emotionally/behaviorally disordered.

Instruments Used for Identification

Selection of specific instruments and techniques is usually left up to the discretion of assessment personnel. Historically, test batteries used in the schools have been oriented toward intellectual and educational assessment (Coulter, Morrow, & Gilliam, 1979), whereas the batteries used by mental health clinicians have been oriented toward projective techniques (Brown & McGuire, 1976). However, a more recent survey of 145 school districts in 27 states suggests that traditional assessment tools are being replaced by observations, interviews, and rating scales (Grosenick, George, George, & Lewis, 1991). In the survey, instruments reported by administrators as most often used in the identification of students

BOX 2-3   Richard[1]

Richard was referred by his fourth grade teacher because of her concerns about his lying, aggression toward peers, noncompliance with school authorities, disruptive classroom behavior, and low academic achievement. Upon questioning, the teacher expressed her belief that Richard was emotionally disturbed and that he should be removed from the regular classroom setting.

Data from classroom observations corroborated the teacher's referral. During instructional periods, Richard was off-task 87 percent of the time. During unstructured recess time, he displayed aggressive behavior an average of every four minutes. Whenever an adult attempted to exercise authority, Richard responded by either denying responsibility or projecting blame. Compliance with adult requests was also charted, with Richard demonstrating compliance approximately 10 percent of the time.

Richard's parents were interviewed to obtain information about his behavior outside of school. They indicated that his behavior at home, in Cub Scouts, and in church was very similar to his behavior at school. However, the parents reported that Richard usually displayed far fewer problem behaviors during organized team sports. A phone call to Richard's soccer coach confirmed the parents' observations. Richard was very athletic and very successful at most sports he tried.

During individual testing, Richard's scores were above average on a standardized test of intelligence. Richard displayed relative strengths in general knowledge and vocabulary. He did very poorly on items involving attention and concentration. Results from an achievement battery were above average in all areas except reading and spelling, which were significantly lower.

Data from personality testing indicated an extremely strong achievement motivation, heightened emotional sensitivity and suspiciousness, low self-esteem, impulsiveness, and mild depression. Richard's test responses also indicated that his emotional security was closely tied to external indicators of success, such as awards and praise. No evidence of severe emotional problems such as sociopathy, thought disorder, or debilitating anxiety was found. Although aggressive themes were common in Richard's responses, they usually surfaced as a reaction to perceptions of frustration or harassment.

Observations, interview data, and test results consistently underscored problems with self-control in the absence of psychopathology; therefore, Richard's teacher and parents were asked to complete a behavior rating scale designed to assess problems associated with attention deficit hyperactivity disorder (ADHD). Richard's scores from both sources indicated extreme levels of hyperactivity, impulsiveness, and distractibility relative to other children his age. These three characteristics are considered the classic triad of symptoms associated with ADHD.

All data just described were presented at a multidisciplinary team meeting attended by Richard's parents and the involved educational personnel. In addition, pertinent information was presented by the school nurse, learning disabilities specialist, school social worker, and speech/language specialist. After discussing all data, the team members agreed upon diagnoses of attention deficit hyperactivity disorder and a learning disability in reading. The team members agreed that because Richard was capable of behaving well under conditions of success (i.e., during soccer) and because personality testing revealed a high achievement motivation coupled with need for external evidence of competence, many of Richard's behavioral and emotional symptoms were secondary to his lack of success in school.

Richard was subsequently placed in a resource room for help with reading. Four short-term interventions also were implemented in order to help Richard decrease impulsive behavior and interact more appropriately with peers: (a) family services consisting of consultation on behavior management issues in the home; (b) behavioral consultation with the regular classroom teacher; (c) individual, cognitive-based therapy to help Richard increase self-control; and (d) placement into a regular education social skills group. Although Richard will likely continue to struggle with problems attendant with ADHD, his school program is now more tailored to his needs, and his teachers and parents are now working together to ensure that he stays on track.

Contributed by Michael C. Kirby, Ph.D., Licensed Psychologist, Mapleton Public Schools, Denver, Colorado.
[1] Selected information in this case study has been altered to preserve confidentiality. The name "Richard" is fictitious.

as E/BD were intelligence tests, direct observation of student behavior, behavior check-lists/rating scales, parent interviews, standardized achievement tests, and student interviews. Anecdotal reports, discipline records, and projective tests were reported as being used "sometimes."

The increased popularity of rating scales to assist in determining behavioral pathology warrants additional mention here. Behavior rating scales are typically completed by teachers or other school personnel familiar with the student whose behavior is to be rated. Items are usually rated on a continuum of frequency or severity, and the rater is asked to compare the student to average or typical students of the same age. In addition to several behavior rating scales that are reviewed in Chapters 3 and 4, two scales have been developed that are based specifically upon the federal definition of emotional disturbance. The Social-Emotional Dimension Scale (SEDS), developed by Hutton and Roberts (1986), is a 32-item scale with 6 factors that relate directly to components of the federal definition: avoidance of peer interaction, avoidance of teacher interaction, aggressive interaction, inappropriate behavior, depressive reaction, and physical/fear reaction. The SEDS total score can be used to identify levels of risk for a student when compared to "typical" children his age.

The Behavior Evaluation Scale-2 (BES-2) (McCarney & Leigh, 1990) is another rating scale based on the federal definition. The BES-2 is composed of 76 items and 5 subscales: learning problems, interpersonal difficulties, inappropriate behavior, unhappiness/depression, and physical fears/symptoms. Problem areas correlating to those outlined in the definition can be identified from the subscales. Components of the federal definition and corresponding subscales from the SEDS and the BES-2 are listed in Table 2-2.

Scores from measures such as these are helpful to the team who must make eligibility decisions for several reasons. First, ratings on the same student from several teachers or school personnel may be obtained, thereby satisfying one requirement for multiple sources of information. Second, when discrepancies occur among these multiple ratings, then assessment personnel can observe and/or interview the individual whose rating was discrepant. Students who pose a problem for only one teacher or only in one class would not be

TABLE 2-2 The Federal Definition and Corresponding Subscales of Behavior Rating Scales

FEDERAL DEFINITION COMPONENTS	SEDS SUBSCALE (HUTTON & ROBERTS, 1986)	BES-2 SUBSCALE (MCCARNEY & LEIGH, 1990)
"inability to learn . . ."		learning problems
"inability to build/maintain satisfactory relationships with teachers and peers"	avoidance of peer interaction avoidance of teacher interaction aggressive interaction	interpersonal difficulties
"inappropriate behavior or feelings under normal circumstances"	inappropriate behavior	inappropriate behavior
"general pervasive mood of unhappiness or depression"	depressive reaction	unhappiness/depression
"tendency to develop physical symptoms or fears . . ."	physical/fear reaction	physical fears/symptoms

considered E/BD. Third, behavior rating scales focus primarily upon observable behavior rather than inferred characteristics, thereby lending some degree of objectivity to the process, although ratings by individuals about other individuals always retain a degree of subjectivity.

Team Decision Making

Eligibility decisions for placement in special education are made by a team composed of educators and other individuals who follow the mandates of federal legislation. The multidisciplinary team must include the parents, the person responsible for assessment, an administrator, an instructional person, and whenever appropriate, the student. Surveys of practices in eligibility decision making indicate that the teams are multidisciplinary in composition and average from five to seven members; individuals most often participating are parents, school administrators, special education teachers, school psychologists, general education teachers, and special education administrators (Gilliam & Coleman, 1981; Thurlow & Ysseldyke, 1980; Ysseldyke & Algozzine, 1982). These surveys also identify some procedural problems in the team decision-making process.

After videotaping more than 30 actual team meetings, Ysseldyke and his colleagues evaluated these meetings thus:

> It was very difficult to find meetings that could be called placement decision-making sessions. Many team meetings were held, but most can be described as meetings to get ready for the meetings to get ready for the meeting. Often, placement decisions were made at the same meetings at which many other kinds of decisions were made. We repeatedly had difficulty attempting to specify decisions that were actually made at meetings because in most instances it was apparent that the decisions were made before the actual meetings took place. We also had difficulty in getting individuals to assume responsibility for the decisions that were made. When we asked people after the meetings, "Who actually made the decision?" nearly all claimed that someone else had been responsible for it and that they, personally, had had little power in the process. We learned to refer to this finding as the "Little Red Hen" phenomenon (When we asked who made decisions, we were consistently told, "Not I!"). (Ysseldyke & Algozzine, 1982, pp. 148–149)

Other difficulties identified by Ysseldyke and his colleagues were minimum participation of general education teachers and lack of congruence between assessment data presented and decisions reached by the teams.

In their survey, Grosenick and her colleagues (Grosenick, George, George, & Lewis, 1991) identified not only the persons but also the factors reported by administrators to be involved in identifying students with emotional/behavioral disorders. Persons most often involved in *eligibility* decisions were special education administrators, parents, and general education administrators; persons making *placement* decisions were E/BD teachers, special education administrators, parents, and general education administrators. According to the survey, the most influential factor in determining both eligibility and placement decisions was the severity of the student's overt behavior and the degree to which that behavior violates normative standards.

Multicultural Considerations

The violation of normative standards as an influential factor in placement decisions is not surprising and is consistent with other research on behavioral deviance. However, it is a cause for concern, especially when considering the relationship between cultural expectations and concepts of deviance. It has been shown that teachers apply different standards or perceptions of ideal behavior to different racial groups (Carlson & Stephens, 1986). Many African Americans and Hispanic Americans have been inappropriately placed in several categories of special education, including classes for students with emotional/behavioral disorders (Park, Pullis, Reilly, & Townsend, 1994). One contributor to inappropriate placement has been the use of culturally biased norm-referenced tests, often in isolation from other important sources of data. Other explanations for misdiagnosis of culturally different students have been cited by Park et al. (1994):

- Lack of understanding by teachers of different learning styles and of the influence of students' cultural backgrounds (Sue, 1988; Sugai, 1988)
- The multiple effects of limited English proficiency on some culturally different students, leading to lower academic performance, lower teacher expectations, and possibly misinterpretation of students' classroom behavior (Argulewicz & Sanchez, 1983)
- Unavailability of instruments needed to assess bilingual students (Ortiz & Maldonado, 1986; Rodriguez, 1988)
- Lack of bilingual special education personnel and appropriate materials (Yee, 1988)
- Development of problem behaviors by culturally different students from inappropriate and frustrating experiences in the classroom

The influence of an individual's cultural background on her behavior and performance in school is pervasive and complex. Sugai (1992) has offered a six-component explanation suggesting that cultural beliefs are primarily transmitted to the child through family values and expectations, family interactions, and child-rearing and management practices of the parents or family unit. He then suggests a number of practical guidelines for assessing whether a culturally different student needs special education services for emotional/behavioral disorders. Included in these guidelines are: (1) use of comprehensive prereferral intervention strategies; (2) a functional analysis of teacher behavior, student behavior, and the setting or context; and (3) examination of the communicative function of behavior, which recognizes that students from culturally different backgrounds may use different behavioral indicators than those expected by the dominant culture. All these suggestions underscore the need to view any student's behavior from within the student's own cultural context.

In summary, the identification procedures of students with emotional/behavioral disorders for special class placement vary from locale to locale, although federal law mandates the general procedures to be followed. The instruments used most often are intelligence tests, behavior ratings/checklists, observations, interviews, and achievement tests. A number of researchers have identified problems with the team decision-making process that is used in special education eligibility and placement decisions. These differences are exacerbated when students from different racial or cultural backgrounds are referred to determine eligibility for E/BD services.

Systematic Screening for Emotional/behavioral Disorders

One promising system that addresses some of the issues inherent in accurate and efficient identification of elementary-aged students with E/BD was developed by Walker and his associates (Walker et al., 1988). This system is a multiple-gating procedure that progressively becomes more time-consuming and precise. It is a three-step procedure. The process begins (Stage 1) by requiring regular education teachers to screen all students in their classrooms on externalizing and internalizing behaviors. In Stage 2, six students who characterize extremes on these two dimensions are targeted for a teacher rating scale that assesses specific critical behaviors as well as frequencies. Students who exceed normative criteria on these scales in Stage 2 are passed on to Stage 3, which requires direct observation of the students in classroom and playground settings. Behaviors targeted for observation are academic-engaged time in the classroom, and amount and quality of social interaction during free time on the playground or during recess. Normative criteria are applied to these observations as a basis upon which to make the final decision about whether the child should then be referred to the multidisciplinary team for a full evaluation. The system is illustrated in Figure 2-1.

This system rectifies some difficulties in the usual identification process. First, it requires teachers to carefully consider all children in their classes and to compare them to a certain set of behaviors rather than nominating a child who is the most personally disturbing. Second, externalizers have historically been identified as emotionally/behaviorally disordered at much higher rates than students who tend toward internalizing. This system insures that socially withdrawn, internalizing children will be considered along with acting out, externalizing children. Third, the system utilizes teacher judgment, which is an underrated and underutilized resource (Walker et al., 1988). Fourth, the multiple-gating procedure provides a comprehensive yet efficient system when compared to usual identification procedures.

The Role of the Special Education Teacher in Identification

The role of the special education teacher in identification varies from school district to school district; it is usually defined by the availability of resources such as administrative and assessment personnel. In some locales, the special education teacher may be involved at all steps of the identification process and may be considered a vital part of the assessment team. In other districts, the special education teacher may be notified that he is receiving a new student—paperwork signed, sealed, and delivered—with no opportunity for any input prior to this notification. According to one survey, special education teachers are involved in screening decisions approximately 48 percent of the time, in placement decisions 85 percent of the time, and in instructional planning 89 percent of the time (Ysseldyke & Algozzine,

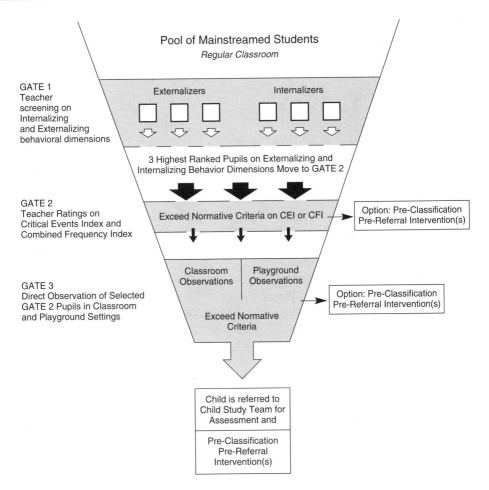

FIGURE 2.1   Systematic Screening for Behavior Disorders

From H. M. Walker et al., (1988). Systematic screening of pupils in the elementary age range at risk for behavior disorders: Development and trial testing of a multiple gating model. *Remedial and Special Evaluation;* 9 (3), 8–14. Reprinted with permission of senior author.

1982). The survey by Grosenick et al. (1992) indicated that teachers of students with emotional/behavioral disorders are often involved in placement decisions after eligibility for placement has been determined. Ideally, the special education teacher should be involved in all three stages of the identification process: during screening, during placement, and certainly during instructional planning. Prior to or upon initial referral, the special education teacher can be a valuable resource to the regular classroom teacher in helping to obtain as much objective data as possible. Possible duties include aiding in behavior observations and behavior recording during class time, helping the teacher develop her own unobtrusive recording system, and making available some of the numerous published checklists and behavior rating scales. Participation in other data-gathering activities may be requested by the evaluator if the student is eventually referred and evaluated.

It is also important for special education teachers to participate in the placement decisions and instructional planning. Data have shown that they do participate in the vast majority of these meetings, and that they are ranked as the most important and influential members by other participants. If these data are a true reflection of practice, then the special education teacher has been assigned a leadership role in the identification process. There are a number of things one can do to prepare for this role: first, become thoroughly aware of one's own personal biases, theoretical orientations, and tolerance levels for certain types of behavior and people; second, be familiar with the specific instruments and measures used for screening and identification; third, have a working knowledge of state and local regulations governing identification procedures; fourth, believe in one's right to voice an opinion among other professionals and have confidence in one's own judgment.

Conclusions

Despite federal regulations that attempt to improve identification procedures, numerous problems continue to plague the field: confusion over terminology and classification systems; inadequacies with the current federal definition; no consensus about what instruments should be used; and unequal participation of team members in the decision-making process. These difficulties are magnified with students from different cultural or racial backgrounds, sometimes resulting in inappropriate referrals and placement. The issue of whether to exclude socially maladjusted students from special education remains controversial, although the professional organization CCBD has spoken for inclusion of these students. On the optimistic side, some positive changes have taken place in identification procedures: the institution of prereferral intervention systems in many districts, availability of multiple-gating procedures such as Walker's systematic screening, and less reliance on projective techniques with more reliance on observational data, interviews, and behavior rating scales from multiple sources.

Key Points

1. Personal and social concepts of deviance determine who gets labeled as E/BD.
2. Terminology used by educators usually differs from that used by mental health professionals, adding to the confusion of the labeling process.
3. The federal definition of emotional disturbance has been adopted by most states but has been roundly criticized as inadequate.
4. Whether to include or exclude students considered socially maladjusted from special education is controversial, with many advocates for including them.
5. The dimensions of chronicity, frequency, and severity should always be considered when determining whether behavior is disordered.
6. The identification regulations provided by most states are very general, resulting in little consistency within or between states in the identification process.
7. Difficulties in identifying students for services for emotional/behavioral disorders

are compounded when students of culturally or racially different backgrounds are referred.

8. Teachers can improve the identification process by offering observational data and information for instructional planning.

Additional Readings

Cultural biases in the identification of students with behavior disorders, by Park, Pullis, Reilly, & Townsend, in Reece Peterson and Sharon Ishii-Jordan (Eds.), *Multicultural issues in the education of students with behavioral disorders,* 1994. Cambridge, MA: Brookline, for a treatise on how understanding or lack of understanding of different cultures can influence perceptions of what is deviant.

Educational assessment of the culturally diverse and behavior disordered student, by George Sugai, in Alba Ortiz and Bruce Ramirez (Eds.), *Schools and the culturally diverse exceptional student,* 1988. Reston, VA: Council for Exceptional Children, for a description of a framework that can be applied to help determine the impact of culture on perceptions of deviance and normalcy.

Implementing a prereferral intervention system: Part I The model, and Part II The data, by J. L. Graden and colleagues, *Exceptional Children, 51,* 1985, for descriptions of how such a system was conceptualized and field-tested in six schools.

Systematic screening of pupils in the elementary age range at risk for behavior disorders: Development and trial testing of a multiple gating model, by Hill M. Walker and colleagues, *RASE, 9,* 1988, for a more detailed description of an innovative screening procedure.

The emotionally disturbed child: Disturbing or disturbed? By B. Algozzine. *Journal of Abnormal Child Psychology, 5,* 1977, for an article on the notion that children's behavior may be more bothersome than pathological.

Who's crazy? II, by C. Michael Nelson. In S. Braaten, R. B. Rutherford, Jr., & C. A. Kardash (Eds.), *Programming for adolescents with behavior disorders.* Reston, VA: Council for Children with Behavior Disorders, 1984, for a treatise on "craziness," which requires the reader to assess self and to question the education process.

Biophysical and Psychodynamic Models

Biophysical Theory:
  Definition and Etiology
  Evaluation Procedures
  Applications

Psychodynamic Theory:
  Definition and Etiology
  Evaluation Procedures
  Educational Applications

Orientation

As a teacher, your personal view of disorders partially determines how you will attempt to instruct and manage students with emotional/behavioral disorders. Before aligning yourself with a particular theoretical model, you should be aware of the alternatives posed by other treatment models. In addition to expanding your range of information and expertise, knowledge of numerous models and techniques enables you to understand and communicate with colleagues and other professionals who are operating from different theoretical bases. The two models presented in this chapter—biophysical and psychodynamic—both view disordered behavior primarily as an internal state of the individual which can be treated either physically or psychologically. Psychiatrists often operate from one or both of these models.

Overview

Although numerous conceptual frameworks have been devised to explain disordered behavior, four major schools of thought seem to prevail: biophysical, psychodynamic, behavioral, and ecological. This chapter and the one that follows provide a descriptive overview of these four models. This chapter covers the biophysical and psychodynamic models, both of which view factors within the child as the primary source of disturbance. Chapter 4 covers the behavioral and ecological models, which view the source of disturbance as the interface of child and environment. Four characteristics of each model will be addressed:

1. Definition and basic view of disturbance[1]
2. Etiology and development of disordered behavior
3. Typical evaluation procedures
4. Educational applications

Biophysical Model

Definition and Basic View

> *The disturbed child is one who because of organic and/or environmental influences, chronically displays: (a) inability to learn at a rate commensurate with his intellectual, sensory-motor and physical development, (b) inability to establish and maintain adequate social relationships, (c) inability to respond appropriately in day to day life situations, and (d) a variety of excessive behavior ranging from hyperactive, impulsive responses to depression and withdrawal. (Haring, 1963, p. 291)*

This definition represents the biophysical view of disordered behavior in its attribution of causality to "organic and/or environmental influences." The biophysical model is basically a medical model that assumes that the problem or pathology lies within the individual. Many advocates of the biophysical viewpoint are from the medical, health, or psychiatric professions who are encouraged by research indicating that many so-called emotional disorders may stem from physiological abnormalities. Some biophysical theorists propose purely biological causes for certain disorders (e.g., autism), whereas other theorists consider the role of a stressful environment in activating dormant biological problems or genetic predispositions (e.g., schizophrenia). In other words, some believe that biological factors rarely operate as constants but depend upon the circumstances under which an individual develops, while others believe that some combination of biological defects ultimately will be found for all mental disorders.

Etiology and Development of Disordered Behavior

Although the research on biological causes of emotional/behavioral disorders is varied and complex, it can be divided into three major categories: *genetic, biochemical/neurological,* and *temperament* factors. Research on the first two factors has been undertaken with more severely impaired populations, primarily autistic and schizophrenic. In this research, children identified as autistic or schizophrenic exhibited many bizarre, repetitive behaviors and were characterized by impaired sensory perception and communication abilities. In fact, characteristics of the syndromes were so similar that much of the literature prior to the 1970s failed to clearly distinguish between the two. It was not until 1977 that a consensual definition of autism was established. Currently, autism is considered a developmental rather than an emotional disorder, and it constitutes a category of special education separate from emotionally/behaviorally disordered.

Although the term *schizophrenia* is currently less often used as a diagnostic term for children, it is still used. The term *pervasive developmental disorder* has become more popular and is sometimes used to describe children with characteristics previously attributed to schizophrenia. Children diagnosed as having schizophrenia or pervasive developmental disorder are included in the federal definition of emotional disturbance. Both of these severely debilitating syndromes will be dealt with in Chapter 10, but possible biophysical causes will be reviewed here.

Genetic Factors

The genetic factor refers to inherited biological characteristics that may cause a predisposition toward disordered behavior. Most of the studies in this area have focused on schizophrenia and have traced prevalence rates among twins and other relatives of diagnosed schizophrenics. A classic study was reported by Kallmann (1956) who followed the biological relatives of all persons with schizophrenia admitted to a hospital during a ten-year period. Follow-up nearly thirty years later indicated that while schizophrenia occurs in about one percent of the population, if one parent were schizophrenic, one-sixth of the offspring were also schizophrenic; if both parents were schizophrenic, more than two-thirds of the offspring were also affected. Similar results were found for siblings, with rates of 85 percent concordance among identical twins, 15 percent among fraternal twins and full siblings, and 7 percent among half-siblings. Other studies of parents (Goldfarb, 1970; Fish & Ritvo, 1979) and siblings (Gottesman & Shields, 1972) have yielded similar results. A more recent study (Gottesman and Shields, 1982) found lower concordance rates, but a similar pattern (42 percent for identical twins versus 9 percent for fraternal twins). Studies of adopted children also suggest a genetic component for some forms of schizophrenia and bipolar depression (Loehlin, Willerman, & Horn, 1988). These and other studies provide strong evidence of a genetic component for schizophrenia. It should be noted that many of these studies dealt with adult schizophrenics and may have limited applicability to childhood onset. However, most authorities currently agree that a predisposing factor may be inherited that renders an individual susceptible to environmental influences. Therefore, both heredity and environment are thought to play interactive roles in the development of schizophrenia.

Biochemical/neurological Factors

Most of the research in this area can be divided into three categories:

- Studies of neurotransmitters, which are chemicals in the brain that relay neural impulses from one neuron to the next
- Organic causes, which are structural abnormalities in the brain and/or unspecified brain dysfunction
- Studies of metabolism, the body's use of chemicals to use and produce energy

Neurotransmitter studies.   Numerous neurotransmitter studies involving the serotonin levels of children with autism have been conducted. Serotonin is a neurotransmitter, a chemical that facilitates transmission of nerve impulses; it is found in minute quantities in the bloodstream where it is carried by platelets. Studies consistently show that children with autism have higher serotonin blood levels and higher platelet counts than children without autism. However, researchers are unsure that the difference is directly related to autism because of methodological problems in the studies (Ritvo, Rahm, Yuwiler, Freeman, & Geller, 1978). They insist that more carefully controlled studies are needed in which subjects are selected according to specific criteria and matched to control for age, racial, and familial factors (Ritvo et al., 1978).

A biochemical cause for schizophrenia also has been suspected for over 100 years, but the exact neurotransmitter has yet to be identified. The neurotransmitter dopamine has been under suspicion due to the reactions of schizophrenics to certain drugs known to affect dopamine activity (i.e., phenothiazines); however, researchers caution that this demonstrated relationship does not prove causality.

Organic causes.   A variety of organic etiologies of autism and schizophrenia have been proposed. Organic causes were posited by Rutter (1965) and Bender (1968) who were pioneers in studying this population of children. Some researchers believe that the autistic child's inability to make associations and establish meaning is neurologically based. Ornitz (1978) has suggested that the vestibular system, which modulates sensory input and motor output "may be responsible for the strange sensorimotor behavior observed in autistic children" (p. 123).

With advanced neuropsychological technology, abnormalities in the brain stem and the cerebellum of youngsters with autism have indeed been found (Ornitz, Atwell, Kaplan, & Westlake, 1985; Ritvo et al., 1986). Based on neuropsychological data, some researchers believe that there is unequivocal evidence for an organic cause of both autism and schizophrenia (Bigler, 1988; Damasio & Maurer, 1978; Dawson, 1983). It should be noted that an organic cause for autism and schizophrenia would not exclude the possibility of neurotransmitter abnormalities; the term *organic* is a more general term that could include a number of specific etiologies, including but not limited to neurotransmitter difficulties. Neurological dysfunction also has been found in patients suffering from depression, indicating a biophysical concomitant of depression that has yet to be specified. As one researcher summarized the state of neuropsychological research into depression, "It seems likely that depressive affect will be found not in one place in the brain, but many. Although this distribution of affective control mechanisms at multiple levels of brain organization causes difficulty for any simple notions of the biology of depression, it also causes the study of depressed affect to be more than the study of an isolated disease process" (D.M. Tucker, 1988, p. 125).

Metabolic factors.   Metabolic factors are proposed by some researchers who believe that schizophrenic, autistic, and other severely disordered children and adults suffer from biochemical disturbances caused by severe vitamin deficiencies (Hoffer & Osmond, 1966; Pauling, 1968; Rimland, 1971). Originally, many researchers claimed that large dosages of vitamin B3 and vitamin C help metabolize adrenaline, which, in pathological cases, can be metabolized by the body into a toxic chemical causing bizarre behaviors. Other researchers reported that behavior of children with autism improved significantly as a function of the amount of vitamin B6 in their diets (Rimland, Callaway, & Dreyfus, 1978). Although proponents are unsure of the specific mechanism through which vitamin therapy works, they remain adamant that it does work.

Whereas studies of vitamin deficiencies and serotonin levels are related to severely disordered behavior, studies of allergies are related to less severe behaviors such as attention deficit hyperactivity disorder (ADHD). The concept of food allergies as a causative factor in ADHD was popularized by Feingold (1975a). Feingold, a pediatric allergist, initially became interested in allergies when treating adverse reactions to aspirin; eventually he and his associates began to suspect widespread allergic reactions to salicylates, a natural compound which is contained in many fruits and which has a structure very similar to aspirin. Combining this hypothesis with known reactions to food additives such as artificial flavors and colorings, Feingold developed a strict diet that he claimed should be successful in alleviating symptoms in "about 50 percent of hyperkinetic-learning disabled children" (1975b, p. 803). The efficacy of both megavitamin therapy and nutrition therapy depends upon alleviation of symptoms. Currently, neither approach can claim undisputed positive results. We will return to a discussion of nutrition therapy later in this chapter.

Allergies to substances other than foods also have been implicated as a causative factor in learning and behavior problems. However, carefully controlled studies by McLoughlin and his colleagues (McLoughlin et al., 1983; McLoughlin, Nall, & Petrosko, 1985) have failed to find differences between allergic and nonallergic students on numerous measures of achievement and behavior.

As with studies on genetic factors, the research on biochemical/neurological factors is promising but not conclusive in determining the etiology of emotional/behavioral disorders. We will return to a more detailed description of efficacy studies in the applications section of biophysical research.

Temperament Factors
Temperament refers to a behavioral style that is an inborn tendency but also highly influenced by the environment. The temperament factor emerges primarily from a longitudinal study begun in 1956 by Thomas, Chess, and Birch. Following a sample of over a hundred children from infancy to adulthood, Thomas and his colleagues (Thomas, Chess, & Birch, 1969; Thomas & Chess, 1977) identified the following nine characteristics of temperament which were stable and endured through maturity: activity level, regularity (of biological functions), adaptability, threshold of responsiveness, intensity of reaction, mood quality, distractibility, persistence, and attention span. From these characteristics, three major patterns of temperament emerged that accounted for 65 percent of the children: (1) *the easy child,* accounting for 40 percent of the sample and characterized by regularity, adaptability, and a positive approach to new stimuli; (2) *the difficult child,* accounting for 10 percent of the sample and characterized by irregularity in biological functions, poor adaptability, and negative and intense moods; and (3) *the slow-to-warm-up child,* accounting for 15 percent of the sample and characterized by a slow but eventually positive adaptability both to change and to new situations. The remaining 35 percent of the sample showed no consistent temperament patterns.

These three categories were not totally predictive of problem behavior. As might be anticipated, the difficult child was more likely to develop problem behaviors, but not all difficult children eventually did so. Thomas and his colleagues believed that with this type of child, interactions between the parent and child were most influential in the development of problem behavior. Parental consistency and pressure toward conformity were especially significant. Moreover, some children characterized as easy or slow-to-warm-up later manifested emotional/behavioral disorders. Overall, the study showed interesting and stable styles of temperament but no clear and indisputable relationship between temperament and eventual problem behavior. Instead, environmental influences such as social pressures and interpersonal relationships were shown to interact with temperament to produce varying results.

The Thomas, Chess, and Birch research was re-evaluated by Buss and Plomin (1985) who concluded that the scales actually measured only two temperament characteristics rather than the nine proposed by the original authors. Buss and Plomin further questioned whether the easy–difficult classification at infancy was predictive of future adjustment, although conceding that temperament ratings at ages four and five do appear to be more reliable. As an alternative schema, Buss and Plomin (1985) propose three aspects of temperament: emotionality, activity, and sociability. Emotionality is the arousal threshold of the infant, especially under conditions of fear or anger. Activity may be loosely defined as the enthusiasm, or vigor and rate at which an infant performs behaviors. Sociability is the tendency to seek the company of others; low sociability connotes a low need to interact rather than shyness, which connotes discomfort or fear in social interactions.

In summary, although there is no agreeement about which schema of temperament most accurately describes and predicts future behavior, most researchers do acknowledge that individuals are born with certain tendencies such as adaptability or intensity; these tendencies can be measured, are stable over time and interact with the environment to produce general patterns of behavior that may be predictable.

Summary of Etiology

Under the biophysical model, disordered behavior is variously attributed to genetic factors, biochemical/neurological irregularities or temperament. Each of these factors has its advocates backed by a body of research; however, none of the advocates can promote definitive conclusions until further research provides clearer answers. Let us now turn our attention to evaluation procedures stemming from the biophysical view.

Typical Evaluation Procedures

Identification of biophysical causes of disorders is usually the domain of medical personnel. Although pediatricians, psychiatrists, and neurologists occupy the central role in making such diagnoses, teachers may be instrumental in detecting potential problems and initiating referrals to medical personnel. In this section, developmental histories and neurological assessment are described.

Developmental Histories

Extensive developmental histories should be a part of evaluations of students manifesting problem behavior because genetic problems, physical trauma, or medical conditions that affect behavior may be revealed. Information on the following conditions which may have influenced the student's physical well-being or development is typically acquired:

1. Prenatal and perinatal conditions: problems or unusual conditions associated with pregnancy or birth
2. Developmental milestones: ages at which the child walked, was toilet trained, talked, and so forth
3. Physical development: severe illness, diseases, or accidents; unusual eating habits, sleep patterns or other behaviors; general activity level
4. Social development: relationships with peers; indications of emotional tension or stress; effective discipline methods and child's reaction to discipline
5. General health: overall physical condition; special health conditions requiring medication; asthma, allergies, diabetes, heart condition
6. Family history: number and age of siblings; divorce and remarriage issues; health or education; problems experienced by parents or siblings; mental health problems of relatives

Experiences that may have caused neurological impairment such as malnutrition, prolonged high fever, severe poisoning, head injuries, or diseases such as meningitis and encephalitis are particularly noteworthy. Since most developmental histories depend on interviews with parents or guardians, school psychologists or other assessment personnel are usually responsible for making this information a part of the student's educational file.

Neurological Assessment
Neurological assessment is an important aspect of biophysical evaluations of disorders because many unusual or bizarre behaviors have neurological bases. Examples are repetitive speech and mannerisms, and overreaction to sensory stimuli such as loud noises or flickering lights. However, neurological assessments are not a routine part of identifying emotional/behavioral disorders in children.

Minimal brain dysfunction, brain damage, and sensorimotor problems are typically diagnosed through some form of neurological testing. Neurological screening is occasionally carried out by trained school assessment personnel, but a neurological evaluation is confined to a neurologist's office. A standard neurological evaluation assesses functioning in the areas of motor skills, coordination, reflexes, mental alertness, sensory discrimination, and integrity of cranial nerves. Except for reflexes, most of these areas are assessed by asking the subject to perform verbal or motor tasks that are quite simple for unimpaired individuals. For example, to check mental alertness, the subject may be asked to demonstrate adequate memory of facts or personal information; to check coordination, the subject may be asked to touch the end of the nose with the index finger; and to check sensory discrimination, the subject may be asked to identify a number being traced in the palm of the hand. If screening measures indicate problems with these or similar tasks, the neurologist may choose to do an electroencephalogram (EEG) or other procedure which sometimes allows the site of dysfunction to be located.

The Halstead-Reitan Battery is a comprehensive neuropsychologic evaluation that assesses cognitive and adaptive ability. It is the best standardized and one of the most widely used batteries of its type. Among its subtests are measures of verbal and nonverbal intelligence, concept formation, expressive and receptive language, auditory perception, time perception, memory, perceptual motor speed, and spatial relations (Strub & Black, 1977). Administration and interpretation of the battery is time-consuming and is limited to trained clinical neuropsychologists.

Another commonly used assessment in this area is the Luria Neuropsychological Investigation. Based upon the work of A.R. Luria, a Russian neuropsychologist, this standardized assessment contains over 260 items covering ten major areas of neuro-psychological functioning, many of which overlap with those of the Reitan. In addition, responses are rated according to accuracy, speed, quality, time lapse, number of trials, or number of responses. Despite its popularity, the Luria has drawbacks in that Luria himself provided no guidelines for standardized administration or interpretation, resulting in few investigations into the reliability and validity of the instrument (C.J. Golden, 1981).

Applications of Biophysical Theory

In the biophysical model, medical interventions are sought when a physiological cause for emotional/behavioral disorders is hypothesized or identified. Medical or health-related personnel are usually responsible for treatment, and the teacher's primary role is observer and monitor of the student's in-school behavior. Two major interventions employed under this model are drug therapy and nutrition therapy. These methods were not developed for exclusive use with individuals with disorders, but each has strong ramifications for behavior change. Both biophysical therapies have been controversial since their introduction to the medical and educational communities. The interested reader is referred to a review article of these and other biophysical therapies by Sieben (1977) and the rebuttal articles by Powers (1977) and Feingold (1977). For the Feingold diet specifically, see Mattes (1983), Kavale and Forness (1983), and a rebuttal by Rimland (1983). A more current review of controlled studies is provided by Pescara-Kovach & Alexander (1994).

Psychopharmacology (Drug Therapy)
Psychopharmacology is the most widely used biophysical intervention. In the recent past, antipsychotic drugs were used to treat schizophrenia and other severe disorders, antidepressants were used to treat major depression, and stimulants were used to treat attention-deficit hyperactivity disorder. However, with the advent of new medications, usage has not been confined strictly to these categories: for example, the newer antidepressants may be used for a variety of childhood problems other than depression. The use of antipsychotics and antidepressants is described in the following paragraphs. The use of stimulant medications with children with ADHD is described in Chapter 6.

The traditional antipsychotics are known by their trade names Haldol, Thorazine, and Prolixin. These drugs work by blocking the neurotransmitter dopamine type 2 receptors in the brain. Although these antipsychotics have been successful in eliminating symptoms such as delusions, hallucinations, and disordered thinking, they have not helped symptoms such as apathy and emotional unresponsiveness. It is estimated that more than 60 percent of patients treated with traditional antipsychotics develop severe motoric side-effects such as rigidity, tremors, spasms, and motor restlessness and agitation (NARSAD Research Newsletter, Summer, 1994). Further, about 20 percent of patients develop tardive dyskinesia, a syndrome of severe tremors, spasms, and motor tics that is potentially irreversible. For this reason, physicians have become increasingly reluctant to prescribe these antipsychotics. Also, this class of antipsychotics does not alleviate symptoms in all persons with schizophrenia.

A new generation of antipsychotics, known as atypical antispychotics, has been developed. Risperdal is the most recently approved, but Clozapine (trade name Clozaril) is the most well-studied of these. It is believed that Clozaril works by blocking a newly discovered dopamine receptor (type 4) in addition to affecting other neurotransmitters. Clozaril may be superior to the traditional antipsychotics in at least two ways. First, the severe motoric side-effects plaguing users of the traditional antipsychotic drugs have not been found with Clozaril, which is particularly important because many schizophrenic patients stop taking their prescribed antipsychotic drugs due to the severity of the side-effects. Second, about one-third of the patients who do not respond to traditional antipsychotics do respond favorably to Clozaril. Despite these advantages, Clozaril is currently used as a last resort because one to two percent of users develop a disorder of the bone marrow that develops quickly, can be lethal, and therefore must be monitored weekly. Therefore, only about 10 percent of those who might benefit from Clozaril are receiving it (Harvard Mental Health Letter, 1992). Researchers who are studying the mechanisms through which Clozaril works are hopeful that they can not only discover other Clozaril-type drugs, but also find a consensus on the key causes of schizophrenia. Although most of the research on antipsychotics has been conducted with adult populations, Clozaril is being tested with children and adolescents, with promising preliminary results (NARSAD Research Newsletter, Spring, 1994).

During hospitalization or residential treatment, medication is often used in conjunction with other interventions such as behavioral programs and therapy. Traditional antipsychotics previously were prescribed for aggression and for stereotypical and self-injurious behavior of children with severe retardation and autism (Gadow, 1986b). However, lithium currently is replacing traditional antipsychotic medications with aggressive and autistic children, and those diagnosed with bipolar disorder.

Antidepressants are another class of drugs that are used with children and adolescents. Antidepressants also act upon neurotransmitters, specifically serotonin and norepinephrine. Although antidepressant drugs have been used effectively with depressed adults since the late fifties, their use with children has been hampered by the question of whether children can experience significant clinical depression. Only recently have professionals agreed that children do in fact experience depression similar to that of adults, characterized by extreme and chronic sadness, withdrawal, changes in appetite and weight, loss of energy, and other behavioral fluctuations.

Antidepressants are now commonly prescribed for depressed children. Previously, the tricyclic compound imipramine (trade name Tofranil) was the most often prescribed antidepressant with children. However, due to the side effects of Tofranil such as possible cardiovascular problems and accidental poisoning from overdosing, Prozac and similar drugs (Zoloft and Paxil) acting upon serotonin are now more commonly used. Welbutrin is also gaining favor because it has no cardiotoxic side-effects. In addition to depression, antidepressants may be prescribed for other childhood problems such as attention-deficit hyperactivity disorder, anxiety, school phobia, and eating disorders.

Nutrition Therapy

The concept of food allergies and the Feingold diet were alluded to in the section on etiology. The Feingold diet (Feingold, 1975b) initially eliminates all foods with the preservatives BHT and BHA, artificial colors and flavorings, and natural salicylates. Among the seemingly nutritious foods containing salicylates are apples, peaches, berries, tomatoes, oranges, grapes, and raisins. Other forbidden items are toothpaste, mouthwash, throat lozenges, cough drops, perfume, and most over-the-counter drugs such as aspirin. After a period of time, some of the foods containing salicylates are reintroduced one by one to check whether there is an adverse reaction. Many children can resume eating these foods, but the artificial additives are never reinstated in the diet. Although Feingold claimed success for only a moderate percentage of ADHD children, the diet received an inordinate amount of publicity because parents often reported dramatic behavior changes and established the Feingold Association, a national network of parents that in 1980 had over 50,000 members.

Research supportive of the diet is reported by Feingold (1975a), Rapp (1978), and T. Rose (1978), and cited by Spring and Sandoval (1976). Some skeptics suggest that reported positive changes are likely the result of placebo effects (Baker, 1980) or increased positive expectations. Others who have reviewed the research supportive of the Feingold diet caution that it is based largely on anecdotal information rather than on well-designed studies with large populations (Myers & Hammill, 1990; Sieben, 1977). Pescara-Kovach and Alexander (1994) reviewed a number of controlled, double-blind studies and concluded thus:

> Though Feingold's research demonstrated his concern for the children's well-being, no absolute or concurrent evidence has emerged in favor of the link between food ingested and adverse behavior. In fact, much of the evidence suggests the contrary. Recent research continues to challenge the link between food additives and behavior. (p. 145)

As with stimulant medication, if undertaken, the Feingold diet should be supervised by competent medical personnel.

Teachers' Role

Biophysical interventions require the services of specialists: physicians, allergists, neurologists, and others. The role of the teacher may initially appear to be restricted to making a referral and following up contacts with the specialists. Although these tasks are important, it is also essential that the teacher help monitor the classroom behavior of a child on medication or on a specialized diet. In order to modify the intervention effectively, the specialist needs both anecdotal and systematic observations from the classroom. Medications are often started on a trial basis, with the dosage too high or too low because physicians cannot predict exactly how a dosage will affect any given child. Fluctuations in behavior as well as symptoms of side effects should be reported both to parents and to the specialist. (If no specific information on side effects is offered to the teacher, he should request it so he will be knowledgeable of what to look for). Often the concerned teacher must take the initiative to maintain contact with specialists such as physicians. There is no substitute for the information a teacher can glean from observing the child on a daily basis in the classroom!

The teacher also can help parents by providing materials on the pros and cons of some of the questionable therapies that may not be standard practice in the medical community. G. Golden (1980) offers guidelines to help parents and teachers identify and critique nonstandard therapies:

1. They are reportedly based on biochemical or neurophysiologic theories that are incongruent with current concepts of the central nervous system.

2. They are said to be absolutely harmless.

3. The children with whom they are supposedly effective are a broad, ill-defined group.

4. The studies cited as supportive research are usually anecdotal and testimonial rather than well-controlled experimental studies.

5. The therapies have an emotional appeal, and their detractors are attacked defensively.

Sieben (1983) goes on to point out that nonstandard therapies may become popular through the media. For example, the author of a new book on a nonstandard therapy may get immediate nationwide coverage on television (e.g., on "Donahue" or "Oprah") or the lecture circuit and therefore become an instant expert without subjecting her theory to peer review or rebuttal.

Parents and teachers would be wise to question any therapies designed to correct learning and behavior problems that exhibit several of these characteristics.

Summary of the Biophysical Model

The biophysical model assumes that there are organic causes of emotional disturbance which can be treated medically or physically. Etiological theories, evaluation procedures, and intervention strategies are summarized in Table 3-1. The research on causative factors is promising but quite inconclusive. Such biophysical interventions as drug therapy and nutrition therapy remain controversial.

The teacher's role is viewed as a liaison to specialists and a daily monitor of the intervention prescribed. Teachers may also provide information to parents regarding advantages and disadvantages of biophysical therapies.

Psychodynamic Model

Definition and Basic View

> *The emotionally disturbed child . . . is so thwarted in satisfaction of his needs for safety, affection, acceptance, and self-esteem that he is unable intellectually to function efficiently, cannot adapt to reasonable requirements of social regulation and convention, or is so plagued with inner conflict, anxiety, and guilt that he is unable to perceive reality clearly or meet the ordinary demands of the environment in which he lives. (Blackham, 1967, p. 73)*

TABLE 3-1   Summary of Biophysical Model

ETIOLOGICAL FACTORS	EVALUATION PROCEDURES
genetic	developmental histories
biochemical/neurological	neurological assessment
temperament	

APPLICATIONS

psychopharmacology (drug therapy)
nutrition therapy (Feingold diet)

The references to "thwarted . . . needs for safety, affection, acceptance, and self-esteem" and the terms "inner conflict, anxiety, and guilt" give this definition a psychodynamic orientation. Psychodynamic theorists are concerned with the needs of the individual. Conflict, anxiety, and guilt also are prime concerns of these theorists, especially psychoanalysts who believe that any of these states may serve as catalysts for personality development. In line with these concerns, evaluation techniques of the psychodynamic model focus on unconscious drives, needs, anxiety, guilt, and conflict. The psychodynamic model is a conglomerate of theories that attempts to explain motivation of human behavior. Falling under this model are the diverse theories of psychoanalysis, ego psychology, phenomenology, Gestalt psychology, and humanistic psychology. Freud's theory of psychoanalytic psychology is the seminal work from which the other branches of psychodynamic thought have emerged. Although arguments may be made for treatment of each of these views as separate and distinct, in this text *psychodynamic* is a broad descriptor that encompasses the other views. Psychodynamic theory will be discussed as two major schools of thought: *psychoanalytic thought* as espoused by Freud and the neo-Freudians Horney and Erikson, and *humanistic thought* as espoused by Rogers and Maslow.

Psychoanalytic thought is unique among psychodynamic theories in its emphasis on unconscious drives that may conflict with conscious desires and thus cause disorders; in contrast, other theories emphasize conscious experiences such as the individual's perception of the environment. In addition, psychoanalytic thought stresses a "predetermined sequence of personality growth" (Rezmierski & Kotre, 1974); that is, there are specific stages through which an individual passes in normal progress to adulthood. Psychoanalysts believe that emotional health depends upon the successful resolution of the conflicts arising during these developmental stages and that disordered emotions and behaviors arise when these conflicts are not resolved. Some humanistic theorists do not share this concept of the importance of sequential developmental stages; rather, they emphasize the importance of self-perception and self-understanding at all stages. Although it is difficult to promote a singular view of psychodynamic theory, a few commonalities may be extracted. The most basic commonality is implied by the definition of the term *psychodynamic,* which literally means the "dynamics of mental activities and processes." All theorists ascribing to the psychodynamic view are concerned about the process of development and change. A second commonality is that anxiety and emotional crises are important motivators of personal growth and self-development. A third commonality is that significant individuals in one's early life play important roles as catalysts or deterrents of personality growth and healthy development. The fourth common concept is the emphasis on intrapsychic reckonings of the individual. Although many psychodynamic theorists recognize the role of the environment in personality development, it is nonetheless the individual's internal perceptions and feelings about that environment—whether conscious or unconscious—that are the focus of intervention.

Etiology and Development of Disordered Behavior

Psychoanalytic Theory: Freud

Sigmund Freud (1856–1939) was a physician whose fascination with the emotional problems of his patients led him to develop a new branch of psychological theory. In addition to being a physician, he was a psychologist, philosopher, scientist, critic, and psychoanalyst. Born in Freiberg in the former Czechoslovakia, Freud moved to Vienna when he was three years old and left when the Nazis entered the city in 1938.

According to Freud, the personality has three major systems of psychic energy, the *id,* the *ego,* and the *superego;* behavior is the result of an interaction among these three systems. The id is the original system that is present at birth and furnishes psychic energy for the other two systems. In other words, the ego is differentiated out of the id, and the superego is differentiated out of the ego. The id represents the inner world of subjective experience and has no knowledge of objective reality. It operates to reduce tension in the organism, that is, to avoid pain and to obtain pleasure; it is said to operate by the *pleasure principle.* The ego develops out of a need to temper the subjective view of the id with the objective world of reality; it is the part of the id that has been modified by the external world. It obeys the *reality principle,* which is characterized by logical and rational thinking. The ego is called the executive of the personality because it controls action by mediating between the real environment and the demands of the id.

The *superego* represents the moral standards imposed upon a child by society, which are enforced by parents and other societal agents. The superego has two aspects: the positive *(ego ideal)* which rewards, and the negative *(conscience)* which punishes. The superego represents the ideal and strives towards perfection. Freud also developed the term *psychic energy* to connote mental activity. He believed that this psychic energy is fluid and is never lost or diminished, but that dynamics of personality are determined by its distribution among the three systems of the id, ego, and superego.

Defense mechanisms are a function of the ego employed to ward off threatening demands of the id and to relieve anxiety. Defense mechanisms are not inherently pathological; in fact, they are used by well-adjusted, mature adults. However, when used excessively, defense mechanisms become debilitating to the personality. They operate unconsciously and deny or distort reality so that the individual is unaware of internal conflict. The principal defense mechanisms are presented in Table 3-2.

Freud postulated five stages of psychosexual development through which a child passes from infancy through adolescence: (1) the *oral stage,* birth to two years of age; (2) the *anal stage,* two to four years; (3) the *phallic stage,* four to six years; (4) the *latency period,* six until puberty; and (5) the *genital stage,* occurring at puberty. The implications of these stages for disordered behavior are based on two of Freud's premises. The first is that the first few years of life determine the formation of personality. The

TABLE 3-2   **Principal Defense Mechanisms of the Ego**

I. Repression—	forcing alarming thoughts or feelings from conscious awareness
II. Projection—	attributing causes of negative impulses or feelings to the external world rather than to oneself
III. Reaction–Formation—	adopting the behavior or attitude opposite to what one really feels
IV. Fixation—	failing to pass into the next stage of psychosexual development
V. Regression—	retreating to an earlier stage of psychosexual development or temporary flight from controlled and realistic thinking

Adapted from Hall (1954), and Hall and Lindzey (1970).

second premise is that abnormal personality development is due to fixations or arrests at specific stages of psychosexual development. A person may become fixated at a stage for a number of reasons, including excessive gratification, excessive deprivation, fear of transition to the next stage, and physical and psychological factors. It is possible for the personality to be arrested in only one developmental area while progressing normally through the remainder of the stages. Examples of adjustment problems resulting from pathological fixations are outlined in Table 3-3.

In summary, Freud viewed abnormal behavior or disordered behavior as arising from the inability to resolve a conflict within a specific psychosexual stage. In his view, when an individual becomes fixated at a given stage, personal adjustment in that area becomes very difficult and the majority of the individual's interpersonal interactions become a replay of the difficulties encountered during that stage.

Neo-Freudian Theory: Horney and Erikson

Karen Horney (1885–1952) was a proponent of neo-Freudian social theory. Along with Harry Stack Sullivan and Erich Fromm, she downplayed Freud's biological orientation and emphasized social factors in the development of abnormal behavior. Central to Horney's theory is anxiety, which stems from a child's feelings of isolation and help-

TABLE 3-3   **Adjustment Problems Based on Fixations at Psychosexual Stages**

I. Oral stage (birth to two years)	Sarcasm, argumentativeness, greediness, acquisitiveness, overly dependent
II. Anal stage (two to four years)	Emotional outbursts such as rages and temper tantrums; compulsive orderliness and overcontrolled behavior
III. Phallic stage (four to six years)	Problems with gender identification
IV. Genital stage (puberty to adulthood)	Narcissism or extreme self-love

Adapted from Hall (1954).

lessness in a world which may be perceived by the child as hostile. A child has a basic need for security which must be supplied by significant others in the child's life through warmth, support, and affection.

According to Horney, as a child struggles with anxiety and the security issue, various behavioral strategies may be tried and eventually a character pattern will be adopted. Horney postulated three such character patterns: (1) moving toward people, characterized by compliance, submissive behavior, and a need for love; (2) moving against people, characterized by arrogance, hostility, and a need for power; and (3) moving away from people, characterized by social avoidance, withdrawal, and a need for independence (Horney, 1937). Emotional and behavioral disorders are viewed as the adoption of one of these rigid patterns to the exclusion of the others, which results in inflexible interpersonal interactions. A basic conflict is experienced by individuals who have adopted a rigid character pattern; such individuals experience severe anxiety when called upon to interact in a manner contrary to the adopted pattern. For example, the person characterized by arrogance and hostility may have a difficult time in giving and receiving affection and warmth. Although healthy people occasionally experience such conflicts, the neurotic person, due to lack of a supportive environment early in life, faces such conflicts on a daily basis. Horney believed that such conflict is avoidable and resolvable if a child is reared in an atmosphere of security, warmth, love, trust, and respect.

Erik Erikson joined theorists such as Anna Freud and Heinz Hartmann in a new conceptualization of the role of the ego in personality development. These theorists view the ego not as an extension of the id, but as autonomous both in origin and function. In other words, the ego is not a passive mediator but an active force with its own energy source. The environment and societal values are central to this new view of the ego, a view that resulted in "the addition of an entire social and cultural dimension to the concept of personality growth" (Rezmierski & Kotre, 1974, p. 209).

Erikson's contribution to the understanding of disordered behavior centers around his concepts of crisis and the importance of crisis resolution during critical periods of development. Erikson proposes eight stages of psychosocial development that roughly parallel Freud's stages of psychosexual development; as implied by the different terminology, Erikson's stages focus on character traits that arise from interpersonal interactions, whereas Freud's stages emphasize character traits arising from experience of a biological or sexual nature. According to Erikson, if the crisis in each stage is not dealt with successfully, the individual will continue to demonstrate behaviors commensurate with that stage, which may be several years below the individual's mental and physical development. Thus, Erikson stresses the developmental nature of personality growth. He further cautions that the successful resolution of a crisis is not a permanent achievement; instead, healthy adults continue to struggle with the issues on a superficial level throughout life. Table 3-4 presents the five psychosocial stages most pertinent to school ages along with adjustment problems stemming from inadequate resolution.

Humanistic Theory: Rogers and Maslow

Carl Rogers and Abraham Maslow share the basic view that human beings are inherently good and capable of actualizing their potential if they can somehow avoid the frustrating and detrimental experiences imposed by society. Rogers asserts that behavior may be

TABLE 3-4   Erikson's Psychosocial Stages

DEVELOPMENTAL PHASE	PSYCHOSOCIAL STAGE	RELATED ADJUSTMENT PROBLEMS
I. Infancy	Trust vs. mistrust	Mistrust of others
II. Early Childhood (age 1-3)	Autonomy vs. shame and doubt	Doubt in oneself and mistrust in environment
III. Play Age (age 3-5)	Initiative vs. guilt	Overdeveloped conscience which prevents independent action; excessive guilt
IV. School Age (age 5-10)	Industry vs. inferiority	Doubt in one's ability to perform adequately for society; feelings of inferiority and inadequacy
V. Adolescence	Identity vs. identity diffusion	Doubt about one's sexual, ethnic, or occupational identity

Adapted from E. H. Erikson (1959).

understood only in terms of the individual's frame of reference, that is, one's personal experiences and perceptions of the world. In order to understand the development of conflict in an individual's world, Rogers (1959) proposes two concepts. The first is the organismic valuing process, which develops from infancy and refers to a regulatory system that tells the infant (organism) how well it is satisfying basic needs. This valuing process leads the infant to select, inasmuch as possible, those experiences that will be positive and enhance the organism, and to avoid experiences that will be negative and debilitating. Thus there exists an innate wisdom for preservation and actualization.

As the infant grows, experiences become differentiated between environment and self, and the young child formulates a concept of the self. As the self-concept emerges, so does a need for positive regard, a universal need for acceptance and respect. The need for positive regard then motivates the developing person to judge personal actions in terms of societal values. Conflict arises when the innate criteria clash with societal values so that the person is torn between the organismic valuing process and the need for positive regard. As Rogers states, disturbance or maladjustment occurs when there is "an incongruence between self and experience" (1959). This incongruence is then usually dealt with either by distortion or denial of the experience. If these strategies fail, a serious breakdown of the self-concept may occur and the individual experiences disorganization characterized by irrational or psychotic behaviors.

Rogers proposes that incongruence can be avoided in an ideal course of development in which the infant receives only unconditional positive regard from the parents. In applying his theory to education, Rogers (1969) states that learning should be self-initiated and congruent with personal experience. The classroom should offer a climate for experiential learning, and the teacher should facilitate the learning process.

Maslow did not address emotional/behavioral disorders in depth, but his theory of human needs and motivation provides a model of health and creativity that has been widely accepted by both psychologists and educators. Maslow (1967) differentiates between basic needs, which are deficiency needs, and meta-needs, which are growth needs. The basic needs of safety, hunger, affection, security, and self-esteem are hierarchical: lower ones must be satisfied by the individual before the higher ones can be attained. Meta-needs such as justice, goodness, beauty, and unity are equally important and are not hierarchical. According to Maslow, only a very few select persons are able to realize and internalize the meta-needs; these self-actualized people are characterized by autonomy, spontaneity, democratic values, creativity, and a resistance to conformity. They are able to transcend rather than tolerate the environment, which is the final step in becoming fully human. Although his theory concentrates on the healthy, self-actualizing being, Maslow does eloquently address disordered behavior:

> *. . . it is now seen clearly that psychopathology in general results from the denial or the frustration or the twisting of man's essential nature. By this conception what is good? Anything that conduces to this desirable development in the direction of actualization of the inner nature of man. What is pathological? Anything that disturbs or frustrates or twists the course of self-actualization. What is psychotherapy, or for that matter any therapy of any kind? Any means of any kind that helps to restore the person to the path of self-actualization and of development along the lines that his inner nature dictates. (Maslow, 1954, pp. 340–341)*

The Psychodynamic Goal: Healthy Development

Although it is difficult to distinguish a singular psychodynamic view of the etiology of problem behavior, it is not difficult to perceive a singular psychodynamic goal of intervention, namely, healthy development. The process by which this goal is attained may be determined largely by variables inherent in the individual, but psychodynamic theorists agree that six basic characteristics are common in development of a healthy personality:

1. *Attitude toward self*—a realistic view of self, including self-esteem
2. *Resistance to stress*—an ability to cope successfully with crises and stressful situations
3. *Autonomy and independence*—a sense of active participation in and partial control of one's life
4. *Interpersonal relations*—awareness and acceptance of others' needs and an ability to establish meaningful relationships with other people
5. *Curiosity, creativity, expressiveness*—the most positive aspects of human potential which find expression when individuals are nurtured rather than frustrated
6. *Cognitive and language skills*—skills necessary for making sense of the world and for successful interaction in an educational environment (Cheney & Morse, 1974).

These characteristics form the basis for psychodynamic interventions, which will be addressed after evaluation procedures are discussed.

Typical Evaluation Procedures

Psychodynamic theory is rich in evaluative instruments such as projective and self-concept measures. Historically, these techniques were liberally used in batteries to identify students with emotional or behavioral disorders, although now they are less commonly used than more objective measures such as direct observations and behavior rating scales. However, projectives may still be widely used as diagnostic tools for individuals in psychotherapy.

Projectives

Projective techniques are based on the premise that, when given a neutral or ambiguous stimulus, a person will project unconscious as well as conscious feelings onto the stimulus. Projectives

> *tend to solicit rich material, depicting the child's perceptions and interpretations of reality. As the child imposes his own cognitive scheme on stimulus materials, he tends to reveal inner thoughts, feelings and attitudes about various aspects of his world. Such tests enable the examiner to secure material which is unobtainable through other means . . . to get at data which the child might guard against revealing, were he asked directly. (Sigel, 1960, p. 360)*

The psychoanalytic premise is that information obtained from projectives comes largely from the subconscious and is therefore untappable by more direct means. As projective techniques draw upon unconscious perceptions of reality, they are less susceptible to intentional distortion or faking. However, this necessary ambiguity and lack of structure also undermines their technical adequacy in that reliability and validity data are very difficult to establish.

Projective instruments are widely used with adults in clinical settings. In their use with children, a developmental factor emerges that adds to the complexity of interpretation. A diagnostic evaluation of *abnormal* child development depends upon the concept of *normal* child development—a loosely defined concept. A child may reveal perceptions of distorted reality due to limited exposure and experience, lack of knowledge, or limited language skills. Therefore the clinician must distinguish between responses which are immature and those which are deviant. Characteristics of the child that must be considered are socioeconomic status, sex, intellectual ability, verbal facility, and fantasy skill (Sigel, 1960). Projective techniques may take the form of elicited drawings, verbal responses to inkblots and pictures, and written responses to sentence stems. Those most commonly used with children will be described.

Rorschach Inkblot Test.   The Rorschach (Rorschach, 1921) consists of ten cards, each containing a symmetrical inkblot; five are black-and-white and five contain color. The cards are presented one by one to the examinee who gives a spontaneous impression of what is seen; the examiner may then start over with the first card and ask which features were most important upon initial impression. Responses are scored according to several categories: which aspects of the blot determined the response (form, movement, color, shading); where the determinant was located; whether the response was human, animal, or inanimate;

whether the response was common or original, and so forth. The number of responses in each category are analyzed to form one basis for conclusions. For example, a high number of color responses is thought to indicate emotionality, and a high number of movement responses is thought to indicate imagination. Analysis of responses for broad categories of information such as reality awareness, self-concept, emotionality, and coping mechanisms may be helpful in personality assessment of children (Halpern, 1960).

Children's Apperception Test (CAT).   The CAT (Bellak & Bellak, 1949) is a series of ten plates, each depicting animal characters. The examinee is shown the pictures one at a time and asked to relate a story about each. The CAT is designed for use with children of ages three to ten and is based on three propositions: (1) that projective techniques allow clinicians to make inferences about personality features; (2) that the animal scenes depicting activities of eating, sleeping, toileting, and punishment are especially relevant to children and thus will elicit accurate information about the way they handle such daily activities in their own lives; and (3) that children would more readily relate to and identify with animals than human figures (Bellak & Adelman, 1960). Children's responses are analyzed for thematic content or commonalities within ten categories: main theme, main hero, main needs of the hero, conception of the environment, view of other figures, significant conflicts, nature of anxieties, main defenses, severity of the superego, and integration of the ego. Interpretation is obviously psychoanalytic in nature, as needs, conflict, anxiety, and guilt are heavily weighted. Two similar measures are sometimes used with children: the *Thematic Apperception Test* (TAT, H.A. Murray, 1943), a technique using pictures of adults and designed for use with adults, and the *Education Apperception Test* (EAT, Thompson & Sones, 1973), which depicts only scenes related to school and achievement.

Sentence completions.   An expanded version of the word association technique, sentence completions consist of sentence stems the examinee is asked to complete. They are commonly used in personality assessment because of the relative ease of administration and interpretation; they may supply the clinician with much information in a short time. Although commercially produced sentence-completion instruments are available, many psychologists develop their own informal measures. Item content is usually aimed at obtaining information about such issues as anxiety, coping skills, and attitudes toward authority figures, siblings, parents, teachers, peers, and schoolwork. Sentence completion measures are generally

TABLE 3-5   A Sampling of Sentence Completion Stems

1. When I can't do something in school, I
2. Most kids in my class think I am
3. I wish my father would
4. When I read out loud, I
5. My greatest fear is
6. My teacher makes me feel
7. I am good at
8. When I get worried, I
9. I wish my mother wouldn't
10. I am happiest when

designed to tap the same areas covered by other projectives, but the clinical interpretation is even less structured and therefore more dependent on the interpreter. Sample sentence stems are presented in Table 3-5 on page 61.

Human figure drawings.   The value of children's drawings in personality assessment lies in the assumption that spontaneous drawings may reveal information that is not distorted by difficulty with language or writing skills nor by deliberate falsification. Many psychologists believe that "drawings speak louder than words," especially in the early developmental stages (Klepsch & Logie, 1982). In addition, drawings are readily obtained, as most children enjoy drawing and do not resist the task. Klepsch and Logie (1982) outline four major projective uses for children's human figure drawings: a measure of personality, a measure of self in relation to others (group drawings), a measure of group values (of racial, cultural, or ethnic groups), and a measure of attitude toward others (drawing teachers or parents, for example). Human figure drawings have also been used to assess a child's developmental status or intellectual ability. Scoring systems for estimating intelligence from figure drawings have been developed by Harris (1963) and by Koppitz (1968).

Test administration consists of presenting the child with a white, unlined sheet of paper and the general directions to "Draw a person, a whole person, not a stick figure or cartoon." No additional directions other than encouragement are given. The drawing may then be scored by a system such as the one used by Koppitz (1968). The 30 emotional indicators in this system fall into one of three categories: (1) items relating to the quality of the drawing, such as size, integration, and symmetry; (2) unusual features such as teeth, crossed eyes, big hands, or monsterlike quality; or (3) omission of essential features such as eyes, mouth, nose, neck, arms, or legs (Klepsch & Logie, 1982). Presence of two or more indicators is considered suggestive of emotional/behavioral disorders. Koppitz also believes that the following three principles are useful in clinical interpretation of human figure drawings in children ages 5-12:

- Regardless of who is drawn, the drawing is a self-portrait and therefore indicative of self-concept.
- The person who is drawn is the person of greatest importance in the child's life at that time.
- Interpretation of the drawing may be twofold, for it may represent actual attitudes and conflicts or wishes (Koppitz, 1968).

Most clinicians do not use drawings as a basis upon which to diagnose emotional/behavioral disorders; rather, they use drawings to formulate hypotheses about emotional issues or conflicts that the child may be unable to verbalize. Such hypotheses may then be confirmed or disconfirmed upon obtaining further information from the child, parents, and possibly teachers. Box 3-1 illustrates how the drawings in Figures 3-1 and 3-2 were used.

Projective techniques are given a critical review by Anastasi (1988), who cites the following points:

1. As a group, projectives make a poor showing when evaluated for technical adequacy, yet they continue to be popular clinical instruments.

BOX 3-1　Interpretation of Human Figure Drawings

Figures 3-1 and 3-2 are the human figure drawings of two boys only three months apart in age. Both were referred for evaluations due to learning problems.

The artist of Figure 3-1 was 7 years, 10 months old and had been retained in first grade due to overall low achievement. He obtained an IQ score of 81 on the Wechsler Intelligence Scale for Children-Revised (WISC-R). He was described as well-behaved and a good kid who always tried hard. His developmental score for the drawing was a little lower than his IQ, and there were three emotional indicators (according to Koppitz' system): poor integration of body parts, transparencies, and hands bigger than the face of the figure. Implications: obtain other drawings now for comparison purposes, obtain other drawings in the future and watch for improvement, explore the child's feelings with him by talking with him and through other self-report measures, explore with teachers and parents their observations about possible emotional difficulties.

Figure 3-2 was drawn by a boy who was 8 years, 1 month old. His IQ as measured by the WISC-R was 111. Although average in math and considered bright by his parents and teachers, he experienced severe reading problems. He was sociable, likable, and described by parents as the negotiator in the family. While his human figure drawing was much more sophisticated than Figure 3-1 and therefore did not reflect abnormal scores according to either the developmental system or the emotional indicators system, it did depict an aggressive incident. Themes of overt aggression were also evident in all three of the other drawings he was asked to complete. His answers to all self-report measures were very appropriate and well within normal ranges; however, the theme of aggression in all four pictures was cause for concern.

Implications: Talk with the child about what was happening in the pictures and why; share concerns with the parents; refer for psychological testing to explore whether the pictures represent harmless fantasy or other issues that need attention.

---

2. The majority of projectives have questionable theoretical rationale and do not meet test standards.

3. Standardization of administration and scoring procedures, adequacy of norms, reliability and validity are all questionable.

4. The validity of the Rorschach Inkblot Test and Human Figure Drawing are particularly suspect.

5. The final interpretation of a projective test may reveal more about background, training, and personal orientation of the examiner than the personality of the examinee.

Anastasi concludes that projectives may best be viewed not as tests but as clinical tools that can provide supplemental information as an interviewing technique. The implications drawn from the drawings in Box 3-1 illustrate this process with Human Figure Drawings.

Self-Report Measures

How one views oneself in relation to others and the environment is a main concern of psychodynamic theorists; thus the construct of self-concept has generated much interest. Although implicit indicators of self-concept may be obtained from projective measures, some instruments have been devised explicitly for this purpose. Two examples are *The Piers-Harris Children's Self-Concept Scale* (Piers & Harris, 1969) and *The Self-Perception Profile for*

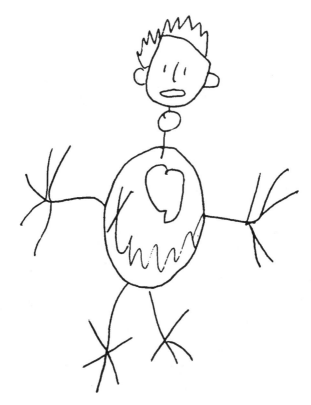

FIGURE 3-1 Human Figure Drawing by Seven-Year-Old Boy

Children (Harter, 1985). The Piers-Harris consists of 80 descriptive items to be answered "Yes" or "No," and six factors: behavior, school status, physical appearance, anxiety, popularity, and happiness. Percentile ranks are available for each of these factors as well as overall self-concept. *The Self-Perception Profile* has 36 items to be rated on a 4-point scale which yields five domains plus general self-esteem: scholastic competence, athletic competence, social acceptance, physical appearance, and behavioral conduct. Harter also asks the respondent to rank the importance of each domain. She maintains that self-concept can vary according to different domains, and further, that a person's poor performance in a domain will only affect self-concept if that domain is important to the person.

Another self-report measure for children and adolescents is the *Index of Personality Characteristics* (IPC; Brown & Coleman, 1988). Although it contains a self-concept subscale, the *IPC* is more comprehensive in scope in that it assesses the child's perceptions of self across four major dimensions: behaviors in academic versus nonacademic settings; perception of self versus perception of others; acting in versus acting out; and internal locus of control versus external locus of control. There are 75 items to which the student responds on a continuum of "Almost always like me" to "Almost never like me." Standard scores are given for each of the eight subscales as well as an overall quotient. The authors emphasize that the *IPC* is to be used as a screening measure rather than an in-depth diagnostic tool.

FIGURE 3-2 Human Figure Drawing by Eight-Year-Old

Sample items are given in Table 3-6. A comparison between these items and those sentence stems listed in Table 3-5 illustrates the more structured nature of measures such as the *IPC* and the open-ended nature of sentence completions.

In summary, a psychologist using psychodynamic techniques might employ projective stimuli such as inkblots or picture cards, or may analyze the child's own drawings. Sentence completions and other self-report measures are also liberally used by psychodynamic psychologists to obtain the child's own perception of his world.

Educational Application

Psychoanalytic theorists had an impact on education in the early part of the twentieth century, as conformity in the classroom came to be viewed by some educators as detrimental to the child's natural development. Educational practices reflecting a more permissive philosophy resulted.

By mid-century, the psychodynamic view had moderated, but the basic tenets remained unchanged. Psychodynamic theorists generally agree that the educational process should be less repressive, more facilitative of emotional expression, and more sensitive to crises

TABLE 3-6   Sample Items from the Index of Personality Characteristics

IPC	Student's Name _____		
Index of Personality Characteristics	School _____		
	Teacher_____		

		Year	Month
Student Response Booklet			
Linda Brown	Date of IPC Testing	_____	_____
Margaret C. Coleman	Student's Date of Birth	_____	_____
	Student's Age at Testing	_____	_____

INSTRUCTIONS

Here is a list of sentences that describe some of the things that students do, and the way that students sometimes feel. Some of these sentences will describe you very well. Others will not describe you at all. If you think a sentence tells something that is *almost always* true of you, fill in the circle or square under ALMOST ALWAYS LIKE ME. If the sentence tells something that is *sometimes* true of you, fill in the circle or square under USUALLY LIKE ME. If the sentence tells something that *usually is not true* of you, fill in the circle or square under USUALLY NOT LIKE ME. If the sentence tells something that is *almost never true* of the way you act or the way you feel, fill in the circle or square under ALMOST NEVER LIKE ME.

	ALMOST ALWAYS LIKE ME	USUALLY LIKE ME	USUALLY NOT LIKE ME	ALMOST NEVER LIKE ME
1. I do good work in school.	○	○	○	○
2. I used to run away from my problems, but now I'm trying to work on them.	○	○	○	○
3. I have run away from home.	❏	❏	❏	❏
4. Most teachers treat me fairly and honestly at school.	○	○	○	○
5. When I'm talking to people, I look at the floor or the ceiling instead of looking at them directly.	❏	❏	❏	❏
6. I sometimes think of things too bad to talk about.	❏	❏	❏	❏
7. When I am punished at school, it's usually because I have been cutting up.	○	○	○	○
8. I get into a lot of trouble at school, but it isn't my fault.	❏	❏	❏	❏
9. I smash things when I'm angry.	❏	❏	❏	❏
10. Other kids talk about me behind my back.	❏	❏	❏	❏
11. I lie more than other kids do.	❏	❏	❏	❏
12. The future seems hopeless to me.	❏	❏	❏	❏
13. I am pleased when other kids get into trouble at school.	❏	❏	❏	❏
14. I have nightmares every few nights.	❏	❏	❏	❏
15. I don't believe in helping someone else unless there's something in it for me.	❏	❏	❏	❏
16. I am an important member of my family.	○	○	○	○

experienced by children (Rezmierski & Kotre, 1974). In accordance, an educational environment should provide not only opportunities for expression and acceptance of conflicts but also active support in dealing with such conflicts as they arise. Three educational applications of psychodynamic theory will be reviewed: humanistic education, a therapeutic milieu, and life space interviewing.

Humanistic Education

Humanistic educators generally view schools as places where development of happy, well-adjusted individuals takes precedence over acquisition of academic skills. Humanistic educators are also vocal about the shortcomings of our current educational system, with the result that some of the more extreme theorists are labeled countertheoretical or radical. Holt and Glasser are proponents of humanistic education who, over 25 years ago, proposed changes in the educational system aimed at reducing failure. In his book *How Children Learn,* Holt (1967) took issue with the sequential skills timetable imposed by the educational curriculum; he proposed instead that children decide for themselves both the pace and the content of their learning and that the teacher become a facilitator rather than a dictator of learning. In *Schools Without Failure,* Glasser (1969) described the atmosphere of failure propagated in our schools by such abuses as A-B-C-D grading systems, use of objective tests and the normal curve, and irrelevant homework. He further suggested that morality issues and social values should be dealt with openly in the classroom. Glasser and Holt shared the humanistic ideals that (1) children have an innate ability to learn independently and creatively; and (2) schoolwork should be relevant to students' daily lives.

These ideals were also espoused by Maria Montessori, who put them into practice by developing a special curriculum and teaching methodology. Many communities have private Montessori schools for elementary-aged children. Box 3-2 gives further information on how the Montessori method applies humanistic principles to the classroom.

A Therapeutic Milieu

Long, Morse, and Newman (1980) articulate a number of principles of the psychoeducational approach, which is heavily steeped in psychodynamic theory. Basically, the psychoeducational approach promotes the view that emotional difficulties can best be resolved through a supportive educational environment and positive learning experiences. The following are condensed from their original list of 18 principles and beliefs:

1. Cognitive and affective processes are in continuous interaction.

2. A special environment must be created so that initially each pupil can function successfully at his level.

3. Teachers must be cognizant of the fact that pupils with emotional/behavioral disorders have a special vulnerability to normal developmental tasks such as competition, testing, learning to share, and so forth.

4. Pupils with E/BD need to associate adult intervention with acceptance and protection, not hostility and rejection.

5. Teachers must listen to pupils and focus on their feelings if academic progress and behavioral change are to occur.

6. Crises are excellent times for teachers to teach and for pupils to learn.

BOX 3-2   A Montessori Classroom

Upon first observation, a Montessori classroom appears to be an unstructured learning environment. There is no teacher standing in front of the classroom directing a lesson; instead, the Montessori guide (teacher) may be sitting in a chair observing the activity of the children or may be on the floor showing a child how to use a set of materials. The children are scattered about the room, some with various materials laid out on the floor, some working in groups or pairs, and others working alone at their tables. It is easy for the observer to see that it is not "math time" or "reading time" because students are working on a total array of subject matter. Juan may be working on a map of Australia, while the two children next to him are learning phonetic sounds. Amanda may be using beads to learn subtraction skills as the child beside her, Erin, is doing long division or algebra.

In actuality, it is a precisely structured or prepared environment that allows this range of activity. Rituals of classroom behavior are established at the primary level (ages 2 1/2 to 6) that foster respect for the classroom, the materials, and the other children. The materials were developed by Maria Montessori in the early 1900s and are a key factor in the success of the Montessori classroom. The materials are used sequentially and are self-correcting. The child must ask the guide for a lesson before using any material. Although the child's interest dictates the selection of the material, the material itself along with the guide's lesson on its proper use will direct the way the material will be used. The materials are designed to lead the child in a natural and logical way from concrete experiences to abstract ideas.

Another unique aspect of the Montessori classroom is that the children are grouped in three-year age spans rather than the traditional one-year span. This arrangement is designed to foster a natural environment in which peer learning occurs between younger and older children. While younger children often rely on the expertise of older children, the older ones benefit from the opportunity to be mentors, tutors, and role models for the younger students.

Maria Montessori believed that learning is a natural process of the child's innate desire to interpret his world. The Montessori classroom is intended to provide a microcosm of the larger world in which the child has the opportunity to master activities ranging from the very practical (sweeping, polishing, gardening) to the abstract concepts of math, science, and language.

Contributed by Debbie Gorence, M.Ed., Behavior Specialist for Austin Independent School District.

These principles form the basis for the general environment or milieu that is needed by students with emotional and behavioral problems. The therapeutic milieu was applied to students in residential settings by Redl (1959a) and Hobbs (1966), and later extended to public school settings by Redl (1966) and Morse (Cheney & Morse, 1974). These educators sought to implement their beliefs that schools can greatly enhance a child's chance for success through careful selection of material, gradation of steps toward a goal, provision of therapeutic teaching, and by ending "demands for perfection" (Cheney & Morse, 1974, p. 341). This individualization process greatly reduces stress in the school environment, thereby providing a supportive atmosphere in which academic and behavioral gains are more easily attained. Appropriate adult role models also are important in milieu therapy.

In addition to individualizing instruction, milieu therapy may require manipulating daily schedules and activities, or involving the entire staff in an intervention plan so that consistent reactions from adults are ensured. Consideration is also given to the physical environment, including space, equipment, and props. Specific changes in the environment may be made on the basis of individual needs, with the result that the student's entire program may be tailored for maximum success. There is a definite emphasis on accommodating the environment to the student.

Life Space Interviewing

The previously reviewed techniques are indirect ones that focus on setting the proper environment; in contrast, the life space interview is a direct intervention technique that focuses on the student. The life space interview (LSI) was pioneered in residential settings as part of a therapeutic milieu for students with emotional/behavioral disorders. The interview is conducted by an adult "who is perceived by the child to be part of his 'natural habitat or life space,' with some pretty clear role and power-influence in his daily living" (Redl, 1965, p. 364). The adult's role is not to exercise authority but to gain an idea of the child's perceptions of a given event.

Redl (1959b) differentiates between two types of life space interviews: *emotional first aid on the spot* and *clinical exploitation of life events*. The primary difference between these two is the goal for the interview, a decision that is made in the initial stages but which, if necessary, may be changed in the middle of the interview. As its title implies, *emotional first aid on the spot* is a temporary support in which the teacher seeks to help the student overcome an immediate obstacle or work through a difficult situation. There is no long-range plan or treatment strategy other than provision of temporary relief and support. In contrast, the intention of *clinical exploitation of life events* is to exploit a momentary experience in order to facilitate long-range goals for a particular student. Consider the following example:

> *The teacher realizes that Sue Ellen is having a particularly bad day, which began with an argument with her mother before she left home this morning. Sue Ellen has a long-standing habit of rationalizing or making elaborate excuses for her obnoxious behavior. When she begins to taunt a classmate, the classmate blows up and a near-scuffle ensues. Arriving at the scene, the teacher may choose simply to break up the argument and talk to Sue Ellen about her difficult day (emotional first aid) or may decide to use the event to illustrate to Sue Ellen her habit of taking out her frustration on others and then excusing it (clinical exploitation).*

Selected subcategories of both types of interviews are briefly described in Table 3-7.

Use of the life space interview in school settings is promoted by Morse (1969b), who recommends it as a problem-solving technique in less serious situations or with students who are experiencing adjustment problems.

Little systematic research on the effectiveness of the LSI has been conducted. Gardner (1990) has questioned the widespread acceptance and practice of the life space interview because of the lack of empirical evidence supporting its effectiveness. Other criticisms by Gardner were:

- That LSI potentially detracts from academic learning time
- That the emphasis on feelings may provide students with excuses for their behavior

TABLE 3-7   Categories and Selected Subcategories of the Life Space Interview (Redl, 1959b)

Emotional first aid on the spot

Drain-off of frustration acidity—sympathizing with a student who is upset at an interruption in scheduling or during a pleasant activity

Support for management of panic, fury, and guilt—providing support during a tantrum or emotional outbursts, and afterward, helping the student gain perspective

Umpire services—helping a student make a decision or mediating in conflicts such as quarrels and fights

Clinical exploitation of life events

Reality rub-in—helping a student to interpret situations clearly and to see the relationship between behavior and its consequences

Massaging numb value areas—appealing to a student's personal value system (e.g., fairness, peer approval)

Reprinted with permission from the *American Journal of Orthopsychiatry*, copyright 1959 by the American Orthopsychiatric Association, Inc.

- That adult attention for inappropriate behavior may serve to increase the behavior rather than help to decrease it

Gardner further suggested that LSI be used as a proactive intervention; that is, it should be used in a preventive way rather than a reaction to an episode of unacceptable behavior. These criticisms were addressed by Long (1990), who maintains that LSI is an effective way to deal with affect and improve behavior. Regarding the academic time issue, Long indicated that LSI usually takes only minutes after the student has calmed down, and that the student in such an emotional state would not be academically engaged anyway. When implemented properly—as part of a continuum of behavioral interventions and as a reaction to emotional flare-ups—Long believes that LSI neither excuses instances of inappropriate behavior nor increases their frequency. One point of agreement between Long, Gardner, and other professionals interested in LSI is that more substantial data are needed about the effectiveness of LSI in a variety of educational settings.

Psychotherapy

The term *psychotherapy* has been used loosely to describe sessions during which someone with emotional stresses or problems talks with someone who is trained in the psychological processes of the human mind. Stricter interpretations would apply psychotherapy only to sessions in which psychodynamic or psychoanalytic principles are applied. The terms *therapy* or *counseling* would be applied to other forms of therapy. In this discussion, psychotherapy is used in its more general sense, i.e., borrowing from Smith and Glass (1977), "The informed and planful application of techniques derived from established psychological principles, by persons qualified through training and experience . . ." (p. 6). Many children with emotional/behavioral disorders receive psychotherapy from either the school counselor or a mental health practitioner outside the school setting.

The effectiveness of psychotherapy has been hotly debated over the years, with early researchers concluding that psychotherapy with both adults (Eysenck, 1965; Rachman, 1971) and children (Levitt, 1963; 1971) was not much better than no treatment. Research in the 70s and 80s with children and adolescents was somewhat more positive, but researchers also underscored the methodological problems with conducting this type of research (Barrett, Hampe, & Miller, 1978; Tramontana, 1980). Goals of psychotherapy typically have been difficult to precisely define and to measure. These researchers used the traditional approach of evaluating the literature from a critical—not statistical—perspective. More recent studies have used meta-analysis, a statistical technique which compares effect sizes of treatment and control groups in the studies. Two of these will be highlighted.

Casey and Berman (1985) reviewed 75 studies comparing psychotherapy with children and adolescents to a control group or to another treatment. They found an effect size of .71, indicating that the average outcome for treated children was .71 of a standard deviation better than that of untreated children. Prout and DeMartino (1986) included only studies of school-based psychotherapy. From 33 studies published between 1962 and 1982, the authors concluded that school-based psychotherapy is "at least moderately effective." Their findings also suggested that group therapy is more effective than individual therapy in the schools, and that behavioral theory (especially cognitive-behavioral) produced stronger effects than other theoretical approaches. Observable behavior and problem-solving skills were most amenable to treatment.

In a critical review of these and other meta-analyses, Kazdin (1993) stated, "The conclusion from each of these analyses has been that psychotherapy for children and adolescents produces effects that exceed changes associated with no treatment (i.e., child therapy is effective)" (p. 646). Kazdin goes on to point out that a number of recent methodological advances have contributed to the positive results. These advances include improved measures of childhood dysfunction and the establishment of normative levels of functioning at different age levels, such as was done by the authors of the *Child Behavior Checklist* (Achenbach & Edelbrock, 1983).

Summary of the Psychodynamic Model

Although the psychodynamic model encompasses varied theories, two major schools of thought—psychoanalytic and humanistic—were delineated in this chapter. Psychoanalytic theorists such as Freud emphasize the role of unconscious drives and conflict in determining personality. Humanistic theorists such as Rogers and Maslow stress the individual's need for accurate self-perception and self-understanding as prerequisites for healthy development. Healthy personality development is a common goal of psychodynamic theorists who are also concerned with the dynamics of self-growth toward that goal. Evaluation procedures arising from this model are projective techniques and self-report measures, which are used widely by psychologists in evaluating emotional problems. In applying psychodynamic principles to education, theorists emphasize the importance of a supportive, therapeutic school environment that encourages students to express and to deal openly with their needs and conflicts. Cognitive and affective issues are given equal status in

TABLE 3-8   Summary of Psychodynamic Model

ETIOLOGICAL FACTORS		EVALUATION MEASURES
Conflict between unconscious drives and conscious desires		Projectives:
Conflict between one's view of self and societal values		*Rorschach Inkblot Test* (Rorschach, 1921)
Excessive use of defense mechanisms		*Children's Apperception Test* (Bellak & Bellak, 1949)
Failure to resolve normal developmental crisis of a biological (psychosexual) or interpersonal (psychosocial) nature		Human figure drawings
		Sentence completions
		Self-report scales
	EDUCATIONAL APPLICATIONS	
	Humanistic education	
	The therapeutic milieu	
	Life Space Interview	
	Psychotherapy	

the classroom. Views of etiology, evaluation measures, and educational applications of the psychodynamic model are summarized in Table 3-8.

Conclusions

Understanding disordered behavior from a biophysical perspective allows educators to appreciate medical interventions that might be helpful primarily with children with pervasive developmental disorder and children who are hyperactive. Many researchers believe that some biologically based cause will eventually be found for many of the severe disorders; various neurotransmitters are suspected in the etiologies of many disorders. Much of the current research points to a combination of genetic predispositions and environmental catalysts in the development of these disorders.

Viewing disordered behavior from a psychodynamic perspective allows educators to understand much of our history in evaluating and treating this population. Freud and other psychodynamic theorists left an unmistakable mark in the treatment of emotional problems. While purely Freudian techniques do not lend themselves to application in educational settings, the majority of early interventions for students with emotional/behavioral disorders in the schools were based on psychodynamic principles. In addition, students may receive psychotherapy from counselors within the schools or from psychologists, psychiatrists, or social workers outside the school setting.

Key Points

1. An understanding of theoretical models is crucial in dealing with students with E/BD because our views, evaluation procedures, and interventions are based on assumptions of these models.
2. The biophysical model assumes that physical/brain-related factors cause many emotional/behavioral disorders that can be treated medically or physically.
3. Much biophysical research has been conducted with neurotransmitters in populations with autism or schizophrenia; much of this research is promising but inconclusive in determining either causes or cures.
4. Teachers are usually only tangentially involved in biophysical interventions such as medication or diet therapy.
5. The psychodynamic model focuses upon personality and the process of emotional growth in individuals.
6. Healthy personality development is a common goal of psychodynamic theorists.
7. Psychodynamic evaluation techniques include projective techniques and self-report measures that are used extensively in diagnosing emotional problems to be worked on in therapy.
8. In contrast to the past, projectives currently are not used extensively to diagnose emotional/behavioral disorders for special education programming.
9. It is important to interpret projective techniques as clinical interview tools rather than tests.
10. Psychodynamic theorists promote humanistic and therapeutic school environments in which emotional and personal growth are as important as academic success.

Additional Readings

A primer of Freudian psychology, by C.S. Hall. New York: World Publishing (Mentor Books), 1954, for a condensation of Freud's theories.

Medical treatment of learning problems: A critique, by R. L. Sieben. In *Interdisciplinary voices in learning disabilities and remedial education.* Austin, TX: Pro-Ed, 1983; A reply to Robert L. Sieben's critique, by H. W. S. Powers. *Academic Therapy, 2,* 1977, 197–203; and a critique of "Controversial medical treatments of learning disabilities," by B. F. Feingold, *Academic Therapy, 2,* 1977, 173–183, for review and rebuttal articles about various biophysical interventions.

Part I: Health and pathology. In *The farther reaches of human nature,* by A. H. Maslow. New York: Viking Compass, 1971, for the views of a well-known humanistic theorist.

Psychotherapy for children and adolescents: Current progress and future directions, by Alan Kazdin, in *American Psychologist,* June, 1993, 644, 648, for an overview of outcome studies and the issues that should be addressed in future research of the effectiveness of psychotherapy for children and youth.

The Feingold diet: A current reappraisal, by J. A. Mattes. *Journal of Learning Disabilities, 16,* 1983, 319–323; Hyperactivity and diet treatment: A meta-analysis of the Feingold hypothesis, by K. A. Kavale & S. R. Forness. *Journal of Learning Disabilities, 16,* 1983, 324–330; and The Feingold diet: An assessment of the reviews by Mattes, Kavale & Forness, by B. Rimland. *Journal of Learning Disabilities, 16,* 1983, 331–333, for review and rebuttal articles on the Feingold diet.

Endnote

1. For illustrative purposes, this author has selected definitions from the literature to represent the models. The authors of the definitions did not create them to represent these specific models, nor do the authors necessarily subscribe to the theoretical model to which their definitions have been attached in this text.

Behavioral and Ecological Models

Behavioral Theory:
> *Definition and Etiology*
> *Evaluation Procedures*
> *Educational Applications*
> *Cognitive-Behavioral Theory*

Ecological Theory:
> *Definition and Etiology*
> *Evaluation Procedures*
> *Educational Applications*

Orientation

The models presented in this chapter view disordered behavior as arising from interactions of the individual with the environment. Yet each model offers something unique to teachers. It is important for you to be familiar with behavioral theory and cognitive-behavioral theory because many classroom management and instructional techniques are based on their principles. Ecological theory is important because it reminds us that in order to effect long-term change in the life of a child, we must try to change not only the child's behavior but also the systems and situations in which the child interacts.

Overview

Two primary theoretical models of disordered behavior are presented in this chapter: behavioral and ecological. Although theorists associated with these models hold somewhat different views of the etiology of deviant behavior, they share the common assumption that the source of deviance lies in the interaction between the individual and the environment. Behavioral theorists focus on events in the environment that maintain an individual's deviant behavior, and ecological theorists believe that both the individual and the environment actively contribute to deviance. In contrast, the previously presented models (biophysical and psychodynamic) assume that the primary source of deviance is either physically or psychologically internal to the individual. The major implication of these assumptions is that treatment under the behavioral and ecological models focuses on changing not only the individual but also the contributing factors in the environment.

Behavioral Model

Definition and Basic View

> *Emotional disturbance consists of maladaptive behavior (Ullman & Krasner, cited in Russ, 1974.) As a learned behavior, it is developed and maintained like all other behaviors. (Russ, 1974, p. 102.)*

This definition indicates that behaviorists view disordered behaviors as learned responses that are subject to laws which govern all behavior. Behaviorists assert that the only differences between many disordered behaviors and normal behaviors are the frequency, magnitude, and social adaptiveness of the behaviors; if certain behaviors were less frequent, less extreme, and more adaptive, they would not be labeled disordered. Therefore, behaviors are not viewed as intrinsically deviant but rather as abnormal to the extent that they deviate from societal expectations.

Behavioral theory is based on principles of learning established primarily in laboratory studies with animal subjects. Behavioral theories are by no means unitary and may appear to have more differences than similarities. Although the differences are unreconciled and there are divisions within divisions of the major theorists, the following assumptions are common to most behavioral theorists:

1. Behavior is reducible to responses or actions that can be observed, analyzed, and measured.

2. Behavior can be controlled through administering reinforcement (rewards) and punishment; therefore, behavior is modifiable through learning.

These assumptions are the basis for a number of distinctive features of the behavioral model. First is the very basic proposition that most human behavior, including maladaptive behavior, is learned and therefore can be "unlearned" and new behaviors learned in its place. Second is the central role of the environment in eliciting and maintaining behaviors. Thus, behaviorists place the utmost importance on the setting in which the behavior occurs and on events immediately preceding and following the behavior. Third, behaviorism is a method that stresses observable behavior; it is not concerned with explaining intrapsychic forces or other reckonings internal to the individual. In this stance, the behavioral model is in direct opposition to the psychodynamic model, which is concerned with concepts of personality growth and the subconscious forces that determine behavior.

Etiology and Development of Disordered Behavior

The simplest and perhaps the most practical way to understand behavioral theory is through its three major divisions: respondent or classical conditioning, operant conditioning, and social learning or modeling.

Respondent (Classical) Conditioning

Three classic experiments are almost always cited as the bases for development of behavioral principles and the applications of those principles to treatment. In 1902, the Russian physiologist Ivan Pavlov observed that dogs in the laboratory began to salivate at cues that it was mealtime, that is, at the sight of the food dish or upon hearing the approach of the person responsible for feeding. Under experimental conditions, Pavlov established that dogs could be conditioned to salivate by pairing a neutral stimulus, a bell, with an unconditioned stimulus, meat powder. An unconditioned stimulus is an event or object that elicits an involuntary response—in this case, salivation. After several pairings, the bell alone elicited salivation in the dogs. Thus, the classical conditioning paradigm was established: an unconditioned stimulus (meat powder) could be paired with a previously neutral or conditioned stimulus (sound of a bell) to elicit a conditioned response (salivation). Learning was defined as the process of conditioning or the association of the bell with food.

The second classic experiment was undertaken by Watson and Raynor (1920) with a child known as "little Albert." At the age of 11 months, little Albert was unusually fearless and showed a fear reaction only in response to loud sounds. By presenting a white rat (neutral or conditioned stimulus) simultaneously with a loud sound (unconditioned stimulus), the experimenters soon induced fear (conditioned response) in the child by presentation of the rat alone. The fear response was demonstrated after only seven pairings and generalized to other objects such as a rabbit, a dog, fur coat, and a Santa Claus mask. The fear response was demonstrated for over a month and in a variety of settings. Learning was again defined as conditioning or association of the rat with the fear-inducing loud sound.

The third classic experiment was conducted by Jones (1924) who worked with Peter, a two-year-old who already feared essentially the same objects that Albert had been conditioned to fear: rabbits, rats, and fur objects. By utilizing a conditioning technique of pairing the presentation of a rabbit with the pleasant activity of eating, over a period of time the experimenter taught Peter to lose his fear response.

These experiments involved reflexes or involuntary responses such as salivation and the startle response, over which the individual or animal had no control. Both Pavlov and Watson believed that all learning takes place through classical conditioning, in which a new stimulus occurs simultaneously with a stimulus already eliciting a reflex response. After numerous pairings, the new stimulus alone will elicit the desired response and thus the organism is said to have learned to respond to novel stimuli or new situations.

Operant Conditioning

E. L. Thorndike and B. F. Skinner have been especially instrumental in establishing and developing operant conditioning theory. Around the turn of the century, Thorndike began a series of laboratory tests with animals which established the basic principles of operant learning. Thorndike placed hungry chickens, dogs, and cats in a "puzzle box" from which they could learn to escape by manipulating levers. Once the animals escaped, they were rewarded with food. From observing and recording the animals' learning on successive trials, Thorndike formulated a "law of effect," which states that a behavior is likely to recur when followed by rewarding consequences and is unlikely to recur when followed by unrewarding consequences or punishment. Thorndike (1932) later rejected the punishment part of this law and retained only the positive part.

Skinner, a Harvard psychologist, developed Thorndike's early formulations to the extent that Skinner's name has become almost synonymous with the term *operant conditioning*. Although Skinner recognized that respondent conditioning plays a role in learned behavior, he believed that the majority of behaviors are developed through operant conditioning, in which new responses are generated by consequences of reinforcement. Operant behavior is a voluntary response that operates on the environment to bring about certain desired consequences (the reinforcement). In operant conditioning, the consequences of behavior are emphasized. In contrast, respondent behaviors are involuntary and elicited by a stimulus that occurs before the behavior occurs.

Reinforcement and punishment are central concepts of operant conditioning theory. The most basic Skinnerian tenet is that the strength of a response increases with reinforcement and decreases without reinforcement or under punishment conditions (the same as Thorndike's original "law of effect"). According to Skinner (1953), reinforcement is the application of an event (for example, giving food) that increases the probability of response. Punishment is the application of a negative event (for example, electric shock) or the withdrawal of a positive event (removal of food) that decreases the probability of a response. Consequently, behavior change is effected through manipulation of reinforcers and punishers in the environment.

Skinner rejected the importance of hypothetical inner causes of behavior, which can neither be proven nor disproven. Although he did not deny the existence of such inner states, he believed that they are useless concepts in behavior change. He further asserted that most deviant behaviors are simply learned through operant conditioning but are deemed pathological by society. Therefore, intervention involves identifying and changing the reinforcers that are maintaining these deviant behaviors. Techniques of behavior modification based on Skinner's concept of operant conditioning are commonly used in educational settings and will be reviewed in the intervention section of this chapter.

Social Learning (Modeling)

Social learning or modeling is a third learning paradigm proposed by behaviorists. In this type of learning, individuals may acquire new responses by observing and subsequently imitating the behavior of other individuals, the "models." Social learning differs from operant and respondent conditioning in that individuals are not required to perform the behavior themselves and no direct reinforcement is necessary for learning to occur (Bandura, 1965a, 1965b).

After watching a model, the observer may be affected in one of three ways: new responses may be acquired, behaviors may become inhibited or disinhibited, or previously learned responses may be facilitated. For example, modeling is often used with students with emotional/behavioral disorders to teach a new social skill such as raising one's hand before speaking out in class. After this behavior has been learned by an individual, it may become inhibited if the teacher responds inconsistently to others in the class who raise their hands before speaking out. Or if the hand-raising behavior was previously learned but not being used by an individual, the teacher's consistent recognition of others' hand-raising may encourage the individual to use the behavior again.

The extent to which the observer is affected depends upon the extent to which identification with the model has occurred. Some of the variables influencing this identification process are age, sex, and status or prestige of the model (Bandura, 1965a). Other factors affecting social learning are whether the model is live or on film (Bandura, 1965a), whether one or more models are observed, and whether the model is punished or reinforced (Bandura, 1977).

According to social learning theorists, negative or maladaptive behaviors as well as positive ones can be learned through exposure to a model. Fears, phobias, and aggressive behavior can be learned vicariously.

Another pertinent area of social learning is that of self-reinforcement in which reinforcement is derived when an individual thinks about his own attitudes and behaviors in positive ways (Bandura, 1968). Thus, the individual's own judgments and personal feelings of merit become important factors in continuation of behaviors not reinforced by others or the environment. Indeed, Bandura believes that an individual's own thoughts and feelings may be powerful enough to override reinforcements readily available in the social environment. Self-reinforcement also can be systematically taught to students as a behavioral self-control technique (Workman, 1982). According to Workman, students can learn to reinforce themselves by merely imagining their involvement in a pleasant and rewarding scene or activity.

In summary, social learning theory proposes that behavior can be learned through observation and vicarious reinforcement. Thus, another dimension is added to behavioral theory by the inclusion of such concepts as vicarious learning and self-reinforcement. These concepts are based on internal mediation processes of the individual; hence, the environmental events that evoke behaviors are not as easily identified as in operant and respondent conditioning.

Typical Evaluation Procedures

In contrast to the biophysical model in which medical personnel are primarily responsible for diagnosis of disturbance, it is the teacher who often occupies a central role in the evaluation process of the behavioral model. Bower aptly describes the situation:

> *The myth still exists that someone, somewhere, somehow, knows how to assess behavior and/or mental health as positive or negative, good or bad, healthy or nonhealthy, and independent of the social context wherein the individual is living and functioning. It is possible that the teacher who focuses on the child's observable behavior in school is closer to an operational reality of mental health than can be determined in an office examination. What a teacher is judging is how a specific behavior affects him as a professional person in a primary social system and how well a child can play the role of student in school. (Bower, 1980, p. 124)*

Checklists and Behavior Rating Scales

Teachers are most often involved during screening in which they are asked to judge whether a student is in need of further evaluation. Two of the primary aids to the teacher in making such a judgment are behavior checklists and behavior rating scales. In addition to providing a specific, somewhat objective structure for rating a student's behavior, these measures may help identify withdrawn or passive children who may be easily overlooked in the classroom.

Several published checklists and rating scales that provide the user with data for comparisons are available. Generally, raw scores are converted into standard scores which allow comparisons among individuals by establishing a range of normalcy. (See Chapter 2 for descriptions of two rating scales based on the federal definition, and one that requires the teacher to consider all children in the classroom in a multiple-gating procedure.)

Two additional examples are the *Devereux Scales of Mental Disorders (DSMD)* (Naglieri, LeBuffe, & Pfeiffer, 1994) and the *Child Behavior Checklist (CBCL)* (Achenbach, 1991). The *CBCL* is widely used in clinical settings and in research. There is a parent form, a teacher form, and a self-report form. The *CBCL* was developed for parents but may be used by others familiar with the individual; it consists of 118 behavior problems items to be rated on a three-point scale and seven social competency items. Its primary scales and subscales are *Internalizing* (anxious obsessive; somatic complaints; schizoid; depressed); *Externalizing* (cruel; aggressive; delinquent); and *Mixed Scale* (immature hyperactive). One of the strengths of the *CBCL* is its provision of different norms for children of different ages and genders. Therefore, the child is judged against standards considered appropriate for his or her age and gender.

The *Devereux Scales of Mental Disorders* consists of 110 items rated on a five-point scale ranging from "never" to "very frequently." There is one scale with different levels for children (ages 5–12) and adolescents (ages 13–18). Like the *CBCL*, the *DSMD* offers various subscales (e.g., depression, anxiety, attention, conduct), that fall under the broader classifications of *Internalizing* or *Externalizing*. In addition, the *DSMD* offers a third classification, *Critical Pathology,* that includes the autism and acute problems subscales. Figure 4-1 shows the profile form of the adolescent version.

Behavior Recording

Behavior observation and recording is another method utilized by behaviorists to identify students with emotional/behavioral disorders. Such recordings are often used as supplemental information to both informal and formal testing procedures. The referring teacher may be asked to keep anecdotal records, but supervisors or assessment personnel generally are responsible for observing and recording behavior of the student in question. Recording involves direct observation of the student in the environment in which the maladaptive behavior occurs, usually the classroom setting. In the technique of time-sampling, the observer chooses several time periods to observe and then records occurrences of one or more specified behaviors. A more difficult and generally less reliable technique is to record every behavior that occurs within very short time periods or intervals. Information derived from behavior recording may be used not only to supplement other information gathered during the diagnostic process, but also to help plan intervention strategies.

Recording obviously involves only those behaviors that are observable and measurable. Such characteristics of behavior as frequency, duration, and type should be considered. For

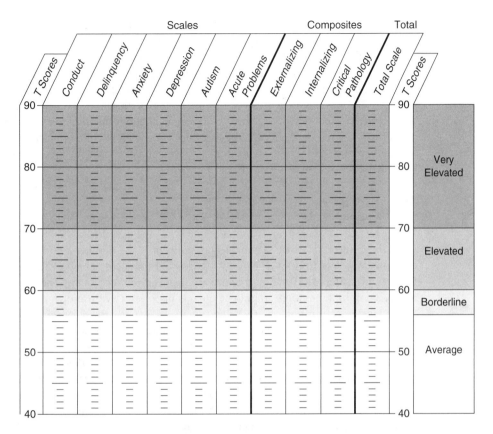

FIGURE 4-1   Profile for the *Devereux Scales of Mental Disorders (DSMD)*, Adolescent Form

Adapted from *Devereux DSMD* Answer Sheet, by J. A. Naglieri, P. A. LeBuffe, & S. I. Pfeiffer (1994). San Antonio: The Psychological Corporation. Reprinted by permission of the publisher and the authors.

example, if a teacher complains about a student's behavior, it may well be that it is the type of behavior (for example, masturbation) which makes it maladaptive or deviant rather than the frequency or number of times it occurs; conversely, the important consideration may be the duration rather than the type of behavior (temper tantrums lasting 20–30 minutes versus temper tantrums lasting 4–5 minutes). In addition to frequency, duration, and type of behavior, other considerations when judging maladaptiveness are whether the behavior is developmentally or age-appropriate, and whether the behavior is situation-specific or occurs across settings.

Educational Application

Behavioral techniques are the most commonly used interventions in classrooms for students with emotional/behavioral disorders. Behavioral techniques can be used in conjunction with other methods; even programs with a heavily psychodynamic orientation toward treatment will often use contracting or a token economy to improve classroom performance. It is perhaps this flexibility plus generally positive results that account for the popularity of behavioral interventions. Although it is beyond the scope of this book to review the massive body of literature on behavioral technology, we will look at the most common applications of behavioral principles to classrooms for students with emotional/behavioral disorders. Applications discussed in the next section are methods to increase behaviors: use of reinforcers, contracting, and token economies. The section following that will delineate methods that are commonly, sometimes controversially, used with students with emotional/behavioral disorders to decrease behaviors.

Methods for Increasing Behaviors

Reinforcers.   A reinforcer is a consequence of a targeted behavior that is intended to maintain or increase that behavior. Reinforcement is the application of a reinforcer. For example, a student finishes a seatwork assignment (targeted behavior) for free time (reinforcer) and is offered a 10-minute break by the teacher (reinforcement). The success of almost all behavioral intervention programs depends upon effective use of reinforcers. The two major classes of reinforcers are *primary* and *secondary*. *Primary* reinforcers are those biologically satisfying to an individual, such as food and liquids. Ice cream, raisins, cookies, crackers, popcorn, fruit, sodas, and the ever-popular M & Ms are examples of primary reinforcers often dispensed in classrooms. Whereas *primary reinforcers* may be necessary with students who are younger or have more severe disabilities, secondary reinforcers usually work with students who are older or have milder disabilities. *Secondary reinforcers* have a value that is learned rather than biological or innate; examples are activities, social rewards, stamps, stickers, and tokens which may be exchanged for something desirable. Use of secondary reinforcers is always preferable to use of primary reinforcers because the goal is eventually to remove any external reinforcement for appropriate behavior.

Preferences for rewards are highly individualistic and the teacher should never assume that a particular reinforcer will be effective with every student. Teachers often prepare a list of acceptable reinforcers (a reinforcement menu) and let the students choose from the list. (Refer to Table 4-1 for examples of reinforcers.) However, the ultimate evaluation of whether a reinforcer works is the effect it has on the target behavior. Only after a reinforcer has been applied and has the desired effect can it be evaluated as truly successful or reinforcing: If it works, it was a reinforcer, and if it doesn't work, it wasn't a reinforcer.

All teachers of students with emotional/behavioral disorders should become proficient at using positive reinforcement. These students often have a history of failure and punishment in the school setting, and the idea of being rewarded for positive deeds rather than punished for negative ones may be novel to them. Contingency contracting and token economies are two methods of applying positive reinforcement in the classroom.

Contingency contracting.   Contingency contracting is a form of instructional or behavior management in which an "if . . . then" contract is made; if the student performs a specific responsibility, then a specific reinforcer is given. Contingencies are based on the Premack principle or Grandma's Law, "First you eat your meat and potatoes" (less probable behavior),

TABLE 4-1   Reinforcers

PRIMARY	SECONDARY	
cereal	Tokens:	Materials:
peanuts	poker chips	balloons
chips	other colored plastic chips	ink stamp pad
ice cream	stars	pennies
Coke	checks	stars
raisins	happy faces	bubbles liquid
fruit	points	badges
popcorn	ink stamps	books
crackers	play money	magazines
candy	hole punch	play dough
M & Ms	paper clips	bookmarks
juice		calendars
other food and drink		puzzles
		stationery or
		writing pads
		toy jewelry
		records
		flash cards
		bean bags
		art supplies

ACTIVITIES/PRIVILEGES

grade or staple papers	typing
teacher's helper for the day	listening to music with headphones
tutor others	using tape recorder
janitorial tasks in class	painting or drawing
sit with teacher	drawing on chalkboard
sit in special spot	skipping nap time
pass out snacks	writing a letter
read to the class	taking photographs
choose story for teacher to read	skipping an assignment or test
class librarian	playing with board games
distribute and collect materials	playing with puppets
being first in line	class Coke break
run errands	
leading an activity	
free time	

"and then you may have dessert" (more probable behavior). Thus, high frequency or valued activities are used to reinforce low frequency or less valued activities. Contingency contracting can be verbal and informal, such as an agreement on how many problems must be completed before free time is allotted. Contracts can also be formal and more complex, such as a written document specifying the behaviors that are disallowed and/or the behaviors that must be demonstrated to earn the reinforcer. The terms of such a contract are usually negotiated between teacher and student, who then sign the contract as a pact.

Contracting is widely used in special education settings and has been effective with a variety of behaviors with students of all ages (Nelson & Rutherford, 1988). However, research studies attempting to validate contracting have generally suffered from methodological flaws. In a review of 35 studies using contracting with students who were delinquent or E/BD, Rutherford and Polsgrove (1981) found a number of such flaws but reached the tentative conclusion that contracting had been effective in aiding behavioral change in many situations. An example of how a simple verbal contract was used with an eight-year-old in a residential treatment center is presented in Box 4-1.

Token economies.   Token economies are often used successfully in the classroom to improve social and academic skills. Tokens play the role that money plays in society, i.e., tokens are inherently worthless; it is what they can buy or be traded for that makes them valuable. Tokens can be poker chips, play money, check marks, stars, points, or any number of other inexpensive, durable objects.

In a token economy, the teacher sets up a system in which accumulated tokens earned for specified behavior can be traded in for selected reinforcers (e.g., finishing 3 math assignments with 90 percent accuracy is worth 6 poker chips that can be traded in for a privilege such as skipping an assignment). Teachers of students with emotional/behavioral disorders often set up token economies in the classroom and then negotiate specific behavioral contracts with individual students.

Advantages of token economies are their flexibility and applicability in a wide range of settings. For example, token economies are often employed in institutional and other residential settings because they can be used by teachers, therapists, and child care workers to reinforce targeted behaviors during school, during therapy, and on the unit. The specific reinforcers and contingencies would obviously differ according to age and sophistication of the students. The variety of reinforcers that can be offered adds longevity to the technique, as the reinforcement menu can be changed as frequently as necessary to sustain interest. In reviews of research, Kazdin (1982, 1983) found that token economies have been used successfully with a wide variety of populations, although not all clients have responded positively. He cautions that long-term gains have yet to be proven.

Methods for Decreasing Behaviors

Punishment.   Punishment is liberally defined here as an act intended to decrease an unwanted behavior in another. As with reinforcement, however, the "proof is in the pudding": an act is truly punishing only if it has the desired effect of decreasing the behavior. Consider, for example, spanking. While universally considered an aversive or punishing act, if spanking does not decrease the behavior the child was spanked for, then it was not truly a punisher for that child.

Child development experts offer many reasons for avoiding use of punishment in teaching children how to behave. Among the reasons often cited are (1) that punishment serves to extinguish behavior only short-term and in the presence of the punisher, and (2) that punishment offers no positive models of what is expected, only what is to be avoided. Regardless of

---

BOX 4-1   Robert's Contract

On the day of admission, Robert broke the psychologist's glasses. Apparently frightened, he would not venture into the open space of a room. Instead, he crouched behind the furniture at every opportunity. This small, blonde, eight-year-old had scratched his own face so badly that there were long, red marks deep in his flesh.

The two teachers to whom Robert was assigned typically "loved" their students into wellness, while teaching them everything from academics to manners to gardening. They were astounded by Robert and his lack of response to them and his classmates; however, they were determined that he would receive all the benefits they had to offer.

Since Robert chose to sit outside the classroom on the floor in the hallway, it was difficult to reward him with his favorite things. Through trial-and-error, it was eventually discovered that Robert responded positively when given certain color crayons—red, blue, black, and green. It was also ascertained that Robert had been severely abused and that his unresponsiveness was primarily due to fear. Therefore, the statement, "It is safe here" was reinforced with Robert as often as possible.

The contract that was implemented was simple: whenever Robert responded positively to his teachers or classmates, he was able to use his favorite crayons. Slowly, but surely, Robert began to respond to others, but he still preferred his safe hallway to the classroom. Still reinforcing, "It is safe here," the teachers placed a desk in the hallway and

daily moved it closer to the door of the classroom. Robert's safety net was slowly changing, and he was accepting it.

After six months of concentrated effort on the part of the teachers, psychologists, and classmates, Robert was able to stay in the classroom. He began to indicate a readiness to learn and an eagerness to participate at an age-appropriate level. We extended the "It is safe here" assurance to other parts of Robert's world, and we emptied the stores of red, blue, black, and green crayons for months!

Throughout my work with a population with emotional/behavioral disorders, the behavioral contract has been a lifesaver. We all have things for which we are willing to work. This basic principle helps eliminate undesirable and inappropriate behaviors, replacing them with socially acceptable ones and providing the client with a chance for a better life in the future.

It is often difficult to identify something for which a client is willing to change a behavior, particularly when that behavior is one that has been a successful tool for him in the past. To be successful in implementing a contract, you must find a meaningful reward, set reasonable expectations for earning the reward, and implement the contract consistently. This simple idea works—don't we all meet certain daily expectations and occasionally modify our behavior so that we can receive our paychecks on a regular basis? I know I do!

Contributed by Sue N. Baugh, M.Ed., Coordinator of Rehabilitation Services, The Devereux Foundation, Victoria, Texas.

---

its effectiveness, punishment is used in public schools. Its use with students with emotional/behavioral disorders has been questioned, and school districts have been sued over its appropriateness with this population. The following sections will address techniques aimed at decreasing behavior that are commonly used with students with E/BD: timeout, in-school suspension, corporal punishment, and physical restraint. Many of these techniques have been questioned in the courts, and the resulting legal constraints are discussed in Box 4-2.

Timeout.   Timeout is the removal of a student for a limited time from a setting that is reinforcing. It is frequently used in programs for students with emotional/behavioral disorders. One survey of E/BD teachers in two states found that 70 percent of the respondents

BOX 4-2   Punishment for Students with Behavior Disorders: Is it Legal?

Several punishment techniques commonly used with students with behavior disorders have been questioned in the courts. Timeout, in-school suspension, and corporal punishment have all been tested. Following is a summary of the courts' findings, along with recommendations for implementation if punishment procedures are to be used:

Timeout

In 1987 *Dickens v. Johnson County Board of Education* was a test case for exclusion timeout, and *Hayes v. Unified School District No. 377* was a test case for seclusion timeout. According to Yell's (1990) analysis of these court decisions, timeout was sanctioned by the courts under the following conditions: schools must have clear written guidelines for timeout procedures, students must know beforehand which behaviors are punishable by timeout, facilities must be adequate, and time spent must be brief and proportionate to the offense. Long periods in timeout without provisions for the student's education would constitute a violation of student rights.

In-school Suspension (ISS)

In *Hayes v. Unified District No. 377,* the court upheld ISS under appropriate conditions: that written procedures outline which behaviors are punishable by ISS and how it will be carried out, that length of time in suspension is related to the offense, and that educational opportunities are provided during the suspension (Yell, 1990). Suspensions of up to five days have been upheld as long as other provisions were met.

Corporal Punishment

In *Cole v. Greenfield-Central Community Schools* in 1986, the court upheld the use of corporal punishment (in this instance, three strokes with the paddle and tape over the mouth). When using corporal punishment, schools must prove that it is part of a comprehensive disciplinary plan that serves an educational function (Yell, 1990). It also must not be excessive in relation to the offense. Although not yet proscribed by the courts, corporal punishment is still controversial and not advocated by a number of professionals concerned with the welfare of students with emotional/behavioral disorders. Use of corporal punishment for E/BD students in public schools is questionable at best and could lead to further litigation.

Legal Principles for Interventions Entailing Punishment

Yell (1990) has analyzed relevant case law and extracted six principles that should be followed when applying punishing procedures with students with E/BD. These principles represent legality as determined by court proceedings to date; moral and ethical issues are less clearly defined. Yell's six principles are as follows:

1. When using punishment, do not violate the student's due process rights. Clearly define the behavior to be punished and the punishing consequences to the student and parents beforehand. Use of a warning to the student before punishment is administered is also advisable.

2. When using punishment, do not violate the educational rights of students. Punishments such as expulsion, serial suspensions, prolonged timeouts and prolonged in-school suspensions have been considered changes in placement by the courts and are therefore illegal.

3. The punishing procedure must have a legitimate educational function. Written guidelines should describe the rationale, specify the intervention, and discuss the anticipated outcome.

4. The punishment must be reasonable. Although open to interpretation, the concept of reasonableness may be satisfied if the rule being enforced was reasonable, the punishment was suited to the offense, the amount of force was not unreasonable, and the punisher demonstrated no personal ill will toward the student.

5. Punishment should be used only if less intrusive interventions have failed. Documentation of this principle helps meet the courts' requirement of reasonableness.

6. Caution is necessary in interpreting case law. Court decisions are not nationally binding unless decided by the Supreme Court.

Although these principles are based on case law, it is advisable for school administrators to consult with school attorneys for updated or locally based information regarding use of punishment with students with E/BD. It is clear that school districts should develop written policies that specify behaviors that are punishable and then detail punishment procedures to be used for these behaviors. To date, courts have upheld punishment procedures that are reasonable, do not interfere with educational rights, and have an educational function. Detailed docu-

used timeout with their students. Reported use decreased with the age of students, with 88 percent of preschool teachers reporting use of timeout, 65 percent at the junior high level, and 51 percent at the senior high level (Zabel, 1986). Some programs have a timeout corner in the classroom that is screened with a partition from the rest of the room (exclusion). However, a separate timeout room (seclusion) may be needed for students with emotional/behavioral disorders, who occasionally may need to be physically separated from their peers until they regain control of their emotions. Also, if students can continue to create a disturbance for the teacher or the remainder of the class after being placed in timeout, then the concept of removal from reinforcement is undermined. Timeout should be used for behaviors that are specified beforehand and only for brief periods of time (e.g., five minutes).

Timeout has generally been effective with students who exhibit disruptive or aggressive behavior and with students with moderate to severe emotional/behavioral disorders. According to a review by Nelson and Rutherford (1988), factors affecting success include level and duration of timeout, whether a warning signal was used, the schedule under which it was administered, and the procedures under which a student is placed in and removed from the timeout setting. There appears to be little consensus in the research about the most appropriate and effective timeout procedures for all students (Polsgrove and Reith, 1983), thereby suggesting that specific timeout procedures should be tailored to fit the individual program.

Some programs with separate timeout rooms allow students who are upset to voluntarily put themselves in timeout in order to allow a cooling down period before returning to classes. In these instances, timeout is not used as punishment.

In-school suspension. As suspension from school as a disciplinary technique for students with disabilities has become controversial, in-school suspensions are becoming more common (Center & McKittrick, 1987). Application of in-school suspensions (ISS) varies, but generally a classroom is designated for ISS with a full-time teacher or aide who supervises the students who bring their regular assignments from class to complete while in ISS. Students are usually not allowed to interact with other students in ISS; otherwise, the ISS loses its punishing feature of removal from interaction with peers. The effectiveness of in-school suspension has not been well-researched, but its legality with students with emotional/behavioral disorders has been upheld, with certain restrictions, in court.

Corporal punishment. Corporal punishment is prohibited by law in many states. Some boards of education prohibit its use regardless of state sanctions. Despite its controversial nature, J. Rose (1984) found that corporal punishment was still being widely used with students with emotional/behavioral disorders in the mid-80s.

Corporal punishment is generally equated with spanking, although slapping, pinching, and shaking may also be considered in this category. Other physically aversive techniques such as application of aversive tastes and odors and electric shock have been used for severely maladaptive behaviors such as self-injurious behavior in lower functioning individuals. While physically aversive techniques have been instrumental in reducing such severe behaviors, their use has been questioned from an ethical standpoint by many parents and professionals. We will return to a more in-depth discussion of aversive techniques in the chapter on severe behavior disorders.

Physical restraint.   Physical restraint is defined here as the application of force to an individual with the purpose of either restricting or redirecting his movement. While it may not be intended to be punitive, it does fit our definition of punishment. This procedure is commonly used in settings for E/BD students; one survey indicated that 71 percent of the teachers of this population use physical restraint with students who display aggressive behavior toward others (Ruhl & Hughes, 1985). Although there are limitations with this procedure, many professionals believe that it is justifiable under two conditions: (1) to prevent harm either to the student (self-injurious behavior) or others, and (2) to enforce prearranged contingencies, such as removal to a timeout area (Schloss & Smith, 1987). Other professionals do not believe that physical restraint or any type of force should be used to enforce timeout.

It is best to have written procedures for use of physical restraint, as most teachers of students with emotional/behavioral disorders will have to deal with aggressive and out-of-control behavior. Teachers also should receive thorough training in the correct use of restraint procedures to minimize the potential for harm. Restraint should be considered as one component of a comprehensive behavior management plan.

Summary of the Behavioral Model
Behaviorists view disordered behavior as learned maladaptive responses. According to this model, behavior has a lawful relationship to the environment, as illustrated by the principles of operant and respondent conditioning. Whereas respondent conditioning occurs because of events preceding behavior, operant conditioning is due to events following behavior. These environmental events are manipulated by behaviorists in order to help change behavior. The impact of social learning, or observation and imitation of others' behavior, is also emphasized. Behavior modification, a system for behavior change based on these learning principles, is used widely in schools. A summary of the behavioral view of etiology, typical evaluation procedures, and educational applications is presented in Table 4-2.

Cognitive-Behavioral Model

The cognitive-behavioral model arose from the work of individuals who believe that the behavioral model only partially accounts for learning and behavior. For example, people often respond differently to exactly the same set of circumstances. Wouldn't behaviorism in its purest form predict that identical circumstances would elicit identical responses? What could account for individual differences in responding? Cognitive-behavioral theorists propose that cognitions or individual differences in thinking are the missing link. Cognitive-behavioral proponents therefore emphasize cognitions or thinking patterns as an important link between environmental stimuli and behavior. Naturally, interventions following from this model focus upon changing distorted thinking patterns and negative self-talk into more productive modes. These interventions can be categorized into: (1) general cognitive techniques such as reality therapy and rational-emotive therapy, and (2) cognitive-behavioral techniques. Each type will be briefly reviewed.

General Cognitive Techniques
Both Glasser's *reality therapy* (1965) and Ellis' *rational-emotive therapy* (1973) are considered cognitive techniques because they are based on the underlying premise that individ-

TABLE 4-2 Summary of the Behavioral Model

ETIOLOGY	EVALUATION PROCEDURES
Respondent (classical conditioning)	Checklists
Operant conditioning	Behavior rating scales
Social learning (modeling)	Behavior recording

EDUCATIONAL APPLICATIONS

Techniques for increasing behaviors:
  use of reinforcers
  contingency contracting
  token economies
Techniques for decreasing behaviors:
  timeout
  in-school suspension
  corporal punishment
  physical restraint

uals can learn to redirect their behavior by changing their thoughts and attitudes. These techniques directly address cognitive processes by attacking illogical and irresponsible thinking. In contrast to traditional therapies, cognitive therapists consider the past irrelevant; their intent is to help individuals understand present and future behavior by restructuring their thinking about it. Cognitive techniques can be implemented in the school setting by therapists, counselors, or teachers who have been trained in their use.

Reality therapy.   In reality therapy, Glasser (1965) emphasizes the *three R's-responsibility, reality,* and *right-and-wrong. Responsibility* is the keystone of reality therapy; Glasser holds the nontraditional view that people become "disordered" because they are irresponsible and therefore they can become "undisordered" by learning to become responsible. Responsible behavior is defined as the ability to meet one's needs without infringing upon the rights of others to meet their needs. *Reality* is an important concept because disordered individuals deny the reality of the world around them; they do not understand or accept the rules and regulations of society, they deny connections between their behavior and its consequences, and they become adept at blaming other people or external events for their difficulties. Reality therapists do not accept rationalizations or excuses as valid justifications for behavior. The third R, *right-and-wrong,* sets reality therapy apart from most other therapies that avoid attaching value judgments to behavior. According to Glasser, disordered or deviant behavior is wrong because it is harmful to the individual or to others. Therefore, the individual must learn to view his maladaptive behavior as wrong and must learn to behave in more adaptive ways.

Glasser (1965) and Towns (1981) have reported successful applications of reality therapy with adolescent populations. Newcomer (1993) recommends its use in settings where the adult has substantial control over the consequences of irresponsible behavior, such as residential settings.

Rational-emotive therapy.   Rational-emotive therapy (RET) was developed by Albert Ellis (1962, 1973) who believes that individuals maintain many maladaptive behaviors through irrational thinking. Although Ellis recognizes the role of environmental and biological factors in the development of behaviors and emotions, his position is that irrational thinking leads to negative emotions and behavior. Rational-emotive therapy is based on the premise that humans are capable of rational thinking and can divest themselves of irrational thought. The "rational" part of RET refers to restructuring one's thinking, and the "emotive" part refers to the resultant changes in emotions.

Ellis (1980) distinguishes between rational and irrational beliefs: rational beliefs are characterized by responsibility to oneself and society; irrational beliefs lead to conflict with other individuals and with society. Ellis contends that people are socialized to adhere to irrational beliefs through messages in the media and from significant people in their lives. Ellis promotes the ABC model for disputing irrational beliefs. The "A" represents an *activating event,* which is unpleasant or bothersome; the "C" represents *consequences,* which are negative emotions, behaviors, or actions. Most people believe that consequences or emotions ("C") are a direct result of an event ("A"). Ellis insists that there is a "B," an intermediate step that represents the *beliefs* one holds about the event, and that it is these beliefs that actually cause the consequences. These "B" statements may be rational statements about the event, which lead to positive or neutral consequences, or may be irrational statements about the event, which generate negative consequences. In RET, the individual learns to recognize and dispute irrational beliefs and to replace them with more adaptive rational beliefs. The following example illustrates the relationship of A, B, and C.

A (EVENT)	B (BELIEF)	C (CONSEQUENCE)
upcoming final exam	irrational: "I'll die if I don't make an 'A' on this exam; nothing is more important"	extreme anxiety
	rational: "I'd like to do well on this exam and it would be nice to get an 'A,' but my personal worth doesn't depend on it."	slight anxiety, confidence

RET has been found to be an effective counseling technique (Smith & Glass, 1977), but Ellis claims success only with populations who have mild emotional difficulties and who are motivated to change their behavior. Towns (1981) suggests that RET is useful with adolescents in coping with cycles of emotional upheaval. RET can be used in the schools in three ways: (1) as a personal mental health program for educators, (2) as a counseling or intervention technique for students with emotional problems, or (3) as an affective curriculum (Zionts, 1985). Webber and Coleman (1988) have described how, using RET, teachers can identify their own maladaptive self-talk that may be interfering with their effectiveness as behavior managers in the classroom.

Cognitive-Behavioral Techniques

Bridging both cognitive and behavioral theories are a number of procedures that collectively have become known as cognitive-behavioral techniques. Very basically defined, cognitive-behavioral techniques refer to the effect that self-talk or inner speech has on an individual's behavior. In contrast to rational-emotive therapy and reality therapy, many of these techniques do not seek to dispute general maladaptive thinking; rather, strategies are provided that can be applied to specific tasks or problems.

Many psychologists adhere to a cognitive-behavioral model and have developed treatments for various emotional and behavioral disorders based on the model. Anxiety disorders, panic disorder, and depression are examples of emotional difficulties that have been successfully treated with cognitive-behavioral techniques. (Refer to Chapter 5 for a description of the cognitive-behavioral model as applied to childhood depression and a case study of how it was used with a ten-year-old girl.) However, this discussion will focus on the applications of cognitive-behavioral techniques to academic and social behavior in the classroom.

Lloyd (1980) has extracted four common attributes of cognitive-behavioral procedures as they are applied to classroom behavior:

1. A self-imposed treatment is taught—for example, self-instruction, self-control, self-evaluation, or self-monitoring.
2. Verbalization is usually a part of the technique.
3. A problem-solving strategy is identified.
4. Modeling is used to teach the technique.

The goal of most cognitive-behavioral techniques is to train students, through self-talk, to develop strategies or to problem-solve for themselves. Such techniques have shown promise for both social and academic improvement. With students with emotional/behavioral disorders, cognitive-behavioral techniques have been shown to improve social adjustment (Larson & Gerber, 1987) and decrease aggressive behaviors (Etscheidt, 1991; Smith, Siegel, O'Connor, & Thomas, 1994), and have been reviewed as promising for social behaviors with this population (Ager & Cole, 1991). The following section highlights several cognitive-behavioral techniques.

Self-management or the ability to regulate oneself with a minimum of external guidance is the goal of most cognitive-behavioral techniques. Three areas in which self-management has proven most successful are: on-task behaviors (for example, complying with teacher directions, working on assignments); academic product behaviors (number of correct math problems on homework or tests); and disruptive behaviors (out-of-seat, verbal threats) (Workman & Hector, 1978). Among the specific self-management techniques are *self-instruction, self-monitoring, and self-evaluation.*

In *self-instruction,* students use self-talk to cue themselves about a specific task and then to give themselves feedback. Self-instruction is a step-by-step verbal guidance technique that is often used to reduce impulsive behavior and to increase on-task behavior with elementary-age students (Workman, 1982).

In *self-monitoring,* students learn to record their performance on a specified behavior.

This technique has been used to increase academic performance and on-task behavior, and to decrease inappropriate behaviors such as out-of-seat. In a review of 27 studies of self-monitoring in special education classrooms, Webber and her colleagues found that self-monitoring was used successfully with students of various ages in increasing attention to task and positive classroom behaviors while also reducing the opposite behaviors (off-task and negative classroom behaviors) (Webber, Scheuermann, McCall, & Coleman, 1993). *Self-evaluation* differs from self-monitoring in that monitoring is a mere tabulation or recording of specific behaviors; evaluation requires students to compare recorded behavior to a standard and to judge its acceptability. For example, in self-evaluation, students may be required to match their own evaluations to those of an observer; they may not be reinforced if their own evaluations do not match, within reasonable limits, those of the observer. This technique with the matching requirement has been successful with samples of students with E/BD in increasing appropriate behavior (Clark & McKenzie, 1989; Rhode, Morgan, & Young, 1983), and in decreasing disruptive behaviors of kindergartners (Fowler, 1986).

Most of the research on cognitive-behavioral techniques is encouraging. Reviews of self-management studies appear to support the use of these techniques as effective in changing academic-related behaviors (e.g., Hughes, Ruhl, & Misra, 1989). In a review of 16 studies of students with emotional/behavioral disorders, Nelson et al. (1991) also found ecouraging results; they report that "the obtained treatment results appear to be durable and . . . may be a viable option to externally managed procedures" (Nelson, Smith, Young, & Dodd, 1991, p. 169). However, Nelson et al. also reported that the positive effects fail to generalize unless specifically programmed. Given the ultimate goal of self-management for most of our students, it seems wise to continue to use cognitive-behavioral techniques in our classrooms.

In summary, the cognitive-behavioral model recognizes the role that thoughts or cognitions play in the development of disordered behavior. General cognitive techniques such as rational-emotive therapy and reality therapy are based on the belief that individuals can learn to redirect their behavior by changing their irrational and irresponsible thinking. Other techniques, collectively known as cognitive-behavioral techniques, also focus upon the link between thoughts and behavior but usually involve specific strategies or problem-solving techniques.

Ecological Model

Definition and Basic View

> *Behavioral disabilities are defined as a variety of excessive, chronic, deviant behaviors ranging from impulsive and aggressive to depressive and withdrawal acts (a) which violate the perceiver's expectations of appropriateness and (b) which the perceiver wishes to see stopped (Graubard, 1973, p. 246).*

Graubard's definition expresses the ecological view in its emphasis on both the perceiver of behavior and the behavior being perceived. The definition establishes that there are two parts to defining problem behavior: some type of behavior must be exhibited and someone must be offended by such behavior. Theorists of this model espouse the view that deviance lies in the interaction of an individual with others (the perceivers) in the environment; hence the term *ecological*.

As applied to human behavior, the ecological model implies that it is meaningless to discuss problems of behavior in isolation from the contexts in which these behaviors arise, since it is these very contexts that define the behavior as a problem. Rhodes (1967) states that the disturbance often lies in the behavioral expectations of those with whom the child must interact. A child may be judged disordered by one person while appearing normal to another, or the child's behavior may be seen as abnormal in one setting but quite normal in another. The predictable result is that children who are judged to be the most disordered are those who uniformly arouse negative reactions in the environments in which they interact with others. Therefore, within the ecological model, behavior is viewed as "disturbing" rather than inherently "disturbed," and emphasis is placed not only on the child but also on other individuals and factors in the child's ecosystem. Therefore, ecological interventions call for a systems approach to treatment.

Etiology and Development of Disordered Behavior

Theory

Rhodes has been a vocal spokesperson for ecological theory; his arguments are persuasive but largely philosophical, as disturbances in ecosystems are difficult to define and assess operationally. According to Rhodes (1970), certain environments may be unable to accommodate the unfolding nature of children, thereby generating disturbance in the ecosystems. This view is in direct opposition to more traditional views that the child should accommodate to the environment rather than vice versa. Rhodes states that a major sign of disturbance is an increase in the amount and intensity of energy that is required by others to interact with the child, or a disturbance in the equilibrium of the ecosystem that calls attention to the child.

To operate from an ecological framework, one must accept that ecosystems rather than children are disordered, and that ecosystems are directly influenced by the culture in which they exist. Rhodes (1967) translates these assumptions into intervention goals: the short-term goal is to intrude into the disordered situation and help modify it, and the long-term goal is to expand the education process to develop functional yet individualistic members of society. Above all, Rhodes (1970) is adamant that we cannot hope to provide effective intervention if we "pluck" a child from a context of disturbance, attempt to fix or change him, and then place the child back into the unchanged environment from which he came.

Ecosystems

Ecosystems are the various environments in which an individual routinely interacts. Components may be tangible or intangible, but they are interrelated and interdependent. People, objects, time, space, and psychological variables are all components of an ecosystem.

Students operate within a number of ecosystems; students with disorders cause "ripples of discomfort" and reverberations within these ecosystems (Rhodes, 1970). The major ecosystems of a student are shown in Figure 4-2. As depicted in the figure, the child participates simultaneously in a number of ecosystems which intersect at some points but which also retain much unshared territory. The larger, more comprehensive ecosystems

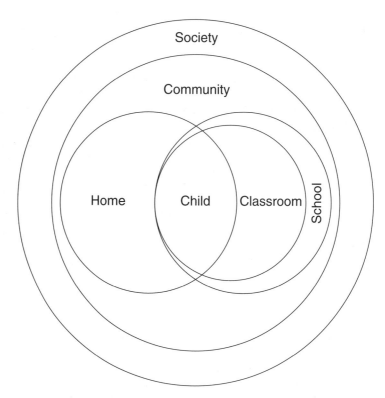

FIGURE 4-2   Ecosystems of the Child

(society and community) have less direct influence on the child than the smaller ecosystems (home and school). The larger ecosystems are also less amenable to change through direct intervention.

Analysis of variables in a child's ecosystem is important for two reasons: (1) to determine whether the variables are contributing to the disturbance, and (2) to determine which contributing variables are amenable to change so that appropriate intervention can be planned. For example, it might be determined that Juan's father's unemployment is causing anxiety in the home, which is having an effect on Juan's frustration tolerance and academic functioning in the classroom. Although dealing directly with parental unemployment (home ecosystem) is outside the domain of education, an analysis of the classroom situation might reveal that Juan would benefit from temporary help by adjusting the length of required assignments and/or providing some individualized tutoring (classroom ecosystem, manipulable variables).

Let us now turn our attention to some variables operating within ecosystems that directly affect student behavior. The variables listed are illustrative and not exhaustive.

Classroom

Teacher-student
teacher attitudes and expectations
class rules

grading system
teacher tolerance level for individual differences
teaching style; e.g., directed learning versus nondirected learning
teacher interaction style
teacher-pupil ratio

Student-peers
peer attitudes: acceptance versus rejection
number of students in class
gender, socioeconomic status (SES), and ethnic composition of class members
general achievement and ability level of class

Physical environment
traditional versus open classroom
light, colorful versus drab
crowded versus spacious
use of props and teaching aids
individual desks versus tables and chairs
arrangement of desks or tables
use of centers

Curriculum
subject areas taught and subject areas stressed
placement in appropriate levels versus placement in inappropriate level
programmed or highly structured versus loose
objectives clearly defined or undefined
subject matter properly sequenced versus haphazard
type of materials used
use of media
lessons individualized or grouped by ability level

School
availability of support personnel
effectiveness of principal
number of students enrolled
general climate and/or atmosphere
school pride
urban, suburban, or rural location
philosophy of discipline
ethnic/SES mix of students
ethnic/SES mix of teachers
number of extracurricular activities
relationship with the community

Home
age, occupation, religion, and SES of parents
intact family versus single-parent home
number and ages of siblings

education level of parents and attitude toward education
philosophy of child-rearing
methods and consistency of discipline
availability of extended family
attractiveness and comfortability of home

Community
urban, suburban, or rural setting
size of town or city
geographic location
ethnic/SES composition
major source(s) of income for workers (farming, industrial, business, etc.)
number of churches and prevailing religious denomination
economic stability
current attitude toward financing education
community pride
number and type of activities available: sports, family functions, theater, concerts, art, etc.

Society
state of economy and economic trends
current attitude toward education
general political climate
current events

Student Contributions

Students also contribute to the workings of ecosystems. Of all the student characteristics that have been shown to influence teacher attitudes and expectations within the classroom, behavior may be the most potent (Kedar-Voivodas & Tannenbaum, 1979; Trevor, 1975). The behaviors that teachers find most disturbing are best described as defiant-aggressive (Algozzine, 1977; Walker, 1979; Gersten, Walker, & Darch, 1988). Such behaviors engender negative attitudes that are often translated into negative teacher-student interactions, thus setting into motion the rippling effect through the ecosystem described by Rhodes.

One of the major criticisms of the ecological theory of disturbance is that it is difficult to assess and apply. The next two sections will offer examples of ecological assessment and of ecological applications to education.

Typical Evaluation Procedures

Ecological Assessment Techniques

Information on ecological assessment has skyrocketed in the past ten years. (As the author was preparing the first edition of this textbook in 1982, she could find only two references that even mentioned the term "ecological assessment.") Basically, ecological assessment refers to the gathering of information from all environments or ecosystems in which a student spends a significant amount of time. A good ecological assessment: (1) describes the environments, (2) lists the demands on the student, including expectations of others in those environments, and (3) defines the skills and behaviors needed by the student to be successful in those environments. Such environments include the home, the neighborhood, the school, and each of the classrooms that a student attends. Some ecological assessments focus only upon the classroom environment. Examples of these are *The Instructional Environment Scale (TIES)* (Ysseldyke & Christenson, 1987) and *Analysis of Classroom and Instructional Demands* (ACID Test) (West, 1990). Both of these measures offer a structure to identify the demands of a particular classroom, including such variables as instructional content/presentation, class rules and teacher expectations, types of evaluations, and grading procedures. The information from these measures can then be used to modify certain aspects of the demands to fit an individual student's abilities or to offer the student additional help in meeting those demands. Educators can conduct their own informal assessments of classroom learning environments without using published measures, but it may be helpful to use these or other measures that have already identified important instructional, motivational, and management variables.

Such assessments and interventions are ecological in scope because they avoid putting all the burden upon the student to adapt to the environment; rather, the importance of a fit or a match between the student and the classroom demands is emphasized. Ecological assessments can be very helpful with all students with emotional/behavioral disorders, but may be particularly important when reintegrating or mainstreaming these students into general education classrooms from more restrictive classrooms. We will return to this important discussion in Chapter 8 under reintegration.

There are also instruments that seek information about an individual from a number of sources and from environments other than the classroom. The *Behavior Rating Profile-2 (BRP-2)* (Brown & Hammill, 1990) is such an instrument. According to its authors, the *BRP-2* is an "ecological/behavioral assessment device" that allows behaviors to be examined in a variety of settings and from several points of view. There are six components of the *BRP-2:* three Student Rating Subscales in which the student responds to a total of 60 self-descriptive items in the areas of home, school, and peers; a Teacher Rating Scale of 30 items; a Parent Rating Scale of 30 items; and a sociogram. Table 4-3 shows these components and respondents. The *BRP-2* is flexible in that one may either utilize input from all the scales or may use any of the scales independently. The instrument can be helpful in defining deviant behavior that is specific to one setting or to one individual's expectations.

Educational Applications

Ecological interventions focus on a single ecosystem or a combination of ecosystems. As mentioned previously, the more intimate ecosystems of the child (classroom, home, and school) are more amenable to direct intervention than the larger ecosystems, which require a systems approach and broad-based cooperative planning.

The educational interventions discussed in this section are not uniquely ecological; many borrow from behavioral and psychodynamic principles. However, each intervention is attempting to make the environment more suitable for the individual student rather than attempting to force the student to fit the environment. In this sense, these interventions are ecological. The targets of change are the student ecosystems of classroom, home, school, and community.

TABLE 4-3 Respondent and Ecology Associated with the BRP-2 Components (Brown & Hammill, 1990)

BRP COMPONENT	RESPONDENT				ECOLOGY		
	Student	Teachers	Parents	Peers	Home	School	Interpersonal
Student Rating Scale: Home	X				X		
Student Rating Scale: School	X					X	
Student Rating Scale: Peer	X						X
Teacher Rating Scale		X				X	
Parent Rating Scale			X		X		
Sociogram				X			X

Used with permission of the publisher, PRO-ED, 8700 Shoal Creek Blvd., Austin, TX 78758

Changes in the Classroom Ecosystem

Physical and psychological adaptations within the classroom may be sufficient to change disturbing interactions of some students. A physical arrangement that has been used successfully in classrooms for students with E/BD includes separate individual and group work areas, a timeout area, and a reinforcement center (Bullock, 1981; Hewett & Taylor, 1980). Use of individual study carrels or screens helps to eliminate distractions when independent work is required. To preserve psychological consistency, a number of clear, concise, enforceable rules are selected and posted on wall charts; to encourage academic success, individualized contracts or task sheets may be arranged. Scheduling and routine are also important parts of the psychological environment; time limits for all daily activities are established and followed. By establishing definite limits, the teacher provides structure and helps students learn to manage time efficiently. Individual adaptations based on ecological assessments can also be made. In such classrooms, the teacher aims to create an atmosphere of acceptance and success rather than the expectation for failure that often surrounds the student with emotional/behavioral disorders.

Changes in the Home Ecosystem

Parents have become increasingly involved with their children's educational programming since the mid-70s. This trend was prompted by the mandates for parental involvement contained in P.L. 94-142 (now IDEA) and encouraged by recognition that home-school planning results in more effective programs. It is being repeatedly demonstrated that parental involvement results in increased student involvement and, ultimately, better grades for those students whose parents keep in close contact with teachers.

The degree of *parental involvement* may range from monthly conferences to comprehensive behavior management systems planned cooperatively and implemented by parents in the home. Parent support groups and parent training programs are often formally organized by educators.

Respite care is a helpful home intervention for parents of individuals with severe emotional or behavioral problems. Additional programs for the children on Saturdays, during after-school hours, and/or through the summer months can alleviate some of the stress inherent in continuous care of these youngsters. The goal is prevention of institutionalization by making the living situation more manageable and comfortable for parents and siblings. Such comprehensive programming often requires a systems approach such as cooperative planning and funding from social agencies working with the school system.

Another potentially effective change in the home ecosystem is that of *family therapy*. Many therapists now take the approach that because all members of a family heavily influence one another, the most effective counseling involves all members of the unit. This interactive influence is especially true for families of students with emotional/behavioral disorders who often have difficulty dealing with the social and emotional problems experienced by these youngsters. Learning to manage such problems as a family unit takes the burden off the individual who is identified as the "patient" and distributes responsibility for change to all members of the family.

Changes in the School Ecosystem

Mainstreaming is an ecological intervention that has been occurring in our schools since the passage of legislation in the mid-70s. Arising from concern with the social ramifications of segregating students with disabilities from those without, mainstreaming required educators to develop plans to ensure that children with disabilities be educated with their nondisabled peers to the maximum extent appropriate; that is, children should be removed from the mainstream of education only when the severity of the disability requires segregation to ensure a satisfactory education. Mainstreaming changed the face of our schools in that students with disabilities were no longer segregated on other campuses or in self-contained classrooms that were usually in the least desirable locations (e.g., boiler rooms, portable trailers). Instead, special educators and general education teachers were required to work jointly to serve these children in various combinations of special education and general education programs.

Recently, a number of educators have been dissatisfied with the concept of mainstreaming or education in the least restrictive environment, and have pushed for full inclusion. Full inclusion is the education of *all children,* regardless of severity of disability, in general education classrooms. Inclusionists recognize that many adaptations in our current system will have to occur to accommodate some individuals with severe disabilities; these accommodations would include the provision of specialists and supports within the general classroom. Full inclusionists advocate abolishing special education in its current form. As this book went to press, full inclusion was a hotly debated issue, with many proponents and many opponents (see Fuchs & Fuchs, 1994; Kauffman, 1993). Opponents generally fear that (a) students with disabilities will receive fewer and less appropriate services in general classrooms, and (b) the inclusion movement is so disassociated from general education that forging an alliance will be difficult, if not impossible. Inclusion is dealt with more fully in Chapter 11.

Both mainstreaming and the full inclusion movement are examples of systems changes in the schools: One has been implemented for almost twenty years now, and the success or failure of the other remains to be seen. Both represent massive changes in the *status quo* of services delivery for students with special needs.

Changes in Home, School, and Community Ecosystems

Project Re-ED is a model program for students with emotional/behavioral disorders that is ecological in scope. The program was conceived by a number of theorists but headed by Nicholas Hobbs, who was motivated by a disenchantment with psychiatric programs for children and youth with disorders. Concerned with the high financial cost and lack of personnel to adequately staff such programs, Hobbs questioned the efficacy of the psychiatric approach:

> *There is a real possibility that hospitals make children sick. The antiseptic atmosphere, the crepe sole and white coat, the tension, the expectancy of illness may confirm a child's worst fears about himself, firmly setting his aberrant behavior. (Hobbs, 1966, p. 1105)*

Hobbs opened Cumberland House in Nashville, Tennessee, and the Wright School in Durham, North Carolina in the early 1960s. There are currently approximately 16 programs throughout the country that operate according to Re-ED principles. These short-term, residential programs are based on the supposition that the most effective treatment is one that intervenes in all ecosystems. The goal, therefore, is not to fix the child and return her to the community, but to make the child's ecosystem fit together more smoothly. The targets for intervention are not only the child but also the child's home, neighborhood, school, social agencies, and community (Hobbs, 1966).

Re-ED's treatment philosophy basically views children as capable of controlling and changing their own behavior to more adaptive ways. Trust in adults and competence in school and other life skills are viewed as the necessary bases from which changes can be made. The child's feelings are recognized and the youngster is taught to express both positive and negative feelings in socially acceptable ways.

School interventions are implemented by teacher-counselors. The teacher-counselor during the day functions much as a public school teacher in academics but performs the additional role of counseling and working to modify maladaptive behaviors. Education takes precedence over psychotherapy, as the ability to achieve academically is considered essential for making the child's school ecosystem work successfully. The night teacher-counselor takes over after school hours and is primarily a support person who supervises group activities and extracurricular activities. Almost all activities are undertaken in small groups, which are considered an important source of both motivation and control.

Another important role is played by the liaison teacher-counselor who assesses the home, school, and community and helps them prepare for the return of the student. In the school, the liaison teacher-counselor collects extensive historical information such as past academic and behavioral records, successful and unsuccessful program modifications, relationships with various school personnel, and so forth. The goal is to plan cooperatively for a smooth reentry. The liaison teacher-counselor is also available as a consultant after reentry into the school. Similar tasks are undertaken in the home and community. Parents are viewed as collaborators in effecting long-term change in their child's life. Beginning with the child's weekend visits early in the Re-ED program, the liaison teacher-counselor maintains close communication with parents and helps them plan changes that will aid the child's adaptation in the home and community. The liaison teacher-counselor also coordinates services with community agencies such as social service departments or mental health centers, which may be essential links to the child's transition. Thus, the liaison teacher-counselor seeks to establish a supportive network in the child's major ecosystems which are conducive to healthy and adaptive functioning.

Changes in the Societal Ecosystem: a Systems Approach

Although changes in society at large are extremely difficult to effect, many professionals concerned about the mental health of our children and adolescents are reaching the same conclusion: all systems working with these children and youth must become more coordinated in their treatment efforts. Saxe, Cross, and Silverman (1988) have written a treatise on this issue entitled, "Children's Mental Health Services: The Gap Between What We Know and What We Do." Saxe and his colleagues estimate that over 11 percent (about 6 to 8 million) of children in the United States need mental health services, yet less than half of these children receive any form of treatment; a much smaller percentage receive the treatment they really need, including support services for the family. These appalling figures translate into several million children who are not being adequately reached by our current systems. To improve this situation, Saxe et al. underscore the need for an ecological approach to formulating policy:

> *Formulation of children's mental health policy is thus inherently difficult because of the interaction between the individual child's vulnerability and risk factors present in that child's environment. Children are highly dependent on their environment; thus, mental health problems depend both on the child and the stresses or support present in his or her family, school, and community. Although for any one child it is difficult to separate individual and environmental factors, to appreciate the range of children's mental health problems, these factors must be described in terms of their interaction. . . Treatment must therefore address conditions in the family, school, and neighborhood, as well as within the child. (pp. 800–801)*

Ecological solutions are required to resolve two major impediments to provision of adequate services for children with E/BD. The first impediment is a lack of a continuum of services, in particular, a lack of community-based services. In many communities, outpatient services are limited, as are family support services such as family counseling, specialized day care, respite care, and therapeutic foster care. Limited options often result in more restrictive placements than may be necessary because the family is unable to keep the child at home without these types of support (National Mental Health and Special Education Coalition, 1989). Also the health care financing system has historically promoted short-term hospitalization (which we know to be ineffective with children whose parents should be involved in treatment) rather than longer-term outpatient treatment and support services (which we know to be effective with these same children). Therefore, drastic changes are needed both in the range of services available and in the philosophies of insurance companies who too often dictate the type and terms of treatment.

A second major impediment to provision of adequate services is lack of interagency coordination. More specific difficulties are cited by the National Coalition (1989):

- Different agencies define the target population differently.
- Different agencies have different eligibility requirements.
- Agencies may blame each other for problems because the lines of responsibility are not clearly defined.
- Vague policies about who pays and who serves can result in children's "falling through the cracks", i.e., no agency takes responsibility for treatment.
- Agencies often do not coordinate or cooperate with other agencies because of turf issues and concerns about agency funding that override concerns for services to children.
- Although public schools have a federal mandate to serve children identified as disordered, no other agencies operate under a legal mandate to provide services.

BOX 4-3   Case Study: Alan: Complex Solutions for Complex Problems

In Texas, as in many states, the legislature became disenchanted with interagency squabbling over eligibility requirements and turf issues. In 1987, it created a commission to develop a model for interagency staffing groups that would coordinate services for children and youth with interagency needs. Eleven state agencies were mandated to establish coordinating groups on the local level; however, in many communities, a number of private, nonprofit agencies and private hospitals also have voluntarily become active members of the groups. These groups, known as Community Resource Coordination Groups (CRCGs), meet on a monthly basis and "staff" the most difficult interagency cases. Plans are made, agencies make commitments for services, and a staff member is assigned to ensure that the plan is implemented. Following is a summary of how one CRCG was able to help Alan; it demonstrates that there are no easy answers, even when all involved agencies are willing to set aside the normal restrictions that guide their work.

Alan was a 14-year-old with a dual diagnosis of mental retardation and mental illness. Specifically, he was diagnosed with conduct disorder, alcohol and substance abuse disorder, and seizure disorder. He had numerous referrals to juvenile court because of assault and public intoxication. He fell through most of the cracks in the system because of his dual diagnosis. The services provided under the auspices of mental retardation were inadequate to address his mental health needs, and the mental health services

were not appropriate for clients with mental retardation. Alan's mother was supportive and willing to try almost anything to get him help.

Alan was referred off and on to CRCG for a period of three years before the group was able to come up with a plan that really worked. The school district applied to the state education agency for community service funds to help keep Alan at home. These funds paid for respite care, a behavior specialist to work at home with Alan's mother and at school with his teachers, and a 1:1 social skills trainer to help Alan control his behavior in school. A nonprofit agency provided case management, juvenile court kept the case open to provide any needed support, and the local mental health/mental retardation authority provided social skills groups and after-school programming. These collaborative efforts have helped maintain Alan in his home for two years without any hospitalizations or detentions.

Despite several false starts, which perhaps is to be expected in difficult cases, the CRCG was finally able to provide services that were intensive enough to help Alan get his behavior under control. Without these efforts at cooperative programming, Alan would no doubt cycle in and out of the state hospital and the courts—indefinitely. CRCG and all similar groups are a very good beginning to overcoming the barriers to interagency collaboration that have traditionally plagued services for children and youth with multiple needs.

Obviously, the issues of an adequate continuum of services and interagency coordination are closely related: if systems can pool their resources and precisely define roles and responsibilities, then a true continuum of services is likely to become available. A systems approach is clearly needed, i.e., one that views (a) emotional/behavioral disorders as the shared responsibility of child-environment, and (b) treatment as the shared responsibility of a number of different systems offering a continuum of coordinated services. These agencies or systems include education, mental health, social services, juvenile justice, and vocational rehabilitation. Models for establishing a systems approach are being developed; one such example is described in Box 4-3. We will return to these issues and the systems approach in Chapter 9.

Summary of the Ecological Model

Ecological theorists believe that it is impossible to define disordered behavior in isolation from the contexts in which the behavior occurs. Disordered behavior is viewed as a disturbance in the equilibrium of a system; therefore, the child is viewed as a part of the problem rather than the owner of the problem. In theory, all components of the disturbed system should be analyzed for contributing factors and then targeted for intervention along with the child. In practice, analyzing and intervening in disturbed systems is difficult and time-consuming. Project Re-ED is one example of an ecologically-based program for students with emotional/behavioral disorders. A systems approach to serving this population is also being touted by the National Mental Health and Special Education Coalition, which is calling for effective interagency cooperation and a true continuum of services that includes family support. The ecological model is summarized in Table 4-4.

Conclusions

Understanding disordered behavior from a behavioral perspective allows teachers to employ a variety of successful interventions in the classroom. Taking data and manipulating either antecedents or consequences to effect behavior change are basic skills needed by all teachers of students with emotional/behavioral disorders. Behavioral interventions should not be viewed as a panacea, however; many useful techniques may stem from other models. A blend of behaviorism and cognitive theory, the cognitive-behavioral model is receiving increasing attention due to the research on successful interventions being conducted with individuals with a number of different emotional/behavioral disorders.

Viewing disordered behavior from an ecological perspective takes some of the pressure off of the children to do all the changing. Although ecological interventions may be difficult to effect, the philosophy underlying this model is an essential one for teachers: only when we truly believe in a systems approach to working with children with emotional/behavioral disorders and their families will we begin to make inroads in their treatment. We will return to a more thorough discussion of the systems approach in Chapter 9.

TABLE 4-4   Summary of the Ecological Model

ETIOLOGY	EVALUATION PROCEDURES

Disturbances in the ecosystems of:
  classroom
  home
  school
  community
  society
	Analysis of Classroom Instructional Demands (West, 1990)
	Behavior Rating Profile-2 (Brown & Hammill, 1990)
	The Instructional Environment Scale (Ysseldyke & Christenson, 1987)

EDUCATIONAL
APPLICATIONS

classroom: physical arrangement, rules
                     contracts, scheduling
home: parent support groups
               parent training groups
               respite care programs
               family therapy
school: mainstreaming,
               inclusion
home/school/community: Project Re-ED
society: provision of continuum of
                   services in community
               interagency coordination

Key Points

1. The basic tenet of behavioral theory is that all behavior, including maladaptive behavior, is learned and therefore can be "unlearned" and new behavior learned in its place.
2. Behavioral theorists effect behavior change by manipulating environmental events that precede or follow the targeted behavior.
3. All teachers of students with emotional/behavioral disorders should be adept at using behavioral techniques to increase desired behaviors and to decrease undesired behaviors in the classroom.
4. Social learning or modeling is useful in teaching social skills.
5. Ecological theorists believe that deviance results from the interactions of an individual with others in the environment; hence, ecosystems rather than individuals are viewed as disturbed or disordered.
6. If ecosystems are disturbed, then we must intervene in the various systems in which students live and interact: classroom, school, home, and community.
7. Although systems changes are difficult to effect, many professionals now agree that

we must provide and coordinate a variety of community-based services to students and their families if we are to truly make changes in their lives.

Additional Readings

Children's mental health: The gap between what we know and what we do, by L. Saxe, T. Cross, & N. Silverman, *American Psychologist, 43*, 1988, 800–807, for a no-nonsense treatise on what we should be doing to provide needed mental health services to our children.

Helping disturbed children: Psychological and ecological strategies, by Nicholas Hobbs, *American Psychologist, 2*, 1966, 1105–1115, for more information on Project Re-ED.

Integrating services for children and youth with emotional and behavioral disorders, by C. Michael Nelson & Cheryll Pearson. Reston: VA: Council for Exceptional Children, 1991, for a reference book on how multiple agencies can work together to plan and offer services to children with E/BD.

Managing behavior series, edited by Vance Hall, includes three practical booklets on understanding and applying behavioral principles in schools and homes. Austin, TX: Pro-Ed, 1983.

The disturbing child: A problem of ecological management, by William C. Rhodes. *Exceptional Children, 33*, 1967, 449–455; and A community participation analysis of emotional disturbance, also by Rhodes. *Exceptional Children, 36*, 1970, 309–314, for seminal writings on the ecological perspective.

The myth of mental illness, by T. Szasz. New York: Hoeber-Harber, 1966, for writings of an author who believes that society *creates* disturbance in individuals.

Using rational-emotive therapy to prevent classroom problems, by Jo Webber and Maggie Coleman, *Teaching Exceptional Children, 21*, 1988, for a short, practical article written for teachers who would like to try RET on themselves to improve classroom management skills.

Chapter 5

Internalizing Disorders

Definition, Characteristics, Etiology, and Treatment of Depression and Anxiety Disorders

A Note on Social Withdrawal

Orientation

Childhood traditionally has been considered a happy, carefree time devoid of the fears and anxieties that are the domain of adults. However, with increased pressures to live between households of divorced parents or with single parents, to "just say no" to drugs, and to otherwise grow up fast, children and adolescents are showing the strain. Children who experience fears, phobias, anxiety, and depression need adult support; for those who cannot function routinely, clinical interventions may be required. Teachers need to be especially keen observers of these characteristics because children are often unable to identify or label internalizing disorders by themselves.

Overview

This chapter addresses internalizing disorders of childhood and adolescence. These disorders tend to be introversive or intrapersonal in nature; in the past, they have been termed "overcontrolled" and "personality disorder." Students with these disorders do not ordinarily present problems of discipline or conformity and therefore historically have not received as much attention in the school setting as externalizing youngsters. However, both educational and mental health professionals are recognizing the debilitating effects of anxiety and depression upon the normal development of children and adolescents. Depression and anxiety disorders are the most prevalent of the internalizing problems. For each of these disorders, this chapter presents an overview of (1) definition, (2) characteristics and symptoms, (3) theories of etiology, and (4) intervention and treatment strategies. Although social withdrawal is rarely seen as a clinical entity separate from other disorders, some concerns about socially withdrawn children are addressed at the end of this chapter.

Depression

The existence of depression in children and adolescents has only recently been accepted by the mental health community. In fact, it was not until the late 1960s that textbooks in psychiatry included chapters on childhood depression (J. M. Golden, 1981). Reasons for questioning its existence related to beliefs about etiology. Early psychoanalytic views held that depression is caused by an overly punitive superego, which results in self-directed aggression manifested in depression (Freud, 1957; Rochlin, 1959). As the superego was thought to become internalized sometime during adolescence, pre-adolescents were thought incapable of experiencing depression.

Overwhelming evidence supports the contention that both children and adolescents experience depression severe enough to interfere with daily functioning. In addition to the traditional markers of sad affect, low self-esteem, and decreased energy level, depressed youngsters may experience apathy or loss of interest in their usual activities and routines, including schoolwork. The federal definition of seriously emotionally disturbed accounts for depressed children in the component, "a pervasive mood of unhappiness or depression." The first two sections of this chapter will clarify the defining characteristics of depression, its prevalence and accompanying symptoms.

Definition and Prevalence

Depression may be defined as "a syndrome of abnormally dejected mood persistent over time that interferes with daily functioning" (Muse, 1990). The current perspective on childhood depression is based upon the belief that children exhibit depressive symptoms paralleling those in adults (American Psychiatric Association, 1994; Kovacs & Beck, 1977; Puig-Antich, 1982). However, many researchers argue for a developmental perspective, which posits that depression manifests itself in different symptoms at different developmental stages (Carlson and Cantwell, 1986; Rutter, Izard, & Read, 1986). For example, as the child gets older, depressive behavior may become more overt and may be manifested in acting out, truancy, running away, and disobedience (Lesse, 1974). Until epidemiological research can clearly establish parameters for depressive symptoms at differing developmental stages, most professionals will continue to define childhood depression by the diagnostic criteria set forth for adults in the DSM-IV (American Psychiatric Association, 1994). This approach is obviously based on the belief that childhood depression is a downward extension of adult depression.

Three primary diagnostic categories of depressive disorders are provided in DSM-IV: *Major Depressive Disorder, Dysthymic Disorder, and Depressive Disorder Not Otherwise Specified.* These categories differ in number, severity, and duration of symptoms, with Major Depressive Disorder being the most severe and Depressive Disorder Not Otherwise Specified, the least severe. Major Depression consists of a prominent and persistent depressed mood *or* loss of interest and pleasure in usual activities. Depressed mood is characterized by symptoms such as "sad, discouraged, down in the dumps," and "hopeless." Children, however, may seem predominantly irritable instead of sad. In addition, at least four of the following symptoms must have been present almost continuously for a period of at least two weeks:

• Change in appetite or weight
• Insomnia or too much sleep
• Psychomotor agitation or retardation
• Loss of interest or pleasure in usual activities
• Loss of energy/fatigue
• Feelings of worthlessness/excessive or inappropriate guilt
• Inability to concentrate
• Recurrent thoughts of death (American Psychiatric Association, 1994).

Further, these symptoms must result in significant distress or impaired functioning. Another type of depression, *bipolar,* may be diagnosed in adolescents and adults; recently, physicians have begun to diagnose it in increasing numbers of children although it was previously thought to be rare in prepubertal children. Bipolar depression was formerly called manic-depressive syndrome because of extreme mood swings from a highly active, agitated, grandiose "manic" state of mind to a dysphoric, "depressed" one. The term *depression* in this chapter will refer to major depression unless otherwise specified.

Prevalence estimates of childhood depression vary widely, primarily due to variation in instrumentation and criteria that are used by researchers. Also, prevalence rates in the general population would be expected to be significantly lower than those in samples of youngsters in special education or clinical treatment. Table 5-1 summarizes a number of prevalence studies. Despite disparities in prevalence rates, these data indicate a few trends. In the general population, adolescents show much higher rates of depression (13–18 percent) than elementary-aged students (from 1.8–5.2 percent). As expected, special samples show

TABLE 5-1 Prevalence Estimates of Depression in Children and Adolescents

Investigation	Sample	% Depressed
Kashani & Simonds (1979)	103 elementary general population	1.9
Kashani et al. (1981)	641 elementary general population	1.8
Lefkowitz & Tesiny (1985)	3020 elementary general population	5.2
Kandel & Davies (1982)	4204 adolescents general population	13
Reynolds (1984)	2800 adolescents general population	18
Alessi (1986)	134 child psychiatric patients	37
Mattison et al. (1986)	158 special ed children	21
	128 special ed adolescents	50
Maag & Behrens (1989)	144 E/BD adolescents	21

significantly higher rates than in the general population (elementary special samples range from 21–37 percent; adolescent special samples range from 21–50 percent). Predictably, studies using more stringent criteria (including DSM criteria and/or clinical interview) usually find lower prevalence rates. For example, Carlson and Cantwell (1979) assessed a sample of psychiatric clients, ages 7 to 17, and found that 60 percent could be classified as having depressive symptoms, 49 percent could be classified as moderately depressed according to a self-report instrument, but only 28 percent could be diagnosed as experiencing major depression according to DSM criteria and a clinical interview. A similar trend was found with a sample of 385 adolescents in the general population, with 13.5 percent reporting mild depression, 7 percent reporting moderate depression, and 1.3 percent reporting severe depression (Kaplan, Hong, & Weinhold, 1984).

Characteristics and Symptoms

The characteristics and symptoms of depression will be discussed under the four categories identified by Kovacs and Beck (1977): *emotional/affective, cognitive, motivational,* and *physical.* Although not mutually exclusive, these categories provide a conceptual framework for viewing depressive symptoms.

The major *emotional/affective* symptoms are dysphoric mood and inability to experience pleasure in activities that were previously enjoyable. Related symptoms are the inability to respond to humor and excessive crying.

The *cognitive symptoms* of negative self-evaluation, guilt, and hopelessness are more prevalent among depressed children than among their nondepressed counterparts. Studies have shown that self-dislike and self-blame are common characteristics (Kashani & Simonds, 1979; Seligman et al., 1984), with one study reporting that 97 percent of the depressed sample exhibited negative self-evaluation (Brumbeck, Dietz-Schmidt, & Weinberg, 1977). Excessive guilt is linked to negative self-evaluation because children who perceive themselves negatively are likely to blame themselves or feel responsible when things do not go well. Hopelessness is related to the child's bleak expectations for the future: things will not change for the better, but they could get worse. It is important to recognize feelings of hopelessness because of the close association with suicidal ideation (Kazdin, French, Unis, Esveldt-Dawson, & Sherick, 1983).

Another cognitive symptom is inability to concentrate, which was found in 77 percent of one sample of depressed adolescent males (Kashani, Heinrichs, Reid, & Huff, 1982). Depressed children may become preoccupied and unable to concentrate on their schoolwork, causing them to fall behind academically. Reported estimates of depressed children who are experiencing academic difficulties range from 48–62 percent (Carlson & Cantwell, 1979; Kaslow, Tanenbaum, Abramson, Peterson, & Seligman, 1983). It is not clear whether this difficulty is related to motivational deficits or inability to concentrate.

Motivational symptoms include social withdrawal and suicidal ideation. Children who are depressed tend to shy away from social interactions (Poznanski, Cook, & Carroll, 1979). The child who withdraws due to depression should be distinguished from the socially isolated child: the former would have been considered socially active prior to the onset of depression, and the latter's behavior would have been consistently withdrawn over time. One study found that over two-thirds of the sample of depressed children had demonstrated decreased social interaction (Brumbeck et al., 1977). Depressed children also tend to think and sometimes talk about suicide (Carlson & Cantwell, 1982).

Physical symptoms may be the most easily observed symptoms of depression in children. Chronic fatigue and depressed energy level may be evident. Depressed children often complain of headaches, stomachaches and other pains. Sleep disorders may be the most common somatic symptom, as one group of researchers found that 92% of their sample of depressed adolescent males reported some type of sleep disorder (Kashani et al., 1982). Both insomnia and hypersomnia (sleeping too much) have been reported. Changes in appetite resulting in weight gain or loss are also a major characteristic. Psychomotor agitation or retardation, referring to abnormal rates in the child's movements, speech, and reaction times, may also be present. Symptoms of depression in children are summarized in Table 5-2.

Related Conditions

In a review of literature on depression in children and adolescents, Hodgman (1985) lists several clinical conditions found to co-exist with depression: conduct disorders, eating disorders, substance abuse, and anxiety disorders.

Two studies assessing major depression in samples of juvenile offenders with conduct disorders have recorded incidences of 15 percent (Alessi, McManus, & Grapente, 1984) and

TABLE 5-2   Symptoms of Depression in Children

Affective/emotional Symptoms
Often looks sad
Complains of feeling sad, blue, or tired
Cries easily
Inability to respond to humor
Loss of interest in previously pleasurable activities

Cognitive Symptoms
Negative self-evaluation
Self-dislike
Self-blame
Excessive guilt
Hopelessness
Difficulty with concentration
Forgetful, failure to complete schoolwork or chores

Motivational Symptoms
Social withdrawal
Suicidal ideation
Poor school performance

Physical Symptoms
Chronic fatigue
Depressed energy level
Insomnia, hypersomnia
Changes in appetite and weight

18 percent (Kashani et al., 1982). These findings may be important because depressive symptoms are not usually associated with acting out behaviors such as are found in conduct disordered populations. Thus, among this population, depression may be manifested in agitated symptoms rather than the classic depressed affective ones. Depression also has been associated with both anorexia nervosa and bulimia. One group of researchers (Katz, Kuperberg, & Pollack, 1984) has suggested that depression and anorexia nervosa are interrelated, perhaps interacting to sustain one another either psychologically or physically. Although bulimic patients have shown a response to antidepressants (Pope, Hudson, & Jonas, 1983), studies linking bulimia to depression are mixed, failing to establish a clear relationship.

Substance abuse may represent attempts by depressed adolescents to cope with dysphoric mood, perhaps clouding the diagnosis of depression in this population. While substance abuse among depressed adolescents has not been sufficiently studied, according to one researcher, the coexistence of depression and alcoholism in many families "is suggestive" (Hodgman, 1985).

Anxiety disorders have also been associated with depression. In fact, the two share many common characteristics and diagnosic criteria, leading researchers and clinicians to wonder whether anxiety and depression are two distinct conditions or a common syndrome. Clark and Watson (1991) conclude that adult anxiety and depression share a common component, that of general affective distress; however, Clark and Watson also found that symptoms of *physiological hyperarousal* were unique to anxiety and that symptoms of *anhedonia* (defined as lack of positive affect) were unique to depression.

Stark and his colleagues (Laurent, Landau, & Stark, 1993; Stark, Humphrey, Laurent, Livingston, & Christopher, 1993) extended this question of differential diagnosis to children and young adolescents. In a sample of fourth through seventh graders, Stark et al. (1993) found that the two disorders are distinct and characterized by unique cognitive, social skills, and family profiles. In another study with the same age group, the two syndromes were differentiated by a number of symptoms. Four symptoms were predictive of depression: feeling unloved, anhedonia, excessive guilt, and depressed mood. One symptom characterized anxiety disorder: worries, especially about future events and academic competence (Laurent, Landau, & Stark, 1993).Thus, there is some preliminary evidence to suggest that despite the overlap in observable symptoms, anxiety and depression do constitute separate syndromes that are identifiable in children, potentially leading to different treatments.

From a medical perspective, Hodgman summarizes the research on related conditions by expressing concerns that an undetermined number of depressed youngsters may not be accurately diagnosed, leading to ineffective treatment attempts. From an education perspective, Forness (1988b) has reviewed literature relevant to the school functioning of depressed children and adolescents and has found it sufficiently lacking in methodological soundness to draw conclusions. Although teachers are not expected to diagnose clinical conditions, it is important to recognize that these conditions may coexist, so that symptoms can be brought to the attention of appropriate personnel.

Etiology and Development of Depression

Researchers have yet to establish the causes of depression, and much of the causal research thus far attempted has focused on adults. There are, however, a number of theories of the etiology of depression, most of which are substantiated by some research. Schools of thought related to the development of depression may be categorized into *biophysical, psychodynamic, behavioral,* and *cognitive* models. A *comprehensive* model that incorporates several aspects of the other models also is presented.

Biophysical Model

The biophysical model includes theories that have explored both biochemical and hereditary etiologies. Biochemical studies with depressed adults have focused primarily on the role of *neurotransmitters,* or chemicals in the brain that facilitate transmission of neural impulses. These studies assess the effects of antidepressant medication, which act by increasing the availability of certain neurotransmitters at critical receptor sites in the brain. The two most frequently targeted neurotransmitters are norepinephrine and serotonin. While some researchers have posited that norepinephrine depletion causes depression, others have argued that serotonin depletion is the culprit, and still others believe that the relationship between the two is the vital factor (Davis, Berger, Hollister, & Barchas, 1978).

Biophysical research with children and adolescents is much scarcer and has dealt primarily with hormones, sleep EEGs, and metabolic secretions (Sellstrom, 1989; Lux, 1990). As Sellstrom points out, biophysical research with children and adolescents is hampered by the many developmental fluctuations caused by normal growth and by puberty. A number of studies have assessed the genetic aspect of depression through studies of adoptions and of twins (identical versus fraternal). These studies generally support the notion of a genetic predisposition to depression in adults (Hodgman, 1985; Kashani et al., 1981). A particularly strong genetic disposition has been found for bipolar depression (Strober & Carlson, 1982; Winokur, Clayton, & Reich, 1984) and for recurring depression. However, these researchers caution that environmental causes are likely necessary for depression to develop, and that current research is inconclusive in identifying a reliable genetic marker (Hodgman, 1985; Cytryn, McKnew, Zahn-Waxler, & Gershon, 1986).

Psychodynamic Model

As mentioned in the beginning of this chapter, many early psychoanalytic theorists maintained that children cannot become depressed because of inadequate superego development. As depression was thought to be caused by a punitive superego and a result of aggression turned inward, children without developed superegos were thought incapable of experiencing depression. However, other psychoanalytic theorists modified this stance by purporting that depression is related to ego rather than superego development (Anthony, 1975; Bibring, 1953), thereby acknowledging that children could in fact become depressed. These ego analyst theorists also believe that the symptoms of depression would vary according to the stage of ego development and that younger children would lack the ego functions of self-observation and self-criticism that are prerequisite to development of depression (Malmquist, 1977). Unfortunately, these views are primarily theoretical and do not lend themselves to empirical study. The psychodynamic view is mentioned here because of its impact on early thought regarding childhood depression and because some mental health workers may base treatment of depression upon an anger-turned-inward paradigm.

Behavioral Model

A behavioral explanation for the development of depression has been formulated by Lewisohn (1974). This model postulates that depression develops when individuals fail to receive positive reinforcement from social interactions with others. According to Lewisohn (1974), the amount of positive reinforcement received by an individual is based upon not only the amount of available reinforcement, but, more importantly, the individual's skill at eliciting it. Therefore Lewisohn and his colleagues propose a causal link between social skills deficits and depression in adults.

This model postulates that when individuals receive a low rate of positive reinforcement for their social behaviors, they become increasingly more passive and nonresponsive, resulting in a dysphoric mood. The dysphoric mood can then lead to secondary symptoms such as low self-esteem, pessimism, and guilt.

Lewisohn & Arconad (1981) have shown that depressed persons do elicit fewer behaviors from others, receive less positive reinforcement, and demonstrate fewer social skills when compared to nondepressed peers. However, it should be noted that these behaviors may exist as a result of depressed behavior rather than as a cause.

Cognitive Models

Cognitive models of depression have been put forth by Seligman (1975) and by Beck (1967, 1974). Seligman and colleagues have formulated a causal theory of depression based upon the concepts of learned helplessness and attributions. Seligman's original model (1975) proposed that individuals become depressed when they believe that they cannot control outcomes in their lives, resulting in the cognitive, emotional, and motivational correlates of depression. This learned helplessness concept was investigated and subsequently reformulated by Seligman and colleagues (Abramson, Seligman, & Teasdale, 1978), who proposed that the key to the development of depression is the attributions about uncontrollable outcomes made by an individual. In other words, the individual must ask himself why the outcomes seem uncontrollable, and the resulting reasons or attributions will determine whether depression will result. Three dimensions of attributions are important in this schema: globality, meaning that the individual believes that he is helpless in a variety of situations; stability, meaning that the individual believes that he will become chronically helpless; and internality, meaning that the individual will attribute reasons for failures to himself.

Beck's (1967) cognitive model of depression is based upon three related concepts: the *negative cognitive triad, negative schemata, and cognitive distortion.* The *negative cognitive triad* refers to the depressed individual's perceptions of the self, the world, and the future. These negative perceptions account for many of the symptoms of depression, e.g., dysphoric mood is viewed as a result of pervasive negative thoughts. Research has substantiated that depressed children do view themselves negatively and that depressed children hold negative expectations for the future, as indicated by hopelessness (Haley, Fine, Marriage, Moretti, & Freeman, 1985; Kazdin, Rodgers, & Colbus, 1986). Beck's second concept, *negative schemata,* refers to stable thought patterns about the self, the world, and the future, the most important of these being negative self-schemata. Several studies support this idea of negative self-schemata in adult depressed subjects (Kanfer & Zeiss, 1983; Roth & Rehm, 1980). Beck's third concept, *cognitive distortion,* is based upon the premise that individuals maintain their negative schemata by faulty information processing: depressed individuals fail to process information that is incongruent with their negative self-schemata. For example, in the Roth and Rehm study cited above, depressed subjects overestimated negative behaviors and underestimated positive behaviors when rating themselves from a videotape. A systematic bias in processing information thus tends to reinforce negative self-schemata and to permeate the thinking of depressed individuals (Lux, 1990). This concept has been supported by researchers who have found that a negative style of information processing is predictive of depressive symptoms (Ingram, 1984; Rush, Weissenburger, & Eaves, 1986).

To summarize, Beck's model (1967, 1974) holds that depression develops as the individual moves from realistic self-appraisal to self-devaluing, from a realistic appraisal of the environment to a negative one, and from a hopeful appraisal of the future to a hopeless one. While various aspects of this cognitive model of depression have been supported by research, the reader should bear in mind that the correlation of negative cognitions and depressive symptoms does not prove causation.

A Comprehensive Model

Stark and his colleagues have extended the work of Beck and others in proposing a more comprehensive model of childhood depression (Stark, Humphrey, Crook, & Lewis, 1990; Stark, Rouse, & Livingston, 1991). Cognitive-behavioral in basic orientation, this model recognizes genetic predisposition, family environment, and the child's own adaptive skills in accounting for the core schemas that determine how the child ultimately will view himself. Stark's research has indicated that depressed children do have negative self-schemata when compared to controls, and that they report receiving more negative messages from both parents about the self, world, and future than either controls or anxious children (Stark, Humphrey, Laurent, Livingston, & Christopher, 1993). From this framework, a multidimensional treatment has been developed that will be described in the next section.

Predisposing Factors

Several studies have shown that, compared to nondepressed parents, depressed parents have offspring with higher rates of depression (Beardslee, Bemporad, Keller, & Klerman, 1983). Maternal depresssion in particular has been implicated in the etiology of childhood depression (Anthony, 1975). However, these studies have not established a causal link between depression in parents and their offspring.

Although a genetic predisposition toward depression has been documented, most researchers believe that environmental factors act as catalysts in its development. Many of these factors are related to losses, stress, or significant changes in the family context (Muse, 1990). Losses refer to such events as death of family members and "loss" of a parent through divorce. Stresses include chronic illness in self or family member, parental unemployment, and family violence or discord. Examples of significant family changes are birth of a sibling and remarriage. Substance abuse by parents, and physical, sexual, or emotional abuse of the child also add to the risk of developing depression. These risk factors are summarized in Table 5-3.

TABLE 5-3   Risk Factors for Depression in Children

Other Family Members with Mental Health Problems
Relatives with depression
Relatives with alcohol problems
Relatives who abuse drugs
Relatives who have been in psychiatric hospital

Important Losses
Death of parent
Death of sibling
Death of other close family
Divorce
Loss of friends because of moving
"Loss" of mother if she returns to work
Death of a pet
Loss of important objects
Loss of home

Chronic Stress in Family
Chronic illness in family member
Chronic illness in the child
Loss of parental job with unemployment
Problems with the law

Child Abuse
Physical abuse
Sexual abuse
Emotional abuse

Any Significant Family Change or Stress
Birth of a sibling
Remarriage
Family violence
Parental discord
Suicide in family or friend

From Muse, 1990. *Depression and suicide in children and adolescents.* Reprinted by permission of Pro-Ed Publishers.

Intervention and Treatment

Research on treatment of depression in children and adolescents may best be described as "in its infancy." Researchers have documented improvement with samples of depressed children and adolescents through psychotherapy, medication, and school-based interventions. However, each of these treatments has its proponents, and consensus has yet to be established as to the most effective treatment or combination of treatments.

Psychotherapy versus Medical Intervention

Psychotherapy for mildly depressed adults and adolescents has been promoted as equal to or superior to other forms of treatment, including medication (Kaplan & Sadock, 1988; Wright & Beck, 1983). According to Hodgman (1985), the best controlled of these studies assessed the effectiveness of cognitive therapy with adults. Muse (1990) suggests that for children whose depression is mild, has clear precipitating stresses and no biological base, psychotherapy is the treatment of choice. For instances of more serious depression, Puig-Antich and Weston (1983) have found limited evidence for effectiveness of psychotherapy with children and adolescents; they suggest that serious depression is not amenable to other treatments until first improved with medication. Hodgman (1985) also suggests that, for more serious cases of depression, a combination of therapy and medication may be most effective. This view is shared by Cantwell & Carlson (1983) and by Gadow (1986a), who support the use of medication in children with physical symptoms and family history of affective disorders.

More doctors are prescribing medications for severely depressed children and adolescents than in the recent past. The use of antidepressants was described in some detail in Chapter 3 under psychopharmacology. To summarize, Imipramine (trade name Tofranil) previously was the most often prescribed, but has recently fallen into disfavor among physicians due to its side-effects. Welbutrin and Prozac are now more commonly prescribed. Also, lithium is often prescribed for the increasing numbers of children and adolescents being diagnosed as having bipolar depression. One concern with antidepressants is the potential for misuse or suicidal overdoses.

School-Based Interventions

A number of school-based intervention studies of depressed children have been based upon cognitive approaches and/or social skills training. For example, Butler et al. compared social skills combined with problem-solving to a cognitive restructuring approach with upper elementary children; both groups improved on a self-report measure of depression as compared to a control group (Butler, Miezitis, Friedman, & Cole, 1980). Likewise, Reynolds and Coates (1986) compared a cognitive-behavioral approach to relaxation training in adolescents and found that both groups significantly improved over a control group on a self-report measure of depression. Other researchers have established the viability of teaching social skills to depressed youngsters (Kratochwill & French, 1984; Schloss, Schloss, & Harris, 1984).

A more comprehensive approach is advocated by Stark and his colleagues. Stark's multidimensional treatment package combines behavioral, cognitive, and affective procedures with parent training and family therapy (Stark, Rouse, & Livingston, 1991). Included in the treatment are procedures for cognitive restructuring, behavioral assignments, problem-solving, self-instructional training, social skills, relaxation exercises, scheduling pleasant activities, anger coping, and games to identify and explore emotions. Both group and individual sessions are used to implement these strategies. Parent training focuses first upon helping parents understand depression and then upon involving them as collaborators in their child's treatment. Among other things, parents are taught to use positive behavior management skills, including praise. Family therapy sessions focus upon communication, family problem-solving, and conflict resolution. Specifically, family interactions that lead to and maintain the child's depressed cognitive schema are targeted for change. One interesting goal of this program is to teach the parents how to help their families have fun.

An example of how these procedures were used to treat a depressed 10-year-old is presented in Box 5-1.

BOX 5-1   Sherry

Sherry was a 10-year-old fourth grader who was enrolled in language arts and math classes for the gifted. She began seeing the school counselor on a regular basis during the second grade. She complained that she hated herself, and was "fat, ugly, and stupid."

Unbeknownst to the counselor, Sherry had first manifested symptoms of depression at the age of four and expressed serious suicidal wishes at the age of six. A visit to the family physician at that time was unproductive. He told Sherry that "you're not fat, you're built strong," and told her parents that there was nothing wrong with her. Unfortunately, Sherry's problems persisted. By the fourth grade, Sherry had very few friends due to her negativity and bad temper. She was seen as a tattle-tale, and generally had very poor social skills. Following an increase in her tantrum behavior and alienation from peers, Sherry finally was referred to the school psychologist. Her parents were at their wits' end, as they had tried everything they knew to help her.

An assessment of Sherry revealed that she was suffering from chronic dysthymic disorder. Although there were only five weeks left in the school year, cognitive behavioral therapy was initiated in the school setting for five sessions, during which Sherry seemed to learn very quickly how to control her mood. She used self-talk to control her anger and engaged herself in pleasant activities as a way to control her dysphoric mood. Cognitive restructuring procedures were introduced, in which she learned to replace some of her negative self-talk with positive self-talk. Both Sherry and her parents noted improvement. Upon returning to school following summer vacation, Sherry's condition was greatly worsened. An episode of major depression was now superimposed on the dysthymia, and she was concurrently experiencing severe separation anxiety. Therapy was resumed; however, Sherry was extremely resistant to the psychological interventions and commonly spent much of her therapy time throwing a temper tantrum or crying for her mother. Systematic desensitization for separation anxiety was not possible since Sherry refused to engage in the relaxation and imagery exercises.

Due to the continued severity of the disorder and a multi-generational family history of depression, Sherry was evaluated for medication and subsequently placed on Prozac. Prozac was chosen because of the favorable response to it by other family members. It produced a marked improvement in her depressive symptoms and especially in her separation anxiety. However, the medication clearly did not eliminate the depressive symptoms; rather, it buffered them and made her much more amenable to psychological treatment. Although her symptoms abated, Sherry continued to miss her mother during school and frequently asked to go to the nurse because she was feeling ill.

Cognitive-behavioral therapy for depression was reinitiated. Sherry was once again taught to use engagement in pleasant activities as a means of coping with dysphoria or anger. A diary was constructed with one page for each day of the week; each page had a list of 25 activities that Sherry most enjoyed doing. In addition, there were 5 blank spaces for her to write in other pleasant activities. An 11-point Likert-type scale ("Worst Ever" to "Best Ever") was placed at the bottom of each page where she rated her mood for the whole day prior to going to bed. Sherry kept the diary with her and self-monitored her engagement in the pleasant activities each day by checking off the ones she engaged in. This activity also led to some cognitive restructuring, as she realized that she actually did a number of enjoyable things every day.

As themes in her thinking were identified, self-monitoring was combined with cognitive restructuring to change the way Sherry was mentally constructing her world. For example, she believed that she was not loved by her parents and, further, that she was unlovable. Sherry generated a list of the criteria that would provide evidence that she was loved by her parents, and that she was in fact worthy of love. (Her parents and the psychologist were quick to note that she was deserving of their love just because she was their child, and if she exhibited all of these desirable behaviors, that was just frosting on the cake. It is important to note that her parents did in fact love her dearly.) These criteria were listed on one side of her diary pages. A paral-

BOX 5-1 *Continued*

lel version of this diary was constructed for her parents. Each night Sherry and her parents were instructed to go through their respective diaries together and to check off the evidence that Sherry was loved and that the parents had in fact demonstrated their love.

In addition, Sherry was taught social skills during sessions and applied them in the classroom. She received quiet and discrete reinforcement from her teacher for engaging in prosocial behaviors.

Cognitive-behavioral family therapy was initiated after the psychologist noted that the parents expected Sherry to act like an adult rather than a 10-year-old. The mother inadvertently responded to challenges to her parenting by blaming Sherry. This tendency led Sherry to feel attacked and as though she were guilty

of being a bad child. Other subtle communications that led to and maintained Sherry's negative self-schema were identified, and her parents were taught to change them. Concurrently, they were taught to be better listeners and to allow Sherry to have an individual personality and to act in a more childlike fashion.

Sherry's mood slowly but continually improved to the point that she generally felt good, her social behavior improved, and she began to like herself. At this writing, the plan is to continue her on the medication until the end of the school year and to discontinue it over the summer.

Contributed by Kevin Stark, Ph.D., Associate Professor in the Department of Educational Psychology, The University of Texas at Austin.

Implications for Teachers

Teachers of students with emotional/behavior disorders will undoubtedly encounter depressed students in their classrooms. Furthermore, teachers should be aware that depression may be significantly underdiagnosed, especially in younger children. The coexistence of other problems such as anxiety, conduct disorders, or substance abuse may mask the accurate diagnosis of depression in older children and adolescents.

Although some students may manifest their depression through agitated behaviors, most depressed individuals will present problems of withdrawal and lack of concentration or motivation in the classroom. These problems likely will be manifested through low rates of social interaction and inability to complete schoolwork. Table 5-4 lists a number of symptoms of depression that may be manifested in the classroom.

For those depressed students being treated by medication, the teacher should routinely confer with the prescribing physician regarding behavioral fluctuations and potential side-effects. For students receiving psychotherapy or counseling, the teacher and therapist should coordinate to reinforce one another's treatment goals. Teachers may want to team with other school personnel (counselors, social workers, or psychologists) in teaching social skills or cognitive techniques in a group format. At this point in our understanding of depression in children and adolescents, cognitive and social skills approaches appear to hold the most promise for educators.

Anxiety Disorders

As with depression, fear and anxiety in children only recently have come to be viewed as a clinical syndrome requiring treatment. As childhood fear and anxiety are often viewed as common and transient, their impact is easily overlooked (Strauss, 1987). However, as Strauss

TABLE 5-4   Symptoms of Depression and their Impact in the Classroom

Motivational impairment	Reduced interest in school work
Anhedonia (lack of positive affect)	Behavioral reinforcers hard to identify
Fatigue	Difficulty finishing assignments
Impaired concentration	Difficulty attending and finishing assignments
Lack of persistence	Failure to complete work
Impaired social relationships	Lack of engagement with teacher or students
Sadness/tearfulness	Withdrawal, alienation from peers, lack of energy for learning
Cognitive biases	Over-perception of failures; tendency to interpret feedback as negative; grades become reinforcers of negative set
Heightened self-consciousness	Difficulty participating in group activities
Irritability/Aggression	Disruptive to rest of class; not engaged in learning process; failure to complete work
Withdrawal	Lack of engagement with others or process; tendency to be ignored

From Stark, K. D., Swearer, S., Delaune, M., Knox, L., & Winter, J. (in press). Depressive disorders. In R. T. Ammerman & M. Hersen, (Eds.), *Handbook of child behavior therapy in the psychiatric setting.* New York: Wiley & Sons. Reprinted with permission of the senior author and John Wiley & Sons, Inc.

asserts, "anxiety in childhood can be intense, distressing, and persistent, thus requiring the attention of professionals" (p. 109).

Definition, Prevalence, and Characteristics

In DSM-IV, only one anxiety disorder specific to children is recognized: separation anxiety. In separation anxiety, the youngster exhibits a pathological fear of leaving a major attachment figure, usually the mother. Separation anxiety may manifest itself as school phobia, and will be discussed in that context. Children and adolescents also can be diagnosed with adult anxiety classifications including generalized anxiety disorder, phobias, and more rarely, obsessive-compulsive disorder and panic disorder.

It may be helpful to distinguish among fear, phobia, and anxiety. Whereas fear can be described as a discrete response to an experience of threat (Kendall et al., 1990), anxiety is "apprehension without apparent cause" (Johnson & Melamed, 1979, p. 107). Phobias can be defined as severe fears, resulting in persistent patterns of avoidance (Barrios & Hartmann, 1988). Phobias appear irrational to observers but nonetheless cause real distress to the phobic individual. Phobias can be further differentiated from fears in that phobias are unrelated to age or developmental stages.

Teachers of students with emotional/behavior disorders may encounter individuals who suffer from excessive anxiety or fears. To a lesser extent, they may also encounter students exhibiting phobias, including school phobia. The remainder of our discussion therefore will be confined to anxiety disorders most commonly manifested in the school setting: generalized anxiety disorder and phobias.

Generalized Anxiety Disorder
The child with this disorder is one who experiences excessive or unrealistic anxiety over a period of time. In addition to appearing nervous or tense, the child may complain of physical

discomfort such as headaches, stomachaches, dizziness, and nausea. Sleep problems are common. The individual with generalized anxiety disorder may be extraordinarily self-conscious and spend inordinate amounts of time worrying about future events, expectations, and competence. She may need excessive reassurance about routine events. In the classroom, extreme anxiety may be manifested over assignments, tests, or other situations in which the student believes her performance may be scrutinized.

Phobias

Before proceeding with a discussion of phobias, it is important to remember that children and adolescents experience fears in the normal course of development. Several studies have established that almost all children experience at least one fear and that many children experience multiple fears. For example, Miller, Barrett, & Hampe (1974) have reported the common fears for differing age levels that are listed in Table 5-5. As illustrated by this and other normative data, children's fears change over time from internal, global, and imaginary content (e.g., ghosts, monsters, the dark) to more external, specific and reality-based content (e.g., school performance, social acceptance). Thus the development of children's fears appears to parallel their cognitive development and increasing perception of reality (Campbell, 1986). Childhood fears may be temporary and are not necessarily precursors to adult fears, although adult phobics report having had more phobias as children than nonphobics (Solyom, Beck, Solyom, & Hugel, 1974). Duration (over two years) and/or intensity (sufficient to be debilitating to routine) can be used as markers to differentiate normal fears from those that need clinical attention (Graziano, DeGiovanni, & Garcia, 1979).

Phobias represent a persistent fear of a specific stimulus. Some of the most common phobias in the general population are of dogs, snakes, insects, mice, closed spaces, heights, and air travel (American Psychiatric Association, 1987). When confronted with the stimulus, the individual has an immediate anxiety reaction, which often involves sweating, difficulty with breathing, and feeling panicky. A phobic individual will therefore go to great lengths to avoid the stimulus. (A well-known example is the television football commentator, John Madden, who travels to football games across the country by bus or train due to his fear of flying). Because of the tendency to avoid the phobic object or situation, phobias may go undetected unless a student is phobic about a stimulus in the classroom.

TABLE 5-5   Common Fears at Different Age Levels

Age	Fears
Birth to 1	Loud noises, loss of support, strangers
1–2	Separation, injury, imaginary creatures
3–5	Dogs, being alone, the dark
6–12	School, injury, natural events, social embarrassment
13–18	Injury, social embarrassment

Adapted from Miller et al., 1974

School Phobia

The phobia most researched among children and adolescents due to its unavoidable impact on the child's life is school phobia. School phobics refuse to come to school, and become extremely anxious and agitated when pressed to attend. Somatic complaints often accompany school refusal. In fact, somatic complaints sometimes signal the onset of school phobia when the student is initially allowed to stay home because of complaints of headaches, stomachaches, dizziness, or other physical problems. The incidence of school phobia is equally distributed between the sexes and among the 5 to 15 age group (Gordon & Young, 1976). School phobia also occurs equally across intelligence levels and is no more prevalent among children with learning problems (Ollendick & Mayer, 1984). It often occurs after changes in the child's life, such as a move to a new school, illness or hospitalization of the child or the mother, or the mother's beginning work (Ollendick & Mayer, 1984). Examples of fears specific to the school setting that have been reported by school phobics include fear of entering a new school, of interpersonal interactions, of tests, of getting sick, and of failure (Ollendick & Mayer, 1984).

Last and her colleagues (Last, Francis, Hersen, Kazdin, & Strauss, 1987) have found it useful to categorize school phobics into two groups: those suffering from separation anxiety disorder and those who are truly phobic of the school situation. The label of "school phobia" historically has been applied to both groups of children, possibly obscuring both etiology and effectiveness of interventions. In their study of 48 children with separation anxiety disorder and 19 school phobics, Last et al. found these differences between groups: children with separation anxiety disorder were more likely to be female, prepubertal, and from families with lower socioeconomic status (SES), while school phobics were more likely to be male, postpubertal, and from higher SES families. In addition, almost all of the separation anxiety disorder sample had other clinical diagnoses, and their mothers were four times more likely to exhibit depression when compared to the mothers of the school phobic sample. However, there were no differences between groups on the number of self-reported fears and anxieties. These findings may indicate a need to more clearly differentiate "true" school phobia from separation anxiety disorders if different treatment approaches are needed.

Physical, Behavioral, and Cognitive Symptoms of Anxiety Disorders

Childhood anxiety is generally viewed as a multidimensional construct manifested at physical, behavioral and cognitive levels (Kendall et al., 1990). Physical and behavioral responses include avoidance, shaky voice, thumb-sucking, nail-biting, perspiration, trembling, flushed face, "butterflies" in the stomach, and gastrointenstinal distress (Barrios & Hartmann, 1988). Increases in autonomic nervous activity also may be present, as was found by Beidel (1988) in a comparison of test-anxious children with controls during test-taking.

Although few would argue that cognitive distress is a major symptom of anxious children, the content of their cognitions has not been agreed upon. Kendall and his colleagues indicate that anxious children seem preoccupied with others' evaluations and negative outcomes, and they exacerbate situations by routinely misperceiving demands of the environment (Kendall et al., 1990). Other researchers have found that anxious children themselves do not report more physiological symptoms (Mattison, Bagnato, & Brubaker,

1988); however, they do report significantly more worries than either depressed or control groups of children (Laurent, Landau, & Stark, 1993).

Relationship to Depression

As mentioned previously, depression and anxiety often coexist. Bernstein and Garfinkel (1986) reported that the majority of their sample of adolescents with anxiety disorder also exhibited major depression. Last (1988) reported that in a sample of 69 children and adolescents with anxiety disorders, about one-third met criteria for major depression. Reviewing these and other data, Last concluded that the coexistence of depression and anxiety may increase with age, i.e., adolescents are more likely than younger children to exhibit both conditions.

Etiology and Development of Anxiety

Behavioral formulations traditionally have been invoked to account for the development of anxiety and fears in children, adolescents, and adults. The principles of operant conditioning, social learning, and classical conditioning have been used to explain the etiology of anxious behavior. A cognitive model developed with anxious adults is a relative newcomer but will be presented because of its implications for treatment. We will first address the etiology of debilitating fears and anxiety, and then will turn to the etiology of school phobia.

Etiology of Anxious and Fearful Behavior

According to operant conditioning principles, fearful and anxious behavior is shaped and maintained by positive environmental responses. For example, if a child evidences fear and receives excessive sympathy or is able to avoid an unpleasant task, the behavior will be strengthened. Bandura (1977) has written extensively on the social conditioning of fears, in which children observe peers or adults in conditioning situations and learn the fear vicariously. For example, a young child witnessing another child being bitten by a dog might vicariously learn to fear dogs. In this example, the child who was bitten could develop an excessive fear of animals through classical conditioning (i.e., the association of pain with the appearance of a dog). Depending on several variables, including the amount of trauma surrounding the event, both children could develop a phobia of dogs or generalize fears to other animals.

Conditioning theories may only partially account for the development of fearful and anxious behavior. Bandura (1977) has discussed the impact of cognitive transmission from parents to children through verbal instructions and information. Rachman (1977) believes that there is a genetic propensity toward development of fears, a supposition that is consonant with the emotional reactivity component of temperament research with children (e.g., Thomas & Chess, 1977). In other words, some children may be born with central nervous systems that predispose them toward fearfulness or anxiety. Unfortunately, little research has been conducted on the role of cognitive or biological factors in the development of anxiety disorders in children and adolescents.

In his work with adults, Beck (1976) developed a cognitive model that explains pathological anxiety as arising from unrealistic perceptions of danger. One or more of four cognitive errors are considered responsible for these unrealistic perceptions:

- Overestimating the probability of a feared event
- Overestimating the severity of the feared event
- Underestimating what one can do about it (coping resources)
- Underestimating what others can do to help (rescue factors)

Beck believes that an individual's perception of danger, realistic or not, sets into motion an "anxiety program" that is a "complex constellation of cognitive, affective, and behavioral changes which we have inherited from our evolutionary past and which were probably originally designed to protect us from harm in a primitive environment" (Clark & Beck, 1988, p. 363). Cognitive therapy is based on this reciprocal relationship between the perception of threat and the resulting anxiety. Cognitive therapy, therefore, deals with one's fears about the cognitive, behavioral, and somatic symptoms of anxiety. The individual's thoughts about his own reactions are the focus of therapy.

Beck suggests that specific cognitive content can be found in each subcategory of anxiety disorder, although this supposition has not been systematically investigated. With phobias, Beck believes that distorted cognitions are exaggerated perceptions of the danger inherent in the object or situation. With generalized anxiety disorder, Beck et al. (Beck, Laude, & Bohnert, 1974) found that the majority of anxiety-related thoughts can be categorized into five divisions: (1) fears of physical injury, illness, or death, (2) fears of mental illness, (3) fears of loss of control, (4) fears of failure, and (5) fears of rejection, domination, or depreciation. In adults, generalized anxiety disorder most often has a gradual onset in individuals who have had long-standing concerns about self-worth and competence (Clark & Beck, 1988).

In summary, although principles of conditioning may account for development of specific fears and phobias, some researchers believe that genetic and cognitive factors also may play a role in the development of anxiety disorders. However, the role of these latter factors currently remains unspecified.

Etiology of School Phobia

The development of school phobia has received ample attention, with schools of thought falling primarily into two camps: psychodynamic and behavioral. Psychodynamic theorists propose that school phobia results from an unresolved mother-child dependency relationship. Due to this unresolved dependency, anxiety for both parties is heightened when they must be separated. The mother is also thought to "unconsciously" reinforce the child's aversion to school by sympathizing and by subtly communicating her desire for the child to remain at home with her. Thus, school phobia is viewed by psychodynamic theorists as a variant of separation anxiety (Ollendick & Mayer, 1984).

Behavioral theories for explaining school phobia fall into the same categories as theories for the etiology of other fears: operant conditioning, social learning, and classical conditioning. However, theorists have been more specific about the mechanisms through which school phobia develops. For example, Yates (1970) suggested that a child learns to fear separation from his or her parents at an early age and to perceive the home as a refuge; while most children grow out of this phase as they begin to interact with others, the budding school phobic develops more anxiety about separation issues. In addition, while the child is not being socially reinforced by the school setting, this anxiety is concurrently being reinforced by the mother's overconcern when the child is not in her company. Thus, like other fears, school phobia is learned and maintained by reinforcers. In other instances of operant conditioning, parents may inadvertently reinforce the child's negative statements about school and/or the child's somatic complaints, resulting in staying home behavior that is much more desirable to the youngster than going to school.

Classical conditioning and social learning principles have also been reported as contributing to the development of school phobia. Some children have become school phobic after experiencing traumatic events at school, and others have become phobic after observing others' phobic behavior and its consequences (for examples, see Jones & Kazdin, 1981). Yates' model (1970) of etiology is more complex. He believes that a variety of precipitating factors may account for the genesis of school phobia, including overdependence on the home as a refuge, lack of reinforcement in the school setting, and anxiety-arousing experiences or traumatic events at school. In this formulation, mother-child relations are only one of many factors contributing to school phobia. This relationship has been explored in studies of anxious children and their families.

Predisposing Factors for Overanxious and School Phobic Children

Few well-designed studies have assessed the relationship between anxious children and their parents. However, one well-controlled study found that of 58 children with anxiety disorder, 83 percent of the mothers had a lifetime history of anxiety disorder and 57 percent presented with anxiety disorder concurrently with their children (Last, 1988). Other studies have found that children of both dysthymic and anxious parents are at increased risk for anxiety disorders when compared to the general population (Cytryn, McKnew, Bartko, Lamour, & Hamovitt, 1982; Turner, Beidel, & Costello, 1987). These and other studies suggest an association of depressive/anxiety disorders in parents and their children, but do not indicate whether this association is specific to the mother-child dyad or a more general family pattern (Last, 1988).

Characteristics of mothers of school phobics have been studied repeatedly. In their review, Gordon and Young (1976) offer a rather unflattering profile of the mother of a school phobic: she had an emotionally deprived childhood, has not adequately resolved her relationship with her own mother, tends to be perfectionistic and neurotic, has no friends or interests outside the family, and has poor relations with her husband. However, even if accurate, this research has few implications for treatment. Perhaps the most consistent and useful finding is a tendency toward maternal overprotectiveness, which may be helpful in planning interventions with families.

Treatment and Intervention

Behavioral approaches constitute the primary interventions with children and adolescents with anxiety disorders. Almost all of this research assesses outcomes with phobias and other subject-specific fears. Much less is written about the child whose anxiety is less well defined or "free-floating." Because school phobia is researched separately from other phobias, methods for reducing fear and anxiety will be addressed first in this section, and interventions with school phobics will be addressed separately.

Fear and Anxiety Reduction

Four primary methods for reducing maladaptive fear and anxiety in children are reported: systematic desensitization, modeling, operant conditioning, and cognitive strategies.

Systematic desensitization.   In systematic desensitization, principles of counterconditioning are used to alleviate symptoms of fear and anxiety. This technique was initially developed by Wolpe in the 1950s; it is predicated on his ideas that phobias are learned fear responses and that anxiety is incompatible with relaxation. According to Wolpe (1958), desensitization involves three basic steps: (1) establishing a hierarchy of fear-invoking stimuli, (2) learning deep-muscle relaxation techniques, and (3) pairing the relaxation state with each of the stimuli on the fear hierarchy. The last step is accomplished by asking the individual to visualize the least-feared stimuli while in a state of deep relaxation; in successive sessions, the client works through the hierarchy until the highest-ranking fear is faced without the accompanying anxiety or fear response. This procedure has been adapted for use with children (e.g., use of scripts and fantasy) and has been used in educational settings.

Systematic desensitization has been applied to a variety of children's fears, including fears of loud noises, separation, school, dogs, the dark, and test-taking (Strauss, 1987). However, its success in treating fears of children and adolescents is not clearly established; this is especially true for children under nine years of age (Morris & Kratochwill, 1987). A number of uncontrolled case examples and some well-designed studies reporting success are available (Strauss, 1987). In one well-designed study, a multiphobic 11-year-old was successfully treated for fears of blood, heights, and test-taking by applying Wolpe's classic systematic desensitization procedure (Van Hasselt, Hersen, Bellack, Rosenblum, & Lamparski, 1979). Other researchers have reported successful treatment of school-related anxieties such as test anxiety, math anxiety, and reading difficulties (Morris & Kratochwill, 1987). These and other studies have led some researchers to conclude that there is enough evidence to warrant the continued use and investigation of systematic desensitization to alleviate fears and anxiety in children (Wells and Vitulano, 1984; Ollendick, 1979). However, its utility with young children is questionable.

Modeling.   Modeling procedures are based on the social learning principles that fears can be both learned and extinguished through vicarious experiences. Bandura (1969), the "grandaddy" of modeling techniques, suggests combining modeling with positive reinforcement to sustain the unfearful response. Bandura (1977) also stressed the importance of cognitive variables such as correcting faulty information and misperceptions about the feared stimuli.

In comparing the success of three types of modeling procedures, Ollendick (1979) found a direct and positive relationship between success and the amount of child involvement in the modeling procedure: symbolic modeling (e.g., by videotape) was less effective than live modeling, and live modeling was less effective than participant modeling, in which the child actually approaches the feared object or situation after observing a model. Also the use of "fearful models" who demonstrate coping strategies to overcome their fear has been shown to be more effective than use of "fearless" models (Meichenbaum, 1971), although this finding has not been consistently replicated (Strauss, 1987).

Modeling has been successful in reducing common childhood fears such as of dogs, snakes, and heights, and of medical procedures such as surgery or dental work (Strauss, 1987). However, little research has focused on modeling as an intervention for school-related fears and anxieties other than social withdrawal (Morris & Kratochwill, 1987).

Operant conditioning techniques.   These techniques are aimed at strengthening approach behaviors and reducing fear responses. The techniques of *positive reinforcement* and *extinction* have been used to achieve these goals (Strauss, 1987). *Positive reinforcement* and other contingency procedures have been applied successfully to specific fears and phobias, e.g., separation anxiety (Patterson, 1965), and fear of the night (Kellerman, 1980). *Extinction* usually involves removing parental attention for avoidance or fearful behavior and is most commonly used in conjunction with another technique. As maladaptive fears are uncommon and idiosyncratic, most of this research is based upon single case studies. In two group studies, positive outcomes for operant procedures were reported, but methodological short-comings preclude drawing definite conclusions (Strauss, 1987).

Cognitive techniques.   The use of cognitive techniques with anxious children and adolescents is a relatively recent approach. A variety of techniques has been employed, almost all of which involve training in self-statements aimed at reducing anxiety related to the feared object or situation. Covert modeling has also been attempted, in which children use imaginative models rather than live or filmed models. Many researchers use a combination of cognitive and behavioral techniques, such as self-statements combined with relaxation.

Much of the research in this area reports clinical treatment of medical-related phobias or severe night fears. Of 16 cognitive-behavioral studies reviewed by Ramirez, Kratochwill, & Morris (1987), only four involved school-related situations: test anxiety, speech anxiety, academic performance anxiety, and evaluation anxiety. In a test anxiety study with tenth graders, researchers compared the effectiveness of cognitive techniques (self-statements) to systematic desensitization and no treatment (Leal, Baxter, Martin, & Marx, 1981). Results indicated that although systematic desensitization was most effective in improving test performance, the cognitive treatment group reported a significant decrease in anxiety compared to the other groups. Thus the complexity of anxiety disorders may dictate that a combination of interventions are necessary to both improve performance and alleviate anxious symptoms.

As Morris and Kratochwill (1987) point out, implementing cognitive procedures with children and adolescents is not easy. Cognitive-based interventions require a certain level of self-awareness and ability to understand both physical and cognitive aspects of anxious behavior. Thus, the child must possess enough cognitive sophistication and behavioral control to apply cognitive techniques in fear-inducing situations. Although cognitive techniques may be limited to subjects with certain prerequisites, the consensus of these researchers is that cognitive techniques in treatment of childhood anxiety are promising despite the current lack of a strong empirical base (Ramirez, Kratochwill, & Morris, 1987; Strauss, 1987; Wells & Vitulano, 1984).

Treatment of school phobia.   Approaches to treating school phobia fall into the same two schools of thought as etiological theories: psychodynamic and behavioral. The *psychody-*

namic orientation to school phobia focuses upon the unresolved dependency relationship between mother and child (Gordon & Young, 1976). Most therapists adhering to this view recommend an immediate if partial return to school for the child, thus breaking the symbiotic relationship and exerting pressure to change. However, the return to school may be done in a step-by-step process, much as behaviorists would proceed. In addition, most psychodynamic therapists would recommend therapy with mother and child or with both parents and child in order to work out the unresolved dependency issues. The school is also viewed as a partner in the intervention process (Gordon & Young, 1976). In a review of five psychodynamically-oriented treatment studies spanning the 1940s, '50s and '60s, Kelly (1973) reports a 92 percent symptom relief rate, suggesting positive results from this approach.

A variety of behavioral techniques also have been employed to treat school phobia. In *operant conditioning,* strategies are intended to increase the positive reinforcement of school attendance while simultaneously decreasing the reinforcement provided by staying at home. Tokens or tangible reinforcers may be used until the child begins to accept the natural reinforcers available in the school environment. A number of successful home-based and school-based contingency-management programs have been reported for school phobic behavior (Ollendick & Mayer, 1984).

Classsical conditioning treatments usually involve variants of systematic desensitization in which the child is taught to relax while using imagery to desensitize himself to the school setting. Many case studies have reported successful treatments of school phobia through variations of systematic desensitization (e.g., P.M. Miller, 1972; Tahmisian & McReynolds, 1971). In a study by Garvey & Hegrenes (1966), a ten-year old boy was cured of school phobia by desensitization procedures. Over a 20-day period, the boy and his therapist went through a sequence of 12 successive approximations, beginning with sitting in a car in front of the school, entering the school (six steps later), being present in the classroom with the teacher only (three steps later), and being in the class with all classmates present (two steps later). At a follow-up two years later the phobic behavior had not recurred. However, in analyzing the study, Ollendick & Mayer (1984) point out that the procedure actually involved several behavioral techniques in that the child was systematically praised for success (operant conditioning) and that modeling was prevalent throughout treatment (social learning). Thus, this study illustrates the successful interaction of several behavioral principles in treating school phobia, and the likely necessity of a multiple rather than a unitary approach (Ollendick, 1979).

Studies utilizing *social learning* or modeling techniques also underscore the importance of multiple strategies, as parent, therapist, and peer models have been used to accompany the school phobic child through a series of graduated steps aimed at getting the child back in school. However, modeling has not been reported as the sole strategy and is most often viewed as part of a more comprehensive treatment program.

In summary, behavioral techniques have been used with varying degrees of success with fearful and anxious children. Successful psychodynamic treatment of school phobia including therapy for dependency issues between mother and child also has been reported. However, much of the clinical literature is devoted to fears and anxieties that are not school-related, with the notable exception of school phobia. It appears that variations of systematic desensitization alone or in combination with other behavioral strategies (reinforcement and modeling) have been the most successful with school-related anxieties. Table 5-6 summarizes general trends for treatment of school-related fears and anxieties.

TABLE 5-6   A Summary of Treatment Techniques for School-Related Fears and Anxieties

Treatment	Presenting Problem
Systematic desensitization	school phobia, test anxiety, math anxiety, reading anxiety
modeling	social withdrawal
positive reinforcement	separation anxiety school phobia
cognitive-behavioral	anxiety related to test-taking, speech, academic performance and evaluation
psychodynamic therapy and treatment	separation anxiety school phobia
social skills training	social withdrawal

Implications for Teachers

Teachers may be unaware that their students have debilitating fears or anxiety unless the students encounter the feared stimuli in the classroom setting. In the case of school phobia, teachers may be asked to participate in certain steps of the hierarchy if systematic desensitization is used.

Systematic desensitization plus other behavioral techniques also may be recommended with other school-related anxieties such as speaking or performing in front of classmates, test anxiety, or subject-specific anxiety (e.g., math anxiety). Usually a behaviorally trained counselor or psychologist will establish the steps of a behavioral program and elicit the aid of the teacher and peers in carrying out the program. Teachers who identify anxious or fearful students in their classrooms should make inquiries about the availability of personnel who can design and implement such programs.

It is more difficult to intervene with children and adolescents whose anxiety is unattached to an object or situation. These youth whose anxiety is "free-floating" may exhibit a variety of somatic complaints and avoidance behaviors. Events that are considered routine to others may cause considerable discomfort to these children, and referral for counseling may be warranted. Children under age 13 who have generalized anxiety disorder are also prone to experience separation anxiety disorder. Remember also that the coexistence of anxiety and depression increases with age from childhood into adolescence, so it may be difficult to detect anxiety in depressed adolescents or vice versa.

A Note on Social Withdrawal

Although the influence of adults upon children's social development has been studied for years, only recently have researchers turned their attention to the impact of peer interactions upon social development (Kendall & Morison, 1984). Experience with peers is viewed as an essential part of socialization and eventual social competence, and early isolation from peers places children at risk for later adjustment problems (Hartup, 1979, 1980).

Definition and Characteristics

Only a small number of children can be described as socially withdrawn without accompanying problems such as depression or anxiety. DSM-IV does not provide a separate clinical category for social withdrawal, but peer problems are an associated feature of several diagnostic categories, most notably, conduct disorders and attention-deficit hyperactivity disorder. In addition, some researchers have found social skills deficits and peer rejection to be characteristic of depressed children (Kennedy, Spence, & Hensley, 1989; Stark et al., 1993).

Socially withdrawn children can be characterized as social isolates, neither initiating contact nor responding to their peers at a normal level (Lyons, Serbin, & Marchessault, 1988). They may seem painfully shy and reticent to talk to anyone in the school setting. They participate in group activities reluctantly if at all and prefer to keep to themselves. Gresham and Evans (1987) reported that between 14 percent and 30 percent of problem children would fall into this category, as they exhibit low frequency of contact with their peers. Two studies have found equal rates of socially withdrawn behavior among boys and girls (Gresham & Evans, 1987; Lyons, Serbin, & Marchessault, 1988). One study concluded that many socially withdrawn children had experienced significantly stressful life events and tended to cope with these events through passivity and withdrawal (Byrnes, 1984). Additionally, these children had difficulties in school, demonstrated low levels of self-esteem, and believed they had little personal power.

The etiology of socially withdrawn behavior is not clear. As mentioned, it can coexist with other budding disorders, such as anxiety and depression. However, child development experts have become increasingly concerned about social withdrawal and have begun to more thoroughly research socially isolated children in schools and preschools. Subjects in these studies are usually identified as socially withdrawn by observation or sociometrics such as teacher and peer nomination. Typically, no clinical diagnoses are sought, so the existence of other clinical problems among these youngsters remains undetermined.

Interventions

A couple of useful frameworks for viewing social withdrawal and planning interventions have emerged from this literature. In a review, Gottman (1977) found two categories of research on socially withdrawn children: studies related to peer acceptance and those related to frequency of interpersonal interactions. Peer acceptance refers to general popularity; however, it may be important to distinguish children who are *rejected* from those who are *ignored*. Children may be rejected due to personal characteristics that may or may not be amenable to change; others may be ignored not because they are unappealing to their classmates but because they do not respond to their classmates' overtures. Several studies have documented that less accepted children are indeed less likely to give and receive positive reinforcement (Kendall & Morison, 1984).

Another framework for viewing social withdrawal is to distinguish children who have *repertoire deficits* from those who have *performance deficits* (Strain, Cooke, & Appolloni, 1976). Repertoire deficits refer to socially inept children who lack the social skills necessary to sustain successful interactions with their peers. Performance deficits refer to those children who possess the prerequisite social skills but are prevented from exhibiting them by such problems as anxiety or low expectancy for reinforcement. According to Kendall & Morison (1984), this distinction may be important because interventions for repertoire deficits would focus on teaching the necessary social skills (sharing, smiling, asking questions), while interventions for performance deficits would focus on the cognitions underlying social interactions (perspective-taking, social problem-solving, self-talk). Kendall and Morison believe that an integration of cognitive and behavioral strategies may be necessary to improve the social interactions of many socially withdrawn youngsters.

In reviewing the literature, Kendall and Morison (1984) found two interventions that have been used primarily with preschool children: use of teacher attention and use of confederate peers. Studies of the impact of teacher attention contingent on interaction with others has shown that although short-term gains in increased interactions have been documented, long-term gains remain questionable. Studies that train one or more confederate peers to initiate and respond positively to socially isolated preschoolers have met with success. Several researchers suggest that both teacher attention and peer confederates should be used to facilitate social interactions, since both are part of the child's natural environment. Other interventions include providing structured group activities, in which social interaction among peers is facilitated by working in small groups on a task with a common goal.

Social skills training has also been undertaken with this population, with mixed results. A study by LaGreca and Santogrossi (1980) seems typical of research in this area. These researchers targeted eight social skills areas to teach to elementary students who had low acceptance ratings by their peers. They combined a social skills training format of modeling, behavioral rehearsal, coaching, feedback, and homework in small groups. Results indicated that although these students improved significantly in performance of the targeted skills, no differences were found on sociometric ratings of acceptance subsequent to the intervention. Other research also suggests that the link between improved social skills and increased peer acceptance is tenuous. In other words, increasing the amount of appropriate social interaction does not nececessarily lead to increased popularity of socially isolated children.

Implications for Teachers

Whether social withdrawal will be more clearly defined and researched as a clinical entity separate from other disorders remains to be seen. It is important, however, that educators recognize the impact of peer relations on social development and later adjustment. When a student is identified as socially withdrawn, teachers may want to ascertain whether (a) the child is rejected or ignored, and (b) whether the child has a repertoire deficit or a performance deficit. These answers then can guide the choice of intervention. It is clear that socially withdrawn children should not be ignored.

Conclusions

We are just beginning to recognize that children and adolescents can suffer from the internalizing disorders of anxiety and depression. There are probably genetic predispositions for development of both disorders, although environmental and family factors may serve as catalysts. One developing body of literature suggests that the individual's cognitions (i.e., faulty information processing) play a role in the development of both anxiety and depression. It is heartening that a variety of treatment approaches are demonstrating that children with these conditions can be helped to overcome their symptoms. Psychotherapy, medication, and cognitive-behavioral approaches have been attempted, with mixed results, with depressed youngsters. Successful treatments for anxiety disorders have included a variety of behavioral and cognitive techniques. In some cases, teachers may be asked to help implement interventions in their classrooms, while in other cases, the child may be treated by a therapist outside the school setting.

Key Points

1. Although mental health professionals have not always believed that children are capable of experiencing depression, it is now commonly held that children and adolescents may experience depression in a manner very similar to that of adults.

2. It is likely that a combination of genetic predisposition, family environment, and the child's coping mechanisms interact to cause depression.

3. Depression has been found to co-exist with other disorders, including conduct disorders, eating disorders, substance abuse, and anxiety disorders; depression may therefore be significantly underdiagnosed in children and adolescents.

4. For youngsters with severe depression and/or family history of depression, medication may be indicated; for others, cognitive-behavioral therapy and social skills training appear promising.

5. Separation anxiety and generalized anxiety disorder may be diagnosed in children and adolescents; although not common, school phobia is likely to be encountered by school personnel.

6. Behavioral principles (classical conditioning, operant conditioning, and social learning) and cognitive models have been used to explain the development of anxious and fearful behavior.

7. Systematic desensitization, modeling, operant conditioning principles, and cognitive techniques have all been applied with some success to anxious and fearful behavior in children.

8. Although social withdrawal is not defined as a separate clinical category, researchers and educators are aware that children need to be able to interact well with their peers in order to develop socially.

Additional Readings

Conceptualization and treatment of social withdrawal in the schools, by Frank M. Gresham and S. E. Evans, *Special Serivces in the Schools, 3,* 1987, 37–51, for a description of school-based interventions of withdrawn behavior.

Depression and suicide in children and adolescents, by Nina Muse. Austin, TX: Pro-Ed, 1990, for a booklet containing practical information for teachers and parents about identifying and working with youth with these problems.

On the edge of darkness, by Kate Cronkite. New York: Doubleday (1994), for a book of interviews with a number of famous people on how it feels to be depressed. The book contains interesting and very powerful descriptions of depression.

The use of visual imagery and muscle relaxation in the counterconditioning of a phobic child: A case study, by P.M. Miller, *Journal of Nervous and Mental Disorders, 154,* 1972, 457–460; and Use of parents as behavioral engineers in the treatment of a school phobic girl, by J. A. Tahmisian & W. T. McReynolds, *Journal of Counseling Psychology, 18,* 1971, 225–228, for case studies in the treatment of phobias in children.

Treatment of depression during childhood and adolescence: Cognitive-behavioral procedures for the individual and family, by Kevin Stark and colleagues. In P.C. Kendall (Ed.), *Child and adolescent therapy : Cognitive-behavioral procedures.* New York: Guilford, 1990, for a description of a comprehensive treatment package for depressed youngsters.

Externalizing Disorders

Definition and Characteristics of:

Hyperactivity and Conduct Disorders

Etiology

Interventions

Orientation

The previous chapter dealt with children suffering from the internalizing disorders of anxiety, depression, and withdrawal, i.e., the kids that hurt on the inside but may not show it on the outside. In sharp contrast are the youngsters who let everybody know what's happening in their lives; in fact, they ***demand*** our attention. Youngsters with conduct disorders demand our attention through actions that are, at best, worrisome acting out behaviors, and at worst, antisocial, aggressive acts that break the law. Hyperactive children demand our attention by twisting, wiggling, fidgeting, interrupting everyone, and performing poorly in school.

Overview

This chapter addresses externalizing disorders of childhood and adolescence. These disorders tend to be extroversive or interpersonal in their manifestations; in the past, they have been called "undercontrolled" and "acting out." Aggressive and delinquent behavior are often associated with hyperactivity and conduct disorders; thus, these youngsters are often in constant conflict with authority, either in school or in the community. For both hyperactivity and conduct disorders, this chapter will address definition and characteristics, etiology and development, and treatment interventions. The role of teachers is also addressed.

Attention-Deficit Hyperactivity Disorder

As with most other syndromes, this disorder historically has been called many names, including minimal brain dysfunction, minimal brain injury, hyperactivity, hyperkinesis, and the current label, *attention-deficit hyperactivity disorder* (ADHD). One writer at the turn of the century even labeled hyperactivity as a "defect in moral control," (Still, 1902). For purposes of this chapter, the terms ADHD and hyperactivity will be used interchangeably.

Definition and Prevalence

Attention-deficit hyperactivity disorder is defined by its core behaviors of *inattention*, *impulsivity*, and *hyperactivity*. These behaviors generally occur across settings and are most noticeable when in-seat and attentive behavior are required, as in the classroom. DSM-IV considers these core behaviors as the essential features when making a diagnosis of ADHD. The following criteria are manifestations of these core behaviors; in order to make a DSM-IV diagnosis, six criteria for inattention *or* six criteria for hyperactivity/impulsivity should have been evident for a period of at least six months and to a maladaptive degree:

> *inattention:*
>
> 1. *fails to give close attention to details/makes careless mistakes*
> 2. *has difficulty sustaining attention to tasks or play*
> 3. *does not seem to listen when spoken to directly*
> 4. *has difficulty following instructions (e.g., fails to finish schoolwork, chores)*
> 5. *has difficulty organizing tasks and activities*
> 6. *avoids tasks requiring sustained mental effort (e.g., homework)*
> 7. *often loses things needed for home or school (e.g., toys, assignments)*
> 8. *is easily distracted*
> 9. *is forgetful*
>
> *hyperactivity:*
>
> 1. *often fidgets or squirms*
> 2. *has difficulty remaining seated*
> 3. *runs or climbs excessively*
> 4. *has difficulty playing or engaging in leisure activities quietly*
> 5. *often talks excessively*
> 6. *is often "on the go"*
>
> *impulsivity:*
>
> 1. *often blurts out answers to questions*
> 2. *has difficulty awaiting turn*
> 3. *often interrupts or intrudes on others*
>   *(American Psychiatric Association, 1994, pp. 83–84).*

It is obvious that these behaviors must be viewed in a developmental context; that is, for any child to be considered hyperactive, these behaviors must be present at a much higher rate than is appropriate for the child's age. Further, some of the symptoms must have been present before age 7, and some impairment from the symptoms must be present in more than one setting.

Prevalence estimates have ranged as high as 20 percent, but a more realistic figure is between 3 and 5 percent (American Psychiatric Association, 1994; Barkley, 1990; Council for Exceptional Children Task Force on Attention Deficit Disorder, 1992). This figure translates into about one hyperactive child per classroom, or between 1.5 and 2.5 million school-age children in the United States. ADHD is much more common in boys, with a male:female ratio of about 6 to 1 (Nussbaum & Bigler, 1990).

Characteristics and Symptoms

Although problems with schoolwork are not listed as specific DSM-IV criteria, the reader can easily ascertain how such problems can arise as a result of these behaviors. The varied classroom manifestations of ADHD will be dealt with in this section. The following clusters of behaviors will be discussed: attending, impulsivity, overactivity, academic performance, and social interaction.

Attending

"He doesn't pay attention" has long been the hue and cry of parents and teachers working with children with ADHD. Research has supported this complaint, as the hyperactive child appears to have problems with both selective and sustained attention (Douglas & Peters, 1979). Selective attention deficiences interfere with the child's classroom functioning because he tends to either focus on inappropriate stimuli and/or to be easily distracted when he is paying attention to the proper stimuli. Both external and internal distraction may be operating. Examples of internal and external distraction commonly seen in the classroom were offered by Fournier (1987): An example of external distraction is the child who cannot be seated by the classroom door because she is distracted by every noise in the hall, even those that are easily screened out by the majority of the class. An example of internal distraction is the child who becomes preoccupied with doodling rather than the class assignment. Larry Silver, a prominent spokesperson for ADHD, has aptly defined the distractibility of these children by describing them as being "at the mercy of their senses." The ability to sustain attention is another requirement for success in the classroom. The inability to sustain attention is illustrated by the child who completes three-fourths of a worksheet and "forgets" the rest, or skips every other row on a sheet of math problems. Poorer performance on repetitious tasks has been found for children with ADHD compared to controls (Hebben, Whitman, Milberg, Andresko, & Galpin, 1981), and the poorer performance is thought to reflect the child's lack of internal controls rather than lack of capability (Draeger, Prior, & Sanson, 1986). Other research suggests that sustained attention may be influenced by external factors such as positive reinforcement (Firestone & Douglas, 1975) or presence of an authority figure (Draeger, Prior, & Sanson, 1986; Nuechterlein, 1983).

Hyperactivity

Increased motor activity may be manifested in a variety of classroom behaviors: being out of seat; wiggling, fidgeting, and constant leg-shaking when seated; pencil-tapping; frequent pencil-sharpening and difficulty keeping hands to self. The analogies to "a motor that is always running" or "an engine that only has one gear—high" appear to be appropriate. Such behaviors present classroom management problems for the teacher because the child is frequently breaking class rules, distracting others, and falling behind in schoolwork.

Impulsivity

Impulsivity refers to a tendency to act without thinking. Many of the DSM-IV criteria describe impulsivity: blurting out answers before the question has been completed, having difficulty with turn-taking, and interrupting others. Although impulsivity has implications for task completion both in the classroom and the home, its most detrimental effect may be on interpersonal relationships. Intrusiveness of verbal interaction (e.g., interrupting or otherwise intruding when socially inappropriate) was found to discriminate hyperactive from nonhyperactive children at a high degree of accuracy (Abikoff, Gittelman, & Klein, 1980). Hyperactive children were found to demonstrate intrusive behavior at higher rates and with greater intensity than nonhyperactive children (Vincent, Williams, Harris, & Duval, 1981).

Academic Performance

There is little doubt that youngsters with ADHD have academic difficulties (Ross & Ross, 1982; Weiss & Hechtman, 1986). The core behaviors of hyperactivity, impulsivity, and attention problems likely interact to produce academic problems (Weiss & Hechtman, 1986). Documented academic problems of students with ADHD include failing grades (Barkley, 1990) and higher levels of grade retention (Cantwell & Satterfield, 1978). They are also prone to underachievement despite intellectual potential.

Social Interaction

Difficulties in social relationships of children with ADHD have become an increasing concern. Research has established that they tend to be deficient in social skills and peer interactions (King & Young, 1981, 1982), attention-seeking (Tallmadge & Barkley, 1983), and less compliant to requests (S. Campbell, 1975). Whether their social interactions are difficult primarily due to their impulsivity and intrusiveness or to other related factors remains to be proven. Some research indicates that aggressive hyperactive children display negative attributional biases when interpreting social situations (Milich & Dodge, 1984). For example, hyperactive aggressive children were more likely to interpret as hostile an ambiguous event such as being hit in the back with a ball. On the other hand, it has been postulated that hyperactive boys with social problems can adequately comprehend social situations but are deficient in generating and acting upon adaptive solutions. Thus, both deficiencies in social perception and generation of adaptive solutions to problems could be contributing to the social problems of children and adolescents with ADHD.

In summary, the symptoms of children with ADHD include a number of problems with attention, impulsivity, and hyperactivity. These core behaviors interact to produce classroom problems in interpersonal interactions and in academic performance. It is important for teachers to recognize these symptoms and to seek help before a negative classroom interaction cycle is set into motion. The hyperactive child in the classroom often elicits teacher behaviors that are more intense, controlling, and negative than usual (Whalen,

Henker, Collins, McAulliffe, & Vaux, 1979). Given the externalized nature of hyperactivity, it may be easy to overlook the internal turmoil experienced by these youngsters, as illustrated in Figure 6-1.

Assessment Procedures

Three types of procedures are used to diagnose ADHD: (1) developmental histories including data from home and school, (2) clinical procedures, and (3) observations and recordings of behavior. It is important to obtain developmental histories because certain factors such as low birth weight, respiratory problems after delivery, and a family history of learning problems have been shown to have an abnormally high occurrence among these children; however, information on behavior observed during the preschool ages of two to five is

**FIGURE 6-1.   A Self-portrait from a "Stressed-out"
7 1/2-year-old with ADHD**

From N. Nussbaum & E. Bigler (1990), *Identification and treatment of
attention deficit disorder,* Austin, TX: Pro-Ed. Reprinted with permission of
the publisher.

considered most important (Safer & Allen, 1976). Most children with ADHD are described by their parents as being restless and inattentive and, to a lesser extent, disruptive, destructive, or temperamental during this period. Safer and Allen consider teacher observations and school history to be more informative even than parental accounts or physicians' judgments because "hyperactivity reaches its peak in a sit-down, all-day classroom situation, an experience routinely observed only by the teacher" (1976, p. 17). In the school setting, the best predictors of attention deficit disorder are conduct grades, evidence of learning problems, and previous and current teachers' ratings of restlessness and inattentiveness.

Clinical procedures are used by pediatric neurologists, pediatricians, psychologists, and other child specialists to diagnose ADHD. Depending upon the specialist, clinical procedures may include assessments of visual-motor skills, intelligence, achievement, and sometimes an electroencephalogram and a pediatric-neurologic examination. If medication is prescribed, it should be based on these clinical findings and information from teacher and parent reports.

Observations and recordings of classroom behavior may be completed by a teacher or other school personnel using a behavior checklist or some type of behavior recording. There are a number of published checklists available for teacher use. On such meaures, the teacher is asked to rate the degree to which a child shows characteristics and behaviors such as impulsivity, disturbing others, fighting, inattention, failing to complete work, tenseness and crying, temper tantrums, or other signs of frustration. Under optimal conditions, more than one teacher's rating on a particular child is obtained. To obtain a behavioral record, a person trained in systematic behavior recording observes the child in the classroom and other school settings. In this procedure, a number of behaviors such as out-of-seat or talking out are usually selected, and for short periods of time, each occurrence is recorded. Recordings of this type may be used to validate or supplement teacher ratings.

ADHD does not constitute a separate special education category. In the past, children and adolescents with ADHD were either labeled as learning disabled or behavior disordered in order to be eligible for special education services. Since 1991, however, they have been eligible for special education services under the category of "other health impaired." Studies both prior to and after 1991 have found a substantial percentage (43 percent to 47 percent) of students in classrooms for emotional/behavioral disorders who have a primary psychiatric diagnosis of ADHD (Mattison et al., 1986; Mattison, Morales, & Bauer, 1992). These findings suggest that regardless of specific identification policies, students with ADHD will continue to be placed in classrooms for students with emotional/behavioral disorders.

Etiology and Development

Theories of etiology and development of ADHD can be categorized into (1) brain-related factors and (2) environmental agents.

Theories of Etiology: Brain-related Factors

The vast majority of research into the etiology of ADHD has centered upon various brain-related hypotheses. You will recall that ADHD previously was called *minimal brain injury* and *minimal brain dysfunction.* The term *minimal brain injury* in particular captured the popular notion of the time that hyperactivity was caused by some type of ill-defined brain damage. It is now generally accepted that a very small percentage of hyperactive children show clear evidence of neurological *damage,* such as abnormal reflexes or loss of sensation (Rutter, 1977). However, some type of neurological *dysfunction* is still believed by many researchers to be a causal factor in ADHD. Among these theories are those implicating (a) neurotransmitters, (b) the reticular activating system of the brain, and (c) developmental lag as causal factors (Nussbaum & Bigler, 1990).

Neurotransmitter disturbances have been hypothesized to cause hyperactivity. The specific systems that have been implicated are the dopamine and norepinephrine systems, which contribute to arousal, alertness, and motor activity; however, the causal link between these systems and hyperactivity is still speculative (Nussbaum & Bigler, 1990).

Reticular activating system problems have also been proposed as causal factors in ADHD (J. H. Rosenthal, 1973). The reticular activating system (RAS) is a group of structures in the brainstem that regulates levels of alertness or arousal. In children with ADHD, the RAS may fail to screen out distracting stimuli in the environment, therefore contributing to the distractibility and inattentiveness of these children. Thus, the RAS acts as a filter mechanism, which may be faulty in these children (Nussbaum & Bigler, 1990). Although some of the stimulant medications used to treat ADHD act by stimulating the RAS, a causal relationship has not been empirically established.

Developmental lag in brain development is another possible causal explanation for ADHD. It is known that the brain matures in developmental stages and that the frontal lobe, which affects the regulation of attention and concentration, does not reach maturity until adolescence. Therefore, this theory posits that the ADHD characteristics of impulsivity and inattention are related to a specific lag in frontal lobe development. For example, a 10-year-old child with frontal lobe immaturity may have the attentional capacity of a 6- or 7-year old (Massman, Nussbaum, & Bigler, 1988). This theory underscores the age-appropriateness of behavior in diagnosing ADHD.

Despite the plausibility of all three brain-related theories, a review of data supports Barkley's conclusion that "The most one can conclude at this point is that neurologic dysfunction of some sort may eventually be shown to play a role in the hyperactivity of some children, although the nature of this dysfunction awaits specification and empirical support," (1984, p. 135).

Theories of Etiology: Environmental Agents

Allergic reactions to toxins and foods are considered under this category. Although sugar, food additives, and fluorescent lighting have all been held accountable for hyperactivity at one time or other by the lay press, none of these has been proven a causal factor for children with ADHD. A very small percentage of youngsters with ADHD have shown hyperactive allergic reactions to certain foods that can be controlled through diet; this topic is treated in greater detail in Chapter 3 under biophysical interventions. Lead poisoning is one toxin that does consistently appear in hyperactive children. Several studies have shown that, among children with elevated blood lead levels, 25 percent to 35 percent are hyperactive (Barkley, 1984). Although these incidence levels were much higher than in control groups, none of the studies addressed lead poisoning as a cause of hyperactivity.

In summary, etiologic factors in the development of hyperactivity are usually assumed to be brain-related or environment-related. These factors are summarized in Table 6-1.

TABLE 6-1 Possible Causes of ADHD

Cause	Comments
Brain-related factors	
Brain dysfunction	Neurotransmitter imbalance
	Faulty "filter mechanism" in the reticular activating system
Lag in brain development	Frontal lobe
Genetic factors	
Family history for ADHD	20% to 30% of all children with ADHD have a parent or sibling with similar problems
Allergic reactions	
Foods, dyes, food additives, environmental toxins	Only a small percentage of children with ADHD show this "allergic-type" reaction

From N. Nussbaum & E. Bigler (1990), *Identification and treatment of attention deficit disorder.* Austin, TX: Pro-Ed. Reprinted with permission of the publisher.

Various theories of brain dysfunction have logical appeal but little evidence to establish them as causal factors. Theories implicating environmental agents also suffer from lack of evidence, although children with high levels of lead in their blood do show a marked increase in incidence of hyperactivity.

Predisposing Factors

Central nervous system difficulties and family variables may predispose youngsters toward manifesting ADHD. It has been established that ADHD is not caused by brain damage per se; however, many studies continue to find various problems such as minor physical anomalies, motor coordination problems, histories of birth complications, and minor EEG abnormalities (Barkley, 1984; Bigler, 1988; Tupper, 1987). Such findings appear to support a correlation between neurological problems and the tendency to display hyperactive behaviors.

A number of familial variables are associated with hyperactivity in children. Some evidence suggests that hyperactive children more often come from families with higher parental alcoholism and clinical problems (Cantwell, 1978). Other research has assessed the social interactions of ADHD children with family members, particularly mothers. Although earlier research showed that mothers of hyperactive children tended to be more controlling, commanding, and negative in their interactions than mothers of nonhyperactives, more recent research indicates that the controlling pattern of the mothers is likely a reaction to, rather than a cause of, their offspring's behavior. The latter research assessed the effects of medication on mother-child interaction styles and found that when the child's behavior improved, mothers' reactions were also less intense (Barkley & Cunningham, 1979). It is generally accepted that hyperactivity runs in families. Between 20 percent and 30 percent of hyperactive children have a parent or sibling who have experienced similar problems (Nussbaum & Bigler, 1990). Researchers have not yet established the specific mechanism through which ADHD is transmitted, but few would dispute the assumption that many children with ADHD inherit a central nervous system that predisposes them toward problems with attention and concentration.

Related Conditions

The two primary conditions associated with ADHD are learning disabilities and conduct disorders. Poor school achievement is almost always associated with hyperactivity. In their review, Weiss and Hechtman (1986) concluded that low school achievement is a common result of the core ADHD behaviors (i.e., impulsivity, inattention, overactivity). The prevalence of learning disabilities among children with ADHD has been estimated as high as 80 percent, but when stringent criteria for learning disabilities are applied, the estimate may drop to as low as 10 to 20 percent (Reeve, 1990). From a clinical perspective, Silver (1987) suggests that hyperactive children are likely to have a specific learning disability in at least one area. Experts do not agree, however, on whether there is a common underlying dysfunction that causes both ADHD and learning disabilities, or whether the ADHD behaviors cause serious achievement problems.

The relationship between hyperactivity and conduct disorders also has been studied. It has been suggested that the hyperactive child is more prone to verbal and physical aggression than other children, thereby demonstrating some of the core behaviors of conduct disorders (Abikoff, Gittelman-Klein, & Klein, 1977). Also, lowered levels of self-control due to impulsivity may predispose these youngsters toward conduct disorders. In two long-term follow-up studies, Weiss and Hechtman (1986) found higher rates of conduct-disordered behavior and antisocial personality disorder among the hyperactive sample than among the controls. While these results would appear to substantiate that ADHD predisposes children to develop conduct disorders, other researchers have pointed out that the Weiss and Hechtman research failed to initially differentiate hyperactive children with conduct disorders from hyperactive children without conduct disorders in the original sample (Satterfield, Hoppe, & Schell, 1982). It is therefore possible that a proportion of the hyperactive sample were displaying concomitant conduct disorders at the time the study began. Longitudinal studies by Lambert and her colleagues (Lambert, 1988; Lambert, Sassone, Hartsough, & Sandoval, 1987) also substantiate that hyperactive children are at risk for developing conduct disorders and have more problems with the juvenile authorities than their nonhyperactive peers.

The research on related conditions can be summarized thus: we do not currently know whether some underlying common cause predisposes youngsters to develop these multiple conditions or whether one disorder causes the others. However, ADHD, conduct disorders, and learning disabilities do coexist at a high rate. Further, it is likely that some students with all three difficulties will find their way into classrooms for students with emotional/behavioral disorders.

Intervention and Treatment

It is not an overstatement to suggest that hundreds and hundreds of studies have assessed treatment outcomes with ADHD youngsters. Its high prevalence relative to other disorders and the visibility of ADHD behaviors at school have likely contributed to this interest in treatment research. The majority of treatments can be categorized as medication therapy, behavior management, or cognitive behavioral techniques. Many studies employed a combination of these techniques such as medication plus behavior management.

Medication

The effects of medication, primarily stimulants, on ADHD behaviors have been widely studied. Stimulants are reported to improve symptoms in approximately 70 percent of hyperactive children (Barkley, 1990). Methylphenidate (Ritalin) is the most commonly prescribed and most studied stimulant. Dexedrine and Cylert are used to a much lesser extent. Stimulants have been shown to have short-term effects on sustained attention, activity level, impulsivity, and classroom behavior (Rapport, 1987). Whether symptom improvement also leads to increased academic achievement is still a point of contention (Gadow, 1983, 1985; Rapport, Stoner, DuPaul, Birmingham, & Tucker, 1985). There is some evidence to suggest that research results on symptom improvement depend largely on which symptoms are studied and which measures are used to document improvement. According to Forness and his colleagues (Forness, Swanson, Cantwell, Guthrie, & Sena, 1992), many studies used only one or two measures and found improvement in one area (e.g., cognitive or behavioral) but not another. For example, higher doses of stimulants may be more effective in controlling classroom behavior but less effective in improving learning than lower doses. On the other hand, lower dosages may not be sufficient to help control behavior (Gadow, 1986c). Forness et al. (1992) studied the effects of Ritalin on six measures of academic, cognitive, and social functioning with a sample of 71 boys with ADHD, ages 7 to 11 years. They concluded that although the disruptive behavioral symptoms do appear to improve significantly, (e.g., response level of around 70 percent), measures of new learning and of oral reading produce favorable responses of only around 50 percent, and tasks such as reading comprehension less than 20 percent. These findings support the need to clearly differentiate the deficits or symptoms that are being targeted for improvement by use of stimulant medication.

The use of stimulant medication to treat excessive activity levels appears to be paradoxical. While the specific mechanism through which these medications work is currently unknown, some researchers speculate that the medications act to stimulate the reticular activating system, the "filtering system" mentioned under theories of etiology. When the RAS is thus stimulated, children with ADHD appear to be better able to focus attention and to act less impulsively.

Side effects of stimulant medication include headaches, stomachaches, insomnia, loss of appetite, irritability or mood swings, and growth inhibition. Most of the side effects disappear naturally within a couple of weeks or in response to adjustments in timing or amount of dosages. Growth inhibition is thought to be related to decreased appetite, which can be ameliorated by giving the medication with or immediately after meals (Nussbaum & Bigler, 1990).

In addition to side effects, there are other drawbacks and criticisms regarding use of medication to treat ADHD. First is a nationwide tendency toward overprescribing, possibly because medication may be viewed as a "sure cure" or a panacea for a host of very difficult behaviors in children. Second, medication can become a crutch for the child and those working with him. For example, the child who becomes psychologically dependent may believe that he can't control himself without the drug. There may also be concerns that children on prescription medication may be prone to later drug abuse, although this assumption has not been borne out by research (Loney, Kramer, & Milich, 1981). Parents and professionals may also tend to let medication replace their management responsibilities.

Third, medication has not always been proven as more effective than behavior management strategies (Myers & Hammill, 1990). These concerns have led some professionals to question whether medication should be used only when other interventions have failed, while others believe that alternative interventions will be more successful when ADHD symptoms are first ameliorated with medication. One study using behavior management as an alternative to medication is reported in Box 6-1.

Behavior Management Strategies

Many behavioral strategies also have been successful in improving the behaviors associated with hyperactivity. Programs using positive reinforcement as well as those using behavior reduction procedures have proven effective. For example, attending behavior of hyperactive children has responded positively to both social reinforcement and a response cost system (Rapport, 1987). On-task behavior has also been increased with a positive reinforcement system (Allyon, Layman & Kandel, 1975). In addition, home-based contingency systems for appropriate classroom behavior have been implemented successfully with these youngsters (Pelham, Schnedler, Bologna, & Contreras, 1980); however, Rapport (1987) cautions that home-based reinforcement may not be effective for those impulsive youngsters with ADHD who have difficulty in delaying gratification. Another potential difficulty with some behavioral programs was identified by Ross and Ross (1982) in their review. These authors concluded that, while many programs were initially successful in changing behavior, the positive gains were not always maintained. Reasons for diminished success were teacher disinterest in continuing the program, inadequacies in the program design, and/or habituation of the children to the reinforcers. One study showed that the teacher also needed reinforcement for maintaining the program: improvement in child behavior fluctuated according to whether the teacher was being reinforced (Brown, Montgomery, & Barclay, 1969). These

---

BOX 6-1 Managing Hyperactive Behavior Without Medication

A study by Rosenbaum, O'Leary, and Jacob (1975) illustrates how both individual and group contingencies can be used in the classroom to curb some of the behavior problems associated with hyperactivity. Ten boys, ages 8 to 12, participated in the study. For those youngsters in the individual contingency program, a target behavior such as staying in seat or completing work was selected. At the end of each hour, if the youngster had complied with the rule, reward cards were distributed by the teacher; these cards could be traded in at the end of the day for candy.

In the group contingency program, the individual could earn rewards for the entire class by following the rules that were set for him. The teacher explained the program to the class and solicited their help by asking them to ignore him when he was behaving badly and to let him know when he was doing well. Hourly reward cards were used that could be traded at the end of the day, but in this case, everyone in the class received a piece of candy for each reward card that was earned by the individual student. Both programs ran for four weeks.

Results indicated that both methods were effective, although teachers much preferred the group method. Follow-up four weeks after the reward was discontinued showed that the students had maintained their improvements in behavior. The authors recommend both group and individual behavior management systems as alternatives to medication for hyperactive children.

studies point to the importance of system variables that may be overlooked when focusing only upon the hyperactive child.

Cognitive-behavioral Interventions

These interventions are based upon a combination of self-talk and problem-solving; with hyperactive children the techniques are usually aimed at increasing attention and decreasing impulsivity. The child is usually taught a set of self-statements or a problem-solving sequence that she practices overtly, and eventually, covertly. Self-talk and self-monitoring have proven helpful to the hyperactive child in specific learning situations (Abikoff, 1985; Craighead, Meyers, & Wilcoxon-Craighead, 1985), and in general classroom and playground behaviors (Abikoff, 1985). However, researchers cite problems in maintaining acquired gains in other settings and over time. Effects of this research are also obscured by the coexistence of hyperactivity with conduct disorders and learning disabilities.

Combination of Treatments

Owing to the intractable and multifaceted nature of ADHD symptoms, the use of combined treatments has become more popular in recent years (Rapport, 1987). Combined treatments also address some of the issues raised by use of medication alone, particularly the tendency toward overreliance on drugs to control or "fix" the behavior.

The most common combination is use of stimulant medication with some behavior management or cognitive-behavioral technique. While some studies have shown superior results with combined treatments, others have failed to increase gains by adding behavioral or cognitive therapy components. Rapport (1983, 1987) has attributed these equivocal results to methodological shortcomings in the research rather than failure of the treatments. Combined treatments appeal to both practitioners and researchers, and therefore probably will continue to be implemented.

In summary, medication appears to improve behavioral symptoms in a large proportion of children with ADHD; however, the drawbacks of side effects and potential overreliance on medication lead many parents and professionals to question its viability. A variety of behavioral and cognitive-behavioral techniques have also been shown to improve symptoms such as attention and impulsivity. Despite the popular appeal of combined treatments, they have not yet been demonstrated as clearly superior to treatments employing single strategies. However, flaws in the studies rather than ineffectiveness of the combined treatments may be responsible for these findings.

Implications for Teachers

Teachers may be more involved in the assessment and remediation of ADHD than with any other of the internalizing and externalizing disorders. Unlike the other disorders, ADHD may cause more problems in the classroom than anywhere else. A teacher may be the first person to point out the age-inappropriateness of the child's behavior to his parents. Teachers may be asked to keep observational data, to complete checklists, and to monitor side effects of medication manifested in the classroom. These are all important tasks and especially necessary if the child is receiving medication. Physicians can only estimate the dosage needed by a particular child and will need feedback from teachers and parents in order to properly adjust the dosage.

Teachers of youngsters with ADHD are also likely to be involved in behavior management programs aimed at improving attention, task completion, and ultimately academic achievement. Such programs may be based on positive reinforcement, a cognitive-behavioral approach or a response cost system. One study of teacher attitudes toward ADHD interventions compared teachers' acceptability ratings of various techniques that could be implemented in their classrooms. Given a choice of a positive reinforcement approach, a cognitive-behavioral strategy, medication therapy, and a response cost strategy, teachers rated the response cost strategy for inappropriate behaviors as most acceptable in their classrooms (Fournier, 1987). Risk to the child, amount of record keeping, and usefulness of the intervention for other behaviors were among the variables influencing teacher ratings.

Because of the incidence of hyperactivity, most teachers will encounter children and adolescents with ADHD in their classrooms. Although the social and emotional needs of these youngsters were not addressed in depth in this section, it is important to realize that these youth may need counseling to help them understand the nature and implications of their problems. Parents may need to increase their behavior management skills and/or may profit from a support group. Teachers may be the only link between some of these parents and the professional community; they are therefore in a position to refer students and their parents to helpful community resources.

Conduct Disorders

Conduct disorder has been used as a catch-all term for a variety of acting out, aggressive, and antisocial acts. It also has been equated with social maladjustment, thus eliciting issues of whether to exclude youngsters so labeled from public school services for students with emotional/behavioral disorders. Many youth with conduct disorders get into trouble with the law, are adjudicated and become labeled delinquent by the courts. It may be helpful to consider that *conduct disorder* is the term of choice for the mental health system, that *social maladjustment* may be used by schools, and that *delinquency* is used by the legal system for those brought before the courts. In addition, the term *antisocial behavior* is a general term used to denote a pattern of willful and repeated violations of societal standards; antisocial behavior is the most common reason for referral of children and youth to mental health services (Reid, 1993). In this context, it is accurate to say that antisocial behavior is commonly exhibited by youth who are labeled conduct disordered, socially maladjusted, and delinquent.

Despite the confusion over terms and eligibility, it is important to understand youngsters with conduct disorders because students with these characteristics do ultimately find their way into classrooms for students with emotional/behavioral disorders in the schools.

Definition and Prevalence

Conduct disorder is composed of a constellation of behaviors, but is best understood as a distinctive pattern of antisocial behavior that violates the rights of others. Some key behaviors are overtly aggressive such as fighting and destroying property, while other key behaviors are more covert such as stealing and lying. DSM-IV emphasizes that individuals with conduct disorders break rules or violate major societal norms across settings: at home, in school, with peers, and in the community. DSM-IV diagnosis lists the following criteria:

Aggression

1. *often bullies, threatens others, or initiates fights*
2. *has used a weapon such as a knife, gun, bat, etc.*
3. *has been physically cruel to people or animals*
4. *has stolen with victim present*
5. *has forced someone into sexual activity*

Destruction of property

1. *has engaged in deliberate fire-setting or destroyed others' property*

Deceitfulness or theft

1. *has broken into houses, buildings or cars*
2. *often lies or cons others*
3. *has stolen without victim present (e.g., shoplifting)*

Serious rules violations

1. *often stays out at night without parental permission*
2. *has run away from home more than once*
3. *is often truant from school (DSM-IV, American Psychiatric Association, 1994, p. 90).*

Oppositional defiant is a separate DSM-IV diagnosis; however, it will be included in this section because it often coexists with conduct disorder and because little is written about the two as distinctly different conditions. Although quite annoying, oppositional defiant behaviors are considered less serious than conduct disorders because they do not violate major norms or the basic rights of others. Oppositional defiant behaviors include: arguing with adults, losing temper, refusing adult requests, blaming others for own mistakes, and deliberately annoying others. Descriptive characteristics include *touchy, angry, resentful, spiteful,* and *vindictive* (American Psychiatric Association, 1994). After perusing these criteria, the reader can readily see that many students with emotional/behavioral disorders could be labeled as oppositional defiant.

It may also be important to distinguish a subgroup of youth with conduct disorders who can be described as not socialized or lacking significant social attachments to family or friends. (As adults, they may be referred to as *psychopathic* or *sociopathic*.) The most salient characteristic of these individuals is their lack of internalization of societal rules, norms, or standards of appropriate behavior toward others; in other words, they do not apply such standards to themselves. They appear to have no conscience and little concept of right and wrong. They may further be described as operating at a low level of moral development: negative behavior is bad if one gets caught and subsequently punished; negative behavior is okay if one doesn't get caught or gets rewarded. Authority and reciprocal relationships with others have little meaning. Due to such attitudes, these individuals are at highest risk for breaking the law, being adjudicated, and continuing persistent patterns of delinquent behavior. These behavior patterns often continue into adulthood, manifested in criminal activity and/or antisocial personality disorder. Several studies have found that aggression, noncompliance, and poor social relationships in children ages 6 to 10 were also evidenced in adolescence along with school failure and delinquency (Camp & Ray, 1984). Thus, once established, these behavior patterns are extremely difficult to change. Individuals who develop conduct disorders in childhood are more likely to continue the behaviors (and become labeled antisocial personality disorder) in adulthood than individuals who develop conduct disorders in adolescence (American Psychiatric Association, 1994). Therefore, early identification and intervention may be essential to working with this population.

Conduct disorders are defined by a number of covert and overt antisocial acts. Walker, Colvin, and Ramsey (1994) assert that antisocial children and youth follow one or more of three distinct paths in developing conduct disorders: covert, disobedient, or overt. A covert path is defined by stealth and is usually directed toward property (vandalism, stealing) or self (substance abuse). An overt path is defined by aggressive behavior and victimization of others (cruelty, fighting), and a disobedient path is characterized by oppositional behavior such as noncompliance with adult requests and rules. Although all three are disruptive and lead to adjustment difficulties, the specific developmental path taken by an individual may dictate a different treatment approach.

The specific behaviors of conduct disorders tend to cluster; in other words, a child who engages in one of these behaviors is likely to engage in others as well. Although one child may not engage in all these behaviors, core behaviors include fighting, temper tantrums, theft, truancy, destroying property, defying or threatening others, and running away (Quay, 1986). Refer to Box 6-2 for brief case studies illustrating the clustering nature of conduct disordered behavior.

Other characteristics of conduct disorders are, not surprisingly, poor interpersonal relations (Carlson, Lahey, & Neeper, 1984) and academic deficiencies (Ledingham & Schwartzman, 1984). In addition, youth with conduct disorders have shown deficiencies in cognitive problem-solving skills such as perspective-taking and identifying alternative solutions to interpersonal problems (Dodge, 1985).

The prevalence of conduct disorders among children has increased over the past few years. In 1987, it was estimated as ranging from 4 to 10 percent (Kazdin, 1987b). In 1994, it was estimated as between 6 and 16 percent for males, and between 2 and 9 percent for females (American Psychiatric Association, 1994). Males most often exhibit conduct disorders prior to puberty, with an average age of onset between 8 and 10; age of onset for females is later, usually between ages 13 and 15 (Toth, 1990).

Children and adolescents with conduct disorders pose a tremendous challenge to society. According to Robins (1981), they also represent one of the most costly groups not only in terms of vandalism and damage, but also because they tend to cycle in and out of the mental health and juvenile justice systems throughout adolescence and into adulthood. These social costs are compounded by the individual misery incurred by persons with antisocial behavior: the youngsters themselves often suffer, as do their families. And when the antisocial behavior takes a violent turn, the victims of crime also suffer. According to Kazdin (1987a), the crimes of murder, rape, robbery, arson, drunk driving, and spouse or child abuse are perpetrated at a much higher rate by individuals with a history of antisocial behavior than by those without such a history. It is important to remember that not all

---

BOX 6-2: Case Studies of Conduct Disorder

CASE STUDY 1: Jeremy

A husband and wife who could not have children adopted Jeremy when he was 3. Jeremy is now 15. He has been very difficult to handle while growing up. He is hyperactive and requires constant attention. When he was younger, he got into everything: wrote on walls, hurt the cat, set fires, and broke various items in the house. Most recently, he has been oppositional and defiant at home. His parents suspect drug use. He is skipping school. He has also been breaking into cars with his peers. This is the first time these individuals have experienced parenthood. They are unsure how to handle this situation, and they do not know how concerned to be about this behavior. Jeremy's mother is worried, but his father is still hoping he will "grow out of it." His father recalls getting into trouble when he was young. The situation is difficult for both parents, and they are constantly in conflict. To make matters worse, Jeremy's father is traveling out of town more frequently on business. Mother cannot handle this situation by herself: She is tired, depressed, and feels abandoned by her husband. The child's behavior worsens as the mother's behavior changes. The problems begin to appear insurmountable to the mother, and she is having difficulty setting any limits.

CASE STUDY 2: Evelyn

Mrs. Harris is a single parent. Her husband left when her two children, Larry and Evelyn, were young. Both children did well in grade school, academically and behaviorally. Mrs. Harris had an opportunity for a better job and relocated her family when Larry was 13 and Evelyn was 16. The job is very stressful. Larry has adjusted well to his new home and school. Evelyn has had more difficulty adjusting. She was in her senior year when they moved. The school is more difficult for her and she has made few friends. She feels isolated and frustrated. Her mother is less available due to work. Mrs. Harris is also struggling with her own mother's recent diagnosis of Alzheimer's disease and has had trouble with anxiousness and depression. Evelyn begins skipping school and smoking marijuana with a group of teens at school who have behavioral problems. She becomes sexually active and sneaks out at night. She keeps these behaviors secret from her mother. She often lies. She begins stealing clothing and cosmetics from a department store. She is arrested for shoplifting, and her mother is called to the police station. Mrs. Harris is very upset and does not know what to do. She feels overwhelmed and unable to make any decisions.

From M.K. Toth (1990), *Understanding and treating conduct disorders,* Austin, TX: Pro-Ed. Used with permission of the publisher.

---

youngsters with conduct disorders are violent or break the law, but a significant portion of them do.

Etiology of Conduct Disorders and Aggression

Although much research has been devoted to identifying predisposing factors, only a couple of behavioral theories have been put forth to explain how conduct disordered behavior (including oppositional behavior) develops. Because aggressive behavior also is so often a part of conduct disorders, theories relating to the development of aggressive behavior will be explored in this section.

Theories of Etiology of Conduct Disorders
Patterson (1976) has developed a "coercion hypothesis" to account for the development and maintenance of behavior leading to conduct disorders. According to Patterson, infants have

a repertoire of coercive behaviors that are highly adaptive in shaping parental responses (e.g., crying when hungry or uncomfortable to get parents' attention). As infants grow older, the majority learn other ways to get their needs met; however, if parents fail to reinforce appropriate social behaviors and/or continue to respond to coercive demands, then a pattern of coercive behavior and responses may be set into motion. For example: mother asks the child to put away his toys; the child whines and refuses; the mother then gives up and does it herself rather than listen to the whining, thus reinforcing the coercive behavior of the child. In a different scenario, if the mother escalates her demand by yelling and becoming aggressive rather than giving up, she may eventually get the child to comply; thus, she is reinforced for her aggressive behavior, and a pattern of negative coercion is still created. Over time, these interactions can establish a pattern of escalating coercion between parent and child that eventually determines the way the child will interact with others.

In-home observations of 27 aggressive and 27 nonproblem boys support this coercive interaction hypothesis, as the aggressive youngsters displayed significantly higher rates of coercive behaviors such as negative commands, disapproval, humiliation, noncompliance, negativism, teasing, and yelling (Patterson, 1976). In return, family members tended to retaliate with equally aversive responses such as criticism and threats.

Although offering a behavioral perspective, Patterson's model also encompasses a family systems orientation in that parents and other family members become a part of the continued coercive pattern over time and therefore become part of the problem. Such an orientation has implications for treatment of the entire family, a topic to which we will return later in this chapter.

Wahler (1976) believes that positive reinforcement can also play a role in the development of conduct disordered behavior. According to this hypothesis, the child's disruptive behavior elicits either verbal or physical attention from the parent, thus inadvertently reinforcing the behavior. In the previous example, the mother might approach the child and quietly try to talk him into putting up his toys by reasoning with him; the positive attention afforded by his refusal would then serve to reinforce the refusal.

These models focus on parent-child interactions; although much less has been written about conduct disordered behaviors in the school setting, these same principles can operate in teacher-child interactions in the classroom (Atkeson & Forehand, 1984).

Theories of Development of Aggression
A number of models explaining the development of aggression have been proposed: (a) a social learning hypothesis, (b) a cognitive hypothesis, and (c) a more comprehensive model including both cognitive and behavioral components. In addition, society has contributed in a very concrete way to the development of aggressive and violent behavior patterns among our children and youth.

Social learning.   A social learning perspective was researched by Bandura (Bandura, Ross, & Ross, 1963), who demonstrated that young children learn aggressive behavior through imitation of aggressive models. These models can be peers, individuals on film or television, and parents (especially those who use physical punishment). There is ample opportunity for today's youngsters to be exposed to aggressive models, particularly in the media. Box 6-3 summarizes several studies on the relationship between watching aggression on TV and

BOX 6-3 Does Watching Televised Aggression Cause Aggressive Behavior?

Soon after television gained popular appeal, critics and parents alike began to express concern about its influence on children. They had good reason: The young seemed especially attracted to the new medium and sat "glued" in front of the TV set for an average of two to three hours daily (Liebert and Poulos, 1976). Concern heightened as aggression and violence became the dominant theme of television entertainment in the 1960s and 1970s. Amid much controversy, researchers took to the laboratory and the field to determine whether the young were adversely affected by their new "babysitter." On the surface the task appeared simple enough. In fact, it was not. Since children are exposed to so many influences, how could the effects of one be isolated? Several years of investigation, employing different methods, were required before the evidence was in.

Experimental laboratory research was conducted in which children's aggression was measured subsequent to their viewing either aggressive or nonaggressive models on television. Overall, compared to control children, those who saw the aggressive examples later displayed similar behaviors (Liebert, Sprafkin, and Davison, 1982; Stein and Friedrich, 1975). This finding held across the age span from early childhood to late adolescence. The studies were compelling because they were experimental in design and well-controlled. They thus established that viewing televised aggression could cause aggression in children under certain conditions. At the same time, however, the laboratory setting raised doubts that the findings would generalize to the "real" world. Researchers attacked this problem with experimental field studies and correlational research.

An example of experimental field research is the work of Stein and Friedrich (1972), which examined the cumulative effects of different TV content on nursery school children. During an initial measurement period the free play of the children, ages 3 1/2 to 5 1/2, was observed and rated. The youngsters were then systematically exposed for a four-week period to either aggressive cartoons (such as Batman and Superman), prosocial programs from

Mister Rogers' Neighborhood, or neutral programming. During this time and during a two-week postviewing period, the children's free-play behavior continued to be observed. Children who were initially in the upper half of the sample in terms of interpersonal aggression exhibited greater aggression when playing if they had been exposed to aggressive programming rather than prosocial or neutral programming. These results were especially important because the effects occurred in a naturalistic setting rather than in a laboratory and because a cause-and-effect relationship could be drawn from the experimental design. Stein and Friedrich found that despite the fact that the children watched less than six hours of television over a four-week period, aggressive behavior, removed in time and setting from the viewing experience, was affected.

Moving even closer to the "real" world has been correlational research, designed to determine the association between aggression in the natural environment and the viewing of television violence. The most extensive work in this area is that of Eron and his colleagues. In the Rip Van Winkle Study, Eron, Huesmann, Lefkowitz, and Walder (1972) studied a sample of 875 children who constituted the entire third-grade population of a semirural county in New York. The researchers found a relationship between the amount of television violence subjects watched when they were 8 or 9 years old and how aggressive they were at the time. Even more interesting was the finding of a relationship between the early television viewing and aggressiveness at age 19. Among the 475 subjects who could be located ten years later, it was found that, for boys, preference for violent television programs during the third grade was significantly related to both peer- and self-rated measures of aggression at age 19. In fact, amount of early viewing of violent television predicted later aggression better than any of the other variables measured, such as IQ, social status, religious practice, ethnicity, and parental disharmony. Another follow-up of these males is in progress.

Meanwhile, Eron and his colleagues have turned to a new population of youngsters. The Chicago

BOX 6-3 *Continued*

Circle Study followed approximately 750 children, ages 6 to 10 years, for three years. Viewing of TV violence was positively associated with aggressive behavior, but this time for both boys and girls. This same finding is showing up in replications of the study in Finland, Poland, and Australia (Eron, 1982). The Chicago Circle Study was also designed to further examine some of the variables and processes implicated in the Rip Van Winkle Study. An interesting picture is emerging of the aggressive child who watches violent television. Observation of aggressive models does cause aggression, but aggressive children also prefer to watch more and more violent TV. It is likely that since aggressive youngsters are unpopular, they spend more time in front of the television set. TV violence may assure them that their own behavior is appropriate and

teach them new coercive techniques. When coercion is used with peers, the youngsters become increasingly unpopular and are driven back to television watching. In addition, aggressive children appear to be low achievers, and they may have fewer resources to deal with the world. They tend to identify strongly with TV characters and thus more readily adopt the violent lessons of the medium. Peer isolation and excessive TV watching may also increase school failure. Thus, a circular process may be operating that involves adoption of aggressive behavior, unpopularity, low achievement, and excessive television watching.

From R. Wicks-Nelson and A. C. Israel (1984), *Behavior Disorders of Childhood.* Englewood Cliffs, NJ: Prentice Hall. Reprinted with permission of the publisher.

subsequent levels of aggression in children and adolescents. Conclusions from these and other studies indicate that aggressive behavior is linked to watching violence on TV, although a direct causal relationship would be difficult to prove.

Cognitive perspective.   Cognitive models have also been developed to explain aggression. Novaco (1978) proposed a cognitive paradigm to explain the relationship of anger and aggression. Angry responses are explained in terms of external cues, internal arousal, cognitions about that arousal, and a behavioral reaction. Novaco stresses that external cues and events play only an indirect role because the cognitions and internal arousal are what eventually determine whether the individual becomes angry. Anger arousal then increases the likelihood of aggressive responses, although there are alternative responses. Children as young as kindergarten-age tend to cognitively appraise events that make them angry (Hill, 1989).

Comprehensive models.   Other researchers promote more comprehensive models suggesting that both cognitive distortions and deficiencies in social problem solving interact to encourage aggressive responding. For example, Dodge (1985) found that aggressive children have shown a tendency to attribute hostile intent to others' actions, especially when the social cues are ambiguous. Aggressive children perceive cues differently and make attributions differently than do nonaggressive children (Lochman, White, & Wayland, 1990). Aggressive youngsters also tend to readily label their internal responses to conflict-producing situations as anger (Garrison & Stolberg, 1983). In addition to these cognitive distortions, aggressive children are deficient in social problem-solving skills. Although findings are mixed as to whether the number or *quantity* of solutions to problems that are generated by aggressive youngsters is deficient, there is little doubt that they display problems with the content or *quality* of the problem solutions they generate (Lochman, White, & Wayland, 1990). In contrast to nonaggressive children, aggressive children consistently generate more action solutions and fewer verbal assertion solutions (Asarnow & Callan, 1985; Lochman & Lampron, 1986). In other words, these kids tend to solve problems by immediate action rather than by trying to talk, which leaves others few choices in interacting with them. Thus, cognitive-behavioral interventions focus upon changing cognitive distortions and upon increasing problem-solving skills.

Social factors.   Societal factors have been implicated as contributing to the increases in youth-perpetrated violence. Of particular concern is that more violent crimes are being committed by younger children, in some cases, pre-teens. One study cited failures of both parents and schools as causal factors (Commission on Violence and Youth, 1993). The commission also cited societal factors such as easy access to firearms, increased use of drugs and alcohol, prevalence of gangs, and exposure to violence in the media. These factors are pervasive in urban and suburban settings, but are quickly spreading to many rural areas that had previously considered themselves immune.

Types of Aggression
Five different types of aggression have been identified by Walker and his colleagues (Walker et al., 1994). In over-aroused aggression, aggressive acts are seen as a side effect of a state of heightened arousal and activity levels such as are often found in youngsters with ADHD. Another type, impulsive aggression, is thought to be neurologically based, unpredictable, and most often manifested in brief episodes. A third type, affective aggression, is spawned by intense anger and rage, such as that suffered by children who have been abused; this aggression is likely to be manifested in violent episodes that may be dangerous and/or destructive. Predatory aggression is related to thought disorders involving paranoia in adolescents and adults; it may involve "settling scores" that are either real or imagined. A fifth type, instrumental aggression, involves the adoption of aggressive tactics to take advantage of others and to get one's way. It is used to intimidate and coerce others. Children and youth who adopt antisocial patterns of behavior (i.e., those with conduct disorders) tend to use instrumental aggression as a means of interacting with others, although affective aggression may be a factor as well. Well-developed, comprehensive intervention plans may help ameliorate all types of aggression. Nonetheless, understanding the specific type may lead to additional interventions such as individual or group therapy for children whose aggression stems from abuse, and use of medication for those whose behavior stems from impulsive or over-aroused aggression.

Predisposing Factors
Two undisputed facts in the study of conduct disorder are (a) that the disorder tends to be stable across time, and (b) that it runs in families (Kazdin, 1987b). Studies have established that aggression is very stable over a ten-year period: test-retest correlations for aggressive behavior range from .60 to .80 (Quay, 1986; Reid, 1993).
    Studies have also shown that antisocial behavior in one's childhood is a good predictor

of antisocial behavior in one's offspring (Huesman, Eron, Lefkowitz, & Walder, 1984; Robins, 1981). Interestingly, this trend continues across generations: children whose grand-parents had a history of antisocial behavior are more likely to evidence antisocial behavior (Glueck & Glueck, 1968).

One explanation for this cross-generational finding is Patterson's coercive behavior model: these patterns of family interaction become routine and are passed from one generation to the next if no intervention occurs. Other explanations are based on hereditary factors, and temperament and bonding issues. Hereditary factors in criminality have been the object of much research; in a review, D. Rosenthal (1975) concluded that heredity and criminality are connected. In reviewing adoption versus twin studies, he concluded that characteristics such as EEG abnormalities and sensitivity to alcohol that predispose one to antisocial and criminal behavior may be inherited. Other evidence suggests that children whose fathers show criminal behaviors and abuse alcohol are at greater risk for developing conduct disorders (Kazdin, 1987a). However, Rosenthal believes that environmental conditions including family factors and social learning are probably instrumental in eliciting the inherited tendencies.

Temperament and bonding problems in infancy have been associated with later conduct and behavior problems. Temperament is an inborn behavioral style that is also influenced by the environment. Defining characteristics of temperament include activity level, mood-iness, intensity of reaction, and ability to adapt to new stimuli (Thomas & Chess, 1977). Parental behavior and responses to the infant, especially the mother's, are influenced by the infant's temperament. Some evidence suggests that infants whose temperaments do not match their mothers' are at increased risk for developing conduct problems (Chess, 1967), perhaps because the quality and closeness of the mother-child interactions are affected. Bonding occurs during the first few months of life and, unfortunately, unless the mother seeks help with her difficult infant very early, the opportunity to intervene and improve the bonding process is lost. In addition, temperament research indicates that infants who have low adaptability and high intensity of emotional reactivity are more prone to develop behavior problems as they grow older (Earls & Jung, 1987). Thus, intense and inflexible temperaments are predictors of childhood problems (Toth, 1990). According to DSM-IV, difficult infant temperament is a predisposing factor to development of conduct disorders (American Psychiatric Association, 1994).

Research with the sociopathic subgroup of individuals with conduct disorders appears to contradict these findings. Some researchers believe that these individuals suffer from *underarousal* of the autonomic nervous system that is thought to cause sensory deprivation, resulting in a need to seek physiological stimulation. Therefore these individuals turn to thrill-seeking and other forms of adventuresome, usually socially unacceptable, behavior to relieve the tiresomeness of routine. Sociopathic individuals have been found to demonstrate lower reactivity and quicker adaptability to stimuli (Hare, 1970; Quay, 1977), as opposed to higher reactivity and slower adaptability cited in the temperament studies. This apparent contradiction may be attributed to the fact that the temperament studies have been linked to problems of conduct, but not conduct disorders *per se*, and not to a subgroup of conduct disordered individuals. Thus, considered together, the temperament and biological research points to inborn tendencies that may predispose an individual to develop patterns of conduct disordered behavior; perhaps modeling and coercive patterns of adult-child interaction are environmental catalysts that bring this predisposition to the surface.

DSM-IV lists a number of predisposing factors that are based on clinical observations about the development of conduct disorders: parental rejection and neglect, inconsistent management with harsh discipline, early institutional living, frequent shifting of parental figures (e.g., foster parents, stepparents), physical or sexual abuse, lack of supervision, difficult infant temperament, large family size, and association with a delinquent peer group (American Psychiatric Association, 1994). Many of these factors can be construed as supportive of the research on parent-child interaction difficulties as well as temperament and bonding problems.

Related Conditions

ADHD and learning problems have been linked with conduct disorders (Kazdin, 1987b; Toth, 1990). The impulsivity, distractibility, and agitated level of activity associated with ADHD can easily lead to problems with self control, which may predispose the individual to a variety of problems in social and academic arenas. If exacerbated by some of the other predisposing factors (e.g., parental rejection and father alcohol abuse), these difficulties can turn into a pattern of antisocial acts. It has been estimated that 50 to 60 percent overlap exists between ADHD and conduct disorders (Barkley, 1990).

Learning problems have also long been associated with conduct disorders; however, whether one causes the other is a subject for conjecture. The relationship between specific learning disabilities and juvenile delinquency has been extensively studied, and two causal theories have been put forth: the school failure theory and the susceptibility theory. The school failure theory indicates that learning disabilities set in motion a chain reaction: learning disabilities cause academic failure that in turn offers motivation for delinquent behavior, i.e., a chance to strike back at society (Keilitz & Dunivant, 1987; Post, 1981). The susceptibility theory posits that correlates of learning disabilities such as lack of impulse control, inability to anticipate consequences, suggestibility, and a tendency to act out directly influence the development of delinquent behavior (Murray, 1976; Post, 1981). From a large, well-designed study commissioned by the U.S. Office of Juvenile Justice and Delinquency Prevention, researchers reported the following conclusions: (1) the relationship between learning disabilities and self-reported delinquency was significant, (2) the incidence of learning disabilities among adjudicated delinquents was high (36 percent), and (3) both the school failure theory and the susceptibility theories were supported (Keilitz & Dunivant, 1987). Thus a strong association between learning disabilities and the propensity to develop delinquent behavior has been established.

In summarizing the development of conduct disordered and aggressive behavior, we should first consider that a number of predisposing factors may be operating: inherited tendencies toward alcohol sensitivity and neurological problems; temperament and bonding difficulties in early interactions between mother and child; later attachment problems with parents and significant adults; and other family and social factors beyond the child's control. Given a combination of these predisposing factors, children who then develop coercive interaction styles with their parents at home and in other settings may be at very high risk for developing conduct disorders. Exposure to aggressive models may also play a role in the development of aggressive behavior. The coexistence of ADHD and learning disabilities with conduct disordered and delinquent behavior should alert educators to the necessity of early identification and intervention with these youngsters.

Intervention and Treatment

In a review of treatment for children with conduct disorders, Kazdin (1987b) introduces the topic thus:

> *The diversity of behaviors that conduct disorder includes, the range of dysfunctions associated with them, and the concomitant parent and family dysfunction present a remarkable challenge for treatment . . . the plethora of available treatments might be viewed as a healthy sign that the field has not become rigidly set on one or two techniques. On the other hand, the diversity of procedures suggests that no particular approach has ameliorated clinically severe antisocial behavior. (p. 187)*

These statements offer an insight about interventions with individuals with conduct disorders: that the complexity of factors contributing to the development and maintenance of these behaviors demands equally complex treatment. So far, we have been unable to find effective interventions that have clear implications for long-term behavior change. However, we have recently begun to recognize the complexity of the problem and to incorporate equally comprehensive interventions.

Comprehensive interventions must involve numerous people who routinely interact with the child in different settings. Since parents, teachers, and peers are the most important socialization agents in the lives of all children, then interventions should include these agents if we are to alter the path of antisocial children who are on their way to developing conduct disorders (Walker et al., 1994). Strategies that include parents (i.e., parent involvement), teachers, and peers (i.e., social skills training) will be reviewed in the remainder of this chapter.

Families that are struggling with issues such as divorce, poverty, abuse, unemployment and drug or alcohol abuse are susceptible to disrupted parenting practices, which in turn often lead to antisocial behavior in young children (Patterson, 1983; Patterson, Reid, & Dishion, 1992). Five parenting practices that, in combination with other factors, have been found to breed antisocial behavior are: harsh and inconsistent discipline, failure to monitor the child's whereabouts, failure to invest time and energy in the child's life, failure to use positive management strategies such as support and limit-setting, and inability to handle conflict within the family (Walker et al., 1994). Interventions with parents usually target these and similar unsuccessful parenting habits. Such interventions include parent training, family therapy, and parent involvement in the school program.

Parent Training in Management Skills

Many variations of parent training exist, but most are focused on breaking the cycle of coercive interactions between parent and child. In accordance, parents must attempt to support prosocial behaviors rather than coercive ones by learning and implementing such skills as using positive reinforcement, negotiating compromises, and using only mild forms of punishment. In this treatment, parents are the clients, and no direct intervention with the child is attempted. Parents must be shown specifically how to use these skills, have a chance to practice them, and be given support and feedback.

The effectiveness of parent training has been evaluated in hundreds of studies with children of varying ages and degrees of problem severity (Kazdin, 1985). Patterson's work with the families of over 200 aggressive youngsters is probably the most concerted effort to prove the effectiveness of parent training with this population. Several of these studies have shown that parent training does result in improvement of children's aggressive behavior. Parent training has been demonstrated as more effective in comparison to other treatments (Patterson, Chamberlain, & Reid, 1982), in bringing the level of problem behaviors within normal range (Wells, Forehand, & Griest, 1980), and as sustaining improvements with noncompliant children up to four years later (Baum & Forehand, 1981).

Factors that appear to limit effectiveness of treatment are length of treatment (optimally, up to 50 or 60 hours) and parental variables such as marital discord and psychopathology (Kazdin, 1985; Strain, Young, & Horowitz, 1981). This treatment obviously makes many demands on parents, including time and a commitment to change habitual ways of interacting with their child. Therefore, parent training is not an option for those students with conduct disorders whose parents are unavailable, unwilling, or unable to make these commitments (Kazdin, 1987b).

Functional Family Therapy

A second promising treatment approach involves the entire family in therapy. Functional family therapy is based on a family systems approach that presupposes that the problem behavior of the child is serving a function in the family, albeit a maladaptive one. The goal, therefore, is to get family members to understand these dynamics in their day-to-day interactions and to alter them to more adaptive ways of communicating with one another. More specific goals are (1) to increase positive reinforcement and reciprocity among family members, and (2) to help them negotiate constructively and learn to identify alternative solutions to conflicts that arise. These goals are actively identified and worked on by family members during sessions with the help of the therapist.

Outcome studies comparing the effectiveness of functional family therapy with other treatments is encouraging, but unfortunately scarce with youth with conduct disorders. Parsons and Alexander (1973; Alexander & Parsons, 1973) compared other types of family therapy to functional family therapy with a group of delinquents and found improved family interaction and lower recidivism rates to juvenile courts 18 months after treatment. Perhaps more impressively, follow-up data 2 1/2 years later showed that siblings of the delinquent group had signficantly lower incidences of juvenile court referrals (Klein, Alexander, & Parsons, 1977). Thus, the positive changes apparently "spilled over" or generalized to other family members as well as the targeted youth.

Parent Involvement in the School Program

The prognosis for positive results with antisocial behavior is greatly enhanced by early intervention that includes a family-school partnership (Reid & Patterson, 1991). Walker et al. (1994) outline a step-by-step approach for involving parents of antisocial children in the school program. Although these authors recognize the difficulties inherent in involving parents of families that are stressed by numerous problems, they also recognize the necessity of doing so. Their strategies include:

- Initiating and maintaining positive interactions through a variety of home-school communicators
- Using a written problem-solving sequence to cooperatively find solutions to problems
- Implementing home-school contracts
- Helping parents with discipline and management strategies at home (specifically, the effective use of timeout, privilege removal, and work chores).

The emphasis throughout all activities is developing a partnership between teacher and parents so that students understand they cannot "get away" with antisocial behavior in either setting. To summarize parent involvement strategies, the literature to date indicates that the most effective interventions help parents identify maladaptive interactions with their children and then offer a means to alter these interactions. Such interventions can be effected through parent training, family therapy, and increased parental involvement in school programs. Each of these techniques has yielded encouraging results, but youth with conduct disorders continue to pose one of the greatest challenges to all professionals.

Social Skills Training

Youngsters with conduct disorders almost always have well-established negative peer and teacher relations. Social skills training emphasizing teacher- and peer-related skills is another component of comprehensive treatment for this population.

Social skills training is treated in some detail in Chapter 7, and the reader is referred there for specific information on selecting and implementing social skills curricula. However, there are several points relative to social skills training with students with conduct disorders that bear mentioning:

1. Social skills training is an important complement to behavior reduction techniques in that it teaches positive alternatives to negative, coercive behavior (Walker et al., 1994). Many students with conduct disorder are totally lacking in positive interaction skills.

2. Social rejection by peers and teachers is a very powerful contributor to the process whereby antisocial behavior develops into conduct disorders (Patterson, 1988). Unfortunately, there is a social perception bias held by peers against aggressive and antisocial students that is extremely difficult to change even after the aggressive behavior improves (Hollinger, 1987; Zaragosa, Vaughn, & McIntosh, 1991). Such findings underscore the need to involve peers in social skills and other interventions.

3. The difficulties in generalization and maintenance of newly acquired social skills are well-established (e.g., Baer, 1981; McGinnis & Goldstein, 1984). Together with the social bias and peer rejection factors described above, these difficulties point to the need to offer opportunities for practice and reinforcement within natural settings. For example, Walker et al. (1994) suggest a playground supervisor who roams the playground and, according to a well-defined set of rules, not only distributes points for positive behavior but also takes points away for instances of negative behavior. Students in each classroom are divided into four or five groups, and the incentive system is based on group performance. Thus, the playground supervision program offers daily opportunities for both reinforcing social skills and punishing negative behavior in a natural setting.

Implications for Teachers

It is clear that teachers should try to establish a strong partnership with parents of students with conduct disorders. Unfortunately, parent involvement may not be feasible for a number of these youths. In such cases, it may be helpful to remember that many aggressive behaviors are maintained by coercive interactions with others, including teachers and peers. Therefore, breaking the coercive interaction cycle at school by refusing to respond coercively is one helpful intervention. Teachers can also implement social skills training that (a) focuses upon teacher- and peer-related skills, and (b) incorporates peers into both the training and reinforcement activities.

The literature on effective interventions with children with antisocial behavior or conduct disorder indicates that a combination of behavioral treatments is needed, including limit-setting, careful monitoring, and a system of both positive and aversive consequences (Kazdin, 1987a, Patterson, Reid, & Dishion, 1992). Special education teachers already employ a variety of behavioral techniques; teachers of students with conduct disorders may want to be certain they include (a) a system for careful monitoring outside the classroom as well as inside the classroom, and (b) aversive consequences (e.g., response cost such as deducting points earned). For further information, the reader is referred to an excellent, comprehensive school-based plan for treatment of these students entitled *Antisocial Behavior in School: Strategies for Practitioners,* by Hill Walker and his colleagues (Walker et al., 1994).

Need for Early Intervention

The stability of antisocial behavior over time leads to the conclusion that early intervention in "budding" conduct disorders may be essential. Young children displaying oppositional defiant and other antisocial characteristics should be identified and worked with as early as possible, even in the preschool years. The child who gets kicked out of one or more preschools for aggressive behavior and who appears to be shaping his parents' behavior rather than vice versa is a good candidate for early intervention. In fact, the argument has been made that, if antisocial behavior has not come under control by the time an individual is eight years old, then it should be viewed as a chronic condition like diabetes: *it cannot be cured, but its symptoms can be managed and controlled only with careful intervention* (Kazdin, 1987a).

Conclusions

Youngsters with ADHD and/or conduct disorders pose a special challenge to teachers because of the provoking, often aggressive nature of their behavior. The coexistence of these disorders and the correlates of learning and social problems frequently require a multifaceted approach to treatment. With ADHD children, a combination of medication and behavior management may prove most effective in ameliorating the symptoms although these techniques will not "cure" hyperactivity. Conduct disorders are stable, persistent, and resistant to treatment. However, early identification and treatment of the child in the context of family interactions may prove to be effective in changing some of the coercive interaction styles of this population. Teachers can focus on parent involvement plus a combination of social skills and selected behavioral techniques that have proven partially effective with students with conduct disorders.

Key Points

1. Children and youth with the diagnosis of ADHD and the core behaviors of impulsivity, inattention, and hyperactivity will find their way into classrooms for students with emotional/behavioral disorders.
2. Teachers may be called upon to assist with the diagnosis of ADHD because of its observability in the classroom.
3. Most professionals now believe that children with ADHD inherit a central nervous system that predisposes them toward problems with attention and concentration.
4. Although studies of stimulant medication treatment for ADHD have proven effective in ameliorating symptoms, some professionals believe that behavior management alone or in combination with medication is the preferred mode of treatment.
5. When a number of predisposing factors are present, a conduct disorder may develop out of a coercive interaction style between child and parent that is subsequently reinforced in the home and other settings.
6. Conduct disorders are stable, persistent over time, and tend to run in families.
7. It is known that conduct disorders require interventions that are multifaceted and comprehensive.
8. We have yet to discover how to effectively help individuals with conduct disorders change their behavior patterns, but promising interventions include early identification, family therapy, parent training, parent involvement in the school program, social skills training, and specific behavior management techniques.

Additional Readings

ADHD: Facts and fallacies, by Ronald E. Reeve, *Intervention in the School and Clinic, 26,* 1990, 70–77, for an overview of ADHD and its implications in the classroom.

Antisocial behavior in the schools: Strategies for practitioners, by Hill Walker, Geoff Colvin, & Elizabeth Ramsey, 1994, Pacific Grove, CA: Brooks-Cole, for a superb, comprehensive treatment of dealing with antisocial behavior and budding conduct disorders through a school-based approach.

Attention-deficit hyperactivity disorder: A handbook for diagnosis and treatment, by Russell Barkley, (1990), New York: Guilford Press, for a practitioner's approach to dealing with children with ADHD.

Conduct disorders and social maladjustments: Policies, politics, and programming, by Frank Wood and his colleagues, 1991, Reston, VA: Council for Exceptional Children, for a monograph describing many of the issues attendant to special education programming for students with conduct disorders.

Identification and treatment of attention deficit disorder, by Nancy Nussbaum and Erin Bigler, Austin, TX: Pro-Ed, 1990, for a practical booklet written for teachers and parents of ADHD children.

Relative efficacy of pharmacological, behavioral, and combination treatments for enhancing academic performance, by K.D. Gadow, *Clinical Psychology Review, 5,* 1985, 523–533, for a review of comparisons of these treatments with ADHD children.

Understanding and treating conduct disorders, by Michele Toth, Austin, TX: Pro-Ed, 1990, for a booklet written for parents and teachers on handling children and adolescents with conduct disorders.

Assessment and Instruction

Evaluation in the Identification Process

Assessment and Instruction
    What to teach
    How to teach

Curriculum
    Affective
    Self-Management
    Social Skills

Orientation

Assessment has always been a paradox to the author: it is boring to read about, but fun to do. It is also a necessary component of good instruction, as we will see in this chapter. An exciting teaching technology has been developed that is successful even with the most difficult-to-teach youngsters. The keys to this successful technology are test–teach–test. This technology applies to both academic and social behaviors, which may be equally important with students with emotional/behavioral disorders.

Overview

This chapter explores assessment and instruction with students with emotional/behavioral disorders with a focus on *what* and *how* to teach these students. First, assessment is defined and differentiated from evaluation. Evaluation procedures used to identify students as emotionally/behaviorally disordered are reviewed. Second, a framework for individualizing instruction for both social behavior and academics is discussed. Under this framework, assessment techniques and curriculum domains for students with E/BD are presented. Finally, a number of commercially available curricula for affective and social behavior are discussed along with guidelines for selecting curriculum and increasing the generalization of acquired skills.

Evaluation in the Identification Process

Educators often use the terms *testing, evaluation,* and *assessment* interchangeably. In this chapter, we will focus on *assessment,* which is the gathering of data for instructional purposes. Because special education is predicated upon individualizing instruction, special education teachers must have a framework for deciding what to teach and how to teach each new pupil. Prior to our discussion of this assessment and teaching process, however, let us review the evaluation process that leads to identification as emotionally/behaviorally disordered.

Evaluation is defined here as the gathering of data for purposes of identifying students as eligible or ineligible for special education. You will recall from Chapter 2 that the special education identification process is based upon tenets from federal law that require multiple criteria and team decisions. However, state education agencies provide few regulations specifying how these tenets should be carried out. The result is little consistency among states or even among school districts within the same state in specific instruments used in identification procedures. However, a few commonalities in the phases of the identification process do exist: Almost all school districts have implemented a sequence of *screening, formal evaluation,* and *team decision making.*

In the screening phase, data are gathered from a number of sources, and a decision is made about whether to continue the referral process to the formal evaluation stage. Data gathered at this phase might include information on language functioning, medical-physical status, results from vision and hearing screening, group achievement test scores, and behavior reports. A third-party observation is usually required; that is, someone other than the regular class teacher observes the child in the classroom setting to gather data on the child's performance and to suggest modifications that might be made to accommodate the child before other steps are taken. A school-based team then should meet to determine whether modifications might be made before a formal evaluation is done. If the team determines that the suggested modifications have been implemented and are not successful, additional modifications can be recommended or a referral for formal evaluation can be made. This practice of documenting modifications and alternatives has become known as *prereferral intervention,* and the extent to which it is implemented in schools varies widely.

The next step in the identification process is *formal evaluation.* Most formal evaluations entail measures of intelligence, achievement, behavior, and socioemotional functioning. Individualized, norm-referenced tests are often used in these evaluations, during which a referred student is taken from the classroom and tested by a psychologist or other qualified person. Results of these testing sessions will then be used to compare the performance of the student on these measures to the performance of a nationally normed sample of students (hence the term *norm-referenced*). A variety of norm-referenced scores may be used for comparison, such as percentile ranks, standard scores, grade equivalents, age equivalents, etc. Such comparisons are almost always made with scores from intelligence and achievement tests.

Norm-referenced scores are also available for many measures of behavior and socioemotional functioning. Teacher checklists and behavior rating scales that yield percentile ranks and other standard scores may be used. Examples are the *Social-Emotional Dimension Scale* (Hutton & Roberts, 1986), the Devereux DSMD (Naglieri, LeBuffe, & Pfeiffer, 1994), and the *Child Behavior Checklist* (Achenbach, 1988), measures that were mentioned previously. The evaluators are looking for deviant scores on these measures, which means that the student has been rated as exhibiting behaviors or characteristics that are considered to be outside the normal range as determined by norm-referenced scores.

Another category of norm-referenced measures often employed in the identification of emotional/behavioral disorders is self-report. Although these measures are susceptible to faking or socially desirable responding, they are often used in an attempt to obtain the student's point of view. Self concept measures such as the *Self-Perception Profile for Children* (Harter, 1985) are popular in this category.

Projective techniques are now used less frequently for identification purposes than in previous years. However, recall from the psychodynamic model that psychologists may use projectives to diagnose emotional problems for treatment in psychotherapy. Unlike the measures just described, projectives do not yield numerical scores that can be compared to a norm group. As explained under the psychodynamic model, projectives are based on the premise that, given an ambiguous stimulus, individuals will project their unconscious as well as conscious feelings onto the stimulus. These feelings will then be analyzed according to a system; classic psychoanalytic systems evaluate themes such as needs, motivations, guilt, anxiety, and fears. Instruments falling into this category are the *Rorschach Inkblot Test* (Rorschach, 1921), *Children's Apperception Test* (Bellak & Bellak, 1949), human figure drawings, and sentence completion measures. Due to the open-ended nature of these instruments, technical adequacy characteristics such as reliability and validity are difficult to establish. These techniques might best be viewed as clinical interview tools rather than formal tests (Anastasi, 1988).

These and other data gathered during the formal evaluation are then written into a report and used to evaluate the student's functioning in the areas of intelligence, achievement, behavior, and socioemotional status. The multidisciplinary team is then reconvened, this time with parents present, to make eligibility and placement decisions. Data gathered during the evaluation are allegedly used to make these decisions, although some researchers have found little congruence between evaluation data and decisions that are made by the teams (Ysseldyke & Algozzine, 1982).

In summary, a variety of norm-referenced measures and other data are used in the evaluation process to identify students as eligible for special education services. While these measures may help the team make eligibility decisions, the majority have minimal application to the classroom setting. Little, if any, information is gained that has implications for academic or behavioral interventions. For example, if told that Gina has a low overall self-concept, was deviant on the Immature and Social Withdrawal subscales of the *Child Behavior Checklist,* and is reading at the 2.8 grade level, does the teacher know how to teach Gina on Monday morning when Gina walks into class for the first time?

Norm-referenced tests offer global descriptors that indicate where a student lies along a continuum of functioning. Little specific information about where to begin or how to approach teaching is gained from these formal evaluations. With norm-referenced achievement tests in particular, "there is no assurance that the items on the test reflect the skills contained in the curriculum used in the classroom," (Blankenship, 1985, p. 233). The remainder of this chapter is devoted to planning instruction of academics and social behavior to students with emotional/behavioral disorders.

Assessment for Instruction

A number of excellent treatises on assessment of students with special needs are available (refer to additional readings at the end of this chapter for recommendations). These books offer information about the purposes and types of assessment, how to assess in the content areas, and specific techniques of assessment. Such information is generic to all students for whom individualizing instruction is a goal, including but not limited to students with emotional/behavioral disorders. After a brief introduction to methods for individualizing instruction, we will focus on one assessment and instructional planning paradigm.

Methods for Individualizing Instruction

Many methods for individualizing instruction have been developed over the years with special needs children. Special instructional programs were developed for children with severe reading disabilities and pioneered in the 1920s and 1930s by Grace Fernald. Fernald developed a multisensory methodology for teaching new words to adolescents who had essentially no word recognition skills. Her work is especially noteworthy because of her interest in the emotional aspects of reading difficulties. In order to alleviate pressure to perform in reading, Fernald (1943) listed four conditions to be avoided: (1) calling attention to emotionally loaded situations by pressuring or pleading with the student to try harder, (2) using methods with which the student has already failed, (3) subjecting the student to conspicuous or embarrassing situations by singling the student out of a group or asking the student to work on age-inappropriate materials, and (4) calling attention to the student's failures rather than his successes and progress. By combining her step-by-step multisensory technique with these and other principles, Fernald was successful in teaching word-learning skills to many children and adolescents with severe reading problems. Although these guidelines may seem basic and commonplace in today's schools, they were quite innovative prior to the practice of individualizing instruction.

Other individualizing methods include the clinical teaching method (Johnson & Myklebust, 1967), precision teaching (Lindsley, 1971), applied behavioral analysis (Lovitt, 1975), and the Exemplary Center for Reading Instruction approach, ECRI, (Reid, 1986). These methods vary in the amount of structure and precision that is required in their application, but they share certain commonalities:

- Active learner involvement
- Planned success experiences
- Immediate feedback and positive reinforcement for the learner
- Overlearning.

In addition, each of the methods follows a basic sequence of steps:

1. Establishment of an instructional objective or behavioral goal
2. Assessment of student skills and deficiencies pertinent to the objective
3. Prescription of a specific plan for teaching the objective
4. Evaluation of success

The last step is especially important because of its emphasis on the success or failure of the *plan* rather than the success or failure of the *student*. The assumption of these techniques is that if a student fails to learn, the teacher must modify either the objective or the manner and/or sequence in which instructional steps are taught. Test-teach-test is implemented on a continuous basis with modifications in teaching at specific points of difficulty for students. Readers interested in developing expertise in one of these methods are referred to the original references in the beginning of this paragraph and to *Diagnosing Basic Skills* (Howell & Kaplan, 1980) and *Applied Behavior Analysis in Education* (Jenson, Sloane, & Young, 1988).

Principle #1: In teaching, we should emphasize the failure of the lesson plan rather than the failure of the student.

What to Teach: Academic and Social Skills

Howell (1985) has indicated that although educators seem to treat academic and social behavior as "two different phenomena," the dichotomy is arbitrary. For example, with social behavior, we are taught to pinpoint behavior, count it, chart it, and evaluate intervention effects. With academic skills, we are taught to schedule time for lessons, specify skill sequences, model correct responses and deliver direct instruction. Howell suggests that the two sets of skills are applicable to both academic and social behavior instruction: teachers of academics should learn to pinpoint skills and monitor skill acquisition closely, and teachers of social behaviors should learn to better clarify curriculum and skill sequences. As teachers of students with emotional/behavioral disorders must be concerned with teaching both types of skills, it makes sense to adopt a single framework of assessment and instruction that applies to behavior as well as to academics.

Zigmond and Miller (1986) have outlined such a framework that conceptualizes the *what to teach* and *how to teach* assessment paradigm: (1) identify curriculum domains, (2) develop specific instructional objectives, and (3) test-teach-test. This framework is summarized in Table 7-1.

What to Teach, Step 1: Identify Curriculum Domains

Selection of curriculum domains for special education students is not an easy process because there is too little time to teach everything these students need to know. In addition to all the content areas, for example, there are daily living/survival skills, vocational and career skills, study skills, social competencies, self management, and self concept or other affective competencies that we may wish to teach our students before

TABLE 7-1   A Framework for Individualizing Instruction

What to Teach, Step 1:
Identify Curriculum Domains
Academic
Social
-social skills
-self-management
-affective/emotional responses

What to Teach, Step 2:
Select Specific Instructional Objectives
use:
observation techniques
criterion-referenced testing
curriculum-based assessment
error analysis
checklists and rating scales

How to Teach
test-teach-test
continuous monitoring

Adapted from Zigmond & Miller, 1986.

they return to mainstream settings or graduate into the real world. We often have to make choices: is it better to graduate a student who knows that Mexico is our neighbor to the south (academic/social studies) or one who can use a city map to navigate across town on public transportation (daily living/social studies)? While we wish that students would exhibit knowledge of both regardless of whether both were specifically taught, the majority of special education students are not proficient at incidental learning and therefore we must plan for them to acquire the competencies and knowledge we wish them to have.

Selection of curriculum domains, then, requires prioritizing competencies. To accomplish this, teachers must identify the ultimate goal of education for their students. Is the ultimate goal for a given student the smooth reintegration of the student back into a mainstream educational setting or is it competence for daily living, perhaps outside an educational setting? In the case of the former, emphasis on study skills, classroom-related behaviors, and achievement in the basic areas of reading, language arts, and math is warranted. In the latter case, academic skills should be related to competence in daily living, vocational and career skills. In this functional approach, decisions on what to teach are based on an assessment of what the child needs to know or do in a target setting (Zigmond & Miller, 1986). Target settings include a mainstream classroom (or less restrictive setting), the school, the home, and the community. Future functioning as well as current functioning are considered.

Principle #2: In curriculum planning, we must first identify the competencies that our students need to acquire to be successful in the environments to which they will return.

Academic achievement and social behavior are the two primary problems of students with emotional/behavioral disorders. Therefore, teachers will want to consider these two major curriculum domains. In this text, the academic domain will be briefly reviewed, as this area is given adequate coverage in other texts for teaching students with mild/moderate disabilities. Students with emotional/behavioral disorders experience the most difficulty in the social domain, and it is this domain that we will emphasize in the discussion that follows.

Academic Domain

Academic competence is the goal of this curriculum area. The definition of academic competence differs according to level of student capability: it may be the attainment of very basic daily living skills for lower functioning students, the acquisition of skills approximating the regular curriculum for high functioning students, or the attainment of functional literacy for students falling somewhere in between the two extremes. The specific content areas for which a special education teacher has primary responsibility should be clearly identified in the student's individual education plan. Math and language arts (reading, spelling, and written composition) are the most common academic responsibilities for special education teachers; however, the reintegration process is facilitated when general education teachers do not absolve themselves of responsibility for the student's instructional program in those areas designated for special education. Whenever possible, these areas should be considered the joint responsibility of general and special education.

Academics is one area in which it may be easy to forget the functionality of the skills we are teaching. Are all academic areas equally important for all students? If a specific skill is next on the scope and sequence chart, is it supposed to be taught regardless of its ultimate usefulness for the student? Consider Ronnie, age 11. Most of the time, not only can you not read his handwriting, but he can't tell you what he has written. Do you work on improving his penmanship by painstaking lessons and practice, or do you teach him to compose on a word processor? How about spelling? If Ronnie can't spell many of the words he wants to use in composition, do you continue to give him weekly lists and try many different methods of helping him retain spelling words? Or do you give him a few basic word lists to keep at his desk for reference and teach him to use a spell checker on the word processor?

The example of Ronnie highlights one of the decisions that must be made in planning an academic curriculum. In the *remedial approach,* the teacher believes that the student can continue to progress if instruction is individualized appropriately. In addition to breaking skills down into instructional objectives and monitoring on a continuous basis, the teacher may try different materials and approaches. The aim is to remediate skill deficits so that the student can progress in a fashion similar to his general education counterparts. In the *compensatory approach,* the teacher decides that, for a given subject or curricular area, the remedial approach is no longer feasible. The teacher then searches for alternative ways to achieve the same or similar goals. In the example of Ronnie's spelling skills, the remedial approach would be to continue having him practice spelling skills, perhaps modifying his program by asking that he learn fewer words per week, showing him how to study with a multisensory method, and having frequent review sessions of previously learned words. The compensatory approach would be to offer him a small list of commonly misspelled words to keep at his desk for reference and teach him to use a spell checker on a word processor. In Ronnie's case, the teacher may decide to combine the two approaches by continuing a multisensory method with a shortened word list each week and teaching him to use a spell checker on the word processor.

Principle #3: Teachers must distinguish between remedial approaches and compensatory approaches to academic instruction and decide which is most feasible for each content area for each student.

Social Domain

The social domain should emphasize skills that help students become socially competent. Social competence has been defined as the ability to "meet personal goals without disrupting others or behaving in self-defeating ways" (Howell, 1985, p. 26). In addition, socially competent persons can communicate and problem-solve while taking good care of themselves physically and emotionally. Howell further indicates that socially competent individuals also contribute to society's goals, if only by refraining from interfering with their attainment.

It is immediately apparent that the majority of students with emotional/behavioral disorders are not, by this definition, socially competent. They are often aggressive and disruptive. Even if they learn to manage these impulses, they may still behave in self-defeating ways. It is in these characteristics that E/BD students differ most from other students and, therefore, it is in this area that teachers need to focus much of their time and attention.

Social competence is the goal of the social domain. To teach social competence, teachers may find the following subdomains useful: *(1) social skills, (2) self management,* and *(3) affective/emotional factors.* These subdomains are depicted in Figure 7-1. Each of these subdomains will be discussed, and in the final section of this chapter, published curricula will be described.

Social skills are those skills used to effectively interact with other people. Such skills can be verbal ones, such as beginning a conversation, or they can be nonverbal and cognitive, such as working independently. Social skills needed by students in mainstream settings are usually task-related, teacher-related, or peer-related. For example, task-related skills include

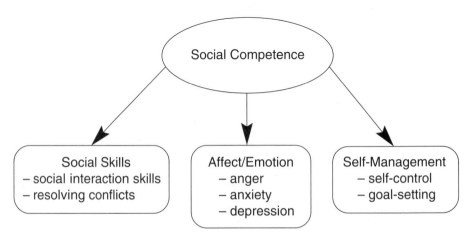

FIGURE 7-1   The Social Competence Domain and Subdomains

following directions and on-task behavior; teacher-related skills include asking and answering questions, and hand-raising before speaking out; and peer-related skills include joining others, having a conversation, and resisting peer pressure. More generic interpersonal skills such as negotiating, coping with conflict, and helping others are also good target behaviors for many students with emotional/behavioral disorders.

Teaching social skills initially may seem easy because social skills are usually described in objective, measurable terms and because so many social skills curricula are commercially available. However, there are at least two reasons to proceed with caution. First, we should distinguish between *controlling* social behavior and *teaching* social behavior (Howell, 1985). A second, related reason for caution is that, although many researchers have been successful in teaching social skills to students in special settings, the generalization of these behaviors to other settings and maintenance over time remains largely unproven. Although we may need to focus on decreasing certain behaviors that interfere with classroom functioning (i.e., controlling behavior), we cannot conclude that controlling students' behavior in one setting will help them behave appropriately in other settings. This consideration is succinctly described by Howell & Kaplan (1980):

> *Unfortunately, in many behavior disorder programs, all we do is control the kid. First we control him in a self-contained classroom. Then we go back to the regular classroom with resource room help and control him there. When school is over, we send him out into the nonclassroom world and are surprised to hear he still has trouble. We incorrectly expect the kid to somehow generalize this classroom experience to completely new settings, but this seldom happens. The reason it doesn't happen is that we, the special education teachers, are the agents of control. The students will have problems in the outside world unless (1) we spend the rest of our lives with them, or (2) we teach them to control themselves. (pp. 270–271)*

The need for self-control is part of the second subdomain of social competence, *self-management*. In self-management, students must be taught to rely on internal controls rather than external ones (such as special ed teachers, parents, or other agents of control). Students with emotional/behavioral disorders experience problems with internal controls for many reasons. First is faulty learning: they simply may never have learned to control themselves because of lack of structure and appropriate modeling of self-control from adults in their lives. Second, they may be prone to impulsivity and are therefore accustomed to acting upon their first impulse regardless of outcomes or consequences. Third, extreme emotional responses even to slight provocation may override these students' abilities to activate self-control.

Self-management is much more than control over one's impulses. It also includes the ability to plan and execute goals. It includes taking responsibility for one's behavior—mistakes and failures as well as successes. Self-management is the goal of all cognitive-behavioral strategies. These include self-assessment, self-instruction, self-monitoring, and self-reinforcement, which were discussed in Chapter 4. Most general problem-solving strategies also attempt to teach self-management.

The third subdomain of social competence is *affective/emotional factors*. This subdomain is defined as those emotional responses to situations that prohibit individuals from acting in a socially competent manner, i.e., from meeting their own goals. Some authors prefer to differentiate affect from emotion by defining *affect* as a more stable characteristic including temperament and pervasive moods, and defining *emotion* as a temporary feeling with physiologic manifestations. These distinctions are likely necessary for purposes such as research; however, for purposes of curriculum planning, it is sufficient to consider the combined impact of affective and emotional states upon behavior.

Anger, anxiety, and depression are examples of three affective/emotional factors that teachers of students with E/BD will routinely encounter. As anger often results in aggressive or disruptive outbursts, it may be the easiest to identify although anger can be manifested in many other forms as well. Anxiety and depression also manifest themselves in a variety of behaviors, ranging from apathetic withdrawal to belligerent noncompliance. In curriculum planning, the teacher is concerned about the impact of these affective/emotional states upon behavior. It is of little use to teach social skills to students who become too easily angered or otherwise upset to use them. Therefore, the teacher will want to assess the affective/emotional status of her pupils and use affective curricula or other techniques accordingly.

The astute reader will have discovered by now that these three subdomains are not mutually exclusive and that many skills will fall under two or all three subdomains. For example, learning to control one's anger is a social skill that addresses an emotional response and is needed for self-management. The reason for classification of subdomains in this chapter is to emphasize the need for assessing and teaching to all three areas of social competence.

Principle #4: Teachers of students with emotional/behavioral disorders must address social competence either through the curriculum or through systematic interventions.

What to Teach, Step 2: Develop Instructional Objectives

Once the curriculum domains have been identified, then the teacher must select the curricula that will address these domains. Next, the teacher must place the student at a suitable place within the curriculum and develop instructional objectives. In order to ascertain which prerequisite skills the student possesses and which prerequisite skills are lacking, the teacher can use a variety of informal assessment techniques such as observation, criterion-referenced measures, curriculum based-assessment, and work-product evaluations (Zigmond & Miller, 1986). Checklists and rating scales can also be used at this step. Each of these methods will be briefly explained.

Observation Techniques
Observation is used most often to identify social needs of students. For example, two of the most useful types of observation are event recording and duration recording because it is often either the frequency or duration of many behaviors that is of concern. In event recording, the frequency of the behavior is tallied: for selected time periods, every occurrence of the behavior is noted. Hitting is an example of a behavior that is often monitored through event recording. Duration recording is used when it is the duration of the behavior rather than the frequency that is of concern (examples are noncompliance and long,

drawn-out tantrums). In duration recording, the beginning and end of the behaviors are carefully documented. Relative to curriculum placement, if a child is experiencing problems with hitting, then placement in a social skills curriculum with "Keeping Hands to Self" or "Keeping out of Fights" would be appropriate. Without observational data of frequency of hitting, the teacher would have difficulty assessing (1) whether the objective is an appropriate place to begin instruction, and (2) when the objective has been met.

Criterion-referenced Testing

In criterion-referenced testing, a child's performance is measured against a predetermined criteria. In contrast to norm-referenced testing in which students are compared to a standard based on others, criterion-referenced testing tells whether a student has met a specific objective. An objective is selected, criteria for mastery are set, and the student is evaluated against the criteria: the student has either mastered the objective or has yet to master it. When used to plan teaching activities, criterion-referenced measures should derive directly from the curriculum or a skills sequence that the teacher intends to use. That is, each item on the measure should correspond to an instructional objective in the curriculum or skills sequence.

Curriculum-based Assessment

Curriculum-based assessment (CBA) is an old method enjoying a comeback under a new name. CBA measures a student's level of achievement in terms of the expected curricular outcomes of the local school (J.A. Tucker, 1985). In other words, to test a student's progress in school, one should test the student in materials from the student's actual curriculum. CBA is similar to criterion-referenced assessment, with the exception that curriculum-based assessment is always performed with materials from the student's actual curriculum. For example, if reading comprehension were to be assessed, passages from the reading textbook used for instruction would be administered along with a set of comprehension questions for each passage (Haring, Lovitt, Eaton, & Hansen, 1978).

A curriculum-based assessment must be developed separately for each curriculum area, e.g., math, reading, and spelling. The scope and complexity of the assessment depend upon the skills to be taught (Blankenship, 1985). Units, chapters, as well as a block of skills from a scope and sequence chart may form the bases for CBAs. Blankenship (1985) has outlined the specific steps in developing CBAs:

- List the skills presented in the selected material.
- Determine whether all important skills are identified.
- Decide if the edited list has skills in logical sequence.
- Write an objective for each skill on the list.
- Prepare test items to assess each listed objective.
- Prepare testing materials for student use, including items.
- Plan how and when to use the CBA; give it prior to instruction on the selected topic.
- Use results to plan instruction by determining which students need prerequisite skills, which students need exposure to the instructional objectives identified, and which students have already mastered the objectives.

The CBA is then readministered periodically throughout the instructional process to modify instruction and to check for long-term retention.

Work-Product (Error Analysis) Evaluations

The teacher also can use the student's work product to help put the student at the appropriate place in the curriculum and determine which instructional objectives are needed next. Error analysis is one method of analyzing the work product that conscientious teachers have been using for years. It can be applied to any subject area in which a written product or work sample is produced. The teacher simply checks the work sample for errors, categorizes the errors, then looks for a pattern among errors. Error analysis is based upon the assumption that the majority of children's errors are not haphazard; rather, they are indicative of a missing link, a particular misconception, or lack of information on the part of the child. Error analysis is an attempt to find the missing link so that the problem can be remediated. Table 7-2 shows an error analysis that was part of a math evaluation for a second grader. In this case, the student showed knowledge of math facts (except in problem c), but consistently subtracted the smaller number from the larger number, regardless of which number was the stated subtrahend in the problem. Error analysis in this case immediately leads to the hypothesis that this student does not understand regrouping in subtraction and likely does not fully grasp the concept of place value. This error analysis should be followed up with specific questions and problems involving the concept of place value and then with instruction in regrouping in subtraction.

Checklists and Rating Scales

There are two types of checklists for assessing academic skills: checklists that are composed of a hierarchy of skills in a selected subject, and problem-oriented checklists that are composed of a listing of potential problems in a selected subject. Both types of checklists are readily available from textbooks, curriculum guides, and publishers of tests in many areas including readiness skills, self-help skills, written and oral language, handwriting, arithmetic, reading, and spelling. Checklists for observation of oral reading problems are very common; most reading tests include checklists of reading difficulties. For maximum efficiency, teachers should choose checklists that derive directly from or have application to the curriculum that they plan to teach.

Checklists are also used to assess the social domain. According to Jenson, Sloane, and Young (1988), assessment of social competencies is somewhat more difficult than assess-

TABLE 7-2 Error Analysis of Subtraction Problems for a Second Grader

(A)		(B)		(C)		(D)	
✓	6 $\underline{-2}$ 4	✓	9 $\underline{-4}$ 5		4 6 $\underline{-1\ 3}$ 3 4	✓	16 $\underline{-4}$ 12

(E)		(F)		(G)	
	2 2 $\underline{-1\ 8}$ 1 6		38 0 $\underline{-9\ 6}$ 31 6		50 0 $\underline{-40\ 2}$ 10 2

ment of academic skills due to the nature of social skills. First, social skills are "opportunity-bound," that is, the actual skills can only be exhibited when the opportunity arises, and not upon request, as reading skills can be. Also, the opportunities for practicing specific social skills are rather infrequent; while a student may work 25 or 30 math problems per day, she may have an opportunity to join in a group only a few times weekly. Due to these limitations, checklists and behavior rating scales are often used as aids to observation in assessing social competencies. Most of the published social skills curricula discussed later in this chapter offer checklists or scales for ascertaining where in the curriculum to place individuals. Use of such placement checklists help to ensure individualization. A portion of the placement test for the ACCESS curriculum is presented in Table 7-3.

Developing Instructional Objectives

As just illustrated, teachers attempting to place students in curriculum with appropriate instructional objectives for both social behavior and academics have at their disposal a variety of informal assessment techniques. Zigmond and her colleagues (Zigmond, Kerr, Brown, & Harris, 1984) have identified a 12-step strategy that utilizes informal assessment techniques. This strategy summarizes the steps a teacher needs to take in deciding what to teach.

TABLE 7-3   ACCESS Placement Test

	Not descriptive or true	Moderately descriptive or true	Very descriptive or true
Area I: PEER-RELATED SKILLS			
Section A: Interpersonal Skills			
1. Listens politely and carefully to others	1 . . . . 2 . . . . 3 . . . . 4 5		
2. Greets other persons (adults, peers) appropriately	1 . . . . 2 . . . . 3 . . . . 4 5		
3. Skillfully joins in with others	1 . . . . 2 . . . . 3 . . . . 4 5		
4. Has extended conversations with peers	1 . . . . 2 . . . . 3 . . . . 4 5		
5. Follows conventional rules in borrowing others' possessions	1 . . . . 2 . . . . 3 . . . . 4 5		
6. Offers assistance when situation calls for it	1 . . . . 2 . . . . 3 . . . . 4 5		
7. Compliments others in an appropriate manner	1 . . . . 2 . . . . 3 . . . . 4 5		
8. Displays an appropriate sense of humor	1 . . . . 2 . . . . 3 . . . . 4 5		
9. Knows how to keep and maintain friends	1 . . . . 2 . . . . 3 . . . . 4 5		
10. Interacts appropriately with the opposite sex	1 . . . . 2 . . . . 3 . . . . 4 5		
Section B: Coping Skills			
1. Negotiates skillfully with peers	1 . . . . 2 . . . . 3 . . . . 4 5		
2. Deals effectively with being left out	1 . . . . 2 . . . . 3 . . . . 4 5		
3. Handles group pressures effectively	1 . . . . 2 . . . . 3 . . . . 4 5		
4. Expresses anger appropriately	1 . . . . 2 . . . . 3 . . . . 4 5		
5. Copes with aggression from others skillfully	1 . . . . 2 . . . . 3 . . . . 4 5		

From H. M. Walker, B. Todis, D. Holmes, & G. Horton. (1988). *The ACCESS Program*. Austin, TX: Pro-Ed. Reprinted with permission of the publisher.

1. Select a curriculum domain to assess.

2. Select or develop a skills hierarchy to represent the domain.

3. Decide where in the hierarchy to begin the assessment.

4. Select or develop a criterion-referenced measure at that level

5. Organize the classroom so that assessment can be done.

6. Administer the criterion-referenced measure and other useful informal measures.

7–9. Evaluate student performance and analyze error patterns to formulate hypotheses about skill deficits.

10. Test hypotheses using informal probes.

11–12. Convert assessment data into instructional goals.

In writing instructional goals, Howell, Kaplan, and O'Connell (1979) suggest these simple steps: choose a specific skill, then specify:

- What the student must do (in observable terms)
- Under what conditions the student will perform
- How well the student must do to pass (mastery)

Example: When given a list of ten sight words from the Scott Foresman primer, the student will correctly pronounce at least eight of ten.

When these steps have been completed, the teacher has short-term instructional goals to guide teaching and writing the individualized education plan.

The Individualized Education Plan (IEP)

Requirement of a written individual education plan (IEP) for each student receiving special education services is an outgrowth of IDEA. The intent of the law is to ensure cooperative planning and documentation of educational services, educational goals, and the annual progress of each student. Although procedures for writing the IEP vary from school system to school system, the law requires that the following people be present when the IEP is written: a representative of the local school system who is knowledgeable about special education, the teacher, parents or guardians, and, when appropriate, the student. Regulations also mandate that each IEP contain the following elements:

- A statement of the student's present level of functioning
- A statement of annual goals, including short-term objectives
- A statement of specific educational services to be provided and extent to which the student will participate in general education
- A timeline for initiation and duration of services, and criteria for evaluation

The format for the IEP is generally determined by the local school system, which provides its own standard form. In addition to the required components, many IEPs also specify those responsible for delivering services, methods and materials to be used, and information on motivation.

For students with emotional/behavioral disorders, educators should include behavioral techniques to be used and possible disciplinary actions; by obtaining parental consent prior to beginning the program, potential problems may be averted. For example, use of a timeout procedure for specified acts of aggression or noncompliance may be agreed upon by parents, teachers, and administrators, and subsequently written into the IEP. When disciplinary actions with students with emotional/behavioral disorders have been litigated, written documentation of disciplinary procedures and actions has been viewed favorably by the courts (Yell, 1990).

Teachers of students with emotional/behavioral disorders also need to be proficient at writing goals for social behavior. Writing realistic goals and objectives may require practice before the teacher experiences a level of proficiency and comfort with the task. Crane, Reynolds, Sparks, and Cooper (1983) recommend the following steps that may help the inexperienced teacher get started:

Step 1. Review all available information on the student, including folders, tests, evaluation reports, teacher reports, discipline reports, observations, and parent concerns.

Step 2. Use this information to decide on broad target areas for behavior change that relate both to the student's needs and to the curriculum that will be used, e.g., on-task, peer interactions, adult interactions, compliance.

Step 3. Select two target areas that are most appropriate for the student. Write at least one annual goal for each target area, more if necessary. In writing the goals, decide which behaviors interfere most with learning. Remember to make the goals realistic and related to the student's present level of functioning.

Step 4. Develop short-term objectives for each annual goal. The objectives must be observable or measurable in some way and must be stated in specific terms. Both the behavior and the expected performance level must be explicit.

Step 5. If counseling is a related service written into the IEP, tie goals in counseling to the annual goals for behavior change so that counseling and instruction supplement each other. An example of an annual counseling goal: "The student will demonstrate use of a problem-solving model to find constructive solutions for dealing with problem situations."

This procedure is illustrated for the student Justine in Box 7-1.

Ideally, the IEP is the culmination of data-gathering and instructional planning for the individual student; it should be a helpful instrument for summarizing plans and monitoring student progress. In reality, many special educators view the IEP as burdensome paperwork that has little relevance to the student's actual program but must be completed to satisfy regulations. However, special education teachers are generally present at IEP meetings (Ysseldyke & Algozzine, 1982) and are expected to contribute to instructional planning decisions (Gilliam & Coleman, 1981). The special education teacher can provide direction to the team if allowed the time for an assessment of the student's skill levels, which can then be translated into long-term and annual goals. A detailed sample IEP is presented for the eight-year-old DeWayne in Box 7-2.

How to Teach: Test-Teach-Test

As special education has been predicated upon the idea that students with disabilities need *special* instruction, the research attempting to match learner characteristics to teaching strategies has been voluminous. However, few reviews of this research reveal substantial support for any attempts to match student type with teaching type (Lloyd, 1984). Instead, as

---

BOX 7-1 IEP Behavioral Goals and Objectives for Justine

Step 1. Review information

Justine, age 7, is in the first grade. Her academic progress this year has been very slow. She frequently sucks her thumb and tries to put her entire hand in her mouth when stressed. Justine is easily distracted; she appears to daydream and often stares out the window or at the floor. She is extremely overweight and usually dirty. She is scorned by her classmates and gets into fights when they call her "Miss Piggy." Justine often tantrums when she does not want to work or play with others. She mumbles to herself and mutters under her breath to her classmates sitting around her.

Step 2. Decide on broad target areas for change.

On-task, motivation and coping, and peer interaction are all appropriate target areas for Justine.

Step 3. Set priorities and select annual goals.

On-task and peer interaction present the most immediate problems for Justine at this time. Annual goals are:

Annual Goal #1. Justine will attend to the assigned task rather than other stimuli. (This goal is the positive alternative for thumbsucking and daydreaming).

Annual Goal #2. When interacting with peers, Justine will exhibit alternative positive behaviors for negative ones. (This goal is the positive alternative for fighting and temper tantrums).

Step 4. Develop objectives for each annual goal that are pertinent to the student's needs.

Annual Goal #1, Attending to Task
  Short-term Objectives
1. Justine will decrease thumbsucking to less than five times per day.
2. Justine will increase independent time-on-task to ten minutes.

Annual Goal #2, Interacting with Peers
  Short-term Objectives
1. Justine will decrease negative physical contact to less than one time per week.
2. Justine will decrease the number of temper tantrums to less than three per week.

Step 5. If counseling is recommended, select a related counseling goal.

Annual Goal for Counseling: Justine will discuss ways she can demonstrate a positive attitude toward peers.

Adapted with permission from *The source book: Behavioral IEPs for the emotionally disturbed*, by C. Crane, J. Reynolds, J. Sparks, & S. Cooper. Houston, TX: Crane/Reynolds, Inc. (1983).

Zigmond and Miller (1986) point out, a teaching technology that appears to be effective with all learners has been established. Among other things, effective teachers model desired behavior, break a goal into component parts and teach each part, teach objectives in many contexts to facilitate generalization, know what types of practice are needed, organize material to promote recall, and use rehearsal strategies, overlearning, and distributive practice as necessary. As mentioned earlier, clinical teaching, precision teaching, applied behavior analysis, and the Exemplary Center for Reading Instruction (ECRI) approach are based on these effective teaching practices.

Given that we have established effective teaching practices, then, Zigmond and Miller contend that we should next ask, "How can good instruction be more responsive to individual differences?" This *how-to-teach* can be answered not by attempting to match learner type to teaching type but by a *test-teach-test* sequence of continual teaching and monitoring. The focus becomes the adaptation of instruction by varying factors such as size of the group, amount of teacher involvement, more explicit instructions, more time, more feedback, and different motivational strategies.

BOX 7-2 DeWayne's IEP

Description and Background Information

DeWayne was recently identified as having an emotional/behavioral disorder and was recommended for placement in the resource room. He is eight years old and in the second grade after having repeated first grade. His second-grade teacher reports that DeWayne is below average in math and is failing reading and language arts; she further describes him as "sullen, uncooperative, and given to alternate bouts of withdrawal and aggressive outbursts." She said that he generally reacts to her attempts to talk with him by completely withdrawing and refusing to talk. While not aggressive toward his classmates, he rarely interacts with them, and they tend to ignore him.

He has severe astigmatism and has been prescribed glasses, which he refuses to wear because they are uncomfortable and make him "nervous." He has broken or lost his glasses so frequently that his mother no longer tries to get him to wear them.

DeWayne lives with his mother and an older sister, aged ten. His parents have been divorced for four years; after the divorce, the father moved to another state and has not contacted the family since then. The mother is working on her college degree and supports the family on her part-time wages as a waitress. According to the mother, DeWayne was very close to his maternal grandmother, who lived next door until her death last year. He formerly spent many evenings and weekends with the grandmother, who gave him a lot of personal attention and helped him with his schoolwork. His mother describes DeWayne as very dependent on her and his sister; his two or three friends are much younger than he is. She also says that DeWayne "doesn't mind very well" and that she "doesn't know what to do with him."

Evaluation for Identification

According to testing by the school psychologist, DeWayne is functioning in the low average range of intelligence. His visual-motor skills are deficient; when asked to copy a printed passage of three sentences, his product was illegible. On the Woodcock-Johnson Tests of Achievement, DeWayne scored at the beginning first-grade level on all reading and written expression subtests, with math being a few months higher.

Measures of behavior and affect showed several areas of concern. On the Achenbach Child Behavior Checklist, teacher report form, scores on the following clusters were deviant: social withdrawal, immature, anxious, inattentive, and aggressive. On the parent report form, he was deviant on the following clusters: social withdrawal, uncommunicative, and depressed. He scored at the tenth percentile for overall self-concept on the Piers-Harris Children's Self-Concept Scale, which was read to him because of his low reading level. Although the psychologist stated that test results were considered valid overall, she also stated that DeWayne's uncooperativeness could have affected test results. Despite frequent breaks and encouragement by the psychologist, DeWayne sometimes refused to do a task or finish one he had started. Because of DeWayne's erratic behavior and visual-motor problems, the psychologist referred him to a neurologist who found distinct abnormalities of left hemispheric functioning and subsequently placed him on an anticonvulsant medication. DeWayne is currently being monitored by the neurologist.

The school psychologist also observed DeWayne during reading class. On several days during the observation period, DeWayne sat with arms folded and head down when he was supposed to be working on independent workbook assignments. He was recorded to be on-task 10 percent of the total time observed.

Identifying Curriculum Domains and Selecting Instructional Objectives

The resource teacher, Ms. Reese, begins her data-gathering the first day DeWayne arrives in the resource room. She notes that when given a worksheet that she is sure DeWayne can do, he only stares at it. She knows that this was his typical behavior in the general education classroom from both the psychologist's observation and from talking with his referring teacher. Ms. Reese believes that reintegration back into the general education classroom is a feasible long-term goal for DeWayne, and she begins to plan the curriculum accordingly. She knows that he has had trouble keeping up with his work in reading, spelling, and math, and that his handwriting is a problem. Because he rarely finishes an assignment and does not relate to his peers, Ms. Reese also selected on-task behavior and peer relations as curriculum areas.

Continued

BOX 7-2 *Continued*

The second, third, and fourth days Ms. Reese begins a curriculum-based assessment in 10-minute periods. In reading, she finds that DeWayne can read the primer stories from his basal reader only because he seems to have memorized them. When given an unfamiliar passage at the same level, he cannot read it. When given word lists at the primer level, he demonstrated a sight vocabulary of fewer than fifteen words. When asked to write some words from a dictated list from his spelling textbook, he spelled correctly only the words "go," "dog," and "can." An error analysis of math computation worksheets from the math curriculum showed that he cannot work addition or subtraction problems requiring knowledge of place value. When shown cards with number facts under ten, DeWayne performed with 100 percent accuracy. Ms. Reese also observed DeWayne's attention span, his preference for certain tasks over others, and his response to praise from her. She now has some idea of how and where to begin instructional planning.

Behaviorally, DeWayne has shown no aggressive outbursts in the four days he has been in the resource room. During assessment, he became very frustrated and refused to talk or attempt tasks when they became difficult for him. Ms. Reese responded by reassuring him and changing tasks. He initiated no conversation with other students in the room but responded when they approached him. He indicated an interest in the reinforcement system and the fact that other students were receiving tokens for completing assignments.

The IEP

Based on information from the school psychologist's report, observations, and the resource teacher's assessment, the following individual education plan was designed for DeWayne:

Summary of Present Levels of Functioning

Reading: preprimer level, sight word vocabulary of fewer than fifteen words

Spelling: functionally, does not spell

Math: knows number facts under 10; counts meaningfully to 20; cannot compute addition and subtraction requiring knowledge of place value; little understanding of concepts of time and fractions

Handwriting: prints name legibly; can copy single words but not sentences legibly

Social/Behavioral: interacts very little with peers and rarely finishes his assigned work

ANNUAL GOALS	EVALUATION CRITERIA
Reading	
Increase sight vocabulary to 50 words or more	Correctly sight reads 50 or more words from his basal reader
To read and comprehend stories from first reader in basal series	Reads and answers comprehension questions with 80 percent accuracy from first reader
Spelling	
Delay formal instruction in spelling until a sight vocabulary of 50 words is demonstrated	
Math	
To work addition and subtraction problems with two- and three-digit numbers	Given ten addition and subtraction problems with two- and three-digit numbers, works with 90 percent accuracy
To show knowledge of time appropriate to his developmental level	Upon request, tells time accurately to the quarter hour
To show knowledge of fractions appropriate to his developmental level	Identifies the terms one-half and one-quarter by pointing on a pie chart
Handwriting	
As sight vocabulary improves, to copy short sentences legibly	Given several short sentences, copies them legibly according to teacher judgment
Social/Behavioral	
To interact appropriately with classmates, both in resource and regular class	Initiates and is able to maintain conversation with resource peers on a daily basis; participates in P.E. with regular class peers and talks to classmates while doing so

BOX 7-2 *Continued*

To complete independent work assignments	According to teacher records, routinely completes 90 percent of independent work assigned in both settings	*Handwriting:*

SHORT-TERM OBJECTIVES

Reading:
Develop a sight vocabulary of 25 words
Develop a sight vocabulary of 50 words
Read and comprehend a short passage (less than five sentences)

Math:
Demonstrate knowledge of place value
Compute two-digit addition problems
Compute two-digit subtraction problems
Compute three-digit addition problems
Compute three-digit subtraction problems
Tell time to the hour
Tell time to the half hour
Tell time to the quarter hour

Handwriting:
Legibly copy single words from sight vocabulary
Legibly copy three- to five-word sentences

Social/Behavioral:
Initiate at least one conversation daily with classmates in resource
Initiate at least one conversation daily in P.E.
Complete one or more independent work assignments daily in the resource room
Complete one or more independent work assignments daily in the general education classroom

Educational Services to be Provided:
Resource services in reading, language arts, and math, three hours daily. DeWayne will participate in math in the general education classroom but will bring his assignments to the resource room for help.

Percent of Time in General Education Classroom:
50 percent

Initiation and Duration of Services:
Resource services begin immediately and continue until a committee review is held in six months.

Consistent monitoring is an essential feature of this teaching paradigm. While some authorities on effective teaching endorse daily monitoring for evaluative purposes, monitoring on a weekly basis has been found to be effective if teachers then use the data to modify instruction (Mirkin, Fuchs, & Deno, 1982). In addition to providing useful instructional information, data from frequent monitoring can be used to offer students specific feedback on a regular basis. Despite the proven value of frequent monitoring, Fuchs, Fuchs, and Warren (1982) found that fewer than 10 percent of the special education teachers they surveyed reported monitoring student progress on a weekly basis.

In summary, individualizing instruction is the hallmark of special education classrooms—it is what makes special education *special*. The effectiveness of many methods for individualizing instruction has been established. Although these methods vary in the amount of structure and precision required, each follows a basic sequence of (a) establishing an instructional objective or behavioral goal, (b) assessing student skills pertinent to the objective, and (c) using frequent evaluation data to modify instruction. Zigmond and Miller (1986) offer a framework for deciding what to teach and how to teach: identify curriculum domains, select specific instructional objectives, and implement a continuous test-teach-test paradigm. These methods emphasize success or failure of the instructional plan rather than success or failure of the student. Jenson, Sloane and Young (1988) have summarized many of these elements of effective educational programs in Table 7-4.

TABLE 7-4   Characteristics of Effective Educational Programs

1. Teachers establish individualized instructional programs by:
   a. Accepting a philosophy of teaching that states that most, if not all, students are capable of learning.
   b. Accepting the philosophy that it is their responsibility as teachers to find the right instructional strategies and materials to facilitate student learning.
   c. Knowing the curriculum they are assigned to teach well enough to identify and sequence specific instructional objectives and to design or obtain appropriate curriculum materials.
   d. Developing an instructional system that allows students to progress at their own pace. Teachers do not move students on to the next sequenced objective until they have mastered the current objective.
2. Teachers use ongoing educational evaluation procedures and instructional decision-making strategies to facilitate student learning by:
   a. Establishing mastery criteria that specify both accurate and fluent performance.
   b. Adopting evaluation strategies that directly and regularly (preferably daily) measure the behavior being taught.
   c. Examining student performance data regularly (at least every six days) and employing decision-making strategies to determine how the student is progressing and what to do next (options include moving to a new objective, changing teaching tactics, or continuing the current program).
3. Teachers employ teaching tactics that maximize student performance by:
   a. Structuring class activities to maximize academic engaged time and increase students' opportunities to respond.
   b. Identifying and utilizing available resources (peer tutors, volunteers) to assist their implementation of instruction tactics.

From Jenson, W. R., Sloane, H. N., & Young, K. R.: *Applied Behavior Analysis in Education.* Adapted and reprinted with permission of the publisher, Prentice Hall, 1988.

Let us now turn our attention to a discussion of curricula that are especially applicable to students with emotional/behavioral disorders.

Curricula for the Social Competence Domain

As alluded to earlier in this chapter, teachers of students with emotional/behavioral disorders face a difficult question: Should academic skills or affective and social concerns take precedence in the educational curriculum? Most special educators agree that neither area should be neglected in favor of the other; however, striking a balance between the two on a daily basis in the classroom poses a challenge. Knoblock (1983) proposes that teachers adopt a "caring curriculum," an outgrowth of humanistic education which emphasizes both academic and emotional development. According to Knoblock:

> *In short, a caring curriculum involves more than teaching. It conveys to students that they are worthy of great consideration; that they can and will become more*

competent; and that the world of ideas, concepts, and information may be of interest and value to them. It also acknowledges that students may face difficult life circumstances, but it creates a learning environment that responds to the human desire for growth. Teachers are often dismayed by the pressures under which many children live: broken homes, poverty, community rejection. Although a caring curriculum cannot solve such problems, it can help structure a student's school experience to foster feelings of self-worth and competence . . . in the context of developing positive relationships with teachers and peers. (1983, pp. 153–154)

In the remainder of this chapter, a number of commercially available curricula for dealing with social and affective issues are reviewed. This author has categorized these curricula into the subdomains of: (a)affective/emotional factors, (b)self-management, and (c)social skills. However, it should be noted that most of the curricula include aspects of all three subdomains. The curricula have been categorized according to their primary focus.

Curricula for the Affective/Emotional Subdomain

Affective curricula can be used preventively, i.e., with entire classes, or with small groups. Where resources allow, they are implemented by school counselors. However, special educators can also use affective curricula in their classrooms.

One affective curricula is based on the principles of transactional analysis (Berne, 1965) and simplified for children in *T.A. for Tots* (Freed, 1973) and *T.A. for Kids* (Freed & Freed, 1977). The purpose of the series is to help young children realize that they are "OK" and to help them relate better to parents and to other adults. Specifically, children are helped to deal with friendship, responsibility, and their emotions of anger, fear, joy, and love. The major instructional materials are books that chronicle numerous childhood difficulties. A third book in the series, *T.A. for Teens* (Freed, 1976) focuses on the adolescent issues of drugs, sex, authority, rebellion, and independence.

Magic Circle (Besell & Palomares, 1970) is a curriculum for developing interpersonal communication skills through small groups. Booklets are provided for preschoolers through sixth graders, but the Magic Circle is the main feature of the curriculum. Daily, children gather in a circle on the floor to discuss a selected topic on human relations. The three major topic areas are: (1) understanding similarities and differences between self and others, (2) identifying and using one's own abilities, and (3) understanding social relationships. Sharing of ideas and experiences is encouraged; interrupting, confronting, and belittling are forbidden. The teacher's role is to present curriculum lessons and to lead Magic Circle discussions.

A third affective curriculum is *Developing Understanding of Self and Others—Revised (DUSO-R)* (Dinkmeyer & Dinkmeyer, 1982). Developed around a central character—*DUSO the Dolphin*—the program provides stories and activities aimed at developing self-concept, responsibility, and decision-making skills. In addition to providing assorted materials and media, *DUSO-R* offers the unique feature of hand puppets and puppet activity cards. Appropriate for kindergarten through fourth grade, *DUSO-R* is organized into three units: developing understanding of self, developing understanding of others, and developing understanding of choices. The authors outline three specific objectives: (1) to help children learn more words for feelings, (2) to teach that feelings, goals, and behavior are related, and (3) to help children learn to express feelings and goals and to talk openly about behavior. In

DUSO-R, the teacher facilitates group lessons and projects, but also takes an active role in helping children to clarify and process their experiences.

The efficacy of affective programs is difficult to evaluate for a number of reasons. First and foremost is the difficulty in measuring affective concepts or constructs, such as "communication skills," "self-concept," and "understanding oneself." The majority of research studies utilize some measure of self-concept, which may be an established, commercially produced instrument or one developed by the authors of the affective program being evaluated. As Medway and Smith (1978) point out, the use of differing definitions and instruments to measure the same concept is not likely to produce consistent or comparable results. A second difficulty is that most of these measures are a form of self-report or self-evaluation. Problems with self-report measures in research include subjects' tendencies to give socially acceptable responses, and great differences across situations and across subjects in their willingness to self-disclose.

Carpenter and Apter (1988) studied several reviews of affective curricula and programs and added these criticisms:

- Differential age responses to a particular curriculum indicate the need to assess student-to-program match rather than applying a program wholesale to a class or group.
- The teacher is a confounding factor in efficacy research because affective issues are greatly influenced by personal variables such as personality.
- Methodological flaws in many studies make it difficult to draw conclusions about the research that has been conducted.

In summary, although special educators recognize the importance of integrating academic with affective concerns in the classroom, the effectiveness of commercial affective curricula remains unproven. However, this state of affairs may reflect inconsistencies in research methodology and program implementation rather than ineffectiveness of the curricula.

Curricula for the Social Skills Subdomain

The importance of social skills in the classroom setting becomes increasingly evident as problems with mainstreaming or reintegrating students with emotional/behavioral disorders have continued. Students who do not make it in the regular classroom are often deficient in the skills that enable them to function as independent learners and to get along with teachers and their classmates. Students who have been in special education programs and are entering mainstream settings have two major adjustments to make: (1) they must meet the teacher's expectations for appropriate social behavior and academic standards, and (2) they must learn to interact with a new peer group (Walker et al., 1983).

The majority of students with emotional/behavioral disorders are deficient in social skills and do not fit either teacher or peer expectations for classroom behavior. (In fact, they are often initially placed in special education because of this deficiency.) In addition, the label of emotional/behavioral disorders has a stigma which often generates negative expectations; thus, the mainstreamed student with emotional/behavioral disorders faces an especially difficult adjustment period in which he must strive to overcome negative expectations and fit smoothly into the regular classroom environment.

The teaching of social skills is important not only to facilitate mainstreaming but also to foster social adjustment and competencies outside the classroom setting (Stephens, 1977). Most social skills curricula offer a variety of communication and coping skills that can be applied to interpersonal interactions in any setting. Two social skills curricula will be described: one that was developed for the elementary population *(ACCEPTS),* and one that is applicable to all age levels *(Social Skills).* References to curricula for adolescent populations will be made. All of the curricula are based on behavioral principles and are implemented through behavioral techniques.

Social Skills in the Classroom

Social Skills in the Classroom (Stephens, 1978) is a basic skills curriculum for individualizing instruction with students with learning and emotional/behavioral disorders. Included are reading and arithmetic curricula for kindergarten through third-grade levels, and a social skills curriculum applicable to any age and grade level. According to Stephens (1977), the *Social Skills* curriculum is "not intended to include every behavior students need to acquire while in school. It is, however, an attempt to assist teachers to consciously and systematically instruct students in social behavior" (p. 120). For each social skill in the curriculum, there is a corresponding behavioral objective, assessment task, and instructional strategy. Stephens offers 136 social skills that are grouped under the following categories and subcategories.[1]

ENVIRONMENTALLY-RELATED BEHAVIORS

Care for Environment	Dealing with Emergency
Lunchroom	Movement around Environment

SELF-RELATED BEHAVIORS

Accepting Consequences	Ethical Behavior
Expressing Feelings	Positive Attitudes toward Self
Responsible Behavior	Self-care

INTERPERSONAL BEHAVIORS

Accepting Authority	Coping with Conflict
Gaining Attention	Greeting Others
Helping Others	Making Conversation

TASK-RELATED BEHAVIORS

Asking and Answering Questions	Attending Behavior
Classroom Discussion	Completing Tasks
Following Directions	Group Activities
Independent Work	On-Task Behaviors
Performing before Others	Quality of Work

As a specific example, under Task-Related Behaviors, four skills are taught under "Quality of Work":

- To turn in neat papers
- To accept correction of school work
- To use teacher's corrections for improving work
- To review work to correct errors

To implement the curriculum with an individual, teachers follow four basic guidelines in the manual:

1. Define the skill to be taught.

2. Assess performance of the skill according to personally acceptable criteria and select a teaching strategy.

3. Implement one of the recommended teaching strategies: modeling, role playing, behavior rehearsing, contingency contracting, or social reinforcement.

4. Evaluate effectiveness of the strategy.

If the student fails to perform the skill at an acceptable level after instruction, Stephens (1977) recommends four possible options. First, the instructional strategy may be changed to a different one. Second, the reinforcement may be changed to a more powerful one and care taken to ensure that the reinforcement immediately follows the behavior. Third, the task may be broken down into smaller steps. Fourth, the student may lack prerequisite skills that require further instruction. (Note that these options reflect the principle of emphasizing failure of the lesson plan rather than failure of the student).

In one study with two elementary and two junior high students, targeted social behaviors showed significant improvement after application of Stephen's principles for teaching social skills (La Nunziata, Hill, & Krause, 1981). Modeling, contracting, and social reinforcement, singly or in combination, were found to be effective instructional strategies.

A Curriculum for Children's Effective Peer and Teacher Skills (ACCEPTS)

The *ACCEPTS* program (Walker et al., 1983) was developed specifically to help youngsters with mild/moderate disabilities acquire the social skills necessary for functioning in a mainstream environment. Two types of skills are emphasized: those that enable the students to function as independent learners in the classroom, and those that contribute to social competence and peer acceptance. A direct instructional approach is used to teach a total of 28 skills appropriate for elementary-age students. The skills related to classroom functioning in *ACCEPTS* were selected according to data gathered from a national sample of teachers who were asked "to rate the importance of 56 adaptive behaviors in facilitating a successful classroom adjustment" (Walker et al., 1983, p. 1). Those behaviors that consistently received the highest ratings were then included in the curriculum; thus, *ACCEPTS* has the advantage of a data-based rationale for its selection of specific skills. The following components are offered in *ACCEPTS:*

- A placement rating scale and procedures to be used for selecting students who need the training
- A nine-step direct instruction procedure to be used with each skill
- Videotapes with positive examples and negative examples for 23 skills activities for one-to-one, small group, large group, or class instruction role-play activities to determine skill mastery
- Behavior management procedures to help teach and maintain the skills
- Scripts for teaching each skill

The authors strongly promote the position that social skills can be most effectively taught through direct instructional techniques coupled with behavior management techniques to strengthen and maintain the skill. They also provide step-by-step guidelines for implementation; the teacher is advised what to do when a student gives an incorrect response or fails to perform a skill to criterion.

The 28 skills are grouped under five major categories:

CLASSROOM SKILLS

Listening to the Teacher	Doing Your Best Work
When the Teacher Asks You to do Something	Following Classroom Rules

GETTING ALONG SKILLS

Using Polite Words	Assisting Others
Sharing	Touching the Right Way
Following Rules	

BASIC INTERACTION SKILLS

Eye Contact	Making Sense
Using the Right Voice	Taking Turns Talking
Starting	A Question
Listening	Continuing
Answering	

COPING SKILLS

When Someone Says "No"	When You Express Anger
When Someone Teases You	When Someone Tries to Hurt You
When Someone Asks You to Do Something You Can't Do	When Things Don't Go Right

MAKING FRIENDS SKILLS

Good Grooming	Smiling
Complimenting	Friendship Making

Other commercially available curricula have been developed for teaching social skills to adolescents. Walker and his colleagues have extended the basic format of their elementary curriculum to include higher level skills for adolescents in The *ACCESS Program* (Walker,

Todis, Holmes, & Horton, 1988). *Skillstreaming the Adolescent* (Goldstein, Sprafkin, Gershaw, & Klein, 1980) offers a manual and a set of training audio-cassettes for the teaching of 50 social skills. Goldstein et al. (1980) use a four-step behavioral format to teach the skills that were developed for use with aggressive, withdrawn, immature, and developmentally delayed adolescents. In addition to beginning and advanced social skills, *Skillstreaming* targets dealing with feelings, dealing with stress, alternatives to aggression, and planning skills.

Selecting a Curriculum

Due to the proliferation of published social skills curricula in the past ten years, new teachers are apt to experience difficulty in deciding which curricula (1) best fit the needs of their students, and (2) incorporate principles of effective instruction. Relative to the first issue, Young and West (1984) have categorized social skills into the following divisions. When selecting a published curriculum, teachers may want to consider the needs of their students relative to these five categories:

- Promoting and developing social interaction, such as asking questions, sharing, inviting others to join in
- Dealing with unpleasant circumstances, such as denying requests, apologizing, and dealing with name-calling, teasing, and accusations
- Resolving conflict, such as negotiating and compromising
- Maintaining social interactions, such as listening, taking turns, and making conversation
- Asserting oneself, such as expressing feelings, expressing concerns, reiterating requests, and saying no

Teachers should be aware of the fallibility of rigidly teaching to the curriculum. In other words, teachers should select, and adapt if necessary, a curriculum that fits the social learning needs of their students rather than selecting a curriculum and rigidly teaching its skill sequence. Teaching to the curriculum is a temptation in the absence of a generally accepted and clearly defined framework for teaching social competence (Howell, 1985). The second issue is evaluating the quality of a curriculum's instructional properties before the curriculum is purchased. A comparison of some of the commercially available curricula on a number of pertinent factors is presented in Table 7-5. Topics and skill areas for each curriculum are listed. In addition, the following instructional properties are examined: teaching methodology, inclusion of assessment measure and specification of acceptable performance criteria, amount of in-class practice, and specific generalization training. Although the curricula have many characteristics in common, a comparison of these variables may help teachers select one which best suits them and their students.

Curricula Addressing All Three Subdomains

Although some of the previously reviewed curricula address more than one subdomain of social competence, the following curricula focus specifically upon all three subdomains:

TABLE 7-5 A Comparison of Four Social Skills Curricula

		Social Skills in the Classroom (Stephens)	ACCEPTS (Walker et al.)	Skillstreaming the Adolescent (Goldstein et al.)	Aggression Replacement Training (Goldstein & Glick)
1.	Population	K–8	K–6	7–12	adolescent JD
2.	Materials	teacher manual (includes everything)	teacher manual optional audio videotapes	teacher manual	teacher manual
3.	Topics (skills)	4 areas/N = 136 (1) environment-related (2) self-related (3) interpersonal (4) task-related	5 areas/N = 28 (1) classroom skills (2) basic interaction skills (3) getting along skills (4) making friends (5) coping skills	6 areas/N = 50 (1) beginning social skills (2) advanced social skills (3) dealing with feelings (4) alternatives to aggression (5) dealing with stress (6) planning skills	(1) 10 social skills (2) 6-step anger control training (3) moral education groups
4.	Teaching methodology	(1) assess (2) evaluate (3) define skill (4) pick a strategy -modeling/role playing -contingency contracting -social reinforcement	9-step "direct instruction" includes teacher scripts, role play activities, and behavior management procedures.	4-step "structured" (1) modeling (2) role playing (3) feedback (4) transfer of training	-structured learning for social skills and anger control -dilemma discussion groups for moral education
5.	Time			60 minutes ideal	60 minutes ideal
6.	Assessment measure?	teacher rating	teacher rating	teacher rating (students can also rate selves)	teacher rating and self rating
7.	Acceptable performance criteria?	teacher rating according to own "personally acceptable" standards	acceptable criteria specified for role play of each skill	performance feedback for each skill	performance feedback for each skill
8.	Amount of in-class practice?	varies; 1–5 suggested activities per skill	3 practice activities per skill; also review and practice at end of skill area	each student role plays situation pertinent to self	each student role plays situation pertinent to self
9.	Specific generalization training?	none; behavior management principles	daily informal contract to try out skill in natural setting	daily homework	daily homework
10.	Efficacy data in manual?	none	2 studies plus results of consumer satisfaction survey N = 160	none	summarizes over 60 studies on structured learning
	Does the curriculum include:				
11.	Task-related skills	N = 43	N = 4	N = 5	none
12.	Self-control?	yes	yes	yes	yes
13.	Self-concept?	yes	no; yes for ACCESS	no	no
14.	"Special" features?		videotapes for modeling, very structured with scripts for teachers	loosely structured teachers make up role plays	unique combination of training in social skills, anger control and moral education

Aggression Replacement Training and *Prepare* by Goldstein and associates, and the *Developmental Therapy* curriculum developed by M. M. Wood and her colleagues. Goldstein and his colleagues have developed curricula for adolescents. *Aggression Replacement Training (ART)* was developed for aggressive, conduct disordered youth (Goldstein & Glick, 1987). *ART* has three major components: social skills training, anger control training, and moral development. The rationale for combining these three components was that, in order to interact in a socially acceptable manner, individuals must (1) possess some basic interaction skills, (2) control impulses and anger well enough to exhibit these skills, and (3) be motivated to use the skills acquired in #1 and #2. Thus, ART addresses social skills, affective responses, and self-management issues. *ART* was piloted with incarcerated, primarily conduct disordered youth, with mixed but promising results (Goldstein & Glick, 1987). Goldstein also developed the *Prepare Curriculum,* a comprehensive curriculum for "teaching prosocial competencies" (Goldstein, 1988). In addition to the components of *ART, Prepare* offers seven other courses:

- Problem solving
- Stress management
- Empathy training
- Situation perception training
- Cooperation training
- Recruiting supportive models
- Understanding and using groups

This comprehensive curricula arose from Goldstein's continued work with a variety of populations exhibiting deficiencies in social competence. It represents his modifications of earlier, simpler curricula. Although efficacy studies of *Prepare* have not been published, Goldstein (1988) believes that *Prepare* adapts well to diverse populations, trainers, and settings.

Mary M. Wood and her colleagues at Rutland Center have developed a curriculum that addresses both affective and academic needs of children with autism and other severe disorders ages 2 to 12 (M. M. Wood, 1975; Wood, Combs, Gunn, & Weller, 1986; Wood & Swan, 1978). *Developmental Therapy* curriculum is based on the assumption that these children need special help in progressing through five normal developmental stages in four basic areas: behavior, communication, socialization, and academics. These four categories constitute the curriculum areas. The five developmental stages describe the individual's degree of involvement with the environment: the stages begin with responding to the environment and move through working with others in groups to taking initiative in new situations.

Each child is individually assessed and placed at the appropriate developmental level within each of the curriculum areas. Activities and materials are selected accordingly. Approximately 150 emotional-developmental milestones are identified and taught through the *Developmental Therapy* curriculum. A very positive aspect of this curriculum is that it integrates the primary needs of the child with emotional or emotional/behavioral disorders into a single curriculum. It also is one of the few curricula that specifically addresses the needs of preschoolers with these problems. The interested reader is referred to *Developmental Therapy in the Classroom* by Wood and her colleagues (Wood et al., 1986).

Issues in Social Skills Training

As social skills training has grown in popularity, many questions about its effectiveness have arisen. Some research has supported the effectiveness of social skills training as an approach to teaching social competence (Van Hasselt, Hersen, Whitehill, & Bellack, 1979; Gresham, 1981, 1982), albeit with limitations (Hollinger, 1987; Sasso, Melloy, & Kavale, 1990; Schloss, Schloss, Wood, & Kiehl, 1986). Three primary issues have surfaced from the research: social validity, negative peer perceptions, and generalization and maintenance concerns.

First is the issue of the *social validity* of the targeted social skills: the skills that are targeted for intervention must be valued not only by the individual but also by others with whom she interacts (Meadows, Neel, Parker, & Timo, 1991). As mentioned previously, authors of some social skills curricula considered social validity by surveying consumers before deciding which skills to include in the curriculum. However, discrepancies may exist in the social skills that are valued by pertinent groups, including special educators, general educators, students with emotional/behavioral disorders, and their peers. For example, Meadows et al. (1991) found that students with emotional/behavioral disorders did not place a high value on skills related to compliance and cooperation with adults, which were rated as valuable skills by both special education and general education teachers. Getting along with adults was also rated higher by their peer group. Thus, Meadows et al. conclude, even if students with emotional/behavioral disorders have certain social skills, they may not be motivated to use the skills because they do not value the skills, i.e., rewards are not great enough or the skills do not meet their needs. Perhaps social skills training will not be effective until the students' values are commensurate with those of the curriculum.

A second major issue in social skills training is that of *negative peer perception.* One of the underlying assumptions of social skills training is that if we are successful in improving the student's interaction skills, then he will be better liked by his peers. Unfortunately, this has not proven true. Social rejection is apparently established early and resistant to change (Coie & Dodge, 1983; Hollinger, 1987). Once negative perceptions have been established, peers are unforgiving and unwilling to change them. In their work, Walker and his colleagues (1994) have concluded that aggressive, antisocial children continue to be socially rejected even after extensive training in social skills, and that "social skills training is a necessary but not sufficient condition for changing the social status" of these students. Strategies aimed at improving the social status of these students include recruiting peers to participate in either the training or in reinforcing target students' behavior.

The third major issue in social skills training is that of *generalization and maintenance.* Educators must be continually asking whether the skills that are acquired by students in special education settings are being transferred to other settings (generalization) and maintained over time (maintenance). Difficulties with mainstreaming students with emotional/behavioral disorders into less restrictive programs are a painful reminder that these students may not be able to demonstrate acquired social skills in settings other than the resource room or self-contained room. Generalization is not a new issue: Redl admonished us in 1959 that our therapeutic environments must approximate the child's natural environment or else the child might be unable to maintain acquired gains. Many techniques to increase the probability of generalization and maintenance of skills have been recommended (e.g., Baer, 1981; Horner, Dunlap, & Koegel, 1988; Kazdin, 1980, McGinnis & Goldstein, 1984). According to Nelson and Rutherford (1988), two general approaches have been identifed. One is the selection and teaching of skills in such a manner that they will not be stimulus-bound, that is, bound to the setting in which they are taught. For example, McGinnis and Goldstein (1984) recommend the daily use of homework in which students must try out the new skill in "real-life" situations and then report to the group. Self-report and self-evaluation are key to the success of homework. Other suggestions include:

- Actually teach the skill in the setting where the skill is to be used or in a setting that is similar.
- Use props to increase the similarity between the teaching setting and the real-world setting.
- Teach the skill in a variety of settings and situations by multiple role plays with a variety of people.
- Use examples and role plays that are relevant to the student's daily life (cited in McGinnis & Goldstein, 1984, and Jenson, Sloane, & Young, 1988).

The second approach is to prepare the environment to reinforce the newly acquired skills. For example, parents, siblings, and receiving teachers can be recruited to reinforce selected behaviors. Given the problems with changing negative peer perceptions, arranging interactions between students with emotional/behavioral disorders and their nondisabled peers may be an especially important and promising area (McConnell, 1987). In addition, preparation of the environment is critical for students who have difficulty with self-management.

Other ways to increase the probability of generalization and maintenance are to apply principles of effective instruction and reinforcement. These include overlearning the skill by repeated practice, systematic withdrawal of instruction and periodic review, and fading the reinforcement to approximate the reinforcement schedules that will be encountered in the natural environment (cited in McGinnis & Goldstein, 1984).

Despite redoubled efforts to address these issues, research demonstrating effective generalization and maintenance of social skills is difficult to conduct and therefore scarce. After reviewing behavioral intervention studies and other reviews of behavioral studies, Nelson and Rutherford (1988) conclude that the "'albatross of generalization' continues to hang around the necks of behaviorists," (p.139).

In summary, social skills training to improve the social competence of students with emotional/behavioral disorders has become increasingly popular. Research indicates that social skills training is promising but should not be considered a panacea for poor social skills or for peer rejection problems. When a teacher undertakes social skills training, she should carefully consider the social validity of the skills being taught and should use strategies to maximize the probability that the skills will used across settings and over time. Recruiting peers without disabilities to participate in such programs may be equally important.

Conclusions

We have developed a successful teaching technology that does not depend upon matching teaching strategy to learner modality. We now know that even hard-to-teach students will learn if we (a) figure out precisely what each student needs to know, (b) teach it by objectives, and (c) monitor whether each objective has been met. This test-teach-test paradigm works for social behavior and academic skills. Another key to successful teaching is to remember the functionality of what is being taught: does the student need this skill in the environment to which he will return outside the special education classroom? For students with emotional/behavioral disorders, social competence must receive equal billing with academic competence in curriculum planning. Numerous published curricula are available for the teacher to use in teaching social skills. In selecting the most appropriate one, teachers must decide which one best fit the needs of their particular students, and whether the curriculum incorporates principles of effective instruction.

Key Points

1. The norm-referenced tests used in formal evaluations for identification purposes typically offer little information for instructional purposes; teachers must do their own assessments for instructional planning.
2. Individualizing instruction involves: (a) selecting an academic or behavioral objective; (b) assessing student skills relative to the objective; (c) teaching the objective; and (d) monitoring success.
3. For students with emotional/behavioral disorders, four principles of effective teaching are:
    a. Emphasize the failure of the lesson plan rather than the failure of the student.
    b. Identify the functional competencies that students need to be successful in the environments to which they will return.
    c. Distinguish between remedial and compensatory approaches to academic instruction.
    d. Address social competence through the curriculum or through systematic intervention.
4. IEPs for students with emotional/behavioral disorders should include a number of annual goals for social behavior as well as academic skills.
5. Teachers of students with emotional/behavioral disorders may want to consider the following curriculum domains of social competence: social skills, self-management, and affective/emotional factors.
6. A variety of excellent social skills and affective curricula are available; however, teachers should remember to match these curricula to individual needs just as they match academic curricula to individual needs.
7. Although social skills training looks promising as an intervention for students with emotional/behavioral disorders, the teacher should be aware of its limitations and should build into the program as many strategies as possible to combat the limitations.

Additional Readings

Assessing the abilities and instructional needs of students, edited by Donald D. Hammill. Austin, TX: Pro-Ed, 1987, for an entire text devoted to individual assessment of content areas and social skills.

Antisocial behavior in schools: Strategies for practitioners, Chapter 8 on social skills training, by Hill Walker, G. Colvin, & E. Ramsey. Pacific Grove, CA: Brooks-Cole, for a comprehensive treatment of the issues teachers should consider when implementing social skills training with students with E/BD.

Diagnosing basic skills: A handbook for deciding what to teach, by Kenneth W. Howell & Joseph S. Kaplan. Columbus, OH: Merrill, 1980, for a guide detailing principles for individualizing instruction.

A task-analytical approach to social behavior, by Kenneth W. Howell, *Remedial and Special Education, 6,* 1985, 24–30, for a discussion of how to apply sound principles of assessment and instruction to social behavior.

Exceptional Children, 52, 1986, for an entire issue devoted to research on effective teaching practices in special education; specifically, see articles by Reid, and by Zigmond and Miller.

How should we individualize instruction—or should we?, by John W. Lloyd, *Remedial and Special Education, 5,* 1984, 7-15, for a review and critique of research attempting to match learner modality to teaching strategy.

Endnote

[1]From *Social Skills in the Classroom by Thomas M. Stephens,* © 1978, All rights reserved. Reprinted by permission of the author and publisher.

A Systems Perspective

The Family System:
    Understanding Parent-Child Dynamics
    Involving Parents

Working with Systems:
    Educational, Social, Juvenile Justice/Correctional, and Mental Health

Orientation

As Rhodes (1970) asserts, we can no longer take a child from a system which is disturbed, attempt to fix the child, place the child back into the unchanged system, and call it satisfactory treatment. Instead, we must attempt to increase the fit between the child and others in the systems in which the child lives and interacts. As a teacher, you can help increase the fit by working closely with parents and with other systems within the community.

Overview

Every child is an inseparable part of a complex web of interrelated systems. For "normal" children, these mini-social-systems function appropriately and may be defined as congruent or balanced. When the systems break down, we term them incongruent or unbalanced. We also tend to place the blame for such incongruence on the child, rationalize our action by labeling the child as emotionally disturbed, and plan our interventions to focus on remediating the identified child's emotional disturbance while neglecting the other aspects of the system. (Apter, 1982, p. 139)

Educators, psychologists, social workers, and other child-care specialists are beginning to recognize the futility of treating the child while ignoring the systems in which he functions

(Apter & Conoley, 1984; Hobbs, 1982; Minuchin, 1970; Rhodes, 1970). Instead, professionals are beginning to advocate a systems or an ecological approach to treatment, which focuses on imbalances or disturbances in systems. The child is seen as a part of the disturbance, and interventions are aimed at promoting changes not only in the child but also in other people and factors in the environment. The goal of a systems approach is to reduce the discrepancy between environmental expectations for a child and the capabilities of that child to fulfill those expectations. According to Apter, such programs are based upon the following assumptions:

1. Each child is an inseparable part of a small social system.
2. Disturbance is not viewed as a disease located within the child, but rather as discordance (a lack of balance) in the system.
3. Discordance may be viewed as a disparity between an individual's abilities and the demands or expectations of the environment—"failure to match" between child and system.
4. The goal of any intervention is to make the system work, and to make it work ultimately without the intervention.
5. Improvement in any part of the system can benefit the system.
6. This broader view of disturbance gives rise to three major areas for intervention:
    a. Changing the child
    b. Changing the environment
    c. Changing attitudes and expectations (Apter, 1982, p. 69).

This chapter promotes a systems approach to programming for students with emotional/behavioral disorders. The focus of the first section is the home, which is the most influential system of a child. The focus of the second section is the education system, which is the second most influential system of a child. The third section emphasizes the community systems that impact the lives of students with emotional/behavioral disorders: social-welfare, juvenile justice/correctional, and mental health. The teacher's role in working with individuals within these systems is emphasized throughout the chapter.

The Family System

Perhaps with no other exceptionality does successful intervention depend so heavily upon parent involvement. Many educators have discovered the futility of trying to change behaviors exhibited at school that are being maintained in the home environment. In contrast, if inappropriate behavior patterns are consistently discouraged in both the home and in school, the student is more likely to choose more appropriate ways of behaving. Cooperative parents and teachers make a formidable team that provides consistency and prevents pitting home against school. For elementary and middle-school students, the home is still a significant source of influence and control. Changes are most easily made in these formative years before loyalties shift from parents and teachers to peers. Parental involvement also enhances counseling efforts with youngsters. Many theorists view parental involvement in counseling sessions with children with emotional and behavioral problems as a necessity.

While recognizing the need to provide consistency between the home and school, teachers must also realize that communicating with parents may not be easy. As illustrated by articles in the 1950s on "refrigerator mothers" in which cold, rejecting parenting was cited as a causal factor in autism, psychologists and educators historically have been willing to blame disordered behavior on disordered homes and poor parenting. Although the idea of poor parenting as a causal factor in autism has been disproven, the belief persisted into the early 1980s that parents of autistic children are responsible for their child's disorder (Gilliam & Coleman, 1982).

Interactions between parents and educators often have been undermined by issues of guilt and blame. Parents of students with emotional problems often feel responsible for or guilty about their child's problems. Educators may unwittingly exacerbate such feelings by pointing out inadequate discipline or management practices in the home, thus setting into motion a guilt-blame cycle that may be difficult to overcome. Teachers of students with emotional/behavioral disorders need to understand these dynamics, as well as research on the role of parenting in the development of behavior problems in children.

Understanding Parent-Child Dynamics

Research on Parenting

Considerable effort has been directed toward identifying parental characteristics and child-rearing practices that are conducive to healthy development. Baumrind's classic research (1971, 1977) identified three basic parenting styles: permissive, authoritarian, and authoritative. Permissive parenting is characterized by a loose, non-demanding style similar to that promoted by the famous pediatrician Benjamin Spock in the 1950s. Permissive parents do not set limits and rarely use punishment, but they may reason with their child. At the other extreme, authoritarian parents value obedience and conformity to a set of standards that is usually based on religious or political beliefs; these beliefs are rigidly adhered to, and little room exists for individual choice or personal freedom. Between these extremes is authoritative parenting, marked by a concern for both obedience and expression of individuality. Authoritative parents often use reason and allow for discussion from the children when setting rules.

These parenting styles have been linked to subsequent behaviors in children. *Overly permissive parenting,* characterized by few demands or limits, has been linked to children who are highly aggressive with low impulse control. Parents who use *severe punishment* (especially physical punishment) as a parenting style may be more likely to produce offspring with higher rates of aggression and delinquency. When punishment is paired with perceived *parental rejection,* the relationship to aggression and delinquency is even more marked. Conversely, when parenting is marked by *warmth,* children are more likely to exhibit good social adjustment and to possess high self-esteem. *Warmth* is characterized by commitment and sensitivity to the child's needs, willingness to spend time with the child, and enthusiasm about the child's accomplishments.

Notably, antisocial children often come from families characterized by divorce, poverty, substance abuse, unemployment, abuse, and other sources of conflict. Under such adverse conditions, effective parenting often falls by the wayside. Patterson and his colleagues have identified parenting practices that have been linked with positive social development in children; further, the inability to carry out such practices has been linked to early development of antisocial and aggressive behavior in children (Patterson, Reed, & Dishion, 1992). The five practices include: (a) fair, consistent discipline, (b) monitoring of the child's whereabouts and activities, (c) positive and supportive behavior management techniques, (d) parent involvement in the child's daily life, and (e) problem solving that models how to deal with conflicts and crises.

Anderson (1981a) also lists several parental variables that have been shown to promote positive social behaviors in children: warmth and responsiveness, consistent discipline, demands for responsible behavior, and purposeful modeling, teaching, and reinforcement of desired behaviors. What parents do with their children may be more important than global personality or attitudinal variables. Further, Anderson emphasizes the reciprocal nature of parent-child interactions. Not only do parents influence their children, but children also shape their parents' behavior: "The child is seen as an elicitor of parent behaviors and as responding in ways which may serve to positively or negatively reinforce parent behavior, or to extinguish or punish it" (Anderson, 1981b, p. 83).

The reciprocal nature of parent-child interactions is particularly applicable to students exhibiting hyperactivity or behavioral excesses. Researchers have found that hyperactive or overactive children tend to elicit more severe disciplinary or controlling behaviors from their parents than do their normal peers (S.B. Campbell, 1973, 1975; Stevens-Long, 1973). In studying parent-child interactions of aggressive children, Patterson (1975; Patterson & Cobb, 1973) observed that an aversive behavior from either party elicits an aversive response and results in a gradual escalation of aversive exchanges. Parents are likely to respond to high frequency or intense behaviors by increasing their efforts at control; in turn, increasing parental control often elicits the child's control behaviors, and a negative pattern becomes established over time.

Although these linkages between parental behavior and child behavior have been consistently demonstrated in research, it should be noted that no parent personality characteristic has been shown to *cause* behavioral pathology. Many children who should be at-risk for developing pathology according to the research in fact turn out to be well-adjusted. In the real world, many other factors may interact to produce or inhibit the development of behavior problems or emotional pathology. On the other hand, parental warmth, limit setting, and involvement in their children's lives have been associated with positive outcomes in children.

Although it has been useful to study families from a dyadic perspective, i.e., the study of two-person relationships, other theorists promote a triadic perspective. This perspective recognizes that many complex factors affect the parent-child relationship. For example, in traditional two-parent families, the mother and father are a social unit of husband and wife whose marital relationship will have an indirect bearing on the child. In single-parent families, the presence or absence of an adult partner will also influence the parent and his relationship with the child. These indirect effects may interact in complex ways to affect family functioning. Recognition of this complexity has led to study of the family as a system.

A Systems Approach to Families

Many professionals advocate a systems approach to working with parents and their children, in which the functioning of the family as a unit is studied. According to Simon and Johnston (1987), many researchers believe that the occurrence of a child's behavioral symptoms are usually related to a change in the family system that disturbs the "delicate balance of daily family functioning" (p. 82). Such changes include the family stresses of divorce, marital conflict, illness, death and loss of employment. One study cited by Simon and Johnston as support of this theory was conducted by Abelsohn (1983) who found that acting-out behavior was a frequent result of parental separation or divorce. "A Mother's Story" presented in Box 8-1 illustrates how an adolescent girl eventually was placed in a residential treatment center partially as a result of her reaction to conditions surrounding the divorce of her parents.

In working with families and family systems, Becvar and Becvar (1988) have identified six characteristics of healthy families:

- A legitimate source of authority, established and supported over time
- A rule system, consistently enforced
- Stable, consistent nurturing behavior
- Effective child-rearing and marriage-maintenance practices
- A set of goals toward which each member of the family works
- Flexibility to adapt to normal developmental changes as well as crises

In addition, researchers have established that healthy families demonstrate shared roles and responsibilities, distinct boundaries (parents are not afraid to act like parents and they allow children to be children), respect for privacy, and opportunities for expression of independence and a wide variety of emotions (Kaslow, 1982). Healthy families also typically have many friends and social relationships outside the immediate family, and such relationships are encouraged for the children. Social isolation, or the absence of such relationships, is common in families that abuse.

A final characteristic of healthy families is clear and congruent communication (Becvar & Becvar, 1988). In these families, verbal and nonverbal communications match so that children do not receive conflicting messages. Disagreement is allowed and individual differences are respected. Effective communication is modeled so that children learn to interact in positive ways with family members and others outside the family.

Systems approaches to developing healthy family relationships can be carried out in a number of ways. Family therapy is one avenue; parent involvement in school programs for parents of students with emotional/behavioral disorders is another. For example, in the On Campus model described by Simon and Johnston (1987), the student and parent(s) must meet with program personnel prior to the student's enrollment. At this orientation meeting, the role of parents and their relationship to the school is outlined; communication and problem-solving procedures are emphasized. After the student is enrolled, family conferences that focus on problem solving and action plans for home and school are held by program personnel as needed. These family conferences are the key systems facet because they (a) recognize that many behaviors are exhibited in both settings; (b) emphasize an action plan, a written contract specifying everyone's responsibilities and consequences; and (c) reinforce the partnership aspect of school-home. To further communication, phone calls are made to parents reporting any cuts or absences. Calls are also made to inform parents of good performance and progress. Academic and behavioral reports are sent to parents as needed: once every three weeks for those students making satisfactory progress, and either daily or weekly for those students needing more support.

BOX 8-1 A Mother's Story

Ms. Brown entered the admissions office, visibly shaken by the procedure she was about to complete. Mary Ann stood close behind her mother with a sullen look on her face. She refused to acknowlege the admissions officer; instead, she gazed out the window in disbelief of what her mother was about to do. Upon request, mother and daughter were seated, and the formalities of the day began. Ms. Brown's hand shook as she signed the forms admitting her daughter into the residential treatment center. Although for a moment she considered backing out, she knew that Mary Ann had already been given too many second chances, and that, as a single parent, her options were limited. She told her story to the admission officer, unaware that her story was typical of the thousands of U.S. teens in psychiatric hospitals and treatment centers across the country.

The Browns had divorced when Mary Ann was 10, concluding several turbulent years of marriage. Mary Ann and her brother Robert remained in their home with their mother, and the father moved into an apartment down the street. The divorce was amicable, and everyone seemed relieved that the new living arrangements were working out so well. For the first year, Mr. Brown sent child support checks regularly and the children spent every week-end with him. At the end of a year, however, Mr. Brown accepted a job in another state. Although he assured the children that they would still come to visit on holidays and summer vacations, they took the news hard.

At first, Mr. Brown did keep in touch through phone calls and packages in the mail. After several months, however, the contacts ceased. At the same time, word drifted back to Ms. Brown that her ex-husband had remarried and was expecting a child with his new wife. Over the next few months, child support checks arrived irregularly. In telephone conversations, Mr. Brown made it clear that he had made a new life for himself that left little room for Robert and Mary Ann. Feeling financial pressure, Ms. Brown took a week-end job to supplement her pay. Mary Ann, now 12, was left to care for her younger brother. After six months of struggling to make ends meet, Ms. Brown was forced to sell the family home and move across town to more afford-

able housing. The children protested, not wanting to leave their neighborhood friends. A sense of loss and abandonment was felt by mother and children.

The difficulties with Mary Ann began on her 13th birthday. Ms. Brown hoped to make up for some of the disappointments of the past year by throwing a birthday party for Mary Ann and inviting some of her "old" friends from their former neighborhood. This idea proved disastrous, as Mary Ann refused to invite her friends to the new home, voicing anger and embarrassment over their predicament. She blamed her mother for the divorce and the loss of her father. Ms. Brown was unprepared for this outburst, as she had hoped to be appreciated for working seven days a week and making sacrifices of her own to keep the family together. After a bitter argument, Mary Ann fled the house.

Things in school were also deteriorating. Although previously an "A" student, Mary Ann now made "Bs" and "Cs" with occasional "Ds". After receiving a call from the principal at work one day, Ms. Brown also learned that Mary Ann had been skipping school. When confronted, Mary Ann lied and stormed to her room, refusing to come out. The next morning Ms. Brown discovered that Mary Ann's bed had not been slept in. Frantic, Ms. Brown called the police to report Mary Ann as a runaway. However, Mary Ann returned of her own accord at mid-morning. Another scene ensued, and Ms. Brown decided that she needed help in dealing with her daughter.

She made an appointment with a counselor at the local mental health clinic. Although Mary Ann begrudgingly accompanied her mother, she refused to cooperate with the counselor. The next several months were difficult. It appeared that Mary Ann no longer wanted to be part of the family. Upon her return from school each day, she would shut herself in her room and listen to loud music or watch television. She rarely ate with the family, preferring to take a plate of food to her room and eat by herself. Although there had been no more incidences of truancy or running away, Ms. Brown continued to worry about her daughter's emotional well-being. Counseling sessions were fruitless. Ms. Brown worried about leaving Mary Ann alone during the

BOX 8-1 *Continued*

days of the upcoming summer vacation; she therefore made arrangements for Mary Ann to spend the summer with her father. This living arrangement proved unsatisfactory from the start. Mary Ann was jealous of her new sister and stepmother. She once again retreated into her room to listen to music. Determined not to fit in and to get back home, she refused to clean up after herself. When her father attempted to set limits, she expressed her anger and hatred toward him, which he in turn blamed on his ex-wife's parenting. Mary Ann began to come and go as she pleased, with grounding proving ineffective because she would sneak out of her window and not return until the early morning ours. On several occasions, Mary Ann took the family car and went joy-riding with several friends who were older than she. Mary Ann was sent back to her mother the day after her stepmother returned to the house to find it full of smoke, loud music, and a number of young people she did not know.

Upon her return home, Mary Ann at first appeared to be doing well at home and school. Her grades improved slightly. In October, however, Ms. Brown made an unannounced home visit at lunch-

time; there she found Mary Ann and a disreputable older boy in her bedroom smoking pot. After a physical confrontation with her mother, Mary Ann ran away and was not found by the police for several days. It was from the juvenile detention center that Ms. Brown had picked up Mary Ann to bring her to the treatment facility.

When it was time to say good-bye, Mary Ann pleaded with her mother not to leave her; when it was obvious that she would indeed have to stay, her pleas turned to anger. She called her mother obscene names, stating that she would never see her again, and for her not to bother to come visit. As Ms. Brown watched her angry daughter disappear behind the locked door of the unit, she succumbed to the familiar sense of pain and loss that had been so prevalent over the past few months. She wondered what had gone wrong and where she had failed. Their lives were not supposed to have turned out this way.

Contributed by Sarah Sims, M.Ed, Psychological Associate, The Devereux Foundation, Texas Center, Victoria, Texas

In summary, many professionals are reaching the conclusion that the most effective approach to working with students with emotional/behavioral disorders is a systems approach. Applied to families, this approach means that educators need to recognize that a student is part of a family unit that strives to maintain its balance. Working with the family as a unit can be undertaken not only in family therapy sessions, but also in school programs. Refer to Box 8-2 for an example of family counseling undertaken by a school psychologist.

Involving Parents

Strategies for Involvement

If special educators are to establish viable teacher-parent relationships, they must accept and abide by two basic tenets: (1) that their role with parents is a consultative one, and (2) that parents should be viewed as individuals, not as a homogeneous group.

The first tenet is that parents must be recognized as experts on their children, while educators must learn to be consultants to parents. Regardless of educational level or parenting skills, almost all parents can offer valuable insights about their child's development and level of functioning. Information on early development, stressful family relation-

BOX 8-2 Paul's Family: Crisis Counseling in the Schools

As an interning school psychologist in a large urban district, I was asked to work with Paul and his family. Paul was a thirteen-year-old seventh grader who was diagnosed as learning disabled. He had difficulty with verbal skills, as evidenced by his speaking in phrases and short sentences in a soft, almost inaudible voice. He had been referred for family counseling due to failing grades and recent incidences of fighting at school. He had also expressed suicidal thoughts to his mother and to school personnel. Paul's drawings were artistic but often depicted violent and bloody death scenes.

Paul's two older brothers, ages 16 and 17, were both in special education classes. The older brother was on probation from juvenile court and had returned to school after dropping out. The younger brother was attending an alternative school for repeated aggressive acts toward others. The only family member apparently doing well in school was the nine-year-old sister. After several attempts, the mother had severed her relationship with the father, a drug and alcohol abuser who was at the time imprisoned on drug charges. My role as therapist was crisis-oriented, geared to a brief therapy problem-solving model of dealing with family needs in six sessions. The intent of this model is to help family members learn how each contributes to preferred behavior (which is the exception), and then to help make these instances commonplace.

It became clear to me very early in the first session that nothing would be easy in this family. The hope of getting a family consensus on a goal for the six sessions was lost in the quagmire of individual concerns. All family members except the daughter seemed depressed. Finally, the mother decided upon a goal: getting Paul to do his chores and his homework. Upon hearing this goal, Paul's brothers retreated into self-absorbed silence and Paul began muttering to himself about "killing someone."

Through the remainder of the sessions, I tried to help the mother see Paul's acting out behavior as his cry for her to provide some stability in his life by demanding that he behave better.

I would like to say that at the end of the counseling sessions, Paul's grades improved, he was getting along better at school, and that his mother had reaffirmed her leadership role in the family. In reality, Paul's grades continued to lag and he was suspended several times for bringing weapons to school. The mother did not appear to have the energy to deal with Paul's challenges or to maintain consistency in discipline. She did indicate, however, that she was able to initiate more conversation of a personal nature with her son; as one example, she was able to talk with him about a situation in which his feelings were hurt. Paul's story does not stop here. When his case was reviewed by school personnel, it was determined that his primary handicapping condition was emotional disturbance. He was placed in a self-contained affective learning class at another school, which has allowed him to get a fresh start in a new environment with an empathic teacher. Meanwhile, I have picked him up in rational-emotive therapy (RET). We are working to expand his understanding of feelings and developing more vocabulary to express those feelings. Through RET, Paul is learning to understand the irrationality of much of his anger and how he creates it. Progress is slow, but Paul wants to change. His teacher is pleased with his schoolwork. In the two months since his reassignment, Paul has missed only one day of school and has not been in any fights.

He may make it yet.

Contributed by Barbara Yonan, who at the time of this writing, was completing an internship as part of the doctoral requirements in school psychology.

ships, and unusual environmental influences may prove crucial in helping the teacher understand the student's current functioning. When information is solicited from parents and their opinions are treated with respect, a bond of trust can be established that lays the groundwork for cooperative planning.

The second tenet is that parents of children with disabilities are not a homogeneous group. Parents differ greatly in the degree to which they participate in educational programming for their children. All parents of students with disabilities have a legal right to participate in decision making regarding their child's placement in special education services and in developing an individualized education program. While some parents communicate regularly with school personnel and are heavily involved throughout special education procedures, others may waive their rights to be actively involved. Similarly, some parents may know very little about alternative special education programs and placements, due process procedures under laws governing special education, and other legal issues; other parents may be well-informed about the law and have definite ideas about what their child's educational program should entail. Some parents are knowledgeable about their child's difficulties and very skilled at managing their child's behavior, while others may need training to develop management skills. The point is that parents have differing levels of awareness and skills that teachers must accommodate when involving parents in education. As Webber and Gilliam (1981) state, "Parents, like children, are individual in their needs. Teachers must individualize their expectations for parents, just as they do for children" (p. 7).

A study by Simpson (1988) supports the need to individualize for parents. Attempting to ascertain the needs of parents, Simpson asked 15 teachers of 161 students with mild disabilities to categorize parental requests for services into five categories: (1) information exchange, (2) consumer and advocacy training, (3) training in home program implementation, (4) counseling and therapy, and (5) parent-coordinated service programs.

Services under the category *information exchange* were requested by the largest percentage of parents; these services included informal feedback, program information, and progress reports. The remainder of services requested were scattered throughout the categories, thereby offering little consistent information about what parents as a group request. This finding suggests that parents do have unique needs and that a comprehensive parent component would offer a variety of services. Although surprisingly no parents of students with emotional/behavioral disorders requested services such as behavior management training or information on parental rights, Simpson cautions that this may reflect a lack of knowledge that such services might be available if requested rather than a lack of interest. In keeping with the tenet that parent involvement and parent services should be individualized as much as possible, a number of alternatives for parent involvement are presented. First, however, the issue of blame will be briefly addressed.

Whose Fault Is It?

Although the issue of blaming parents was alluded to earlier, it warrants additional attention. Few readers probably identified with the belief that "refrigerator mothers" can cause autism. However, many educators can fall into the trap of *"if only"*— *"if only* the parents were more interested"; *"if only* the parents would be consistent in discipline"; *"if only* there were a father in the home," etc. These statements represent a subtle form of blame; i.e, if only the parents were somehow different or better parents, then teaching students with emotional/behavioral disorders wouldn't be so hard. While this may be partially true, engaging in this type of thinking may also predispose the teacher to seeing the parent as an adversary rather than a partner. Further, the teacher may be tempted to absolve himself of responsibility for helping students achieve their behavioral and academic potential.

Simon and Johnston (1987) offer a good example of this blaming cycle. As they describe it, school personnel may easily fall prey to common misperceptions about single parents. Realizing that single parenting is often fraught with difficulties, school personnel may view the single parent as responsible for many of his child's behavior problems. This perception may be cemented when the single parent inevitably has difficulty scheduling and even making conferences—the parent then becomes labeled as indifferent or irresponsible. As the relationship between the home and school deteriorates, the child is caught in the cycle: the school becomes more frustrated, the parent is viewed as more uncooperative, the child shows more behavior problems, and the school complains more about the parent.

Special Considerations for Nontraditional and Multicultural Families

Single-parent families are rapidly becoming the *status quo* rather than the exception. In 1970, 84 percent of school-age children lived in two-parent homes; by 1988, the percentage had dropped to 73, indicating that approximately one in four or five children is being reared by a single parent (Lefrancois, 1992). Single-parent families often experience many difficulties, including lack of emotional support from a partner for the remaining parent, absence of a same-sex role model for children to emulate, and severe financial stress. Financial stress is worst in households headed by single mothers. According to the U.S. Bureau of the Census, the median income of mother-only families ($8,574) is less than half the median income of father-only families ($20,000), and less than one-fourth of the median income of two-parent families ($34, 573) (1990).

Other "nontraditional" family configurations that are becoming more common are families in which both parents work, and families in which grandparents are rearing their grandchildren. It has been estimated that in the 1990s, 80 percent of married women with children under 6 years of age will become employed outside the home (Frost, 1986). Finding adequate and affordable child care for preschoolers and after school care for older children becomes stressful for many families. Extended care also puts additional demands upon the children to behave themselves in settings outside the home for most of their waking hours. Additionally, parents who have chronic and severe problems with substance abuse, unemployment, and/or maintaining their mental health are increasingly turning their children over to their own parents to rear. Sensitivity to the special issues in these nontraditional families is essential in building partnerships between home and school.

Working with families of different ethnic, racial, or cultural backgrounds also calls for special consideration from teachers. Children and youth from African American and Hispanic homes may be overrepresented in classes for students with emotional/behavioral disorders in various parts of the country (Sugai, 1988), indicating a lack of sensitivity on the part of the educational system in dealing with these youth. Each of us is so socialized by our respective cultures that it becomes difficult to know just how sensitive to others' cultural practices we actually are. For example, the following have been suggested as basic values promoted by the dominant United States culture:

1. Importance of individualism and privacy
2. Belief in the equality of all individuals
3. Informality in interactions with others
4. Emphasis on the future, change, and progress

5. Belief in the general goodness of humanity
6. Emphasis on the importance of time and punctuality
7. High regard for achievement, action, work, and materialism
8. Pride in interactional styles that are direct and assertive (Althen, 1988)

These values are general but may affect a teacher's interactions, her behavior and her assumptions about others' behavior. Some of these values also have direct implications for classroom performance. Experts in cross-cultural competence assert that the first step in becoming culturally sensitive is to be aware of one's own culture and its impact on beliefs, attitudes, and actions. Cultural self-awareness then becomes a bridge to understanding other cultures (Lynch, 1992).

The culturally competent individual also understands that communication often differs from culture to culture. Particularly important are nonverbal behaviors and the meanings attributed to them by various cultures. Eye contact, facial expressions, proximity and touching, gestures, and other body language such as posture and body position may have very different meanings for persons from different cultures. For example, one researcher found that although members of different cultures claimed to recognize 70 to 100 percent of gestures from other groups, these members correctly interpreted the gestures at rates as low as 30 percent (Schneller, 1989).

Lynch (1992) offers a number of suggestions for improving cross-cultural communication:

- *Respect individuals from other cultures.*
- *Make continued and sincere attempts to understand the world from others' points of view.*
- *Remain open to new learning.*
- *Be flexible.*
- *Have a sense of humor.*
- *Accept ambiguity.*
- *Approach others with a desire to learn (pp. 51–52).*

These suggestions and others in the remainder of this chapter for involving parents are applicable to families of all cultural backgrounds. Although it may be important to understand the influence of certain aspects of an individual's cultural background, it is equally important to avoid stereotyping on that basis. As mentioned, successful teachers individualize expectations for parents and avoid blaming parents for their children's difficulties.

Staying in Touch

Teachers can encourage parental involvement in many ways. For parents who are interested in learning more about management techniques, teachers can be instrumental in setting up parent education groups. Parents who are experiencing high levels of stress may improve their coping skills by participation in a support group or in counseling. Each of these options is discussed in the following pages.

Staying in touch on a routine basis is essential. Ideally, parents should be involved in their child's school program in an ongoing, systematic way that was illustrated by the On

Campus program. While this degree of involvement is not always possible, there are some creative ways to stay in touch with parents. Taking advantage of technology can save time—examples are using microcomputers to generate daily or weekly parent reports and using telephone answering machines to record daily assignments. In the latter case, parents call a number to get the day's classwork or homework assignment; this tactic can be effective when students are especially "forgetful."

Many teachers find it helpful to make the student responsible for a daily notebook to be carried between home and school each day. Notes of communication and assignments are written in this notebook; teachers and parents can sign it each day to ensure its passage back and forth. Contingencies (penalties) can be set up for students who fail to keep the notebook updated.

Parent Groups

Organized parent groups are usually one of two types: (1) support groups, established to provide a support system among parents who have similar concerns, or (2) educational groups, established for the purpose of giving information or teaching specific skills. Support groups serve the function of getting parents together, often on an informal basis, to discuss concerns and frustrations relating to parenting and the education and management of their children. The impetus of support groups may come either from teachers or parents, but can be successful only if parents take an active role in sharing their needs and concerns. It is often a good idea for teachers to take very passive roles in parent support groups so that parents feel free to provide their own leadership. Support groups can also be structured according to the needs and desires of the group; for example, parents may want to bring in guest speakers on a certain topic and then break out into smaller discussion groups (Miller and Hudson, 1994).

Educational parent groups are usually conducted much like classes or workshops, with a specific agenda and a set number of meetings at a regular time and place. Educators, psychologists, social workers, and other child specialists are generally responsible for organizing and conducting these groups. Topics such as behavior management in the home and improving parent-child communication are offered.

Parent Counseling

Many parents need more support than can be provided by empathetic teachers or by parent groups. Individual or family counseling may be particularly indicated for parents of students with E/BD, who usually face stressful situations on a daily basis. Parents may become so overwhelmed by financial problems, marital stress, or the day-to-day responsibilities of managing a family that the additional stress of their child's behavior problems becomes too much to handle (e.g., recall Mary Ann from the case study in Box 8-1).

Although teachers should lend a sympathetic ear to parents, it is beyond the scope of teacher responsibility—and training—to provide counseling services. However, the teacher is often in a position to be the first to recognize a plea for help and can be instrumental in making a referral. Some signals that may indicate a need for professional counseling are:

Parents are experiencing a period of unusual financial difficulty, marital discord, or other emotional upheaval.

Parent(s) routinely expresses feelings of helplessness or depression.

Parent(s) feels out of control of the child.

Child is habitually in trouble with the juvenile authorities.

Parent(s) chronically appears to be under a high level of stress.

Parent(s) is beginning to impose upon the teacher's time (at home or at school) with personal problems.

In order to make appropriate referrals, teachers should become familiar with community resources that offer counseling and other psychological services. It is a good idea to know the background and training, credentials, and theoretical orientation of counselors and therapists to whom referrals are made. Many counselors and therapists specialize in school-related problems, child psychology, or family therapy; it is best to match parental needs to the specialty area of professionals. Teachers can be of most benefit to parents by helping them gain a realistic picture of their child's capabilities and behavior relative to school functioning, which is best accomplished in face-to-face conferences. Conferencing skills will be addressed in the next section.

Conferencing Skills

Getting Them There

The first step in conducting an effective parent conference is often overlooked: getting the parent to attend. A number of barriers may be operating, including parent feelings of alienation from the school, inconvenient meeting times, and meetings that consistently fail to meet the needs of parents (Alexander, Kroth, Simpson, & Poppelreiter, 1982). In one survey of parents of secondary students with mild disabilities, parents who failed to attend any school conferences indicated problems with the following:

Transportation

Babysitting

Scheduling—night of week was not convenient

Questionable worth of meetings

Belief that the school was too concerned about paperwork, i.e., getting parents to complete forms (Hamilton & Koorland, 1988)

With these general considerations in mind, teachers of students with emotional/behavioral disorders may be able to find the times, places, and formats that suit the parents of their particular group. Once suitable times for meetings have been established, the next step is to establish and maintain good communication with one another. To communicate effectively with parents in conferences, teachers should be skilled in building relationships, setting goals for each conference, and dealing with conflict.

Relationship Building

The quality of parent-teacher conferences largely depends upon the teacher's ability to develop a relationship based upon mutual trust. Kroth and Simpson (1977) have listed four factors that aid teachers in building trust with parents. First is the teacher's willingness to take risks: when teachers feel capable and confident in dealing with others, they are more inclined to become involved and to share some responsibility with parents. Second is the joint establishment of clear expectations for parents: when parental responsibilities are clearly defined and agreed upon, the probability of follow-through is much increased. A third way to develop trust is to know the capabilities and constraints of the parents so that unrealistic expectations do not arise. For example, Kroth and Simpson note that parents may fail to attend meetings because they do not have transportation, or may fail to respond to a written memo because it is not written in their language or at their reading level. The teacher should not assume that failure to respond is indicative of lack of caring. A fourth way to develop trust is to provide feedback and reinforcement, especially if parents are involved in behavior management programs with their children. Teachers will find it easier to communicate effectively with parents if they are good active listeners. An active listener knows how to encourage the conversant to talk. The active listener reflects and clarifies the other's message and evidences a body posture that indicates interest (eye contact, nodding, and so forth). Teachers should try to balance speaking time—neither parent nor teacher should monopolize the conversation. Teachers should also try to avoid using jargon and "talking at" parents without heeding their reactions.

Setting Goals
Parent conferences are usually called for three reasons: to get information, to give information, or to problem-solve. Although any given conference may cover all three categories, the teacher should have a specific goal in mind for every conference. The initial interview with parents of a student is often primarily for gathering information about family and home factors that affect the student's functioning. Kroth and Simpson (1977) suggest the following interview format:

- *Statement of the problem.* Elicit parents' assessment of and feelings about their child's difficulties; if the parental assessment differs drastically from the professional assessment, try to ascertain why the discrepancy exists and, if necessary, give the parent more information.
- *Developmental history.* If unavailable in the student's records, get a complete developmental history including conditions around birth, developmental milestones, illnesses and injuries, and any unusual conditions that may have affected the child's development. If a developmental history is available, it is good to explore the parents' perceptions of the effect of some of the past difficulties on the child's current behavioral and cognitive functioning.
- *Personality history.* Encourage parents to discuss their child's personality factors such as extreme likes and dislikes, and attitudes toward peers, school, family, and home. Behavior patterns relative to tantrums, accidents, activity level, sleep patterns, reaction to parental discipline, or emotional difficulties should be explored. Ask parents to note some of the child's strengths.
- *Sociological information.* Tactfully ascertain information about the home that will help in understanding and planning for the child. Such information may include cultural, ethnic, and religious background of the family, other languages spoken in the home, ages and gender of siblings, parental attitudes and child-rearing practices, and the hours

that parents are available for child supervision and for participation in conferences or other school activities.

- *School history.* Ask parents to share information about relationships with previous teachers and programs; find out what interventions were successful in the past.
- *Parental goals and expectations.* Explore the parents' expectations for you as the teacher and for the current educational program. Compare their responses to your own plans. Discuss long-term goals for the child's future and compare parental goals to the child's capabilities.

A second type of interview focuses upon giving information to parents. Such information may be general program information, an explanation of special education policies, or a special intervention for which the teacher wants to enlist parental permission or help. In other information-giving interviews, teachers may set up a home-school report system or give a progress report. Teachers should carefully prepare factual information and should solicit the backing of their principal when policies are being explained or unusual interventions are being suggested.

To report progress, most teachers of students with emotional/behavioral disorders institute some form of parent-school communication other than the routine report card. Daily, weekly, or biweekly notes have been used successfully in home-based reinforcement systems. Teachers may also phone parents to give them progress reports; parents of students with E/BD are often shocked to receive positive reports about their child over the telephone, as they are much more accustomed to receiving negative reports. Regardless of which reporting system is used, teachers should schedule periodic parent conferences in order to give information about academic and behavioral progress.

A third type of interview involves problem solving. It is not unusual for teachers and parents to find themselves in disagreement over various facets of the student's program. Some of the most common causes of conflict are: different opinions or values, thwarted needs, resentment of authority, and feelings of inadequacy or jealousy (Institute for Parent Involvement, 1980). Regardless of the cause, conflicts are best resolved by obtaining as much information as possible, analyzing the information, and then generating possible solutions.

Dealing with Conflict

When parents become frustrated or angry, the teacher may become the outlet for their aggression. Upon being verbally attacked, one's initial reaction is to counterattack or to defend oneself vehemently; both reactions are counterproductive to further communication. The Institute for Parent Involvement (1980) offers some very specific guidelines for handling aggressive parents:

1. Use active listening to convey interest; write down the parents' complaints.
2. Exhaust parents' list of complaints; ask if they have any to add to the list. Ask them to clarify any complaints that are too general or vague.
3. Ask parents for suggestions for solving the problems they have brought up; write these down also.
4. Respond to loud talking by speaking softly.
5. Avoid arguing, explaining, or defending yourself, as this often feeds aggression.

Adhering to these guidelines will often diffuse the parents' frustration or anger; it is difficult for them to remain angry at someone who is earnestly and quietly attending to their complaints. Often the initial complaint is not the real problem, which may never surface unless the lines of communication are kept open.

Do's and Don'ts

The development of trust and the enlistment of parents as partners rather than adversaries are keys to successful teacher-parent relationships. Setting a goal, organizing information, and preparing ahead of time for parent conferences are ways to enhance communication during the conference. In addition, Simpson (1990) offers the following tips:

DO'S
Maintain a sense of humor.
Be accepting of yourself and the parents with whom you work.
Be positive and sincere.
Demonstrate respect for the parents.
Listen.
Use language that the parents can understand.

DON'TS
Attempt to have all the answers.
Argue with parents.
Make agreements or promises that you may not be able to keep.
Patronize parents.
Make moralistic judgments.
Minimize what the parents have to say about their youngster.

A Summary Checklist

Table 8-1 contains a conference checklist that can be used for planning and evaluating parent conferences. The preconference section gives reminders for preparing the interview—including a reminder for arranging a pleasant physical environment. During the conference, the teacher is reminded to state the purpose of the interview, to encourage information sharing, to summarize, and to end the conference on a positive note. The postconference section offers suggestions for follow-up with parents, students, and other involved school personnel.

In summary, teachers who view parents as partners in the educational process are likely to effect changes in a student's life at home and at school. All educators need to be skilled at communicating with parents in conferences. Other opportunities for parent involvement should be individualized to match the capabilities and interests of parents. In keeping with systems theory, the goal of parent involvement is to make adjustments in the home and with the family as a unit that will accommodate the child and make the system work more smoothly. Parents and teachers together should decide whether participation in activities such as parent groups will be both realistic and beneficial.

TABLE 8-1   Conference Checklist

PRECONFERENCE

_____	1.	NOTIFY
		PURPOSE, PLACE, TIME, LENGTH OF TIME ALLOTTED
_____	2.	PREPARE
		REVIEW CHILD'S FOLDER
		GATHER EXAMPLES OF WORK
		PREPARE MATERIALS
_____	3.	PLAN AGENDA
_____	4.	ARRANGE ENVIRONMENT
		COMFORTABLE SEATING
		ELIMINATE DISTRACTIONS

CONFERENCE

_____	1.	WELCOME
		ESTABLISH RAPPORT
_____	2.	STATE PURPOSE
		TIME LIMITATIONS
		NOTE TAKING
		OPTIONS FOR FOLLOW-UP
_____	3.	ENCOURAGE INFORMATION SHARING
		COMMENTS
		QUESTIONS
_____	4.	LISTEN
		PAUSE ONCE IN A WHILE!
		LOOK FOR VERBAL AND NONVERBAL CUES
		QUESTIONS
_____	5.	SUMMARIZE
_____	6.	END ON A POSITIVE NOTE

POSTCONFERENCE

_____	1.	REVIEW CONFERENCE WITH CHILD, IF APPROPRIATE
_____	2.	SHARE INFORMATION WITH OTHER SCHOOL PERSONNEL, IF NEEDED
_____	3.	MARK CALENDAR FOR PLANNED FOLLOW-UP

Reprinted with permission from the University of New Mexico Institue for Parent Involvement, Albuquerque, New Mexico.

The Education System

The education system may be the second most important system in the lives of students with emotional/behavioral disorders because of the potential for impacting their daily lives. This section describes educational services, known as a continuum of services, that are offered in a variety of settings. These settings are briefly reviewed, and the difficulties in moving students from one placement to another are addressed.

A Continuum of Services

Alternative placements in special education were conceptualized by Reynolds (1962) in the Cascade Model, which presented a continuum of services ranging from regular classroom (least restrictive setting) to residential schools (most restrictive setting). Students are to be moved to more restrictive environments only as necessary and moved to less restrictive environments as soon as possible.

The full continuum of services for E/BD students is presented in Figure 8-1. This continuum can be divided into two categories: (1) *integrated,* which means that the student spends most of the day with the regular classroom teacher who has primary responsiblity for the student; and (2) *segregated,* which means that a student spends the majority of time with a special education teacher who has primary responsibility for instruction. The next five sections of this chapter describe the most common settings for E/BD students and teacher roles within those settings. Advantages and disadvantages of each setting are summarized in Table 8-2.

Hospitals

Students being served in hospital settings generally fall into one or more of the following categories: suicidal, drug-dependent, violent, psychotic, or exhibiting organic impairments accompanied by bizarre behavior and requiring medication. Chronic runaways and adjudicated youth are occasionally placed in hospital settings by the courts for security and treatment purposes. Students are usually placed in highly restrictive settings because they require close medical supervision or protection of self or others.

Day schools with low teacher-pupil ratios are often provided in hospital settings. Typically, hospital day schools are heavily influenced by medical and psychological staff. Total treatment programs for individuals that include the classroom setting may be worked out by psychiatrists and then implemented by teachers. Teachers in hospital settings therefore must be adept at working with psychological and medical personnel and at being members of a multidisciplinary team.

Special Schools: Residential and Day

Students served in special schools are usually those exhibiting such severe emotional or behavioral problems that they are deemed unable to function in the public school environment but do not need the close supervision provided in the hospital setting. Special schools may be day schools or residential schools and may be either privately or publicly funded. A major advantage of special schools is that the environment can be more tightly structured

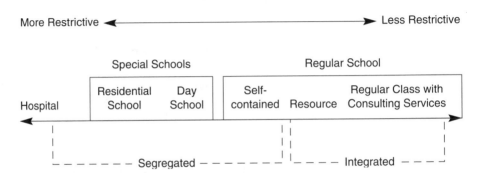

FIGURE 8-1   Placements for Students with Emotional/Behavioral Disorders

TABLE 8-2 A Comparison of Settings for Students with E/BD

	HOSPITALS	SPECIAL SCHOOLS (RESIDENTIAL/DAY)	SELF-CONTAINED	RESOURCE ROOM	CONSULTING SERVICES
advantages	security/protection constant availability of medical and psychological staff equipped to handle emergencies	environment tightly structured consistency between "home" and school program (resdiential schools only) multidisciplinary staff	small teacher-pupil ratio environemnt controlled by one teacher	less restrictive environment while providing individualized help	least intrusive student maintained in regular classroom
disadvantages	stigma restrictive environment total segregation loss of personal liberties	difficulty in returning to regular school campus segregated from nondisabled	lack of opportunity to interact with and model peers without disabilities	sometimes supplants regular classroom curriculum	no direct service provided

than in regular schools because the entire staff usually operates under the same behavioral plan. Day and evening staff of residential schools should coordinate so that the students operate under the same regulations and expectations for 24 hours a day.

In addition to specially trained teachers, special schools are staffed with multidisciplinary staff, usually a physician or nurse, a psychologist and/or psychiatrist, counselors, social workers and child care workers. The evening staff generally includes trained counselors who are available to deal with crises that may arise during the evening hours. The team concept is advocated and staffings are common, in which all team members jointly work out objectives and assign responsibility for carrying out those objectives with individual students.

As in the hospital setting, the teacher in a special school must learn to work on a daily basis with personnel from different disciplines such as medicine and psychology. Effective programs depend upon cooperative planning and mutual support among staff members.

The major disadvantage of special schools and hospitals is the difficulty involved in returning students to regular education campuses. Reintegration of BD students into less restrictive settings has become a major concern of educators and will be dealt with later in this chapter.

Regular School: Self-Contained

Students are usually placed in self-contained classrooms in regular schools because they (a) can be safely maintained at home, (b) are deemed able to function in the public schools, but (c) need more structure and/or specialized instruction than can be provided on a part-time basis. In this setting, students are segregated rather than mainstreamed and therefore have less contact with regular education teachers and peers without disabilities. By staying with one teacher for the majority of the day, students are not exposed to inconsistency or the different expectations of several different teachers. Some students with emotional/behavioral disorders need the consistency and structure provided in this setting.

Regular School: Resource

Students with emotional/behavioral disorders who are placed in resource settings usually exhibit milder behavior or emotional difficulties and need less academic remediation than those students placed in self-contained programs. While being mainstreamed in the regular classroom for most of the day, the student can still receive individualized help in the resource room.

Students who are placed in a resource room spend the majority of their time in a regular classroom but are "resourced out" for periods ranging from 30 minutes to two or more hours a day. For example, the resource teacher may have the primary responsibility for both language arts and math instruction for some students, while for others, the resource program may be limited to math only. Although the resource room is supposed to supplement regular classroom instruction, it most often supplants or replaces the regular instructional program in those designated academic areas. Reasons for this replacement role are (1) conflicts with daily scheduling between the regular class and the resource room, and (2) the willingness of regular education teachers to turn over their instructional responsibility to specialists. The resource teacher should promote the supplementary role by encouraging the regular education teacher to include the special student in his instruction whenever possible.

Resource rooms may be either *categorical,* which serves only one disability type, or *cross-categorical,* which serves special education students with different labels such as learning disabled, mentally retarded, and emotionally/behaviorally disordered. Many educators prefer the categorical because it conforms to the definitions of disability conditions, and teachers are usually certified in one of the disability conditions; others prefer the cross-categorical because it allows grouping of students by instructional needs rather than special education label.

Regular Classroom with Consulting Services

In this setting, students are placed full-time in the regular classroom, and the special education teacher provides direct services to the students' teachers. This placement represents the least restrictive setting on the continuum of services, and students who are placed here have been judged as capable of meeting regular education requirements if some allowances or modifications are made. In most consulting models, it is the regular class teacher rather than the student who is the direct recipient of services. Consultation focuses on instructional and management strategies, but the latter is of more concern to teachers of many students with emotional/behavioral disorders. Consultation services may be used in place of a pullout program (i.e., resource or self-contained), or may be used to help reintegrate a student into the regular classroom after she has been in a more restrictive setting.

Although there are many proponents of the consultation model, it has yet to be implemented on a large scale. We will return to the consulting model later in this chapter.

In summary, the placements on the continuum of services are designed to meet the needs of students who have different characteristics. Ideally, placement decisions should be based on the severity of behavioral difficulties and the degree of academic deficiency exhibited by the student. In reality, a true continuum of services may not be available in every community, and when available, placements may be determined by finances rather than student need (National Mental Health and Special Education Coalition, 1989).

Reintegration

The ultimate goal for any program serving E/BD students should be to ensure that each individual student can function in the setting that is least restrictive for her. Thus, special education teachers must address the potential for each student's placement: if the setting is a hospital or residential school, perhaps the next step is to help the student function in a day school or self-contained program. If the setting is a self-contained program, the next step for students may be integration into a resource class or a regular class with consulting services. Any experienced special education teacher can attest that although these goals are worthwhile, they are not easily attained. Barriers to reintegration and some guidelines to aid the process are discussed in the next sections.

Barriers to Reintegration

Research over the years consistently shows that students with emotional/behavioral disorders are rated as the least accepted and the most negatively stereotyped of all exceptionalities (Haring, Stern, & Cruickshank, 1958; Kingsley, 1967; Parish, Dyck, & Kappes, 1979; Vaac

& Kirst, 1977). Among the beliefs held by general education teachers were that they would be unable to manage E/BD students in their classrooms, and that these students would have a detrimental effect on their peers without disabilities in a regular classroom setting.

These results are consistent with research on teacher attitudes toward consultation services. When teachers perceive that the problem lies within the child, they often want the child to be removed from the regular classroom rather than to be asked to make modifications or adjustments. Resistance by teachers and administrators has been cited by experts as a major barrier to consultation services (Idol & West, 1987).

One study (Algozzine & Curran, 1979) showed that when teachers were asked to predict the school success of hypothetical E/BD students in a mainstream setting, their responses varied as a function of their tolerance levels for behavior. The authors concluded that a "goodness of fit," the matching of teacher attitude to child behavior, can greatly influence the child's chances for success in that classroom.

Guidelines for Reintegration

Montgomery (1982) offers one set of guidelines for teachers whose goal is to reintegrate their students into a less restrictive setting. According to Montgomery, the program itself should be structured to foster student growth along four dimensions:

1. *From rigid to flexible scheduling.* As the student is able to handle independent learning situations, more free time is allowed and the schedule becomes more flexible.

2. *From external to internal control.* Initially, external reinforcers may be necessary; heavy supervision and planning are done for the student. Structure is lessened as the student becomes more responsible.

3. *From short-term to long-term goals.* The student may initially be able to complete only short assignments or to work for very short periods of time. Extension of work periods to approximate those in regular classrooms and delay of rewards become program objectives.

4. *From segregation to integration.* Although the student may initially need the structure and control imposed in the segregated clssroom, the long-term goal is to wean the student from dependency on external controls so she can function in integrated settings.

Some school districts are attempting to ease the reintegration process through transition classes. These classes focus on independent behaviors and socialization skills that should facilitate a student's transition from a segregated class with a small teacher-pupil ratio to an integrated setting in which a student must be more independent.

Following the "goodness of fit" idea, special education teachers also can attempt to match student skills with the demands of the setting into which they are to be integrated (Algozzine & Curran, 1979). The following questions might be asked of the receiving teacher:

- What reading level and other academic skills are prerequisites for successful functioning in the new class?
- Is information presented primarily in lecture format or are students expected to gain most of the information by reading their textbooks?
- Is the class grouped by ability or is everyone required to do the same level of work?

- How much and what kinds of individual help are available if needed?
- What academic-related behaviors (for example, hand-raising, on-task) are required to function smoothly?
- What social skills (taking turns, not talking in class) are needed?
- What classroom rules are posted and enforced?

These and other requirements may be determined through direct observation or by asking the teacher. Most teachers are pleased to identify the crucial skills that are needed for success in their classrooms if the purpose is to teach those skills to incoming students.

Structured inventories with detailed questions about classroom rules and requirements for success have been published (Fuchs, Fernstrom, Scott, Fuchs, & Vandermeer, 1994; Welch, 1994). In addition, Walker and Rankin (1980) have devised an assessment instrument for the specific purpose of facilitating mainstreaming for students with E/BD. *Assessment for Integration into Mainstream Settings (AIMS)* is designed to help identify: (1) the skills required in the receiving setting; (2) maladaptive social skills that the receiving teacher finds unacceptable; and (3) technical assistance needed by the receiving teacher in order to teach and manage the child's behavior. Walker and his associates have developed a corresponding social skills curriculum *(ACCEPTS)* aimed at teaching behaviors needed for functioning in an integrated setting. Skills taught in *ACCEPTS* are one of two types: those identified by teachers as critical to "successful classroom adjustment" or those which contribute to "social competence and peer acceptance. The ACCEPTS curriculum is described more fully in Chapter 7.

A teacher of students with emotional/behavioral disorders may be employed in any one of the settings from the continuum of services and therefore will probably deal with the issue of helping students make the transition into a less restrictive setting. Planning for these transitions on both an individual basis and a program-wide basis is essential to the success of the program. Some of the problems with reintegration and the skills needed to counteract them are also relevant to other social systems in the community.

Social Systems

Three major systems other than education may impact the lives of students with emotional/behavioral disorders: social-welfare, juvenile justice/correctional, and mental health (see Figure 8-2). If teachers are to take a systems approach to programming, they should know something about how these systems work.

Social/Welfare System

A variety of social services are provided to eligible families, including health services, family planning, housing services, emergency aid, and protective services for minors. Services are delivered primarily through caseworkers who decide eligibility and devise service plans for families. Families of children with emotional/behavioral disorders may become clients of the social-welfare system for reasons unrelated to the child, or they may become clients as a result of reported abuse, neglect, or exploitation of that child. Children are rarely direct

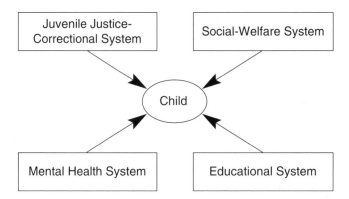

FIGURE 8-2   Systems Impacting Students with Emotional/Behavioral Disorders

(Adapted with permission from *Troubled Chidren/Troubled Systems* by Stephen J. Apter. Copyright 1982, Pergamon Press)

recipients of social services unless it is protective services that may result in legal removal from the home.

Social caseworkers are more likely to be interested in a child's school functioning if abuse or neglect is suspected or if parental custody is in question. Because the teacher is in the position to observe on a daily basis, the teacher may be asked to make judgments about the child's general emotional state or physical welfare. Further, in most states teachers are required by law to report suspected abuse to child protective services. Alarming rates of child injury and death due to family violence should serve as the impetus for complying with such laws. Although no reliable statistics are currently available on the percentage of youngsters with E/BD who have been physically or sexually abused, it is common for therapists to uncover instances of abuse with their clients who have been brought to therapy for other presenting problems. Concerns about physically abused children relative to a systems perspective are discussed in Box 8-3, and concerns about sexually abused children are discussed in some detail in "Special Issues," Chapter 11.

Teachers and caseworkers together can gain a clearer picture of the child's total environment and be better equipped to plan interventions. Although their duties vary, many caseworkers coordinate all social services received by a family; therefore the caseworker generally has a network among other agencies that can be valuable when searching for resources to provide additional services to a child or adolescent. Teachers should not be reluctant to contact caseworkers to help find pertinent community resources.

Juvenile Justice/Correctional System

The alarming trend in increasingly violent crimes being committed by increasingly younger children has swept the nation, leaving few communities immune. Even small towns, once considered refuges from "big city" crimes, have been shocked by episodes of children killing other children. One source documented that violent crime (homicide, sexual assault, robbery, aggravated assault) among juveniles has increased threefold in the last six to seven years

---

BOX 8-3 Child Abuse: Whose Responsibility?

We have all had the experience of reading about specific instances of child abuse that have occurred in our communities; some of us also have either read about or known children who died as a result of abuse. When these deaths occur, the media really gets interested: What were the circumstances? What was the psychological profile of the person who killed the child? How many times had this person abused the child before? Had it ever been reported to child protective services? Why wasn't the child removed from the home? etc.

Unfortunately, we know the answers to these questions because they are identical for so many cases in which children are routinely or severely abused. For instance, we know that many abusers were themselves abused as kids, that they tend to be immature and not prepared for the responsibility of taking care of children, that they suffer from frequent personal crises, and may use drugs or alcohol. We know that abusers tend to repeat the abuse when stressed. We know that in many cases, suspi-

cion of child abuse was reported to the authorities who may have investigated but not found just cause to remove the child from the home. (Although parents are the most frequent child abusers, relatives and the parent's friends and lovers also abuse). In many instances, child protective workers are so overworked that they can investigate only those reports in which the child's life is reported to be endangered.

When children die from repeated abuse, it is easy to point a finger—at the killer, at child protective services, at society, at the "system" that can allow such a thing to happen. We have discussed a systems orientation in this chapter. An important facet of a systems orientation is not allowing children to "fall through the cracks" because we think it is someone else's responsibility. How much responsibility beyond reporting it can teachers take when they suspect child abuse? What can teachers do about suspected sexual abuse, neglect, and emotional abuse? Whose responsibility is it?

(Texas Juvenile Probation Commission, 1993). Figure 8-3 illustrates the frequency of all crimes committed by juveniles in one state during the course of one year.

Analysis of juvenile referrals suggests that the continual rise in violent crime is directly related to two factors: extensive growth in gang-related crimes and increased substance abuse-related crimes. We will return to the important issues of gangs and substance abuse in the chapter on adolescents.

Many youth with emotional/behavioral disorders have histories of arrests or other incidences of lawbreaking. The police and the courts have discretionary powers that allow great latitude in dealing with juvenile offenders. Before making a court referral, police can use a number of alternatives, such as verbal warnings with release to parent custody, referral to a social agency, or temporary custody at the police station. According to one report, about half of all juvenile arrests are dealt with by police and never reach the courts (Atwater, 1983). When a youngster is taken to court for an offense, the judge may let him off with a warning, give him probation, or assign him to a restricted setting such as a group home, halfway house, detention center, or correctional facility. For example, in 1992 in Texas, 136,415 juveniles ages 10 to 17 who were arrested for offenses were handled in the following ways: 48 percent were counseled, diverted, or dismissed by juvenile probation, 20 percent were dismissed or disposed of by the court, 16 percent were handled by informal adjustment procedures, 14 percent were assigned to court-ordered probation, and 2 percent were committed to the correctional system (Texas Juvenile Probation Commission, 1993). Thus, by the time a

TEXAS JUVENILE PROBATION COMMISSION

TEXAS JUVENILE CRIME CLOCK

One Delinquent Conduct Referral *to a Juvenile Probation Department* Every 6½ Minutes

One Violent Crime Referral Every 73 Minutes

One Homicide Referral Every 28 Hours

One Sexual Assault Referral Every 6 Hours

One Robbery Referral Every 4 Hours

One Aggravated Assault Referral Every 3 Hours

One Property Crime Referral Every 15 Minutes

One Burglary Referral Every 38 Minutes

One Theft Referral Every 36 Minutes

One Motor Vehicle Theft Referral Every 73 Minutes

One Other Delinquent Referral Every 14 Minutes

One Other Felony Referral Every 70 Minutes

One Other Non-Felony Delinquent Referral Every 17 Minutes

FIGURE 8-3   Texas Juvenile Probation Commission

From Texas Juvenile Probation Commission, Eleventh Annual Report, *The Second Decade*. October 1993, Austin, TX.

juvenile offender is assigned to probation or a correctional facility, he has usually been arrested and/or taken to juvenile court several times.

Depending on the severity and chronicity of their offenses, many juvenile offenders are still placed in detention centers (short-term) or youth correctional facilities (long-term). As in adult correctional facilities, the alleged goal of these juvenile treatment centers is rehabilitation of the individual for a productive life in the mainstream of society. Unfortunately, institutionalized youth often become more antisocial during their incarceration, resulting in low rates of rehabilitation. Recognizing the ineffectiveness of incarceration as a rehabilitative experience, many correctional programs are offering alternatives such as group homes, juvenile boot camps, and intensive supervision programs marked by close surveillance, home detention, and electronic monitoring.

The public education system is usually responsible for youth placed in community-based programs. The teacher often will need to work with parents, houseparents, or probation officers on matters of school attendance and other conditions of probation. The correctional system is responsible for the education of juveniles placed in institutional settings. For juvenile offenders who are identified as disabled, state education agencies are legally responsible for monitoring the quality of education and ensuring that the safeguards of federal law are met. However, in many states, educational programs within correctional facilities are the responsibility of corrections, mental health, or human service agencies other than education (Rutherford, Nelson, & Wolford, 1986). Teachers should be aware of the potential clash between the custodial and educational functions of the correctional system, which may exacerbate the difficulties in ensuring delivery of quality education for the handicapped offender (Rutherford et al., 1986).

A comprehensive data base detailing the state of the art for special education in juvenile corrections has not been established. A study by Rutherford et al. (1986) cited several problems based on a survey of 15 state directors of correctional education. There was considerable variability among states in the numbers of certified special education teachers employed, and a shortage of certified teachers relative to the population with disabilities. Also cited were a lack of special education assessment procedures and lack of functional skills curricula. Three special education program prototypes were reported: self-contained, resource, and mainstream with regular correctional education.

Some specific recommendations for special educators wanting to work with correctional educators were offered by Coffey (1983), who suggested the following: (1) offering to train and assist court and correctional personnel in needed areas, particularly ramifications of laws governing special education; (2) assisting in developing model programs that can be disseminated; and (3) joining the Correctional Education Association.

Since the mid-1980s, an increased concern over the identification and education of juvenile offenders has been evidenced and will likely continue. One model program utilizing a systems approach to educating and rehabilitating delinquent youth is described in Box 8-4.

Mental Health System

It is a certainty that teachers of students with emotional/behavioral disorders will at some time come in contact with members of the mental health system. Psychologists or psychiatrists are usually responsible for diagnosing emotional/behavioral disorders; they may subsequently

---

BOX 8-4 STRIVE: Help with Emotional/Behavioral Disorders

One of the most challenging groups of students with disabilities is juvenile offenders with E/BD. The complex needs of these students can be met only through cooperative programming by schools, human service agencies, and law enforcement officials. STRIVE[1] in Sheboygan, Wisconsin, is one such program.

After three years of joint planning among various agencies, STRIVE began operating in 1980 and has since served over 200 youth. The program is a comprehensive self-contained program for adolescents ages 12–21 with emotional/behavioral disorders, 97 percent of whom are juvenile offenders. It employs six teachers certified in emotional disturbance, eight aides, four full-time social workers, a social work supervisor, a job training specialist, a secretary, and an administrator.

Truancy is a major contributor to juvenile crime. Therefore, STRIVE takes extensive measures to ensure 100 percent attendance. Staff ride the buses to school with students in order to provide counseling and assistance in transit. If a student refuses to come to school, staff obtain parental permission, enter the home, and firmly escort the reluctant student to the bus. If a student disappears from home or school, a search is undertaken that involves personnel from all involved agencies including law enforcement. When the student is found, his/her school day begins and runs its full course, regardless of the time of day or night.

Lack of education and meaningful employment are additional contributors to juvenile crime. As a result, assistance is provided to STRIVE students to help them obtain high school diplomas or the general equivalency diploma (GED). All students are also enrolled in a job training program consisting of four progressive components: individual assessment/career awareness, job responsibilities, job station, and community involvement.

As one of the primary goals is to maintain students in their homes, the program provides assis-

tance and support to parents through the social workers who work directly with the families via systems theory and family-based services.

A 1987 follow-up study indicated that approximately 150 students had received services from STRIVE. Of this sample, 85 percent had either graduated from high school or received their GED, 87 percent had passed all of the required minimum competency tests, and 75 percent were employed full-time in the community. Although almost all students had previously been involved in serious juvenile crime, only 7 % committed serious crimes after leaving the program, and only three individuals were incarcerated in adult penal institutions.

Interviews further substantiate the success of the STRIVE program. As one former student put it, "Do I like the STRIVE program? Hell, no! I hated it when I was there, but if it wasn't for the program I would not be working today, and I would probably be dead from drugs." Employers report that they look forward to employing STRIVE students because they possess many skills lacking in other workers. Police officers report a substantial reduction in the number of criminal activities.

The success of STRIVE is the result of a strong partnership among the schools, the department of human services, the police department, and private business. Even after eleven years, continuation of the partnership is a challenging and difficult task. However, it is an unavoidable task if we are to have a significant impact on the lives of juvenile offenders with emotional/behavioral disorders.

Contributed by Michael Weber, Ph.D., former STRIVE administrator and current Superintendent, Glenwood City Schools, Wisconsin
[1]STRIVE is an acronym for Sheboygan Area Treatment for Reintegration Through Involvement in Vocation and Education.

---

see students in individual or group therapy. In many states, social workers also are licensed therapists, as are licensed professional counselors. Some school systems contract with therapists in private practice for such services, while others depend upon the personnel in their local mental health centers for these services. The centers are usually staffed by psychologists, psychiatrists, social workers, and licensed professional counselors, who may vary widely in background, training, and theoretical orientation. Outpatient services also vary but usually include diagnostic services, psychotherapy or counseling, chemotherapy, group therapy, and consultation to parents and local school systems. Many centers have outreach programs aimed at promoting mental health and preventing alcohol and drug abuse. Mental health agencies are increasingly turning to schools as the site of services delivery, especially support groups and substance abuse prevention groups. Depending on local resources, inpatient services may be provided in hospitals, halfway houses, or other residential settings.

Two mental health interventions for children and youth with emotional/behavioral disorders that have been popular over the years are institutionalization and use of medication. Based upon the recommendation of child specialists, youngsters with E/BD may still be placed in institutional settings or prescribed psychotropic medication. As Hobbs (1982) points out, these practices are contrary to a systems orientation because each isolates the child as the sole focal point of intervention:

> *Often wisdom lies simply in* not *doing something that may impede the restoration of the ecosystem, such as institutionalizing the child or prescribing tranquilizing drugs. Both of these acts create abnormal situations; they cut off or distort feedback of information needed to modify or redirect behavior, and thereby impair an essential component of the regulatory process in all living systems. From an ecological perspective, the widespread practice of sending disturbed children out of a state for treatment elsewhere makes no sense at all. This convenient but expensive practice makes it impossible to build a sustaining eco-system for the child and thus impedes a return to normal patterns of development. (Hobbs, 1982, p. 186)*

Of course, there are exceptions such as suicidal, violent or other maladaptive behavior that indicate an urgent need for drastic measures such as hospitalization or medication. However, the conventional wisdom appears to be changing in favor of keeping children in the home environment and local community whenever possible by providing the family with sufficient support and resources needed to maintain the child at home. Backed by federal legislation and public health funding, this trend is called *family preservation* and is available—but not limited—to children with emotional difficulties. Services falling under *family preservation* include developmental screening, information and referral, improvement of parenting skills, family therapy, case management services, parent support groups, drop-in centers, and emergency and routine respite care. States and local communities may also develop plans for other services tailored to the specific needs of families in their area. Family preservation recognizes the importance of helping the family maintain its integrity as a unit capable of caring for itself. The nationwide trend toward family preservation programming should also result in fewer out-of-home placements for children and youth with emotional/behavioral disorders, resulting in declining enrollments in institutions and residential treatment centers.

Systems Changes

A number of obstacles inherent in the education, social, juvenile justice, and mental health systems have traditionally impeded services delivery:

Services not tailored to the needs of individual clients
Poor working relationships among agencies
Decision makers who do not perceive the need for services
Lack of appropriate planning for services
Prohibitive cost of mental health services
Inability to reach potential clients
Political and social resistance to change
Medical model that focuses on pathology rather than preventative services
Lack of clear definition of mental health
Services that dehumanize and frustrate clients (Apter, 1982).

The need for systems changes, i.e., changes in the ways in which services are conceptualized and delivered, has garnered national attention. In 1984, the National Institute of Mental Health funded a technical assistance program, CASSP (Child and Adolescent Service System Program) to guide the work of states and communities trying to effect systems change in mental health services for children. The CASSP model is a set of principles for planning and delivering such services. CASSP is based on a number of important assumptions:

- The system of care must be child-centered and family-driven.
- Services should be community-based.
- Real interagency coordination and cooperation are essential.
- Services must be culturally sensitive.
- The youngsters with the most severe disorders must be served by the system.
- A balance of least restrictive to most restrictive options should be maintained.

In addition, the basic guiding principles of CASSP promote early identification and prevention services, case management for integrated services, individualization of services, and emphasis on transition to adult service systems. Due to the funding of statewide development grants, CASSP has aided in systems changes in many states by attacking the very obstacles just outlined. Figure 8-4 illustrates this child-centered, multiagency approach, and Box 8-5 describes how one community has implemented these principles.

Another needed systems change is a more effective use of resources. One-to-one treatment programs reach only a small segment of the population and are not cost-effective: there will never be enough trained specialists in any of the systems to deal on an individual basis with the social, legal, and mental health problems existing in our society. Hobbs (1982) estimated that if all the psychiatrists and clinical psychologists and one-third of the social workers and psychiatric nurses in this country were available to work with children with E/BD, their individual caseloads would be approximately 360 children at any given time. Some school systems and mental health systems are attempting to combat this problem by shifting to a consultation model in which trained personnel give direct services to a mediating person (such as a teacher or counselor) who can then use the acquired skills with a number of others. The purpose of the consultation model is to build a broader base of expertise within the system.

By adopting a consultation model, school districts can make inroads toward changing the system to better accommodate not only students with E/BD, but also other students with

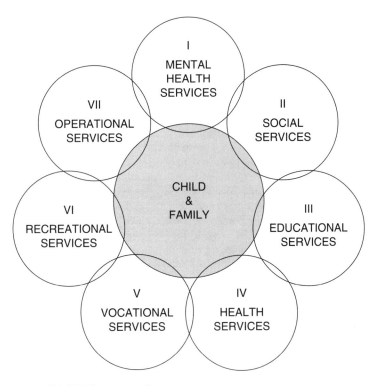

FIGURE 8-4   CASSP Framework

special needs. In the next section, we will consider various roles, including consulting, that can be taken by special education teachers with a systems orientation.

The Teacher's Role

Teacher as Consultant

Proponents of a consultation model within schools suggest that consultation can not only build a broader base of expertise within the system (West & Idol, 1987), but also can reallocate resources from the traditional test-and-place sequence to a refer-and-consult sequence (Graden, Casey, & Christenson, 1985). However, even proponents of consultation are aware of its limitations: that increased expertise of regular educators as a result of consultation has not been clearly established in research (Carter, 1989), and that resistance to the process on the part of teachers and administrators may impede its adoption in many school districts (Idol & West, 1987).

Despite these limitations, enthusiasm persists for the special education teacher in a consulting role. Consultation with general education teachers is touted as means to "(a) improving communication between general and special education, (b) collaborating on instructional programs for handicapped students in mainstreamed settings, (c) sharing the

BOX 8-5 A Children's Mental Health Partnership

Faced with limited funding for children's mental health services, communities across the country have sought interagency collaboration as a means of pooling resources and stretching dollars. In Travis County, Texas, children and families have benefited from a state-initiated collaboration that has brought local mental health providers and families together to develop a comprehensive community-based system of services.

The Travis County Children's Mental Health Partnership has its roots in a legislative appropriation of over $22 million that began in the 1992 biennium and has continued to be funded. Nine state agencies were mandated to work together to develop a community-based range of mental health and related services for children with serious emotional, behavioral, and mental disorders. The program is administered at the state level by an interagency management team and a project director. Similarly, each local project is administered by a project director and a community management team composed of representatives of the nine participating agencies. These agencies and departments include health, child protective and regulatory services, education, juvenile justice, juvenile corrections, early childhood intervention, rehabilitation, mental health, and the alcohol and drug abuse commission.

Each local community management team is charged with (a) ensuring a continuum of preventive, early intervention, and treatment services, (b) improving the coordination and delivery of services to children and their families, (c) identifying unmet needs and developing programs to meet those needs, and (d) ensuring that services are family-focused and culturally comprehensive. Implicit is the idea that by coordinating and streamlining services among agencies, finances will be maximized, i.e., more and better services will result from the same limited resources.

The community management team and a parent advisory group meet monthly to review progress and plan for the future. In Travis County, the community management team identified gaps in services and decided to offer the following programs:

• Parents as Teachers provides in-home training for parents of children up to three years of age.

• School-based Services, offered on a pilot basis to students in two schools, include both school- and home-based therapeutic interventions.

• Family Preservation Program provides home-based intervention to families in which there is a child at risk for removal from the home due to a mental health problem. Services include family therapy, individual therapy, group therapy, crisis intervention, case coordination, advocacy, and parent training skills. When a child is returning from out-of-home care, reunification services are provided.

• Child and Adolescent Psychiatric Emergency Team provides crisis assessment and intervention around the clock, seven days a week, to youth who are experiencing a psychiatric emergency. A walk-in clinic and a mobile unit both can respond wherever the crisis is occurring. Follow-up services are available for 30 days.

• Therapeutic Foster Care serves children and youth in need of a structured home environment.

After two years in operation, the members of the community management team seem to have developed an informal camaraderie. In addition, the prevailing mentality seems to have shifted from turf issues to a focus on what can be done to meet the needs of the children and their families. Although more work remains to be done, many of the barriers to providing these much-needed services are gradually being overcome.

Contributed by Ann Stanley, Project Director, and Maggie Coleman, Community Management Team member

expertise of the special educator, and (d) facilitating effective instruction for low achieving students" (Carter, 1989, p. 235).

Within this framework, the consulting teacher is viewed as a support person who shares information. Consultation is viewed as an ongoing relationship that should be handled as a peer relationship rather than a leader-follower relationship. Duties of the consulting teacher include: observation in the classroom; assessment; help with creating lesson plans, management strategies, and the individual education plan; locating needed materials; in-class demonstration sessions, and suggestions for other modifications in the general education program.

The role of the consulting teacher may be the most demanding of all possible teacher roles because of the sensitive nature of this position within the social system of the school. The school is a self-contained community with its own rules and regulations, some of which are verbalized, some of which are "understood." Montgomery (1982) offers an excellent description of these political realities, which include (1) territoriality of teachers, who assume responsibility for and ownership of their assigned group of students, and (2) the view that consultants are imposed by the system rather than invited by the regular teacher and are therefore intruders rather than helpers. Montgomery offers some suggestions for overcoming these barriers. The consulting teacher can help overcome territoriality by referring to the special education students as belonging to the general education classroom teacher and by being unobtrusive when visiting in the general education classroom. When observing, the consulting teacher can increase acceptance by simple courtesies such as obtaining prior permission, not taking notes, staying seated in one place rather than moving about the room, and offering the teacher positive feedback. It is helpful to have a written job description so that everyone has a clear idea of what the consulting teacher is supposed to do. To be successful, the consulting teacher must be the ultimate diplomat and must be skilled at pointing out both the positive aspects of the regular program as well as needed modifications.

Despite philosophical support for the consulting model among special educators, the reality is that consultation has not been widely adopted in the public schools (Idol-Maestas & Ritter, 1985; Idol & West, 1987). Most proponents agree that consultation requires specific training and that the consulting teacher is more than a resource teacher who spends time consulting (Huefner, 1988). It appears that colleges and universities must make a systems change and begin to teach consultation as a special education role before it can become a viable option for school districts.

Teacher as Liaison

Another role that is essential for teachers from a systems perspective is that of liaison among the many individuals who are involved in the lives of their students. As previously mentioned, students with emotional/behavioral disorders are likely to be involved in systems other than education, such as juvenile justice, social-welfare, and/or mental health. Coordinating services between these agencies may not be in the job description of the special education teacher, but if progress is to be made in the lives of the students, someone has to assume that role. Although the special education teacher may need not to serve as a formal case manager, he can keep in touch with representatives of the other agencies so that he is aware of services being offered and problems in other settings.

The liaison role requires many of the diplomatic skills mentioned under the consulting role. Although there are many similarities between the two roles, the consulting teacher works within the social system of the school, and the liaison teacher works with other social systems in the community. As Hobbs (1982) has indicated, a liaison

> *. . . is interested in what it is that keeps ecosystems from working; she is not interested in what is wrong with people—not the child, or the parents, or teachers, or others. The question is: What needs to be changed in order for the system to work reasonably well? (p. 217)*

Apter (1982) offers some general suggestions for teachers who wish to fulfill a liaison role:

> *Work with the Child*
>   *Build new competencies.*
>   *Change priorities.*
>   *Obtain necessary resources.*
>   *Find more appropriate settings.*
> *Work with the Adults*
>   *Alter perceptions.*
>   *Raise or lower expectations.*
>   *Increase understanding or knowledge.*
>   *Restructure activities.*
> *Work with the Community*
>   *Bring more resources into the school.*
>   *Allow more entry into community.*
>   *Develop coordinating ties.*
> *Develop New Roles*
>   *Consulting teacher.*
>   *Diagnostic-prescriptive teacher.*
>   *"Linking" person (liaison).*
> *Develop New Program Models*
>   *Community education/schools.*
>   *Outdoor education.*
>   *Alternative public schools.*
>   *Focus on prevention.*
>   *Teach "mental health."*
>   *Preventive mainstreaming. (Apter, 1982, pp. 70–71)*

Although the specific activities undertaken by liaison teachers will vary, it is important for these teachers to embody a systems orientation. The key to a systems orientation is attitudinal: respect for the goals of other systems, a nonterritorial view of services, and a willingness to share both the responsibilities and rewards for providing services. When planning programs and services for students with emotional/behavioral disorders, representatives from all the systems—education, social, juvenile justice, and mental health—have many opportunities to extend these courtesies to one another.

Teacher as Part of a Social System

Nelson (1983) has articulated a number of suggestions for the teacher who recognizes the need to work both within and outside the education system for the benefit of her students. Nelson cautions that a prerequisite for effective collaboration is that the teacher must have already established credibility as a teacher who models good instruction and behavior management; i.e., if her students often create disturbances within the building, not many teachers will want to work with her. Nelson's recommendations for working with school personnel include:

1. *Be visible within the school.* Visibility can be increased by accepting all "general ed" duties such as cafeteria duty or club sponsorship, working and socializing where other teachers work and socialize rather than staying confined to your room, and creating opportunities for your students to mix with other students and staff.

2. *Recruit reinforcement for yourself.* Learn about all your colleagues in the school and enlist their aid for tasks they can easily perform (e.g., the janitor may build a study carrel for you). Offer support to those who are also working with your students.

3. *Encourage the school administration to reinforce your students and the staff who work with them.* Principals often set the tone for the entire school's attitude toward students with special needs. Ask the vice principal or disciplinarian to praise or reward your students when warranted, thereby serving as a source of positive reinforcement as well as punishment.

4. *Find reinforcing activities for your students around the school that involve other school staff.* Examples are intramural sports and clubs. Be prepared to assist when interaction problems arise.

5. *When asking for assistance from others, be specific.* If asking a teacher to "watch" one of your students outside your classroom, list specific behaviors that you have been working on, such as pushing, pulling or other physical contact with peers.

When working with persons outside the school from the other systems, Nelson (1983) offers the following:

1. *Be aware of political realities.* Although it is natural for dedicated teachers to assume that they are primarily responsible for their students' salvation, this view is not generally held by human service agencies. Credibility must be established through helping these systems attain their goals and refraining from designing interventions that may conflict with those of other agencies.

2. *Practice underdogmanship.* Give credit to others even when you have been instrumental in a student's success. For example, credit the probation officer even if you devised a successful plan to decrease shoplifting.

3. *Avoid language barriers.* All human service systems are full of technical language and acronyms that serve as a type of shorthand within the system but are alienating to professionals outside the system. For example, practice not saying "IEP" or using the term "task analysis" when talking to other professionals outside education.

4. *Take the responsibility to initiate and maintain contact wih other agencies.* Don't wait for others to contact you and inform you about what's happening with your students.

Be persistent in maintaining contact and don't mistake others' lack of initiative as indifference. The caseloads of social workers, child protective caseworkers, probation/parole officers, and publicly funded mental health workers often approach the impossible.

5. *Clarify the roles and responsibilities of various agencies in writing.* Have a multi-agency committee devise an individualized, written plan outlining what services are to be provided to the student, who is responsible for following through, and timelines.

Conclusions

A systems approach to intervention requires changes in students' homes and in their communities. Although working with parents of students with emotional/behavioral disorders may not be easy, it is important that teachers work with parents whenever possible by offering several alternatives for involvement. Also, many of these youngsters have multiple problems that necessitate the involvement of several community systems with them and their families. Professionals from all systems are recognizing the futility of providing fragmented services and are becoming very vocal about providing a community-based continuum of services that is coordinated by case managers. To operate effectively within systems, teachers must be aware of political realities—both within the school and relative to other community agencies.

Key Points

1. Research on parenting styles suggests that the parent-child relationship is best viewed as a reciprocal one, with each party shaping the behavior of the other.
2. A systems approach to working with families assumes that the child with emotional/behavioral disorders is a symptom of difficulties with the family system that can best be rectified through working with all family members as a unit.
3. Because parents of students with E/BD have historically been blamed for their children's difficulties, it is important for teachers to avoid blaming statements when talking with or about the parents.
4. The first step in parent conferencing is getting them there.
5. Within the education system, reintegration of students from more restrictive to less restrictive settings is fraught with difficulties.
6. The ability to work with professionals from other community systems is an important skill for teachers of students with emotional/behavioral disorders; more and more frequently, multiagency systems approaches are being implemented across the country.
7. Teachers operating from a systems perspective can fill consultant or liaison roles.
8. Effective special education teachers recognize their place in the mini-social system of the school and are able to create their own bridges to other people and resources within the system.

Additional Readings

Conferencing with parents of exceptional children, by Richie Simpson, 1990. Austin, TX: Pro-Ed, for a practical guide to conferencing and working with parents.

Doing things differently: Issues & Options, by M. McLaughlin, P. Leone, S. Warren, and P. Schofield, June, 1994. The Center for Policy Options in Special Education, College Park, MD: University of Maryland, for the very latest thinking on how to restructure services for E/BD children. Four specific issues are addressed: designing interagency services delivery, including families, establishing outcomes for students, and improving personnel training.

Integrating services for children and youth with emotional and behavioral disorders, by C. Michael Nelson and Cheryll Pearson, 1991. Reston, VA: Council for Exceptional Children, for a handbook describing some of the issues (and solutions) to interagency programming for students with E/BD.

Special education programming in juvenile corrections, by Rob Rutherford, C. Michael Nelson, and Bruce Wolford, *Remedial and Special Education, 7,* 1986, 27–33 for an article describing the relationship between the two systems.

The fact and fiction of consultation, by J.F. Carter, *Academic Therapy, 25,* 1989, 231–242, for a research-based overview of the consulting teacher model in special education.

$$C \quad h \quad a \quad p \quad t \quad e \quad r \quad \mathit{9}$$

Adolescents

Developmental Changes

Dealing with Adolescent Issues:
Drop-outs, Sex, Drugs, Gangs, Self-destructive Behavior

Interventions:
Career Training, Behavioral Strategies, Counseling and Groups

Orientation

The fine line between deviant and nondeviant behavior during adolescence is implied by Morse's observation that "All secondary teachers are teachers of disturbed adolescents" (1969a, p. 442). It is common for today's adolescent to experiment with drugs and sex and to evidence many other forms of behavior that can be characterized as "borderline deviant." In addition to experimenting, which is a normal part of adolescence, adolescents with emotional/behavioral disorders evidence extremeness of behavior and maladaptive coping patterns which result in their being labeled. If you plan to teach this population, you should be prepared to deal with numerous problems that are not as often found in younger children.

Overview

The mere use of the term *adolescence* generally evokes images of awkwardness, self-consciousness, and conflict. Adolescents typically experience a period of rapid changes in physical, cognitive, and social development which they enter into as children and emerge from as adults. The first section of this chapter explores some of the major issues plaguing adolescents during these years and causing friction between them and the adults in their lives. The primary adolescent issues that educators must deal with in the schools are related to dropping out, sex, drugs, gangs, and self-destructive behavior.

Experimentation is a natural part of adolescent development. The majority of adolescents experiment and then eventually adopt social behaviors that allow them to function as young adults in society. In contrast, adolescents with emotional/behavioral disorders fail to learn coping strategies that allow them to adapt. Behavioral and counseling interventions are often necessary to help them learn more acceptable ways of coping.

Although development of educational services for adolescents with E/BD has lagged behind services for children with E/BD, many school systems have established successful model programs for this population. A prevocational model program for adolescents with emotional/behavioral disorders is reviewed at the end of the chapter.

Defining Adolescence and Emotional/behavioral Disorders in Adolescence

Adults sometimes cynically regard adolescence as a "disease" that only time can cure, suggesting that parents would do well to bury their offspring at age 12 and dig them up again at age 20. At the same time, some critics contend that adolescence has become artificially prolonged as a "tribal subculture," so that there is little assurance of adulthood even at 20. (Atwater, 1983, p. 1)

Adolescence is a developmental period of the human growth cycle occurring between the ages of approximately 12 and 20. For most individuals, it is an awkward period in which they are no longer considered children but have not yet attained adult status. The onset of adolescence is generally considered to be marked by the rapid physiological changes occurring during puberty. The demise of adolescence is less well-defined by markers such as legal independence and the acquisition of adult responsibilities. There is no clearly defined upper limit of adolescence, or age at which individuals officially pass over from adolescence into adulthood. Unlike many primitive cultures which clearly separate childhood from adulthood by ceremonial rites of passage, our modern culture allows the individual nearly a decade of preparation for the responsibilities of adulthood. Adolescence is best defined as the period of transition from childhood to adulthood, a period of flux in which the adolescent may act as mature and responsible as any adult on one day and then revert to childish behavior the next. Adolescence is a time in which individuals redefine their identities based on rapidly changing potential in many areas of their lives.

Developmental Changes

Studies of the modern adolescent reveal upheaval in three developmental areas: physical, cognitive, and personal-social.

Physical

Rapid changes in physical development mark the onset of puberty and the adolescent period. Hormonal secretions from the hypothalamus and pituitary gland are responsible for physiological changes manifested in growth spurts of height and weight, and in sexual maturation. Girls generally become sexually mature and capable of reproduction between ages 11 and 13, and reach their approximate adult height and weight at about age 15 or 16. Boys mature sexually at age 13 or 14 and reach their approximate adult stature at age 17 or 18. Commensurate changes in skeletal and muscular structure also occur during this period. Such drastic physiological changes in the adolescent require an adjustment in body image which may be reflected in self-concept. As they attempt to adjust mentally to their rapidly developing physiques, adolescents can become preoccupied with physical characteristics and attractiveness. They are sensitive to societal standards of beauty and are often highly self-critical. Girls tend to be more concerned about their physical appearance than boys who tend to be more concerned about physical competence or prowess. Another issue is the age at which an individual matures; while early maturers may be thrust into social situations which they are not yet prepared to handle, late maturers often experience undue anxiety about their development.

Cognitive Changes

In addition to physiological changes, the onset of puberty generally is accompanied by an increasing capacity for complex and abstract thought. In Piaget's theory of cognitive development, adolescence corresponds with the stage of *formal operational thought*. Formal thought is marked by the ability to think abstractly and to hypothesize. In contrast to the previous childhood stage of concrete thought, which is limited to perceived reality, formal thought encompasses hypothetical possibilities (Inhelder & Piaget, 1958). This shift from the real to the possible enables an individual to generate and discard hypotheses (hypothetico-deductive reasoning), much like the scientist does. For example, younger children usually generate a single explanation for an event based on their perception, and they are unable to discard this explanation even when subsequent experience proves them wrong; the child's perception *is* her reality. Adolescents in the formal operations stage are able to discard an explanation when it fails to fit the facts and are able to generate other possible explanations. Hypotheses are secondary to reality (Inhelder & Piaget, 1958). Other characteristics of formal thought include increased flexibility and imagination, and capacity for logic and propositional thought ("if-then" hypotheses).

Some implications of formal thought in adolescents are summarized by Atwater (1983):

> *The emergence of abstract thought at this age helps to explain much characteristic adolescent behavior. For one thing, it helps to explain why adolescents become so idealistic and romantic on the one hand, yet more critical and cynical on the other. It also explains why adolescents are so busy clarifying their own identity, yet suffer from the accompanying conflicts and confusion. The newly discovered capacity for abstract thought may also explain the characteristic self-centeredness of this stage of life. (p. 72)*

Although formal thought generally is acquired between the ages of 12 and 16, there is much variation among individuals in capability for formal thought. Some adolescents and adults never attain it. Most cognitive development theorists, including Piaget (1972), now recognize that formal thought is not automatically attained, but can be facilitated through appropriate educational experiences. Effects of social class and intelligence on the acquisition of formal thought have been found to be negligible (Kuhn & Angelev, 1976; Neimark, 1975).

Personal and Social Changes

Along with physical and cognitive changes, adolescents experience tremendous upheaval in personal ideology and social relationships. The old rules of childhood suddenly don't work any more. The adolescent is thrust into a period of experimentation with new rules, new roles, and an emerging concept of a new self. Three major personal-social changes that occur during this period are noteworthy: searches for identity, independence, and peer approval.

The *search for identity* involves the individual's attempt to integrate the old childhood self with potential for a new adult self. Erikson (1968) dubbed this phenomenon "identity versus role confusion" and included it as the fifth stage of the eight stages of psychosocial development, as discussed in Chapter 3. According to Erikson, the search for self is a normal developmental process that may reach crisis proportions but must be resolved if optimal personal growth is to be attained. Conflict, anxiety, self-doubt, and experimentation are all part of the process as adolescents try to find out who they are and what distinguishes them as individuals from their peers. This period is also marked by egocentrism or extreme self-centeredness, during which individuals may become painfully self-conscious. This acute self-consciousness is illustrated by Elkind's (1974) concept of the *imaginary audience,* in which adolescents feel as though they are constantly being watched and evaluated by everyone as if on stage and performing for an audience. A preoccupation with others' perceptions is the major outcome of this stage of egocentrism.

A certain degree of role confusion is unavoidable as the individual tries out various points of view and periodically adopts new styles of interacting, but role confusion is detrimental when it becomes so extreme that the individual loses the boundaries of self. Extreme role confusion and loss of sense of self are frequently found among adolescents with severe disorders (e.g., psychosis). Another difficulty is the adoption of a negative identity, which often happens when adolescents have no positive role models to emulate (Hauser, 1972). Many youth from impoverished communities or unhappy homes turn to delinquency or gangs as ways to establish an identity, albeit an unacceptable one by society's standards.

A second major issue for adolescents is the *development of independence* or autonomy. While not wanting to jeopardize the emotional security provided by the home, the adolescent constantly struggles to establish a legitimate identity separate from parents. Increased self-sufficiency and decision making are a large part of independence, yet adolescents do not consistently manifest these skills even when acquired; rather, an individual may be unusually mature and self-sufficient in one moment and quite dependent the next. Such fluctuations make teenagers' behavior difficult to predict and sometimes exasperating for adults to deal with.

Open rejection of parental values and questioning of authority are classic symptoms of developing independence. The home is typically the focal point of conflict over independence issues, as the adolescent wants to have more decision-making power, to be afforded some privileges, and generally to take more control of her life. Issues that cause conflict in most families of adolescents are dress, use of the family car, dating, daily chores, school performance, and use of drugs (Atwater, 1983). The parents' sense of authority and the adolescent's sense of increasing autonomy are challenged by the almost daily conflicts that arise over these issues. Various influences on parent-child conflicts are summarized in Table 9-1.

TABLE 9-1   Some Influences on Parent-Adolescent Conflicts

AGE: Although the number of conflicts tends to decrease with age, older adolescents pose more serious conflicts involving the use of the car, sex, or drugs.

SEX: The frequency and type of conflict tend to vary by sex. According to one study, family problems made up 22 percent of the difficulties reported by adolescent girls, but only 10 percent of those reported by boys. Parents are more likely to have conflicts with their sons over taking care of property or use of cars.

SOCIAL CLASS: The type of conflict often reflects social-class values. Working-class families tend to worry more about their teenagers' being obedient, polite, and staying out of trouble in school. Middle-class families tend to be more concerned about their teenagers' taking the initiative, being competitive, and doing well in school.

FAMILY SIZE: The larger the size of the family, the more parent-adolescent conflicts occur, and the more often parents use force in settling such conflicts. However, this is true mostly for middle-class families; the efforts to control conflicts do not vary with the size of working-class families.

PARENTAL AUTHORITY AND FAMILY ATMOSPHERE: An unhappy marriage or home life tends to increase parent-adolescent conflicts; unhappily married, authoritarian parents evoke the most conflicts.

TOPICS: Common sources of conflicts are dress, daily chores, use of the car, dating, and use of cigarettes or alcohol. Other conflicts of special concern to both generations are staying out late and school performance, especially failure at school. Some of the most heated conflicts occur over sex and drugs.

A third and extremely important change that occurs in the lives of adolescents is the *shift in allegiance from family to peers*. Peer approval supersedes most other social aspirations at this point in the individual's development. An inordinate amount of time is spent in cultivating friendships and dating relationships, and for many teenagers the telephone becomes an essential instrument for gathering information about the rapidly changing social scene at school.

The adolescent's emerging identity is closely allied with peer approval and acceptance. Social acceptance is generally based on social conformity; to be "in," one must speak, dress, look, and act like everyone else. Although the styles change over the years, each generation creates a "fringe" element, which is the ultimate adolescent statement of identity through conformity. (Consider the beatniks of the fifties, the hippies of the sixties, preppies of the seventies, and punks of the eighties.) The generation gap is often purposefully widened by use of lingo and slang.

In addition to seeking acceptance from the larger peer group, many adolescents seek further support from cliques, which are small, informal groups of friends who do things together. These cliques are loosely structured but usually identifiable within a school or neighborhood setting. While some cliques are based on common interests such as music or sports, others are based on popularity or status within the system. Gangs also fulfill the adolescent need for peer acceptance.

Although all adolescents experience some degree of pressure from peers, the amount of needed peer approval varies widely. The ultimate resolution of the need for peer acceptance depends in part on the quality of the parent-adolescent relationship. With parents who are perceived as nonsupportive, rejecting, or punitive in other ways, the individual may respond with a total shift of allegiance from family to the peer group. For adolescents whose parents are perceived as understanding and supportive, a gradual transition can be made from total reliance on the family to a more balanced sense of self-acceptance, which includes but is not limited to peer approval. This transition may not be complete until the individual is well into adulthood. The need for peer approval has a strong impact on motivation and therefore has many implications for the classroom setting, which will be addressed later in this chapter.

In summary, the entire adolescent experience is best viewed as a normal developmental process of identity redefinition. As Schmid and Slade note, all adolescent behavior is an "experimentation to successfully adapt to the demands of life," and is meaningful when viewed in this context (1981, p. 369). The struggles between parent and teenager, and between teacher and teenager over issues such as school attendance, grades, and social behavior are all part of adolescent experimentation. While most adolescents experience stress and exhibit some deviant behavior, they eventually learn the skills that will enable them to cope in an adult world. In contrast, adolecents with E/BD fail to develop these adaptive coping patterns.

The Adolescent with Emotional/behavioral Disorders

What distinguishes adolescents with E/BD from their peers? It is often difficult to determine exactly what constitutes maladaptive, disordered, or deviant behavior during adolescence. McDowell and Brown (1978) note that many definitions of emotional/behavioral disorders include inability to establish appropriate relationships with others, and demonstration of behaviors that fail to meet the expectations of others. Since these characteristics are often found in normal adolescents, deviance in adolescents is more appropriately defined by the frequency or severity of the offending behavior (McDowell, 1981). As in childhood psychopathology, the extremeness of behavior can be considered an underlying characteristic of adolescent psychopathology.

Other researchers have attempted to define emotional/behavioral disorders in adolescents more clearly by identifying specific dimensions of problem behavior. In two studies, researchers asked parents of adolescents referred for mental health services to rate their children on behavior checklists. Results yielded two dimensions of problem behavior: *internalizing* (keeping feelings of distress inside, resulting in depression or psychosomatic symptoms) and *externalizing* (striking out at others or the environment), which have also been identified with younger children (Achenbach & Edelbrock, 1979; L.C. Miller, 1980). In another study, Epstein, Cullinan, and Rosemier (1983) asked teachers to rate the behaviors of adolescents with E/BD and those without E/BD on the BPC, *Behavior Problem Checklist* (Quay & Peterson, 1967). The BPC is composed of four dimensions: Conduct Disorder, Personality Problem, Inadequacy-Immaturity, and Socialized Delinquency; it has been used extensively with children with emotional/behavioral disorders. Epstein et al. (1983) found that adolescents with E/BD were rated as significantly more maladjusted on the Conduct

Disorder and Personality Problem dimensions only; there were no significant differences in ratings on Inadequacy-Immaturity and Socialized Delinquency. Conduct Disorder is characterized by aggressive, hostile, and contentious behavior, and Personality Problem is characterized by anxious, withdrawn, and introvertive behavior. These results are consistent with previous investigations with adolescents that found the two primary dimensions of externalizing and internalizing.

In a review of long-term, follow-up studies, Safer and Heaton (1982) found that children with moderate-to-serious behavior problems were likely to manifest the same difficulties in adolescence and sometimes in adulthood. Based upon research to date, one might surmise that children with emotional/behavioral disorders grow into adolescents with emotional/behavioral disorders, and if the cycle is not broken, into adults with emotional/behavioral disorders. Some adolescents with E/BD are also juvenile offenders.

Dealing with Adolescent Issues in the Schools

Taking into account the extremeness of behavior that is typical of students with emotional/behavioral disorders, educators should expect routinely to be confronted with nonattendance, sex-related problems, substance abuse, gangs, and delinquent and self-destructive behavior. Although the author recognizes that many of these problems, particularly substance abuse and suicide, are also relevant to preadolescents, the issues will be dealt with in a manner that is applicable to younger students as well as adolescents. Prevalence of the problems, ramifications, and possible interventions within the schools are addressed in this section.

Dropping Out

Although compulsory attendance laws have been in effect in most states for several decades, many adolescents do not attend school on a regular basis. Educators traditionally have been unable, through coercion or other means, to motivate a certain proportion of adolescents to regularly attend classes.

Estimates of chronic nonattendance or absenteeism at the junior high level range from 1 percent to 2 percent in middle-class neighborhoods to 15 percent in inner-city schools (Safer & Heaton, 1982). Students in the general population who are chronically absent tend to be male, minority, older, from lower socioeconomic (SES) homes, and have learning problems (Berg, 1985; Fogelman, Tibbenham, & Lambert, 1980). Farrington (1980) found that low attenders are also characterized by social isolation, depression, and problems with discipline. In a study of adolescents with severe emotional/behavioral disorders, Hagborg (1989) found that only student SES and behavioral adjustment distinguished high attenders from low attenders. Gender, race, and age characteristics did not distinguish groups in this population as they did in the general population. High rates of absenteeism are accompanied by school failure and, eventually, high drop-out rates. The drop-out rate for the general population seems to have stabilized at 25 percent. Unfortunately, the drop-out rate for students with emotional/behavioral disorders is over 50 percent , which means that we are losing one out of every two of these students before they graduate (Wagner, 1991). This percentage is not only twice that of the general population, but it is also much higher than for any other special education category.

Factors associated with failure to stay in school generally fall into two broad categories: (1) poor academic performance, especially failure of one or more grades; and (2) family/economic issues such as teenage motherhood, single parent families, and disadvantaged family background necessitating teen employment. The largest contributor to the drop-out rate for female adolescents is pregnancy (Strobino, 1987).

In an effort to keep students in school, many communities have aided schools in developing dropout prevention programs. Services provided through these programs vary but often include individual and peer counseling, tutoring, and social services to families of high-risk students. Some communities offer special classes to teenage parents and on-campus day care services. In addition, many communities have alternative schools or alternative programs for students who do not fare well under the traditional educational system or who have dropped out and wish to re-enroll. For students who have dropped out but wish to obtain the equivalent of a high school diploma, community colleges are a good resource. As students with emotional/behavioral disorders are at risk of dropping out, teachers should become familiar with drop-out prevention/alternative programs offered in their own communities and schools.

Sex-related Problems

It is estimated that 12 million adolescents are sexually active (LeFrancois, 1992). An increasing number of adolescents are becoming sexually active at younger ages, a fact easily explained from a sociological perspective. More permissive attitudes toward sex and trends toward accepting a greater number of options for sexual expression have permeated U.S. culture since the mid-twentieth century. Improved forms of contraception, including the birth-control pill, have made sexual experimentation more appealing to many adolescents. However, despite easier access to information and increasing availability of contraceptives to today's youth, the problems accompanying sexual activity such as premarital pregnancy and sexually transmitted disease have continued to increase. According to one source, more than half of all teen-agers do not use contraception at the time of first intercourse, and a third continue to have intercourse without contraception (Arnett, 1990). These adolescents either remain ignorant about contraceptive information or do not seek out contraceptive devices for a number of reasons, including embarrassment, trusting to luck, and fear of adult reprisal.

Teen Pregnancy

For thousands of adolescents each year, the failure to use contraceptives results in pregnancy. Teen-age mothers account for about 1,000,000 births each year, and the rate for unmarried teen-age mothers giving birth has risen dramatically since 1970 (U.S. Bureau of the Census, 1990). Teen parents are obviously the least prepared emotionally or financially to provide for the needs of an infant or to provide a stable home environment for a growing child. More "high-risk" infants are born to adolescent mothers than to older mothers, thereby increasing the pressures of parenthood. Risk of child abuse increases dramatically under such adverse conditions. The younger the woman, the more likely she is, either single or married, to keep the child. One source estimated that only 4 percent of adolescent mothers give up their infants for adoption (News and Reports, 1981). Although marriage has traditionally been the most socially acceptable option, abortions have also been sought by a large number of adolescents: about 400,000 U.S. teens have abortions each year (Masters, Johnson, & Kolodny, 1988).

Adolescent females most likely to become pregnant are those from homes with a high degree of family disruption (Hogan & Kitgawa, 1985) and who also have the following characteristics: minority status, low socioeconomic status, low achievement and occupational aspirations, and living in a single-parent household (Polit, 1985). One of the most consistent predictors of adolescent pregnancy is low academic achievement, accompanied by low aspirations for employment. It is clear that many teen-age mothers, once they drop out of school, do not return. Thus, they are at-risk for additional pregnancies and inability to take care of themselves financially over the long term. Many experts on teen pregnancy therefore believe that sex education and pregnancy prevention programs must include training of skills related to choosing and gaining appropriate employment (Paget, 1988).

Sexually Transmitted Diseases

Another problem associated with adolescent sexual activity is sexually transmitted disease (STD). Sexually active adolescents are at risk of contracting one of the three most common STDs: gonorrhea, chlamydia, or herpes. Gonorrhea is especially insidious because its symptoms may go unnoticed, resulting in infertility in women and sterility in men. Although a relatively new disease, chlamydia is now the most common STD, with estimates running as high as 10 percent of sexually active females (Lefrancois, 1992). Chlamydia is also insidious, often without symptoms in the early stages; although it can be treated with antibiotics, many women become infertile before the condition is diagnosed. Herpes is a viral infection that is also reaching epidemic proportions and can affect fertility and newborn infants.

Acquired immune deficiency syndrome (AIDS) is another sexually transmitted disease that has reached epidemic proportions among segments of the U.S. population. The fact that AIDS often leads to debilitating illness and death has been well-publicized. AIDS is acquired primarily through direct sexual contact or through injections with a needle contaminated with the virus. Experts assure us that the percentage of AIDS victims acquiring the virus through contaminated blood transfusions has decreased since the implementation of screening donors' blood before accepting it. Having several sexual partners increases the risk of contracting AIDS if precautions are not taken. Although many adolescents are knowledgeable about symptoms and effects of sexually transmitted diseases, a sizeable percentage do not know how to prevent its transmission or what treatment is available in most states without parental permission. Roscoe and Kruger (1990) report that adolescents seem to be knowledgable about AIDS and how it is transmitted; however, only one-third have changed their sexual practices accordingly.

Sexuality Issues

Students with emotional/behavioral disorders may be more susceptible to difficulties with sexuality than their peers. The primary difference in sexual development between adolescents with emotional/behavioral disorders and their peers probably lies in the psychosocial domain (Adrian, 1990). While adolescents with emotional/behavioral disorders usually do not differ from their peers in physical development or the variety of sexual relations they experience, their psychosocial development may have been impaired by many factors, including difficult parent/child relationships, parental substance abuse, conflicting subcultural norms and values, and sexual abuse (Adrian, 1990). They also may experience more conflict than other adolescents over body image and attractiveness. Thus, relating to the opposite sex and developing healthy attitudes toward sexuality may be more difficult for these youth. Realmuto and Erickson (1986) found that adolescents with emotional/behavioral disorders tended to: (1) equate the capacity for sexual intercourse with maturity, (2) equate sexual relationships with personal desirability, and (3) view contraception as an authoritative and punitive demand.

Delinquent sexual behavior among adolescents has not been sufficiently researched to draw many conclusions. Sexual misbehavior by females consists primarily of nonviolent contact with willing male partners, and the only distinctive form of sexual delinquency for female adolescents is prostitution (Erickson, 1984). On the other hand, delinquent sexual behavior by males may either be violent, as in rape, or nonviolent, as in exhibitionism. Child molestation is another sexual offense usually instigated by males. Although there are few empirical studies solely with adolescent sex offenders, there is some evidence that sexual assaults, including rape, are more linked to aggression and to antisocial tendencies than to specific sexuality problems (Erickson, 1984; Lewis, Shanok, & Pincus, 1979). This finding also holds true with adult offenders. Erickson (1984) argues that "there is little that is unique about sexual delinquency, male or female. Arguments in favor of specialized programs must be based on the inadequacy of regular programs (for juvenile offenders) in dealing with sexual matters" (p. 31).

Dealing with Gay and Lesbian Issues

Inclusion of this topic is not meant to imply that gay and lesbian sexual orientations constitute emotional/behavioral disorders. Rather, students with emotional/behavioral disorders who are also gay or lesbian are likely to experience additional stresses related to their sexual orientation. And, as it is generally accepted that ten percent of the population is gay or lesbian (Tievsky, 1988), it is almost a certainty that teachers of students with emotional/behavioral disorders will encounter many gay and lesbian students during their teaching careers.

The basic issue with gay and lesbian youth is not what causes their orientation, whether it is right or wrong, better or worse than a heterosexual orientation; the basic problem is how society reacts to it (Mallon, 1992). And the stresses associated with societal stigmatization make gay and lesbian youth especially vulnerable to psychological problems such as chronic depression, substance abuse, school failure, and relationship problems (Mallon, 1992). Many leave their homes either by force or by choice and turn to foster homes or the streets to live. Further, the suicide rate is higher among gay and lesbian adolescents than among their heterosexual peers.

Adding to these difficulties is the fact that sexual orientation usually emerges during adolescence, and many mental health professionals consider sexual experimentation with same-sex individuals a part of heterosexual identity development. Therefore, therapists and counselors may ignore such adolescent disclosures, or worse, may hasten to assure the adolescent that same-sex encounters are a "normal" part of heterosexual experimentation, thereby inadvertently confirming the "abnormality" of gay and lesbian orientations.

Another difficulty is that many gay and lesbian adolescents feel that they must hide their identities. Martin (1982) describes gay and lesbian adolescents as members of a minority group because they are subjected to prejudice; unlike members of other minority groups, however, there is no supportive subculture and usually no support at home to help ameliorate the effects of prejudice and stigma. There is also the unique mistaken belief that gay and lesbian youth choose their orientation and therefore could change their sexual orientation if they so chose. Little wonder that most report feelings of extreme isolation (Hunter and Schaecher, 1990). Following are excerpts from a newspaper article by a high school senior about the isolation of "growing up gay":

> *Growing up gay and not being able to tell everyone is like hell. It's very hard to have to keep it to yourself . . . My friends would look at girls and I would look at my friends. By then, I knew I could not tell them the truth. I had heard the jokes about gays and I was afraid of what might happen. I went through elementary and junior high school lying to all my friends, but the hardest thing was lying to my parents. My parents have a real problem with gays. My dad says they're sick and AIDS is what they deserve to get. It hurts me to think this is the way they feel. What they don't know is that they're talking about their own son . . . I have to think twice before I do everything. I have to watch what I stare at, how I talk, what I say, and how I walk and behave. Trying to worry about these things and juggle my classes is too much to bear.* (Los Angeles Times, *1994*)

The prejudice and resulting isolation has become so widespread in some locations that alternative programs or campuses have been set up for gay and lesbian youth. Examples are the Harvey Milk School, a segregated campus in New York, and Project 10, a drop-out prevention program for gay and lesbian adolescents in the Los Angeles Unified School District. Project 10 offers nonjudgmental counseling, support, and information. Similar projects have been started across the country.

What can teachers do? They can help by being sensitive to the particular problems experienced by gay and lesbian adolescents and by knowing local resources that are available to help ameliorate the feelings of isolation. One cannot assume, for example, that all counselors or therapists will handle gay and lesbian disclosures appropriately. Teachers should know which counselors are sensitive to these issues and then can make referrals when needed. Teachers can search out local support groups. In addition, discussion of successful role models would be helpful. Finally, teachers should neither model nor tolerate slurs, homophobic jokes, and other prejudiced remarks.

Sex Education

Many sex-related problems could be minimized if adolescents were better informed about sex-related issues. Although it is argued by some that the home is the proper place for such information to be dispensed, the majority of adolescent students report that their parents do not give them the information they need. Minimal information needed by adolescents includes facts on sexual anatomy and functioning, sexually transmitted disease, birth control, abortion, and informative discussions on such anxiety-provoking issues as masturbation and gay and lesbian orientation. Most experts agree that in addition to providing factual information, sex education programs should also explore sexual values and attitudes.

In the recent past, the majority of states had laws that either prohibited or restricted sex education in the schools, primarily due to a vocal minority of parents who did not want the schools to deal with sex education. The advent of AIDS has helped reverse this trend: in the 1980s, the number of states *requiring* sex education to be taught in public schools increased from 3 to 23 (Hackett, 1990). This mandate to teach sex education in many states is a distinct reversal from the earlier prohibitions and offers educators an opportunity to address sexuality as a part of basic human relationships.

Sex education should be a part of all adolescent treatment programs. In many locales, Planned Parenthood organizations have sex education materials appropriate for use with adolescents. Sex education programs should encourage self-expression while teaching responsibility for one's sexual behavior (Knopp, 1982). For male adolescent sex offenders, Erickson (1984) suggests that a well-trained male staff member take a detailed sexual history in order to demystify sexual issues and to establish a relationship in which the adolescent can begin to express sexual concerns. Erickson warns that with adolescent offenders, premature attempts to explore sexual issues in coeducational groups may increase resistance rather than promote growth. With groups of nonoffenders, however, coeducational discussion may facilitate more comprehensive understanding of sexuality issues.

Despite its controversial nature, sex education in the public schools should be addressed. Advocates believe that public school sex education can increase knowledge (Kirby, 1984), improve decision making (S. Gordon, 1983), improve self-esteem (Crooks & Baur, 1983), and ultimately decrease unwanted pregnancies (Zabin et al., 1988). A common argument against sex education—that increased knowledge leads to increased sexual experimentation—has not been validated. What have been validated are increasing numbers of premarital pregnancies and incidences of sexually transmitted disease among the adolescent population. It should be clear to educators and parents alike that the ostrich approach—of pretending that if we don't talk about sex the problems will go away—is untenable.

Substance Abuse

Prevalence

Experimentation with mood-altering drugs is a hallmark of adolescence. Unfortunately, drug use has crept downward into middle schools and even into the early elementary grades. Availability of many drugs on the street, tolerant attitudes toward underage drinking, and misuse of prescription drugs may account for much of the drug use among today's children and adolescents. The drugs most widely used by high school students are alcohol, tobacco, and marijuana. Amphetamines, cocaine, crack, inhalants, and miscellaneous other drugs are used to a much lesser extent by this age group. Among high school seniors, a study conducted by the National Institute on Drug Abuse in 1992 showed a decline in the number admitting to "illegal drug use in the past month": 25 percent compared to 39 percent in 1979. Although this decline appears encouraging, the researchers also found that one of every two high school students used an illicit drug before graduation, that 37 percent have smoked marijuana, and that 10 percent have tried cocaine (National Institute on Drug Abuse, 1992). Table 9-2 shows

TABLE 9-2   Self-Reported Drug Use Among Adolescents

	8th Grade	10th Grade	12 Grade
	Percent		
LIFETIME:			
Alcohol	70.1	83.8	88.0
Been Drunk	27.0	50.0	65.0
Cigarettes	44.0	55.0	63.0
Marijuana	10.2	23.4	36.7
Inhalants	17.6	15.7	17.6
Cocaine	2.3	4.1	7.8
Crack	1.3	1.7	3.1
Hallucinogen	3.2	6.1	9.6
Stimulants	10.8	13.2	15.4
LSD	3.0	6.0	9.0
LAST 30 DAYS			
Alcohol	25.0	43.0	54.0
Been Drunk	8.0	21.0	32.0
Cigarettes	14.0	21.0	28.0
Marijuana	3.0	9.0	14.0
Inhalants	4.0	3.0	2.0
Cocaine	.5	0.7	1.4
Crack	0.3	0.3	0.7
Hallucinogen	0.8	1.6	2.2
Stimulants	2.6	3.3	3.2
LSD	0.6	1.5	1.9

Source: *National Institute on Drug Abuse (1992). A Comparison of Drug Use Among 8th, 10th, and 12th Graders from NIDA's High School Senior Survey; Monitoring the Future study.*

the patterns of self-reported drug use of students from a study of eighth, tenth, and twelfth graders.

Few would deny that drug use among adolescents is a cause for concern. Alcohol, which is legal after a certain age and socially acceptable by many standards, is the most widely used and misused drug by teenagers and even pre-teens. Recent surveys show that the first drinking experience in the United States today usually occurs around age 12, and that over a third of fourth graders report peer pressure to try beer, wine, or liquor (Genaux, Likens, & Morgan, 1993). Not only are kids drinking at earlier ages, but also an alarming number of youth are drinking at a rate that suggests serious problems:

- 37 percent of one sample of high school seniors reported engaging in "heavy drinking," i.e., 5 or more drinks in a row over a two-week period (Johnston, O'Malley, & Bachman, 1988).
- In a survey of 27,000 New York junior and senior high students, 13 percent admitted attending classes while "high" or "drunk" from alcohol (Genaux, Likens, & Morgan, 1993).

- Approximately 10 percent of all youngsters between the ages of 12 and 17 are now or will become alcoholics, and approximately 30 percent will exhibit continued use of alcohol (Schmid & Slade, 1981).

In addition to physical and psychological dependency caused by alcohol are the dangers of driving while intoxicated. Studies have shown that alcohol use has been a factor in almost half of all fatal car accidents, and the majority of these involve drivers under the age of 21. Such statistics have encouraged some states to raise the legal drinking age to 21; currently, more than half the states require a person to be 21 before he can legally purchase alcohol.

Another legal and socially acceptable drug is tobacco, or more specifically, nicotine. Since the adverse publicity surrounding the Surgeon General's Report in 1965 linking cigarette smoking to lung cancer, the incidence of smoking among youth has declined. However, tobacco use still has a sizeable following. In 1988, 19 percent of the high school seniors in one study reported that they smoked on a daily basis (Johnston, O'Malley, & Bachman, 1988). Cigarettes are known to be physically addicting and to be highly carcinogenic, causing lung ailments and several forms of oral cancer.

Another drug favored by adolescents is marijuana. Popularized by hippies and the college crowd of the 1960s, marijuana became a common part of the U.S. drug scene. Although still illegal, it has become more socially acceptable and has been touted by many as less harmful than cigarettes or alcohol. However, marijuana use does have drawbacks. Habitual use often results in lowered academic performance because of its effects on concentration and memory. High levels of marijuana ingestion also impair motor performance and ability to maneuver a car in traffic. The most detrimental effect of marijuana is the psychological dependency it fosters, and for this reason many experts discourage its use by adolescents (National Institute on Drug Abuse, 1980).

Crack cocaine has made inroads into the child and adolescent population in the past few years. Previous to the development of crack, which is a low-grade, inexpensive form of cocaine, few adolescents could afford the higher grade quality of cocaine, which was considered an upper-class drug due to its expense. In many locations, crack is now being sold to elementary and middle school kids as well as high school students. Crack is especially dangerous because it is psychologically addictive and deprives the user of the normal drives to eat, rest, and take care of himself.

Numerous other drugs are used by adolescents with less frequency than alcohol, tobacco, or marijuana, but with great potential for damage. "Hard" drugs such as heroin are not likely to be used frequently by this age group because of the expense. Amphetamines and sedatives are more likely to be misused by adolescents because of availability through prescriptions. Amphetamines ("speed," "uppers") are commonly prescribed for weight loss, and sedatives ("downers," barbiturates, and tranquilizers) may be prescribed to alleviate anxiety or to promote sleep. The prescribed use of sleeping pills and tranquilizers has become so widespread among middle- and upper-class families that many adolescents need only to shake down their mothers' purses or to raid the family medicine cabinets for a ready supply. In addition, mild amphetamines are available over the counter in the form of diet pills. The major dangers resulting from misuse of amphetamines and sedatives are physical and psychological addiction, overdosing, and potentially lethal effects of mixing the drugs with alcohol. Amphetamine use, although not physically addicting, can be psychologically addicting and can cause depression, aggressiveness, and other undesirable psychological states.

Risk Factors and Characteristics

A number of high-risk factors have been identified by researchers attempting to decrease drug abuse among adolescents. Several of these risk factors are associated with parental attitudes or parental use. For example, if there is a history of alcoholism in the family, the risk of an adolescent male's abuse of alcohol is doubled (Hawkins & Catalono, 1988). Risk factors outside the home include lack of commitment to school, academic failure (especially in grades 4–6), friends who use, and pronounced feelings of alienation and rebelliousness (Hawkins & Catalono, 1988). Antisocial behavior, evidenced in early childhood as well as in early adolescence, has a marked correlation with substance abuse. These and other characteristics are summarized in Table 9-3.

In addition to these risk factors are a number of characteristics of substance abusers that teachers can use to help identify individuals who may be abusing:

- Psychosomatic symptoms
- Poor diets
- Sleep disturbances
- Inability to handle social experiences
- High number of stressful life events
- Belief in the magical power of the substance
- Serious disturbances in moral and character development
- Risk-taking behavior and intellectual curiosity
- State-dependent learning, in which material learned while under the influence of chemicals is not available when sober
- Depression and suicidal ideation
- Low self-esteem (Johnson, 1988).

TABLE 9-3   Risk Factors for Adolescent Substance Use

1. Family history of alcoholism, especially males (2 times greater)
2. Family management problems
   - poorly defined roles
   - little monitoring
   - inconsistent & excessively severe discipline
3. Early antisocial behavior, hyperactivity
4. Parental drug use and positive attitudes towards use
5. Academic failure (4–6 grade level)
6. Little commitment to school
7. Alienation, rebelliousness, lack of social bonding to society
8. Antisocial behavior in early adolescence
9. Friends who use
10. Favorable attitudes toward drug use
11. Early first use of drugs

Adapted from *Preparing for the Drug Free Years,* by J. D. Hawkins and R. F. Catalano. Seattle: Developmental Research and Programs, Prevention Resource Center, 1988.

These characteristics and risk factors bear a remarkable resemblance to characteristics of students with emotional/behavioral disorders, thereby placing these students at very high risk for substance abuse. One group of researchers surveyed drug and alcohol use by almost 300 high school students in both special education and general education settings. The researchers found that students with emotional/behavioral disorders in restrictive settings reported using a much wider range of drugs and were more likely to be currently using cigarettes, alcohol, and marijuana than their peers in less restrictive settings and in general education classes (Leone, Greenberg, Trickett, & Spero, 1989). Additionally, numerous studies of adolescent psychiatric patients indicate a strong relationship between substance use/abuse and emotional problems such as depression (Leone, 1991).

Effects of Substance Abuse

The damaging effects of drug misuse are not limited to physiological side effects. For adolescents who are trying to learn to cope with life and who are struggling to become adults, the psychological side effects can be especially deleterious. Chronic or heavy use of drugs can postpone these struggles, which are an essential part of the transition from childhood to adulthood. Drug-dependent adolescents make little progress toward becoming responsible, functioning members of society. Students who are occasional users may suffer only temporary difficulties, but they are more likely than nonusers to have problems in school or on the job. Educators can play an important role in detecting and helping ameliorate drug misuse.

Substance Abuse Education

It is a temptation to react emotionally or moralistically to the topic of drug abuse among children and adolescents. The drug abuse programs of the early sixties reflected this moralistic tone. Many of these school- and community-based programs utilized scare tactics such as having ex-addicts or police condemn the use of drugs. Often, misinformation or biased information was given in hopes of discouraging drug use. Unfortunately, the effect of most of these efforts was to undermine the credibility of drug education programs and to further entrench adolescents against "the establishment." Due to the shortcomings of early programs, subsequent programs began to avoid moralizing and to focus upon providing accurate, unbiased information. Many programs also began to incorporate activities in values clarification in order to help students make their own decisions and take responsibility for them. More recently, programs have returned to a moralistic note, a campaign against any use of drugs.

Research on the effectiveness of substance abuse prevention has yielded few consistent results. According to Leone (1991), we are currently unable to determine whether school-based substance abuse prevention programs have been successful in changing actual student consumption of controlled substances. Leone asserts that most prevention efforts have continued in the "Just say no" vein; that is, prevention efforts focus upon the individual to the exclusion of powerful contextual and cultural influences. Some researchers (Pentz et al., 1989; Wallack and Corbitt, 1990) argue that successful prevention efforts must expand to cover multiple environmental influences (schools, family, peer group, the community) as well as the individual. Wallack and Corbitt (1990) believe that effective prevention programs share the following characteristics:

- Drug problems are viewed as complex.
- An integrated approach is taken.
- Long-term planning is utilized.
- The idea is understood that information about drugs is necessary but not sufficient to change behavior.

In developing a substance use prevention curriculum specifically for special education students, Morgan (1993) reviewed the literature to determine successful strategies. Morgan found that effective school-based programs:

- Focus on knowledge, attitudes, and behavior that influence use
- Are based on theoretical models that include: awareness of pressures to use, attitudinal inoculation to those pressures, and rehearsal of strategies to overcome those pressures
- Build general life skills such as communication, resistance, and decision-making, etc.
- Target families and communities for intervention
- Recognize the need for long-term, intensive involvement for high-risk kids.

In summary, the latest research on substance abuse prevention indicates that we must move beyond teaching decision-making skills and providing information about drugs, alcohol, and tobacco. Effective programs must also begin to (a) target the context as well as the individual, (b) offer specific strategies for resisting peer pressure to use controlled substances, and (c) provide opportunities for youth to practice resistance skills. An example of a program that incorporates these principles is described in Box 9-1.

Most substance abuse education programs have a prevention focus and may not be suitable for students who are already into heavy or chronic drug use. In such cases, other intervention measures are necessary. Leone (1991) and Johnson (1988) take the hard-line position that teachers and other direct-care professionals are contributing to students' substance abuse problems when they ignore suspected use or abuse.

Jardin and Ziebell (1981) offer guidelines for teachers to follow when they suspect a student of having a drug problem. Before action is taken, however, Jardin and Ziebell warn that two things must be clearly understood by all involved parties. First is a clear statement of school policy about legal issues regarding drug possession and *observed* use of drugs on the school grounds. Second, when the student is only *suspected* of drug abuse, the issue is one of treatment and not of discipline. Once these issues are clearly articulated, teachers may take action in the following sequence:

Identification.   The most accurate clue to drug use is a drastic and sustained change in a student's attitude, temperament, work habits, work quality, or grades. The teacher should solicit information from other school personnel before a suspicion is voiced. The teacher should also describe the resulting unacceptable behaviors to the student and obtain the backing of an administrator before further action is taken.

Parent Conference.   The purpose of meeting with the student's parents is to define the problem, to obtain parental input about what steps they intend to take, to get the parents' opinion about the role the school should take, and to get a commitment to try a plan of action.

BOX 9-1 RESIST: A Substance Use Prevention Program

RESIST is a curriculum to prevent the use of alcohol, tobacco, and other drugs by students in special education. It is one of the few prevention programs specifically for students with disabilities. Developed by Daniel Morgan and his colleagues at Utah State University, RESIST has both elementary and secondary curricula. RESIST is based on theoretical premises and on current research about effective strategies in prevention. Among the premises are that an effective program must include: (a) awareness of pressures to use alcohol, tobacco, and other drugs; (b) attitudinal inoculation to those pressures; and (c) active practice of skills and strategies to overcome those pressures.

RESIST emphasizes the following messages:

• Drug use is not normal or healthy behavior.
• Most youths do not use drugs.
•One can lead a full and exciting life with many friends without using.
•Students help themselves and their communities by staying drug-free.

Similar to many social skills curricula, RESIST is a combination of instruction, discussion, and practice of skills. Based on sound instructional principles, it incorporates the following: direct instruction, role-playing, homework, parent involvement activities, behavior management procedures, and correction procedures. A typical lesson includes all of these components.

One unique feature of RESIST is that it teaches and reinforces a number of resistance skills:

• Resist with a reason ("I don't like the taste/smell").
• Say "no thanks."
• Use humor ("I can't afford to kill any brain cells.").
• Change the subject ("Did you see the game last night?").
• Leave the situation ("No" and walk away).
• Avoid the situation.
• Ignore.

• Be a broken record ("No thanks . . . No thanks. . . . No thanks").
• Stalling for time ("Not right now/ Maybe later").

In addition to basic resistance skills, lessons focus on information and practice in resisting each of the individual drugs: alcohol, tobacco, marijuana, cocaine, crack, inhalants, and hallucinogens. For example, the lesson overview on "Resisting Pressure to Use Alcohol," contains the following elements: review previous homework, address facts about alcohol and drinking, discuss reasons not to use alcohol, role play situations involving pressure to drink alcohol, quiz on alcohol facts, homework assignment, and hand-out for parents.

Although a relatively new program, preliminary data from field-testing RESIST are encouraging. Parents, teachers, and participating students rated the program favorably. Pre- and post-tests indicate that students both improved their attitudes and increased their knowledge of the risks of using alcohol, tobacco, and other drugs. Inconsistent results were obtained when students were asked to rate their own drug use in the past 30 days; however, there was a sizable decrease in self-reported recent use of alcohol among high school students with mild disabilities.

One interesting finding is that although RESIST specifically emphasizes the idea that most students do not use drugs, tobacco, and alcohol, the majority of students continue to overestimate drug use among their peers. According to the authors of RESIST, we need to direct more attention to student perceptions and expectations about peer drug use.

Sources: Morgan, D.P. (1993). *RESIST: A curriculum to prevent the use of alcohol, tobacco, and other drugs by students in special education.* Logan, UT: Utah State University, and Morgan, D., Likins, M., Friedman, S., & Genaux, M. (1994). *A preliminary investigation of the effectiveness of a substance use prevention program for students in special education programs.* Logan, UT: Utah State University.

Family Conference.   A family conference that includes the student and a school representative should be held as soon as the parents come up with a plan of action. The proposed plan should be parent-initiated and school-supported.

Follow-up.   If outside help for the student is part of the plan, the teacher should check on whether it has been obtained. Continued contact with parents is essential, and if representatives from the mental health or juvenile justice systems have become involved, the teacher should maintain periodic contact with them.

Gangs, Delinquency, and the Juvenile Offender with Emotional/behavioral Disorders

In this section, we will explore issues related to gangs and law-breaking among adolescents. First, the research on juvenile offenders and the relationship between education and corrections will be described. Next, the prevalence of gangs, reasons for joining gangs, and a few community-based solutions will be discussed.

Juvenile Offenders with E/BD

Research on the juvenile offender with emotional/behavioral disorders is scarce. The bulk of related research in special education literature is devoted to: (a) the characteristics of juvenile offenders who are not specifically labeled emotionally/behaviorally disordered, or (b) the necessity of coordinating services between the educational and juvenile justice systems.

Studies clearly identifying juvenile offenders with emotional/behavioral disorders are difficult to conduct primarily due to the different classification systems used by the education, mental health, and correctional systems (Gilliam & Scott, 1987). For example, many juvenile offenders are labeled as conduct disordered by psychologists using the DSM system; however, many professionals in the education system have equated "conduct disordered" with "socially maladjusted" and therefore can exclude these youth from special education services. Although there is a recent movement to prevent exclusion of the socially maladjusted in the educational definition, such problems with definition and terminology have historically hampered efforts to conduct prevalence studies of individuals with emotional/behavioral disorders among adjudicated populations.

If students are not labeled by the special education system prior to incarceration, then chances may be slim for their being referred for special education afterward. As Gilliam and Scott (1987) point out, correctional staff have little motivation to make such referrals because they may see few differences between inmates who are labeled and those who are not. In addition, the facility may not have segregated classes for individuals with emotional/behavioral disorders; therefore, both labeled and unlabeled students are likely to be served in the same classroom.

Despite these difficulties in identifying offenders with emotional/behavioral disorders, some prevalence estimates have been made. One national survey indicated that 35 percent of the juvenile inmates were identified as having emotional/behavioral disorders (Eggleston, 1984), while others have found prevalence estimates around 16 to 17 percent for the offender with E/BD (Morgan, 1979; Young, Pappenfort, & Marlow, 1983). Either of these estimates is cause for alarm. When applied to the total estimate of 150,00 incarcerated youth under age 22 (Murphy, 1986), the resulting number of juvenile offenders with emotional/behavioral disorders falls between 25,000 and 52,500. Also, when compared to the general population prevalence estimates of approximately 2 percent, the magnitude of emotional problems among this population becomes evident.

Unfortunately, prevalence estimates shed little light on the characteristics of juvenile offenders with emotional/behavioral disorders and how they may differ from other populations. For example, although not all conduct disordered youth break the law, juvenile offenders may differ from conduct disordered/behaviorally disordered youth as a group primarily by the fact that the juvenile offenders have been caught breaking the law enough times to become adjudicated. Preliminary findings by Coleman and Gilliam (1990) indicated no significant differences between a sample of incarcerated juvenile offenders with emotional/behavioral disorders and non-labeled incarcerated offenders on 13 behavioral and personality measures. While the sample was too small (N = 37) to draw conclusions or to generalize to larger segments of the population, the authors question whether results of follow-up studies with larger numbers would differ. Zionts (1980) also found no differences between inner city delinquents and non-delinquents on five self-reported affective variables. It appears that until researchers can distinguish between juvenile offenders with emotional/behavioral disorders and those without, it would be presumptuous to differentiate methods of instruction or management for this group. Box 9-2 offers a teacher's point of view about managing students with emotional disorders and juvenile offenders in the same classroom.

Gangs

The Problem.   Adolescents with emotional/behavioral disorders, especially those with diagnoses of conduct disorder, are at risk for becoming involved in gangs or delinquency. A gang is a group of persons who identify with one another by a common name and sign, and who break the law or behave in antisocial ways (Donnelly & Suter, 1994). Once confined primarily to the largest cities in the United States, gangs have now spread into suburban and small communities in almost all 50 states. The massive migration to smaller communities is believed to be related primarily to expanding the turf for drug trafficking (Huff, 1992). According to one national survey, law enforcement officials in 35 cities professing to have problems with gangs identified nearly 1500 different gangs with over 120,600 members (Spergel, 1993).

Youths who are most at-risk for becoming involved in gangs and delinquency are those from neighborhoods in which poverty and crime are rampant, and from homes in which substance abuse and violence are routine. In addition, these youth often have established histories of behavior problems and academic failure in school.

Gangs are popular and difficult to combat because they serve basic socialization and survival functions. When families and schools are unable to meet the needs of these children and youth, gangs become an attractive alternative. Youths join gangs for many reasons, including acceptance, recognition, sense of belonging, status, power, shelter, food, clothing, nurturing, and respect (Conley, 1993). Unemployment is also a large factor; in many cities where gangs are a problem, job opportunities for which potential gang members would qualify are scarce. In fact, Huff (1992) emphasizes that to combat gangs, legal job opportu-

BOX 9-2 A Teacher's Experience

It was bound to be an interesting year for me because it was the first year I'd taught in a public school since my college days. For three and one-half years I'd taught in a psychiatric setting with doctors, social workers, psychologists, nurses, nutritionists, child-care workers, and what would later seem like a cast of thousands for support services. That year I was teaching in one of the largest and poorest school districts in the state, in an area of town where people were highly transient. I was assigned to a self-contained classroom for junior high school students with serious emotional/behavioral disorders.

From the information in my students' folders I learned that I would have one of the most ethnically diverse groups imaginable, including a Polynesian American and an American Inuit. As it turned out, ethnicity was not a problem in developing cooperative work groups. The problem in group interaction seemed to arise from the fact that my students were evenly divided between those with a very tenuous contact with reality, and those who had a firm grasp on reality but chose to walk on the fine edge with the local police. The other little twist was that of my ten students, only one was female.

Early on, my aide and I knew that we would have to watch our delinquent group very carefully because they began to manipulate and "borrow" from the less discerning students. We addressed the problem through careful seating arrangement, giving each student a single desk with some sort of barrier to limit visual contact with other students where academic work was to be completed. We structured group activities so that the more vulnerable of our students never worked with our more cunning students unless they were under the direct supervision of the aide or the teacher. We also worked very hard to foster friendships between the students, and eventually some of our delinquent students became very protective of the others.

Our group activities had to be carefully designed so that competition did not become a destructive dynamic. Team members were chosen by the aide or the teacher. Most of the activities were cooperative, but those that were competitive had rules about such things as "seeing how long we can keep the ball in bounds" or giving points for assists.

Some days, the electricity in the air was just too tense to try to involve the group in a game; on such days, science lessons might be adjusted to include a nature walk. The key element in all our planning was flexibility. There were a lot of beautiful lesson plans that were put on hold because the students' needs shifted so quickly.

The most difficult adjustment for me was dealing with the isolation and lack of support personnel. I was accustomed to working in a setting where everyone was dealing with handicapped children and trying to promote each child's potential. In the public school setting, not only were there no psychologists, no social workers, no child-care workers, but there were no other special education teachers on my side of the building! I was the only faculty member who ate lunch with her students, and frequently the only adult to be seen in the cafeteria at noon. When I talked with the principal about mainstreaming my students, she painfully admitted that there were only three teachers in the building who would give my students a chance—and two of them taught the same subject.

There may be a dozen solutions to the problem of not having support personnel, but I only found one that worked—looking for help outside the school system. By the end of the fall semester, I knew most of the juvenile probation officers in that section of town. I met with or called the students' parents at least once a week, even if it was a chat at the curb or a five-minute phone call. I checked with the local United Fund office to locate as many social service agencies as I could, and then I developed friendships with some of the staff members. Within my building, I used any excuse I could find to bring other teachers into my room so that they could see for themselves that we were just another class. When a student was having a good day, he might earn the privilege of running errands, not only for me but also for the other teachers in our area. Before too long, teachers on our hall were asking why such a nice child was in my class.

There weren't any miracle cures in our class, but there were some significant changes. All of the students managed to stay out of the juvenile detention facilities for the year. None of the furniture was damaged. One student gave up being a mountain lion during free time. One young man learned to eat with a knife and fork and to stop talking to the plastic alligator he kept in his pocket. Three of our students did go to mainstream class, but only one progressed to the point of not needing the support of a self-contained class the next year. Although we would have liked to have seen more progress, I know how hard all of us had to work to achieve these goals.

Contributed by Dona Stallworth, Ph.D., former teacher and current special education consultant, Region XIII Education Service Center serving central Texas.

nities must not only be available, but also must be able to compete with illegal opportunities such as drug trafficking.

Solutions.   Obviously there are no simple solutions to gangs and juvenile crime because they are intertwined with a myriad of societal problems. Arrest and prosecution of gang members have not proven to be a deterrent to gang membership; in fact, among some gangs, arrests are viewed as honors. A strategy that has been adopted by community-based programs is to identify active gang members and try to supplant gang-related activities with positive activities and skills. Prevention programs are similar, except that they target youth who are at-risk but have not yet joined a gang. A survey of gang-plagued cities concluded that the most effective approaches to date have been a combination of tight law enforcement, provision of opportunities such as remedial education and job training, and community mobilization in which a variety of neighborhood groups coordinate efforts to help (Spergel, 1990).

As discussed in Chapter 8, it is important to work with the various systems involved with these youth. On a personal level, teachers can help by establishing relationships with individuals from law enforcement and juvenile justice who are also working with students involved in gangs and delinquent activities. On a systems level, teachers who are concerned about their students' involvement in gangs can also volunteer for interagency task forces or community mobilization groups to help combat the problem. School buildings, playgrounds, and gyms are ideal places for community programs to offer after-school activities as positive alternatives to gang activities (e.g., midnight basketball).

Self-Destructive Behavior

Youngsters with emotional/behavioral disorders may be prone toward self-destructive behaviors such as suicide and severe eating disorders.

Suicide

The most extreme form of self-destructive behavior is suicide. Adolescent suicide has increased dramatically over the past 20 years; it is the third leading cause of death among youth ages 15 to 24 (Kaplan & Saddock, 1988). The suicide rate for adolescents ages 15 to 19 has been placed at 8.7 per 100,000 (Davis, Sandoval, & Wilson, 1988). Many more attempted suicides take place. In a review of several studies, it was found that between 9 and 13 percent of high school students report that they themselves have attempted suicide (Davis, Sandoval, & Wilson, 1988). While adolescent females attempt suicide more often than their male counterparts, adolescent males successfully kill themselves four times more often (Muse, 1990).

Researchers have attempted to identify factors contributing to adolescent suicide. The acute onset of so many developmental changes during the adolescent years may create increased susceptibility. Chronic depression has also been linked with suicidal behavior, although depression is likely a correlate rather than a cause of suicide. In other words, the factors that cause an individual to be depressed may also eventually lead to suicide. Another factor is alienation, or a feeling of irreparable aloneness, which may be manifested through broken romances, little contact with peers, poor communication or conflict with parents, and divorce of parents. Other recurrent themes in suicide victims are feelings of being helpless and powerless, and unresolved feelings over loss of a parent or other close relative at an early age. Psychotic adolescents also may be at high risk for attempting suicide, as auditory hallucinations commanding suicide have been reported among both psychotic adults and adolescents. Some experts estimate that 60 percent of the adolescents who commit suicide in this country are suffering from some type of mental disorder (Blumenthal, 1985).

Table 9-4 lists a number of risk factors that may predispose children and adolescents toward suicidal behavior. These risk factors include substance abuse, familiarity with suicide, recent loss of family member or friend, chronic illness, and access to lethal means. Also increasing the probability of suicide attempts are a history of physical or sexual abuse and close association with a person who has died by suicide (Muse, 1990). Additional signals are progressive isolation from social contact and a long history of social problems that worsens in adolescence.

Teachers and other significant adults in the lives of teenagers can play key roles in suicide prevention. Adolescents who talk about suicide must be taken seriously, as they are at higher risk for attempting it, especially if a specific method is mentioned. Experts caution that no suicide threat is an idle threat, because it is always a plea for help. Konopka (1983)

TABLE 9-4   Risk Factors for Suicide

Emotional/Behavior Problems
Depression
Impulsive personality
Alcohol abuse
Drug abuse
Other serious psychiatric illness

Decreased Inhibition
Alcohol intoxication
PCP intoxication
Hallucinogen intoxication

Suicide Is Familiar
Suicide threats
Previous suicide attempts
Family member has attempted suicide
Completed suicide in family member
Recent publicized suicide in community

Severe Stress
Recent significant loss
Chronic illness
Public humiliation or threat thereof

Access to Lethal Means
Prescription drugs at hand
Street drugs easy to obtain
Guns and ammunition in home
Has time alone to carry out plan

indicates that adults in a preventive role must be able to maintain open, honest communication and to accept strong emotions, both positive and negative. Guetzloe (1988) offers some pragmatic suggestions for school personnel in working with potentially suicidal youth. These youth may be overwhelmed by a series of events over which they have little or no control; by identifying specific areas and making even a small positive change, the students can be shown that all is not hopeless. For example, dropping a class, removing the threat of punishment or entering into a peer support group may relieve some of the pressure perceived by the individual. Guetzloe also recommends addressing problems relevant to suicidal behavior in the individual education plan; for example, if the student is highly stressed, provide training in relaxation, problem-solving, and other coping skills.

One interesting note from research on suicide prevention is that students themselves are the most likely to know who among them is suicidal. This finding has led some schools to set up peer counseling programs, in which students are trained to make referrals within the school system. Although there is some evidence for "contagion," i.e., one suicide encouraging others, research suggests that contagion is more likely to occur when the first suicide is not discussed openly, thereby denying adolescents the opportunity to voice their feelings and regain some sense of control (Davis, Sandoval, & Wilson, 1988). School personnel will also want to contact parents and refer to a mental health professional in the event of threatened or attempted suicide. It is important to remember that the single best predictor of subsequent attempts is whether the adolescent is able to maintain communication with others.

Eating Disorders

Two self-destructive eating disorders, *anorexia nervosa* and *bulimia,* are more prevalent among adolescent girls than among other populations. The incidence has steadily increased over the past two decades, with as many as 18 to 20 percent of school-age youngsters suffering from one or both disorders (Phelps & Bajorek, 1991).

Anorexia nervosa is a self-imposed restriction of eating that results in severe, sometimes life-threatening, weight loss. It is ten times more common in girls than in boys, and is most likely to occur in adolescent girls around age 14 or 15. Unfortunately, mental health professionals are reporting increasing numbers of cases in preadolescents, including children as young as 7 (Phelps & Bajorek, 1991). If untreated, cases of the disorder are likely to continue into adulthood.

The cause of anorexia is currently unknown. Anorexics have been characterized as over-controlled and meticulous and as coming from overcontrolled homes, which engendered emotional conflict. It is more practical to view anorexia as a phobia of being overweight or fat. Anorexia usually begins with dieting, which becomes an obsession; consequently, the individual loses all perspective of appropriate body weight. Even when abnormally thin, the individual cannot lose the fear of becoming fat and therefore does not resume normal eating habits. It has not been determined whether most anorexics are overweight before they begin dieting. Some studies have indicated that many anorexics were not overweight but began dieting for reasons of their own, without external suggestions or provocation.

There is some evidence that anorexia has a biochemical basis, which also may be responsible for the anxiety and depression found in individuals suffering from anorexia

(Fava, Copeland, Schweiger, & Herzog, 1989; Garfinkel & Garner, 1987). One study has found that both anorexics and bulimics lack the ability to absorb zinc, a trace metal that is essential to a variety of internal processes (Warren, 1990). Subjects' symptoms improved with zinc supplements, suggesting that a biochemical abnormality may in fact be causally related to these eating disorders. Other studies have found changes in neurotransmitters among anorexics (Fava et al., 1989; Kaplan & Woodside, 1987).

Although the mortality rate has decreased in the past few years since anorexia has been more readily diagnosed and treated, as many as 15 percent of the anorexia population die from complications or from suicide (Hsu, 1980). Treatment is complicated, usually involving behavioral interventions with a goal of realistic weight gain followed by cognitive-behavioral interventions aimed at changing irrational beliefs and distorted body image. Numerous drugs have been tried in treating anorexic symptoms; however, to date, no drug has been found effective in treating anorexia (Fava et al., 1989).

Bulimia is an eating disorder in which the individual eats an abnormally large amount of food and then induces vomiting or uses laxatives to remove the food before it can be digested. For this reason, it is often called the "binge-and-purge" syndrome. Bulimia differs from anorexia in that bulimics are often of normal weight; thus their abnormal eating habits may not be known to others. Bulimia may be characterized as a form of obsessive-compulsive behavior: bulimics cannot rid themselves of the idea of going on a food binge (obsessive), and once the food has been ingested, cannot resist the urge to get it out of their system (compulsive). Although individuals with bulimia may be of normal weight and appear healthy, they can suffer a number of physical ailments related to constant vomiting and/or use of laxatives. In addition, persons with bulimia recognize their aberrant eating habits and therefore suffer more anxiety, depression, and guilt about the disorder than persons with anorexia (Johnson, Steinberg, & Lewis, 1988).

Researchers have found that a cognitive-behavioral approach (coupled with response prevention of vomiting) is highly effective in treating individuals with bulimia (Phelps & Bajorek, 1991). This approach is a step-by-step procedure aimed at eliminating the secrecy, gradually shaping dietary behavior through self-monitoring, and gradually introducing binge foods. Faulty cognitions regarding food and body image are also targeted (Fairburn, 1981). Some success has also been reported with drug therapy, specifically with tricyclic antidepressants and phenelzine (a monoamine oxidase inhibitor) in the treatment of individuals with bulimia (Fava et al., 1989).

If teachers suspect that a student is experiencing either of these eating disorders, referral to a local mental health program specializing in these disorders should be made. Support groups for adolescents with eating disorders and their parents are also available in many communities.

Interventions with Adolescents with Emotional/behavioral Disorders

Over the years, program development for adolescents with emotional/behavioral disorders has received much less attention than program development for younger children. One factor impeding program development for adolescents with E/BD is the lack of clear-cut research on the effectiveness of specific approaches to dealing with important issues such as career preparation, sex-related problems, and drug abuse. Despite these factors, a growing interest in developing model programs and researching the efficacy of specific interventions for this population has become evident. The remainder of this chapter explores career education alternatives and behavioral and counseling interventions that hold promise for dealing with the adolescent with emotional/behavioral disorders.

Career Education and Prevocational Training

Career education is viewed as a comprehensive curriculum area, and prevocational training is viewed as instruction in specific job-related skills. In this section, a general career education model is discussed, followed by a model prevocational program for adolescents with severe emotional/behavioral disorders.

Career Education

It is a common belief that career education programs can not only increase motivation to stay in school, but also can prepare students for employment upon graduation. In reality, however, career education suffers from a confusing history and from a lack of unity in program development and implementation. Despite the fact that career education for students with disabilities is backed by federal legislation, services to this population are sporadic. Follow-up studies of students with mild disabilities indicate that career education is falling short of its goal: unemployment, underemployment, and poor wages are common among this population after graduation (Montague, 1987).

Brolin and Kokaska (1979) conceptualize three major competency areas within a career education curriculum: (1) daily living skills, (2) personal-social skills, and (3) occupational guidance and preparation. Twenty-two competencies in these three skill areas are outlined in Table 9-5. According to these authors, career education includes skills for functioning independently and for sustaining interpersonal relationships on the job and in the community.

Career education is viewed as a body of knowledge that is best taught on a developmental basis from kindergarten through graduation. Most career specialists recommend that career education begin in kindergarten and continue through the elementary years with an emphasis on awareness and exploration of career possibilities. In the junior and senior high years, students should receive more specific instruction in developing work habits, acquiring specific occupational skills, and seeking employment. Many employers regard basic communication skills and interpersonal skills as more important than technical skills (Wilms, 1984). Students with emotional/behavioral disorders are therefore at particular risk for failure at job placements, and instruction in job-related interpersonal skills should be emphasized with this population. Montague (1987) has identified crucial job-related interpersonal skills that include understanding instructions, asking a question, asking for help, accepting criticism, offering assistance, and accepting assistance. Such skills have been taught successfully in a controlled setting; however, problems persist in the ability of these youth to routinely perform these skills on the job.

The role of the special education teacher in career education varies according to the roles assumed by other personnel in the system. Few special education teachers have the

TABLE 9-5 Career Education Curriculum Competencies

DAILY LIVING SKILLS
1. Managing family finances
2. Selecting, managing, and maintaining a home
3. Caring for personal needs
4. Raising children, family living
5. Buying and preparing food
6. Buying and caring for clothes
7. Engaging in civic activities
8. Utilizing recreation and leisure
9. Getting around the community (mobility)

PERSONAL-SOCIAL SKILLS
10. Achieving self-awareness
11. Acquiring self-confidence
12. Achieving socially responsible behavior
13. Maintaining good interpersonal skills
14. Achieving independence
15. Achieving problem-solving skills
16. Communicating adequately with others

OCCUPATIONAL GUIDANCE AND PREPARATION
17. Knowing and exploring occupational possibilities
18. Selecting and planning occupational choices
19. Exhibiting appropriate work habits and behaviors
20. Exhibiting sufficient physical-manual skill
21. Obtaining a specific occupational skill
22. Seeking, securing, and maintaining employment

background to carry out comprehensive career development programs. However, special education teachers can work on the social skills aspect of job training and can ensure that their students' individual education plans (IEPs) include career-oriented objectives. Two examples of how career education goals can be written into IEPs are given in Table 9-6.

A Model Prevocational Program

One model for a successful prevocational program for adolescents with severe behavior disorders was reported by Gable (1984). Participants were youths ages 15 to 17 in a psychiatric residential setting in Virginia. Problems leading to residential placement were reported as "aggressive acting-out behavior, immature withdrawn behavior, self-injurious behavior, theft, chronic disruption or school avoidance, sexual acting-out, runaway, and other delinquency status offenses" (Gable, 1984, pp. 59–61). The youths were also reported to evidence severe academic retardation in relation to their intellectual ability. The prevocational program consists of three major components: (1) an academic-remedial curriculum, (2) a social skills curriculum, and (3) prevocational training/work experience. The academic curriculum is based on functional, life-related skills. Within the academic framework, participants are rated daily on amount of participation, work accuracy and attitude, and

TABLE 9–6 Examples of Career Education Goals in IEPS

CURRICULUM AREA	MATHEMATICS	LANGUAGE ARTS
ANNUAL GOAL:	Rita will increase her skills in the basic mathematical processes of addition, multiplication, subtraction, and division.	Beth will increase her written language skills.
SHORT-TERM OBJECTIVE:	Given a series of 10 one-digit multiplication problems, Rita will compute correct answers with 90% accuracy.	Given a specific subject, Beth will demonstrate the ability to organize ideas in written paragraph form, beginning with a topic sentence.
CAREER EDUCATION ACTIVITY:	Cut out newspaper advertisements and coupons for grocery store items. Use them as the basis for math problems and such related activities as budgeting and planning a simple meal. Place related coupons and teacher- or student-made worksheets in separate manila envelopes. Students may assist in the collection of materials and in writing problems. Examples: (1) Select and list items totaling no more than $5 to take on a picnic. (2) Find the cost of two loaves of bread. (3) Find the coupon that tells the cost of a can of pork and beans. Multiply to find the cost of five cans.	Have students take turns assuming responsibility for a Weekly Career Report. Using a simple interview form as a guide, interview a parent, neighbor, or community acquaintance regarding her or his occupation, work location, type of activities performed during the work day, and any other interesting information desired. Use the information gathered to write short reports in paragraph form. One report is presented in class each week, then posted on a class or school bulletin board. Students will benefit from role-playing interviews in class before trying one on their own.

From J. S. Lamkin, *Getting Started: Career Education Activities for Exceptional Students (K-9)*. (1980). Reston, VA: The Council for Exceptional Children.

independence or self-maintenance. The social skills curriculum is composed of interpersonal skills needed to function in a work setting. Students are rated daily on five competencies: following directions, using appropriate language, interacting with peers, interacting with adults, and exhibiting self-control. The prevocational component includes activities ranging from seeking employment to actual work experiences. The program offers instructional units developed for specific jobs, and the students are given ample time to master basic job-related skills in these units before being placed in a work setting. Some work settings are on-campus, while others are community-based. After only one year of operation, program evaluation results were encouraging: participants showed appreciable academic gains and maintained an acceptable level of work performance and behavior in 94 percent (31 of 33) of the placements. Anecdotal reports also suggested that participants evidenced more age-appropriate behaviors and more responsibility than they did prior to their participation in the program.

To summarize, it is important that teachers of adolescents with E/BD make provisions for instruction in job-related skills, which include interpersonal communication as well as vocational and technical skills. Teachers can easily incorporate career education objectives into IEPs. Another option is to gear the total curriculum, including academic objectives, toward prevocational training as illustrated in the model program.

Behavioral Interventions

Utilization of behavioral techniques with adolescents warrants special consideration. It is generally not too difficult to find reinforcers for a child, and, between parents and teachers, the child's environment may be fairly easily arranged to control reinforcement. In contrast, adolescents have much more control over their environment, and many of the reinforcers that worked in childhood no longer work in adolescence. It may be difficult for teacher and student to mutually agree upon suitable reinforcers, as adolescents may name reinforcers that are either illegal or unethical (alcohol or pornography, for example). Another factor is the emergence of peer group influence as a major motivator for adolescents, which may diminish the adolescent's need for adult approval. Adolescents with emotional/behavioral disorders in particular often do not place a premium on the usual social incentives, which may further limit the range of possible reinforcers.

Despite these potential difficulties, token economy and contingency management systems appear to be useful with this population. Towns (1981) reviewed research in this area and found that token economies that were successful with adolescents fall into three categories: those utilizing *home-based reinforcement systems,* those using *group contingencies,* and those using *self-determined reinforcement.* Home-based reinforcement systems can have a powerful effect on in-school behavior if parents and teachers work out a cooperative plan. Typical targeted behaviors in home-based systems include completing homework and other study behaviors, and typical reinforcers include watching television and social privileges in the home and community. Due to the influence of peer pressure among adolescents, *group contingencies* may be more successful than individual contingencies. In group contingencies, reinforcement is dependent upon the cooperation of every member of the group: if any member fails to exhibit the agreed upon behavior, then no one receives the reinforcement. Group contingencies have been applied successfully with adolescents with emotional/behavioral disorders to behaviors such as on-task in the classroom and school attendance. *Self-determined reinforcement* allows students either to choose from a teacher-approved list or to negotiate reinforcers with the teacher. Although self-determined reinforcement is always good practice, it may be essential to getting adolescents "hooked" into a behavior management plan.

Token systems are based upon contingency management, which is in turn based upon the Premack Principle: that high probability behaviors can be used to increase low probability behaviors (Premack, 1965). High probability behaviors of adolescents include listening to music, watching videos, eating, talking to one another, playing pinball or video games, and participating in sports or other recreational activities. Low probability behaviors include studying, completing classwork, and finishing homework. Although token economies have been successful with adolescents with emotional/behavioral disorders, teachers may choose to forego tokens and to implement a simplified contingency management system whereby the student is presented with an "If-then" proposition. ("If you finish your class assignment" [low probability behavior] "then you may listen to music through the headphones" [high probability behavior]).

Another promising avenue for educators is teaching self-control and self-management techniques to adolescents. Behavioral self-control and other forms of cognitive behavior management are especially important with adolescents because these techniques emphasize the shift from external to internal controls. The shift to internal controls becomes important as the individual matures and experiences more choices and options, while at the same time fewer restrictions are imposed by adults in the environment. Although tight environmental controls are used in the highly structured classrooms of many adolescent programs, the individual must learn to cope with increasing demands for independence if she is to be able to leave the program and be successful on her own. An emphasis on student self-control and student responsibility for outcomes also helps eliminate the power struggles between teacher and student so often found in adolescent classrooms.

Several self-management techniques have been implemented successfully with adolescents with emotional/behavioral disorders. Disruptive behavior has decreased with self-rating intervention (Smith, Young, West, Morgan, & Rhode, 1988), and on-task behavior has been improved with self-recording (Blick & Test, 1987; Lloyd & Hilliard, 1989; Smith et al., 1988). Although problems with generalization and maintenance of behavioral gains persist, self-management techniques with this population are promising. Social skills training is another important consideration in programming for adolescents with emotional/behavioral disorders. In addition to the benefit of increasing the probability of successful mainstreaming, social skills training can foster the development of social competence outside the classroom setting. Development of social competencies is especially important for adolescents with emotional/behavioral disorders, who have been characterized as "socially nearsighted" and as lacking in social judgment. Moreover, mixing with peers is an important competency for all adolescents to whom peer acceptance is one crucial determinant of self-worth. The concept of social skills training and two social skills curricula appropriate for adolescents were outlined in Chapter 7.

Counseling Techniques and Classroom Groups

Techniques employed in individual therapy sessions vary according to the preference and training of the therapist, but most focus upon some combination of self-understanding and the changing of behaviors that are maladaptive to the individual. Although family therapy has been available for years, only recently have researchers begun to view it as necessary for effecting long-term change in the life of a child. Because friction between parent and child is a normal part of the adolescent developmental phase, parent involvement in therapy is especially important for this age group. In fact, one study found a moderately high success rate for adolescents in therapy whose parents were involved in some part of the treatment plan, and a 100 percent failure rate for adolescents whose parents were not involved at all (Rosenstock & Vincent, 1979).

Another form of counseling especially effective with adolescents is group therapy. Group therapy may yield more satisfactory results than individual therapy for adolescents for several reasons. A strong allegiance to peers and need for peer approval is one factor. This strong identification with peers can be both a source of support and a source of pressure to conform to the group's ideas and values. With some adolescents, there is the additional factor of rebellion against adults or authority figures. Such an attitude, when coupled with an exaggerated need for privacy, often leaves an adult therapist with a sullen, non-communicative client. Therefore, group therapy is often a better outlet for adolescents than individual therapy. Group therapy for adolescents usually focuses upon a common theme, such as groups for individuals at risk for substance abuse or dropping out.

Teachers can implement group sessions in the classroom on a routine basis. These groups should be considered class meetings rather than group therapy. Coleman and Webber (1988) suggest that groups can be used to accomplish two major goals: (1) groups allow students and teacher to openly deal with sources of conflict that may be causing surface behavior problems, and (2) groups help shift control from external (teacher) to internal (students themselves). In other words, a group process allows students to analyze and manage their own actions and reactions.

BOX 9-3 Ham Bone and the Group Process[1]

The group described below was part of a prevention program funded by the state commission on alcohol and drug abuse and administered by the local child guidance center in two middle schools. The purpose of the eight-week groups was to provide experiential exercises to enhance social skills, problem-solving skills, and self-esteem. Students can be referred by counselors, teachers, administrators, parents or self.

One group consisted of 8 African-American 6th graders. Groups typically have ethnic balance; however, referrals determined the group composition. During the first meeting, the students signed a contract establishing ground rules for the group. They also played some "icebreaker" games. Two of the male students were absent at this meeting, but both showed up for the second meeting. One of these was about six inches taller and much stockier than the rest of the group; during introductions, he announced that his name was "Ham Bone." During icebreaker activities, Ham Bone repeatedly called the other students "nigger" and other racial epithets. He was unnecessarily rough and refused to hold hands during one activity because he "wasn't a fag."

According to the group contract, put-downs were not forbidden, but it was agreed that the group would discuss them. When Ham Bone's slurs were discussed, the other students responded that it didn't matter because "words can't hurt."

At the third session, Ham Bone and another student refused to participate in a trust-building activity. At the next session, the group confronted both students about their refusal to participate and decided that those who refused to participate should return to their classes. Ham Bone did participate in that day's activity, which was another trust-building activity using a blindfold. He also followed the group rules and refrained from name-calling. During the following sessions, Ham Bone continued to participate and his bullying and other negative behavior continued to decrease. During a particularly challenging problem-solving activity, Ham Bone reverted to his old behaviors of dominating and name-calling, but the group acted protective toward him and scapegoated another male group member. At the last session, Ham Bone was a model of considerate and cooperative behavior. He expressed concern about another student, was attentive during discussion, and volunteered to do helpful tasks. He also expressed frustration that the girls, who were giggling and whispering among themselves, were not abiding by the group guidelines. Ham Bone and the group had come to terms with one another.

Contributed by Beth Dennis, MSSW-CSW, and Rebecca Brown, M.A., therapists with the Austin Child Guidance Center
[1]The Texas Commission on Alcohol and Drug Abuse furnished financial support to the activity described in this publication. This does not imply the Commission's endorsement or concurrence with statements or conclusions contained therein.

Students should feel that the meetings are a forum during which they may speak freely and honestly. The teacher should also take an active part and provide direction to the group and support to those who may feel threatened. Ground rules should always be established and maintained. Box 9-3 illustrates how one group incorporated a recalcitrant member into its ranks.

Conclusions

Children who are labeled emotionally/behaviorally disordered do not tend to "grow out of it" as they approach adolescence; in fact, their behaviors may become more intense and have more serious ramifications. All adolescents become more egocentric and experience identity crises; many experiment with behavior that is deviant. These experiences are intensified for the adolescent with emotional/behavioral disorders, who has even fewer coping skills than his peers. School may be the only place that many of these kids will have access to the help they need with issues related to staying in school, drugs, alcohol, gangs, sex, and self-destructive behavior. Providing support while helping your students sort out all the confusion may be the most important thing you can do as a teacher. Viewing the adolescent as a child searching for an adult identity may be a helpful framework.

Key Points

1. Adolescence is an awkward period in which individuals are no longer children and not quite adults.
2. Struggles for identity, independence, and peer approval are the hallmarks of normally developing adolescents.
3. Research has failed to document pathology in adolescence that differs from pathology in childhood, suggesting that children with emotional/behavioral disorders grow into adolescents with emotional/behavioral disorders.
4. Teachers of adolescents must routinely deal with problems related to dropping out, drugs, gangs, sex, and self-destructive behavior such as eating disorders and suicide.
5. Although the effectiveness of school-based substance abuse education in reducing actual consumption has not been established, it is essential that educators continue to deal with substance use and abuse.
6. The content of sex education programs in the schools is the subject of much controversy; however, with the skyrocketing incidence of sexually transmitted diseases and teen-age pregnancies, schools must continue to deal with sex-related issues.
7. Recognizing the importance of peer approval to adolescents, teachers may want to use group sessions and group contingencies instead of individual ones.
8. Self-management becomes increasingly important during the teen-age years, as parents, teachers, and other authority figures have less and less control over the adolescent's environment.

Additional Readings

Alcohol and other drugs: Use, abuse and disabilities, by Peter Leone, 1991, Reston, VA: Council for Exceptional Children, for a handbook describing (a) the prevalence of these problems among exceptional children and youth, (b) strategies for practitioners, and (c) suggestions for program development.

Behavior problems? Try groups! by Maggie Coleman and Jo Webber, 1988, *Academic Therapy,* 23, pp. 265–274, for an article written for teachers who would like to try groups with adolescent students.

Depression and suicide in children and adolescents, by Nina Muse, Austin, TX: Pro-Ed, 1990, for a practical handbook for teachers and parents about identifying symptoms of depression and preventing suicide.

How to motivate adolescents: A guide for parents, teachers, and counselors, by L. Nielsen, Englewood Cliffs, NJ: Prentice Hall, 1982, for a handy paperback on motivating this difficult-to-motivate group.

Suicide and depression: Special education's responsibility, by Eleanor Guetzloe, *Teaching Exceptional Children, 20,* 1988, 25–28, for a discussion on what special educators should be doing about depression and suicide.

The management of sexual issues in adolescent treatment programs, by G.M. Realmuto & W.D. Erickson, *Adolescence, 21,* 1986, 347–356, for tips on how to deal with sexual issues with adolescents with emotional and behavioral problems

Chapter 10

Severe Behavior Disorders

CO-AUTHORED BY JO WEBBER

Defining Severe Behavior Disorders

What to Teach

How to Teach

Special Issues:
   Self-Injurious Behavior
   Communication/language
   Independent Living
   Working with Parents

Orientation

Jordi is diagnosed "childhood schizophrenic."
"He drank his milk slowly, watching her as she did the dishes.
Then she asked, 'How was it, Jordi?'
'The man was the same on the train.'
'What man?'
'The man who sat.'
'Who sat, Jordi?'
'The big stranger.'
'But how was school, Jordi?'
'School, pool, fool, tool. So jiggle, jiggle.'
He took the jiggler out of his pocket and left the house. The sun was going down, and he felt cold. He went back to the house and put on his sweater. Then he dangled the jiggler and waited.
The jiggler took him all over the neighborhood. He checked all the places —the tower, the busy street, the subway station. All of it was like before.

Then it was dark, and he felt the jiggler lead him home.
After supper he was very tired. He went to his room and fell asleep."
(From Lisa & David/Jordi, T. I. Rubin, 1962, p. 22)

Overview

Psychotic, schizophrenic, autistic . . . professionals disagree over what constitutes a severe behavior disorder and even whether use of the term is justifiable. However, few professionals deny that a group of children and adolescents exists for whom the more traditional methods of special education and therapy are unsuccessful: these children exhibit severely maladaptive behaviors and are very low functioning in cognitive and social domains. Many of these children are nonverbal, deficient in basic self-help skills, and engage in self-stimulatory or self-injurious behavior.

The premise of this chapter is that children with these characteristics require modifications in their educational programs that are quite different from those required by children with less severe disorders. Such modifications include developing a curriculum oriented toward addressing behavioral deficits (i.e., communication) by teaching functional skills, and reducing behavioral excesses (i.e., self-abuse) through behavior modification. The first section of this chapter defines the behavioral and cognitive characteristics of this population, and the second section delineates the needed modifications in curriculum and instruction. The third section addresses four major issues of concern to teachers of students with severe behavior disorders: (1) eliminating self-stimulatory and self-injurious behavior, (2) developing communication and social skills, (3) transition planning for independent living and possible employment, and (4) dealing with the special concerns of families.

Defining Severe Disorders

The label *severe behavior disorders* generally has been accepted as a generic or umbrella term for children with severely debilitating disturbances in affect or behavior. However, controversy has arisen over whether subclassifications of severely disordered behavior are helpful. Most researchers now believe that autism and schizophrenia constitute two separate syndromes worthy of diagnostic labels (Freeman & Ritvo, 1981; Kanner, 1943; Neel, 1979), although historically the two have been considered inseparable. Currently, children with severe behavior disorders might be classified as having a pervasive developmental disorder (PDD), the most severe form being autism, or they may be labeled as schizophrenic, with onset in childhood (Harvard Mental Health Letter, 1990). Controversy has plagued research in this area since autism and childhood schizophrenia were first identified: the group of children whom Bender (1942) studied and labeled as "childhood schizophrenics" were clinically similar to those identified as "autistic" by Kanner (1943). Bender used medically oriented diagnostic criteria such as difficulties with central nervous system integration and functioning. Although Kanner used behavioral criteria in describing autism, the symptoms he described could be manifestations of central nervous system dysfunction (inappropriate responses to objects, stereotypical or repetitive actions, disinterest in relating to people, insistence on "sameness" in the environment). Adding to the confusion, Bleuler (1911/1950) used the term *autistic* to refer to the withdrawn state of schizophrenics, and Goldfarb (1961, 1964) outlined nine diagnostic criteria for childhood schizophrenia, seven of which are also characteristic of autism. One current theory proposes that autism, PDD, schizophrenia with childhood onset, adult schizophrenia, and schizotypal personality are forms of a single illness with differences dependent on severity and age of onset (Harvard Mental Health Letter, 1990).

Autism

Definition

Despite the confusion, schizophrenia and autism are currently considered to be separate and distinct syndromes. Autism was included in the original P.L. 94-142 definition of emotional disturbance but was removed in 1981 and placed under the category of "Other Health Impaired." The American Psychiatric Association has categorized autism as a "Pervasive Developmental Disorder" since 1980 in their Diagnostic and Statistical Manual of Mental Disorders (DSM). These changes in diagnostic classification systems were a result of two trends: (1) updated research which suggests that autism is a biochemically or neurologically based disorder rather than an emotional disorder, and (2) a political move backed by parents and other advocacy groups to remove autism from the category of emotional disorders.

Beginning in the early seventies, a proliferation of research on autism emerged, due largely to advances in medical research technology and the successful application of behavior modification principles to severely maladaptive behaviors. As a result of coalescing this research on autism, the national advocacy organization adopted a definition of autism in 1977. This definition was recently revised:

> *Autism is a severely incapacitating lifelong developmental disability that typi-cally appears during the first three years of life. The result of a neurological disorder that affects functioning of the brain, autism and its behavioral symp-toms occur in approximately 15 out of 10,000 births. Autism is four times more common in boys than girls. It has been found throughout the world in families of all racial, ethnic, and social backgrounds. No known factors in the psychological environment of a child have been shown to cause autism. . . Autism is a behav-iorally defined syndrome. Some behavioral symptoms of autism include:*
> *(a) Disturbances in the rate of appearance of physical, social, and language skills.*
> *(b) Abnormal responses to sensations. Any one or a combination of senses or reponses are affected: sight, hearing, touch, balance, smell, taste, reaction to pain, and the way a child holds his or her body.*
> *(c) Speech and language are absent or delayed, while specific thinking capaci-ties may be present.*
> *(d) Abnormal ways of relating to people, events and objects. (Autism Society of America, 1994, p. 3).*

This definition has implications for causal theories, particularly the psychogenic theory. Touted by several of the early researchers in this area (Bettelheim, 1959; Goldfarb, 1961;

Kanner, 1943; Szurek, 1956), the psychogenic theory suggested that negative personality characteristics of parents are causal factors in the development of autism. Terms such as *cold, unresponsive, rejecting,* and *personality disordered* were cited as parental characteristics that caused children to become totally withdrawn from social interaction. However, subsequent research has not borne out the psychogenic theory. Research that refutes this stance can be divided into two categories: (1) that which finds no significant differences between parents of psychotic or autistic children and parents of normal children (e.g., Creak & Ini, 1960; Peck et al., 1969; Rutter et al., 1971), and (2) that which supports a physiological or biochemical causation of autism (e.g., Courchesne, 1988; DesLauriers & Carlson, 1969; Hutt, Hutt, Lee, & Ounsted, 1964; Ornitz, 1978; Rimland, 1971; Ritvo, Rahm, Yuwiler, Freeman, & Geller, 1978; Ritvo, 1988). This research is reflected in the definition's statement that autism is a result of a neurological disorder that affects brain functioning. Parental pathology has effectively been ruled out as a causal factor in the development of autism.

The diagnostic criteria offered by the current Diagnostic and Statistical Manual (DSM-IV, American Psychiatric Association, 1994) are similar to those offered in the definition. For a diagnosis of autism, DSM-IV requires behaviors that are (a) characteristic of impairment in social interaction, (b) characteristic of impairment in communication, and (c) repetitive and stereotyped patterns. Delays in symbolic or imaginative play are also mentioned as diagnostic indicators.

A rating scale based upon both the definition and DSM-IV criteria has been developed to aid in diagnosing individuals with autism. The *Gilliam Autism Rating Scale, GARS* (Gilliam, 1995) is described in Table 10-1.

Etiology

The etiology of autism was discussed in Chapter 3 under the biophysical model. Biochemical correlates have been found in numerous neurotransmitter studies, especially those showing elevated levels of the neurotransmitter serotonin in children with autism; however, these studies do not establish causality. Abnormalities also have been found in the brainstem and the cerebellum of children with autism (Ornitz et al., 1985; Ritvo et al, 1986).

More recently, Courchesne and his colleagues documented abnormalities of the cerebellum in a study of 50 subjects with autism compared to 50 subjects without disabilities (cited in Autism Research Review International, 1994a). Using magnetic resonance imaging (MRI) techniques, Courchesne et al. found that 86 percent of the autistic subjects showed underdevelopment of specific areas of the cerebellum, and 12 percent showed signficant overdevelopment of the same areas. The researchers reported that the degree of impairment correlates with the degree of cerebellar abnormality. Further work by Corchesne and his colleagues suggests that the cerebellum may affect the ability to shift attention, thus partially accounting for the inability of persons with autism to blend a number of perceptions into a coherent whole. For example, this difficulty might explain the inability of autistic persons to interact socially in that normal social interactions would be perceived as a group of disconnected fragments made up of gestures, facial expressions, and vocal information. In related work, Courchesne has found that 43 percent of subjects with autism had parietal lobe defects, which may explain the tendency toward stimulus overselectivity discussed in the next section. The specific causes of such cerebellar abnormalities are unknown, but include

TABLE 10-1   Subtests and Selected Items from the *Gilliam Autism Rating Scale*

Stereotyped Behaviors
1. Avoids establishing eye contact (i.e., looks away when eye contact is made).
2. Stares at hands, objects, or items in the environment for at least 5 seconds.
5. Licks inedible objects (e.g., person's hand, toys, books, etc.)
8. Spins objects not designed for spinning (e.g.,saucers, cups, glasses, etc.)
9. Rocks back and forth while seated or standing.

Communication
15. Repeats (echoes) words verbally or with signs.
17. Repeats words or phrases over and over.
22. Fails to initiate conversations with peers or adults.
24. Uses pronouns inappropriately (refers to self as he, you, she, etc.)
27. Uses gestures instead of speech or sign to obtain objects.

Social Interaction
31. Resists physical contact from others (doesn't seem to like hugs, pats, being held, or other close contact).
32. Non-imitative of other people when playing.
36. Looks through people (i.e., shows no recognition that a person is present).
39. Does things repetitively, ritualistically.
40. Becomes upset when routines are changed.

Developmental Disturbances (manifested in first 36 months of life)
43. Did the child walk in the first 15 months of life?
48. Did the child reach out or prepare to be picked up when the parent attempted to lift the child?
49. Did the child smile at parents or siblings when played with?
50. Did the child cry when approached by unfamiliar persons during the first year?
54. Did the child appear to be deaf to certain sounds but hear others?

From Gilliam. J. E. (1995). *Gilliam Autism Rating Scale*. Austin TX: Pro-Ed. Reprinted by permission of the author and the publisher. Copyright 1995.

the usual etiologies of genetic defects, infections, toxic exposure, lack of oxygen, and metabolic disorders. The damage apparently occurs before or shortly after birth (Autism Research Review International, 1994a).

Characteristics Related to Learning

Characteristics unique to children with autism that are directly related to learning include *stimulus overselectivity, diminished motivation, self-stimulatory behaviors,* and *abnormal responses to reinforcement* and other consequences (Simpson & Regan, 1988).

Stimulus overselectivity.   This concept refers to restricted attention to the environment. Children with autism usually do not attend to people, but obsessively attend to sensory stimuli and objects. For example, while many do not willingly respond to another person's voice or give eye contact, they may spend unusually long periods of time staring at flickering lights or spinning objects. They appear overresponsive or underresponsive to pain, touch, or changes in temperature or lighting because they can only respond to a few of the stimuli available to them. It appears that they see, hear, and feel things much differently than children without autism. Thus, a teacher who points to a picture in order to assist the student in matching a picture to a word might have only succeeded in teaching the student to match the word to her pointing finger.

Diminished motivation.   Most children are naturally motivated to explore new environments and try new behavior in order to meet their needs. Children with autism are not motivated in this way. For example, a child with autism who is hungry might become agitated but not point to the food, look for food, or even grab at the food in order to get it. Thus there may be very few productive responses from these students (i.e., no attempt to communicate, try out a new toy, ask for help, etc.), resulting in fewer opportunities to reinforce behavior and diminishing motivation to learn.

Self-stimulatory behaviors.   Behaviors such as rocking, spinning objects, hand-flapping, and gutteral noises are non-productive behaviors and interfere with the learning of productive behaviors. Children with autism will spend hours engaged in self-stimulatory behavior to the exclusion of the rest of the world. Reasons for engaging in self-stimulation will be addressed later in the chapter, but it is obvious that these behaviors must be reduced or eliminated in order for the child to be able to attend to learning tasks.

Responses to reinforcement.   Reinforcers, a primary tool in motivating children to learn, are very difficult to find for children with autism. These children do not like many things available in the environment (e.g., praise, toys, TV), preferring, instead, to engage in self-stimulatory behavior. According to behavior learning theory, the motivation for students to learn new responses (e.g., talking, reading, toileting) comes from receiving desirable stimuli (e.g., praise, privileges, status, materials) after correct responding.

   Motivating a student with autism demands creativity on the part of the teacher. One example of a reinforcer not usually found in other classrooms is letting the student drink water after eating crackers. Even if an effective reinforcer is found, the student may not connect appropriate behavior with receiving the reinforcer. For instance, a teacher may require the student to say "drink" in order to receive the water. But if he says "drink," looks to the right, and flicks his fingers before the teacher gives him a sip, then he might connect finger-flicking with the water, and not know to say "drink" the next time he wants water.

   Children with autism often react uniquely to punishment by responding as though it were reinforcing. One type of punishment, timeout, allows more time to self-stimulate. The administration of pain might also provide desired sensory input. Removing rewards is also often ineffective because autistic children find so few things rewarding. Therefore, teachers must keep detailed behavioral data in order to determine which reinforcers and which punishers will work to motivate an individual student to learn.

Other Characteristics

Other characteristics that make working with this population challenging include resistance to change, speech and language deficits, and below-average intelligence. The insistence on sameness in the environment identified by Kanner (1943) in his original study means that any change in routine, however slight, is potentially upsetting. For example, the breakfast table must be set with exactly the same utensils, the same route to school must always be taken, and the same bus driver must always be present. If there is any change, the child may become very upset, throw tantrums, and insist on having it done "the right way."

Although some children with autism are highly verbal, speech is usually nonexistent or severely delayed and appears to have little communicative value for the majority of this population. The symbolic use of language is lacking, as evidenced by the absence of imaginative play in younger children and failure to understand the use of symbols in older children. Echolalia, which is parrotlike repetition of words and sentences, and pronoun reversal (for example, use of "I" for "he" or use of "he" to mean "everyone") are common. Receptive language is also usually very poor, resulting in an inability to understand others at a basic level. Thus, comprehensive language difficulties at both functional and symbolic levels are a central characteristic of autism. Language capabilities often exhibited by children with autism are illustrated in Box 10-1.

The intelligence of children with autism has been misinterpreted in the past, largely due to the existence of splinter skills among some autistic children. While functionally retarded, some youngsters have displayed remarkable rote memory for television commercials, poems, speeches, songs, or other long passages requiring high levels of memorization. The young man with autism portrayed by Dustin Hoffman in the movie *Rainman* demonstrated such a splinter skill in his complex mathematical abilities. Such skills led Kanner (1943) and others to hypothesize that these children actually have normal-to-superior cognitive abilities that are masked by emotional and communication problems. However, subsequent research has shown: (1) the majority of children with autism score in the moderately retarded range on intelligence tests (Bartak & Rutter, 1973; DeMyer, 1979), (2) that such scores are reliable over time for children with IQs under 50 (Baker, 1979; Rutter, 1978) but more variable with higher functioning children (Schopler & Dalldorf, 1980), and (3) that IQ and the language level combined with IQ are the best predictors of potential functioning for an autistic individual (DeMyer, 1979; Lovaas, Koegel, Simmons, & Stevens, 1972; Rutter, 1978; Schopler & Dalldorf, 1980). Generally, the prognosis for children with autism is poor (American Psychiatric Association, 1980). Approximately one in six will achieve independent living and competitive employment; another one in six will make minimal social adjustment needing supervision; and two-thirds will remain severely disabled, usually residing in institutions.

Schizophrenia

Definition and Characteristics

As mentioned previously, the terms *autism* and *childhood schizophrenia* were first used in the early forties and were often used interchangeably in research. It is therefore difficult to trace the development of the concept of childhood schizophrenia as a syndrome separate from autism. Realizing the limitations of an adult model of schizophrenia imposed on children, the psychiatric and psychological communities deleted childhood schizophrenia as a category in their classification system in the late seventies and early eighties. In addition, they classifed autism as a pervasive developmental disorder.

However, many professionals believe that schizophrenia can be found in children. Although the onset of schizophrenia generally occurs in adolescence or young adulthood, some children do exhibit symptoms similar to adult schizophrenia. Despite the fact that

---

BOX 10-1 A Glimpse into a Classroom for Children with Autism

He gleefully sat spinning the saucer on the tiled floor. As the saucer vibrated to a stop, his eyes danced with excitement and he sang his nonsensical tune, "ee-ah, ee-ah, ee-ah." As he sang, he rocked back and forth, seemingly oblivious to the others in the room. When the saucer stopped, he picked it up and with almost artistic skill flipped it into another rapid rotation. Infrequently his eyes would dart to other children in the room, but only as if to confirm their position about him, never to establish contact. As if it were a magnet, the spinning saucer compelled his attention. Again the song, "ee-ah, ee-ah, ee-ah."

In a corner the teacher was saying, "Joey, touch red," indicating a red block on the desk top. With almost forced effort, Joey began to lift his hands from his lap. When his hands were above the desk, he quickly slapped the block off the desk top.

"Joey, no" the teacher said firmly.

As if on cue, the boy made his hand into a fist and pounded his ear repeatedly. His facial expression never changed as the teacher grabbed his wrist and placed his hand on his lap.

"No hitting," she said. Placing another red block on the desk, she repeated, "Touch red."

Again Joey started to respond, then slapped the block off the desk.

Immediately he jammed the back of his hand against his mouth and began biting it.

Alone at a desk, the girl was busy placing a shiny washer on a large bolt. As she completed this action she picked up a nut and, with a quick rotation of her fingers, skillfully threaded the nut onto the bolt and placed it into a box of other similarly dressed bolts.

"Good working, Mary," her teacher complimented. At a table in the front of the room, the teacher's aide was speaking to a handsome child who seemed to be attending closely.

"What's your name?" the aide asked.

"What's your name?" the child responded in a monotone.

"No, listen now. Tommy, what's your name?"

"Tommy, what's your name?" the child echoed.

"Okay, Tommy, let's take a break. Do you want to play?"

"Want to play?" he said, as he jumped up. It was mid-morning and time for a break for everyone in the class.

Contributed by Jim Gilliam, Ph.D., Associate Professor of Special Education, The University of Texas at Austin.

---

schizophrenia is a label for adults in the DSM-IV, children may be so classified if they fit the diagnostic criteria. Childhood-onset schizophrenia is much rarer than adult-onset, occurring at about one-sixtieth the rate. It is considered more severe than adult schizophrenia, as adults may have psychotic episodes that come and go, but children most often experience chronic difficulties (NARSAD Research Letter, 1994). Children exhibiting severe language difficulties and bizarre behaviors may also be diagnosed with pervasive developmental disorder (PDD) if their symptoms do not clearly match those of schizophrenia or of autism. The federal definition of emotional disturbance outlined in federal law allows for the inclusion of children with schizophrenia. The following characteristics are typical of children with schizophrenia:

1. *Inappropriate affect.* Affect and emotions are inappropriate for given situations and may change rapidly with no apparent reason. May exhibit little or no affect, or be highly anxious or explosive.

2. *Disinterest in surroundings* and *deterioration* from previous levels of functioning. Loses interest in self-care and in interacting with others. May stop eating, bathing, or taking any care in dressing. Parents, friends, and teachers may get only a minimal response. Usually a deterioration of functioning, that is, skills and behaviors previously attained are no longer evident.

3. *Variable behavior.* Inappropriate behaviors or symptoms may come and go; periods of normalcy are interspersed with periods of bizarre behavior, during which strange language and inappropriate affect are evident.

4. *Inappropriate speech.* May be highly verbal and have experienced normal language development, but speech becomes disjointed or bizarre. Voice tone or pitch may change drastically or child may exhibit echolalia. May talk to self. May use nonsense words or put words together in a sentence that doesn't make sense. In extreme cases, child may create his own language of nonsense words. Such language deterioration usually reflects disorganized thought processes.

5. *Delusions or hallucinations.* A hallmark of adult schizophrenia, which may or may not be present in childhood schizophrenia. Delusions and hallucinations will usually begin by age seven. Delusions are totally irrational false beliefs. Examples of rather common delusions are the beliefs that one is actually a famous personality (Jesus Christ and Napoleon are popular choices for adults) or feelings of persecution (for example, "Others can steal my thoughts and use them to harm me"). Hallucinations may be either visual or auditory; some children with schizophrenia report having conversations with voices that sometimes tell them to do things.

Etiology

The genetic predisposition toward schizophrenia and the positive response of persons with schizophrenia to antispychotic drugs were briefly discussed in Chapter 3. To recap, we know that a susceptibility to schizophrenia runs in families, and we know that antipsychotic drugs act on the neurotransmitter dopamine, which results in alleviation of the most distressing symptoms of schizophrenia such as hallucinations and disordered thinking. Currently, we do not know exactly how the genetic predisposition is passed from generation to generation, and we do not know why schizophrenic individuals apparently have elevated levels of dopamine. The search for specific gene markers is underway, but it is thought that a combination of markers may be responsible. It is further speculated that the combination of markers may vary from family to family, therefore possibly accounting for the influence of the environment in determining which of the "genetically predisposed" individuals will eventually develop schizophrenia. Current thinking on etiology can be summarized thus:

> *The best present scientific guess is that a defect in the genetic control of fetal brain development results in a structural abnormality that makes a person vulnerable to schizophrenia later in life, either because of environmental influences or because of changes in the maturing brain, including the hormonal flood of puberty (Harvard Mental Health Letter, 1992, p. 2)*

Differential Diagnosis

Some children with schizophrenia experience distorted perceptions of sensory stimuli such as light and touch, and some exhibit hyperactivity or repetitive motor activity such as body rocking or hand movement. These symptoms are also typical of children with autism which has added to the confusion in making differential diagnoses. However, there are a few differences that help distinguish between autism and schizophrenia. First is the age of onset. By definition, autism occurs in the first 36 months of life, and symptoms such as highly irregular sleep patterns, aversiveness to being touched, held, or cuddled, and abnormal patterns of development in speech and motor skills during the first three years are usually noted by parents. In contrast, schizophrenia is rarely diagnosed until age four or five, after much normal physical, cognitive, and social development has already occurred; it is much more commonly diagnosed in adolesence or adulthood. A second point of differential diagnosis is the occasional presence of delusions and hallucinations in children with schizophrenia and the absence of these symptoms in children with autism. A third point of differential diagnosis is in language usage. Although children with schizophrenia may use language inappropriately or in a bizarre manner, they generally have a grasp of the syntax and the function of language. Children with autism are often mute, echolalic, or characterized by a severe language delay. Even after careful language programming, many autistic children fail to understand the functional use of language.

A fourth point is that most children with schizophrenia naturally relate to people and the environment, although on a sporadic basis and sometimes in a bizarre manner. In contrast, children with autism are more attentive to objects and sensory stimuli in the environment than they are to other people; they must often be taught to attend to human voices and to make eye contact. Bettelheim (1967) described this difference by remarking that the schizophrenic child withdraws from his world but the autistic child never enters it.

A fifth point is that children with schizophrenia, as a group, tend to have higher IQs than children with autism. On tests of cognitive functioning, autistic children often excel in short-term memory and visual-motor coordination, whereas children with schizophrenia find it more difficult to filter out distractions and organize sensory data (American Psychiatric Association, 1980). On the other hand, autistic children will often struggle on tests requiring abstract thinking and normal language.

Additionally, children with schizophrenia show more emotion such as anger, fear, and worry, and they have more physical complaints. They tend to have more psychiatric disorders in their families. Schizophrenia in childhood predisposes the individual toward schizophrenia in adulthood.

Although teachers may be asked to describe a child's functioning level or to keep behavioral data, the differential diagnosis of severely disordered behaviors is primarily the domain of psychologists and psychiatrists. Whether a child is labeled as autistic or schizophrenic will have little bearing on the educational program that is designed and implemented by the special education teacher. Instead, the teacher should focus on educationally relevant characteristics.

In summary, specific labels for severe disorders such as schizophrenic or autistic rarely provide the classroom teacher with information for instructional planning. Instead, for this population, the teacher must evaluate each student's functioning in a number of areas and plan instruction based on refined behavioral techniques. Classroom planning for students with severe behavior disorders is the focus of the next section, and it is here that the special needs of these students become most evident.

Programming for Students with Severe Disorders

Working with students with severe behavior disorders poses a challenge for educators not only in the heterogeneity among individuals but also in the variability of functioning within individuals. Skill development in autistic children is particularly varied. For example, a child with autism may possess excellent rote memory or read at a basic level yet be unable to go to the bathroom without help. Other special problems with this population are serious behavior problems and extreme deficits in communication. Receptive and/or expressive language may be severely impaired; when coupled with lack of motivation and disinterest in the environment, such deficits can impede even basic development. As a result, these students are often functionally retarded in most situations inside and outside the classroom.

Deciding What to Teach

The first step in deciding what to teach is to identify specific *behavioral excesses* (e.g., self-stimulation, self-abuse, tantrums) and specific *behavioral deficits* (e.g., language and social skills deficits) unique to each student. This assessment process should include a review of records, interviews with parents and previous teachers, behavior checklists, and informal observational recording. After these data are gathered, the second step is to develop goals and objectives both for reducing behavioral excesses and for teaching new behavior in the deficient areas. The third step is to check for social validity. Do significant people in the child's environment think it is important for the child to learn the skills to be taught?

Deciding which behavioral excesses should be addressed is usually not difficult because bizarre behavior is so visible and disturbing. Deciding which behavioral deficits to address can be accomplished in two ways: (1) curriculum can be developed by evaluating a student's performance in traditional curricular areas, or (2) it can be developed by evaluating a student's day-to-day performance in many settings and creating a completely unique curriculum for each student. Both types of curriculum development will be addressed.

Traditional Curriculum Development

A program for students with severe behavior disorders should include six basic curricular areas: *prerequisite skills, language-communication, self-help, social, cognitive,* and *prevocational/vocational.* A teacher can either examine published curricula or create her own curricular sequences. Each student should be assessed as to which skills in the selected sequence have been mastered. The skills next in the sequence for each area then constitute the curriculum. Each of the traditional curricular areas is addressed in the following sections.

Prerequisite skills.   Some children will lack basic prerequisite behaviors for learning that must be taught before other curricular areas can be addressed. These behaviors include sitting, attending, eye contact, and responding to simple commands (Simpson and Regan, 1988). These behaviors may take several days or weeks to teach, but little progress will be made until these basic responses are present. Additionally, simple imitation and discrimination tasks must be mastered. For example, the student should be able to copy motor movements such as raising arms above the head, and discriminate by shape, size, sound, color, etc., before more complex training can begin.

Language/communication. Communication skills of this group can be very baffling, as some students have well-developed language abilities, while others are totally nonverbal; some have fairly high receptive language but minimal expressive language, and others are echolalic or have well-developed speech but attach no meaning whatsoever to the words. The primary goal of this curriculum area is to provide the individual with a means of communicating with others, whether it be through speech and language development, sign language, or with a communication board. A minimum level of communication is obviously a prerequisite for establishing a teacher-student relationship and moving to other curricular areas. If a student is language disordered, the services of speech therapists or language therapists are usually included in the student's individualized program; however, if a specialized language program is to be effective, it must be incorporated into the child's daily classroom experiences by the special education teacher. The issue of teaching communication skills to this population is dealt with later in this chapter under "Special Issues."

Self-help. The major goal of teaching self-help skills is to enable a child to function independently in everyday life. Areas in self-help include toileting, dressing, eating, and safety. Student mastery of objectives within the self-help area usually requires the teacher to task-analyze and/or to model the desired skill. Many published curricula for students with severe disablties include task analyses or specific behavioral programs for teaching self-help tasks such as tying shoelaces, zipping jackets, brushing teeth, and toileting. Along with communication development, this curricular area should take precedence with lower functioning students.

Social. The teaching of social skills to students with severe disorders is predicated upon minimal communication skills and the absence of interfering negative behaviors. In addition to their disinterest in the environment, many of these children engage in self-stimulatory behavior, self-injurious behavior, or repetitive motor activity. Examples are rocking or whirling the body, hand-flapping, head-banging, and arm-biting. Such extreme behaviors obviously interfere with socialization and should be controlled or eliminated. The elimination of negative behaviors should be followed by the direct teaching of positive social skills such as responding to another's statements, introducing oneself by name, smiling and initiating conversation. All age-appropriate conversational and behavioral skills that enable the child to fit more easily into the peer group or the community are desirable teaching objectives.

Cognitive. Some students with severe disorders are able to attain functional literacy, that is, to read, write, and compute numbers well enough to get along in society. (Estimates of functional literacy range from third-grade levels to eighth-grade levels, with many experts choosing sixth-grade as criterion level.) In very rare cases, students with severe behavior disorders are able to complete a high school curriculum and maintain themselves in college. With students who are higher functioning, academic skills may constitute a feasible and separate curriculum area. For example, a reading objective of demonstrating literal comprehension may be appropriate.

However, the majority of this population are unable to attain functional literacy and are operating at a preacademic level. Imitation and discrimination tasks, basic counting, and matching tasks are a few examples of basic cognitive skills. For these students, it is best to infuse cognitive tasks into other areas of the curriculum such as prevocational or self-help (For example, discriminating between a shirt and a sock, or recognizing basic sight words in public: "Women," "Men," "Wet Floor"). In making this decision for an individual, the teacher should consider the student's age, intelligence, and language level. For adolescents who have not progressed beyond the preacademic level, it is more helpful to spend instructional time on vocational and survival skills than on isolated readiness skills.

Prevocational/vocational.   Prevocational and vocational training is a necessity for this population if integration into the community is to become a reality. Communication and social skills are necessary but not sufficient for adults with severe disorders to be able to maintain themselves independently or semi-independently in the community; some means of financial support is also necessary. The goal of prevocational training is to prepare students, at a young age, to demonstrate job-related behavior. Common objectives of prevocational training are general skills such as complying with requests, following directions, staying on task, and completing tasks, and specific skills such as using tools, sorting objects, or matching samples.

Vocational training addresses actual job tasks that can earn money. Students learn to perform tasks such as woodwork, assembly tasks, and cleaning. Vocational programming for this population differs from vocational training for students with mild behavior disorders and is addressed in more detail under "Special Issues."

Environmental Curriculum Development

A second way to determine what to teach these students is to bypass traditional curricular areas and create a curriculum unique to the individual student. This type of curriculum is based on what the student needs to learn to be able to function in all aspects of his life. The teacher is required to first assess the student's environmental demands and then match goals and objectives to deficient areas. Listed below are steps for the teacher to follow in order to develop this type of curriculum.

1. List all the environments in which the student must function in his daily life (e.g., home, school, neighborhood park, etc.). Eliciting the help of parents in this process is a necessity.

2. List all sub-environments of each major environment (e.g., bathroom, classroom, hall).

3. List all activities that need to be performed in the sub-environments (e.g., toileting, washing hands, drying hands). This might require the teacher to spend time analyzing what a person without disabilities does in the bathroom or classroom.

4. List the skills necessary for each activity (e.g., pulling pants up and down for toileting, turning water on and off). Determine prerequisite skills necessary for the entire activity to be performed.

5. Task analyze each skill. The process of task analysis or breaking down a skill into smaller instructional components will be addressed in the next section.

6. Implement instruction (Brown et al., 1979).

This method of developing a functional curriculum may preclude the traditional curricular areas mentioned earlier. Proponents of this method claim that skills selected through a functional approach are the most relevant to the student's life. Additionally, the generalizability of functional skills is increased because people will naturally reinforce the student for performing relevant tasks. On the other hand, a teacher usually does not have time to assess all possible environments for each student and often will resort to traditional curricula for convenience.

One method of combining traditional and environmental curriculum development is suggested by McGinnis (1982). Educators who are using traditional curricular areas should consider the environmental domains in which students will be expected to function as adults. These include the home, community, vocational or work setting, and settings in which adults with disabilities are expected to spend leisure time and to interact with adults without disabilities. Thus, skills that need to be taught are skills that will be needed in one or more of these environments. For instance:

Community functioning	Using public transportation
	Using pay telephones
	Recognizing street signs
	Comprehending dangerous situations
Home functioning	Self-help in eating and dressing
	Preparing meals
	Doing household chores
Vocational functioning	Being on time
	Completing tasks
	Traveling to and from work
Recreational functioning	Absence of self-stimulating behaviors
	Interest in and ability to ride a bike, play table games, electronic games, or pinball, swim, watch TV, use books and magazines, do artwork
Interacting with adults without disabilities	Greeting others
	Asking appropriate questions
	Dealing with frustration (McGinnis, 1982)

McGinnis advocates that teachers use a grid format to help develop objectives in the traditional curricular areas for each of the basic environmental domains. A grid using five traditional curricular areas and five environmental domains advocated in this text is presented in Table 10-2.

Regardless of which method of curriculum development is chosen, the teacher will need to consider the functionality of the curriculum.

A Functional Curriculum

The prognosis for independent functioning for schizophrenic or autistic adults is quite poor; it is estimated that 75 percent of autistic adults will spend their lives in institutional placements (DeMyer, 1979) and the majority of schizophrenics will spend most of their adult lives in and out of psychiatric hospitals. If this trend of institutionalization is to be reversed,

TABLE 10-2 **Development of Curricular Objectives**

Curriculum Areas	Home	Community	Vocational	Recreational	Interacting with Nondisabled
Language/ Communication					
Self-Help					
Social					
Academics					
Vocational					
	Home	Community	Vocational	Recreational	Interacting with Nondisabled

Domains

From "An Individual Curricula for Children and Youth with Autism," by Ellen McGinnis, 1982. In C. R. Smith, J. Grimes and J. Freilinger (Eds.). *Autism: Programmatic Consideration*, pp. 170–207. Des Moines: Iowa Department of Public Instruction. Reprinted by permission.

educators must prepare students with severe disabilities to function as independently as possible. This goal has been dubbed the "criterion of ultimate functioning," which requires that programs for persons with disabilities focus on skills that allow optimal independent functioning in the least restrictive environment (Brown, Nietupski, & Hamre-Nietupski, 1976; Donnellan, Mesaros, & Anderson, 1985). In other words, not only broad curricular areas but also specific instructional objectives should be selected according to plans for long-range functioning of the individual in the community. When selecting objectives to meet the criterion of ultimate functioning, Brown et al. (1976) suggest that the following questions be answered:

1. Why should we engage in this activity?
2. Is this activity necessary to prepare students to ultimately function in complex heterogeneous community settings?
3. Could students function as adults if they did not acquire the skill?
4. Is there a different activity that will allow students to approximate realization of the criterion of ultimate functioning more quickly and more efficiently?
5. Will this activity impede, restrict, or reduce the probability that students will ultimately function in community settings?

6. Are the skills, materials, tasks, and criteria similar to those encountered in real life? (p. 9)

Although such questions are vitally important for adolescents with severe disorders who are nearing the end of their educational program, it is also important to consider these questions when program planning for students who are younger and have milder disorders.

The concept of functional skills has been further developed by Donnellan (1980) and by McGinnis (1982). In determining future usefulness of a skill, Donnellan (1980) advocates asking the question, "If this child does not learn to perform this skill, will someone have to do it for him?" (p. 71). For instance, if a child does not learn to cut up meat at dinner or brush his teeth before bedtime, someone else will have to do it for him; however, if a child fails to recite the alphabet or sort blocks by color, no one will have to help the youngster complete the task. McGinnis (1982) cites several examples of functional and nonfunctional activities that are age-appropriate for adolescents:

NONFUNCTIONAL ACTIVITIES	*FUNCTIONAL ACTIVITIES*
a. Counting pegs and blocks	Counting silverware, money for a purchase
b. Pointing to hands	Shaking hands
c. Sorting paper pieces; matching colored blocks	Matching and sorting silverware into drawer tray; sorting clothing or coins; sorting materials such as nuts and bolts (needed in sheltered workshop settings)
d. Placing pegs in a pegboard	Placing coins in a vending machine or a washing machine at the laundry
e. Reading basal text	Reading bus schedules, menus, street signs, recipes, TV guides, etc.

As illustrated by the examples, *functional* does not mean *nonacademic;* basic academic skills such as counting and reading are very functional when applied to situations which the student encounters in everyday life. Also, tasks are not inherently functional or nonfunctional: placing pegs in a pegboard is functional if the goal is to teach the student to play a game such as cribbage. The information about Daryl in Box 10-2 illustrates the importance of focusing on functional skills.

Deciding How to Teach

Due to their unique learning characteristics, students with severe disorders require different instructional methodology from that required for students with mild-moderate disabilities. It was not until the 1960s that educators and psychologists began to experience success in teaching behavioral and academic skills to students with severe disorders, and it was not until the 1970s that successful model programs were established in the public schools (Koegel & Rincover, 1974; Kozloff, 1975). The success of these programs has been due largely to the increasing sophistication in applying behavioral techniques to a number of particularly difficult areas such as the acquisition of language skills (Lovaas, 1966) and

BOX 10-2 Daryl

Eighteen years old (30–49 IQ). Been in school twelve years. Never been served in any setting other than elementary school. He has had a number of years of "individual instruction." He has learned to do a lot of things he couldn't do before!

• Daryl can put 100 pegs in a board in less than 10 minutes with 95 percent accuracy—but he can't put quarters in a vending machine.

• Upon command, he can can touch his nose, shoulder, leg, foot, hair and ear; he's still working on wrist, ankle, and hips—but he can't blow his nose when needed.

• He can now fold primary paper into halves and even quarters—but he can't fold his clothes.

• He can string beads in alternative colors and match it to a pattern—but he can't lace his shoes.

• He can sing his ABC's and tell the names of all the upper case letters with 80 percent accuracy—but he can't tell the men's room from the ladies' room at McDonald's.

• He can sit in a circle and sing songs and play "Duck, Duck, Goose,"—but nobody else his age in our neighborhood seems to want to do that.

I guess he's just not ready yet.

Adapted from the TASH Newsletter, December, 1987

elimination of self-injurious behaviors (Lovaas & Simmons, 1969; Wolf, Risley, & Mees, 1964). Establishing a basic form of communication and eliminating self-injurious or self-stimulating behaviors are obviously important areas of learning. Because so many children with severe disorders experience problems in these two areas, each topic is treated separately under "Special Issues" later in this chapter. This section delineates techniques that have been found to be effective in overcoming learning problems in this population.

Countering Overselectivity

As mentioned earlier, one important learning problem of children with autism is stimulus overselectivity. Stimulus overselectivity is defined by Stainback and Stainback (1980) as attention to limited aspects of a task. Overselectivity has a pervasive detrimental effect on learning, as the tendency to focus on one (often irrelevant) aspect of a task or characteristic of an object interferes with generalization. For instance, a teacher may be attempting to teach the concept of the number five with five green blocks; while the teacher is attempting to instill an association between the word "five" and the five blocks, the student is focusing on the color green. If the materials were changed to five yellow or to multicolored blocks, the student would no longer associate the word "five" with the five blocks. In other words, the student's overselectivity caused attention to an irrelevant aspect of the task (color) and prevented learning the concept (five) and generalizing to another situation (given multicolored blocks).

The teaching of students with autism therefore requires that measures be taken to counteract tendencies toward overselectivity. Educators have found that varying the learning environment in systematic ways can help overcome overselectivity and promote generalization of acquired skills (Sailor & Guess, 1983). Irrelevant attributes of the task (i.e., color when trying to teach number, shape when trying to teach color) must be varied. In addition, aids that are used to assist with initial learning (teacher prompts such as pointing or giving directions) must be systematically applied and faded. Prompts and cues work best when they are present within the task demand as opposed to giving the child a separate prompt such as pointing (Schreibman, 1975; Rincover, 1978). For instance, the five blocks in the above example would be placed on a card with the number 5 on it. Different colored blocks and various objects could be introduced as "five" on the card to prevent the student from focusing on irrelevant attributes of the task.

Increasing Motivation

Another learning problem common to children with autism is diminished motivation. These students display little or no goal-directed behavior and are virtually unmotivated to learn behaviors necessary to function in life. Ferster (1961) originally wrote of success in motivating autistic individuals through the principles of positive reinforcement. The use of positive reinforcement has been shown to motivate these students to learn language, self-help skills, school-related behaviors, and work skills (Koegel, Rincover, and Egel, 1982). Due to the fact that children with autism respond uniquely to consequences, very powerful reinforcers such as food have been necessary for motivational purposes. However, food as a reinforcer has limited usefulness for a couple of reasons: it causes satiation (the individual tires of it easily), and has restricted generalizability in that the child may refuse to perform unless food is offered. Thus, continued research into effective reinforcement techniques has been necessary.

One method of increasing the effectiveness of positive reinforcement is to provide a reinforcer as part of the behavior that is being required of the student. This method is called *direct response reinforcement* (Koegel and Williams, 1980). For example, while teaching the child the color green the teacher says, "Open the green box." Within the box is a favorite piece of candy. Another method of effective reinforcement is the provision of sensory stimuli (tickling, music, vibrations, flashing lights, etc.) rather than food reinforcers. These types of reinforcers cause less satiation (Rincover, Newson, & Carr, 1979) and seem to be more powerful motivators.

It has also been found that if the tasks, commands, and reinforcers are frequently varied, autistic students seem more motivated to work (Koegel, Rincover, & Egel, 1982). Rather than asking a student to stand up ten times in a row, the teacher could request her to stand up, put hands up, touch nose, sit down, and point to green; the student would then receive tickles, lights, rubs, a raisin, and bubbles for correct responding. Koegel and Egel (1979) found that providing task success has positive effects with autistic learners. As with all learners, repeated failure dampens motivation. Teachers must not only encourage their students to complete tasks, but also task analyze skills into steps small enough to promote success.

Another technique that can increase the power of reinforcers is that of sensory extinction (Rincover et al., 1979). This technique requires the teacher to mask the sensory input that the child receives from self-stimulation. Masking means that the sensory input is no longer available through self-stimulation. An example is to put tape on a light switch to prevent it from making noise if the child enjoys the sound of the switch flicking. Another example is to put gloves on a child who receives tactile stimulation from flicking his fingers so he cannot feel his fingers passing over each other. Once sensory input is decreased from self-stimulation, the provision of sensory input by the teacher becomes a more powerful motivator.

Discrete Trial Format

A teaching strategy that has proven successful for teaching new skills to children with autism is the discrete trial format (Donnellan-Walsh, Gossage, LaVigna, Schuler, & Traphagen, 1976). Based on research which suggests that these children attain greater achievement under highly structured conditions, the discrete trial format can be applied to any teaching task. In the discrete trial format, the teacher specifies three things: (1) the discriminative stimulus (teacher's instruction to the student), (2) the desired student response (student behavior), and (3) the consequence (teacher's behavior that follows the student response). For example:

DISCRIMINATIVE STIMULUS	STUDENT RESPONSE	CONSEQUENCE
"Do this."	Imitates teacher extending hand	Praise and sip of orange juice

In the example, the teacher attempts to instill a basic imitation skill, which can be built upon later to teach a variety of communication and social skills. In the initial stages, the stimulus should remain the same until the student demonstrates that the task has been acquired; after competence has been demonstrated, the stimulus should be varied and the consequences (reinforcement) should be systematically thinned to encourage generalization. Part of the discrete trial format is a brief interval of three to five seconds between trials which allows the teacher to record the response and reinforce the response if appropriate. The interval also provides a break that identifies each trial as discrete or separate from other trials of the same task.

Prompting

Because of communication and language problems, children with severe disorders often need to be prompted to begin or to complete a task. Instructional prompts are purposefully added to the learning situation in order to assure correct responses (McGinnis, 1982). Prompts range from demonstrating to physically guiding the child through the activity. Dorsey (1980) outlines a hierarchy of prompts that moves from the most intrusive to the least intrusive:

full manual guidance > partial manual assistance > gesture > verbal > demonstration.

For instance, a teacher using the prompt hierarchy to help a child learn the self-help skill of cutting food at mealtime might go through the following sequence:

1. Put hands over child's hands on the utensils and manually guide the cutting.
2. Put hands over the child's hands on the utensils and begin the motion of cutting.
3. Gesture or pretend to cut the food.
4. Give the direction, "Cut up your food."
5. Actually cut up the food on own plate while child watches.

The process of providing progressively less assistance is called *prompt fading*. Prompting is often necessary for initial learning. Teachers should always choose the least intrusive prompt that is successful and should fade the prompt as soon as possible because of these students' tendency toward overselectivity. If the student remains dependent upon teacher prompting, then the skill has not been mastered.

Generalization and Maintenance

Generalization of acquired skills across settings and maintenance of skills over time pose a special concern with children with severe disorders. Studies with these children have shown that generalization does not occur unless adaptations are made in the instructional program (Koegel & Rincover, 1974; Stokes & Baer, 1977; Strain, Kerr, & Ragland, 1979). Due to characteristics including a tendency toward overselectivity, many students with severe disorders become stimulus-bound; that is, they demonstrate the skill only in one setting, in the presence of one teacher, or to a specific cue or set of directions. Or a student may show the behavior once or twice in another setting, but for some reason does not maintain it. Therefore, in programs for this population, special adaptations may be necessary that are not necessary for students with less severe disorders. Some of the techniques already alluded to in this section help children generalize and maintain the skills they are taught. The next two sections address additional techniques that enhance generalization and maintenance of learning for this population.

Promoting generalization.   It takes specific planning and instruction to guarantee that a student with a severe disorder will generalize appropriate behaviors to the real world. Some techniques that have been found to be effective are:

   1. *Sequential modification.* Once a reinforcement strategy has been successful in the classroom for maintaining a certain response, the same reinforcement technique must be applied in other settings. Lovaas, Koegel, Simmons, and Long (1973) used this technique when they trained parents to reinforce their children for self-help, communication, and social skills that had been taught in the classroom.

   2. *Introduction of natural reinforcers.* It is helpful to select behaviors to teach that will result in naturally occurring reinforcers. These behaviors previously have been described as functional behaviors. Smiling is a behavior that will receive social reinforcement (smiles) from others in the generalized environment. Additionally, teachers must teach the student to respond to natural reinforcers (i.e., smiles, grades in a regular classroom, praise at home) by pairing these reinforcers with those that the student naturally prefers.

   3. *Train sufficient exemplars.* The examples or stimuli used by the teacher must be varied in order to prevent students from becoming stimulus-bound. Sprague and Horner (1984) trained students with severe disabilities to use vending machines by providing training on many different kinds of machines (different places for coins, different colors, different sizes, different handles, etc.). It is also important to teach a skill in a variety of settings with a variety of trainers so that the student will be able to perform the behavior under many similar conditions.

   4. *Program common stimuli.* Once a student has demonstrated a skill in the classroom or training setting, the teacher begins to make the classroom more like the generalized setting. For instance, Koegel and Rincover (1974) trained autistic children to follow directions in a very structured, one-to-one setting. Wanting the children to be able to follow directions in the mainstream classroom, they gradually introduced more children to the training setting. The classroom was then made to look like the mainstream classroom. A variation of this technique is to introduce into the next setting a stimuli that has maintained the student's behavior in a previous setting. For example, if it is found that the student follows directions when sitting at a certain desk in the training setting, then she will more probably follow directions in the new setting if the familiar desk is present (Koegel & Rincover, 1974).

5. *Mediate generalization.* If the child is able to monitor her own behavior, then self-recording and self-evaluation techniques can enhance generalization. For example, the student can be taught to record the time spent on-task in the mainstreamed setting, and then report back to the special education teacher for reinforcement. Self-monitoring works best with higher functioning students; if the student is lower functioning , this technique will not be feasible.

Promoting maintenance.   Once a student has acquired and generalized a behavior, the teacher becomes interested in how to get the student to maintain the behavior over time. Training others to reinforce behaviors is one way of ensuring maintenance. Training the student to respond to natural social reinforcers is another way. Two other techniques can also be effective:

1. *Manipulate the schedule of reinforcement.* When teaching a new behavior, the teacher should provide "thick" schedules of reinforcement, that is, the student should be reinforced for every correct response. But when the teacher is interested in maintenance, an intermittent schedule of reinforcement is required. The reinforcement schedule must be thinned to such a degree that the student does not know exactly when or in which setting it will occur. Thus, realizing that reinforcement will be forthcoming but unable to predict exactly when it will occur, the student will continue the behavior (Alberto & Troutman, 1989). Slot machines work on this premise.

2. *Use indiscriminable contingencies.* Noncontingent reinforcement is another technique for maintaining behaviors. In noncontingent reinforcement, no single behavior is reinforced systematically, but the child sometimes receives a reward for "acting appropriately," terminology that includes many different behaviors. Students tend to repeat all behaviors that received reward in the past because they are unaware of which specific behavior caused the reinforcement to be delivered. Thus, students will continue to perform many appropriate behaviors over long periods of time (Koegel and Rincover, 1977).

In summary, the special needs of students with severe disorders become apparent when their educational programs are planned. Teachers must make decisions not only about what to teach but also about how to teach this population. In deciding what to teach, educators must take into consideration special problems in the traditional areas of communication, self-help, and social skills; along with cognitive development and prevocational/vocational training, these three areas generally constitute curricular areas for these students. Teachers must also consider the student's environmental demands. When deciding how to teach, educators should be familiar with the special techniques that have proven successful with autistic and other special populations. Specific curricular objectives and activities for each individual should be applied against the criterion of ultimate functioning: will the learning of this particular objective enable the individual to function more independently in the future? Box 10-3 illustrates how two teachers tackled this problem with nine-year-old Tommy.

BOX 10-3 Tommy

Tommy was a nine-year-old boy diagnosed with autism and mental retardation. When we met Tommy he had been living in the children's unit of a state hospital for several years. He went on periodic home visits with his mother and sisters. His mother reported that he had been impossible to handle from an early age. He spent most of his time running in circles and throwing furniture. He was large for his age and sometimes aggressive—pulling hair, hitting, stomping, and grunting—which made him generally unpopular with the staff. Having no language, Tommy seemed to lash out in frustration and anger. He also had a self-stimulatory behavior of flapping objects against the palm of his hand. He would grab anything that would make a good flapper (wallboard, pieces of wood, combs, brushes, etc) and flap them vigorously. He was preoccupied with obtaining flappers, which were usually taken away from him.

We were assigned by the school district as teachers on Tommy's unit. We initiated a program for Tommy by delineating four target areas: attending to task, language, prevocational skills, and lowering self-stimulation and aggression. The teaching staff liked Tommy from the beginning. We found him to have a delightful sense of humor and to be very responsive to training, which made teaching him reinforcing to us.

The language program consisted of teaching Tommy signs for his favorite objects and activities: "flapper, Mother, want, go, bus, eat, hamburger, school, work, drink," etc. Through trial-by-trial training, Tommy mastered these signs quickly and began to use them to make his wishes known. His aggression subsequently decreased. He learned two- and three-word sentences in the two years that we worked with him. He laughed more and seemed to have fun. His mother was thrilled to communicate for the first time with her child, and she wanted to spend more time with him.

Tommy became one of our star students. He usually worked up to one hour at a time. He even prompted other students to respond to teacher directions. In the prevocational program, he mastered nut-and-bolt-assembly, collating, sorting, envelope stuffing, cooking, table setting, and leisure time activities. He would sign "Time for work" at the designated time and then work with little feedback until the task was completed. He received pennies for his work, which he exchanged for a quarter and then bought a soft drink.

Since flapping was his favorite activity, instead of extinguishing it, we gave him a cloth bag with "Flappers" written on the side. He was told that he could keep five flappers in the bag, and that when he earned free time, he could have the bag. During school he had to place this bag on a shelf until he earned it. If we left the unit, he was told to take one flapper and keep it in his pocket until given permission to use it. This strategy brought his self-stimulatory behavior under control.

This program was of benefit to everyone who worked with Tommy. The staff spent less time taking away flappers, fending off aggression, and trying to guess what he wanted. More time was spent communicating with Tommy and he became more popular.

This training program continued until Tommy was 16. After he left the children's unit, his journey was erratic. There was no system for transition to the adolescent unit, so he was isolated on a unit, received little training, and again became feared and unpopular among the staff. Fortunately, this situation was short-lived. Tommy's mother had him placed in a private group home with a sheltered workshop. He still flaps. His mother still brings him home on weekends and he still uses sign language. Today he is paying part of his room and board from the $375 he earns each month assembling piecework. As we said earlier, Tommy was one of our stars.

Contributed by Jo Webber, Ph.D, Associate Professor at Southwest Texas State University and Debbie Gorence, M.Ed., Behavior Specialist with Austin Independent School District.

Special Issues

In addition to the different curricular emphases and instructional methodology required by students with severe behavior disorders, there are other issues that set this population apart from students with mild and moderate disorders. Although many issues are worthy of consideration, this discussion is limited to four that are basic to the success of any educational program for this population: (1) eliminating self-stimulatory and self-injurious behavior, (2) developing language-communication skills, (3) implementing a vocational/independent living program, and (4) working with the families of students with severe disorders. This discussion is not intended as comprehensive coverage but is intended to highlight some of the questions and special problems inherent in dealing with these issues.

Self-stimulating and Self-injurious Behavior

Some of the most maladaptive behaviors that distinguish children with severe disorders from those with mild disorders are self-stimulation and self-injurious behavior. In the past, youngsters exhibiting these conditions were often placed in physical restraints in restrictive settings such as hospitals or residential centers; with the advent of mainstreaming and increased sophistication in behavioral technology, many students exhibiting these behaviors can be found in public school programs. It is important for teachers who plan to work with this population to be aware of the special problems posed by such behaviors and of some of the behavioral techniques that have proven successful in dealing with them.

Some students with severe disorders engage in self-stimulating behaviors that interfere with social contact. These repetitive, stereotypical behaviors are usually motoric (for example, hand-flapping or object-spinning) or vocal (screeching or repeating a sound such as "ah-ah-ah-ah. . .") and serve no obvious function other than sensory stimulation for the individual. However, self-stimulating behaviors have an inverse relationship to learning (Koegel & Covert, 1972) and must be replaced with more adaptive behaviors if optimal learning and social functioning are to take place.

Similar to self-stimulation, self-injurious behavior usually occurs at high rates or with high intensity, but unlike self-stimulation, it results in injury to the individual. Common examples are arm-biting, head-banging, eye-poking, hair-pulling, and slapping or scratching self. Despite the physical damage inflicted by such behavior, many individuals continue to self-injure on a daily basis.

Causal Factors

Many researchers have attempted to identify the cause of self-injurious behavior. Carr (1977) reviewed the literature on the motivation of self-injurious behavior and formulated five major hypotheses: (1) the *positive reinforcement hypothesis,* which suggests that the immediate social attention received by self-injuring individuals is the motivating factor; (2) the *negative reinforcement hypothesis,* which suggests that individuals injure themselves to escape an unpleasant situation, such as an adult's demand; (3) the *self-stimulation hypothesis,* which indicates that individuals perform self-abusive acts in order to provide sensory stimulation; (4) the *organic hypothesis,* which states that self-injurious behavior is the product of an aberrant physiological process; and (5) the *psychodynamic hypothesis,* which proposes psychological causes (for example, guilt) for self-injury. From this research, it appears that self-injurious behavior is a very complex behavior with multiple causative factors, and that with any given individual, one or more of the factors could be operating. Sasso and Reimers (1988) offer screening guidelines to help determine exactly what is maintaining an individual's aberrant behavior and offer a process for determining which intervention technique would be most effective for elimination of the behavior in the classroom.

Techniques

Over the past two decades, a variety of behavioral techniques have been successfully applied to suppressing or eliminating self-stimulating and self-injurious behavior. Among these are *punishment, overcorrection, response-cost,* and variations of *differential reinforcement.*

Punishment has been defined as the application of aversive stimuli or the removal of rewarding stimuli. It has been highly successful with both self-stimulating and self-injurious behavior. Aversive stimuli such as electric shock, shouting, and slapping the hand or thigh have proven effective in reducing a variety of self-stimulating behaviors (Baumeister & Forehand, 1972; Bucher & Lovaas, 1968; Koegel & Covert, 1972; Lovaas & Simmons, 1969; Risley, 1968). Electric shock has also effectively eliminated self-injurious behavior in a number of individuals with severe disorders (Corte, Wolfe, & Locke, 1971; Tate & Baroff, 1966; Young & Wincze, 1974). Tanner and Zeiler (1975) report the successful suppression of self-injurious behavior (face-slapping) in a young autistic woman by inducing her to smell an ammonia capsule, and Myers and Deibert (1971) report successful suppression of self-injurious behavior (head-banging) by delaying meals and withdrawing food during meals whenever the behavior occurred.

Although highly successful, the use of aversives—especially electric shock—with this population has been questioned. In 1988, the Autism Society of America proposed that punishment resulting in pain or dehumanization not be used with individuals with developmental disabilities (Autism Society of America, 1988). The argument is that alternative positive reductive procedures are effective and that punishment has several negative side-effects (McGee, Menolascino, Hobbs & Menousek, 1987; Smith, 1988). Additional arguments are that: (1) punishment reduces behavior but teaches no new behavior; (2) punishment elicits aggression and/or withdrawal; and (3) positive procedures have better generalizability. A final argument is that many people find punishment to be morally objectionable.

In contrast, proponents of punishment claim that positive procedures do not always work and that children with severe disorders have a right to appropriate and effective behavioral treatment (Council for Children with Behavioral Disorders, 1989; Rimland, 1988). Prohibiting all punishment procedures would mean that a mother could not say "no" to her child, or a teacher could not remove tokens when a child acts inappropriately. Research has shown that when used appropriately, punishment can keep a child from severely harming himself (Myers & Deibert, 1971). Proponents of punishment consider themselves pro-choice; they claim that behavioral techniques should be based on individual need and not restricted by "misinformed do-gooders" (Rimland, 1988). In light of this controversy, a few punishment techniques appropriate for school use and a few positive reductive techniques will be discussed.

Overcorrection is a punishment procedure developed by Foxx (1971) and Foxx and

Azrin (1973) that has been effective with autistic and lower functioning populations who have not responded to other forms of reinforcement or punishment. Overcorrection involves the application of an exaggeration of an experience that acts as an aversive in order to reduce inappropriate behavior. There are two types of overcorrection: (1) correcting the environmental consequences of an inappropriate behavior (restitution), and (2) practicing an appropriate behavior that is incompatible with the inappropriate behavior (positive practice).

The first, restitution, is necessary only if the behavior has affected the environment in a negative way (for example, repeated self-induced regurgitation or feces smearing). In these cases, the individual might have to clean the soiled area, take a shower, wash his clothes, dress, and then clean the bathroom. Positive practice procedures have also been used to reduce self-injurious and self-stimulatory behaviors. For example, Kelly and Drabman (1977) reported elimination of eye-poking behavior in a visually handicapped preschooler. Each time the child poked his eye, his arms were raised and lowered repeatedly to his sides without touching his face or eyes; this positive practice was coupled with verbal praise and eventually resulted in elimination of the behavior. Other researchers reduced self-stimulating hand-clapping by requiring the child to hold his hands by his side for long periods of time after a hand-clap (Foxx and Azrin, 1973). In most instances of overcorrection, periods in which the maladaptive behavior does not occur are intermittently reinforced (for example, reinforcement for periods of non-eye-poking and non-clapping). Overcorrection has the added benefit of instilling a positive behavior while decreasing a negative one.

Also a punishment technique, *response-cost* is the removal of reinforcers in order to reduce behavior. It can be thought of as a system of fines. The child is given tokens, money, food, etc. for appropriate behavior but must forfeit some of these for inappropriate behavior. Reponse-cost will act as a reductive technique only if the tokens, money, or food are truly reinforcing. The teacher could also remove a privilege or a favorite object. If a student is allowed to manipulate a favorite object for a short period of time when work is complete, the teacher could remove the object or reduce the time whenever the student shows self-abuse. Response-cost has the advantage of producing fewer of the negative side-effects of punishment.

Differential reinforcement is based on the premise that teaching appropriate positive behaviors will result in the reduction of inappropriate behaviors without any of the negative side effects of punishment. There are four basic types of differential reinforcement that can easily be used in the classroom:

1. DRO. *Differential reinforcement of other behavior* is a method of reinforcing the student for periods of time that any behavior occurs other than the inappropriate behavior. In other words, the student is reinforced for periods of time during which she displays no self-stimulation or self-abuse. The period of time can be 10 seconds, 10 minutes, or entire days. For instance, in order to reduce head-banging, a student could receive a reinforcer (preferably a powerful one, such as a favorite food) after each 10-second interval that no head-banging is displayed. If the student bangs her head, then the timer would be reset to a new 10-second interval. After success with 10-second intervals, the intervals would be gradually lengthened (Carr, Robinson, Taylor, & Carlson, 1990).

2. DRI. *Differential reinforcement of incompatible behaviors* requires that the teacher identify a specific behavior that is incompatible with the inappropriate behavior and systematically reinforce it. An example would be reinforcing quiet hands in order to decrease hand-flapping. Another example is to reinforce a student who is coloring (both hands on the paper with crayon moving across the paper) instead of face-slapping (Carr et al., 1990).

3. DRL. *Differentially reinforcing lower rates* of an inappropriate behavior can also work to reduce behavior. For example, a student who is engaging in self-stimulation an average of 20 minutes during each hour is told that if she keeps the self-stimulation to 15 minutes in an hour, she will receive a reinforcer. The time is gradually lowered to an acceptable level (e.g., 5 minutes per hour).

4. DRC. *Differential reinforcement of communicative behavior* is based on the assumption that self-stimulation and self-abuse might be forms of nonverbal communication (Carr, 1985; Carr & Durand, 1985). Thus, if a teacher suspects that a student wants something, then an appropriate way of asking for it through signs or speech is provided and reinforced. Or if a teacher suspects that the student is self-abusing in order to get out of a frustrating situation, then the teacher shows him the sign for "finished" or "out" and subsequently permits the student to leave the situation when the sign is used rather than when self-abuse occurs.

A combination of reinforcement of appropriate behaviors with mild punishment also has been effective in reducing severely maladaptive behaviors (Repp & Deitz, 1974; Repp, Deitz, & Speir, 1974). Repp and Deitz (1974) reduced the face-scratching self-injurious behavior of a young institutionalized female by rewarding periods of non-face-scratching with candy and by giving a verbal reprimand when face-scratching did occur. These studies yield results similar to those combining reinforcement of incompatible behaviors with a time-out procedure (Ausman, Ball, & Alexander, 1974; Bostow & Bailey, 1969). In these studies, the combination of a positive technique with a punishment technique was more effective than the application of a single technique. Also, researchers are discovering that pairing punishment with differential reinforcement is helpful in avoiding some of the shortcomings of punishment, such as temporary elimination of the behavior and failure to generalize.

Although punishment and differential reinforcement techniques have proven successful in eliminating self-stimulation and self-injurious behaviors, researchers are concerned about generalization and maintenance in settings other than the classroom. Many of the procedures do not generalize outside the training setting unless generalization tactics are built into the program (Kissel & Whitman, 1977). As in planning for generalization of instruction, teachers must also systematically plan for the generalization of behavior reduction.

Communication/language Development

The majority of children with severe disorders have limited communication skills. Although the type and the severity of the problem differ widely from individual to individual, autistic children as a group are characterized by mutism, echolalia, and severe language delay. Schizophrenic children may create their own vocabularies or use nonsense words or sentences. Other children with severe disorders may have highly developed vocabularies but temporary or prolonged lapses in ability to use language to communicate with others. Some children with severe disorders are characterized by adequate receptive language skills but deficient expressive skills; that is, they understand what is said to them but they cannot express themselves verbally. It is estimated that 50 percent of children with autism will never utilize speech for communication (Alpert & Rogers-Warren, 1985). The language difficulties of this population are idiosyncratic; therefore, as with other curriculum areas, language development programs must be tailored to to fit the needs of the individual.

The Function of Language

Echolalia and other peculiar language difficulties of children with autism were not successfully remediated until the sixties when a number of researchers began using operant conditioning techniques to teach speech to these youngsters (Hewett, 1965; Lovaas, 1966; Risley & Wolf, 1967). In most behavioral treatment programs, common speech sounds and grammatical structures were targeted and taught through imitation, reinforcement, and punishment procedures. Thus, functional language training for nonverbal children has consisted mainly of a limited number of self-help phrases that are elicited in certain contexts or in response to specific cues. As McLean and Snyder-McLean (1982) state:

> *An analysis of most of our existing language treatment programs for severely handicapped students would lead one to believe that the primary functions of human communication systems are to name things, indicate desired food items or objects, and to request permission to "go bathroom." While such functions are surely included in children's communicative repertoires, they are far from adequate to represent a full appreciation of the basic function of communication in human societies. (p. 211)*

Although operant conditioning of speech sounds and phrases was a definitive beginning in helping nonverbal youngsters acquire speech, many language experts believe that language therapy should focus on the individual's ability to generalize acquired language skills to other settings (Mirenda & Iacono, 1988), and to use speech spontaneously for communication purposes (McLean & Snyder-McLean, 1982). Before such language programming can be accomplished, educators must clearly distinguish the concepts of speech, language, and communication. Speech is the oral or verbal production of sounds; language is the use of a symbol system that can be verbal or nonverbal; communication is the exchange of information between people, which can take any number of forms (smile, gesture, a look, writing, words, and so forth). Therefore, communication is a social tool that allows an individual to interact with others; speech and language are means of communication, and it is the ability to communicate through whatever means that should be the focus of training in this area.

Alternative Systems

Various systems are used to teach children with severe disorders to communicate, and teachers often must be proficient at alternative and augmentative communication systems. Alternative communication systems used with autistic students include manual sign language in conjunction with speech (Creedon, 1973); symbols (McLean & McLean, 1974); word cards (Ratusnik & Ratusnik, 1974); computerized devices (Colby, 1973) and pictorial communication boards or books (Mirenda & Santograssi, 1985; Reichle & Brown, 1986). Although language therapists may be responsible for designing a comprehensive language development program and may provide direct services on a routine basis, teachers obviously must be able to communicate with students as a prerequisite to teaching all other skills. Language development is therefore incorporated into all curricular areas of the program for the nonverbal or language-delayed child.

As previously mentioned, sign language in conjunction with speech (total communication) is one alternative for teaching children with severe disorders to communicate. Although the usefulness of sign language in nonschool settings is being questioned, it is still often taught to children who are unable to use verbal language. Two basic sign systems are used: a sign-concept system, American Sign Language (AMESLAN), and a sign-word system, Signing Exact English (SEE 11). The SEE system translates into exact English, including grammatical structure components, and therefore may be better for students who have some verbal skills, who are learning to read, or who may become very proficient in signing (Marcott-Radke, 1981).

The reader who is interested in language and/or communication development is referred to McLean and Snyder-McLean (1982) and to Stainback and Stainback (1980) who raise important issues and provide conceptual frameworks for communication training for this population. A controversial newcomer to the field, facilitated communication, is treated in some detail in Box 10-4.

Vocational/Independent Living Programming

Trends Toward Independent Living
Prior to 1970, prevocational and vocational programming for students with severe behavior disorders was rare if not nonexistent. However, beginning in the late sixties and continuing into the eighties, three trends encouraged educators to begin programming for this population

---

BOX 10-4 Facilitated Communication: Does It Work?

What is Facilitated Communication?

A relatively new alternative communication technique, *facilitated communication,* has been at the center of controversy since its induction in this country. Facilitated communication, or FC, as it has come to be known, consists of a trained facilitator who places his hand over the hand of the individual who then types out her own thoughts, ideas, and answers to questions. Crossley (1988) pioneered this technique in Australia with approximately 30 individuals with severe impairment; she reported that with facilitated communication, these individuals expressed unexpectedly high levels of comprehension and literacy. In the United States, Crossley's facilitated communication

technique was adopted by Biklen and his colleagues at Syracuse University. Biklen (1990, 1992) has indicated that many individuals with severe impairments have a condition known as global apraxia that prohibits their communicating effectively despite adequate intelligence and communication abilities. In other words, these individuals are cognitively competent but trapped in their uncommunicative bodies. Biklen has claimed successes similar to Crossley's with 21 individuals with severe impairments (Biklen & Schubert, 1991). Unfortunately, the successes that were reported for these individuals were based on anecdotal evidence rather than objective data (Simpson & Myles, in press-a).

BOX 10-4 *Continued*

What Does the Research Say?

A number of independent researchers have attempted to repeat the successes reported by Crossley and Biklen through empirical research studies. Many of these researchers set up conditions under which the facilitator is given one set of instructions or questions (i.e., through headphones) while the individual being facilitated receives another, different set of instructions or questions. These conditions are obviously designed to ascertain whether the facilitator is somehow, perhaps unconsciously, influencing the typed responses. For example, in one sophisticated study of this type, Simpson and Myles (in press-a) set forth five conditions:

1. Set work, such as typing student's name from a model and random numbers from 0 to 9
2. Questions with answers known to the teachers who were trained and serving as facilitators (e.g., "Is it snowing outside today?")
3. Questions with answers unknown to the teacher/facilitators (e.g., answers based on age-appropriate stories read to the students but not to the teacher/facilitator)
4. Affective questions (e.g., "Why were you angry when you came into class today?")
5. Five minutes for spontaneous typing (e.g.,"Type whatever you want to.")

Subjects were 18 individuals with autism. The study was conducted 5 days per week for 15 weeks. Simpson and Myles concluded that subjects "universally failed to respond to FC as per the celebrated claims" of the proponents of FC. The subjects were unable to use their communication devices (Canon communicators) to generate anything above their identified cognitive levels. In addition, they were unable to answer questions at a level higher than chance unless the teacher/facilitator was also familiar with the answers. Simpson and Myles (in press-b) have also reviewed 14 other empirically-based studies attempting to validate FC. Sample sizes ranged from 1 to 23 and a wide variety of test conditions were used. Results of these studies were again very clear that individuals being facilitated were unable to generate either a) information unknown to their facilitators, or (b) communications of an extraordinary nature. An additional study was undertaken by Cardinal and Hanson and reported in Autism Research Review International (1994b). Again, in a carefully developed research design, 43 individuals with autism, retardation, and other developmental disabilities were tested for FC effects. The facilitated task was to type a word from a flash card selected from a list of 100 words; the word to be typed was unknown to the facilitator. After six weeks of training three times a week, one-third of the individuals were able to correctly type the given word on at least three of five trials.

What Can We Conclude from the Research?

Rimland reports that there have been 44 controlled studies of FC with almost 400 subjects, only 50 of whom have shown any ability to facilitate (Autism Research Review International, 1994b). He further asserts that we are perhaps assessing two different phenomena: FC Type I, which consists of one- or two-word responses and usually requires a significant amount of training, and FC Type II, which is reported by Crossley, Biklen, and others. FC Type II is described as occurring very quickly and as attaining a level of literacy far above the known competencies of the individual. So far, only poor to moderate successes of FC Type I have been validated by empirically-based research. Simpson and Myles (in press-b) caution that there are several critical issues that parents and professionals should consider when deciding whether to pursue FC with an individual. Supplanting other successful communication methods with FC is probably not a good idea until FC can be validated. More important, perhaps, is the relevance and feasibility of FC over the life span. For example, is it reasonable to assume that one-to-one facilitators will always be available to the individual, and if so, will they promote independent functioning of the individual as an adult?

In summary, it is clear that FC is not a cure for severe impairments in communication abilities of individuals with autism, mental retardation or other developmental disabilities. It is not clear, yet, whether FC should be considered as a helpful alternative communication tool with this population.

Written by the author in collaboration with Rich Simpson, Ph.D., and Brenda Myles, Ph.D., University of Kansas, Department of Special Education.

that would enhance the probability of employment and independent living in the community. First was a nationwide push toward deinstitutionalization, the practice of helping adults with disabilities to maintain themselves independently or semi-independently in community settings rather than in institutions. Deinstitutionalization has affected special education by requiring educators to redouble their efforts to graduate young adults who are functioning independently despite their disabilities. This type of programming is called *transition programming* because it is concerned with transition from school to the world of work. Transition programming recently has been established as a national priority by the Office of Special Education and Rehabilitative Services (OSERS). Thus, secondary teachers dealing with students with severe disorders need to prepare them for meaningful work instead of custodial institutionalization or non-work day programming (Edwards & Siler, 1988). If individuals can contribute financially to their own support by functioning in competitive employment or some type of sheltered workshop setting, the chances of their remaining in the community are much increased.

The second trend affecting transition programming for this population was the development by Gold (1972, 1973) and others of successful vocational training programs for low functioning individuals. By task-analyzing the component parts of tasks into small, discrete units and using reinforcement, Gold (1972) was able to teach adults with moderate and severe disabilities to perform such complex tasks as assembling 24-part bicycle brakes. Educators began to realize that with the proper combination of instruction and reinforcement, these individuals are capable of learning tasks that are functional and for which they can be paid. Also, more sophisticated assessment of autistic individuals revealed a suitability for vocational training: although persons with autism generally perform poorly on abstract, symbolic, and logical tasks, they do tend to perform well on tasks requiring manipulative, visual-spatial, and short-term rote memory skills (American Psychiatric Association, 1980), all of which are helpful in performing a variety of vocational tasks.

A third trend that has affected transition programming is the notion of supported competitive employment for individuals with severe disabilities who could not enter competitive employment without long-term assistance (Wehman & Kregel, 1985). Supported competitive employment differs from competitive employment in that permanent follow-along staff support is provided to workers in order to enhance job success and retention (Wehman & Kregel, 1988). Supported competitive employment differs from sheltered workshops in that the worker is placed in an integrated rather than a segregated work setting while earning at least minimum wage. The Rehabilitation Act Amendments of 1986 have provided grants for the establishment of supported employment programs.

Wehman and Kregel (1988) list several components necessary for successful supported competitive employment programs:

1. Job development or locating appropriate jobs. This can be done by vocational personnel in high schools or by vocational specialists trained to deal with populations with severe disabilities.

2. Job placement or the appropriate matching of the person to the job. This matching of a difficult-to-place individual to an appropriate placement is a crucial component and can save hours of future on-site training (Rusch, 1986; Wehman, 1986).

3. Job-site training by the staff person, also known as a job coach or employment specialist. This person must possess expertise and creativity in order to work successfully with students with severe disorders.
4. Assessment, which is an ongoing process to determine how the new worker is performing.
5. Job retention, which involves advocacy and procedures to ensure long-term job maintenance. This includes, most importantly, a long-term commitment to ensure employment and to re-placement if needed. (p. 2)

Much has been written about the success of supported competitive employment of individuals with developmental disabilities (Bellamy, Mank, Rhodes, & Albin, 1986; Donnellan, LaVigna, Zambito, & Thredt, 1986; McCarthy, Fender, & Fender, 1988) and much of the success is related to the classroom preparation of these individuals before job placement begins.

Prevocational/vocational Training
Vocational training for persons with severe disorders must be designed at a much more basic level than vocational training for persons with mild or moderate disorders. In designing this training as part of the transition plan, the classroom teacher needs to consult with vocational specialists, job coaches and employment specialists, rehabilitation personnel, and with parents in order to ensure that the training will be the best preparation for future employment and independent living in the student's community. Once the transition plan has been developed, the teacher will know which skills need emphasis. Classroom training may include basic motor and discrimination skills, social skills, self-help and communication skills, and compliance as it directly relates to employment and to independent living needs.

Whenever possible, prevocational/vocational skills should be taught in the settings in which the skills are to be used. Community-based programming for adolescents with severe disorders assures that the skills will generalize and be maintained, thus becoming functional and useful to the individual. Many secondary teachers of this population spend most of the school day with their students outside of the school building (i.e., riding buses, buying things in stores, cooking in the home, etc.).

A basic prevocational/vocational training model for classroom teachers will be described in the remainder of this section. This model is derived from a training program for children and youth with autism (see Table 10-3) developed by Regan, Jones, Holzschuh, and Simpson (1982). This overview is intended for illustrative purposes only; interested readers should refer to Regan et al. for comprehensive information on designing a prevocational/vocational training program.

Assessment.   An overall profile of strengths and weaknesses of each individual should be compiled for each of the following areas: language level, cognitive-intellectual, behavioral or work habits, and personal-social. Work habits to be assessed include the ability to stay on task, to work without supervision, and to follow verbal directions. Personal-social skills include self-help skills and the ability to get along with others in a work setting.

Prevocational skills.   Skills that are prerequisite to vocational performance should be assessed and taught if necessary. Regan et al. (1982) outline four areas: (l) motor develop-

TABLE 10–3 Basic Components of a Voactional Program

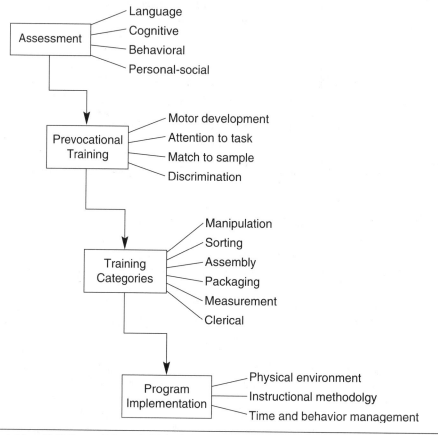

Adapted from M. K. Regan, C. Jones, R. Holzschuh, and R. L. Simpson, Autism Teacher Training Program (Kansas City, KS: University of Kansas Medical Center), 1982.

ment, including skills in grasping, wrist rotation, eye-hand coordination, and imitation of motor movement; (2) attention to task, preferably uninterrupted for five to ten minutes; (3) match to sample, making a product that matches a given sample, whether it be sorting objects or arranging objects according to a model; and (4) discrimination, using objects according to function, given verbal or visual cues.

Training tasks and task categories. Selecting specific training tasks for the vocational program should carry the same considerations as selecting instructional objectives in other curriculum areas: all should be applied against the criterion of ultimate functioning. The following questions may be especially helpful in selecting vocational skills to be taught:

1. Does the skill transfer to community job opportunities?
2. Will mastery of the skill facilitate assimilation into the community?

3. Is it feasible to teach the skill in a classroom setting?
4. Is it feasible to teach the skill to a given student, in view of the student's strengths, deficits, and learning potential? (Regan et al., 1982, p. 24)

It is also helpful to organize tasks by categories so that types of tasks or skill clusters rather than isolated skills are learned. Six categories of vocational tasks are common:

- Manipulation—performing physical operations on materials, perhaps using tools
- Sorting—separating large numbers of objects according to a predetermined classification
- Assembly—putting parts of objects together, sometimes using tools
- Packaging—putting a prescribed set of materials into boxes, bags, etc.
- Measurement—using standard units of volume, weight, and length
- Clerical—filing, alphabetizing, stuffing envelopes, stapling, collating, and other office work (Regan et al., 1982)

Program implementation.   To implement a prevocational/vocational program, the teacher must set up the environment, choose appropriate instructional methodology, and manage the behavior and productivity of the students. The physical environment should approximate a work setting and should be stocked with a variety of cheap, safe, dispensable work materials. Instructional methodology is similar to that used for instruction in other curricular areas. After analyzing each specific prevocational and/or vocational task into its component parts, the teacher may want to use one or more of the following methods: modeling, prompting, picture cues, and forward or backward chaining, which involves mastery of a single step in a hierarchy of steps toward completing a complex task. Each of the methods has advantages and disadvantages and will be better suited to certain tasks than to others.

The teacher must be sure to structure the students' time and productivity. Provisions should be made for signing in and signing out, taking breaks, recording the amount of work accomplished by each individual, and reinforcing productivity through a token system or with actual money. If the token system or money is not understood by a student, tangible reinforcers should be paired with the token/money until the student learns the concept. Working for money is a crucial concept for success on the job.

In summary, prevocational/vocational training and transition programming is necessary for optimal functioning of individuals with severe disorders. With proper assessment and training, many of these adolescents and adults are capable of productivity in a work setting and semi-independent or independent living in the community. Vocational goals should be set toward competitive employment or supported competitive employment and a transition plan should be developed for adolescents with objectives toward that end. Community-based instruction and the development of functional skills will greatly assist in the integration of young adults with severe disorders into their communities.

Working with Families of Individuals with Severe Disorders

Although the issue of parental involvement in education was explored in Chapter 8, parents of students with severe disorders have some special needs that warrant further consideration.

It is not unreasonable to suggest that the more severe the disorder, the more stress is created in the home. Children with autism or schizophrenia often create an unrelenting drain on their parents' time and energy. For example, many of these children have heightened activity levels and highly erratic sleep patterns, perhaps sleeping only a couple of hours before getting up to roam about the house at night. Motivated by curiosity, they may take apart, damage, or destroy furniture, appliances, mechanical objects, and other household goods. Many have no regard for safety and therefore cannot be left alone even for short periods of time.

Not only are these children difficult to live with but historically the parents have been blamed for causing the disorder. Leo Kanner (1943) originally speculated that children were autistic because parents "were strongly preoccupied with abstractions of scientific, literary, or artistic nature, and limited in genuine interest in people" (p. 250). At one time, Bettelheim (1950) went so far as to suggest that children with severe disorders needed a "parentectomy," that is, institutionalizing children so that parents could be replaced with staff considered more caring and competent.

Family Stressors

The sources of stress for parents and families of these children are real and constant. Some of the major stressors are briefly reviewed: managing behavior, lack of respite time, disrupted family functioning, and concerns over the future.

Managing behavior.   For obvious reasons, parents are concerned about compliance, that is, having their child obey their directions and instructions. For psychotic children who are nonverbal and oppositional, compliance can be a very difficult concept to teach. For children who are not safety-conscious, noncompliance can be very dangerous: they may burn, cut, or otherwise injure themselves while unattended even for a few minutes. Another major area of management is self-help skills; as children with severe disorders grow older, they may not naturally acquire skills in eating and dressing that are easily acquired by normally developing children. For these children, it is especially important for teachers and parents cooperatively to plan and implement behavior management programs. If behavioral programs are not carried out in both home and school settings, there is little chance that the skills will generalize to other settings or be maintained over time. Teachers can be particularly helpful by teaching family members problem-solving strategies so that they can become self-sufficient and less overwhelmed (Simpson & Webber, 1991).

Lack of respite time.   The erratic activity levels and sleep patterns of many of these children can leave parents chronically exhausted. The usual respites of evenings out and vacations may not be feasible due to difficulties in acquiring babysitting services. Even family outings may not be possible when the child does not function well in large groups or with strangers. Such a schedule leaves parents with little time to invest in other family members or to pursue personal interests.

Disrupted family functioning.   The inordinate amounts of time and energy required by the child with severe behavior disorders inevitably disrupt family functioning. In families that have adapted well, continuous compromises and flexibility are required of each family member. Unfortunately, many marriages do not survive the strain, as over half of the marriages of parents of children with disabilities end in divorce (Raaz, 1982), as compared to about a 35 percent divorce rate in the general population. Many of the stages through which families normally develop, such as sibling relationships, personal growth of the parents, and marriage renewal are thwarted by the presence of a child with so many special needs (Handleman & Harris, 1986). Thus, individual and group counseling, sibling support groups, crisis intervention services, and parent support groups are often necessary for these families.

Concerns over the future.   Even for parents who cope successfully with their child in the home and manage to maintain their child in quality educational programs, the question of the future looms large. No states are required to extend public education programs for students beyond the age of 21, and few offer adequate day or residential treatment programs for adults with severe disorders which are funded from other sources, either public or private. For parents of children and adolescents who will not be able to maintain themselves independently, the question of future caretaking is burdensome. For many, institutionalization is the only feasible alternative.

The issue of institutionalization is a difficult and ever-present one. Parents who decide to place their child out of the home must deal with both their own feelings of inadequacy and guilt and with the criticisms of others. Because of these constraints, some parents wrestle with the decision for years, even when it is the best alternative for both the child and themselves. Other parents may decide upon residential or institutional placement of children who potentially could be maintained at home simply because they can no longer cope with the pressures.

Roles for Educators

Educators can play three major roles in helping ease the difficulties of these parents. The first role is advocacy for respite care programs, which include babysitting services, after-school care, weekend care, summer educational programs, summer camps, and recreational programs or other alternative day-care programs. Respite care programs are designed to meet the needs of individuals with severe disorders and remove the burden of caretaking from the family for a few hours. Most state agencies do not view such services as a public responsibility; therefore, in many cases respite care services are limited or unavailable. In a plea for more respite care services, Raaz (1982) cites parent/advocate Ruth Sullivan's rationale for state provision of respite care:

> *The cure for lack of respite is known, yet there is still a tremendous psychological resistance to the idea that the state has a moral responsibility to help families who need respite services. If we think of government as an extension of persons and families, providing for us, by our permission, what we cannot do for ourselves as efficaciously (e.g., roads, bridges, schools, parks, postal services, airport terminals), then we should have no problem in expecting government to*

provide to families in a crisis, no matter how long, what it does routinely for other citizens' convenience and pleasure. (Sullivan 1979, p. 114)

Second, the teacher can provide training to parents. This training might include knowledge of effective teaching strategies, reinforcement techniques, effective behavior management programs, strategies for enhancing communication and self-help skills, and knowledge of community resources that might be helpful. Not all parents will be receptive to training, and teachers should not assume that every parent needs training. Many parent training programs have been published that may be useful for planning (Hall, 1981; Dangel & Polster, 1984, Jenson, 1985; Handleman & Harris, 1986).

The third major role of educators is that of a concerned professional who is willing to listen to parents and to offer support and guidance. Many parents want to be informed and involved with their child's education. According to Sullivan (1976), parents of children with severe disorders want an equal role with professionals "in assigning their child's priorities and planning his future" (p. 44). Too often, educators assume that they know what is best for the child and plan the child's IEP and assign home training duties without first consulting the parents about the parents' priorities for the child. A truly successful educational program for all children combines educators' and parents' priorities for skill development and orients activities toward agreed-upon long-range goals for that child's life.

Conclusions

Teachers planning to work with students with severe behavior disorders should be aware of the special demands of working with this population. Many basic prerequisites to learning that are acquired incidentally by other children may have to be carefully programmed for these children. Characteristics that affect learning are stimulus overselectivity, unique responses to reinforcers, basic communication deficits, and a tendency toward self-stimulatory or self-injurious behavior. Countering these difficulties in the classroom often requires a degree of precision in planning and teaching not usually found in other classrooms. Although these students do respond well to operant conditioning techniques, teachers may have to be unusually creative in finding reinforcers that elicit and maintain the students' interests. A special issue is whether the use of punishment is warranted with students who exhibit self-injurious behavior.

Key Points

1. Although children with autism are under the rubrics of "pervasive developmental disorder" and "other health impaired" rather than "emotional disturbance," they were included in this text because of the many special modifications they require in the classroom.
2. Five basic curriculum areas for this population are: language/communication, self-help, social, academics, and vocational.
3. The importance of the "criterion of ultimate functioning" cannot be overemphasized—remember Daryl and Tommy.

4. Children with autism have unique learning characteristics that require specialized teaching technology.

5. A number of techniques have been successfully used to eliminate self-stimulatory and self-injurious behavior: punishment, overcorrection, response-cost, and differential reinforcement.

6. In order to communicate, the teacher of students with severe disorders may need to learn an alternative communication system such as signing.

7. Parents of children with severe disorders such as autism and schizophrenia face very difficult problems such as lack of respite care and the prospect of institutionalization.

Additional Readings

Criterion of ultimate functioning, by L. Brown, J. Nietupski, and S. Hamre-Nietupski. In *Hey, Don't forget about me!* Edited by M.A. Thomas. Reston, VA: The Council for Exceptional Children, 1976, for a discussion of basic issues in selecting curriculum and instructing individuals with severe disabilities.

Educating children with severe maladaptive behaviors, by Susan Stainback and William Stainback, New York: Grune & Stratton, 1980, for more comprehensive information in all areas of programming for this population (including an excellent chapter on teaching language to the nonverbal child).

Parents and families of children with autism, by Rich Simpson and Jo Webber, In *Collaboration with parents of exceptional children,* Edited by M.J. Fine. New York: Clinical Psychology Press, (1991), for more information about the special problems these parents face.

Strategies for promoting augmentative and alternative communication in natural contexts with students with autism, by P. Mirenda and T. Iacono, *Focus on Autistic Behavior, 3(4),* 1988, 1–16, for an overview article of alternative communication strategies.

Teaching the autistic series, edited by Stephen C. Luce and Walter P. Christian, Austin, TX: Pro-Ed, 1980–82, for a series of six booklets on how to deal with the special problems of autistic youngsters.

The resolution on aversives, by the Autism Society of America in *The Advocate, 20 (3),* 1988; and Don't ban aversives, by Bernard Rimland, *The Advocate, 20 (4),* 1988, for the pros and cons of using aversive techniques with this population.

Chapter 11

Special Issues

The Developing Child:
  Effects of Substance Exposure
  Effects of Sexual Abuse

Suspension, Expulsion, and Inclusion Issues

Orientation

> In this special issues chapter, we will explore three questions relevant
> to the education of students with emotional/behavioral disorders that
> have received increasing attention in the popular press: What can we as
> special educators expect from children who have been exposed to
> drugs in utero? What is the impact of sexual abuse on the socio-
> emotional development of children and adolescents? And last, will we
> even need special education if the "full inclusion" movement succeeds?

Overview

This chapter could have been titled "Special Issues of the 1990s." The society in which we are living today offers special challenges that were unheard of in previous decades. This is certainly true of the prevalence of substance abuse, and crack cocaine in particular. Sexual abuse of children and adolescents is not new, but there is an increased public awareness of the scope of the problem and the need to deal with it as a society. The issue of inclusion seems to represent the inevitable voice of radical reform: When educators and others have finally seemed to secure the basic educational rights of children with disabilities, voices of dissent are raised to say that we are doing it all wrong and should basically start over. This chapter will explore each of these issues, because teachers of children with emotional/be-havioral disorders will have as their students those children who have been substance-exposed and those who have been sexually abused. The issue of full inclusion is dealt with because teachers will need to be informed when they are called upon to advocate for their students if full inclusion replaces the traditional continuum of services in their local districts.

Substance-Exposed Infants and Young Children: Behavioral Effects

The massive increase in use of illegal drugs, particularly cocaine, among all segments of U.S. society in the past decade or so has led the media to explore its ramifications. These ramifications include increased gang activity and drug-related violence, and the ill effects of chronic drug abuse on families. In families where the drug culture is prevalent, it permeates all aspects of family life, subsequently affecting the children. Direct involvement of the children themselves in substance abuse, gangs, and violence were dealt with in Chapter 9 on adolescents. Also affecting the developing child are the drug habits of the mother, particularly the drugs ingested by the mother during pregnancy.

The media has portrayed problems of substance exposed infants as epidemic in nature; further, they have emphasized the extreme difficulties suffered by "cocaine babies" (Schutter & Brinker, 1992). Although media coverage has raised some legitimate questions, it has also given rise to misconceptions about the scope and the severity of the problem. This Special Issues section will explore what the research says. Specifically, the following topics will be addressed: scope of the problem; the impact of various drugs upon the fetus, neonate, and infant; the psychosocial environment of the developing child; and the characteristics of young children who have been exposed *in utero* to drugs. The importance of comprehensive, family-centered intervention and implications for teachers also will be discussed. Although the long-term effects of substance exposure on child development have yet to be documented, it is certain that some of these children will exhibit behavior and learning problems that will bring them into special education classrooms with labels of "emotional/ behavioral disorder."

Prevalence

Unfortunately, the media has not exaggerated the increase in cocaine use by all segments of society: It is prevalent across socioeconomic, ethnic, and age levels. Cocaine is thought to be the drug of choice by women of child-bearing age. At least seven studies have established that between 10 and 30 percent of women use cocaine during pregnancy (cited in Vincent, Poulsen, Cole, Woodruff, & Griffith, 1991). However, another study found that between 13 and 16 percent of pregnant women used any kind of illicit drug or alcohol (Chasnoff, Landress, & Barrett, 1990).

These statistics are at odds because the exact incidence of drug use among pregnant women is difficult to document. Self-report figures are obviously low because of the unwillingness of mothers to admit to drug use during pregnancy. There are no laws requiring routine testing for drugs with pregnant or delivering women; however, hospitals doing routine toxicology tests have found higher incidence of general drug abuse than hospitals relying on patients' reports (Chasnoff, 1989). For these and other reasons, the reported incidence of substance abuse varies widely, and the true incidence of substance abuse, including cocaine, is probably underestimated.

Effects of Substance Exposure

Prenatal and Perinatal Outcomes

These two areas of substance abuse effects have been studied extensively. Several researchers have documented maternal lifestyle problems such as poor nutrition and little or no prenatal care that exacerbate problems in substance-exposed fetuses. Several studies have indicated that between 60 and 70 percent of cocaine-abusing pregnant women received no prenatal care. Other related health issues are increased risk for infectious diseases (Chasnoff, 1987) and vitamin deficiencies (Ryan, Ehrlich, & Finnegan, 1987).

Some evidence indicates that cocaine can precipitate labor, but there is disagreement over whether it is a causal factor in prematurity (Schutter & Brinker, 1992; Vincent et al., 1991). However, some evidence exists that cocaine-exposed infants may have a fetal death rate that is twice as high as other drug-exposed infants, and four times higher than nonexposed infants (Ryan et al., 1987). Cocaine evidently also increases the risk of sudden infant death syndrome (SIDS), as Chasnoff and associates have found incidence rates ranging from 8 to 15 percent among cocaine-exposed infants, compared to 5 percent among narcotic-addicted women and to 0.5 percent among the general population (Chasnoff, Burns, & Burns, 1987; Chasnoff, Hunt, Kletter, & Kaplan, 1989).

Other detrimental effects on the developing fetus have been noted, including spontaneous abortion, fetal distress during labor and delivery, intrauterine strokes, intrauterine growth retardation, and low birth weight (Schutter & Brinker, 1992; Vincent et al., 1991). Low birth weight and growth retardation in particular have been associated with cocaine in several studies. Some of these difficulties may be detected at birth, while others manifest themselves later in the developing child.

A Note on Fetal Alcohol Syndrome

Researchers have been able to identify a definite condition caused by fetal exposure to alcohol: fetal alcohol syndrome (FAS). It is estimated that 5 percent of all birth defects are correlated with alcohol exposure and that alcohol abuse is the leading cause of mental retardation in the United States (Davis, 1994). An FAS diagnosis has three major criteria: (a) specific facial features that may include small head size, flat midface and nasal bridge, and protruding forehead; (b) growth deficiency, and (c) central nervous system damage. A related condition, fetal alcohol effects (FAE) is diagnosed when two of the three criteria are present. According to Davis (1994), it is often the distinctive facial features that are lacking in children with FAE, and they may therefore go undiagnosed and untreated. Children with fetal alcohol effects may look normal and have normal IQs but have learning disabilities and share many of the behavioral characteristics of children with fetal alcohol syndrome. These characteristics (consistent with central nervous system damage) include irritability and slow development as infants; and poor coordination, distractibility, low impulse control, poor social skills, and needing one-to-one attention as school-age children. Current prevalence estimates indicate that one in every 500 to 700 babies is born with FAS, and one in 300 to 350 has FAE (Davis, 1994).

Experts in this area believe that, with the possible exception of FAS, it is difficult to demonstrate that specific drugs are associated with specific outcomes due to the facts that most substance abusers are multiple drug users, and many risks to the fetus are common to many different drugs. In addition, fetal factors and other maternal factors such as nutrition and prenatal care interact to obscure predictions. One area needing more research is that of fetal resilience, as it is known that some infants who have been exposed *in utero* to substance abuse do not show subsequent problems.

The remainder of this review will present research on children who may generally be characterized as *substance exposed*. The term *substance exposed* may include illicit drugs as well as alcohol. Further, many researchers have attempted to isolate the effects of cocaine exposure; therefore, some studies are reported for cocaine-exposed infants and children.

Newborns, Infants, and Toddlers

Much of the early research does not support extreme developmental deficits in substance-exposed babies, as one might expect. What has been documented, however, is a plethora of behavioral characteristics that basically describe how well the baby interacts with his environment and learns from it; these characteristics are collectively known as *neurobehavioral characteristics* (Vincent et al., 1991). According to a number of researchers, substance-exposed babies are most likely to show delays or differences in this area. Neurobehavioral characteristics are a primary concern because they dictate how a child will ultimately learn and form relationships with people.

Newborns or neonates who have been substance exposed often respond irritably to the normal caregiving activities of feeding, diapering, and bathing. They may show irregular eating and sleeping patterns. They are easily agitated and not easily consoled or comforted. They may startle easily, and be hypersensitive to certain stimuli such as sounds and lights. Low thresholds for stimulation and inability to process multiple stimulation have been shown in cocaine-exposed toddlers up to two years old (van Baar, 1990). In addition, substance-exposed infants may show unusual muscle tone or tremors. Their neurologically-based behavior may be described as disorganized.

These characteristics add up to babies that are difficult to handle, both physically and psychologically. They do not respond normally to caregivers' attempts to console them, offering the caregiver little positive reinforcement for interacting in a loving manner with them. Therefore, the attachment and bonding process may be disrupted. Many child development specialists believe that early attachment to the mother or a primary caregiver is essential in building positive relationships in later life. The experiences of Stacy, a 24-year-old pregnant mother trying to kick her crack habit, illustrate many of these problems in mothering substance exposed children. Stacy's story is presented in Box 11-1.

One study specifically assessed attachment in 18-month-old children who were exposed to multiple drugs. In comparison to a drug-free group, these

BOX 11-1 Stacy

Stacy was a 24-year-old woman who had been in and out of drug rehabilitation programs since she was fifteen. Five months pregnant with her third child, she re-entered a day treatment program for substance-abusing pregnant mothers. Stacy had been in the program before; she returned with a desperate desire to keep the child she was about to have. Stacy's first two children were premature and had been born with significant levels of crack in their blood system. Each child had eventually been removed from her custody due to neglect and suspicions of abuse. Stacy acknowledged that her drug use was preventing her from being the mother she wanted to be, but she expressed little hope of making real changes. Like the majority of women in the program, Stacy had been "strongly advised" to attend the program by the courts, who were threatening to remove her next baby at time of birth if there were evidence of substances in the baby's system. Although she seemed to have little energy or motivation, she stated upon entering the program that she felt this was her only hope. Her mother was refusing to trust or help her any longer, and she would soon be on the streets if she did not get help. Basically, Stacy had reached "the bottom."

When she began the program, she appeared lifeless and depressed. She rarely spoke. The staff who had worked with her during previous pregnancies were skeptical that she would remain in the group and really work toward recovery. However, Stacy attended the meetings faithfully and slowly began to participate. She seemed most responsive to discussions about children and childrearing. The program provided her with a place to experience herself as a mother, capable of loving and caring for herself. She described it as a window into a separate world, separate from her drug addiction and the community which places drugs at the central point of their existence. As Stacy responded to the treatment, and improvements were noted, the staff began to hope that she would make it out of the cycle she had been in for so long. Their hopes also centered on Stacy's unborn child, who may have been spared the cycle of being born with a fragile system already damaged by the cruel impact of crack.

The component of the program which seemed to have the greatest impact on Stacy was the emphasis placed on the infant, and on teaching the mothers the importance of bonding, especially with those infants fetally exposed to drugs. Stacy learned about the long-term impact crack can have on a baby's development, not only physically, but also psychologically. She related her own experiences with her children, describing their infant cries as "piercing" and very difficult to soothe. She complained that her babies did not respond like she had expected and often would not calm down even when fed and dry. Like many of the mothers, Stacy expressed the belief that the infants had become spoiled and began to ignore their persistent crying or, on occasion, became physically abusive in an attempt to make them stop.

In the program, Stacy learned about the relationship between the substances in the babies' systems and their persistent crying. She learned that by not responding to the baby, she was affecting the important bond between her and her baby, which is essential to the baby's growth and development. She learned that the baby may develop a lack of trust in the mother and the outside world, which contributes to a sense of helplessness. The child may continue to seek outward stimulation and fail to learn that self-soothing is possible. Stacy related that as her children grew, they were often overly active, inattentive, clingy, and fearful of her absence. She described her mounting frustrations and her need to escape, typically through drugs, in order to relieve her own feelings of helplessness in trying to care for such difficult children. As she escaped through drugs, she learned that this habit perpetuated the child's fearfulness and clinging behavior. . . . and so the cycle continued until the abusiveness between Stacy and her children was interrupted by the Department of Human Services. Stacy lost custody of her children. The children experienced another break in trust and bonding as they were removed from their mother's care.

The cycle which Stacy and her children experienced represents the increasing trend in a culture which is so dominated by drugs. Although both Stacy and her children could be considered victims in such difficult circumstances, it is the children who continue to suffer the effects of both physiological and psychological abuse. As many of these toddlers enter childhood, their perceptions of the world have been damaged and their ability to trust others has been compromised. This lack of trust continues to manifest itself in children's behavioral and emotional functioning, and can often compromise the very relationships they are so desperately seeking to establish.

Contributed by Ann Kelley, a doctoral candidate in school psychology at the University of Texas at Austin who worked in the substance abuse program during her internship.

toddlers demonstrated deficits in intellectual functioning, emotional expression, quality of play, and organization of attachment behavior (Howard, Beckwith, Rodning, & Kropenske, 1989). However, when the researchers compared the attachment security of the toddlers, no differences were found between groups. Thus attachment behavior of drug-exposed infants is another area in need of further research.

The Importance of the Psychosocial Environment

Early research on substance-exposed infants has pointed to the importance of the postnatal social environment in determining positive outcomes. Some researchers believe that the postnatal environment is as important as other factors (e.g., Bradley, 1989; Lipsitt, 1988). The psychosocial environments into which many of these children are born will be briefly described.

It is known that the majority of substance-abusing pregnant women were abused and neglected as children (Vincent et al., 1991). In one study, as many as 83 percent reported having had a parent who was a substance abuser and 70 percent had been sexually abused before age 16; these percentages were much lower in nonaddicted samples matched for socioeconomic status (Fieg, 1990). Women with abusive histories have a tendency to continue living in abusive and exploitative relationships; some become involved in prostitution in order to support their drug habit. Due to these and other activities associated with the drug culture, some may be incarcerated.

In addition, many substance-abusing parents belong to a drug culture that is marked by poverty, poor nutrition, and educational or intellectual limitations (Poulsen, 1991). Poulsen also reported that many substance-abusing mothers are single parents or live with drug-abusing partners who offer little emotional or financial support. When they do decide to "go clean" (often for their children's sake), they have no support because their social milieu is defined by the drug culture. And many do not understand child development; they may misinterpret their babies' behavior. It is not difficult to see that mothers living under such conditions are unable to meet their own needs, much less those of their children, in a healthy way. Women fitting this profile "bring a host of biological and environmental risk factors to their pregnancy in addition to substance abuse," (Vincent et al., 1991, p. 4). Of course, many pregnant women who abuse drugs and alcohol do not fit this profile: they may be, on the surface, indistinguishable from other pregnant women who are working, going to school, and/or rearing families. Nonetheless, the psychological correlates of substance abuse in the mother may put the young child at risk due to inadequate caregiving.

Substance-Exposed Young Children

Most child development specialists now agree that much of development is accounted for—not by biology alone, nor by environment alone but—by the interaction between the two. This interaction is central to the study of preschoolers who have been substance exposed. It is important to realize that by the time a child is three or four, it is virtually impossible to ascertain whether the characteristics and behavior displayed by these children are due to drug effects or to a poor environment (Vincent et al., 1991). A complex interplay between the two is most likely responsible.

There is no typical profile of a substance-exposed child. However, it can be said with some authority that children who were substance-exposed are at risk for developmental difficulties and for school failure. Some substance-exposed children will have several of the characteristics described, while others will have few or none at all. The research to date does indicate that the majority show normal development in social, emotional, and intellectual areas. However, problems in language development and attention have been noted by several researchers (Griffith, 1991; Griffith, Chasnoff, & Freier, 1990; van Baar, 1990). According to a review by Vincent et al. (1991), other marked characteristics that have been found are: inability to regulate and control their behavior, less task persistence, decreased frustration tolerance, and low thresholds to overstimulation. The reader can easily relate these characteristics to those described in the neonate as irritable, hypersensitive to stimuli, and unable to process multiple stimulation. The reader can also probably easily translate these into learner characteristics that will cause these children to have problems in the classroom. Further, research to date suggests that these children have difficulty reading social cues and therefore have peer problems.

Intervention

The body of research on large numbers of substance-exposed children is relatively recent. Longitudinal studies or those following cohorts of these children into their adolescence are needed. However, the information we currently have is very clear on a number of points. First, there is no typical profile of substance-exposed children, due to many uncontrolled variables. During gestation, these variables include exposure to multiple drugs, and the nutritional and prenatal care of the mother. After birth, many substance-exposed children display a number of neurobehavioral characteristics that may be best described as hypersensitive and disorganized; however, many substance-exposed children do not display these characteristics. Second, the psychosocial environment of the child, beginning in infancy and continuing throughout childhood, is of paramount importance in determining how these children will develop. Third, for children born into families that are part of the drug culture, the prognosis is poor due to impoverished environments and the inadequate caregiving many of them receive. It is difficult, if not impossible, to distinguish the effects of substance exposure *in utero* from the detrimental effects of inadequate care. Fourth, experts agree that multiple agencies providing family-centered services are needed to improve the psychosocial environments, and, ultimately, developmental outcomes for these children.

A multi-agency, multidisciplinary systems approach was discussed in Chapter 8, as was the need to form parent-teacher partnerships. These approaches are also needed with the population of young children who show detrimental effects of substance exposure. Agencies such as public health, vocational rehabilitation, early childhood education, mental health, substance abuse programs, and in some cases, corrections and child protective services, may work with these families. A variety of services may be needed, including but not limited to: specialized medical care, substance abuse treatment, family therapy, babysitting and respite care, prenatal care, home health care, infant-parent interaction programs, early childhood intervention, speech, occupational and physical therapy, vocational and job procurement assistance, specialized foster care, life skills instruction, and obtaining food, clothing, and household supplies on a routine basis (Vincent et al., 1991).

The key to providing services that are coordinated and tailored to fit individual families' needs is the individual family service plan (IFSP). The IFSP is a coordinated treatment plan that views the family as a unit rather than a group of isolated individuals, each needing something different. Another key to effective services delivery is the treatment of families as capable of determining their own needs and priorities. Once the family has identified its needs, the agencies can assist by providing the resources to meet those needs.

Implications for Teachers

Again, research to date offers some guidelines for educating young children who have been substance exposed; we do not yet know what these children will need as they grow into adolescents. Vincent et al. (1991) assert that substance-exposed children do not need a specialized curriculum or teaching methodology; instead, they need application of what is already known about early intervention. For example, routine, rituals, and rules should provide a safe and predictable classroom environment; experiential learning should be a major part of the curriculum; and the child-adult ratio should be small enough to promote attachment and nurturing (Cole et al., 1989). Given the self-regulatory difficulties experienced by some of these children, it is also important to have a management plan for situations in which the child begins to lose control.

Vincent et al. (1991) summarize the essential role of teachers:

> *As educators, we cannot change the prenatal exposure, but we can give children support and new skills for dealing with the world in which they live. If we form a cooperative partnership with their families and other community agencies, we can work to change the social situation in which they live. We can be effective in helping children and families function in the educational mainstream. (p. 20)*

Sexual Abuse of Children and Adolescents

Currently, no nationwide data are available on the percentage of students with emotional/behavioral disorders who have been sexually abused. However, one study of adolescents in programs for E/BD found that 74 percent of the females and 21 percent of the males reported having experienced sexual abuse; these statistics compare to 20 percent of females and 1 percent of males in a matched sample of adolescents without disabilities (Miller, 1993). These percentages are high, but not surprising because of the significant short-term and long-term behavioral and affective problems exhibited by victims of sexual abuse. In this section of the Special Issues chapter, we will explore some of the research related to sexual abuse: definition and incidence, who is likely to abuse, who is likely to be abused, the dynamics of abuse, and its numerous effects. A brief overview of treatment issues and implications for teachers will also be addressed.

Definition and Incidence

Sexual abuse can be defined as any interaction between a child and adult in which the child is used for sexual stimulation of either that adult or another person. Sexual abuse also can be committed by a person who is not an adult (i.e., under the age of 18) if the person is significantly older than the victim or in a position of power over the victim. Sexual abuse acts include fondling, sodomy, oral stimulation, involving the child in masturbation, sexual intercourse or penetration with an object, and other forms of sexual molestation. Sexual exploitation usually refers to acts inflicted upon a child by a person responsible for the child's care; such acts include permitting the child to engage in sexual acts or prostitution, and permitting the child to photographed or filmed in a pornographic manner. Such acts can be legally prosecuted as child sexual abuse. However, it is important to recognize that more subtle forms of inappropriate sexual behavior also may affect the child and lead to similar symptomatology. Examples include suggestive language, sexual innuendos, and being viewed while naked, i.e., when changing clothes or taking a bath.

The actual incidence of sexual abuse is the subject of much debate. For obvious reasons, it is difficult to obtain accurate statistics. Data are usually gathered from two sources: reports of numerous agencies, and large surveys of adults who self-report about their pasts. Even these sources are subject to extreme underreporting: some researchers suggest that the actual incidence of child sexual abuse is 5 to 10 times the reported incidence (Tsai & Wagner, 1978). Nonetheless, there appears to be some consensus that between one-fourth and one-third of all children have some sexual experience with an adult (Mrazek, 1980).

Who Abuses and Who is Abused?

Upon hearing the term "sexual abuse," many of us project this scenario: a scraggly stranger offers candy to an unsuspecting child on the playground in order to lure the child into the bushes or a car where perverted acts are carried out. Although this does unfortutnately happen, it is the exception in child sexual abuse cases. It is far more likely that a child will be sexually abused by a relative, friend of the family, neighbor, or some authority figure with legitimate routine access to the child. In fact, 75 to 80 percent of sexual abuse cases occur within this "affinity system" (Finkelhor, 1979), and only about 7 percent are molested by strangers (Tsai, Feldman-Summers, & Edgar, 1979).

Within the family, brother-sister incest is thought to be the most common, although father-daughter incest is the best-documented form. Brother-sister incest is likely greatly underreported and is not generally considered as harmful unless there is a discrepancy between the ages or power of the siblings (Finkelhor, 1980). Mother-daughter, mother-son, and same-sex sibling incest are rarely reported. There is great variation among estimates of the types of incest, with the result that no reliable statistics are available. The majority of perpetrators are males (Lindholm & Willey, 1983). It has long been thought that girls were much more likely to be abused than boys. However, it has been reported that a significant number of male perpetrators were themselves abused as children, and many researchers now believe that sexual abuse of boys may be as common as that of girls.

The peak ages for reported sexual abuse are between the ages of 8 and 13 (Waterman & Lusk, 1986). Some professionals believe that these ages are inflated, particularly in cases of incest, in which the abuse begins at an early age and continues for several years. Also, in cases of long duration, the victim may not clearly remember the age at which he or she was first abused. Also, there appears to be an alarming trend toward sexual abuse of preschoolers;

for example, in one large metropolitan area, over one-fifth of the sexual abuse cases reported in one year were children under the age of five (Waterman & Lusk, 1986).

Socioeconomic status does not appear to be a factor. Again, it was previously thought that sexual abuse was more common among families with lower SES; however, this misconception was probably due to more families with lower SES being reported to authorities. Families with more financial resources have often been able to handle the incidences without being reported either to child protective agencies or law enforcement agencies (Waterman & Lusk, 1986).

The Dynamics of Abuse

Sgroi (1982) has described the dynamics of sexual abuse in five identifiable phases. In Phase I, *engagement,* the abuser has to figure out a way to engage the child in sexual activity without getting caught. There are four main strategies that abusers use in order to get the child engaged in such activities. The first is *enticement,* such as using bribes or rewards, or telling the child they are going to play a game. Second is the strategy of *entrapment,* which is threatening the child in a nonviolent way or making him feel obligated, i.e., "You owe me this because of what I've done for you." A third strategy is to *threaten* the child with force or harm, either to the child or a third party such as a sibling or parent. The fourth strategy is the use of *physical force* or use of *drugs* or *alcohol* to lower the child's resistance. It is important to realize that children cooperate because of their subordinate position to adults and because they lack the cognitive ability and emotional maturity to understand sexual behavior. It is important not to confuse cooperation with consent.

Phase II, according to Sgroi (1982), consists of the *sexual interaction* itself. Phase III is the *secrecy* phase, in which abusers use a variety of strategies to ensure that the child will not tell. Strategies used to keep the secret are usually related to the engagement strategy, (i.e., "Keeping our secret is part of the game," or "If you tell, I'll hurt your sister."). The majority of children do not tell after the first abusive incident, which unfortunately some-times results in adults' blaming them or in the children's blaming themselves when the abuse is disclosed. In Phase IV, the *disclosure* phase, the abuse may be accidentally disclosed or purposefully disclosed by the child. In cases of accidental disclosure, the child may react with silence, denial, or alarm because he fears that the abuser will hold him responsible for telling. And interestingly, when children choose to tell, their primary reason is usually not to stop the abuse. Rather, reasons are often ones adults view as unworthy, such as anger with the abuser for something other than the abuse and subsequent revenge. Such reasons may cause adults to doubt the credibility of the child's account. Phase V is the *suppression* phase, which begins when others begin to investigate. The abuser will typically deny the abuse or try to blame the child as a liar or seducer. Other adults, sometimes adults in positions of power, will support the abuser. Often the child will join in suppression by recanting or refusing to talk further. These factors underscore the need for investigators who are both knowledgable about and sensitive to child sexual abuse dynamics.

Effects of Sexual Abuse

The numerous long-term and short-term effects of sexual abuse on the child's socioemotio-nal development have been the subject of much study. The literature to date can be summarized under five headings: affective, psychosomatic, cognitive or school-related, behavioral, and other effects (Lusk & Waterman, 1986).

Affective Effects.   *Guilt or shame* has been reported by over a dozen studies as a common reaction by victims of child sexual abuse. Children tend to blame themselves, and may feel particularly guilty if their families broke up after a disclosure of incest (Lusk & Waterman, 1986). Also, as children grow older and gain a clearer picture of cultural taboos against sexual abuse and incest, their guilt may in fact intensify rather than lessen (Rosenfeld, Nadelson, & Krieger, 1979). *Anxiety* has also been documented by numerous researchers, both with preschoolers and with older children. Anxiety can be manifested in a variety of ways, including psychosomatic symptoms, and extreme levels of fears or phobias (Lusk & Waterman, 1986). A third major affective reaction is *depression.* Some authors believe that ongoing sexual abuse will almost invariably result in chronic depression (Blumberg, 1981), and others have observed depressed symptoms in victims ranging from preschoolers through adults. *Anger* is a fourth common affective reaction to sexual abuse that has also been noted in victims of all ages.

Psychosomatic Symptoms.   In addition to the acutal physical trauma that may be suffered by sexual abuse victims, many demonstrate psychosomatic symptoms such as stomachaches, headaches, encopresis, enuresis, and hypochondria. Changes in eating or sleeping habits, difficulty sleeping, and recurrent dreams or nightmares may occur.

Cognitive/School-Related Effects.   Many school-aged children demonstrate difficulties in school that may be related to their sexual abuse histories. Problems with concentration on academic tasks have been noted (Johnston, 1979). Other professionals believe that sexually abused children may develop feelings of powerlessness (Jiles, 1981) or "helpless victim" mentalities (Knittle & Tuana, 1980; Summit, 1983). As a function of the abusive situation in which the victims were in fact helpless, these feelings of being powerless and helpless can pervade the victims' social and school-related interactions.

Behavioral Effects.   In their review, Lusk & Waterman (1986) cite a litany of aggressive or acting out behaviors that have been found with children who have been sexually abused: hostile-aggressive behavior, antisocial behavior, delinquency, stealing, tantrums, and substance abuse in older children. In contrast, other studies have found introvertive or withdrawn behaviors in sexual abuse victims: withdrawal into fantasy and regressive behavior such as a return to early childhood fears (Lusk & Waterman, 1986). A third category of behavioral effects is precocious or inappropriate sexual behavior for the child's age and developmental level.

Other effects.   Other effects that have been noted among this population are self-destructive behaviors, psychopathology, and problems with self-esteem and interpersonal functioning. Professionals working with abuse victims have reported numerous self-destructive behaviors in their clientele. Acts of self-punishment or a "masochistic orientation" to life have been noted by Brooks (1982) and others. Also, tendencies toward suicidal ideation and suicide attempts have been noted, both during the abusive period and later in life.

The relationship between sexual abuse and serious psychopathology is not clear. Some researchers believe that it is related to character disorder, multiple personality, and psychotic symptoms. It is estimated that between 20 and 50 percent of child sexual abuse victims develop some form of psychopathology (Lusk & Waterman, 1986).What is clear, however, is that sexual abuse affects self-esteem and interpersonal relationships; both short-term and long-term effects have been noted. Numerous studies have established poor self-concepts or inadequate self-identities among victims of sexual abuse. Interpersonal difficulties have been noted both with peers (Sgroi, 1982) and with long-term heterosexual relationships (Boatman, Borkan, & Schetky, 1981). Although many reasons have been proposed for these interpersonal difficulties, some researchers believe that a basic lack of trust stemming from the abuse permeates the victim's personal interactions.

Mediating Factors and Treatment

Mediating Factors. Waterman and Lusk (1986) have identified factors that seem to mediate the harmful effects of sexual abuse, causing some children and adolescents to suffer less trauma than others. Two separate but related mediating factors are the degree of family psychopathology and the child's emotional health prior to the abuse. If the family climate or the child is characterized by pathology, then the child is at greater risk for psychological trauma. A third mediator is the relationship of the child and the offender. Most professionals believe that the closer the relationship, the more harmful the effects, although one exception probably is sibling incest (Nakashima & Zakus, 1979). A fourth mediating factor is age or developmental level of the child, although experts do not agree on whether sexual abuse is more harmful for preschoolers or for older children. Neither do they agree on whether sexual abuse is more harmful for boys or for girls. Degree of guilt is a fifth mediating factor, with older children apparently suffering more guilt than younger children, hence increasing their trauma because they feel partially responsible. A final mediating factor proposed by Waterman & Lusk (1986) is the degree of support and assurance provided by parents after the abuse is disclosed; overreaction or lack of support increases the trauma.

Treatment. Victims of sexual abuse have differential reactions, as the effects of abuse are mediated by these factors and doubtless many others that remain undocumented. Thus, treatment must be tailored to meet the individual needs of the child and her family. However, therapy or counseling for the child and family is always indicated. Most professionals agree that some type of family systems therapy is needed (Waterman, 1986). There is disagreement, however, over the timing of conjoint family therapy in cases of incest; many therapists believe that much individual therapy is needed before the family can meet as a unit (Waterman, 1986). In cases of incest, the perpetrator must apologize to the child, take responsibility for failure to protect him, and offer reassurance that abuse will never recur.

Other avenues are individual therapy and group therapy for adolescents. Younger children may be involved in play therapy or art therapy, either in groups and/or individual sessions. Specific treatment issues may vary according to whether the abuse was perpetrated by a family member or someone outside the family. Guilt, fear, depression, and impaired self-esteem are treatment issues for most if not all victims of sexual abuse; with incest, additional issues relate to trust, repressed anger, and blurred boundaries and role confusion

(Porter, Blick, & Sgroi, 1982). Not surprisingly, the best predictors for positive outcomes of treatment for the child appear to be the degree of parental concern for the child and the degree of parental involvement in treatment (Waterman, 1986). A therapist's experience with one teenage victim of incest is presented in Box 11- 2.

Implications for Teachers

There are a number of behavioral indicators of sexual abuse of which teachers and child care professionals should be aware. Although singly, any of these indicators may be the result of something other than sexual abuse, several of these indicators together suggest that the child or adolescent may have experienced sexual abuse:

- Abrupt changes in behavior such as loss of appetite, sleep disturbance, failing school-work
- Inappropriate seductive behavior with classmates, teachers, and other adults
- Knowledge of or unusual interest in sexual matters inappropriate to child's age and developmental level
- Promiscuity
- Anger directed anywhere and everywhere
- Reluctance to be with a certain person
- Regressive behavior
- Depression, withdrawal, few friends
- Extreme passivity and compliance
- Repeated running away

If a child or adolescent chooses to disclose a sexual abuse incident to you, try to support the individual by indicating you believe her and by not overreacting to the disclosure. You should find a private place to talk, tell her you will do what you can to protect and support her, but you should not promise not to tell. All states require adults to report suspected child abuse or neglect, which includes sexual abuse. While most states protect the identity of the source, it is possible that the reporting source will be asked to testify if the case comes to court. If you do receive a disclosure, it is important for you to be supportive, and report it to the authorities whose responsibility it is to investigate the veracity of the disclosure.

Teachers can be helpful in the classroom in a number of ways. Most special education teachers anchor their classrooms around providing success-oriented experiences and improving self-esteem. Such factors may be crucial with these children. It may be helpful also to establish a relationship with the child's therapist, with parental permission, so that the teacher can be aware and supportive of special issues being dealt with in therapy sessions. For example, the impaired ability to trust may be an issue and it would be helpful for the teacher to give the student some "space." Another example may be that the therapist is working on getting the individual to acknowledge and express repressed anger toward the offender; in such cases, the teacher may be more understanding if some of the new-found ability to express anger spills over into the classroom. If the child has recently been involved in sexual abuse and is not in therapy, the teacher may, after conferring with the parents, want to make a referral or to facilitate an on-campus referral to the counselor.

BOX 11-2 Cassie: A Victim of Sexual Abuse

Cassie entered my office quietly with a shy smile. She was an attractive fifteen year old who looked older than her years. Cassie had been admitted to the residential treatment facility three months prior to my taking a position there as supervisor and therapist. Her history indicated that she had been sexually abused by her father beginning at age three, and that he had recently been convicted and imprisoned as a result of her outcry. Cassie's younger brother, age 12, and sister, age 7, both continued to live with their mother. While the family continued to contact her on a sporadic basis, it was clear that their support and loyalty remained with the father.

Despite her turbulent past Cassie was able to present herself very well. Her intelligence and charm made her a favorite with her teachers. Being popular and assuming a leadership role with her peers came easily as well. It was only later, as her responsibilities and stressors increased, that cracks began to appear in her carefully constructed facade.

In the initial phase of treatment Cassie was able to talk about her past in a very detached and mechanical way, all the while maintaining that she had worked through her problems and that "*that* part of her life was behind her." Typical of dissociative phenomena, she often would appear to be somewhere else, unaware of her immediate surroundings. Nevertheless, she functioned quite well. She continued with school, became active in the girls' softball team, and got a part-time job working evenings and weekends.

As time went on, Cassie began acting out in ways to "test " our relationship. At times she became verbally aggressive both at school and at home. Slamming doors and throwing books underscored her frustration. In further attempts to alienate me as well as others, she would withdraw into a stony silence refusing to acknowledge anyone except for a contemptuous glance. She quit her part-time job, her grades began to slip, arguments with authority figures increased, and she determinedly strived to sabotage herself at every turn.

When her efforts didn't succeed in proving that I would abandon her as her family had, a slow transformation began taking place. She began truly working in therapy, taking risks in giving voice to what had been her worst nightmare, allowing herself to feel the rage and loss that she had suffered and ultimately role-playing a confrontation with both her father and her mother regarding the abuse.

Her progress was by no means consistent. Intermittent crises threatened to undermine the gains that she had made. She was involved in a close relationship with a young man by the name of Mark whom she met shortly before beginning therapy. The normal ups and downs of an adolescent relationship could throw her into the depths of depression. Cassie was caught up in the fantasy that Mark would be her savior. She believed that they would marry and create the kind of family that she longed for and had never had. The issues she was dealing with in therapy impacted her relationship with Mark, just as their relationship affected her participation in therapy. Mark came in for couples therapy in addition to Cassie's individual work.

I had first focused on helping Cassie objectively see that she was not to blame and that she had done nothing to warrant the abuse and betrayal of her childhood. As she began to rightfully shift responsibility away from herself, her ability to separate intimacy and shame increased. Cassie's growing self-confidence enabled her to become more self-reliant and realistic regarding her future goals. Over time my role as her therapist evolved from utilizing an active, directive approach to that of giving gentle support.

After eighteen months of hard work and determination to confront and work through the issues of her past, Cassie graduated from high school and set out on her own. She has the potential to accomplish whatever she puts her mind to. I can only hope that she'll continue to draw on her incredible inner strength and the tools that she has learned to do just that.

Contributed by Vicki Knowles, M.A., LPC.

In summary, there is a very good chance that teachers of children and youth with emotional/behavioral disorders will work with those who have been sexually abused. In fact, our best estimates indicate that about one-third to one-fourth of all children in this country are at risk for at least one sexual abuse incident. It is far more likely that the offender will be a family member or friend of the family than a stranger. The long-term and short-term effects of sexual abuse include guilt, anxiety, depression, psychosomatic symptoms, school-related problems, withdrawn behavior, and a variety of aggressive or acting out behaviors. A number of factors are thought to mediate the effects of sexual abuse such that individual children may react in very different ways. However, teachers should be aware that certain school-related issues of concentration on task, impaired self-esteem, a "helpless" mentality, and interpersonal difficulties are common reactions to abuse. Understanding these students' behavior from the perspective of a victim may help teachers formulate better instructional and management plans in the classroom.

Suspension, Expulsion, and Full Inclusion of Students with E/BD

This third and final section explores both legal and philosophical issues attendant to educating students with emotional/behavioral disorders. Legal parameters for using suspension and expulsion as discipline tools have been determined by litigation. The courts have also been asked to help determine parameters of full inclusion placements. Recent litigation in these areas is summarized. The chapter closes with a discussion of ethical and practical considerations about full inclusion and students with E/BD.

The Legality of Suspension and Expulsion

Two common interventions for students with emotional/behavioral disorders in public schools are suspension and expulsion. Suspension of a student by the principal is effective for periods of up to ten days and, as established by litigation, it must be accompanied by a parent conference and a hearing. Expulsion is the exclusion of a student for a longer period of time, generally a term, semester, or a year. Expulsions also must be accompanied by a hearing. In several studies attempting to ascertain major reasons for school suspensions, nonattendance and antisocial behaviors consistently were ranked in the top three (Safer, 1982). Neither the logic of suspending students for not coming to school nor the effectiveness of suspension as a disciplinary tool has been established. Expulsions generally are given for more serious infractions such as violent behavior, or illegal acts such as possession of drugs or weapons.

The use of suspension and expulsion as disciplinary measures for students with emotional/behavioral disorders has been questioned ethically and legally. Because laws regarding education for individuals with disabilities have not dealt with disciplinary issues, a number of lawsuits have forced the courts to provide guidelines that balance the rights of individuals with disabilities with the rights of public schools to maintain safe and orderly environments for all students. Yell's (1989) review of litigation of numerous cases involving suspension and expulsion of handicapped students yielded five principles:

1. *Temporary suspensions may be used to discipline students with disabilities.* Short-term suspensions (less than 10 days) do not constitute change in placement and therefore do not invoke the procedural safeguards of IDEA. Serial suspensions or suspensions of more than 10 days have been considered expulsions by the courts.

2. *Expulsions and lengthy suspensions are changes in educational placement that invoke procedural safeguards.* In these situations, all procedural safeguards outlined by IDEA for changes in educational placement must be observed.

3. *A trained and knowledgeable group of people must determine whether the misbehavior is causally related to the disabling condition. If a relationship exists, the student cannot be expelled.* This decision should be made by a group such as the IEP team; it cannot be a unilateral administrative decision.

4. *Due process procedures must be applied when expelling or suspending students with disabilities.* Even when suspended for 10 days or less, students must be given a hearing in which evidence from both sides can be given. This principle applies to all students, those with disabilities and those without disabilities.

5. *School districts may opt to place a disruptive student in a more restrictive setting.* Movement to a more restrictive setting is a viable option that invokes due process procedures.

An additional landmark case involved the suspensions of two students with E/BD in the San Francisco public schools. *Honig vs. Doe* was heard by the U.S. Court of Appeals and, eventually, by the Supreme Court who issued a ruling in January of 1988. In addition to upholding many of the five principles just outlined, the courts held that before an IEP team can recommend that a student with a disability be expelled, the team must consider results of an independent evaluation. The most controversial portion of the ruling, however, involved the "stay-put" provision, which means that during during the pendency of any hearings, the student must remain in his or her educational placement unless both the school and the parents agree otherwise. The court ruled that normal disciplinary measures could still be used, including temporary suspension up to 10 days. If the student is considered dangerous, the school has these 10 days in which to seek change of placement or to enlist the aid of the courts if necessary.

Yell (1989) offers a model upon which to base policy decisions for discipline of students with disabilities. He suggests that, when making decisions, the IEP team or a similar designated group answer the following questions: (1) Is the behavior a threat to the student or others? (2) Is the misbehavior a manifestation of the disabling condition? and (3) Is the disabled student's current placement appropriate?

It should be noted that although courts have restricted suspensions and expulsions as disciplinary tools with students with disabilities, these actions are not prohibited as long as legal rights of the students are adhered to. The general intent of the courts appears to be to prevent school officials from using suspension and expulsion as measures to exclude students with disabilities from school for lengthy periods without providing them with due process under IDEA.

Legal Issues and Inclusion

Full inclusion is a term generally used to refer to the idea of eliminating placements in special education and a call for all students to be educated in general classroom settings. There is a movement afoot in the nation today that is pressing for full inclusion of all children and youth with disabilities, i.e., that all children should be educated in general education classrooms, with appropriate supports and services. Relevant issues and ramifications of full inclusion for students with emotional/behavioral disorders will be addressed in the next section of this Special Issues chapter. However, legal provisions governing special education may sometimes get lost in all the rhetoric involved in this movement. Therefore, current legal provisions established by legislation and litigation will be briefly described.

Federal Law (IDEA) and Inclusion.   The provisions of the Individuals with Disabilities Act (IDEA) must be adhered to once an individual is identified as having a disability. According to Lewis, Chard, & Scott, (1994), IDEA clearly stipulates that (a) placement decisions should be made according to each individual student's needs, and not according to available space or trends; and (b) school districts that adopt a full inclusion policy without consideration of each child's individual needs may be placing themselves in jeopardy. It is up to the courts to decide how the regulations in IDEA will be interpreted for individual school districts making decisions for individual students.

Central to understanding the legal aspects of full inclusion is understanding the least restrictive environment, or LRE, as it is called. Placement decisions in special education are to be based upon the concept of least restrictive environment. Lewis et al. (1994) point out that LRE is a set of decision-making guidelines and not a "place." However, the concept of LRE assumes that there is a continuum of placements available, ranging from more restrictive settings such as a residential or hospital, to less restrictive settings such as resource rooms on general education campuses. The setting or placement itself is secondary to ensuring that eligible students obtain their educational objectives as determined by the multidisciplinary team in the individualized education plan.

Court Rulings on Placement and Inclusion.   As of this writing, the U.S. Circuit Courts of Appeals were the highest courts to hear cases questioning full inclusion principles. None of the cases have involved students with emotional/behavioral disorders. In 1989, the Fifth Circuit Court of Appeals heard *Daniel R.R. v. State Board of Education.* Daniel was a kindergartner with developmental delays; Daniel's parents requested a full-day placement in general education, and the school district recommended full-day placement in special education, with lunch and recess with his peers without disabilities. The Fifth Circuit ultimately upheld that Daniel would not benefit from general education placement. In so doing, the court determined that reviewing courts must first assess whether the individual's educational needs can be met, with supports and services, in the general education classroom. The court stipulated that the effect of the individual on the operation of the class must also be considered. Second, according to the Fifth Circuit, reviewing courts must determine whether the district is providing an appropriate, integrated environment.

The Eleventh Circuit Court of Appeals heard *Greer v. Rome City School District* in 1991, and extended the findings of *Daniel R.R.* to include an excessive cost factor: If the cost of educating a child in general education would have an impact on the education of other children, then it is an inappropriate placement (Lewis et al., 1994). Two other court cases (*Oberti v. Clementon School Board,* 1993; *Sacramento City Unified School District, Board of Education v. Holland,* 1994) have upheld general education placements for students with developmental disabilities. These cases have generally been interpreted as supportive of full inclusion.

However, it should be noted that the courts considered not only the appropriateness of the educational opportunities available to the individual in the general classroom, but also the impact of the individual upon the teacher and others in the classroom. It should further be noted that none of the individuals in these cases had significant emotional or behavioral problems, and did not pose a management problem for the general education teacher. Full inclusion cases for students with emotional/behavioral disorders who may pose management problems have yet to be heard by the courts.

While courts are in the process of clarifying the least restrictive environment on a case-by-case basis, some educators themselves are calling for an overhaul of the system, i.e., the full inclusion movement. Following is a speech by the 1994 President of the Council for Children with Behavioral Disorders, who explains the context of the full inclusion movement relative to other educational reform and offers some very specific advocacy roles fo teachers of students with E/BD.

Caring for Students with Emotional and Behavioral Disorders Amidst School Reform by (Jo Webber)[1]

Reform, revolution, and change characterize the world today. Some political systems are disintegrating and some are re-integrating. Passive observation of these transformations confirms that change is often accompanied by strife, fanaticism, struggle, and, sometimes, hope and reason. And so it goes in the United States. We elected our current President to bring about domestic change and this change is penetrating our social service and educational agencies. Here, too, change has brought strife, fanaticism, and struggle. The hope is that the current social reform will result in better services for children and youth with disabilities, particularly those with emotional and behavioral disorders. If this is to occur, however, it is essential to proceed reasonably and carefully with reflection, attention to detail, and effective problem solving (Kauffman, 1993).

Social Policy and Students with Emotional/Behavioral Disorders
Some of the new and proposed social policies directly affect children and youth with emotional/behavioral disorders (E/BD). President Clinton's proposed health care plan would have made mental health treatment available to all Americans, not just those who can afford it. One can only speculate as to what effect that would have had on services for young people with or at-risk for E/BD, but it seemed to be addressing a significant area of need. Additionally, the National Institute of Mental Health (NIMH) specially targeted young people with E/BD by providing states with funding to develop and implement a comprehensive system of mental health services known as the Child and Adolescent Service System Program (CAASP; Stroul & Friedman, 1986). To date, 35 states have received such funding.

The Juvenile Justice System, usually a key player after students have developed problems, appears ready to take a proactive role. U.S. Attorney General Janet Reno, recognizing that "America would rather build prisons than invest in a child" (MHA/Texas, 1993, p. 1), is moving her agency toward preventing crime by intervening with very young children who are at risk. This proactive stance can only enhance what social service and education agencies are already trying to do—empower families and care for children.

Within the Department of Education, progressively more funding has been designated for drug-free schools, drop-out prevention programs, and various at-risk populations. The Individuals with Disabilities Education Act (IDEA) has been reauthorized for students with disabilities and the Office of Special Education Programs (OSEP) is specifically targeting students with E/BD by formulating a national agenda for improving educational outcomes for children and youth with and at risk of developing serious emotional disturbance (Webber, 1993). These young people stand to gain substantially better services if intervention efforts remain coordinated and organized.

State and local education agencies have also been contemplating change and the recent frenzy of restructuring activity in the schools is receiving much attention. The general public and corporate America have become increasingly vocal in their criticism of public schools, and opinions about what is wrong and suggestions for fixing the schools abound. The current change process has seemingly pitted parents against educators, educators against each other, and everyone against legislators (Olson, 1993). Funding formulas, goals, curricula, strategies, teacher training, school calendars, and school administrations are in various states of alteration across the country.

The role of special education in the school reform movement remains unclear. Some people think special educators should take a leadership role; others believe special education should take only a support role, but for those of us who care about children and youth with E/BD it needs to be an advocacy role. Caring for students with E/BD amidst the change and restructuring means that we need to guarantee their "right" to the most effective treatment and/or education. This guarantee has to do with informed decision making for each student, with quality educational practices—with accountability and with the availability of a full range of treatment options and choices. Ensuring this guarantee may be the essential work for all of us in the coming years.

Concepts and Terminology

Trying to make sense of current changes in the schools and establishing our role is made more difficult by confusing terminology and concepts. Perhaps some clarification is necessary. In 1975, with the passage of P.L. 44-142 (now known as IDEA), the notion of quality educational programs for students with disabilities was introduced. One section of that legislation mandated that these students be placed in separate classes and schools *only* when their education could not be achieved satisfactorily in general education classrooms, even with special services and aids. This process came to be known as *mainstreaming*. Special education has been criticized for not adhering to the mainstreaming philosophy. There is evidence to suggest that parallel educational systems have developed, that special education students are predominantly served in pull-out programs with different curricula, that labeling has had a detrimental effect on the students, and that special education costs too much (e.g., Institute on Community Integration, 1991; Rogers, 1993; U. S. News, 1993; TASH, 1993). In fact, among special educators, the term mainstreaming has become somewhat obsolete and indicative of unenlightenment. Interestingly enough, however, the concept of mainstreaming is a driving force in general education reform.

A second special education movement came in the late 1980s. The *regular education initiative* (REI) was proposed for students with mild disabilities who were to be merged into general education with adapted curriculum and strategies delivered by well-trained general education teachers (Wang & Walberg, 1988). REI proponents advocated a merger of funding and administrative structures along with strategies such as cooperative learning, consulting-teacher models, peer facilitation, and teacher assistance teams. This merger was described as an expansion of, not supplanting, the continuum of special education services (Trent, 1989).

REI critics, however, pointed out that general education had already failed to success-fully educate students with mild disabilities and that research did not support the notion that special education had failed and needed to be changed (Kauffman, 1991). It was also pointed out that some students with mild disabilities achieved more in pull-out programs and that approaching reform purely from a teacher-deficit model was a simplistic answer to a rather complex issue (Trent, 1989).

Building upon the original maxims of mainstreaming and REI, the current special education restructuring movement is known as the *full inclusion* movement. Proponents of full inclusion primarily address the plight of students with mental retardation, partic-ularly those with severe multiple disabilities (Gartner & Lipsky, 1989; Stainback & Stainback, 1991; TASH, 1993). They state, however, that special education has failed for all of its students primarily because of the location in which these students have received instruction and, therefore, all special education students must now be served in general education classrooms. Supporters of full inclusion advocate eliminating individ-ualized education plans (IEPs), labels, and pull-out options so that special education students will have the same choices that we all have. These reformers say that diversity is normal and fully including all special education students into general education class-rooms is an issue of morality, acceptance, respect, and coming together as equals (Flynn, 1993). Rather rigid and zealous about their philosophy, many full-inclusion proponents rely on emotional images and generally hostile advocacy techniques to make their points. They appear to be very critical of the "old guard" or those who disagree with them (Kauffman, 1993).

Critics of the full inclusion movement have pointed out that:

- Functional curricula and community-based instruction may be sacrificed for students served in general education classrooms.
- Individualized planning may be compromised for this notion of maximum exposure.
- Placement has gained too much importance.
- Historical research has been ignored.
- We cannot speak about "all special education students" and provide effective individ-ualized instruction.
- The movement is a fanatical one rather than a logical one (Kauffman, 1993).

In response to this aggressive movement, many special education organizations (e.g., The Council for Exceptional Children, the Council for Children with Behavioral Disorders, the

Council of Administrators of Special Education, the Council on Learning Disabilities, and the CEC Division on Mental Retardation and Developmental Disabilities) have prepared position statements supporting the preservation of a full continuum of services, hoping to protect the major tenets of IDEA and to prevent the wholesale dumping of special education students into general education classrooms.

Only recently, however, has full inclusion been criticized by general educators. Albert Shanker, president of the American Federation of Teachers, called for a "moratorium to stop the helter-skelter, even tumultuous rush toward full inclusion," (Austin American-Statesman, 1993, p. A6). He further stated that placing students who cannot function into an environment that does not help them is a disservice to them and to other students in that classroom. He claimed that school districts see this as a budget-cutting option, that teachers are not adequately trained to cope with the students, and that special services needed by the special education students are no longer available.

While these instances of special education restructuring were conceptualized by special educators, there is also a current move by general educators to restructure special education as it reforms all of education. This movement, known as *inclusion* or the *inclusive schools movement,* has been supported primarily by general education administrators (e.g., National Association of State Boards of Education, 1992; Rogers, 1993) and is seen by many special educators as support for full inclusion.

However, the inclusion movement is much broader in scope and has not advocated the demise of pull-out options nor the inclusion of all students in general education classrooms. Inclusive schools work on the assumption that schools have failed and need to be reconceptualized to teach all children and to teach to the whole child. Not unlike mainstreaming, inclusion "refers to the commitment to educate each child, to the maximum extent appropriate, in the school and classroom he/she would otherwise attend" (Rogers, 1993, p. 1).

This notion is one of many cornerstone concepts of the school reform literature. The inclusive school's literature (e.g., National Association of State Boards of Education, 1992; Olson, 1993; Rogers, 1993) additionally advocates:

1. Heterogeneous grouping (side-by-side learning for multiage diverse classes)
2. Bringing support services to the child (including the provision of multiagency support)
3. A personalized approach to educating students (all students get what they need)
4. Outcomes-based education and performance assessment (goals, objectives, and behavioral measurement)
5. A developmental approach (take students where they are and move them unlabeled, ungraded and self-paced where they need to go)
6. Varied curricula (de-emphasizing academics in favor of character development, strategy learning, and critical thinking)
7. Lower student-teacher ratios
8. Adapted strategies including multimodal presentations, computer-based instruction, cooperative learning, peer tutoring, no-cut athletic policies, and team teaching
9. Team problem solving and decision making, including site-based management and total quality management

Many of these reform activities have been part of special education since the inception of P.L. 94-142 in 1975. For years, special educators have been attempting to promote school-wide acceptance of special education students while providing effective instructional strategies to students who are challenging to teach. These strategies, based on a combination of developmental, cognitive, and behavioral theories, included individualized instruction, identification of annual outcomes, performance-based assessment, multiage grouping, functional and affective curriculum, lower student-teacher ratios, multimodal presentations, related services, and team decision making.

It seems that general educators are trying to reform all of education to be more like special education. Unfortunately, the connection between general education reform and special education has not been widely recognized and special education is still seen by many as a failure (*U.S. News,* 1993). Regardless, special educators should be striving to assist general education in their effort to provide "exceptional" education for all students while actively protecting students with disabilities in the process.

School Reform and Students with E/BD

Certainly, the schools have their work cut out for them. Critics of school reform (e.g., Citizens for Excellence in Education) have called heterogeneous grouping, cooperative learning, peer tutoring, and ungraded systems "dumbed-down" learning (Olson, 1993). Behavior modification has been called brainwashing. Whole language strategies are seen as a plot to keep children from learning how to read and write, and outcome-based education is seen as a "big brother" move to dictate what students ought to think and believe. In addition to this formidable opposition, schools are now serving more students with complex problems (e.g., hungry, poor health, abused, unsupervised, suicidal, pregnant, violent, armed, bisexual, on drugs, and neurologically impaired). More students have or are at risk for mental illness and more students are in need of social services than ever before (Department of Health and Human Services, 1989). A most challenging subgroup of these students is served by special education as students with emotional or behavioral disorders.

Students with E/BD, who are often characterized by attention deficits, immature behavior, anxiety, low academic achievement, social skills deficits, depression, aggression, antisocial behavior, and/or disordered thinking also tend to be poor and come from single-parent families (Knitzer, Steinberg & Fleisch, 1990). Many of these students are abused or neglected and live in "fragmented" living arrangements. About 42 percent of students with E/BD drop out of school and many have arrest records. In order to educate students with such complex problems, Knitzer and others (1990) recommended that school programs provide responsive, intensive intervention approaches, including:

- Access to meaningful mental health services, including crisis intervention, group discussions, consistent behavior management strategies, and intensive case management
- Strong support structures for their teachers
- Strong expectations that families will participate in their child's school life facilitated by case managers, school-family liaison personnel or mental health personnel stationed in the classroom

- High-intensity school-based interventions for sexual and physical abuse and substance abuse

These authors further recommended a full scope of mental health and educational services to be available to at-risk students (including, but not limited to, general education classrooms, self-contained classrooms, day schools, day treatment, and partial hospitalization programs). Curricula should address not only behavior management, but also social skills training, academic remediation, self-control, and affective development. Collaborative programs between schools, mental health agencies, and juvenile justice agencies were deemed essential.

Given the characteristics of these students and a view of what is necessary to adequately serve them, it seems ludicrous to assume that *all* students should be placed in general education classrooms as a matter of policy. It seems so ludicrous, in fact, that it is hardly worth discussion. Instead, those of us who care for children and youth with E/BD should review the recommendations put forth for these students and their families (e.g., Knitzer et al., 1990) and work through collaborative efforts to promote a comprehensive system of mental health and educational services. Within the inclusive schools movement, we should support the notion of ownership of these students by all educators, thus reducing the tendency to push them out. At the same time, we need to ensure quality special education services by providing relevant IEPs, pertinent curricula, consistent behavior management, therapeutic crisis intervention, quality instruction, mental health services, a safe environment, and support for administrators and teachers.

Caring for Students with E/BD Amidst Reform

The first step in caring for students with E/BD during this time of change is to accept the role of advocate. This means neither resisting change totally nor being passive in the face of ill-conceived recommendations. Instead, it means being guided by the needs of individual students. Advocates for children and youth with E/BD will be pitted against some special educators who may insist on "dumping" these students into hostile, inadequate situations, and also against some general educators who may want to exclude these students from school altogether. The road will not be easy or clear. Perhaps the following list of suggested actions may act as an advocacy guide and assist with this endeavor.

To advocate for children and youth with E/BD it will be necessary to:

- Protect their right to the most effective treatment and education by expanding—not condensing—the range of choices available to these students regarding curriculum, intervention, and treatment strategies, services, and placements.
- Protect their right to an individualized team-decision-making process that first inspects a student's needs, prescribes curriculum and strategy adaptations, and only then addresses the best location to obtain an education.
- Resist the move to talk about all special education students needing a particular strategy. Recognizing individual differences ensures the appropriateness of an education.
- Resist being bullied by zealots into losing sight of what is best for each student. Encourage fanatical reformers to practice their own notion of inclusion by accepting diverse viewpoints and refraining from punishing those who disagree with them.
- Keep what has worked in special education and expand it to others who can benefit.

Smaller student-teacher ratios, individualized planning and instruction, creative strategies, relevant curricula, skill training, parent involvement, team decision making, and support services have been found to improve educational outcomes.

- Strengthen special education's empirical base (Kauffman, 1993) and use it to make decisions. Acting purely on emotion and choosing change only for the sake of change can do great damage to students.
- Question those practices that may not work, be willing to change them, and be accountable for choosing effective teaching practices. Are our identification practices valid? Have we a clear definition for our population? Are we relying too heavily on a curriculum of control and questionable level systems and neglecting sound instruction? Are we using too many dittos and giving too much free time? Have we created reinforcement junkies? Are we reluctant to let go of our students? Are we actively facilitating our students' integration into larger society? Conducting reviews of instructional practices and the quality of available services can promote continued improvement.
- Prepare students to succeed in general education. Assess the general education setting for necessary behaviors, directly teach those behaviors along with self-control techniques, use behavior management strategies that will transfer easily, train healthy thinking, provide mental health support, and accomplish transition at a reasonable pace.
- Protect students with E/BD in general education settings. These students have traditionally been excluded from school altogether. General educators usually have little tolerance for their behavior and often become angry and frustrated. Trying to reintegrate students who have already failed in general education is more difficult than integrating students (e.g., those with multiple physical disabilities) who have not previously been served by general education. Also, protect students from the undue frustration, anxiety, embarrassment, and anger that might result from large student-teacher ratios, fast-paced irrelevant curriculum, failing grades, and outright ridicule and/or rejection. Protect them also from harsher punishments that might be developed if other alternatives become unavailable.
- Commit to professional growth and development so as to be knowledgeable and assertive advocates.
- Promote the ownership of all children in school, the acceptance of people's humanity, the creation of supportive communities, the valuing of cooperation, and interdependence. These are noble notions and worthy of consistent attention.
- Work to ensure that a full range of mental health services is available to students with E/BD and their families, preferably in or around the school. This means supporting the CASSP and OSEP agendas, promoting interagency collaboration and case management, and remaining focused on the needs of students and their families.

Conclusions

As Kauffman (1993) so aptly stated:

In a world of rapidly changing social institutions and conventions, special education is being subjected to enormous pressures for change. Special education's

*future—and the futures of the students who are its primary concern—will largely
be determined by responses to these pressures. (p. 6)*

It seems wise to proceed carefully and gauge the effects of any change on the students
for whom we are responsible. It might be necessary to actively resist some recommended
changes. Instead, wisdom dictates preserving what is valid about special education—improving areas that have been neglected, and expanding the range of educational and mental
health services available to students with E/BD. Change can be exciting and promising,
particularly if it is well planned. Taking care of students with E/BD means advocating, not
abdicating; it means being responsible, reflective reformers.

Key Points

1. Although there is no typical profile of a substance-exposed child, these children are
   at risk for developmental disabilities and school failure.
2. Some substance-exposed neonates display hypersensitive and disorganized characteristics; as preschoolers, some display problems in language development, attention,
   and ability to regulate and control their behavior.
3. Experts agree that the psychosocial environment of these children, beginning in infancy, is of paramount importance in determining how they will develop.
4. Effective interventions must involve multiple agencies that help the family improve
   the psychosocial environment.
5. Children are much more likely to be sexually abused by someone in the family's affinity system than by a stranger.
6. Many researchers now believe that sexual abuse of males is as common as that of females.
7. Dozens of studies have attempted to document the numerous short-term and long-
   term effects of sexual abuse on children; perhaps the clearest findings are that self-
   concept and interpersonal relationships are damaged.
8. Among the factors thought to mediate effects of sexual abuse are parental support
   and involvement in therapy subsequent to the disclosure.
9. Litigation to date indicates that, with restrictions, school officials may use suspension and expulsion as disciplinary tools with students with E/BD as long as the students are provided due process under IDEA.
10. Although litigation to date has been interpreted as being supportive of full inclusion,
    the courts have mandated that effects of the individual with a disability upon the
    teacher and others in the classroom be considered. Court cases thus far have involved
    individuals with developmental disabilities who were not posing behavior or discipl-
    ine problems.
11. Caring for students with E/BD in the midst of education reform means advocating
    for their rights to the most effective treatment and education.

Additional Readings

Born substance exposed, educationally vulnerable, by L.J. Vincent, M.K. Poulsen, C.K. Cole,
G. Woodruff, & D.R. Griffith, 1991, Reston, VA: Council for Exceptional Children, for a

handbook neatly summarizing the research on substance-exposed children and offering strategies for educators.

Drug and alcohol exposed: Implications for special education for students identified as behaviorally disordered, by Anne Bauer, 1991, *Behavioral Disorders, 17,* 72–79, for an article summarizing the effects of substance exposure and offering implications specifically for teachers of students with E/BD.

How we might achieve the radical reform of special education, by Jim Kauffman, 1993, *Exceptional Children, 60,* 6–16, for a thoughtful and thought-provoking response to pressures of proponents of full inclusion and other reform movements.

Inclusive schools movement and the radicalization of special education reform, by Doug Fuchs and Lynn Fuchs, 1994, *Exceptional Children, 60,* 294–309, for another thoughtful treatment of the full inclusion movement and its implications for all of special education.

Sexual and physical abuse among adolescents with behavioral disorders: Profiles and implications, by Darcy Miller, 1993, *Behavioral Disorders, 18,* 129–138, for results of a survey of adolescents with E/BD who self-report their experiences with abuse.

Endnote

[1]This presentation was given by Jo Webber as a keynote address for the First General Session of the CCBD Forum on Inclusion, held in St. Louis, MO, October 1, 1993. It was published in L.M. Bullock & R.A. Gable (Eds.) *Monograph on inclusion: Ensuring appropriate services to children and youth with E/BD-I.* Reston, VA: Council for Children with Behavioral Disorders. Reprinted with permission of the author and the publisher.

References

Abelsohn, D. (1983). Dealing with the abdication dynamic in the post-divorce family: A context for adolescent crisis. *Family Process, 22*, 359–383.

Abikoff, H. (1985). Efficacy of cognitive training interventions in hyperactive children: A critical review. *Clinical Psychology Review, 5*, 479–512.

Abikoff, H., Gittelman, R., & Klein, D. F. (1980). Classroom observation code for hyperactive children: A replication study. *Journal of Consulting and Clinical Psychology, 48*, 555–565.

Abikoff, H., Gittelman-Klein, R., & Klein, D. F. (1977). Validation of a classroom observation code for hyperactive children. *Journal of Consulting and Clinical Psychology, 45*, 772–783.

Abramson, L. Y., Seligman, M. E. P., & Teasdale, J. (1978). Learned helplessness in humans: Critique and reformulation. *Journal of Abnormal Psychology, 87*, 49–74.

Achenbach, T. M. (1966). The classification of children's psychiatric symptoms: A factor-analytic study. *Psychological Monographs, 80*, (No. 615).

Achenbach, T. M. (1978). Psychopathology of childhood: Research problems and issues. *Journal of Consulting and Clinical Psychology, 46*, 759–776.

Achenbach, T. M. (1991). *Child behavior checklist.* Burlington, VT: Department of Psychiatry, University of Vermont.

Achenbach, T. M., & Edelbrock, C. S. (1978). The classification of child psychopathology: A review and analysis of empirical efforts. *Psychological Bulletin, 85*, 1275–1301.

Achenbach, T. M., & Edelbrock, C. S. (1979). The Child Behavior Profile: II. Boys aged 12–16 and girls aged 6–11 amd 12–16. *Journal of Consulting and Clinical Psychology, 47*, 223–233.

Achenbach, T. M., & Edelbrock, C. S. (1981). Behavioral problems and competencies reported by parents of normal and disturbed children aged 4 through 16. *Monographs of the Society for Research in Child Development, 46*, (Serial No. 188).

Achenbach, T. M., & Edelbrock, C. S. (1983). *Manual for the child behavior checklist.* Burlington, VT: University of Vermont Department of Psychiatry.

Adrian, S. E. (1990). *The effects of a formal sexuality education program on the self-esteem of adolescents labeled emotionally disturbed.* Unpublished doctoral dissertation, The University of Texas at Austin.

Ager, C. L., & Cole, C. L. (1991.) A review of cognitive-behavioral interventions for children and adolescents with behavioral disorders. *Behavioral Disorders, 16*, 276–287.

Aiello, B. (1976). Especially for special educators: A sense of our own history. *Exceptional Children, (42)*, 244–252.

Alberto, P. A., & Troutman, A. C. (1989). *Applied behavioral analysis for teachers.* (3rd ed.). Columbus, OH: Merrill.

Alessi, N. E. (1986). *DSM-III diagnosis associated with childhood depressive disorders.* Paper presented at American Academy of Child Psychiatry, Los Angeles, CA.

Alessi, N. E., McManus, M., & Grapente, W. L. (1984). The characterization of depressive disorder in serious juvenile offenders. *Journal of Affective Disorders, 6*, 9–17.

Alexander, J. F., & Parsons, B. V. (1973). Short-term behavioral intervention with delinquent families: Impact on family process and recidivism. *Journal of Abnormal Psychology, 81*, 219–225.

Alexander, R., Kroth, R., Simpson, R., & Poppelreiter, T. (1982). The parent role in special education. In R. McDowell, G. Adamson, and F. Wood (Eds.), *Teaching emotionally disturbed children.* Boston: Little, Brown.

Algozzine, B. (1977). The emotionally disturbed child: Disturbed or disturbing? *Journal of Abnormal Child Psychology, 5*, 205–211.

Algozzine, B., & Curran, T. J. (1979). Teachers' predictions of children's school success as a function of their behavioral tolerances. *Journal of Educational Research, 72*, 344–347.

Allyon, T., Layman, D., & Kandel, H. J. (1975). A behavioral-educational alternative to drug control of hyperactive children. *Journal of Applied Behavior Analysis, 8,* 137–146.

Alpert, C. L., & Rogers-Warren, A. K. (1985). Communication in autistic persons: Characteristics and intervention. In S. F. Warren & A. K. Rogers-Warren (Eds.), *Teaching functional language.* (pp. 123–155). Austin, TX: Pro-Ed.

Althen, G. (1988). *American ways—A guide for foreigners in the United States.* Yarmouth, ME: Intercultural Press.

American Psychiatric Association (1980). *Diagnostic and statistical manual of mental disorders* (3rd ed.). Washington, DC: Author.

American Psychiatric Association (1987). *Diagnostic and statistical manual of mental disorders-Revised (DSMIII-R).* (3rd ed., revised). Washington, DC: Author.

American Psychiatric Association (1994). *Diagnostic and statistical manual of mental disorders-IV (DSMI-IV).* (4th ed.). Washington, DC: Author.

Anastasi, A. (1988). *Psychological testing* (6th ed.). New York: Macmillan.

Anderson, C. W. (1981a). Parent-child relationships: A context for reciprocal developmental influence. *The Counseling Psychologist, 4,* 35–44.

Anderson, C. W. (1981b). The handicapped child's effects on parent-child relations: A useful model for school psychologists. *School Psychology Review, 10,* 82–90.

Anthony, E. J. (1975). Childhood depression. In E. J. Anthony & T. Benedek (Eds.), *Depression and human existence* (pp. 231–277). Boston: Little-Brown.

Apter, S. J. (1982). *Troubled children/troubled systems.* Elmsford, NY: Pergamon Press.

Apter, S. J., & Conoley, J. C. (1984). *Childhood behavior disorders and emotional disturbance.* Englewood Cliffs, NJ: Prentice Hall.

Arbuthnot, J., & Gordon, D. A. (1986). Behavioral and cognitive effects of a moral reasoning development intervention with high-risk behavior-disordered adolescents. *Journal of Consulting and Clinical Psychology, 54,* 208–216.

Argulewicz, E. D., & Sanchez, D. (1983). The special education evaluation process as a moderator of false positives. *Exceptional Child, 49(5),* 452–454.

Arnett, J. (1990). Contraceptive use, sensation seeking, and adolescent egocentrism. *Journal of Youth and Adolescence, 19,* 171–182.

Asarnow, J. R., & Callan, J. W. (1985). Boys with peer adjustment problems: Social cognitive processes. *Journal of Consulting and Clinical Psychology, 53,* 80–87.

Associated Press. (1990, February 14). Survey shows fewer students using drugs. *Daily Texan,* p. 8.

Atkeson, B. M. & Forehand, R. (1984). Conduct disorders. In E. J. Mash & L. G. Terdal (Eds.), *Behavioral assessment of childhood disorders* (pp. 185–219). New York: Guilford.

Atwater, E. (1983). *Adolescence.* Englewood Cliffs, NJ: Prentice Hall.

Ausman, J., Ball, T. S., & Alexander, D. (1974). Behavior therapy of pica with a profoundly retarded adolescent. *Mental Retardation, 12,* 16–18.

Austin American-Statesman (1993, December 16). *Educator: Integration doesn't serve disabled* [Interview with Albert Shanker]. p. A6.

Autism Research Review International (1994a). *More evidence links autism, cerebellar defects. 8* (2). Austin Research Institute: San Diego, CA.

Autism Research Review International (1994b). *Facilitated communication: Long-awaited study reported. 8*(2). Autism Research Institute: San Diego, CA.

Autism Society of America (1988). The resolution on aversives. *The Advocate, 20*(3) 1–2. Silver Spring, MD: Author.

Autism Society of America (1994). Definition of autism. *The Advocate 26*(2), 3. Silver Spring, MD: Author.

Baer, D. M. (1981). *How to plan for generalization.* Austin, TX: Pro-Ed.

Baker, A. M. (1979). Cognitive functioning of psychotic children: A reappraisal. *Exceptional Children, 45*, 344–348.

Baker, A. M. (1980). The efficacy of the Feingold K-P diet: A review of pertinent empirical investigations. *Behavioral Disorders, 6*, 32–35.

Bandura, A. (1965a). Behavior modifications through modeling procedures. In L. Krasner & L. P. Ulman (Eds.), *Research in behavior modification* (pp. 310–340). New York: Holt, Rinehart & Winston.

Bandura, A. (1965b). Vicarious processes: A case of no-trial learning. In L. Berkowitz (Ed.), *Advances in experimental social psychology* (Vol. 2). New York: Academic Press.

Bandura, A. (1968). Social learning interpretation of psychological dysfunctions. In P. London & D. Rosenhan (Eds.), *Foundations of abnormal psychology*. New York: Holt, Rinehart & Winston.

Bandura, A. (1969). *Principles of behavior modification*. New York: Holt, Rinehart, & Winston.

Bandura, A. (1977). *Social learning theory*. Englewood Cliffs, NJ: Prentice Hall.

Bandura, A., Ross, D., & Ross, S. A. (1963). Vicarious reinforcement and imitative learning. *Journal of Abnormal and Social Psychology, 67*, 601–607.

Barkley, R. A. (1977). The effects of methylphenidate on various types of activity level and attention of hyperkinetic children. *Journal of Abnormal Child Psychology, 4*, 327–348.

Barkley, R. A. (1984). Hyperactivity. In E. J. Mash, & L. G. Terdal (Eds.), *Behavioral assessment of childhood disorders* (3rd ed., pp. 127–184). New York: Guilford.

Barkley, R. A. (1990). *Attention-deficit hyperactivity disorder: A handbook for diagnosis and treatment*. New York: Guilford.

Barkley, R. A., & Cunningham, C. E. (1979). The effects of Ritalin on the mother-child interactions of hyperactive children. *Archives of General Psychiatry, 36*, 201–208.

Barrett, C. L., Hampe, I. E., & Miller, L. (1978). Research on psychotherapy with children. In S. L. Garfield & A. E. Bergin (Eds.) *Handbook of psychotherapy and behavior change* (2nd ed.) (pp. 411–436), New York: Wiley.

Barrios, B. A., & Hartmann, D. B. (1988). Fears and anxieties. In E. J. Mash and L. G. Terdal (Eds.) *Behavioral assessment of childhood disorders* (Second edition, pp. 196–264). New York: Guilford Press.

Bartak, L., & Rutter, M. (1973). Special education treatment of autistic children: A comparative study. I. Design of study and characteristics of units. *Journal of Child Psychology and Psychiatry, 14*, 161–179.

Baum, C. G., & Forehand, R. (1981). Long-term follow-up assessment of parent training by use of multiple outcome measures. *Behavior Theory, 12*, 643–652.

Baumeister, A. A., & Forehand, R. (1972). Effects of contingent shock and verbal command on body rocking of retardates. *Journal of Clinical Psychology, 28*, 586–590.

Baumrind, D. (1971). Current patterns of parental authority. *Developmental Psychology Monographs, 4*, 1.

Baumrind, D. (1977). Some thoughts about child-rearing. In S. Cohen & T. J. Comiskey (Eds.), *Child development: Contemporary perspectives*. Itasca, IL: F.E. Peacock.

Beardslee, W. R., Bemporad, J., Keller, M. B., & Klerman, G. L. (1983). Children of parents with major affective disorders: A review. *American Journal of Psychiatry, 6*, 282–299.

Beck, A. T. (1967). *Depression: Clinical, experimental and theoretical aspects*. New York: Harper & Row.

Beck, A. T. (1974). The development of depression. In R. Friedman & M. Katz (Eds.), *The psychology of depression: Contemporary theory and research*. (pp. 3–20). Washington, DC: Winston.

Beck, A. T. (1976). *Cognitive therapy and the emotional disorders*. New York: International Universities Press.

Beck, A. T., Laude, R., & Bohnert, M. (1974). Ideational components of anxiety neurosis. *Archives of General Psychiatry, 31*, 319–325.

Becvar, D. S., & Becvar, R. J. (1988). *Family therapy: A systemic integration*. Boston: Allyn & Bacon.

Beidel, D. C. (1988). Psychophysiological assessment of anxious emotional states in children. *Journal of Abnormal Psychology, 97,* 80–82.

Beilin, H. (1959). Teachers' and clinicians' attitudes toward the behavior problems of children: A reappraisal. *Child Development, 39,* 9–25.

Bellak, L., & Adelman, C. (1960). The children's apperception test (CAT). In A. I. Rabin & M. R. Haworth (Eds.), *Projective techniques with children*. New York: Grune & Stratton.

Bellak, L., & Bellak, S. S. (1949). *Children's apperception test*. Larchmont, NY: C.P.S., Inc.

Bellamy, G. T., Mank, D. Rhodes, L. E., & Albin, J. M. (1986). Supported employment. In W. E. Kiernan & J. A. Stark (Eds.) *Pathways to employment for adults with developmental disabilities* (pp. 129–138). Baltimore: Paul H. Brooks.

Bender, L. (1942). Schizophrenia in childhood. *Nervous Child, 1,* 138–140.

Bender, L. (1954). Current research in childhood schizophrenia. *American Journal of Psychiatry, 110,* 855–856.

Bender, L. (1968). Childhood schizophrenia: A review. *International Journal of Psychiatry, 5,* 211.

Bentzen, F. A., & Petersen, W. (1962). Educational procedures with the brain-damaged child. In W. T. Daley (Ed.), *Speech and language therapy with the brain-damaged child*. Washington, DC: Catholic University Press.

Berg, I. (1985) Annotation: The management of truancy. *Journal of Child Psychology and Psychiatry, 26,* 325–331.

Berkowitz, P. H. (1974). Pearl H. Berkowitz. In J. M. Kauffman and C. D. Lewis (Eds.), *Teaching children with behavior disorders: Personal perspectives*. Columbus, OH: Merrill.

Berkowitz, P. H., & Rothman, E. P. (1960). *The disturbed child: Recognition and psychoeducational therapy in the classroom*. New York: New York University Press.

Berne, E. (1965). *Games people play*. New York: Grove Press.

Bernstein, G. A., & Garfinkel, B. D. (1986). School phobia: The overlap of affective and anxiety disorders. *Journal of the American Academy of Child Psychiatry, 2,* 235–241.

Bessell, H., & Palomares, V. (1970). *Magic Circle/Human Development Program*. San Diego, CA: Human Development Training Institute.

Bettelheim, B. (1950). *Love is not enough*. Glenco. NY: Free Press.

Bettelheim, B. (1959). Joey: A mechanical boy. *Scientific American, 200,* 116–127.

Bettelheim, B. (1967). *The empty fortress*. New York: Free Press.

Bibring, E. (1953). The mechanism of depression. In P. Greenacre (Ed.), *Affective disorders: Psychoanalytic contribution to their study* (pp. 13–48). New York: International Universities Press.

Bigler, E. D. (1988). *Diagnostic clinical neuropsychology*. Austin, TX: University of Texas Press.

Biklen, D. (1990). Communication unbound: Autism and praxis. *Harvard Educational Review, 60* (3), 291–314.

Biklen, D. (1992). Typing to talk: Facilitated communication. *American Journal of Speech and Language Pathology, 1*(2), 15–17.

Biklen, D., & Schubert, A. (1991). New words: The communication of students with autism. *Remedial and Special Education, 12,*(6), 46–57.

Billings, A. G., & Moos, R. H. (1983). Comparisons of children of depressed and nondepressed parents: A social-environmental perspective. *Journal of Abnormal Child Psychology, 11,* 463–486.

Blackham, G. J. (1967). *The deviant child in the classroom*. Belmont, CA: Wadsworth.

Blakenship, C. S. (1985). Using curriculum-based assessment data to make instructional decisions. *Exceptional Children, 52,* 233–238.

Bleuler, E. (1950). *Dementia praecox on the group of schizophrenics* (J. Zinkin, Trans.). New York: International University Press. (Originally published, 1911.)

Blick, D. W., & Test, D. W. (1987). Effects of self-recording on high-school students' on-task behavior. *Learning Disability Quarterly, 10,* 203–213.

Blumberg, M. L. (1981). Depression in abused and neglected children. *American Journal of Psychotherapy, 35,* 342–355.

Blumenthal, S. (1985, April 30). *Testimony before the United States Senate Subcommittee on Juvenile Justice.* Washington: U.S. Department of Health and Human Services.

Boatman, B., Borkan, E. L., & Schetky, D. H. (1981). Treatment of child victims of incest. *American Journal of Family Therapy, 9,* 43–51.

Bostow, D. E., & Bailey, J. B. (1969). Modifications of severe disruptive and aggressive behavior using brief time-out and reinforcement procedures. *Journal of Applied Behavior Analysis, 2,* 31–37.

Bower, E. M. (1961). *The education of emotionally handicapped children.* Sacramento, CA: California State Department of Education.

Bower, E. M. (1969). *Early identification of emotionally handicapped children in school* (2nd ed.). Springfield, IL: Thomas.

Bower, E. M. (1980). Slicing the mystique of prevention with Occam's razor. In N. J. Long, W. C. Morse, & R. G. Newman (Eds.), *Conflict in the classroom: The education of emotionally disturbed children* (4th ed.). Belmont, CA: Wadsworth.

Bower, E. M. (1982). Defining emotional disturbance: Public policy and research. *Psychology in the Schools, 19,* 55–60.

Bower, E. M., & Lambert, N. M. (1962). *A process for in-school screening of children with emotional handicaps.* Princeton, NJ: Educational Testing Service.

Bradley, R. (1989). Home environment and cognitive development in the first year of life. *Developmental Psychology, 25,* 217–235.

Breier, A., Charney, D. S., & Heninger, G. R. (1984). Major depression in patients with agoraphobia and panic disorder. *Archives of General Psychiatry, 41,* 1129–1135.

Brolin, D. E., & Kokaska, C. J. (1979). *Career educaton for handicapped children and youth.* Columbus, OH: Merrill.

Brooks, B. (1982). Familial influence on father-daughter incest. *Journal of Psychiatric Treatment and Evaluation, 4,* 117–124.

Brophy, J. E. (1977). *Child development and socialization.* Chicago: Science Research Associates.

Brown, J., Montgomery, R., & Barclay, J. (1969). An example of psychologist management of teacher reinforcement procedures in the elementary classroom. *Psychology in the Schools, 6,* 336–340.

Brown, L., Branston, M. B., Hamre-Nietupski, S., Pumpian, I., Certo, N., & Gruenwald, L. (1979). A strategy for developing chronological age appropriate and functional curricular content for severely handicapped adolescents and young adults. *Journal of Special Education, 13,* 81–90.

Brown, L., Nietupski, J., & Hamre-Nietupski, S. (1976). Criterion of ultimate functioning. In M. A. Thomas (Ed.), *Hey, don't forget about me!* Reston, VA: The Council for Exceptional Children.

Brown, L. L., & Coleman, M. C. (1988). *Index of Personality Characteristics.* Austin, TX: Pro-Ed.

Brown, L. L., & Hammill, D. D. (1990). *Behavior Rating Profile-2: An ecological approach to behavior assessment.* Austin, TX: Pro-Ed.

Brown, L. L., & Sherbenou, R. J. (1981). A comparison of teacher perceptions of student reading ability, reading performance, and classroom behavior. *The Reading Teacher, 34,* 557–560.

Brown, W. R., & McGuire, J. M. (1976). Current psychological assessment practices. *Professional Psychology, 7,* 475–484.

Brumbeck, R. A., Dietz-Schmidt, S., & Weinberg, W. A. (1977). Depression in children referred to an educational diagnosis center—Diagnosis, treatment and analysis of criteria and literature review. *Diseases of the Nervous System, 38,* 529–535.

Bucher, B., & Lovaas, O. I. (1968). Use of aversive stimulation in behavior modification. In M. R. Jones (Ed.), *Miami symposium on the prediction of behavior, 1967: Aversive stimulation.* Coral Gables, FL: University of Miami Press.

Bullock, L. M. (1981). *Basic principles of establishing programs for the seriously emotionally disturbed,* Project S.E.D. Austin, TX: Education Service Center, Region XIII.

Buss, A. H., & Plomin, R. (1985). *Temperament: Early developing personality traits.* Hillsdale, NJ: Erlbaum.

Butler, L., Miezitis, S., Friedman, R., & Cole, E. (1980). The effect of two school-based intervention programs on depressive symptoms in preadolescents. *American Educational Research Journal, 17,* 111–119.

Byrnes, D. A. (1984). Forgotten children in classrooms: Development and characteristics. *The Elementary School Journal, 84,* 271–281.

Camp, B. W., & Ray, R. S. (1984). Aggression. In A. W. Meyers & W. E. Craighead (Eds.), *Cognitive behavior therapy with children.* (pp. 315–348). New York: Plenum.

Campbell, S. B. (1973). Mother-child interaction in reflective, impulsive, and hyperactive children. *Developmental Psychology, 8,* 341–349.

Campbell, S. B. (1975). Mother-child interaction: A comparison of hyperactive, learning disabled, and normal boys. *American Journal of Orthopsychiatry, 45,* 51–56.

Campbell, S. B. (1986). Developmental issues. In R. Gittelman (Ed.), *Anxiety disorders of childhood* (pp. 24–57). New York: Guilford.

Cantwell, D. P. (1978). Hyperactivity and antisocial behavior. *Journal of the American Academy of Child Psychiatry. 17,* 252–262.

Cantwell, D. P., & Carlson, G. A. (1983). *Affective disorders in childhood and adolescence: An update.* New York: Spectrum Publications.

Cantwell, D. P., & Satterfield, J. (1978). The prevalence of academic underachievement in hyperactive children. *Journal of Pediatric Psychology, 3,* 168–171.

Carlson, C. L., Lahey, B. B., & Neeper, R. (1984). Peer assessment of the social behavior of accepted, rejected, and neglected children. *Journal of Abnormal Child Psychology, 12,* 189–198.

Carlson, G. A., & Cantwell, D. P. (1979). A survey of depressive symptoms in a child and adolescent psychiatric population. *American Academy of Child Psychiatry, 18,* 587–599.

Carlson, G. A., & Cantwell, D. P. (1982). Diagnosis of childhood depression: A comparison of the Weinberg and DSM-III Criteria. *Journal of the American Academy of Child Psychiatry, 21,* 247–250.

Carlson, G. A., & Cantwell, D. P. (1986). Developmental issues in the classification of depression in children. In M. Rutter, C. E. Izard, & P. B. Read (Eds.), *Depression in young people: Developmental and clinical perspectives.* (pp. 399–434). New York: Guilford.

Carlson, P., & Stephens, T. (1986). Cultural bias and the identification of behaviorally disordered children. *Behavioral Disorders, 11,* 191–198.

Carpenter, R. L., & Apter, S. J. (1988). Research integration of cognitive-emotional interventions for behavior disordered children and youth. In M. C . Wang, M. C. Reynolds, & H. J. Walberg (Eds.) *Handbook of special education: Research and practice* (Vol. 2). New York: Pergamon.

Carr, E. G. (1977). The motivation of self-injurious behavior: A review of some hypotheses. *Psychological Bulletin, 84,* 800–811.

Carr, E. G. (1985). Behavioral approaches to language and communication. In E. Schopler & G. Mesibov (Eds.), *Current issues in autism: Volume 3. Communication problems in autism* (pp. 37–57). New York: Plenum.

Carr, E. G., & Durand, V. M. (1985). Reducing behavior problems through functional communication training. *Journal of Applied Behavior Analysis, 18,* 111–126.

Carr, E. G., Robinson, S., Taylor, J. C., & Carlson, J. I. (1990). *Positive approaches to the treatment of severe behavior problems in persons with developmental disabilities: A review and analysis of reinforcement and stimulus-based procedures* (Monograph No. 4). Seattle: The Association for Persons with Severe Handicaps.

Carter, J. F. (1989). The fact and fiction of consultation. *Academic Therapy, 25,* 231–242.

Casey, R. J., & Berman, J. S. (1985). The outcome of psychotherapy with children. *Psychological Bulletin, 98*, 388–400.

Center, D. B., & McKittrick, S. (1987). Disciplinary removal of special education students. *Focus on Exceptional Children, 20*, 1–8.

Chasnoff, I. J. (1987). Perinatal effects of cocaine. *Contemporary Obstetrics and Gynecology, 29*, 163–179.

Chasnoff, I. J. (1989). Drug use and women: Establishing a standard of care. *Annals of the New York Academy of Sciences, 562*, 208–210.

Chasnoff, I. J., Burns, K. A., & Burns, W. J. (1987). Cocaine use in pregnancy: Perinatal morbidity and mortality. *Neurotoxicology and Teratology, 9*, 291–293.

Chasnoff, I. J., Hunt, C. E., Kletter, R., & Kaplan, D. (1989). Prenatal cocaine exposure is associated with respiratory pattern abnormalities. *American Journal of Diseases of Children, 143*, 583–587.

Chasnoff, I. J., Landress, H., & Barrett, M. (1990). The prevalence of illicit drug or alcohol use during pregnancy and discrepancies in mandatory reporting in Pinellas County, Florida. *New England Journal of Medicine, 322*, 1202–1206.

Cheney, L., & Morse, W. C. (1974). Psychodynamic interventions in emotional disturbance. In W. C. Rhodes & M. L. Tracy (Eds.), *A Study of child variance* (Vol. 2). Ann Arbor, MI: The University of Michigan Press.

Chess, S. (1967). The role of temperament in the child's development. *Acta Paedopsychiatrica, 34*, 91–103.

Clarizio, H. F., & McCoy, G. F. (1976). *Behavior disorders in children* (2nd ed.). New York: Thomas Y. Crowell.

Clark, D. M., & Beck, A. T. (1988). Cognitive approaches. In C. G. Last & M. Hersen (Eds.) *Handbook of anxiety disorders* (pp. 362–385). New York: Pergamon.

Clark, L. A., & McKenzie, H. S. (1989). Effects of self-evaluation training of seriously emotionally disturbed children on the generalization of their classroom rule following and work behaviors across settings and teachers. *Behavioral Disorders, 14*, 89–98.

Clark, L. A., & Watson, D. (1991). Tripartite model of anxiety and depression: Psychometric evidence and taxonomic implications. *Journal of Abnormal Psychology, 100*, 316–336.

Coffey, O. D. (1983). Meeting the needs of youth from a corrections viewpoint. In S. Braaten, R. B. Rutherford, Jr., & C. A. Kardash (Eds.), *Programming for adolescents with behavioral disorders* (pp. 79–84). Reston, VA: Council for Children with Behavioral Disorders.

Coie, J. D., & Dodge, K. A. (1983). Continuities and changes in children's social status: A five-year longitudinal study. *Merrill-Palmer Quarterly, 29*, 261–262.

Colby, K. M. (1973). The rationale for computer-based treatment of language difficulties in non-speaking autistic children. *Journal of Autism and Childhood Schizophrenia, 2*, 182–197.

Cole, C., Ferrara, V., Johnson, D., Jones, M. Schoenbaum, M., Tyler, R., Wallace, V., & Poulsen, M. (1989). *Today's challenge: Teaching strategies for working with young children prenatally exposed to drugs/alcohol.* Los Angeles, CA: Los Angeles Unified School District.

Coleman, J. C. (1964). *Abnormal psychology and modern life.* Glenview, IL: Scott, Foresman.

Coleman, M. C. (1986). *Behavior disorders: Theory and practice.* Englewood Cliffs, NJ: Prentice Hall.

Coleman, M. C., & Gilliam, J. E. (1983). Disturbing behaviors in the classroom: A survey of teacher attitudes. *Journal of Special Education, 17*, 121–129.

Coleman, M. C., & Gilliam, J. E. (1990). Preliminary findings: Differences between behavior disordered juvenile offenders and non-BD juvenile offenders. *Unpublished manuscript.* Austin, TX: The University of Texas.

Coleman, M. C., & Webber, J. (1988). Behavior problems? Try groups! *Academic Therapy, 23*, 265–274.

Commission on Violence and Youth. (1993). *Violence and youth.* Washington, DC: American Psychological Association.

Conley, C. H. (1993). *Street gangs: Current knowledge and strategies.* Washington, DC: U.S. Department of Justice, National Institute of Justice.

Conners, C. K. (1970). Symptom patterns in hyperkinetic, neurotic, and normal children. *Child Development, 41,* 667–682.

Conners, C. K., & Werry, J. S. (1979). Pharmacotherapy. In H. C. Quay & J. S. Werry (Eds.), *Psychopathological disorders of childhood* (2nd ed.). New York: Wiley.

Corte, H. E., Wolfe, M. M., & Locke, B. J. (1971). A comparison of procedures for eliminating self-injurious behavior of retarded adolescents. *Journal of Applied Behavior Analysis, 4,* 201–213.

Coulter, A., Morrow, H., & Gilliam, J. E. (1979). *Emotional disturbance: Diagnostic procedures and eligibility determination* (Report to Texas Education Agency, Austin, TX).

Council for Children with Behavioral Disorders (1989). *Policy statement of behaviorally disordered children's rights to appropriate and effective behavior reduction procedures.* Reston, VA: Council for Exceptional Children.

Council for Children with Behavioral Disorders: Executive Committee (1987). Position paper on definition and identification of students with behavioral disorders. *Behavioral Disorders, 13,* 9–19.

Council for Exceptional Children: Task Force on Attention Deficit Disorder (1992). *Children with ADD: A shared responsibility.* Reston, VA: Author.

Courchesne, E. (1988). Hypoplasia of cerebellar vermal lobules VI and VII in autism. *New England Journal of Medicine, 318(21),* 1349–1354.

Craighead, W. E., Meyers, A. W., & Wilcoxon-Craighead, L. W. (1985). A conceptual model for cognitive-behavioral therapy with children. *Journal of Abnormal Child Psychology, 13,* 331–342.

Crane, C., Reynolds, J., Sparks, J., & Copper, S. (1983). *The source book: Behavioral IEPs for the emotionally disturbed.* Houston: Crane/Reynolds.

Creak, M., & Ini, S. (1960). Families of psychotic children. *Journal of Child Psychology and Psychiatry, 3,* 501–504.

Creedon, M. (1973). *Language development in nonverbal autistic children using a simultaneous communication system.* Paper presented at the meeting of the Society for Research in Child Development, Philadelphia.

Crooks, R. & Baur, K. (1983). *Our sexuality* (2nd ed.). Menlo Park, CA: Benjamin/Cummings Publishing.

Crossley, R. (1988, October). *Unexpected communication attainments by persons diagnosed as autistic and intellectually impaired.* Unpublished paper presented at International Society for Augmentative and Alternative Communication, Los Angeles, CA.

Cruickshank, W. M. Bentzen, F. A., Ratzeburg, F. H., & Tannhauser, M. T. (1961). *A teaching method for brain-injured and hyperactive children.* Syracuse: Syracuse University Press.

Cullinan, D. & Epstein, M. H. (1985). Behavioral interventions for educating adolescents with behavior disorders. *The Pointer, 30,* 4–7.

Cullinan, D., Epstein, M. H., & Lloyd, J. A. (1983). *Behavior disorders of children and adolescents.* Englewood Cliffs, NJ: Prentice Hall.

Curran, D. K. (1987). *Adolescent suicidal behavior.* Washington: Hemisphere.

Cytryn, L., McKnew, D. H., Bartko, J. J., Lamour, M., & Hamovitt, J. (1982). Offspring of parents with affective disorders: II. *Journal of the American Academy of Child Psychiatry, 21,* 389–391.

Cytryn, L., McKnew, D. H., Zahn-Waxler, C., & Gershon, E. S. (1986). Developmental issues in risk research: The offspring of affectively ill parents. In M. Rutter, C. E. Izard, & P. B. Read (Eds.), *Depression in young people: Developmental and clinical perspectives.* New York: Guilford.

Damasio, A. R., & Maurer, R. G. (1978). A neurological model for childhood autism. *Archives of Neurology, 35,* 777–786.

Dangel, R. F., & Polsterm, R. A., (1984). Winning! A systematic, empirical approach to parent training. In R. F. Dangel & R. A. Polster (Eds.), *Parent training: Foundations of research and practice* (pp. 166–174). New York: Guilford.

Davis, D. (1994). *Reaching out to children with FAS/FAE.* West Nyack, New York: Simon & Schuster.

Davis, J. M., Sandoval, J., & Wilson, M. P. (1988). Strategies for the primary prevention of adolescent suicide. *School Psychology Review, 17,* 559–569.

Davis, K. L., Berger, P., Hollister, L. E., & Barchas, J. D. (1978). Cholinergic involvement in mental disorders. *Life Sciences, 22,* 1865–1871.

Dawson, G. (1983). Lateralized brain dysfunction in autism: Evidence from the Halstead-Reitan neuropsychological battery. *Journal of Autism and Developmental Disorders, 13,* 269–286.

DeMyer, M. K. (1979). *Parents and children in autism.* New York: Wiley.

Department of Health and Human Services. (1989). *Year 2000 National Health Objectives.* Washington, DC: Author.

DesLaurier, A., & Carlson, C. F. (1969). *Your child is asleep.* Homewood, IL: Dorsey.

Despert, J. L. (1965). *The emotionally disturbed child—Then and now.* New York: Robert Brunner.

Dinkmeyer, D., & Dinkmeyer, D., Jr. (1982). *Developing understanding of self and others—Revised.* Circle Pines, MN: American Guidance Service.

Dodge, K. A. (1985) Attributional bias in aggressive children. In P. C. Kendall (Ed.), *Advances in cognitive-behavioral research and therapy* (Vol. 4, pp. 73–110). Orlando: Academic Press.

Donnellan, A. (1980). An educational perspective on autism: Implications for curriculum development and personnel development. In B. Wilcox & A. Thompson (Eds.), *Critical issues in educating autistic children and youth.* U.S. Department of Education, Office of Special Education.

Donnellan, A., LaVigna, G., Zambito, J., & Thredt, J. (1986). A time-limited intensive program model to support community placement for persons with severe behavior problems. *Journal of TASH, 10(3),* 123–131.

Donnellan, A. M., Mesaros, R. A., & Anderson, J. L. (1985). Teaching students with autism in natural environments: What educators need from researchers. *Journal of Special Education, 18,* 505–522.

Donnellan-Walsh, A. (1976). *Teaching makes a difference: A guide for developing successful classes for autistic and other severely handicapped children.* Administrative manual. Sacramento, CA: California State Department of Education.

Donnellan-Walsh, A., Gossage, L. D., LaVigna, G. W., Schuler, A., & Traphagen, J. D. (1976). *Teaching makes a difference: A guide for developing successful classes for autistic and other severely handicapped children.* Santa Barbara, CA: Santa Barbara Public Schools.

Donnelly, P., & Suter, K. (1994). *Juvenile gangs: It's not the Sharks and Jets anymore.* Austin, TX: Texas Juvenile Probation Commission.

Dorsey, B. (1980). *Teaching for autistic child—the use of prompts.* Unpublished paper, Iowa City: The University of Iowa.

Douglas, V. I. & Peters, K. (1979). Toward a clearer definition of the attention deficit of hyperactive children. In G. Hale & M. Lewis (Eds.), *Attention and the development of cognitive skills.* New York: Plenum.

Draeger, S., Prior, M., & Sanson, A. (1986). Visual and auditory performance in hyperactive children: Competence or compliance. *Journal of Abnormal Child Psychology, 14,* 411–424.

Durant, W. (1939). *The life of Greece.* New York: Simon & Schuster.

Durant, W. (1961). *The story of philosophy: The lives and opinions of the great philosophers of the western world.* New York: Simon & Schuster.

Earls, F., & Jung, K. (1987). Temperament and home environment characteristics as causal factors in early development of childhood psychopathology. *Journal of American Academy of Child and Adolescent Psychiatry, 26,* 491–498.

Edwards, L. L., & Siler, M. E. (1988). Classroom evaluation for secondary level students with autism. *Focus on Autistic Behavior 3(2)*, 1–8.

Eggelston, C. R. (1984). *Results of a national correctional/special education survey.* Paper presented at the Correctional/Special Education National Conference, Arlington, VA.

Elkind, D. (1974). *Children and adolescents* (2nd ed.). New York: Oxford University Press.

Ellis, A. (1962). *Reason and emotion in psychotherapy.* New York: Lyle Stuart.

Ellis, A. (1973). *Humanistic psychotherapy: The rational-emotive approach.* New York: Julian.

Ellis, A. (1980). An overview of the clinical theory of rational-emotive therapy. In R. Grieger & R. Boyd (Eds.), *Rational-emotive therapy.* New York: Van Nostrand Reinhold.

Epstein, M. H., Cullinan, D., & Rosemier, R. A. (1983). Behavior problems of behaviorally disordered and normal adolescents. *Behavioral Disorders, 8,* 171–175.

Epstein, M. H., Kinder, D., & Bursuck, B. (1989). The academic status of adolescents with behavioral disorders. *Behavioral Disorders, 14,* 157–165.

Erickson, W. D. (1984). Sexual behavior disorders in adolescents. In S. Braaten, R. B. Rutherford, Jr., & C. A. Kardash (Eds.), *Programming for adolescents with behavioral disorders.* Reston, VA: Council for Children with Behavioral Disorders.

Erikson, E. H. (1959). Identity and the life cycle. In G. S. Klein (Ed.), *Psychological issues.* New York: International University Press.

Erikson, E. H. (1968). *Identity: Youth and crisis.* New York: W.W. Norton & Co.

Eron, L. D. (1982). Parent-child interaction, television violence, and aggression in children. *American Psychologist, 37,* 197–211.

Eron, L. D., Huesman, L. R., Lefkowitz, M. M., & Walder, L. O. (1972). Does television violence cause aggression? *American Psychologist, 27,* 253–263.

Etscheidt, S. (1991). Reducing aggressive behavior and improving self-control: A cognitive-behavioral training program for behaviorally disordered adolescents. *Behavioral Disorders, 16,* 107–115.

Eysenck, H. J. (1965). The effects of psychotherapy. *Journal of Psychology, 1,* 97–118.

Eysenck, H. J. (1973). Learning therapy and behavior therapy. In T. Millon (Ed.), *Theories of psychopathology and personality.* Philadelphia: Saunders.

Fairburn, C. G. (1981). A cognitive-behavioral approach to the treatment of bulimia. *Psychological Medicine, 11,* 707–711.

Farrington, D. (1980). Truancy, delinquency, the home, and the school. In L. Hersov & I. Berg (Eds.), *Out of school.* (pp. 49–64). New York: Wiley.

Fava, M., Copeland, P. M., Schweiger, U., & Herzog, D. B. (1989). Neurochemical abnormalities of anorexia nervosa and bulimia nervosa. *American Journal of Psychiatry, 146,* 963–971.

Federal Register (1981, January 16). Washington, DC: U.S. Government Printing Office.

Feingold, B. F. (1975a). *Why your child is hyperactive.* New York: Random House.

Feingold, B. F. (1975b). Hyperkinesis and learning disabilities linked to artificial food flavors and colors. *The American Journal of Nursing, 75,* 797–803.

Feingold, B. F. (1977). A critique of "Controversial medical treatments of learning disabilities." *Academic Therapy, 13,* 173–183.

Fenichel, C. (1974). Carl Fenichel. In J. M. Kauffman & C. D. Lewis (Eds.), *Teaching children with behavior disorders: Personal perspectives.* Columbus, OH: Merrill.

Fernald, G. (1943). *Remedial techniques in basic school subjects.* New York: McGraw-Hill.

Ferster, C. B. (1961). Positive reinforcement and behavioral deficits of autistic children. *Child Development, 32,* 437–456.

Fessler, M. A., Rosenberg, M. S., & Rosenberg, L. A. (1991). Concomitant learning disabilities and learning problems among students with behavioral/emotional disorders. *Behavioral Disorders, 16,* 97–106.

Fieg, L. (1990). *Drug exposed infants and children: Service needs and policy questions.* Washington, DC: Department of Health and Human Services.

Finkelhor, D. (1979). Sexual socialization in America: High risk for sexual abuse. In J. M. Samson, Ed.), *Childhood and sexuality*. Montreal: Editions Etudes Vivants.

Finkelhor, D. (1980). Sex among siblings: A survey on prevalence, variety, and effects. *Archives of Sexual Behavior, 9*, 171–194.

Firestone, P., & Douglas, V. I., (1975). The effects of reward and punishment on reaction times and automatic activity in hyperactive and normal children. *Journal of Abnormal Child Psychology, 3*, 288–297.

Fish, B., & Ritvo, E. R. (1979). Psychoses of childhood. In J. D. Noshpitz (Ed.), *Basic handbook of child psychiatry, Vol. 2*. New York: Basic Books.

Florida Department of Education (1983). *A resource manual for the development and evaluation of special programs for exceptional students: Affective curriculum for secondary emotionally handicapped students*. Tallahassee, FL: Author.

Flynn, G. (1993, October). *Address by the president of TASH*. Address given at the LBJ Center, Southwest Texas State University, San Marcos, TX.

Fogelman, K., Tibbenham, A., & Lambert, L. (1980). Absence from school: Findings from the national child development study. In L. Hersov & I. Berg (Eds.), *Out of School* (pp. 25–48). New York: Wiley.

Foley, R. M., & Epstein, M. H. (1992). Correlates of the academic achievement of adolescents with behavioral disorders. *Behavioral Disorders, 18*, 9–17.

Forness, S. R. (1988a). Planning for the needs of children with serious emotional disturbance: The national special education and mental health coalition. *Behavioral Disorders, 13*, 127–132.

Forness, S. R. (1988b). School characteristics of children and adolescents with depression. In R. B. Rutherford, Jr., C. M. Nelson, & S. R. Forness (Eds.), *Issues of Severe Behavior Disorders in Children and Youth* (Vol. 10), 177–203. Boston: Little, Brown.

Forness, S. R., Bennett, M. A., & Tose, B. A. (1983). Academic benefits in emotionally disturbed children revisited. *Journal of the American Academy of Child Psychiatry, 22*, 140–144.

Forness, S. R., Frankel, F., Caldon, P. L., & Carter, M. J. (1980). Achievement gains of children hospitalized for behavior disorders. In R. B. Rutherford, Jr., A. G. Prieto, & J. E. McGlothlin (Eds.), *Severe behavior disorders of children and youth*. (Vol. 3, pp. 34–40). Reston, VA: Council for Children with Behavioral Disorders.

Forness, S. R., Swanson, J. M., Cantwell, D. P., Guthrie, D., & Sena, R. (1992). Response to stimulant medication across six measures of school-related performance in children with ADHD and disruptive behavior, *Behavioral Disorders, 18*, 42–53.

Fournier, C. F. (1987). *Teacher perceptions of impact of hyperactivity on classroom situations and on ratings of intervention acceptability*. Unpublished doctoral dissertation: University of Texas.

Fowler, S. A. (1986). Peer-monitoring and self-monitoring: Alternatives to traditional teacher management. *Exceptional Children, 52*, 573–581.

Foxx, R. M. (1971). *The use of overcorrection procedure in eliminating self-stimulatory behavior in a classroom for retarded children*. Unpublished doctoral dissertation, Southern Illinois University.

Foxx, R. M. (1977). Attention training: The use of overcorrection avoidance to increase the eye contact of autistic and retarded children. *Journal of Applied Behavior Analysis, 10*, 489–499.

Foxx, R. M., & Azrin, N. H. (1973). The elimination of autistic self-stimulatory behavior by over-correction. *Journal of Applied Behavior Analysis, 6*, 1–14.

Freed, A. M. (1973). *T. A. for tots*. Sacramento: Jalmar Press.

Freed, A. M. (1976). *T. A. for teens*. Sacramento: Jalmar Press.

Freed, A., & Freed, M. (1977). *T. A. for kids* (Rev. ed.). Sacramento: Jalmar Press.

Freeman, B. J., & Ritvo, E. R. (1981). The syndrome of autism: A critical review of diagnostic systems, follow-up studies, and the theoretical background of the behavior observation scale. In J. E. Gilliam (Ed.), *Autism: Diagnosis, instruction, management, and research*. Springfield, IL: Thomas.

Freud, S. (1957). Mourning and melancholia. In J. Strachey (Ed. and Trans.), *The standard edition of the complete psychological works of Sigmund Freud* (Vol. 14). London: Hogarth Press. (Original work published 1917).

Frost, J. L. (1986). Children in a changing society: Frontiers of challenge. *Childhood Education, 62,* 242–249.

Fuchs, D., Fernstrom, P., Scott, S., Fuchs, L., & Vandermeer, L. (1994). Classroom ecological inventory: A process for mainstreaming. *Teaching Exceptional Children, 26,* 11–1.

Fuchs, D., & Fuchs, L. S. (1994). Inclusive schools movement and the radicalization of special education reform. *Exceptional Children, 60,* 294–309.

Fuchs, L. S., Fuchs, D., & Warren, L. M. (1982). *Special education practice toward evaluating student progress toward goals* (Research Report No. 81). Minneapolis: University of Minnesota, Institute for Research on Learning Disabilities.

Gable, R. (1984). A program for prevocational instruction for adolescents with severe behavioral disorders. In S. Braaten, R. B. Rutherford, Jr., & C. A. Kardash (Eds.), *Programming for adolescents with behavior disorders.* Reston, VA: Council for Children with Behavior Disorders.

Gadow, K. D. (1983). Effects of stimulant drugs on academic performance in hyperactive and learning disabled children. *Journal of Learning Disabilities, 5,* 290–299.

Gadow, K. D. (1985). Relative efficacy of pharmacological, behavioral, and combination treatments for enhancing academic performance. *Clinical Psychology Review, 5,* 523–533.

Gadow, K. D. (1986a). Fundamental concepts in pharmacotherapy: An overview. In K. D. Gadow (Ed.), *Children on medication: Epilepsy, emotional disturbance, and adolescent disorders* (pp. 1–19). San Diego: College-Hill.

Gadow, K. D. (1986b). Emotional disturbance. In K. D. Gadow (Ed.), *Children on medication: Epilepsy, emotional disturbance, and adolescent disorders* (pp. 99–135). San Diego: College-Hill.

Gadow, K. D. (1986c). *Children on medication, Vol. 1. Hyperactivity, learning disabilities, and mental retardation.* Austin, TX.: Pro-Ed.

Gardner, R., III. (1990). Life space interviewing: It can be effective, but don't. . . . *Behavioral Disorders, 15,* 111–119.

Garfinkel, P., & Garner, D. (1987). *The role of drug treatments for eating disorders.* New York: Brunner/Mazel.

Garrison, S. R. & Stolberg, A. L. (1983). Modification of anger in children by affective imagery training. *Journal of Abnormal Child Psychology, 11,* 115–130.

Gartner, A., & Lipsky, D. K. (1989). *The yoke of special education: How to break it.* Rochester, NY: National Center on Education and the Economy.

Garvey, W. P., & Hegrenes, J. R. (1966). Desensitization techniques in the treatment of school phobia. *American Journal of Orthopsychiatry, 36,* 147–152.

Genaux, M., Likins, M., & Morgan, D. (1993). Teacher's desk reference: substance use prevention in special education, (2nd ed.). Logan, UT: Utah State University.

Gersten, R., Walker, H. M., & Darch, C. (1988). Relationships between teachers' effectiveness and their tolerance for handicapped students. *Exceptional Children, 54(5),* 433–438.

Gilliam, J. E. (1995) *Gilliam Autism Rating Scale.* Austin, Tx: Pro-Ed.

Gilliam, J. E., & Coleman, M. C. (1981). Who influences IEP committee decisions? *Exceptional Children, 47,* 642–644.

Gilliam, J. E., & Coleman, M. C. (1982). A survey of knowledge about autism among experts and caregivers. *Behavioral Disorders, 7,* 189–196.

Gilliam, J. E., & Scott, B. K. (1987). The behaviorally disordered offender. In C. M. Nelson, R. B. Rutherford, Jr., & B. I. Wolford, (Eds.), *Special education in the criminal justice system.* Columbus, OH: Merrill.

Glasser, W. (1965). *Reality therapy: A new approach to psychiatry.* New York: Harper & Row.

Glasser, W. (1969). *Schools without failure.* New York: Harper & Row.

Glueck, S., & Glueck, E. (1968). *Delinquents and nondelinquents in perspective.* Cambridge, MA: Harvard University Press.

Gold, M. W. (1972). Stimulus factors in skill training of the retarded on a complex assembly task: Acquisition, transfer, and retention. *American Journal of Mental Deficiency, 76,* 517–526.

Gold, M. W. (1973). Research on the vocational rehabilitation of the retarded: The present, the future. *International Review of Research in Mental Retardation* (Vol. 6). New York: Academic Press.

Golden, C. J. (1981). A standardized version of Luria's neuropsychological tests: A quantitative and qualitative approach to neuropsychological evaluation. In S. B. Filskov & T. J. Bell (Eds.), *Handbook of clinical neuropsychology.* New York: Wiley.

Golden, G. (1980). Nonstandard therapies in the developmental disabilities. *American Journal of Diseases of Children, 134,* 487–491.

Golden, J. M. (1981). Depresson in middle and late childhood: Implications for intervention. *Child Welfare, 60,* 457–465.

Goldfarb, W. (1961). *Childhood schizophrenia.* Cambridge, MA: Harvard University Press.

Goldfarb, W. (1964). An investigation of childhood schizophrenia. *Archives of General Psychiatry, 11,* 621–634.

Goldfarb, W. (1970). Childhood psychosis. In P. H. Mussen (Ed.), *Carmichael's manual of child psychology, Vol. 2.* New York: Wiley.

Goldstein, A. P. (1988). *The Prepare Curriculum.* Champaign, IL: Research Press.

Goldstein, A. P., & Glick, B. (1987). *Aggression Replacement Training.* Champaign, IL: Research Press.

Goldstein, A. P., Sprafkin, R. P., Gershaw, N. J., & Klein, P. (1980). *Skillstreaming the adolescent.* Champaign, IL: Research Press.

Good, T. L., & Grouws, D. (1972). *Reaction of male and female teacher trainees to descriptions of elementary school pupils* (Tech. Rep. No. 62). Center for Research in Social Behavior, Columbus, MO: University of Missouri.

Gordon, D. A., & Young, R. D. (1976). School phobia: A discussion of aetiology, treatment and evaluation. *Psychological Reports, 39,* 783–804.

Gordon, S. (1983–84). The case for moral sex education. *Impact, '83–'84,* 2.

Gottesman, I. & Shields, J. (1972). *Schizophrenics and genetics: A twin study vantage point.* New York: Academic Press.

Gottesman, I.I., & Shields, J. (1982). *The schizophrenic puzzle.* New York, Cambridge University Press.

Gottman, J. M. (1977). Toward a definition of social isolation in children. *Child Development, 48,* 513–517.

Graden, J. L., Casey, A., & Bonstrom, O. (1985). Implementing a prereferral intervention system: Part II. the data. *Exceptional Children, 51,* 487–496.

Graden, J. L., Casey, A., & Christenson, S. (1985). Implementing a prereferral intervention system: Part I. the model. *Exceptional Children, 51,* 377–384.

Graham, P. (1979). Epidemiological studies. In H. C. Quay & J. S. Werry (Eds.), *Psychopathological disorders of childhood* (2nd ed.). New York: Wiley.

Graubard, P. S. (1973). Children with behavioral disabilities. In L. Dunn (Ed.), *Exceptional children in the schools.* New York: Holt, Rinehart & Winston.

Graziano, A. M., DeGiovanni, I. S., & Garcia, K. A. (1979). Behavioral treatment of children's fears: A review. *Psychological Bulletin, 86,* 804–830.

Gresham, F. (1981). Social skills training with handicapped children: A review. *Review of Educational Research, 51,* 139–176.

Gresham, F. (1982). Misguided mainstreaming: The case for social skills training with handicapped children. *Exceptional Children, 48,* 422–433.

Gresham, F. M. & Evans, S. E. (1987). Conceptualization and treatment of social withdrawal in the schools. *Special Services in the Schools, 3,* 37–51.

Griffith, D. (1991, May). *Intervention needs of children prenatally exposed to drugs.* Congressional testimony before the House Select Committee on Special Education.

Griffith, D. R., Chasnoff, I. J., & Freier, C. (1990, April). Second and third year follow up studies. In B. Karmel (Chair), *Cocaine exposure: Neurofunctional consequences for the fetus and infant.* Invited symposium conducted at the 7th International Conference on Infant Studies, Montreal.

Grosenick, J. K., George, N. L., George, M. P., & Lewis, T. J. (1991). Public school services for behaviorally disordered students: Program practices in the 1980s. *Behavioral Disorders, 16,* 87–96.

Guetzloe, E. (1988). Suicide and depression: Special education's responsibility. *Teaching Exceptional Children, 20,* 25–28.

Hackett, L. (1990, April 8). Experts want sex education restructured. *Austin American-Stateman,* p. E12.

Hagborg, W. J. (1989). A study of persistent absenteeism of severely emotionally distrubed adolescents. *Behavioral Disorders, 15,* 50–56.

Haley, G. M. T., Fine, S., Marriage, K., Moretti, M. M., & Freeman, R. J. (1985). Cognitive bias in depression in psychiatrically disturbed children and adolescents. *Journal of Consulting and Clinical Psychology, 53,* 535–537.

Hall, C. S. (1954). *A primer of Freudian psychology.* New York: William Collins Publishers.

Hall, C. S. & Lindzey, G. (1970). *Theories of personality* (2nd ed.). New York: Wiley.

Hall, M. C. (1981). *Responsive parenting.* Shawnee Mission, KS: Responsive Management.

Halpern, F. (1960). The Rorschach test with children. In A. I. Rabin & M. R. Haworth (Eds.), *Projective techniques with children.* New York: Grune & Stratton.

Hamilton, K. & Koorland, M. A. (1988). Factors affecting program attendance by parents of exceptional secondary students. *Teaching: Behaviorally Disordered Youth, 4,* 16–19.

Hammill, D. D. (1976). Defining "learning disabilities" for programmatic purposes. *Academic Therapy, 12,* 29–37.

Handelman, J. S., & Harris, S. L. (1986). *Educating the developmentally disabled: Meeting the needs of children and families.* San Diego: College-Hill.

Hare, R. D. (1970). *Psychopathy: Theory and research.* New York: Wiley.

Haring, N. (1963). The emotionally disturbed. In S. Kirk & B. Weiner (Eds.), *Behavioral research on exceptional children.* Washington, DC: The Council for Exceptional Children.

Haring, N. G., Lovitt, T. C., Eaton, M. D., & Hansen, C. L. (1978). *The fourth R: Research in the classroom.* Columbus, OH: Merrill.

Haring, N. G., & Phillips, E. L. (1962). *Educating emotionally disturbed children.* New York: McGraw-Hill.

Haring, N. G., Stern, G., & Cruickshank, W. (1958). *Attitudes of educators toward exceptional children.* New York: Syracuse University Press.

Harris, D. B. (1963). *Children's drawings as measures of intellectual maturity.* New York: Harcourt, Brace Jovanovich.

Harter, S. (1985). *The Self-Perception Profile for Children.* Denver, CO: The University of Denver.

Hartup, W. W. (1979). The social worlds of childhood. *American Psychologist, 34,* 944–950.

Hartup, W. W. (1980). Peers, play, and pathology: A new look at the social behavior of children. In T. Field, S. Goldberg, D. Stern & A. Sostek (Eds.) *High-risk children and infants: Adult and peer interactions.* New York: Academic Press.

Harvard Mental Health Letter (1990). *Childhood psychoses. 6(11),* pp. 1–3. Harvard Medical School Health Publications Group: Boston, MA.

Harvard Mental Health Letter (1992). *Schizophrenia: The present state of understanding, Part II. 8(12),* pp. 1–5. Harvard Medical School Health Publications Group: Boston, MA.

Hauser, S. T. (1972). Black and white identity formation: Aspects and perspectives. *Journal of Youth and Adolescence, 1,* 113–130.

Hawkins, J. D., & Catalono, R. F. (1988). *Preparing for the drug-free years* (2nd ed.). Seattle: Developmental Research and Programs.

Hebben, N. A., Whitman, R. D., Milberg, W. P., Andresko, M., & Galpin, R. (1981). Attention dysfunction in poor readers. *Journal of Learning Disabilities, 14,* 287–290.

Hewett, F. (1965). Teaching speech to autistic children through operant conditioning. *American Journal of Orthopsychiatry, 35,* 927–36.

Hewett, F. M. (1968). *The emotionally disturbed child in the classroom.* Boston: Allyn & Bacon.

Hewett, F. M. (1974). Frank M. Hewett. In J. M. Kauffman & C. D. Lewis (Eds.), *Teaching children with behavior disorders: Personal perspectives.* Columbus, OH: Merrill.

Hewett, F. M., & Taylor, F. D. (1980). *The emotionally disturbed child in the classroom: The orchestration of success* (2nd ed.). Boston: Allyn & Bacon.

Hill, S. M. (1989). *A study of the cognitive specificity hypothesis: Anger and depression in children and adolescents.* Unpublished doctoral dissertation, The University of Texas at Austin.

Hobbs, N. (1966). Helping disturbed children: Psychological and ecological strategies. *American Psychologist, 21,* 1105–1115.

Hobbs, N. (1974). Nicholas Hobbs. In J. M. Kauffman & C. D. Lewis (Eds.), *Teaching children and behavior disorders: Personal perspectives.* Columbus, OH: Merrill.

Hobbs, N. (1975a). *Issues in the classification of children.* San Francisco: Jossey-Bass.

Hobbs, N. (1975b). *The futures of children: Categories, labels, and their consequences.* San Francisco: Jossey-Bass.

Hobbs, N. (1982). *The troubled and troubling child.* San Francisco: Jossey-Bass.

Hodgman, C. H. (1985). Recent findings in adolescent depression and suicide. *Developmental and Behavioral Pediatrics, 6,* 162–169.

Hoffer, A., & Osmond, H. (1966). Nicotinamide adenine dinucleotide (NAD) as a treatment of schizophrenia. *Journal of Psychopharmacology, 1,* 79–95.

Hoffman, E. (1974). Treatment of deviance by the educational system: History. In W. C. Rhodes & S. Head (Eds.), *A study of child variance* (Vol. 3). Ann Arbor, MI: University of Michigan.

Hogan, D. P., & Kitgawa, E. (1985). The impact of social status, family structure, and neighborhood on the fertility of black adolescents. *American Journal of Sociology, 90,* 825–855.

Hollinger, J. D. (1987). Social skills for behaviorally disordered children as preparation for mainstreaming: Theory, practice, and new directions. *Remedial and Special Education, 8,* 17–27.

Holt, J. (1967). *How children learn.* New York: Pitman.

Horner, R. H., Dunlap, G. & Koegel, R. L. (Eds.). (1988). *Generalization and maintenance: Lifestyle changes in applied settings.* New York: W. W. Norton & Co.

Howard, J., Beckwith, L., L., Rodning, C., & Kropenske, V. (1989, June). The development of young children of substance abusing parents: Insights from seven years of intervention and research. *Zero to Three,* 8–12.

Howell, K. W. (1985). A task-analytical approach to social behavior. *Remedial and Special Education, 6,* 24–30.

Howell, K. W., & Kaplan, J. S. (1980). *Diagnosing basic skills: A handbook for deciding what to teach.* Columbus, OH: Merrill.

Howell, K. W., Kaplan, J. S., & O'Connell, C. Y. (1979). *Evaluating exceptional children.* Columbus, OH: Merrill.

Hsu, L. K. (1980). Outcome of anorexia nervosa: A review of the literature (1954 to 1978). *Archives of General Psychiatry, 37,* 1041–1043.

Huefner, D. S. (1988). The consulting teacher model: Risks and opportunities. *Exceptional Children, 54,* 403–413.

Huesman, L. R., Eron, L. D., Lefkowitz, M. M., & Walder, L. O. (1984). Stability of aggression over time and generations. *Developmental Psychology, 20,* 1120–1134.

Huff, C. R. (1992). *Juvenile justice and public policy: Toward a national agenda.* New York: Lexington Books.

Hughes, C. A., Ruhl, K. L., Misra, A. (1989). Self-management with behaviorally disordered students in school settings: A promise unfulfilled? *Behavioral Disorders, 14,* 250–262.

Hunter, J., & Schaecher, R. (1990). Lesbian and gay youth. In M. J. Rotherram-Borus, J. Bradley, & N. Obolensky (Eds.) *Planning to live: Evaluating and training suicidal teens in community settings* (297–316). Tulsa, OK: University of Oklahoma Press.

Hutt, S., Hutt, C., Lee, D., & Ounsted, C. (1964). Arousal and childhood autism. *Nature, 204,* 908–909.

Hutton, J. B., & T. G. Roberts. (1986). *Social-emotional dimension scale.* Austin, TX: Pro-Ed.

Idol, L., & West, J. F. (1987). Consultation in special education (Part II): Training. *Journal of Learning Disabilities, 20,* 474–494.

Idol-Maestas, L., & Ritter, S. (1985). A follow-up study of resource/consulting teachers. *Teacher Education and Special Education, 8,* 126–134.

Ingram, R. E. (1984). Toward an information-processing analysis of depression. *Cognitive Therapy and Research, 8,* 443–478.

Inhelder, B., & Piaget, J. (1958). *The growth of logical thinking from childhood to adolescence.* New York: Basic Books.

Institute for Parent Involvement (1980). *Strategies for effective parent-teacher interaction.* Albuquerque, NM: University of New Mexico.

Institute on Community Integration, University of Minnesota (1991). Feature issue on inclusive education. *IMPACT, 4*(3), 1–24.

Jardin, R. A., & Ziebell, P. W. (1981). Adolescent drug and alcohol abuse. In G. Brown, R. L. McDowell, & J. Smith (Eds.), *Educating adolescents with behavior disorders.* Columbus, OH: Merrill.

Jenson, W. R. (1985). Skills preference in two different types of parenting groups. *Small Group Behavior, 16,* 549–555.

Jenson, W. R., Sloane, H. N., & Young, K. R. (1988). *Applied behavior analysis in education: A structured teaching approach.* Englewood Cliffs, NJ: Prentice Hall.

Jiles, D. (1981). Problems in the assessment of sexual abuse referrals. In W. Holder (Ed.), *Sexual abuse of children.* New York: Pergamon Press.

Johnson, C. L., Steinberg, S., & Lewis, C. (1988). Bulimia. In K. Clark, R. Parr, & W. Castelli (Eds.), *Evaluation and management of eating disorders: Anorexia, bulimia, and obesity* (pp. 187–228). Champaign, IL: Life Enhancement Publications.

Johnson, D. J., Myklebust, H. R. (1967). Learning disabilities: Educational principles and practice. New York: Grune & Stratton.

Johnson, J. L. (1988). The challenge of substance abuse. *Teaching Exceptional Children, 20,* 29–31.

Johnson, S. B., & Melamed, B. G. (1979). The assessment and treatment of children's fears. In B. B. Lahey & A. E. Kazdin (Eds.), *Advances in clinical child psychology* (Vol. 2, pp. 107–139). New York: Plenum Press.

Johnston, L. D., O'Malley, P. M., & Bachman, J. G. (1988). *Illicit drug use, smoking, and drinking by America's high school students, college students, and young adults, 1975–1987.* Rockville, MD: National Institute on Drug Abuse, Division of Research.

Johnston, M. S. K. (1979). *Nonincestual sexual abuse of children and its relationship to family dysfunction.* Paper presented at the Fourth National Conference on Child Abuse and Neglect. Los Angeles.

Jones, M. C. (1924). A laboratory study of fear: The case of Peter. *Pedagogical Seminary, 31,* 308–315.

Jones, R. T., & Kazdin, A. E. (1981). Childhood behavior problems in the school. In S. M. Turner, K. S. Calhoun, & H. E. Adams, (Eds.), *Handbook of clinical behavior therapy.* New York: Wiley-Interscience.

Kallman, F. J. (1956). The genetics of human behavior. *American Journal of Psychiatry. 113,* 496–501.

Kandel, D. B., & Davies, M. (1982). Epidemiology of depressive mood in adolescents. *Archives of General Psychiatry, 39,* 1205–1212.

Kanfer, R. & Zeiss, A. M. (1983). Depression, interpersonal standard setting, and judgements of self-efficacy. *Journal of Abnormal Psychology, 92,* 319–329.

Kanner, L. (1943). Autistic disturbance of affective contact. *Nervous Child, 2,* 217–250.

Kanner, L. (1949). Problems of nosology and psychodynamics of early infantile autism. *American Journal of Orthopsychiatry, 19,* 416–426.

Kanner, L. (1957). *Child psychiatry* (3rd ed.). Springfield, IL: Thomas.

Kanner, L. (1962). Emotionally disturbed children: A historical review. *Child Development, 33,* 97–102.

Kaplan, A. S., & Woodside, B. (1987). Biological aspects of anorexia nervosa and bulimia nervosa. *Journal of Consulting and Clinical Psychology, 55,* 645–653.

Kaplan, H. I., & Sadock, B. J. (1988). Epidemiology of depressive symptoms in adolescents. *Journal of American Academy of Child Psychiatry, 23,* 91–98.

Kaplan, S. L., Hong, G. K., & Weinhold, C. (1984). Epidemiology of depressive symptoms in adolescents. *Journal of American Academy of Child Phychiatry, 23,* 91–98.

Kashani, J. H., Heinrichs, T. F., Reid, J. C., & Huff, C. (1982). Depression in diagnostic subtypes of delinquent boys. *Adolescence, 17,* 943–949.

Hashani, J. H., Husain, A., Shekim, W. O., Hodges, K. K., Cytryn, L., & McKnew, D. H. (1981). Current perspectives in childhood depression: An overview. *American Journal of Psychiatry, 138,* 143–153.

Kashani, J. H., & Simonds, J. F. (1979). The incidence of depression in children. *American Journal of Psychiatry, 136,* 1203–1205.

Kaslow, F. (1982). Profile of the healthy family. *The Relationship, 8* (1), 9–25.

Kaslow, N. J., Tanenbaum, R. L., Abramson, L. Y., Peterson, C., & Seligman, M. E. P. (1983). Problem-solving deficits and depressive symptoms among children. *Journal of Abnormal Child Psychology, 11,* 497–502.

Katz, J. L., Kuperberg, A., & Pollack, C. P. (1984). Is there a relationship between eating disorder and affective disorder? New evidence from sleep tracings. *American Journal of Psychiatry, 141,* 753–759.

Kauffman, J. M. (1991). Restructuring in sociopolitical context: Reservations about the effects of current reform proposals on students with disabilities. In J. W. Lloyd, N. N. Singh, & A. C. Repp (Eds.), *The regular education initiative: Alternative perspectives on concepts, issues, and models (pp. 57–66).* Sycamore, IL: Sycamore.

Kauffman, J. M. (1993). How we might achieve the radical reform of special education. *Exceptional Children, 60,* 6–16.

Kauffman, J. M., & Kneedler, R. D. (1981). Behavior disorders. In J. M. Kauffman & D. P. Hallahan (Eds.), *Handbook of special education.* Englewood Cliffs, NJ: Prentice Hall.

Kaufman, A. S., Swan, W. W., & Wood, M. M. (1979). Dimensions of problem behaviors of emotionally disturbed children as seen by their parents and teachers. *Psychology in the Schools, 16,* 207–217.

Kavale, K. A., & Forness, S. R. (1983). Hyperactivity and diet treatment: A meta-analysis of the Feingold hypothesis. *Journal of Learning Disabilities, 16,* 324–330.

Kazdin, A. E. (1980). *Research design in clinical psychology.* New York: Harper & Row.

Kazdin, A. E. (1982). The token economy: A decade later. *Journal of Applied Behavior Analysis, 15,* 431–445.

Kazdin, A. E. (1983). Failure of persons to respond to the token economy. In E. B. Foa & P. M. G. Emmelkamp (Eds.), *Failures in behavior therapy* (pp. 335–354). New York: Wiley.

Kazdin, A. E. (1985). *Treatment of antisocial behavior in children and adolescents.* Homewood, IL: Dorsey Press.

Kazdin, A. E. (1987a). *Conduct disorders in childhood and adolescence.* Newbury Park, CA: Sage.

Kazdin, A. E. (1987b). Treatment of antisocial behavior in children: Current status and future directions. *Psychological Bulletin, 102,* 187–203.

Kazdin, A. E. (1993). Psychotherapy for children and adolescents: Current progress and future research directions. *American Psychologist, 48,* 644–657.

Kazdin, A. E., French, N. H., Unis, A. S., Esveldt-Dawson, K., & Sherick, R. B. (1983). Hopelessness, depression, and suicidal intent among psychiatrically disturbed inpatient children. *Journal of Consulting and Clinical Psychology, 54,* 241–245.

Kazdin, A. E., Rodgers, A., & Colbus, D. (1986). The hopelessness scale for children: Psychometric characteristics and concurrent validity. *Journal of Consulting and Clinical Psychology, 54,* 241–245.

Kedar-Voivodas, G., & Tannenbaum, A. J. (1979). Teachers' attitudes toward young deviant children. *Journal of Educational Psychology, 71,* 800–808.

Keilitz, I., & Dunivant, N. (1987). The learning disabled offender. In C. M. Nelson, R. B. Rutherford, Jr., & B. I. Wolford (Eds.), *Special education in the criminal justice system.* Columbus, OH: Merrill.

Kellerman, J. (1980). Rapid treatment of nocturnal anxiety in children. *Journal of Behavior Therapy and Experimental Psychiatry, 11,* 9–11.

Kelly, E. W. (1973). School phobia: A review of theory and treatment. *Psychology in the Schools, 10,* 33–42.

Kelly, J. A., & Drabman, R. S. (1977). Generalizing response suppression of self-injurious behavior through an overcorrection punishment procedure: A case study: *Behavior Therapy, 8,* 468–472.

Kendall, P. C., Chansky, T., Friedman, M., Kim, R., Kortlander, E., Sessa, F. M., & Siqueland, L. (1990). Treating anxiety disorders in children/adolescents. In P. C. Kendall (Ed.), *Child and Adolescent Therapy: Cognitive-Behavioral Procedures.* (pp. 131–157). New York: Guilford.

Kendall, P. C., & Morison, P. (1984). Integrating cognitive and behavioral procedures for the treatment of socially isolated children. In A. W. Myers & E. W. Craighead (Eds.), *Cognitive Behavior Therapy with Children.* (pp. 261–288). New York: Plenum Press.

Kennedy, E., Spence, S. H., & Hensley, R. (1989). An examination of the relationship between childhood depression and social competence amongst primary school children. *Journal of Child Psychology and Psychiatry, 30,* 561–573.

Kessler, J. W. (1966). *Psychopathology of childhood.* Englewood Cliffs, NJ: Prentice Hall.

King, C. A., & Young, R. D. (1981). Peer popularity and peer communication patterns: Hyperactive versus active but normal boys. *Journal of Abnormal Child Psychology, 9,* 465–482.

King, C. A., & Young, R. D. (1982). Attentional deficits with and without hyperactivity: Teacher and peer perceptions. *Journal of Abnormal Child Psychology, 10,* 483–496.

King, T. R. (1980). The complex relationships among selected family, educational, and cultural variables and sex to specific indicators of juvenile delinquency. In R. B. Rutherford, Jr., A. G. Prieto, and J. E. McGlothlin (Eds.), *Severe behavior disorders of children and youth.* Reston, VA: Council for Children with Behavioral Disorders.

Kingsley, R. (1967). Prevailing attitudes toward exceptional children. *Education, 87,* 426–430.

Kirby, D. (1984). *Sexuality education: An evaluation of programs and their effects, Volume 1.* Atlanta: U.S. Department of Health and Human Services.

Kissel, R. C., & Whitman, T. L. (1977). An examination of the direct and generalized effects of a play-training and overcorrection procedure upon the self stimulatory behavior of a profoundly retarded boy. *AAESPH Review, 2,* 131–146.

Klein, N. C., Alexander, J. F. & Parsons, B. V. (1977). Impact of family systems intervention on recidivism and sibling delinquency: A model of primary prevention and program evaluation. *Journal of Consulting and Clinical Psychology, 45,* 469–474.

Klepsch, M., & Logie, L. (1982). *Children draw and tell: An introduction to the projective uses of children's human figure drawings.* New York: Brunner/Mazel.

Knittle, B. J., & Tuana, S. (1980). Group therapy as primary treatment for adolescent victims of intrafamilial sexual abuse. *Clinical Social Work Journal, 8,* 236–242.

Knitzer, J. (1982). *Unclaimed children.* Washington, DC: Children's Defense Fund.

Knitzer, J., Steinberg, Z., & Fleisch, B. (1989). *At the schoolhouse door: An examination of programs and policies for children with behavioral and emotional problems.* New York: Bank Street College of Education.

Knoblock, P. (1983). *Teaching emotionally disturbed children.* Boston: Houghton Mifflin.

Knopp, F. (1982). *Remedial intervention in adolescent sex offenses: Nine program descriptions.* Syracuse, NJ: Safer Society Press.

Koegel, R. L., & Covert, A. (1972). The relationship of self-stimulation to learning in autistic children. *Journal of Applied Behavior Analysis, 5,* 381–387.

Koegel, R. L. & Egel, A. L. (1979). Motivating autistic children. *Journal of Abnormal Psychology, 88,* 418–426.

Koegel, R. L., & Rincover, A. (1974). Treatment of psychotic children in a classroom environment: Learning in a large group. *Journal of Applied Behavior Analysis, 7,* 45–49.

Koegel, R. L., & Rincover, A. (1977). Research on the difference between generalization and maintenance in extra-therapy responding. *Journal of Applied Behavior Analysis, 10,* 1–12.

Koegel, R. L., Rincover, A., & Egel, A. L. (1982). *Educating and understanding autistic children.* Boston: College-Hill.

Koegel, R. L., & Williams, J. A. (1980). Direct vs. indirect response reinforcer relationships in teaching autistic children. *Journal of Abnormal Child Psychology, 8,* 537–547.

Konopka, G. (1983). Adolescent suicide. *Exceptional Children, 49,* 390–394.

Koppitz, E. M. (1968). *Psychological evaluation of children's human figure drawings.* New York: Grune & Stratton.

Kovacs, M. & Beck, A. T. (1977). An empirical-clinical approach toward a definition of childhood depression. In J. G. Schulterbrandt & A. Raskin (Eds.), *Depression in childhood: diagnosis, treatment, and conceptual models.* (pp. 1–25). New York: Raven Press.

Kozloff, M. A. (1973). *Reaching the autistic child: A parent training program.* Champaign, IL: Research Press.

Kozloff, M. (1975). *Educating children with learning and behavior problems.* New York: Wiley.

Kratochwill, T. R., & French, D. (1984). Social skills training for withdrawn children. *School Psychology Review, 13,* 331–338.

Kroth, R. L., & Simpson, R. L. (1977). *Parent conferences as a teaching strategy.* Denver, CO: Love.

Kuhn, D., & Angelev, J. (1976). An experimental study of the development of formal operational thought. *Child Development, 47,* 696–706.

LaGreca, A. M., & Santogrossi, D. A. (1980). Social skills training with elementary school students: A behavioral group approach. *Journal of Consulting and Clinical Psychology, 48,* 220–227.

Lambert, N. M. (1988). Adolescent outcomes for hyperactive children. *American Psychologist, 43,* 786–799.

Lambert, N. M., Sassone, D., Hartsough, C. S., & Sandoval, J. (1987). Persistence of hyperactivity symptoms from childhood to adolescence and associated outcomes. *American Journal of Orthopsychiatry, 57,* 22–32.

Lamkin, J. S. (1980). *Getting started: Career education activities for exceptional students (K–9).* Reston, VA: The Council for Exceptional Children.

Laneve, R. S. (1979). Mark Twain School: A therapeutic educational environment for emotionally disturbed students. *Behavioral Disorders, 4,* 183–192.

La Nunziata, L. J., Hill, D. S., & Krause, L. A. (1981). Teaching social skills in classrooms for behaviorally disordered students. *Behavioral Disorders, 6,* 238–246.

Larson, K. A., & Gerber, M. M. (1987). Effects of social metacognitive training for enhancing overt behavior in learning disabled and low achieving delinquents. *Exceptional Children, 54,* 201–211.

Last, C. G. (1988). Anxiety disorders in childhood and adolscence. In C. G. Last & M. Hersen (Eds.) *Handbook of anxiety disorders* (pp. 531–540). New York: Pergamon.

Last, C. G., Francis, G., Hersen, M., Kazdin, A. E. & Strauss, C. C. (1987). Separation anxiety and school phobia: A comparison using DSM-III criteria. *American Journal of Psychiatry, 144,* 653–657.

Laurent, J., Landau, S., & Stark, K. D. (1993). Conditional probabilities in the diagnosis of depressive and anxiety disorders in children. *School Psychology Review, 22,* 98–114.

Leal, L. L., Baxter, E. G., Martin, J. & Marx, R. W. (1981). Cognitive modification and systematic desensitization with test anxious high school students. *Journal of Counseling Psychology, 28,* 525–528.

Ledingham, J. E., & Schwartzman, A. E. (1984). A 3-year follow-up of aggressive and withdrawn behavior in childhood: Preliminary findings. *Journal of Abnormal Child Psychology, 12,* 157–168.

Lefkowitz, M. M., & Tesiny, E. P. (1985). Depression in children: Prevalence and correlates. *Journal of Consulting and Clinical Psychology, 53,* 647–656.

Lefrancois, G. R. (1992). *Of children* (7th ed.). Belmont, CA: Wadsworth.

Leone, P. E. (1991). *Alcohol and other drugs: Use, abuse and disabilities.* ERIC/OSEP Special Project, ERIC Clearinghouse on Handicapped and Gifted Children. Reston, VA: The Council for Exceptional Children.

Leone, P. E., Greenberg, J. M., Trickett, E. J., & Spero, E. (1989). A study of the use of cigarettes, alcohol, and marijuana by students identified as "seriously emotionally disturbed." *Counterpoint, 9(3),* 6–7.

Lesse, S. (1974). Depression masked by acting out behavior patterns. *American Journal of Psychotherapy, 28,* 352–361.

Levitt, E. E. (1963). Psychotherapy with children: A further evaluation. *Behavior Research and Therapy, 60,* 326–329.

Levitt, E. E. (1971). Research on psychotherapy with children. In S. L. Garfield & A. E. Bergin (Eds.) *Handbook of psychotherapy and behavior change* (pp. 474–493), New York: Wiley.

Lewis, D. O., Shanok, S. S., & Pincus, J. H. (1979). Juvenile male sexual assaulters. *American Journal of Psychiatry, 136,* 1191–1196.

Lewis, K. A., Schwartz, G. M., & Ianacone, R. N. (1988). Service coordination between correctional and public school systems for handicapped juvenile offenders. *Exceptional Children, 55,* 66–70.

Lewis, T. J., Chard, D., & Scott, T. M. (1994). Full inclusion and the education of children and youth with emotional and behavioral disorders. *Behavioral Disorders, 19,* 277–293.

Lewisohn, P. M. (1974). A behavioral approach to depression. In R. J. Friedman & M. M. Katz (Eds.), *The psychology of depression: Contemporary theory and research.* New York: Wiley.

Lewisohn, P. M., & Arconad, M. (1981). Behavioral treatment of depression: A social learning approach. In J. F. Clarkin & H. I. Glazer (Eds.), *Depression: Behavioral and directive intervention strategies.* New York: Garland Press.

Liebert, R. M., & Poulos, R. W. (1976). Television as a moral teacher. In T. Lickona (ed.), *Moral development and behavior.* New York: Holt, Rinehart, & Winston.

Liebert, R. M., Sprafkin, J. N., & Davison, E. (1982). *The early window: Effects of television on children and youth.* New York: Pergamon.

Lindholm, K., & Willey, R. (1983). Child abuse and ethnicity: Patterns of similarities and differences (Occasional Paper No. 18). Los Angeles: UCLA Spanish Speaking Mental Health Research Center.

Lindsley, O. (1971). Precision teaching in perspective. *Teaching Exceptional Children, 3*, 114–119.

Lipsitt, L. (1988). Infant mental health: Enigma or brilliant breakthrough. *Child Behavior and Development Letter, 7, 9*.

Lloyd, J. (1980). Academic instruction and cognitive behavior modification: The need for attack strategy training. *Exceptional Education Quarterly, 1*, 53–63.

Lloyd, J. W. (1984). How shall we individualize instruction—or should we? *Remedial and Special Education, 5*, 7–15.

Lloyd, M. E., & Hilliard, A. M. (1989). Accuracy of self-recording as a function of repeated experience with different self-control contingencies. *Child & Family Behavior Therapy, 11(2)*, 1–14.

Lochman, J. E. & Lampron, L. B. (1986). Situational social problem-solving skills and self-esteem of aggressive and nonaggressive boys. *Journal of Abnormal Child Psychology, 14*, 605–617.

Lochman, J. E., White, K. J., & Wayland, K. K. (1990). Cognitive-behavioral assessment and treatment with aggressive children. In P. C. Kendall (Ed.), *Cognitive Behavioral Therapy with Children and Adolescents.* New York: Guilford.

Loehlin, J. C., Willerman, L., & Horn, J. M. (1988). Human behavior genetics. *Annual Review of Psychology, 39*, 101–133.

Loney, J. P., Kramer, J., & Milich, R. (1981). The hyperkinetic child grows up: predictors of symptoms of delinquency and achievement at follow-up. In K. Gadow & J. Loney, (Eds.), *Psychosocial aspect of drug treatment for hyperactivity* (pp. 232–252) Boulder, CO: Westview Press.

Long, N. J. (1990). Comments on Ralph Gardner's "Life space interviewing: It can be effective, but don't . . .," *Behavioral Disorders, 15*, 119–125.

Long, N. J., Morse, W. C. & Newman, R. G. (1965). *Conflict in the classroom: The education of emotionally disturbed children.* Belmont, CA: Wadsworth.

Long, N. J., & Newman, R. G. (1965). Managing surface behavior of children in the school. In N. J. Long, W. C. Morse, & R. G. Newman (Eds.), *Conflict in the classroom: The education of emotionally disturbed children.* Belmont, CA: Wadsworth.

Los Angeles Times (Jan. 6, 1994). Growing up gay. *OC High Student News & Views.*

Lovaas, O. I. (1966). Program for establishment of speech in schizophrenic and autistic children. In J. K. Wing (Ed.), *Early childhood autism: Clinical, educational, and social aspects.* London: Pergamon Press.

Lovaas, O. I. (1977). *The autistic child.* New York: Irvington.

Lovaas, O. I., & Simmons, J. (1969). Manipulation of self-destruction in three retarded children. *Journal of Applied Behavior Analysis, 2*, 143–157.

Lovaas, O. I., Koegel, R., Simmons, J., & Long, J. S. (1973). Some generalization and follow-up measures on autistic children in behavior therapy. *Journal of Applied Behavior Analysis, 6*, 131–166.

Lovaas, O. I., Koegel, R., Simmons, J., & Stevens, J. (1972). Some generalizations and follow up measures on autistic children in behavior therapy. *Journal of Applied Behavior Analysis, 34*, 17–23.

Lovitt, T. C. (1975). Applied behavior analysis and learning disabilities. Part I: Characteristics of ABA, general recommendations, and methodological limitations. *Journal of Learning Disabilities, 8*, 432–443.

Lusk, R., & Waterman, J. (1986). Effects of sexual abuse on children. In K. MacFarlane & J. Waterman (Eds.), *Sexual abuse of young children: Evaluation and treatment.* New York: Guilford Press.

Lux, M. G. (1990). *The impact of several familial variables on the development of children's depressogenic style of thinking.* Unpublished doctoral dissertation. The University of Texas at Austin.

Lynch, E. W. (1992). Developing cross-cultural competence. In E. W. Lynch & M. J. Hanson (Eds.), *Developing cross-cultural competence* (pps. 32–59). Baltimore, MD: Brookes.

Lyons, J., Serbin, L. A., & Marchessault, K. (1988). The social behavior of peer-identified aggressive, withdrawn, and aggressive/withdrawn children. *Journal of Abnormal Child Psychology, 16* 539–552.

Maag, J. W., & Behrens, J. T. (1989). Epidemiologic data on seriously emotionally disturbed and learning disabled adolescents: Reporting extreme depressive symptomatology. *Behavioral Disorders, 15,* 21–27.

Mahler, M. S. (1952). On child psychosis and schizophrenia. *Psychoanalytic Studies of the Child, 7,* 286–305.

Mallon, G. (1992). Gay and no place to go: Assessing the needs of gay and lesbian adolescents in out-of-home care settings. *Child Welfare, LXXI,* 547–556.

Malmquist, C. P. (1977). Childhood depression: A clinical and behavioral perspective. In J. G. Schulterbrandt & A. Raskin (Eds.), *Depression in childhood: diagnosis, treatment, and conceptual models.* New York: Raven Press.

Marcott-Radke, A. (1981). A multipurpose communication system: Modified for the autistic total communication (M.A.T.C.). In J. E. Gilliam (Ed.), *Autism: Diagnosis, instruction, management, and research.* Springfield, IL: Chas. C. Thomas.

Marshall, A. E., & Heward, W. L. (1979). Teaching self-management to incarcerated youth. *Behavioral Disorders, 4,* 215–226.

Martin, A. D. (1982). Learning to hide: The socialization of the gay adolescent. In S. C. Feinstein, J. G. Looney, A. Schartzberg, & A. Sorosky, (Eds.) *Adolescent psychiatry: Developmental and clinical studies* (pp. 234–243). Chicago: University of Chicago Press.

Maslow, A. H. (1954). *Motivation and personality.* New York: Harper & Row.

Maslow, A. H. (1967). A theory of metamotivation: The biological rooting of the value life. *Journal of Humanistic Psychology, 7,* 93–127.

Massman, P. J., Nussbaum, N. L., & Bigler, E. D. (1988). The mediating effect of age on the relationship between Child Behavior Checklist hyperactivity scores and neuropsychological test performance. *Journal of Abnormal Child Psychology, 16,* 89–95.

Masters, W. H., Johnson, V. E., & Kolodny, R. C. (1988). *Human sexuality* (3rd ed.). Boston: Little, Brown.

Mastropieri, M., Jenkins, V., & Scruggs, T. (1985). Academic and intellectual characteristics of behavior disordered children and youth. In R. B. Rutherford, Jr. (Ed.), *Severe behavior disorders of children and youth.* (Vol. 8, pp. 86–104). Reston, VA: Council for Children with Behavioral Disorders.

Mattes, J. A. (1983). The Feingold diet: A current reappraisal. *Journal of Learning Disabilities, 16,* 319–323.

Mattison, R. E., Bagnato, S. J., & Brubaker, B. H. (1988). Diagnostic ability of the Revised Children's Manifest Anxiety Scale in children with DMS-III anxiety disorders. *Journal of Anxiety Disorders, 2,* 147–155.

Mattison, R. E., Humphrey, J., Kales, S., Handford, H. A., Finkenbinder, R. L., & Hernit, R. C. (1986). Psychiatric background and diagnosis of children evaluated for special class placement. *Journal of the American Academy of Child Psychiatry, 25,* 514–520.

Mattison, R. E., Morales, J., & Bauer, M. A., (1992). Distinguishing characteristics of elementary school boys recommended for SED placement. *Behavioral Disorders, 17,* 107–114.

McCarney, S. B., & Leigh, J. E. (1990). *Behavior Evaluation Scale-2.* Austin, TX: Pro-Ed.

McCarthy, J. M., & Paraskevopoulos, J. (1969). Behavior patterns of learning disabled, emotionally disturbed, and average children. *Exceptional Children, 36,* 69–74.

McCarthy, P., Fender, K., & Fender, D. (1988). Supported employment for persons with autism. In P. Wehman & M. S. Moon (Eds.), *Vocational rehabilitation and supported employment.* Baltimore: Paul H. Brooks.

McClure, G., Ferguson, H. B., Boodoosingh, L., Turgay , A., & Stavrakaki, C. (1989). The frequency and severity of psychiatric disorders in special education and psychiatric programs. *Behavioral Disorders, 14,* 117–126.

McConnell, S. R. Entrapment effects and the generalization and maintenance of social skills training for elementary school students with behavioral disorders. *Behavioral Disorders, 12,* 252–263.

McDowell, R. L. (1981). Adolescence. In G. Brown, R. L. McDowell, & J. Smith (Eds.), *Educating adolescents with behavior disorders.* Columbus, OH: Merrill.

McDowell, R. L., & Brown, G. B. (1978). The emotionally disturbed adolescent: Development of program alternatives in secondary education. *Focus on Exceptional Children, 10,* 1–15.

McGee, J. J., Menolascino, F. J., Hobbs, D. C., & Menousek, P. E. (1987). *Gentle teaching: A non-aversive approach to helping persons with mental retardation.* New York: Human Sciences Press.

McGinnis, E. (1982). An individualized curriculum for children and youth with autism. In C. R. Smith, J. P. Grimes, & J. J. Freilinger (Eds.), *Autism: Programmatic considerations.* Des Moines, IA: State Department of Public Instruction.

McGinnis, E., & Goldstein, A. P. (1984). *Skillstreaming the elementary school child.* Champaign, IL: Research Press.

McLean, J. E., & Snyder-McLean, L. K. (1982). Communication: New perspectives on assessment and treatment. In C. R. Smith, J. P. Grimes, & J. J. Freilinger (Eds.), *Autism: Programmatic considerations.* Des Moines, IA: State Department of Public Instruction.

McLean, L. P., & McLean, J. E. (1974). A language training program for non-verbal autistic children. *Journal of Speech and Hearing Disorders, 39,* 186–194.

McLoughlin, J. A., Nall, M., Isaacs, B., Petrosko, J., Karibo, J., & Lindsey, B. (1983). The relationship of allergies and allergy treatment to school performance and student behavior. *Annals of Allergy, 51,* 506–510.

McLoughlin, J. A., Nall, M., & Petrosko, J. (1985). Allergies and learning disabilities. *Learning Disabilities Quarterly, 8,* 255–260.

Meadows, N., Neel, R. S., Parker, G., & Timo, K. (1991). A validation of social skills for students with behavioral disorders, *Behavioral Disorders, 16,* 200–210.

Medway, F. J., & Smith, R. C. (1978). An examination of contemporary elementary school affective education programs. *Psychology in the Schools, 15,* 260–269.

Meehl, P. (1969). Schizotaxia, schizotypy, schizophrenia. In A. Buss (Ed.), *Theories of schizophrenia.* New York: Lieber-Atherton, 21–46.

Meichenbaum, D. (1971). Examination of model characteristics in reducing avoidance behavior. *Journal of Personality and Social Psychology, 17,* 298–307.

MHA/Texas. (1993). Kids in trouble. *Mental Health Advocate, 11(2),* 1.

Milich, R. & Dodge, K. A. (1984). Social information processing in child psychiatric populations. *Journal of Abnormal Child Psychology, 91,* 183–198.

Miller, D. (1993). Sexual and physical abuse among adolescents with behavioral disorders: Profiles and implications. *Behavioral Disorders, 18,* 129–138.

Miller, L. C. (1967). Louisville behavior checklist for males, 6–12 years of age. *Psychological Reports, 21,* 885–896.

Miller, L. C. (1980). Dimensions of adolescent psychopathology. *Journal of Abnormal Child Psychology, 8,* 161–173.

Miller, L. C., Barrett, C. L., & Hampe, E. (1974). Phobias of childhood in a prescientific era. In A. Davids (Ed.), *Child personality and psychopathology: Current topics.* (Vol. 1). New York: Wiley.

Miller, P. M. (1972). The use of visual imagery and muscle relaxation in the counterconditioning of a phobic child: A case study. *Journal of Nervous and Mental Disease, 154,* 457–460.

Miller, S. P., & Hudson, P. (1994). Using structured parent groups to provide parental support. *Intervention in School and Clinic, 29,* 151–155.

Minuchin, S. (1970). The use of an ecological framework in the treatment of a child. In J. E. Anthony & C. Koupernik (Eds.), *The child in his family.* New York: Wiley.

Mirenda, P. & Iacono, T. (1988). Strategies for promoting augmentative and alternative communication in natural contexts with students with autism. *Focus on Autistic Behavior, 3(4),* 1–16.

Mirenda, P. & Santograssi, J. (1985). A prompt-free strategy to teach pictorial communication system use. *Augmentative and Alternative Communication, 1,* 143–150.

Mirkin, P. K., Fuchs, L. S., & Deno, S. L. (1982). *Considerations for designing a continuous evaluation system: An integrative review* (Monograph No. 20). Minneapolis: University of Minnesota, Institute for Research on Learning Disabilities.

Montague, M. (1987). Job-related socialization training for mildly to moderately handicapped adolescents. In R. B. Rutherford, Jr., C. M. Nelson, & S. R. Forness (Eds.), *Severe behavior disorders of children and youth.* Boston: Little, Brown.

Montgomery, M. D. (1982). Educational services for emotionally disturbed children. In J. L. Paul & B. C. Epanchin (Eds.), *Emotional disturbance in children: Theories and methods for teachers.* Columbus, OH: Merrill.

Mooney, C. & Algozzine, R. (1978). A comparison of the disturbingness of behaviors related to learning disability and emotional disturbance. *Journal of Abnormal Child Psychology, 6,* 401–406.

Morgan, D. J. (1979). Prevalence and types of handicapping conditions found in juvenile corrections: A national survey. *Journal of Special Education, 13,* 283–295.

Morgan, D. P. (1993). *RESIST: A curriculum to prevent the use of alcohol, tobacco, and other drugs by students in special education.* Logan, UT: Utah State University.

Morgan, D. P., Likins, M., Friedman, S., & Genaux, M. (1994). *A preliminary investigation of the effectiveness of a substance use prevention program for students in special education programs.* Logan, UT: Utah State University.

Morris, R. J., & Kratochwill, T. R. (1987). Dealing with fear and anxiety in the school setting: Behavioral approaches to treatment. *Special Services in the Schools, 3,* 53–68.

Morse, W. C. (1969a). Preparing to teach the disturbed adolescent. In H. W. Harshman (Ed.), *Educating the emotionally disturbed: A book of readings.* New York: Thomas Y. Crowell.

Morse, W. C. (1969b). Training teachers in life space interviewing. In H. Dupont (Ed.), *Educating emotionally disturbed children: Readings.* New York: Holt, Rinehart & Winston.

Mrazek, P. B. (1980). Sexual abuse of children. *Journal of Child Psychiatry and Psychology and Allied Disciplines, 21,* 91–95.

Murphy, D. M. (1986). The prevalence of handicapping conditions among juvenile delinquents. *Remedial and Special Education, 7,* 70–71.

Murray, C. A. (1976). *The link between learning disabilities and juvenile delinquency: Current theory and knowledge.* Washington, DC: U.S. Goverment Printing Office.

Murray, H. A. (1943). *Thematic Apperception Test.* Cambridge: Harvard University Press.

Muse, N. J. (1990). *Depression and suicide in children and adolescents.* Austin, TX: Pro-Ed.

Myers, J., & Deibert, A. (1971). Reduction of self-abusive behavior in a blind child by using a feeding response. *Journal of Behavior Therapy and Experimental Psychiatry, 2,* 141–144.

Myers, P. I., & Hammill, D. D. (1990). *Learning disabilities: Basic concepts, assessment practices, and instructional strategies* (4th ed.). Austin, TX: Pro-Ed.

Naglieri, J. A., LeBuffe, P. A., & Pfeiffer, S. I. (1994). *Devereux Scales of Mental Disorders.* San Antonio: Psychological Corporation.

Nakashima, I. I., & Zakus, G. (1979). Incestuous families. *Pediatric Annals, 8,* 300–308.

NARSAD Research Newletter (1994, Spring), *A profile of Judith Rapoport, M.D.* National Alliance for Research on Schizophrenia and Depression Research Fund: Great Neck, NY.

NARSAD Research Newletter (1994, Summer). *Promising medications on the horizon.* National Alliance for Research on Schizophrenia and Depression Research Fund: Great Neck, NY.

National Association of State Boards of Education (1992). *Winners all: A call for inclusive schools.* Alexandria, VA: Author.

National Association of State Directors of Special Education (1986). *SED Findings: Project Forum and Decision Resources Corp.* Washington, DC: Author.

National Institute of Mental Health (1990). *National Plan for Research on Child and Adolescent Mental Disorders.* Rockville: MD.: Author.

National Institute on Drug Abuse (1980). *Review of evidence on effects of marijuana use.* Washington, DC: U.S. Government Printing Office.

National Institute on Drug Abuse (1992). *A comparison of drug use among 8th, 10th, and 12th graders. NIDA's high school senior survey: Monitoring the Future.* Washington, DC: U.S. Government Printing Office.

National Mental Health and Special Education Coalition (1989, April 4). *Statement to the House Committee on Select Education.*

Neel, R. (1979). Autism: Symptoms in search of a syndrome. In F. Wood & Lakin (Eds.), *Disturbing, disordered, or disturbed?* Minneapolis: Department of Psychoeducational Studies, University of Minnesota.

Neimark, E. D. (1975). Intellectual development during adolescence. In F. D. Horowitz (Ed.), *Review of child development research* (Vol. 4). Chicago: University of Chicago Press.

Nelson, C. M. (1983). Beyond the classroom: The teacher of behaviorally disordered pupils in a social system. In R. B. Rutherford, Jr. (Ed.), *Severe behavior disorders of children and youth.* Tempe, AZ: Arizona State University.

Nelson, C. M., & Rutherford, R. B. Jr. (1988). Behavioral interventions with behaviorally disordered students. In M. C. Wang, M. C. Reynolds, & H. J. Walberg (Eds.) *Handbook of special education: Research and practice* (Vol. 2). New York: Pergamon.

Nelson, C. M., Rutherford, R. B., Jr., & Wolford, B. I. (1987). *Special education in the criminal justice system.* Columbus, OH: Merrill.

Nelson, J. R., Smith, D. J., Young, R. K., Dodd, J. M. (1991). A review of self-management outcome research conducted with students who exhibit behavioral disorders, *Behavioral Disorders, 16,* 169–179.

Newcomer, P. L. (1993). *Understanding and teaching emotionally disturbed children and adolescents (2nd edition).* Austin, TX: Pro-Ed.

News and Reports. (1981). *Children Today, 10,* 28.

Novaco, R. (1978). Anger and coping with stress. In J. Forety & D. Rathjen (Eds.), *Cognitive behavior therapy: Research and application.* New York: Plenum Press.

Nuechterlein, K. H. (1983). Signal detection in vigilance tasks and behavioral attitudes among offspring of schizophrenic mothers and among hyperactive children. *Journal of Abnormal Psychology, 92,* 4–28.

Nussbaum, N., & Bigler, E. (1990). *Identification and treatment of attention deficit disorder.* Austin, TX: Pro-Ed.

Ollendick, T. H. (1979). Fear reduction techniques with children. In M. Hersen, R. M. Eisler, & P. M. Miller (Eds.), *Progress in behavior modification* (Vol. 8). New York: Academic Press.

Ollendick, T. H., & Mayer, J. A. (1984). School phobia. In S. M. Turner (Ed.), *Behavioral theories and treatment of anxiety* (pp. 367–411). New York: Plenum.

Olson, L. (1993). Who's afraid of O.B.E.? *Education Week, XIII*(15), 25–27.

Ornitz, E. (1978). Neurophysiologic studies. In M. Rutter & E. Schopler (Eds.), *Autism: A reappraisal of concepts and treatment.* New York: Plenum.

Ornitz, E. M., Atwell, C. W., Kaplan, A. R., & Westlake, J. R. (1985). Brainstem dysfunction in autism. *Archives of General Psychiatry, 42,* 1018–1025.

Ortiz, A., & Maldonado, C. E. (1986). Recognizing learning disabilities in bilingual children: How to lessen inappropriate referrals of language minority students to special education. *Journal of Reading, Writing, and Learning Disabilities International, 2(1),* 43–56.

Parish, T., Dyck, N., & Kappes, B. (1979). Stereotypes concerning normal and handicapped children. *The Journal of Psychology, 102,* 63–70.

Park, E. K., Pullis, M., Reilly, T., & Townsend, B. L. (1994). Cultural biases in the identification of students with behavioral disorders. In R. L. Peterson & S. Ishii-Jordan (Eds.), *Multicultural issues in the education of students with behavioral disorders.* Cambridge, MA: Brookline.

Parsons, B. V. & Alexander, J. F. (1973). Short-term family intervention: A therapy outcome study. *Journal of Consulting and Clinical Psychology, 41,* 195–201.

Patterson, G. R. (1965). A learning theory approach to the treatment of the school phobic child. In L. P. Ullmann & L. Krasner (Eds.), *Case studies in behavior modification.* New York: Holt, Rinehart & Winston.

Patterson, G. R. (1975). The aggressive child: Victim and architect of a coercive system. In E. J. Mash, L. A. Hamerlynck, & L. C. Handy (Eds.), *Behavior modification in families.* New York: Brunner/Mazel.

Patterson, G. R. (1976). The aggressive child: Victim and architect of a coercive system. In E. J. Mash, L. A. Hamerlynck, & L. C. Handy (Eds.), *Behavior modification and families.* New York: Brunner/Mazel.

Patterson, G. R. (1983). *Longitudinal investigation of antisocial boys and their families: Research* (Grant from the National Institute of Mental Health). Eugene, OR: Oregon Social Learing Center.

Patterson, G. R. (1988). Family process: Loops, levels, and linkages. In N. Bolger, A. Caspi, G. Downey, & M. Moorehouse (Eds.), *Persons in context: Developmental processes* (pp. 114–151). New York: Cambridge University Press.

Patterson, G. R., Chamberlain, P., & Reid, J. B. (1982). A comparative evaluation of a parent-training program. *Behavior Therapy, 13,* 638–650.

Patterson, G. R. & Cobb, J. A. (1973). Stimulus control for classes of noxious behavior. In J. S. Knutson (Ed.), *The control of aggression: Implications from basic research.* Chicago: Aldine.

Patterson, G. R., Reid, J. B., & Dishion, T. J. (1992). *Antisocial boys (Vol. 4): A social interactional approach.* Eugene, OR: Castalia.

Pauling, L. (1968). Orthomolecular psychiatry. *Science, 160,* 265–271.

Peck, H., Rabinovitch, R., & Cramer, J. (1969). A treatment program for parents of schizophrenic children. *American Journal of Orthopsychiatry, 19,* 592–598.

Pelham, W. E., Schnedler, R. W., Bologna, N. C., & Contreras, A. J. (1980). Behavioral and stimulant treatment of hyperactive children: A therapy study with methylphenidate probes in a within-subject design. *Journal of Applied Behavior Analysis, 13,* 221–236.

Pentz, M. A., Dwyer, J. H., MacKinnon, D. P., Flay, B. R., Hansen, W. B., Wang, E. U. I., & Johnson, C. A. (1989). A multicommunity trial for primary prevention of adolescent drug use. *Journal of the American Medical Association, 261,* 3259–3266.

Pescara-Kovach, L. A., & Alexander, K. (1994). The link between food ingested and problem behavior: Fact or fallacy? *Behavioral Disorders, 19,* 142–148.

Peterson, D. R. (1961). Behavior problems of middle childhood. *Journal of Consulting Psychology, 25,* 205–209.

Phelps, L., & Bajorek, E. (1991). Eating disorders of the adolescent: Current issues in etiology, assessment, and treatment. *School Psychology Review, 20,* 9–22.

Piaget, J. (1972). Intellectual evolution from adolescence to adulthood. *Human Development, 15,* 1–12.

Piers, E., & Harris, D. (1969). *The Piers-Harris Children's Self-concept Scale.* Nashville: Counselor Recordings and Tests.

Polit, D. (1985). *A review of the antecedents of adolescent sexuality, contraception, and pregnancy outcomes.* Jefferson City, MO: Humanalysis, Inc.

Polsgrove, L., & Reith, H. J. (1983). Procedures for reducing children's inappropriate behavior in special education settings. *Exceptional Education Quarterly, 3,* 20–33.

Pope, H. G., Hudson, J. I., & Jonas, J. M. (1983). Bulimia treated with imipramine: A placebo-controlled, double blind study. *American Journal of Psychiatry, 140,* 554–558.

Porter, F. S., Blick, L. C., & Sgroi, S. M. (1982). Treatment of the sexually abused child. In S. M. Sgroi (Ed.), *Handbook of clinical intervention in child sexual abuse.* Lexington, MA: D.C. Heath.

Post, C. H. (1981). The link between learning disabilities and juvenile delinquency: Cause, effect, and "present solutions." *Juvenile and Family Court Journal, 32,* 58–68.

Poulsen, M. (1991). *Schools meet the challenge: Educational needs of children at risk due to substance exposure.* Sacramento: Resources in Special Education.

Powers, H. W. S., Jr. (1977). A reply to Robert L. Sieben's critique. *Academic Therapy, 2,* 197–203.

Poznanski, E. O., Cook, S. C., & Carroll, B. J. (1979). A depression rating scale for children. *Pediatrics, 64,* 442–450.

Premack, D. (1965). Reinforcement theory. In D. Levine (Ed.), *Nebraska Symposium on Motivation.* Lincoln: University of Nebraska Press.

Prinz, R., Connor, P., & Wilson, C. (1981). Hyperactive and aggressive behaviors in childhood: Intertwined dimensions. *Journal of Abnormal Child Psychology, 9,* 191–202.

Prout, H. T., & DeMartino, R. A. (1986). A meta-analysis of school-based studies of psychotherapy. *Journal of School Psychology, 24,* 285–292.

Puig-Antich, J. (1982). Major depression and conduct disorder in prepuberty. *Journal of the American Academy of Child Psychiatry, 21,* 118–128.

Puig-Antich, J., and Weston, B. (1983). The diagnosis and treatment of major depressive disorder in childhood. *Annual Review of Medicine, 34,* 231–245.

Quay, H. C. (1966). Personality patterns in pre-adolescent delinquent boys. *Educational and Psychological Measurement, 26,* 99–110.

Quay, H. C. (1972). Patterns of aggression, withdrawal and immaturity. In H. C. Quay & J. S. Werry (Eds.), *Psychopathological disorders of childhood.* New York: Wiley.

Quay, H. C. (1975). Classification in the treatment of delinquency and antisocial behavior. In N. Hobbs (Ed.), *Issues in the classification of children* (Vol. 1). San Francisco: Jossey-Bass.

Quay, H. C. (1977). Psychopathic behavior. In I. C. Uzgiris & F. Weizmann (Eds.), *The structuring of experience.* New York: Plenum.

Quay, H. C. (1986). Conduct disorders. In H. C. Quay & J. S. Werry (Eds.) *Psychopathological disorders of childhood* (3rd ed., pp. 35–72). New York: Wiley.

Quay, H. C., Morse, W. C., & Cutler, R. L. (1966). Personality patterns of pupils in classrooms for the emotionally disturbed. *Exceptional Children, 32,* 297–301.

Quay, H. C., & Peterson, D. R. (1967). *Manual for the Behavior Problem Checklist.* Champaign, IL: Children's Research Center. Mimeographed.

Quay, H. C., & Peterson, D. R. (1987). *Manual for the Revised Behavior Problem Checklist.* Coral Gables, FL: Author.

Raaz, N. (1982). Working with parents of students with autism. In C. R. Smith, J. P. Grimes, & J. J. Freilinger (Eds.), *Autism: Programmatic considerations.* Des Moines, IA: Department of Public Instruction.

Rachman, S. (1971). *The effects of psychotherapy.* Oxford: Pergamon.

Rachman, S. (1977). The conditioning theory of fear acquisition: A critical examination. *Behaviour Research and Therapy, 15,* 375–387.

Ramirez, S. Z., Kratochwill, T. R., & Morris, R. J. (1987). Childhood anxiety disorders. In L. Michelson & L. M. Ascher (Eds.), *Anxiety and stress disorders: Cognitive-behavioral assessment and treatment.* (pp. 149–175). New York: Guilford.

Rapp, D. J. (1978). Does diet alter hyperactivity? *Journal of Learning Disorders, 11,* 383–389.

Rapport, M. D. (1983). Attention deficit disorder with hyperactivity: Critical treatment parameters and their application in applied outcome research. In M. Hersen, R. Eisler, & P. Miller (Eds.), *Progress in behavior modification* (pp. 219–298). New York: Academic.

Rapport, M. D. (1987). Attention deficit disorder with hyperactivity. In M. Hersen & V. B. Van Hasselt (Eds.), *Behavior therapy with children and adolescents* (pp. 325–361). New York: Wiley.

Rapport, M. D., Stoner, G., DuPaul, G. J., Birmingham, B. K., & Tucker, S. (1985). Methylphenidate in hyperactive children: Differential effects of dose on academic, learning, and social behavior. *Journal of Abnormal Child Psychology, 13,* 227–244.

Ratusnik, C. M., & Ratusnik, D. L. (1974). A comprehensive communication approach for a ten year old non-verbal autistic child. *American Journal of Orthopsychiatry, 44,* 396–403.

Realmuto, G. M. & Erickson, W. D. (1986). The management of sexual issues in adolescent treatment programs. *Adolescence, 21,* 347–356.

Redl, F. (1959a). The concept of a therapeutic milieu. *American Journal of Orthopsychiatry, 29,* 721–734.

Redl, F. (1959b). The concept of the life space interview. *American Journal of Orthopsychiatry, 29,* 1–18.

Redl, F. (1965). The concept of the life space interview. In N. J. Long, W. C. Morse, & R. G. Newman (Eds.), *Conflict in the classroom: The education of emotionally disturbed children.* Belmont, CA: Wadsworth.

Redl, F. (1966). *When we deal with children.* New York: Free Press.

Redl, F., & Wineman, D. (1957). *The aggressive child.* New York: Free Press.

Reeve, R., & Kauffman, J. (1978). The behavior disordered. In N. G. Haring (Ed.), *Behavior of exceptional children* (2nd ed.). Columbus, OH: Merrill.

Reeve, R. E. (1990). ADHD: Facts and fallacies. *Intervention in School and Clinic, 26,* 70–77.

Regan, M. K., Jones, C., Holzschuh, R., & Simpson, R. L. (1982). *Autism teacher training program: Vocational training program: Vocational training for autistic children/youth.* Kansas City, KS: University of Kansas Medical Center.

Reichle, G., & Brown, L. (1986). Teaching the use of a multipage direct selection communication board to an adult with autism. *Journal of the Association for Persons with Severe Handicaps, 11,* 68–73.

Reid, E. R. (1986). Practicing effective instruction: The exemplary center for reading instruction approach. *Exceptional Children, 52,* 510–519.

Reid, J. (1993). Prevention of conduct disorder before and after school entry: Relating interventions to developmental findings. *Development and Psychopathology, 5*(1/2) 243–262.

Reid, J. & Patterson, G. R. (1991). Early prevention and intervention with conduct problems: A social interactional model for the integration of research and practice. In G. Stoner, M. Shinn, & H. M. Walker (Eds.), *Interventions for achievement and behavior problems* (pp. 715–740). Silver Spring, MD: National Association of School Psychologists.

Reilly, T. F., Ross, D., & Bullock, L. M. (1980). The contemporary adolescent delinquent: Intellectual or impulsive? In R. B. Rutherford, Jr., A. G. Prieto, & J. E. McGlothlin (Eds.), *Severe behavior disorders of children and youth.* (Vol. 3, pp. 71–82). Reston, VA: Council for Children with Behavioral Disorders.

Reinert, H. R. (1976). *Children in conflict.* St. Louis: C. V. Mosby.

Renner, J. W., & Stafford, D. G. (1976). The operational levels of secondary school students. In J. W. Renner, D. G. Stafford, A. E. Lawson, J. W. McKinnon, F. E. Friot, & D. H. Kellogg, *Research, teaching, and learning with the Piaget model.* Norman, OK: University of Oklahoma Press.

Repp, A. C., & Deitz, S. M. (1974). Reducing aggressive and self-injurious behavior of institutionalized children through reinforcement of other behaviors. *Journal of Applied Behavior Analysis, 7,* 313–325.

Repp, A. C., Deitz, S. M., & Speir, N. C. (1974). Reducing stereotypic responding of retarded persons by the differential reinforcement of other behavior. *American Journal of Mental Deficiency, 79,* 279–284.

Reynolds, C. J., Salend, S. J., Beahand, C. L. (1989). Motivating secondary students: Bringing in the reinforcement. *Academic Therapy, 25,* 81–90.

Reynolds, M. C. (1962). Framework for considering some issues in special education. *Exceptional Children, 28,* 367–370.

Reynolds, W. M. (1984). Depression in children and adolescents: Phenomenology, evaluation, and treatment. *School Psychology Review, 13,* 171–182.

Reynolds, W. M., & Coates, K. I. (1986). A comparison of cognitive-behavioral therapy and relaxation training for the treatment of depression in adolescents. *Journal of Consulting and Clinical Psychology, 54,* 1–8.

Rezmierski, V., & Kotre, J. (1974). A limited review of theory of the psychodynamic model. In W. C. Rhodes & M. L. Tracy (Eds.), *A study of child variance* (Vol. 1). Ann Arbor, MI: The University of Michigan Press.

Rhode, G., Morgan, D. P., & Young, K. R. (1983). Generalization and maintenance of treatment gains of behaviorally handicapped students from resource rooms to regular classrooms using self-evaluation procedures. *Journal of Applied Behavior Analysis, 16,* 171–188.

Rhodes, W. C. (1967). The disturbing child: A problem of ecological management. *Exceptional Children, 33,* 449–455.

Rhodes, W. C. (1970). A community participation analysis of emotional disturbance. *Exceptional Children, 36,* 306–314.

Rhodes, W. C., & Tracy, M. L. (Eds.) (1974). *A study of child variance* (3 vols.). Ann Arbor, MI: The University of Michigan Press.

Rich, H. L. (1979). Classroom interaction patterns among teachers and emotionally disturbed students. *Exceptional Child, 26,* 4–40.

Rimland, B. (1971). The effect of high dosage levels of certain vitamins on the behavior of children with severe mental disorders. In D. R. Hawkins and L. Pauling (Eds.), *Orthomolecular psychiatry.* San Francisco: W. H. Freeman.

Rimland, B. (1983). The Feingold diet: An assessment of the reviews by Mattes, by Kavale and Forness and others. *Journal of Learning Disabilities, 16,* 331–333.

Rimland, B. (1988). Don't ban aversives. *The Advocate, 20(4),* 12–14.

Rimland, B., Callaway, E., & Dreyfus, P. (1978). The effect of high doses of vitamin B_6 on autistic children: A double-blind crossover study. *American Journal of Psychiatry, 135,* 472–475.

Rincover, A. (1978). Variables affecting stimulus fading and discriminative responding in psychotic children. *Journal of Abnormal Psychology, 88,* 235–246.

Rincover, A., Newson, C. D., & Carr, E. G. (1979). Using sensory extinction procedures in the treatment of compulsivelike behavior of developmentally disabled children. *Journal of Counsulting and Clinical Psychology, 47,* 695–701.

Risley, T. (1968). The effects and side effects of punishing the autistic behaviors of a deviant child. *Journal of Applied Behavior Analysis, 1,* 21–34.

Risley, T., & Wolf, M. (1967). Establishing functional speech in echolalic children. *Behavior Researh and Therapy, 5,* 73–88.

Ritvo, E. (1988). Ask the experts: The ADVOCATE interviews Dr. Edward Ritvo. *The ADVOCATE, 20(2),* pp. 1, 4.

Ritvo, E., & Freeman, B. J. (1977). National Society for Autistic Children: Definition of autism. *Journal of Pediatric Psychology, 4,* 146–148.

Ritvo, E., Freeman, B. J., Scheibel, A. B., Duong, T., Robinson, H., Guthrie, D., & Ritvo, A. (1986). Lower Purkinje cell counts in the cerebella of four autistic subjects: Initial findings of the UCLA-NSAC autopsy research report. *American Journal of Psychiatry, 143,* 862–866.

Ritvo, E., Rahm, K., Yuwiler, A., Freeman, B. J., & Geller, E. (1978). Biochemical and hematologic studies: A critical review. In M. Rutter & E. Schopler (Eds.), *Autism: A reappraisal of concepts and treatment.* New York: Plenum.

Robins, L. N. (1981). Epidemiological approaches to natural history research: Antisocial behaviors in children. *Journal of the American Academy of Child Psychiatry, 20,* 566–580.

Rochlin, G. (1959). The loss complex. *Journal of American Psychoanalytic Association, 7,* 299–316.

Rodriguez, R. F. (1988). *Bilingual special education is appropriate for Mexican-American children with mildly handicapping conditions.* ERIC Clearinghouse on Rural Education and Small Schools. ERIC Document Reproduction Service No. ED 293679.

Rogers, C. (1959). A theory of therapy, personality, and interpersonal relationships, as developed in the client-centered framework. In S. Kock (Ed.), *Psychology: A study of a science* (Vol. 3). New York: McGraw-Hill.

Rogers, C. (1969). *Freedom to learn.* Columbus, OH: Merrill.

Rogers, J. (1993, May). The inclusive revolution. *Phi Delta Kappa Research Bulletin,* pp. 1–6.

Rohrkemper, M. M., & Brophy, J. E. (April 1979). *Classroom strategy study: Investigating teacher strategies with problem students.* Paper presented at the annual meeting of the American Educational Research Association, San Francisco.

Rorschach, H. (1921). *Psychodiagnostics: A diagnostic test based on perception.* New York: Grune & Stratton.

Roscoe, B., & Kruger, T. L. (1990). AIDS: Late adolescents' knowledge and its influence on behavior. *Adolescence, 25,* 39–48.

Rose, J. (1984). Current use of corporal punishment in American public schools. *Journal of Educational Psychology, 76,* 427–441.

Rose, T. (1978). The functional relationship between artificial food colors and hyperactivity. *Journal of Applied Behavior Analysis, 11,* 439–446.

Rosenbaum, A., O'Leary, K. D., & Jacob, R. G. (1975). Behavioral intervention with hyperactive children: Group consequences as a supplement to individual contingencies. *Behavior Therapy, 6,* 315–323.

Rosenfeld, A. A., Nadelson, C. C., & Krieger, M. (1979). Fantasy and reality in patients' reports of incest. *Journal of Clinical Psychiatry, 40,* 159–164.

Rosenstock, H. A., & Vincent, K. R. (1979). Parental involvement as a prerequisite for successful adolescent therapy. *Journal of Clinical Psychiatry, 40,* 132–134.

Rosenthal, D. (1975). Heredity in criminality. *Criminal Justice and Behavior, 2,* 3–21.

Rosenthal, J. H. (1973). Neurophysiology of minimal cerebral dysfunctions. *Academic Therapy, 8,* 291–294.

Ross, D. M., & Ross, S. A. (1982). *Hyperactivity: Research, theory, and action.* New York: Wiley.

Roth, D. & Rehm, L. P. (1980). Relationships among self-monitoring processes, memory, and depression. *Cognitive Therapy and Research, 4,* 149–157.

Rubin, R. A., & Balow, B. (1971). Learning and behavior disorders: A longitudinal study. *Exceptional Children, 38,* 293–299.

Rubin, R. A., & Balow, B. (1978). Prevalence of teacher identified behavior problems: A longitudinal study. *Exceptional Children, 45,* 102–111.

Rubin, T. I. (1962). *Lisa & David/Jordi.* New York: Random House.

Ruhl, K. L., & Hughes, C. A. (1985). The nature and extent of aggression in special education settings serving behaviorally disordered students. *Behavioral Disorders, 10,* 95–104.

Rusch, F. R. (1986). *Competitive employment issues and strategies.* Baltimore: Paul H. Brooks.

Rush, A. J., Weissenburger, J., & Eaves, G. (1986). Do thinking patterns predict depressive symptoms? *Cognitive Therapy and Research, 10,* 225–236.

Russ, D. F. (1974). A review of learning and behavior theory as it relates to emotional disturbance in children. In W. Rhodes & M. L. Tracy (Eds.), *A study of child variance* (Vol. 1). Ann Arbor, MI: The University of Michigan Press.

Rutherford, R. B., Jr., Nelson, C. M., & Wolford, B. I. (1986). Special education programming in juvenile corrections. *Remedial and Special Education, 7,* 27–33.

Rutherford, R. B., & Polsgrove, L. J. (1981). Behavioral contracting with behaviorally disordered and delinquent children and youth: An analysis of the clinical and experimental literature. In R. B.

Rutherford, A. G. Prieto, & J. E. McGlothlin (Eds.) *Severe behavior disorders of children and youth,* (Vol. 4). Reston, VA: Council for Exceptional Children.

Rutter, M. (1965). The influence of organic and emotional factors on the origins, nature, and outcome of childhood psychosis. *Developmental Medicine and Child Neurology, 7,* 518–528.

Rutter, M. (1977). Brain damage syndromes in childhood: Concepts and findings. *Journal of Child Psychology and Psychiatry, 18,* 1–21.

Rutter, M. (1978). Language disorder and infantile autism. In M. Rutter & E. Schopler (Eds.), *Autism: A reappraisal of concepts and treatment.* New York: Plenum.

Rutter, M., Bartak, L., & Newman, S. (1971). Autism: A central disorder of cognition and language? In M. Rutter (Ed.), *Infantile autism: Concepts, characteristics, and treatment.* London: Churchill.

Rutter, M., Izard, C. E., & Read, P. B. (1986). *Depression in young people: Developmental and clinical perspectives.* New York: Guilford.

Ryan, L., Ehrlich, S., & Finnegan, L. (1987). Cocaine abuse in pregnancy: Effects in the fetus and newborn, *Neurotoxicology and Teratology, 9,* 295–299.

Safer, D. J. (1982). Varieties and levels of interventions with disruptive adolescents. In D. J. Safer (Ed.), *School programs for disruptive adolescents.* Baltimore: University Park Press.

Safer, D. J., & Allen, R. P. (1976). *Hyperactive children: Diagnosis and management.* Baltimore: University Park Press.

Safer, D. J., & Heaton, R. C. (1982). Characteristics, school patterns, and behavioral outcomes of seriously disruptive junior high school students. In D. J. Safer (Ed.), *School programs for disruptive adolescents.* Baltimore: University Park Press.

Sailor, W., & Guess, D. (1983). *Severely handicapped students: An instructional design.* Boston: Houghton Mifflin.

Sasso, G. M. & Reimers, T. M. (1988). Assessing the functional properties of behaviors: Implications and applications for the classroom. *Focus on Autistic Behavior, 3(5),* 1–16.

Sasso, G. M., Melloy, K. J., & Kavale, KA. (1990). Generalization, maintenance, and behavioral covariation associated with social skills training through structured learning. *Behavioral Disorders, 16,* 9–22.

Satterfield, J. H., Hoppe, C. M., & Schell, A. M. (1982). A prospective study of delinquency in 110 adolescent boys with attention deficit disorder and 88 normal adolescent boys. *American Journal of Psychiatry, 139,* 797–798.

Saxe, L., Cross, T., & Silverman, N. (1988). Children's mental health: The gap between what we know and what we do. *American Psychologist, 43,* 800–807.

Schloss, P. J., Schloss, C., & Harris, L. (1984). A multiple baseline analysis of an interpersonal skills training program for depressed youth. *Behavioral Disorders, 9,* 182–188.

Schloss, P. J., Schloss, C. N., Wood, C. E., & Kiehl, W. S. (1986). A critical review of social skills research with behaviorally disordered students. *Behavioral Disorders, 12,* 1–14.

Schloss, P. J., & Smith, M. A. (1987). Guidelines for ethical use of manual restraint in public school settings for behaviorally disordered students. *Behavioral Disorders, 12,* 207–213.

Schlosser, L., & Algozzine, B. (1979). The disturbing child: He or she? *The Alberta Journal of Educational Research, 25,* 30–36.

Schmid, R., & Slade, D. (1981). Adolescent programs. In R. Algozzine, R. Schmid, & C. D. Mercer (Eds.), *Childhood behavior disorders: Applied research and educational practice.* Austin, TX: Pro-Ed.

Schneller, R. (1989). Intercultural and intrapersonal processes and factors of misunderstanding: Implications for multicultural training. *International Journal of Intercultural Relations, 13,* 465–483.

Schopler, E., & Dalldorf, J. (1980). Autism: Definition, diagnosis, and management. *Hospital Practice, 15(6),* 64–68.

Schreibman, L. (1975). Effects of within stimulus and extra-stimulus prompting on discrimination learning in autistic children. *Journal of Applied Behavior Analysis, 8,* 91–112.

Schroeder, L. B. (1965). A study of relationships between five descriptive categories of emotional disturbance and reading and arithmetic achievement. *Exceptional Children, 32,* 111–112.

Schultz, E., Salvia, J., & Feinn, J. (1974). Prevalence of behavioral symptoms in rural elementary school children. *Journal of Abnormal Child Psychology, 1,* 17–24.

Schutter, L. S., & Brinker, R. P. (1992). Conjuring a new category of disability from prenatal cocaine exposure: Are the infants unique biological or caretaking casualties? *Topics in Early Childhood Special Education, 11(4),* 84–111.

Seligman, M. E. (1975). *Helplessness: On depression, development, and death.* San Francisco: Freeman.

Seligman, M. E., Peterson, C., Kaslow, N. J., Tanenbaum, R. L., Alloy, L. B., & Abramson, L. Y. (1984). Attributional style and depressive symptoms among children. *Journal of Abnormal Psychology, 93,* 235–238.

Sellstrom, E. A. (1989). *Schematic processing and self-reference in childhood depression.* Unpublished doctoral dissertation, The University of Texas at Austin.

Sgroi, S. (1982). *Handbook of clinical intervention in child sexual abuse.* Lexington, MA: D.C. Heath.

Sieben, R. L. (1977). Controversial medical treatments of learning disabilities. *Academic Therapy, 2,* 133–147.

Sieben, R. L. (1983). Medical treatment of learning problems: A critique. In *Interdisciplinary voices in learning disabilities and remedial education.* Society for Learning Disabilities and Remedial Education. Austin, TX: Pro-Ed.

Sigel, I. (1960). The application of projective techniques in research with children. In A. I. Ragin & M. R. Haworth (Eds.), *Projective techniques with children.* New York: Grune & Stratton.

Silver, L. B. (1987). *Attention deficit disorders. Booklet for parents.* Summit, NJ: CIBA.

Simon, D. J., & Johnston, J. C. (1987). Working with families: The missing link in behavior disorder interventions. In R. B. Rutherford, Jr., C. M. Nelson, & S. R. Forness (Eds.), *Severe behavior disorders of children and youth.* Boston: Little, Brown.

Simpson, R. L. (1988). Needs of parents whose children have learning and behavior problems. *Behavioral Disorders, 14,* 40–47.

Simpson, R. L. (1990). *Conferencing parents of exceptional children.* Austin, TX: Pro-Ed.

Simpson, R. L., & Myles, G. S. (in press-a). Effectiveness of facilitated communication with children and youth with autism. *Journal of Special Education.*

Simpson, R. L., & Myles, B. S. (in press-b). Facilitated communication and children and youth with disabilities: An enigma in search of a perspective. *Journal of Special Education.*

Simpson, R. L., & Regan, M. (1988). *Management of autistic behavior.* Austin, TX: Pro-Ed.

Simpson, R. L., & Webber, J. (1991). Parents and families of children with autism. In M. J. Fine (Ed.), *Collaboration with parents of exceptional children.* (pp. 239–256). Brandon, VT: Clinical Psychology Press.

Skinner, B. F. (1953). *Science and human behavior.* New York: Macmillan.

Smith, C. R., Wood, F. H., & Grimes, J. (1988). Issues in the identification and placement of behaviorally disordered students. In M. C. Wang, M. C. Reynolds, & H. J. Walberg (Eds), *Handbook of special education: Research and practice* (vol. 2, pp. 95–123). Oxford: Pergamon.

Smith, D. J., Young, K. R., West, R. P., Morgan, D. P., & Rhode, G. (1988). Reducing the disruptive behavior of junior high school students: A classroom self-management procedure. *Behavioral Disorders, 13,* 231–239.

Smith, M. D. (1988). Statement supporting the ASA resolution on the use of aversives. *The Advocate, 20(4),* 10–11.

Smith, M. L., & Glass, G. V. (1977). Meta-analysis of psychotherapy outcome studies. *American Psychologist, 32,* 752–760.

Smith, S. W., Siegel, E. M., O'Connor, A. M., & Thomas, S. B. (1994). Effects of cognitive-behavioral training on angry behavior and aggression of three elementary-aged students. *Behavioral Disorders, 19,* 126–135.

Solyom, I., Beck, P., Solyom, C., & Hugel, R. (1974). Some etiological factors in phobic neurosis. *Canadian Psychiatry Association Journal, 19,* 69–78.

Spergel, I. (1990). *National youth gang suppression and intervention research: Problem response.* Washington, DC: Office of Juvenile Justice and Delinquency Prevention.

Spergel, I. (1993). *Comprehensive strategy for serious and chronic offenders.* Washington, DC: Office of Juvenile Justice and Delinquency Prevention.

Sprague, G. R., & Horner, R. H. (1984). The effects of single instance, multiple instance, and general case training on a generalized vending machine use by moderately and severely handicapped students. *Journal of Applied Behavior Analysis, 17,* 273–278.

Spring, C., & Sandoval, J. (1976). Food additives and hyperkinesis: A critical evaluation of the evidence. *Journal of Learning Disabilities, 9,* 560–569.

Stainback, S., & Stainback, W. (1980). *Educating children with severe maladaptive behaviors.* New York: Grune & Stratton.

Stainback, W., & Stainback, S. (1991). A rationale for integration and restructuring: A synopsis. In J. W. Lloyd, N. N. Singh, & A. C. Repp (Eds.), *The regular education initiative: Alternative perspectives on concepts, issues, and models* (pp. 226–239). Sycamore, IL: Sycamore.

Stark, K. D., Humphrey, L. L., Crook, K., & Lewis, K. (1990). Perceived family environments of depressed and anxious children: Child's and maternal figure's perspectives. *Journal of Abnormal Child Psychology, 18,* 527–547.

Stark, K. D., Humphrey, L. L., Laurent, J. L., Livingston, R., & Christopher, J. C. (1993). Cognitive, behavioral, and family factors in the differentiation of depressive and anxiety disorders during childhood. *Journal of Consulting and Clinical Child Psychology, 61,* 878–886.

Stark, K. D., Rouse, L. W., & Livingston, R. (1991). Treatment of depression during childhood and adolescence: Cognitive-behavioral procedures for the individual and family. In P. C. Kendall (Ed.), *Child and adolescent therapy: Cognitive-behavioral procedures.* (pp. 165–206). New York: Guilford.

Stein, A. H., & Freidrich, L. K. (1972). Television content and young children's behavior. In J. P. Murray, E. A. Rubinstein, & G. A. Comstock (Eds.), *The battered child.* Chicago: University of Chicago Press.

Stein, A. H., & Freidrich, L. K. (1975). Impact of television on children and youth. In E. M. Hetherington (Ed.) *Review of Child Development Research.* Chicago: University of Chicago Press.

Stephens, T. M. (1977). *Teaching skills to children with learning and behavior disorders.* Columbus, OH: Merrill.

Stephens, T. M. (1978). *Social skills in the classroom.* Columbus, OH: Cedars Press.

Stevens-Long, J. (1973). The effects of behavioral context on some aspects of adult disciplinary practice and affect. *Child Development, 44,* 476–484.

Still, G. F. (1902). The Coulstonian lectures on some abnormal physical conditions in children. *Lancet, 1,* 1163–1168.

Stokes, T. F., & Baer, D. M. (1977). An implicit technology of generalization. *Journal of Applied Behavior Analysis, 10,* 349–368.

Strain, P. S., Cooke, T. P., & Appolloni, T. (1976). *Teaching exceptional children: Assessing and modifying social behavior.* New York: Academic Press.

Strain, P. S., Kerr, M. M., & Ragland, E. U. (1979). Effects of peer-mediated social initiations and prompting/reinforcement procedures in social behavior of autistic children. *Journal of Autism and Developmental Disorders, 9,* 41–54.

Strain, P. S., Young, C. C., & Horowitz, J. (1981). Generalized behavior change during oppositional child training: An examination of child and family demographic variables. *Behavior Modification, 5,* 15–26.

Strauss, A. A., & Lehtinen, L. E. (1947). *Psychopathology and education of the brain-injured child.* New York: Grune & Stratton.

Strauss, C. C. (1987). Anxiety. In M. Hersen & V. B. Van Hasselt (Eds.) *Behavior therapy with children and adolescents.* (pp. 109–136). New York: Wiley.

Strober, S., & Carlson, G. (1982). Bipolar illness in adolescents with major depression. *Archives of General Psychiatry, 39,* 549–555.

Strobino, D. (1987). Health and medical consequences. In C. Hayes, & S. Hofferth (Eds.), *Risking the future: Adolescence, sexuality, pregnancy, and childbearing* (pp. 107–123). Washington, DC: National Academy Press.

Stroul, B. A., & Friedman, R. M. (1986). *A system of care for severely emotionally disturbed children and youth.* Washington, DC: Georgetown University Child Development Center, CASSP Technical Assistance Center.

Strub, R. L., & Black, F. W. (1977). *The mental status examination in neurology.* Philadelphia: F. A. Davis.

Sue, S. (1988). Sociocultural issues in the assessment and classroom teaching of language minority students. *Cross-cultural Special Education Series* (Vol.3). Sacramento, CA: California State Department of Education.

Sugai, G. (1988). *Educational assessment of the culturally diverse and behaviorally disordered student: An examination of critical effect.* Paper presented at the Ethnic and Multicultural Symposium, Dallas, TX. ERIC Document Reproduction Service No. ED 2298706.

Sugai, G. (1992). Educational assessment of the culturally diverse and behavior disordered student: An examination of critical effect. In A. A. Ortiz & B. A. Ramirez (Eds.), *Schools and the culturally diverse exceptional student: Promising practices and future directions* (pp. 63–75). Reston, VA: Council for Exceptional Children.

Sullivan, R. C. (1976). The role of the parent. In M. A. Thomas (Ed.), *Hey, don't forget about me!* Reston, VA: The Council for Exceptional Children.

Sullivan, R. C. (1979). The burnout syndrome. *Journal of Autism and Developmental Disorders, 1,* 113–114.

Summitt, R. (1983). The child sexual abuse accommodation syndrome. *Child Abuse and Neglect, 7,* 177–193.

Szurek, S. (1956). Childhood schizophrenia symposium: Psychotic episodes and psychotic maldevelopment. *American Journal of Orthopsychiatry, 25,* 519.

Tahmisian, J. A., & McReynolds, W. T. (1971). Use of parents as behavioral engineers in the treatment of a school phobic girl. *Journal of Counseling Psychology, 18,* 225–228.

Tallmadge, J. & Barkley, R. A. (1983). The interactions of hyperactive and normal boys with their fathers and mothers. *Journal of Abnormal Child Psychology, 11,* 565–580.

Tanner, B. A., & Zeiler, M. (1975). Punishment of self-injurious behavior using aromatic ammonia as the aversive stimulus. *Journal of Applied Behavior Analysis, 8,* 53–57.

TASH Newsletter (1993, October). *Issue watch: Education reform—Senate subtext is inclusion.* pp. 10–12.

Tate, B. G., & Baroff, G. S. (1966). Aversive control of self-injurious behavior in a psychotic boy. *Behavior Research and Therapy, 4,* 281–287.

Texas Juvenile Probation Commission. (1993). *Eleventh annual report of the Texas Juvenile Probation Commission.* Austin, TX: Author.

Thoma, S., Rest, J., & Barnett, R. (1986). In J. Rest (Ed.), *Moral development: Advances in research and theory.* New York: Praeger.

Thomas, A., & Chess, S. (1977). *Temperament and development.* New York: Brunner/Mazel.

Thomas, A., Chess, S., & Birch, H. (1969). *Temperament and behavior disorders in children.* New York: New York University Press.

Thompson, J. M., & Sones, R. A. (1973). *Education Apperception Test.* Los Angeles: Western Psychological Services.

Thorndike, E. L. (1932). *The fundamentals of learning.* New York: Teacher's College.

Thurlow, M. L., & Ysseldyke, J. E. (1980). *Factors influential on the psychoeducational decisions reached by teams of educators* (Research Report No. 25). Minneapolis: University of Minnesota Institute for Research on Learning Disabilities.

Tievsky, D. L. (1988). Homosexual clients and homophobic social workers. *Journal of Independent Social Work, 2,* 51–62.

Toth, M. K. (1990). *Understanding and treating conduct disorders.* Austin, TX: Pro-Ed.

Towns, P. (1981). *Educating disturbed adolescents: Theory and practice.* New York: Grune & Stratton.

Tramontana, M. G. (1980). Critical review of research on psychotherapy outcome with adolescents: 1967–1977. *Psychological Bulletin, 88,* 429–450.

Trent, S. (1989). Much to do about nothing: A clarification of issues on the Regular Education Initiative. *Journal of Learning Disabilities, 22,* 23–25.

Trevor, W. (March 1975). *Teacher discrimination and self-fulfilling prophecies.* Paper presented at the annual meeting of the American Educational Research Association.

Trippe, M. (1966). *Educational therapy.* Seattle, WA: Special Child Publications.

Tsai, M., Feldman-Summers, S., & Edgar, M. (1979). Childhood molestation: Variables related to differential impacts on psychosexual functioning in adult women. *Journal of Abnormal Psychology, 88,* 407–417.

Tsai, M., & Wagner, N. N. (1978). Therapy groups for women sexually molested as children. *Archives of Sexual Behavior, 7,* 407–417.

Tucker, D. M. (1988). Neuropsychological mechanisms of affective self-regulation. In M. Kinsbourne (Ed.), *Cerebral hemisphere function in depression.* Washington, DC: American Psychiatric Press.

Tucker, J. A. (1985). Curriculum-based assessment: An introduction. *Exceptional Children, 52,* 199–204.

Tupper, D. E. (1987). *Soft neurological signs.* Orlando: Grune & Stratton.

Turner, S. M., Beidel, D. C., & Costello, A. (1987). Psychopathology in the offspring of anxiety disorders patients. *Journal of Consulting and Clinical Psychology, 55,* 229–235.

U.S. Bureau of the Census (1990). *Statistical abstracts of the United States 1990* (110th ed.), Washington, DC: U.S. Government Printing Office.

U.S. Department of Education (1986). *Eighth annual report to Congress on implementation of the Education of the Handicapped Act, Vol. I,* Washington, DC: Author.

U.S. Department of Education, Office of Special Education Programs (1993). *Fifteenth annual report to Congress on the implementation of the Individuals with Disabilities Act.* Washington, DC: Author.

U.S. News and World Report (1993, December 13). *Separate and unequal,* pp. 46–60.

Vaac, N. A., & Kirst, N. (1977). Emotionally disturbed children and regular classroom teachers. *Elementary School Journal, 77,* 309–317.

van Baar, A. L. (1990). Development of infants of drug dependent mothers. *Journal of Child Psychology and Psychiatry, 31,* 911–920.

Van Hasselt, V., Hersen, M., Bellack, A. S., Rosenblum, N., & Lamparski, D. (1979). Tripartite assessment of the effects of systematic desensitization in a multi-phobic child: An experimental analysis. *Journal of Behavior Therapy and Experimental Psychiatry, 10,* 51–56.

Van Hasselt, V. B., Hersen, M., Whitehill, M. D., & Bellack, A. S. (1979). Social skills assessment and training for children: An evaluative review. *Behavior Research and Therapy, 17,* 413–437.

Vincent, J. P., Williams, B. J., Harris, G. E., & Duval, G. C. (1981). Classroom observations of hyperactive children: A multiple validation study. In K. D. Gadow & J. Looney (Eds.), *Psychological aspects of drug treatment for hyperactivity* (pp. 207–248). Boulder, CO: Westview Press.

Vincent, L. J., Poulsen, M. K., Cole, C. K., Woodruff, G., & Griffith, D. R. (1991). *Born substance exposed, educationally vulnerable.* Reston, VA: Council for Exceptional Children, ERIC/OSEP Special Project.

Wagner, M. (1991, September). *Drop outs with disabilities: What do we know? What can we do?* Menlo Park: SRI International.

Wahler, R. G. (1976). Deviant child behavior within the family: Developmental speculations and behavior change strategies. In H. Leintenberg (Ed.), *Handbook of behavior modification and behavior therapy.* Englewood Cliffs, NJ: Prentice Hall.

Walker, H. M. (1979). *The acting-out child: Coping with classroom disruption.* Boston: Allyn & Bacon.

Walker, H. M., & Buckley, N. K. (1973). Teacher attention to appropriate and inappropriate classroom behavior: An individual case study. *Focos on Exceptional Children, 5,* 5–11.

Walker, H. M., & Buckley, N. K. (1974). *Token reinforcement techniques: Classroom applications for the hard to teach child.* Eugene, OR: E-B Press.

Walker, H. M., Colvin, G., & Ramsey, E. (1994). *Antisocial behavior in school: Strategies for practitioners.* Pacific Grove, CA: Brooks-Cole.

Walker, H. M., McConnell, S., Holmes, D., Todis, B., Walker, J., & Golden, N. (1983). *The Walker Social Skills Curriculum: The ACCEPTS Program.* Austin, TX: Pro-Ed.

Walker, H. M., & Rankin, R. (1980). *Assessment for Integration into Mainstream Settings (AIMS).* Eugene, OR: Social Behavior Survival Project, Center on Human Development.

Walker, H. M., Severson, H., Stiller, B., Williams, G., Haring, N., Shinn, M., & Todis, B. (1988). Systematic screening of pupils in the elementary age range at risk for behavior disorders: Development and trial testing of a multiple gating model. *Remedial and Special Education, 9(3),* 8–14.

Walker, H. M., Todis, B., Holmes, D., & Horton, G. (1988). *The ACCESS program.* Austin, TX: Pro-Ed.

Walker, J. E., & Shea, T. M. (1980). *Behavior modification: A practical approach for educators* (2nd ed.). St. Louis: C. V. Mosby.

Wallack, L., & Corbett, K. (1990). Illicit drug, tobacco, and alcohol use among youth: *Trends and promising approaches in prevention. Youth and drugs: Society's mixed messages* (pp. 5–29). (OSAP Monograph No. 6). Washington, DC: U.S. Department of Health and Human Services. (DHHS Publication No. ADM 90-90-1689).

Wang, M. C., & Walberg, H. J. (1988). Four fallacies of segregationism. *Exceptional Children, 55,* 128–137.

Warren, J. (1990, June 24). Zinc helps anorexics, study shows. Knight-Ridder News Service. *Austin American Statesman,* D4.

Waterman, J. (1986). Overview of treatment issues. In K. MacFarlane & J. Waterman (Eds.), *Sexual abuse of young children: Evaluation and treatment.* New York: Guilford Press.

Waterman, J., & Lusk, R. (1986). Scope of the problem. In K. MacFarlane & J. Waterman (Eds.), *Sexual abuse of young children: Evaluation and treatment.* New York: Guilford Press.

Watson, J. B., & Raynor, R. (1920). Conditioned emotional reactions. *Journal of Experimental Psychology, 3,* 1–14.

Webber, J. (1993, August). President's message. *Council for Children with Behavioral Disorders Newsletter, 2,* 4.

Webber, J., & Coleman, M. (1988). Using rational-emotive therapy to prevent classroom problems. *Teaching Exceptional Children, 21* (1), 32–35.

Webber, J., & Gilliam, J. E. (1981). *Working with parents.* Project S.E.D. Teacher Training Module. Austin, TX: Education Service Center, Region XIII.

Webber, J., Scheuermann, B., McCall, C., & Coleman, M. (1993). Research on self-monitoring as a behavior management technique in special education classrooms: A descriptive review. *Remedial and Special Education, 14,* 38–56.

Wehman, P. (1986). Competitive employment in Virginia. In F. R. Rusch (Ed.), *Competitive employment issues and strategies* (pp. 23–34). Baltimore: Paul H. Brooks.

Wehman, P. & Kregel, J. (1985). A supported work approach to competitive employment of individuals with moderate and severe handicaps. *Journal of the Association for Persons with Severe Handicaps, 10(1),* 3–11.

Wehman, P. & Kregel, J. (1988). Supported competitive employment for individuals with autism and severe retardation: Two case studies. *Focus on Autistic Behavior 3(3),* 1–14.

Weiss, G. & Hechtman, L. T. (1986). *Hyperactive children grown up: Empirical findings and theoretical considerations.* New York: Guilford Press.

Welch, M. (1994). Ecological assessment: A collaborative approach to planning instructional interventions. *Intervention in School and Clinic, 29,* 160–164.

Wells, K. C., Forehand, R. & Griest, D. L. (1980). Generality of treatment effects from treated to untreated behaviors resulting from a parent training program. *Journal of Clinical Child Psychology, 9,* 217–219.

Wells, K. C., & Vitulano, L. A. (1984). Anxiety disorders in childhood. In S. M. Turner (Ed.), *Behavioral theories and treatment of anxiety* (pp. 413–433). New York: Plenum.

Wender, P. H. (1971). *Minimal brain dysfunction in children.* New York: Wiley.

Werry, J., & Quay, H. C. (1971). The prevalence of behavior symptoms in younger elementary school children. *American Journal of Orthopsychiatry, 41,* 136–143.

West, J. F. (1990). *Analysis of classroom and instructional demands.* Austin, TX: Institute for Learning and Development.

West, J. F., & Idol, L. (1987). School consultation (Part I): An interdisciplinary perspective on theory, models, and research. *Journal of Learning Disabilities, 20,* 388–408.

Whalen, C. K. & Henker, B. (1980). The social ecology of psychostimulant treatment: A model for conceptual and empirical analysis. In C. K. Whalen & B. Henker, (Eds.), *Hyperactive children: The social ecology of identification and treatment.* New York: Academic Press.

Whalen, C. K., Henker, B., Collins, B. E., McAulliffe, S., & Vaux, A. (1979). Peer interaction in a structured communication task: Comparisons of normal and hyperactive boys and of methylphenidate (Ritalin) effects. *Child Development, 50,* 388–401.

Wickman, E. K. (1928). *Children's behavior and teachers' attitudes.* New York: Commonwealth Fund.

Will, M. C. (1986). Educating children with learning problems: A shared responsibility. *Exceptional Children, 52,* 411–415.

Wilms, W. (1984). Vocational education and job success: The employer's view. *Phi Delta Kappan, 65,* 347–350.

Winn, C. (1969). Adolescent suicidal behavior and hallucinations. In G. Caplan & S. Lebovici (Eds.), *Adolescence: Psychosocial perspectives.* New York: Basic Books.

Winokur, G., Clayton, P. J., & Reich, J. (1984). *Manic-depressive illness.* St. Louis, MO: Mosby.

Wolf, M. Risley, T., & Mees, H. (1964). Application of operant conditioning procedures to the behavior problems of an autistic child. *Behavior Research and Therapy, 1,* 305–312.

Wolpe, J. (1958). *Psychotherapy by reciprocal inhibition.* Stanford, CA: Stanford University Press.

Wood, F. H. (1979). Defining disturbing, disordered, and disturbed behavior. In F. H. Wood & K. C. Lakin (Eds.), *Disturbing, disordered or disturbed? Perspectives on the definition of problem behavior in educational settings.* Minneapolis: Advanced Training Institute, University of Minnesota.

Wood, F. H., Cheney, C. O., Cline, D. H., Sampson, K., Smith, C. R., & Guetzloe, E. C. (1991). *Conduct disorders and social maladjustments: Policies, politics, and programming.* Reston, VA: Council for Exceptional Children.

Wood, M. M. (1975). (Ed), *Developmental therapy.* Baltimore: University Park Press.

Wood, M. M., Combs, C., Gunn, A., & Weller, D. (1986). *Developmental therapy in the classroom,* (2nd ed.), Austin, TX: Pro-Ed.

Wood, M. M., & Swan, W. W. (1978). A developmental approach to educating the disturbed young child. *Behavioral Disorders, 3,* 197–209.

Workman, E. A. (1982). *Teaching behavioral self-control to students.* Austin, TX: Pro-Ed.

Workman, E. A., & Hector, M. (1978). Behavior self-control in classroom settings: A review of the literature. *Journal of School Psychology, 16,* 227–136.

Workman, E. A., Helton, G. B., & Watson, P. J. (1982). Self-monitoring effects in a four year old child: An ecological behavior analysis. *Journal of School Psychology, 20,* 57–64.

Wright, J. H., & Beck, A. T. (1983). Cognitive therapy of depression: Theory and practice. *Hospital and Community Psychiatry, 34,* 1119–1127.

Yates, A. J. (1970). *Behavior therapy.* New York: Wiley.

Yee, L. Y. (1988). Asian children, *Teaching Exceptional Children 20(4),* 49–50.

Yell, M. (1990). The use of corporal punishment, suspension, expulsion, and timeout with behavior disordered students in public schools: Legal considerations. *Behavioral Disorders, 15,* 100–109.

Yell, M. L. (1989). Honig vs. Doe: The suspension and expulsion of handicapped students. *Exceptional Children, 56,* 60–69.

Young, J. A., & Wincze, J. P. (1974). The effects of the reinforcement of compatible and incompatible alternative behaviors on the self-injurious and related behaviors of a profoundly retarded female adult. *Behavior Therapy, 5,* 614–623.

Young, K. R., & West, R. P. (1984). *Parent training: Social skills manual.* Logan: Utah State University.

Young, T. A., Pappenfort, D. M., & Marlow, C. R. (1983). *Residential group care, 1966 and 1981: Facilities for children and youth with special problems and needs.* Preliminary Report of Selected Findings from the National Survey of Residential Group Facilities. Chicago: School of Social Service Administration, University of Chicago.

Ysseldyke, J. E., & Algozzine, B. (1982). *Critical issues in special and remedial education.* Boston: Houghton Mifflin.

Ysseldyke, J. E., & Christenson, S. L. (1987). *The Instructional Environment Scale.* Austin, TX: Pro-Ed.

Zabel, M. (1986). Timeout use with behaviorally disordered students. *Behavioral Disorders, 12,* 15–21.

Zabin, L. S., Hirsch, M. B., Streett, R., Emerson, M. R., Smith, M., Hardy, J. B., & King, T. M. (1988). The Baltimore pregnancy prevention program for urban teenagers: I. How did it work? *Family Planning Perspectives, 20,* 182–187.

Zaragosa, N., Vaughn, S., & McIntosh, R. (1991). Social skills intervention and children with behavior problems: A review. *Behavioral Disorders 16,* 260–275.

Zigmond, N., Kerr, M. M., Brown, G., & Harris, A. L. (1984). *School survival skills in secondary school age education students.* Paper presented at the annual meeting of the American Educational Research Association, Baton Rouge, LA.

Zigmond, N., & Miller, S. E. (1986). Assessment for instructional planning. *Exceptional Children, 52,* 501–509.

Zionts, P. (1980). The relationship of five affective variables with regard to inner-city juvenile delinquents and inner-city non-delinquents and a national norm group: Implications for school curriculum and placement. In R. B. Rutherford, Jr., A. G. Prieto, and J. E. McGlothlin (Eds.) *Severe behavior disorders of children and youth.* Reston, VA: Council for Children with Behavioral Disorders.

Zionts, P. (1985). *Teaching disturbed and disturbing students.* Austin, TX: Pro-Ed.

Index

ABC model, in rational-emotive therapy, 90
Abikoff, H., 138, 143, 146
Abuse:
  sexual:
    case studies in, 318
    defined, 312–313
    dynamics of, 314
    effects of, 314–316
    incidence of, 312–313
    mediating factors in, 316
    perpetrators of, 313–314
    teaching implications of, 317–319
    treatment of, 316
    victims of, 313–314
  substance:
    case studies in, 250, 263
    characteristics of, 247–248
    in depression, 112
    education in, 248–251
    prevalence of, 244–247
    risk factors in, 247–248
Academic domain, 169–170
Academic functioning:
  in attention-deficit hyperactivity, 138
  in emotional/behavioral disorders, 28–29
ACCEPTS curriculum, 186–188
ACCESS curriculum, 175
Achenbach, T.M., 25–26, 71, 80, 165, 238
Acquired immune deficiency syndrome (AIDS), 241
Adolescence:
  counseling in, 262–264
  developmental changes in:
    cognitive, 235

personal and social, 236–238
    physical, 234–235
  disorders in:
    eating, 256–257
    emotional/behavioral, 238–239
  interventions in:
    behavioral, 261–262
    career education as, 258–259
  school issues in:
    dropping out as, 239–240
    gay and lesbian, 242–243
    sex-related, 240–244
    suicide in, 254–256
Advocacy roles, 327–328
Affective/emotional curriculum, 171–172, 183–184
Aggression (*see also* Conduct disorders)
  case studies in, 152–153
  criteria for, 148
  etiology of, 150–156
  factors in, 154–156
  types of, 154
Aggression Replacement Training curriculum, 190
AIDS (acquired immune deficiency syndrome), 241
Alcohol:
  adolescent abuse of, 245–246
  fetal exposure to, 307–308
Algozzine, B., 29, 30, 38–39, 96, 165, 177, 216
Allergies, in attention deficit hyperactivity disorder, 47
American Psychiatric Association, 20, 108–109, 121, 137, 148, 149, 155, 156, 270, 273, 276, 296
Americans with Disabilities Act, 12

Amphetamine abuse, 246–247
Analysis of Classroom and Instructional Demands (ACID Test), 97
Anhedonia, in depression, 112
Anorexia:
  in adolescence, 256
  in depression, 112
Antidepressants, 51, 113, 117
Antipsychotics, 50–51
Antisocial behavior (*see* Conduct disorders)
Anxiety disorders:
  in child sexual abuse, 315
  depression and, 112, 123
  etiology of, 123–125
  generalized, 120–121
  interventions in, 125–129
  in neo-Freudian theory, 56–57
  phobias as, 121–122
  prevalence of, 120–122
  symptoms of, 122–123
Apter, S.J., 195, 196, 223–224, 228
Assessment:
  case studies in, 178–181
  curriculum-based, 173–174
  defined, 164
  instructional objectives in, 172–176
  techniques in:
    checklists as, 174–175
    criterion-referenced testing as, 173
    error analysis as, 174
    observation as, 172–173
Attention-deficit hyperactivity:
  assessment in, 139–140
  brain-related factors in, 140–141
  characteristics of, 137–139
  conditions related to, 143

defined, 136–137
environmental agents in, 141–142
interventions in:
  behavior management as, 145–146
  cognitive-behavioral, 146
  medications as, 144–145
predisposing factors in, 142
teaching implications of, 146–147
treatments for, 146
At the Schoolhouse Door, 14–15
Atwater, E., 234, 235, 236–237
Authoritarian parenting, 197
Autism:
  biophysical model of, 45, 47
  case studies in, 274
  defined, 269–273
  etiology of, 270–271
  learning in, 271–273
  psychogenic theory of, 269–270
Autonomy:
  in adolescence, 236
  in healthy personality, 59
Aversives, in self-injurious behavior, 290

Bandura, A., 79, 123, 126, 151
Barkley, R.A., 137, 142, 144
Beck, A.T., 108, 110, 114–115, 116, 123–124
Beers, Clifford, 7
Behavior(s):
  in attention-deficit hyperactivity, 145–146
  decreasing, 84–88
  increasing, 82–84
  rating of, 80
  recording of, 80–81
  in schizophrenia, 275
  self-stimulatory, 272, 289–292
  in sexual abuse, 315
Behavioral model (*see* Models, behavioral)
Behavior Evaluation Scale–2 (BES–2), 35
Behavior Problem Checklist, 238–239
Behavior Rating Profile–2 (BRP–2), 97
Bender, Lauretta, 8
Bettelheim, Bruno, 8
Biophysical model (*see* Models, biophysical)
Bipolar depression, 109
Bower, E.M., 10, 17, 21, 27, 28, 29, 79
Brain-related factors, in attention-deficit hyperactivity, 140–141
Brown, L.L., 19, 64–65, 97
Bulimia:
  in adolescence, 257
  in depression, 112

Cantwell, D.P., 108, 110, 111, 117, 142
Career education, 258–259
Carlson, G.A., 108, 110, 111, 117
Cascade Model, of educational services, 211–215
Case studies:
  in abuse:
    sexual, 318
    substance, 250, 263, 309
  in assessment, 178–181
  in autism, 274
  in conduct disorders, 150, 152–153
  in contingency contracting, 85
  in depression, 118–119
  in ecosystems, 102
  in emotional/behavioral disorders, 30–31, 32, 34
  in facilitated communication, 294–295
  in family systems, 200–202
  in juvenile offenders, 222, 253
  in mental health services, 226
  in severe behavior disorders, 288
Chasnoff, I.J., 306, 307, 311
Checklists:
  in assessment, 174–175
  in behavioral model, 80
  in parent conferences, 210–211
Child and Adolescent Service System Programs (CASSP), 15, 224, 322
Child Behavior Checklist, 71, 80
Children's Appperception Test (CAT), 61, 165
Children's Behavior and Teachers' Attitudes, 7–8
Child sexual abuse (*see* Abuse, sexual)
Chronicity, of emotional/behavioral disorders, 27
Classrooms:
  as ecosystem, 94–95, 98
  engineered, 10–11
Clozapine, 51
Cocaine abuse, 246
Coercion hypothesis, of conduct disorders, 150–151
Cognitive-behavioral model (*see* Models, cognitive-behavioral)
Cognition (*see also* Skills, cognitive)
  adolescent changes in, 235
  in child sexual abuse, 315
  distortions of, 114–115
  therapy of, in anxiety, 124, 127
Coleman, M.C., 30, 36, 64–65, 90, 92, 177, 197, 252, 262
Compensatory approach, to academic curriculum, 169–170

Conditioning:
  in anxiety, 123, 127
  in behavioral model, 77–78
  in school phobia, 128
Conflict in the Classroom, 11
Conduct disorders (*see also* Aggression)
  in attention-deficit hyperactivity, 143, 156
  case studies in, 150, 152–153
  conditions related to, 156
  defined, 26, 147–150
  etiology of, 150–156
  interventions in:
    family therapy as, 158
    parent training as, 157–158
  learning disorders in, 156
  parent involvement in, 158–159
  prevalence of, 147–150
  teaching implications of, 160
Conferencing skills, for parents, 207–211
Consulting services, 215, 225–227
Contingency contracting, 82–85
Cooperation, interagency, 14–15
Corporal punishment, 87
Correctional system, 218–221
Counseling:
  for adolescents, 262–264
  for parents, 206–207
Counterconditioning, in anxiety, 126
Court rulings:
  on behavioral disorders, 11–12
  on placement and inclusion, 321–322
Crack cocaine abuse, 246
Criterion-referenced testing, 173
Curriculum:
  academic, 169–170
  affective/emotional, 171–172, 183–184
  assessment based on, 173–174
  comprehensive, 188–190
  instructional objectives of, 172–176
  selection of, 188
  in severe behavioral disorders, 279–282
  in social competence, 170–172, 182–188, 191–192
  in substance abuse, 250
Curriculum for Children's Effective Peer and Teacher Skills (ACCEPTS), 186–188
Cylert, in attention-deficit hyperactivity, 144

Daniel R.R. v. *State Board of Education*, 321–322
Day schools, 212–214
Defense mechanisms, 55

Delinquency (*see* Conduct disorders)
Delivery of services, 14
Delusions, in schizophrenia, 275
Demonology, 2
Depression:
    anxiety and, 112, 123
    case studies in, 118–119
    characteristics of, 110–111
    in child sexual abuse, 315
    conditions related to, 111–112
    defined, 108–110
    interventions in, 116–119
    models of:
        behavioral, 114
        biophysical, 113
        cognitive, 114–115
        comprehensive, 115
        psychodynamic, 113
    predisposing factors in, 115
    prevalence of, 108–110
    symptoms of, 110–111
    teaching implications of, 119
Desensitization, systematic, 126, 129
Destruction of property, 148
*Developing Understanding of Self
    and Others—Revised*, 183–184
Development:
    in adolescence, 234–238
    disorders of:
        in attention-deficit hyperactiv-
            ity, 141
        pervasive, 45
        psychosexual, 55–56
Developmental Therapy curriculum,
    190
*Devereux Scales of Mental Disor-
    ders (DSMD)*, 80–81
Deviance (*see* Behavior disorders)
Dexedrine, in attention-deficit hyper-
    activity, 144
Diagnostic and Statistical Manual,
    20–21, 270
Differential reinforcement, 291
Direct response reinforcement, 284
Discrete trial format, in autism, 285
Disturbed Child, The, 10
Dix, Dorothea, 6
Dropping out, 239–240
Drug abuse (*see* Abuse, substance)
Dysthymic disorder, 108–109

Eating disorders, 256–257
Ecological model (*see* Models, eco-
    logical)
Ecosystems, 93–103
Edelbrock, C.S., 25–26, 71, 238
Educating Emotionally Disturbed
    Children, 10
Education Appreception Test (EAT),
    61

Education of All Handicapped Chil-
    dren Act, 12, 23–25
Ego, in psychoanalytic theory, 55
Emotional/behavioral disorders (*see
    also* Behavior disorders)
    in adolescence, 238–239
    advocacy roles in, 327–328
    case studies in, 30–31, 32, 34
    concepts of, 18–22
    defined, 22–25
    dimensions of, 26–28
    factors of, 25–26
    identification of:
        instruments for, 33–36
        multicultural considerations in,
            37–38
        procedures in, 31–33
        screening in, 38
        teacher role in, 38–40
        team decision making in, 36–37
    in juvenile offenders, 251–252
    prevalence of, 29–31
    sex ratio of, 29–31
    school policy and, 322–323
    school reform and, 326–328
    sociological parameters of, 21–22
Emotionally disturbed, defined, 21
Emotions, in human behavior, 3
Engineered classroom, 10–11
Environmental curriculum, 279–280
Erikson, Erik, 57
Error analysis, 174
Evaluation (*see* Assessment)
Exemplary Center for Reading In-
    struction, 178
Exposure, substance (*see* Substance
    exposure)
Expulsion, of behavior disordered
    students, 319–320
Externalizing disorders:
    in adolescence, 238–239
    attention-deficit hyperactivity as,
        136–147
    of conduct, 147–160
    emotional/behavioral, 25–26
    rating of, 80

Facilitated communication, 294–295
Family system (*see* Systems,
    family)
Fear (*see* Anxiety disorders)
Federal guidelines, in emotional/be-
    havioral disorders, 33
Feingold, B.F., 47, 50, 52
Fenichel, Carl, 8
Fetal alcohol syndrome, 307–308
Formal evaluation, 164
Formal operational thought, 235
Forness, S.R., 28, 50, 112, 144
Freud, Sigmund, 55–56

Fromm, Erich, 56–57
Full inclusion movement, 324–325

Galen, 3
Gangs, 252–254
Gay and lesbian issues, in adoles-
    cence, 242–243
Generalization and maintenance:
    in severe behavior disorders, 286–
        288
    in social skills curriculum, 191–
        192
Generalized anxiety disorder, 120–
    121
Genetic factors:
    in behavior disorders, 45
    in schizophrenia, 275
Gilliam Autism Rating Scale, 270
Gilliam, J.E., 30, 33, 36, 177, 197,
    203, 251, 252
Greek views, of behavioral disor-
    ders, 2–3
Greer v. *Rome City School District*,
    321–322
Group contingency reinforcement
    systems, 261
Group hysteria, 4

Haldol, 50
Hallucinations, 275
Halstead-Reitan Battery, 49–50
Haring, N.G., 44, 171, 215
Hewett, Frank, 10–11, 18–19, 98
Hobbs, Nicholas, 10, 19, 20, 68, 100,
    196, 223, 224
Home-based reinforcement systems,
    261
Home ecosystem, 95–96, 98–101
Homosexuality, 242–243
Honig v. *Doe*, 320
Horney, Karen, 56–57
Hospital of St. Mary of Bethlehem,
    4
Hospitals:
    educational services in, 212
    mental, 4–5
How Children Learn, 67
Howe, Samuel Gridley, 6
Howell, K.W., 165, 170, 171, 176
Human figure drawings, 62–63
Humanism, 57–59, 67
Hyperactivity (*see* Attention-deficit
    hyperactivity)

Id, in psychoanalytic theory, 55
Imaginary audience, in adolescence,
    236
Imipramine, in depression, 51, 117
Impulsivity:
    in aggression, 154

in attention-deficit hyperactivity, 138
defined, 136
Inadequacy-immaturity, defined, 26
Inappropriate affect, in schizophrenia, 274
Inattention, defined, 136
Incest, 313–314
Inclusion, legal issues in, 321–322
Independent living, programming in, 294–299
Index of Personality Characteristics, 64–65
Individualized education plan, 176–177, 180–181
Individuals with Disabilities Education Act, 12, 23–25, 321
In-school suspension, 87
Instinct, 3
Institutionalization, in severe behavior disorders, 301
Instruction:
    individualized education plan in, 176–177, 180–181
    methods of, 177–183
Instructional Environment Scale, The (TIPS), 97
Intelligence:
    in autism, 273
    in emotional/behavioral disorders, 28–29
Interagency cooperation, 14–15
Internalizing disorders:
    in adolescence, 238–239
    anxiety as, 119–129
    depression as, 108–119
    emotional/behavioral, 25–26
    rating of, 80
    social withdrawal as, 110–111, 129–131
Interpersonal relations, 59, 138–139
Interviewing, life space, 69–70
Involvement, parent (*see* Parents, involvement of)
Itard, Jean, 5

Juvenile justice/correctional system, 218–221, 322–323
Juvenile offenders, emotional/behavioral disorders in, 251–252

Kanner, L., 6, 7, 27, 268, 270, 272, 273, 300
Kaplan, J.S., 171, 176
Kashani, J.H., 110, 111, 112, 113
Kazdin, A.E., 71, 84, 110, 114, 125, 149, 154, 158, 160
Koegel, R.L., 11, 282, 286, 287, 289

Language skills (*see* Communication/language skills)
Latency period, 55
League School (New York), 8
Learning, social (*see* Social learning)
Learning:
    disorders of:
        in attention-deficit hyperactivity, 143
        in autism, 271–273
        conduct disorders in, 156
    social:
        in aggression, 151–153
        in behavior model, 78–79
        in school phobia, 128
Legislation, in behavioral disorders, 11–12
Liaison, teacher as, 227–228
Life space interviewing, 69–70
"Little Albert," in classical conditioning experiments, 77
Long, N.J., 11, 67, 70
Lovaas, O.I., 11, 282–283, 286, 290
Luria Neuropsychological Investigation, 50

Magic Circle, 183
Mainstreaming, 99, 323
Maintenance (*see* Generalization and maintenance)
Manic depressive disorder, 108–109
Marijuana abuse, in adolescence, 246
Maslow, Abraham, 57–59, 71
Maternal depression, 115
Medical intervention:
    in attention-deficit hyperactivity, 144–145
    in depression, 116–117
Mental health system, 221–223
Metabolic factors, 46–47
Methylphenidate, in attention-deficit hyperactivity, 144
Milieu, therapeutic, 67–69
Mills v. *Board of Education of District of Columbia*, 11–12
Mind That Found Itself, A (Beers), 7
Minimal brain injury (*see* Attention-deficit hyperactivity)
Modeling:
    in anxiety, 126–127
    in behaviorism, 78–79
Model programs, in behavior disorder therapy, 7–11
Models
    behavioral:
        application of, 81–88
        defined, 76
        of depression, 114
        etiology in, 77–79
        evaluation in, 79–81

of school phobia, 128
biophysical:
    biochemical factors in, 45–47
    defined, 44
    of depression, 113
    developmental histories in, 48–50
    drug therapy in, 50–51
    genetic factors in, 45
    neurological factors in, 45–47
cognitive-behavioral:
    of aggression, 153
    of attention-deficit hyperactivity, 146
    of depression, 114–115
    rational-emotive therapy in, 90
    reality therapy in, 88–90
    self-management in, 91
ecological:
    application of, 97–103
    defined, 92–93
    etiology in, 93–96
    evaluation in, 96–97
psychodynamic:
    application of, 65–71
    defined, 53–55
    of depression, 113
    etiology in, 55–59
    evaluation in, 60–63
    goal of, 59
    humanistic theory in, 57–59
    neo-Freudian theory in, 56–57
    projective techniques in, 60–63
    psychoanalytic theory in, 55–56
    of school phobia, 127–128
    self-report measures in, 63–65
Montessori, Maria, 67
Morse, W.C., 67, 68, 69, 233
Motivation:
    in autism, 272, 282
    in depression, 110–111
    in engineered classroom, 11
Multicultural considerations, 37–38, 204–205

National Association for Retarded Citizens, 8–9
National Institute of Mental Health, 10, 15, 224, 322
Negative cognitive triad, 114–115
Negative peer perception, 191
Negative reinforcement hypothesis, 289
Negative schemata, 114–115
Nelson, C.M., 84, 192, 221, 229–230
Neo-Freudian theory, 56–57
Neurobehavioral characteristics, of substance exposure, 308–310
Neurological factors, 45–50
Neurotransmitters

in attention-deficit hyperactivity, 141
in behavior disorders, 46
in depression, 113
Nicotine abuse, 246
Nondiscriminatory testing, 33
Nontraditional families, 204–205
Norm-referenced, defined, 164

Oberti v. *Clementon School Board*, 322
Observation techniques, 172–173
Oppositional defiant, as conduct disorder, 148
Organic causes:
in biophysical model, 46
in self-injurious behavior, 289
Overcorrection, 290–291
Overselectivity, 271–272, 283–284

Parents (*see also* Systems, family)
conferencing skills for, 207–211
counseling for, 206–207
involvement of:
in conduct disorders, 157–159
current status of, 14
in ecological model, 98
in emotional/behavioral disorders, 33
strategies for, 201–203
in substance abuse, 249–251
teacher role in, 205–206
styles of, 197–198
support groups for, 206
Peer acceptance, 130
Perinatal outcomes, of substance exposure, 307
Personality:
healthy, 59
histories of, 208
problems of, 26
Pervasive developmental disorder, 45
Phobia, school, 122–129
Physical restraint, 88
Physiological hyperarousal, 112
Piers-Harris Children's Self-Concept Scale, The, 63–64
Pinel, Philippe, 5
Plato, 3
Positive reinforcement hypothesis, 289
Pregnancy, in adolescence, 240–241
Prepare Curriculum, 190
Prereferral intervention, 31–33, 164
Prerequisite skills, in severe behavior disorders, 277
Prevocational training:
model programs in, 259–261
in severe behavior disorders, 279–282, 297–299

Primary reinforcers, 82
Process for In-School Screening of Children with Emotional Handicaps, A, 10
Projective techniques, 60–63, 165
Project Re-ED, 10, 100–101
Prolixin, 50
Prompting, in autism, 285–286
Prozac, in depression, 51, 117
Psychoanalytic theory, 55–56
Psychodynamic hypothesis, in self-injurious behavior, 289
Psychodynamic model (*see* Models, psychodynamic)
Psychogenic theory, of autism, 269–270
Psychopathic disorder, 148–149
Psychopharmacology, 50–51
Psychosexual development, 55–56
Psychosomatic symptoms, of child sexual abuse, 315
Psychotherapy, 70–71, 116–117
Public Law 93–112, 12
Public Law 94–142, 12, 23–25
Punishment:
in behavioral model, 78, 84–87
in self-injurious behavior, 290

Quay, H.C., 29, 149, 154, 155, 238

Rainman, 273
Rating scales, 80, 174–175
Rational-emotive therapy (RET), 90
Reality therapy, 55, 88–90
Recording, of behavior, 80–81
Redl, F., 8, 68, 69, 70
Regan, M.K., 271, 277, 297–299
Regular education initiative, 324
Rehabilitation Act, 12, 296
Reinforcement:
in autism, 272
in increasing behaviors, 82
in increasing motivation, 284
in operant conditioning, 78
in promoting generalization. 286
Reintegration, as educational goal, 215–217
Remedial approach, to academic curriculum, 169–170
Repertoire deficits, 130–141
Residential schools, 212–214
RESIST curriculum, 250
Resource schools, 214–215
Respite care, 98–99
Respondent conditioning, 77
Response-cost, as punishment, 291
Restitution, in overcorrection, 291
Restraint, physical, 88
Rimland, B., 47, 50, 270
Rincover, A., 282, 284, 286, 287

Ritalin, in attention-deficit hyperactivity, 144
Ritvo, E., 29, 45, 46, 268, 270
Rogers, Carl, 57–59
Rorschach Inkblot Test, 60–61, 165
Rush, Benjamin, 5
Rutherford, R.B., Jr., 84, 192, 221
Rutter, M., 46, 108, 141

Sacramento City Unified School District Board of Education v. Holland, 322
Santa Monica Project, 10–11
Schizophrenia:
in biophysical model, 45
as severe disorder, 273–276
Schools:
consulting services in, 215
day, 212–214
as ecosystem, 95, 99–101
phobia in, 122–129
residential, 212–214
resource, 214–215
Schools Without Failure, 67
Screening:
defined, 164
for emotional/behavioral disorders, 38
Secondary reinforcers, 82
Seguin, Edouard, 6
Self-contained schools, 214
Self-help skills, 278
Self-management:
in adolescence, 262
in cognitive-behavioral model, 91
in social curriculum, 171
Self-Perception Profile for Children, 63–64, 165
Self-report measures, 63–65
Self-stimulatory behavior, 272, 289–292
Sentence completions, 61–62
Seriously emotionally disturbed, defined, 21, 23
Serotonin, in autism, 47
Service continuum, in education system, 211–215
Severe behavior disorders (*see* Behavior disorders, severe)
Severity, of emotional/behavioral disorders, 27
Sex education, in adolescence, 243–244
Sex ratio, of emotional/behavioral disorders, 29–31
Sex-related issues, in adolescence, 240–243
Sexual abuse (*see* Abuse, sexual)
Sexually transmitted diseases, 241

Shakespeare, William, on mental illness, 4–5
Simpson, R.L., 207, 208, 210, 271, 277, 300
Single-parent families, 204
Social changes, in adolescence, 236–238
Social competence curricula, 170–172, 182–188
Social-Emotional Dimension Scale (SEDS), 35, 165
Social factors, in aggression, 154
Social interaction, 59, 138–139
Socialized delinquency, 26
Social learning:
  in aggression, 151–153
  in behavior model, 78–79
  in school phobia, 128
Social maladjustment (*see* Conduct disorders)
Social-role expectations, 22
Social skills:
  in conduct disorders, 159–160
  curriculum for, 167–172, 184–188, 191–192
  in severe behavior disorders, 278
Social Skills in the Classroom, 186–187
Social validity, 191
Social/welfare system, 217–218
Social withdrawal, 110–111, 129–131
Societal ecosystem, 96, 101–103
Sociopathic disorder, 148–149
Stark, K.D., 112, 115, 117, 130
Stimulants, in attention-deficit hyperactivity, 144
Stimulus overselectivity, in autism, 271–272, 283–284
Stress, 59, 115
Subcultures, 22
Substance exposure (*see also* Abuse, substance)
  case studies in, 309
  effects of, 307–310
  interventions in, 311–312
  prevalence of, 306–307
  psychosocial environment in, 310
  teaching implications in, 312
  in young children, 310–311
Suicide, 110–111, 254–256

Sullivan, Harry Stack, 56–57
Superego, 55
Supported employment, in transition programming, 296–297
Suspension, of behavior disordered students, 87, 319–320
Systematic desensitization, 126, 129
Systems:
  changes in, 223–225
  education:
    reintegration goals of, 215–217
    services of, 211–215
  family:
    approach to, 198–201
    case studies in, 200–202
    multicultural, 204–205
    nontraditional, 204–205
    parent-child dynamics in, 197–201
    severe disorders in, 299–302
  juvenile justice/correctional, 218–221, 322–323
  mental health, 221–223
  social/welfare, 217–218
  teacher role in, 229–230

T.A. for Kids, 183
T.A. for Teens, 183
T.A. for Tots, 183
Task analysis, in transition programming, 296
Teacher role:
  in attention-deficit hyperactivity, 146–147
  in biophysical model, 52–53
  in conduct disorders, 160
  in consulting, 225–227
  in identification, 38–40
  as liaison, 227–228
  in parental involvement, 205–206
  in school phobia, 129
  in severe behavior disorders, 301–302
  in sexual abuse, 317–319
  in social system, 229–230
  in social withdrawal, 131
  in substance exposure, 312
  in systems, 229–230
Teaching Method for Brain-Injured and Hyperactive Children, A, 9–10

Team decision making, in behavior disorder therapy, 36–37
Teen pregnancy, 240–241
Temperament factors, in biophysical model, 47–48
Terminology, in emotional disturbances, 19–21
Testing:
  criterion-referenced, 173
  in emotional/behavioral disorders, 33
  in psychodynamic model, 60–63
Thematic Apperception Test (TAT), 61
Therapeutic milieu, 67–69
Thorazine, 50
Timeout, 85–87
Tofranil, in depression, 51, 117
Token economies, 84
Token reinforcement systems, 261–262
Training:
  prevocational/vocational:
    model programs in, 259–261
    in severe behavior disorders, 279–282
Tranquilizer abuse, in adolescence, 246–247
Transition programming, in severe behavior disorders, 296

Victor ("wild boy of Averyon"), 5
Vocational training:
  model programs in, 259–261
  in severe behavior disorders, 279–282, 297–299

Walker, H.M., 26, 30–31, 39, 96, 154, 157, 159, 160, 184, 186–188, 191, 217
Waterman, J., 315, 316, 317
Webber, J., 90, 92, 203, 262, 300, 323
Welbutrin, in depression, 117
Withdrawal, social, 110–111, 129–131
Wright School (Durham, NC), 100

Ysseldyke, J.E., 36, 38–39, 97, 165, 177

Zoloft, 51